GENERATIONS OF PRIESTS

GENERATIONS OF PRIESTS

Thomas J. McGovern

with a foreword by
Cardinal George Pell

To Fr Michael Witt,
With best wishes for a fruitful
New Year.
Tom McGovern

OPEN AIR

14 January 2011

Set in 10 pt on 13 pt Janson for
OPEN AIR
an imprint of Four Courts Press
7 Malpas Street, Dublin 8, Ireland
http://www.fourcourtspress.ie
and in North America for
FOUR COURTS PRESS
c/o ISBS, 920 N.E. 58th Avenue, Suite 300, Portland, OR 97213.

With ecclesiastical permission
+Diarmuid, Archbishop of Dublin, 5 October 2009

A catalogue record for this title
is available from the British Library.

ISBN 978-1-84682-256-8 hbk
978-1-84682-257-5 pbk

Printed in England
by MPG Books, Bodmin, Cornwall.

Contents

In grateful memory of
His Holiness Pope John Paul II
(1920–2005)
who ordained me to the priesthood
on Trinity Sunday, 6 June 1982
in St Peter's basilica, Rome

Foreword

Cardinal George Pell, archbishop of Sydney

FR MC GOVERN IS ALREADY the distinguished author of several books on priesthood and on priestly celibacy. *Generations of Priests* is a rather different book – dramatic and existential rather than spiritual and theological. Newman, he tells us, is profoundly affected by the Church Fathers 'because they are saints who come alive in their writings and he is thus able to establish a very personal relationship with them.' This accurately describes *Generations of Priests* too: its vivid writing invites its readers into a very personal relationship with the ten priests whose lives he explores.

There are what Saul Bellow called 'axial lines'[1] going through these priests – all of them are challenged and inspired by the newness of the Gospel, applying it with what Pope Benedict calls 'the knowledge of love' to their hard times. All of them deeply experience their weakness, and focus on the Cross, which opens them out to God's mercy. As priests, they live intrinsically relational ministries, where their unique vertical and sacramental relationship with God, is expressed in their horizontal relationship with the hierarchy, with their fellow priests, and with those they serve.

While many of Fr McGovern's ten are bishops, and two are popes, all are characterized by a truly Christian democracy of service. The one among them who was neither pope, nor bishop, nor cardinal – the simple Curé d'Ars – most clearly defines the essence of the priesthood as 'the love of the heart of Jesus'. As Pope Benedict has noted, 'only in this way can we cooperate effectively in the mysterious "plan of the Father" which consists in "making Christ the heart of the world"! This plan is accomplished in history as Jesus gradually becomes the Heart of human hearts, beginning with those called to be closest to him: namely his priests.'[2]

These ten priests, spanning 1500 years, can be seen as unfolding an array of virtues that we priests need today. For example, we are told that John Chrysostom is often seen as *Doctor Eucharistiae*, reminding us that 'it is not

1 The phrase is used in Saul Bellow's novel, *The Adventures of Augie March*. 2 Benedict XVI, Homily on the opening of the Year for Priests, 19 June 2009.

man who causes what is present to become the Body and Blood of Christ, but Christ himself who was crucified for us.'

John Fisher, in the prayer he wrote while awaiting death in the Tower of London, draws us into his heart-to-heart dialogue with the Father: 'Whither should I rather go than to my Father, to my most loving Father, to my most merciful Father, to him that of his infinite love and mercy hath given me boldness to call him Father?'

Oliver Plunkett, himself preparing for a similar fate, reminds us that our courage in the face of harsh if not lethal criticism is rooted in the courage of Christ himself – as he wrote to his fellow prisoner and spiritual director, Fr Maurus: 'I have considered that Christ by his fears and passion merited for me to be free of fear.'

John Vianney's humility and readiness to forgive is beautifully expressed in his answer to a letter from a priest from a neighbouring parish, pointing out that 'when a man knows as little theology as you do, he should not go into the confessional.' The Curé d'Ars replied: 'Most dear and most venerated confrère, what good reasons I have for loving you! You are the only person who really knows me. Since you are so good and kind as to take an interest in my poor soul, do help me to obtain the favour for which I have been asking for so long a time, that being released from a post which I am not worthy to hold by reason of my ignorance, I may be allowed to retire into a little corner, there to weep over my poor life. What penances there are to be undertaken! how many expiations there are to be offered! how many tears to be shed.' It's no surprise that his humility won over his critic.

John Henry Newman accurately diagnosed a religious flabbiness that is still with us: 'Liberalism in religion is the doctrine that there is no positive truth in religion, but that one creed is as good as another, and this is the teaching that is gaining substance and force daily. It is inconsistent with any recognition of any religion, as *true*. It teaches that all are to be tolerated, for all are matters of opinion. Revealed religion is not a truth, but a sentiment and a taste; not an objective fact, not miraculous; and it is the right of each individual to make it say just what strikes his fancy.'

The life of John Baptist Lamy reads like an adventure story, marked by a word we don't use much these days, but as essential as ever: zeal. A typical moment is described by Fr McGovern: 'He arrived at Granite Creek on Christmas Eve. One of miners put his cabin at the bishop's disposal where snow blew through the cracks. On Christmas Day he said Mass for about twenty-five miners kneeling on the night-time's snow. The altar was improvised from old planks set up within the cabin. Only a few men could kneel inside the cabin – the rest were outside in the cold. It was so cold that a fire was lit in the cabin, and several times Lamy had to bring the chalice with its frozen wine and water to be thawed out by the stove.'

St Pius X towards the end of his life wrote an encyclical letter on priesthood born from his own life of priestly service: 'there is abundant evidence from every age that even the humblest priest, provided his life is adorned with overflowing sanctity, can undertake and accomplish marvellous works for the spiritual welfare of the People of God.'

Clement von Galen is probably most famous for his defence of the defenceless – his sermons against the National Socialist state's euthanasia policies: 'Once admit the right to kill unproductive persons, then none of us can be sure of his life. A curse on men and on the German people if we break the holy commandment "Thou shalt not kill."' As Fr McGovern notes, 'Von Galen's words had a powerful effect. By the end of August [1941] the program for euthanasia had been suspended, but not before 100,000 people had been killed in this manner.'

Josemaría Escrivá, like the other ten priests, has many virtues, one of them being his close, day-to-day relationship with our Lady, expressed in this 1970 prayer: 'O Lady, all I can offer you now – I have nothing else – are thorns, the thorns embedded in my heart; but I am sure that through you they will turn into roses … Grant that in us, in our hearts, roses may blossom all through the year, little roses, the roses of daily life, ordinary roses but filled with the perfume of sacrifice and love. I deliberately say little roses, because they are what suit me best, because all through my life I have only dealt with ordinary, everyday things, and even then I often haven't been able to finish them; but I am sure that it is in this ordinary, daily activity, that your Son and you await me.'

And from John Paul the Great we can find a profound respect from a celibate priest for the married state – all the more profound, because he was celibate: 'In this domain I have received more graces than battles to fight. A day came when I knew for certain that my life would not be fulfilled in the human love the beauty of which I have always felt deeply. As a pastor, I have had to prepare many young people for marriage. My status as priest has never separated me from them; on the contrary, it has brought me closer to them and has helped me to understand them better … The fact that my path differs from theirs did not make me a stranger; quite the contrary.'

This book could be read as a handbook for living the priesthood in a difficult time. Through the often heroic lives of these priests, we are introduced to rich insights from Church and secular history and imaginative pastoral practices – many as relevant now as when practiced by their ten protagonists. There is an excellent interweaving too, with various papal or ecclesial writings on priesthood, indications of Fr McGovern's experience as a spiritual director.

Because the ten priests are saints, or at least on the way to sainthood, their stories will also be invaluable to catechists and an inspiration to all Christians living in our age, which is no less exciting or exacting than the times experienced by these outstanding men.

Introduction

In March of 2009[1] His Holiness Benedict XVI announced that he was convoking a jubilee year for priests, to begin on 19 June 2009, the 150th anniversary of the death of the Curé of Ars. The purpose of this special year is to make the role and the mission of the priest in the Church and in contemporary society better known, and 'to achieve a complete identification of the priest with his mission'.[2] It is the Holy Father's expectation 'that this year will be an opportunity for interior renewal for every priest and, consequently, a year of firm reinvigoration in the commitment to his mission'.[3] He encourages us to let ourselves 'be totally won over by Christ … this was the goal of the entire ministry of the holy Curé of Ars, whom we shall invoke in particular during the Year for Priests; may it also be the principal objective for each one of us'.[4]

How can we suggest that the priest of today can somehow model his life and ministry on the example of the Curé of Ars who exercised his priesthood over 150 years ago, in very different social and historical circumstances? The reason is that the essence of the Catholic priesthood always remains the same, because it is an ontological participation in the priesthood of Jesus Christ 'who is the same yesterday, today, and forever' (Heb 13:8).

I had completed this book, *Generations of Priests*, before the special Year of the Priest was inaugurated. However, in light of what the Holy Father expects of priests for this jubilee year, I feel that the book will be helpful in attaining these objectives. It deals not only with the Curé of Ars, but also with nine other priests who at different stages of Church history committed themselves fully to follow Christ as labourers in his vineyard. I think it will be seen that these men – St John Chrysostom, St John Fisher, St Oliver Plunkett, Cardinal Newman, Archbishop John Baptist Lamy, St Pius X, Blessed Cardinal Clement von Galen, St Josemaría Escrivá, Pope John Paul II – although very contrasting in personality and following very different paths, have several elements in common arising from the holiness of their lives. Thus we find in all a deep personal love for Christ, a willingness to sacrifice themselves generously

1 Benedict XVI, Address to the members of the Vatican Congregation for the Clergy, 16 March 2009. 2 Ibid., Letter to priests, 16 June 2009. 3 Ibid., Address, 1 July 2009. 4 Ibid., Homily inaugurating the Year for Priests, 25 June 2009.

for the salvation of souls, a great loyalty to the Magisterium, and a rich human sensibility. Their whole lives were identified with the specific mission each had received.

On the other hand they are men of very different temperaments, men of their own time and culture. I am not in any way suggesting that the priests recalled in these pages are a fully representative selection of the great variety of men who have followed Christ down through the centuries. They are primarily the result of my own historical and theological interests, and thus have all the inherent limitations for such a basis of selection. Yet, on the other hand, I think it will be seen that each of them reflects the perennial aspects of the priesthood, whether we are considering a fourth-century bishop such as John Chrysostom, or a modern twentieth-century defender of the faith like Clement von Galen.

The objective of this book is to highlight the supernatural call to the priesthood and its fruitful expression in the lives of men who responded with great generosity to their vocation. They followed Jesus Christ with passion and zeal, and were ready to sacrifice everything to defend the rights of the Church and of souls. Their minds and hearts were imbued with Christ's teaching, which is reflected in the holiness of their lives and their commitment to winning new disciples for the Lord. While this book has relevance for anyone interested in Church history, it is meant primarily for priests and those preparing for the priesthood. It is hoped that by recalling the lives of these great men, from different periods of history, those who read it will be convinced once again of the marvellous works which God can achieve through his priests, and of the exceptional graces which he places in their hands.

thomasmcgovern@eircom.net

CHAPTER ONE

St John Chrysostom (345–407)

JOHN CHRYSOSTOM was born at Antioch in Syria some time between 344 and 347, of a noble and well-to-do Christian family. His father, Secundas, was a distinguished military officer who died while John was still in his infancy. His mother, Anthusa, was an exceptional woman, to whom John pays tribute in his book *On the priesthood.*[1] Although she was widowed at the early age of twenty, she refused all offers of marriage in order to devote herself exclusively to the formation of her son and his older sister. Deeply religious herself, she saw to it that he received a thorough instruction in piety. She sent him to the best secular schools in Antioch, where he followed the programme of studies customary at the time, and had very able teachers, among them the well-known Libanius. From Libanius John acquired the skills for a career in law and rhetoric, as well as a love of the Greek language and literature.

Although he was brought up as a Christian, John was not baptized until 369. Such deferment of baptism was the common custom during the second half of the fourth century, even among the very pious. John was admitted as a catechumen in 366. Meletius, bishop of Antioch, who discerned that John was a young man of exceptional intelligence, allowed him to accompany him continually over the next three years. Meletius, who baptized John in his twenty-third year, exercised an important influence on him when his religious education was completed. John also began to live a life of strict mortification at home and would have withdrawn from the world but for the sake of his mother who begged him not to make her a widow again.

The teaching of Meletius was supplemented by that of Diodorus, a remarkable man of learning, who was one of the directors of the religious school which the young John attended at this time. Under his guidance John began to withdraw from the pursuit of classical and profane studies and to

1 *On the priesthood: a treatise in six books* by St John Chrysostom, translated by Patrick Boyle, CM (Westminster, MA, 1943). For bibliography on Chrysostom, see J.N.D. Kelly, *Golden Mouth: the story of John Chrysostom, ascetic, preacher, bishop* (London, 1995); D. Attwater, *St John Chrysostom: the voice of gold* (Milwaukee, 1939).

apply himself more and more to the study of Scripture. This was the Diodorus who founded the exegetical school of Antioch, which was less preoccupied with allegory than the school of Alexandria was, and more inclined to accept the literal or historical sense of Scripture. This is the spirit which inspired Chrysostom in his scriptural commentaries. In 375, after the death of his mother, John could now indulge his strong desire to live an ascetic life of fasting and prayer in the caves outside Antioch. However, he carried this to such an extreme that after two years his health was so impaired that he had to return to Antioch to recover his strength.

It was probably about 381 that Meletius made him a deacon. Meletius died at Constantinople that same year while presiding at the second ecumenical council, and the aged Flavian succeeded to the see of Antioch. In 386 Flavian ordained John a priest, and it is from that year that his importance to Church history begins. As deacon he had engaged in assisting with liturgical functions, in caring for the sick and the poor, and in the instruction of catechumens. We will see how this varied pastoral experience is consistently reflected in his preaching in subsequent years. Chrysostom's lifetime saw the development of monasticism in the East. He came to prominence when Christianity was emerging from the great crisis of Arianism, and when the barbarians were beginning to make settlements within the confines of the Roman empire. It was, to say the least, a period of challenge and change.

John was a man of great apostolic zeal who was fearless in proclaiming the Gospel. He was a real pastor of souls and, above all, a great preacher. His contemporaries, and subsequent authorities, regarded him as the greatest orator of the Greek Church. He was declared a doctor of the Church by St Pius V in 1568, and patron of preachers by St Pius X. His literary output exceeded all the writers of the Greek Church – in the West only Augustine compares with him. What is so attractive about Chrysostom's writings is not only their content but their easy oratorical style. His sermons, which were often an hour long, didn't tire his listeners because his brilliant sense of imagery and his deep understanding of human psychology helped to hold the attention of his audience, who often broke out into spontaneous applause. Part of his preaching skill lay in his ability to mix exegetical discourse with commentary on contemporary events and practical moral exhortation. His sermons breathe the realism of a man who is conversant with all the follies of the human heart, as well as the optimism of a pastor who is convinced of the transforming power of divine grace. His writings, as one of his biographers describes it, 'give a clear presentation of the age in which he lived. It is the picture of a society in the main no longer heathen but not yet properly Christian; of many people living under conditions of grinding want, and many more in a state of formal slavery; of a rapacious fiscal system administered by corrupt officials; of a selfish and predatory governing class, and of considerable insecurity of life and property'.[2]

QUALITIES OF THE PRIEST

It was about this time (between 381 and 386) that John wrote the most famous of his works, his treatise *On the priesthood*. It has always been regarded as a classic text on the subject because of the sublimity of its thought and the elegance of its style. His purpose in this work is to describe the dignity of the Catholic priesthood, the challenges that it involves, and the way to exercise this office faithfully and effectively. It is made up of six books composed in the form of a dialogue, a method of instruction which, initially developed by Plato, was adopted by the Fathers to teach aspects of Christian philosophy and Christian moral life.

In the early part of the treatise John describes some of the qualities which the priesthood requires. The priest must be the good shepherd of the people entrusted to his care. The sheep, he says, are under attack from many different sides and the shepherd will have to account to God for any who are lost. Changing the metaphor, he sees the priest as the physician of souls who needs insight to identify their infirmities and skill to apply the appropriate medicine. Great diligence, patience and perseverance are required to bring the straying sheep back to the right path. In reading the homilies of Chrysostom we can see that he is speaking from experience. He uses all the resources of his priesthood, and the great natural gifts given him by God, to persuade the people of Antioch to leave behind their sinful ways and embark on the road to Christian holiness. There are many very impressive passages in the treatise on the greatness of the priesthood, but one of the most eloquent must surely be the following:

> For the office of the priesthood is executed upon earth, yet it ranks amongst things that are heavenly, and with good reason. For it was neither an angel or an archangel nor any created power, but the Paraclete Himself that established that ministry, and commanded that men yet abiding in the flesh should imitate the functions of angels. Wherefore it behoves the priest to be as pure as if he stood in heaven itself amidst those Powers ... For when you behold the Lord immolated and lying on the altar, and the priest standing over the sacrifice and praying, and all the people purpled by the precious blood, do you imagine that you are still on earth amongst men?

2 Attwater, ibid., p. 2.

> For if you consider what it is for a man yet clothed in flesh and blood to approach that pure and blessed nature, you will easily understand to what a dignity the grace of the Holy Spirit has raised priests. For by them these things are accomplished, and others not inferior to these pertaining to our redemption and salvation … It is to priests that spiritual birth and regeneration by baptism is entrusted. By them we put on Christ, and are united to the Son of God, and become members of that blessed Head. Hence we should regard them as more august than princes and kings, and more venerable than parents. For the latter begot us of blood and the will of the flesh, but priests are the cause of our generation from God, of our spiritual regeneration, of our true freedom and sonship according to grace.[3]

For all of these reasons, he tells us, the powers of the priesthood must be approached with great awe and reverence. Doubtless such eulogizing of the priesthood would be considered by some as naked clerical triumphalism. But there are few more accurate theological observers than Chrysostom, and to understand the nature of the Catholic priesthood we do well to pay attention to what he says about it.

There is no doubt that, more than anybody else, the writings and apostolic achievements of St Paul inspired the eloquence of Chrysostom. It is clear that he conceived an extraordinary love and admiration for the Apostle of the Gentiles. He is amazed at his magnanimity, his sufferings, his zeal for the Gospel. And so it is not surprising that he is moved when he finds that even St Paul, who was made a sharer of God's secrets, was filled with fear and trembling when he considered the great responsibilities of his calling (cf. 2 Cor 11:3).

VIRTUES OF THE PRIEST

The office of the priesthood requires 'great prudence, – and even more than prudence – great grace from God, good morals, purity of life and more than ordinary virtue'.[4] The priest has to be forewarned against the insidiousness of vainglory, ambition for honours, preaching to please, servility towards the rich, and lack of courage to rebuke or admonish. Chrysostom writes elsewhere about prudence in the selection of candidates for the priesthood. 'It is not after the first test, or the second, or the third', he warns, 'that you should lay on hands, but when you have thought deeply on the matter and studied it carefully.'[5] John has a very high estimate of the virtues required of a priest – they

3 See *On the priesthood*, pp 40–4. 4 Ibid., p. 48. 5 *Homily on 1 Tim* 5:22.

should be such that they enlighten the souls of all who come to him for assistance. His behaviour should be above reproach. While the sins of ordinary people, even though public, do no great harm, the sins of the priest are conspicuous to all, and even though the things they fail in are small, they can seem great to others. For he says, 'all measure the gravity of a sin, not by the gravity of the act but by the dignity of him who commits it.'[6]

Consequently the priest needs to be particularly vigilant to lead an upright life so as not to be a cause of scandal to others. Even one small fault, he claims, can cast a shadow on the rest of his actions because people tend to judge him by higher standards. Along with piety he should, especially if he is a bishop, be a man of great prudence. In summary 'he ought to be grave yet not haughty, awe-inspiring yet kind, full of authority yet affable, no acceptor of persons yet condescending, humble yet not servile, strong yet meek, that he may be able with ease to cope with all the difficulties' that can arise, promoting the building up of the Church at all times, and doing nothing through partiality.[7] He has interesting instructions about how to deal with poor widows, and gives practical indications replete with human and supernatural wisdom about how to care for consecrated virgins.

EUCHARIST AND SACRIFICE

In our own day Chrysostom has often been referred to as *Doctor Eucharistiae*.[8] This is because he is an outstanding witness to the doctrine of the Real Presence of Christ in the Eucharist and its sacrificial character:

> To show the love He has for us He has made it possible for those who desire, not merely to look upon Him, but even to touch Him and consume Him and to fix their teeth in his flesh and to be commingled with Him; in short, to fulfil all their love.[9]

Here he transfers to the substance of the Body and Blood of Christ what is strictly true only of the accidents of bread and wine, in order to make the truth of the Real Presence and the identity of the Eucharistic Sacrifice with the Sacrifice of the Cross as clear as possible. Many references to this effect could be culled from the writings of Chrysostom. The 'Eucharist should be approached with awe and devotion', with 'reverence and trembling'. The con-

6 *On the priesthood*, p. 58. 7 Ibid., p. 66. 8 Cf. J. Quasten, *Patrology*, vol. III (Utrecht, 1966), p. 479. 9 *Homily on John*, no. 46, p. 469, in St John Chrysostom, *Commentary on St John the Apostle and the Evangelist*, vol. I (nos. 1–47), vol. II (nos. 48–88) (Washington, DC, 1960). Subsequent references to this commentary will be abbreviated after the style *John no. 46*, p. 469.

secrated wine is 'the awe-inspiring blood'; it 'is the same as what flowed from the side of Christ'. The Eucharist is also 'a fearful and holy Sacrifice'; and so, pointing to the altar, he can say 'Christ lies there slain'.[10] The sacrificing priest is Christ himself and the consecration takes place the moment that the words of consecration are pronounced:

> It is not man who causes what is present to become the Body and Blood of Christ, but Christ himself who was crucified for us. The priest is the representative when he pronounces those words, but the power and the grace are those of the Lord. 'This is my Body,' he says. This word changes the things that lie before us; and as that sentence 'increase and multiply', once spoken, extends through all time and gives to our nature the power to reproduce itself; even so the saying 'This is my Body', once uttered, does at every table in the Churches from that time to the present day, and even till Christ's coming, make the sacrifice complete.[11]

He admonished his congregation to give much more importance to interior preparation to receive the Eucharist:

> Is it not ridiculous, he asks, to be so meticulous about bodily things when the feast draws near, as to get out and prepare your best clothes days ahead …, and to deck yourself in your finest, all the while paying not the slightest attention to your soul, which is abandoned, besmirched, squalid and utterly consumed by desire …?[12]

And so he reminds those approaching the altar: 'Reflect, O man, what sacrificial flesh you take in your hand! to what table you will approach. Remember that you, though dust and ashes, do receive the Body and Blood of Christ.'[13]

Commenting on the passage of Scripture, 'and Jesus entered the Temple' (Mt 21:12), he encourages the Antiochenes to visit the Blessed Sacrament: 'This was proper to a good son: to enter immediately into the house of his Father to render due honour to Him there – just as you, who should imitate Jesus, whenever you enter a city should first of all go to the church.'[14]

PREACHING

As is to be expected in a man of Chrysostom's talents and experience, he gives particular importance to the ability to preach well. At a time when the Church,

10 Quasten, *Patrology*, vol. III, p. 480. **11** *Hom. 1 de prodit. Iudae*, no. 6. **12** *Homily* 6. **13** *Hom. in nat. Dom.*, no. 7. **14** *Catena aurea*, III, p. 14.

as a consequence of Vatican II, has given renewed emphasis to the liturgy of the Word and its exposition, his assessment of the role of preaching in the pastoral function of the Church is of particular relevance. He points out how the Apostles, to leave themselves free to get on with the business of preaching, appointed deacons to take care of widows. By means of preaching, he says, the soul that is sick by reason of false doctrine is restored to health. Many enemies of the spiritual life can be dealt with by effective preaching, enemies such as the false doctrines of the Arians, Manichaeans, Sabellians, etc. During the whole of the fourth century, religious struggles had troubled the empire and found their echo at Antioch. Even the Catholics themselves were separated by the schism between the orthodox and Arian bishops.

By considering his own homiletic style we see what he means by effective preaching. This reflects the exegetical tradition of the School of Antioch which focused primarily on the literal and historical meaning of the inspired text. At the same time he draws out the spiritual meaning of his text with great facility, applying it in a very practical way to the needs of his congregation. His knowledge of Scripture is encyclopaedic, ranging freely and with equal facility among the books of the Old and the New Testaments. During the twelve years he spent in Antioch as a priest, he was an indefatigable preacher. Every day in Lent and at least once a week at other periods of the year he preached to the people. His sermons were solid and practical as well as being eloquent. He had a great understanding of his audience as is evident from the practical details of life he discourses on. He is trenchant in his criticisms but is always the good shepherd who tries to win back souls to conversion and forgiveness.[15]

Antioch at that time was a city of over 200,000 people, more than half of whom were Christian. Since the city of Antioch was a great centre of government and administration, Christianity spread there almost from the beginning. The seed of Christ's teaching was carried to Antioch by some disciples from Cyprus and Cyrene, who fled from Jerusalem during the persecution which followed on the martyrdom of St Stephen. They preached the teaching of Jesus not only to the Jewish colony, but also to the Greeks or Gentiles, and soon large numbers were converted. The mother church of Jerusalem sent Barnabas to confirm them in the faith. There he laboured with St Paul for a whole year with such success that the followers of Christ were acknowledged as forming a distinct community, 'so that at Antioch the disciples were first named Christians' (Acts 11:26). Their charity was exhibited by the offerings sent to the famine-striken brethren in Judea. St Peter himself came to Antioch

15 Typical of his teaching under this heading is the following: 'For though God has been offended, yet he is still our Father; and even though He has been provoked to anger, He remains fond of his children. One thing only does he seek, which is not vengeance for our offences, but rather true repentance and the conversion of our hearts' (*Homilies on St Matthew*, 22:5).

probably about the year 44, and lived there for some time. Antioch soon became a centre of missionary activity, and a central point of all Christian interests in the East.

The people flocked to hear John preach, both Christians and pagans. Although they were eager to hear the word of God, we can see the Antiochenes reflected in the Johannine homilies warts and all. These Christians were surrounded by a pagan culture in a city renowned for its wealth, for the splendour of its buildings, its baths, circus and theatre. A broad avenue, with four rows of columns forming covered porticos on each side, traversed the city from east to west for several miles. Its most attractive pleasure resort was the beautiful grove of laurels and cypresses called Daphne, some four or five miles west of the city. The population included a great variety of races. There were Macedonians and Greeks, native Syrians and Phoenicians, Jews and Romans. However, it remained always predominantly a Greek city. Its luxury was well known. In such circumstances Christian morals were always endangered, so it is not surprising then that in his sermons Chrysostom frequently inveighs against the attractions and the licence of the theatres, against vainglory, luxury and the display of wealth. Because of his concern for the poor, he inculcated the obligation of alms-giving and pleaded the cause of the destitute with exceptional eloquence and earnestness. One commentator sums Chrysostom up as follows:

> The combination of all the qualities of an orator: ease, pathos, sublimity, has rendered St John Chrysostom the greatest orator of the early Church, the most illustrious exponent of that memorable epoch. The works of Chrysostom are the most complete course of sermons that antiquity has handed down to us. Throughout them you perceive a great knowledge of the heart of man, a charity truly evangelical. The whole Christian civilization of the East lives again in the eloquent pages of the orator of Antioch.[16]

Bossuet, no mean preacher himself, regarded Chrysostom as the greatest of Christian orators. He calls him 'the most illustrious of preachers, and beyond question the most eloquent that ever taught the Church'.[17] His method was homiletic and consequently varied and popular in structure, and very down to earth in terms of practical application. Preaching for him was a labour of love – his one purpose was the moral conversion of his audience. He taught, rebuked, encouraged and enlightened at the same time. Everything was

16 J. Villemain, *Tableau de l'éloquence Chrétienne au quatrième siècle*, p.144, quoted in Preface to *On the priesthood*, p. xvi. **17** *Sermon sur la parole de Dieu*, quoted by Boyle, in his introduction to *On the priesthood*, p. xvii.

geared towards the reformation and conversion of his congregation. The popularity of John's preaching was due to his outstanding command of language and, doubtless, in part due to his reputation as a castigator of the rich and the privileged. However, its effectiveness was due primarily to Chrysostom's personal holiness, to the fact that he was obviously a man of God. As in many other respects, St Paul was the exemplar of the preacher Chrysostom aspired to be. He offered him to priests as the perfect role model of Christian eloquence. His admiration and veneration for the Apostle of the Gentiles is unbounded.

John emphasizes two characteristics of the effective preacher: the priest should eliminate all desire for praise, and should develop a talent for oratory. 'A priest', he says, 'should have for his people the sentiments of a father for his tenderest children. And as we are not concerned when children insult and strike us, and lament, nor are we elated when they laugh and rejoice with us; so a priest ought not to be elated by the praise of the people, nor cast down by their unreasonable dispraise.'[18] He makes the point that a talent for oratory is not usually one that a man has naturally, but rather one that comes as a result of education. It is also a talent, he says, that has to be worked at constantly through the study of Scripture. In his own preaching he demonstrates that he was always developing his capacity for imagery and allegory, which gave such impact to his homilies. His sermons are replete with a deep knowledge of the inspired text, the history of the Church and secular history. He was also a keen student of psychology, with a deep knowledge of human nature, not only of its limitations but aided by grace, of its capacity for heroic virtue as well.

ACTIVE AND CONTEMPLATIVE VOCATIONS

In Book VI of his treatise *On the priesthood* John contrasts the active life of what was then the secular priesthood with the contemplative life of the monks. He draws the interesting conclusion that the priestly apostolate in the middle of the world requires a greater degree of holiness, especially in what relates to the virtue of holy purity.

One of John's first extant writings refers to celibacy. As a young man he lived, as we have seen, a monastic lifestyle and had among his companions Theodore, the future bishop of Mopsuestia. At one stage Theodore left the community and announced his intention of marrying a girl called Hermione, a development that came as a great shock to Chrysostom who was ardently committed to the monastic ideal. He wrote a letter of remonstrance to

18 *On the priesthood*, p. 110.

Theodore, appealing to him to return and pointing out how human nature with the help of God's grace can rise above itself:

> The beauty of his beloved ever so enthralled no lover as God loves and longs for the beauty of the human soul. You at present are altogether taken up with Hermione's loveliness, but you can, if you will, give to your soul a beauty as far exceeding that of her body as Heaven surpasses earth. Spiritual beauty alone is real and lasting.[19]

After a period of uncertainty Theodore returned to the monastic way of life, and was later ordained priest and bishop. We get a glimpse here of the powerful and persuasive language of even the young Chrysostom, but also an awareness of his still immature perception of the vocation of marriage.

He shows his great humanity and prudence in analyzing the dangers which the priest in the world has to confront by comparison with the monk:

> Though he needs greater purity, he is exposed to greater dangers, which may sully him unless he uses constant vigilance, and great attention to hinder them access to his soul. For beauty of countenance and affected airs, and studied gait, the tone of the voice, painting of the eyes and cheeks, arrangement of tresses, colouring of the hair, costly raiment, varied ornaments of gold, beautiful gems, the fragrance of perfumes and the like, which the female sex affect, are capable of making an impression on the mind, unless it be hardened by great austerity and self restraint.[20]

He was obviously well aware of all the female lures used to attract the attention of men and is at times harsh in his judgement about them. A woman has a right to look well, to be truly feminine in appearance – her beauty is a reflection of the perfection of God. However, more than condemning women for being true to themselves, he is above all pointing out to the priest the need for custody of the eyes so as not to cause his heart to be divided in relation to God. He sees the need for purity of life especially in relation to the Eucharist:

> What purity, what piety shall we require of him? Think what those hands ought to be which perform such a ministry; what the tongue which pronounces those words; how much more pure and holy than aught we can imagine that soul should be which receives so great a spirit. At that moment the angels attend on the priest, and the whole

19 Attwater, p. 17. **20** *On the priesthood*, p. 121.

> sanctuary and the space around the altar is filled with the heavenly powers to honour Him who lies thereon. And this is credible from the nature of the sacrifice then offered.[21]

One of the dangers for the priest's purity of life is overfamiliarity with women, and, consequently, prudence is required in visiting the sick, consoling in sorrows, and assisting in difficulties.[22]

JOHN CHRYSOSTOM AS APOLOGIST

We get a good idea of John's ability and competence in defending the doctrine of the Church from two of his apologetic works, the *Discourse on Blessed Babylas and against the Greeks*[23] and the *Demonstration against the pagans that Christ is God.*[24] Basically he realizes that the pagans will reject any proof for Christ's divinity if it starts with a recounting of his miracles. He has therefore to find as a basis for his arguments something which even the pagans will admit. And what is that? They will, he says, agree that the family of Christians came from Christ, and that through them Christ founded churches throughout the world. His point is that it is not in the character of a mere man to bring so much of the earth under his spiritual sway in so short a time, nor is it attributable to a human being to call man to such lofty ideals, men who previously were often engaged in an evil way of life. Only a person of divine power could have brought about such a complete change in man's behaviour. Only a man who is God could have persuaded them to give up deeply cherished ancestral customs and laws and substitute an easy-going life by an austere lifestyle. This success continues in spite of present and past persecutions.

The second stage of Chrysostom's argument is that all that Christ did had been foretold by the prophets. A fulfilled prediction is a proof of power and thus the fulfilment of the predictions concerning Christ confirm that he had a divine power. Among the different prophecies about Christ, John gives special

21 Ibid., p. 125. **22** 'Now in all this the wicked one can easily find an opportunity of effecting an entrance, unless a man guards himself with the greatest care. For the look not merely of a lewd, but even of a modest, woman disturbs and makes an impression on the mind; flattery softens, honours enslave, and love, the cause of all good things, springs up and becomes the source of every evil to those who do not use it rightly. Sometimes, too, continual cares blunt the edge of the mind, and make him who had wings become heavier than lead, and passion attacks and envelopes as it were in darkness all within' (ibid., p. 135). **23** *Discourse on Blessed Babylas and against the Greeks*; The Fathers of the Church, 73 (Washington DC, 1985), translated by Margaret A. Schatkin, pp 75–152 (subsequently referred to as *Babylas*). **24** *Demonstration against the pagans that Christ is God*, published in the same volume as *Babylas*, The Fathers of the Church, 73, translated by Paul W. Harkins, pp 187–262 (subsequently referred to as *Pagans*).

importance to the role of the Cross – how what was the greatest of human ignominies turned out to be the most glorious crown of victory. The Cross had always been a symbol of shame and a curse, but now one can see it everywhere, both in public places and in private homes. How is it that people are so eager to obtain a portion of this Cross, and to wear this symbol of the greatest shame? The answer must be in the great power of the man who was crucified. Previously they loathed it; now they encase relics of it in gold and wear it about their necks.[25]

> For this symbol of death – and I shall not stop repeating this over and over again – became the foundation of many blessings, a wall to make us secure on every side, a timely trap to catch the devil, a rein to hold in check the demons, a muzzle against the power of our adversaries. This sign has destroyed death, this sign has shattered hell's gates of brass and crushed iron bars. It has destroyed the stronghold of the devil, it has cut the sinews of sin. The Cross has rescued the whole world, which was lying under condemnation, and has rid us of the calamity which God was sending down upon our human nature.[26]

Another element in John's argument was to turn to Christ's own predictions and to show that their fulfilment is proof of his divine power. Specifically he takes Christ's predictions concerning the Church and the Temple to prove his point. Starting from the promise of the Petrine ministry, 'upon this rock I will build my Church, and the gates of hell shall not prevail against it' (Mt 16:16), he shows how miraculously this prediction has come true. All the old pagan altars, rites and festivals are gone and have been replaced by new altars all over the known world, even as far as the British Isles.

> Think, he suggests, what it means to have converted so many nations, to have won over so many peoples, to have destroyed ancestral customs, to have torn out deep-rooted habits, to have driven out, like the dust before the wind, the tyrannous rule of pleasure and the power and strength of evil.[27]

Yet all this was done through eleven poor, unlettered men who spoke a strange language. And it was achieved in the face of persecution on every side. Christian teaching was opposed by imperial edicts, and it had to overcome deeply ingrained pagan ways and customs.

25 Cf. *Pagans*, pp 228–9. **26** Ibid. **27** Ibid., p. 239.

> The new way, he tells us, drove them from luxurious living and led them to fasting; it drove them from the love of money and led them to poverty; it drove them from wanton ways and led them to temperance; it drove them away from anger and led them to mildness; it drove them away from envy and led them to kindliness; it drove them from the broad way and the wide street and led them onto a way which was narrow, straight, and steep, despite the fact that they were used to a wide road.[28]

But all this was achieved through the power of Christ who said, 'I will build my Church.'

The Church, he says, did not go in search of an esoteric brand of men who lived on the margins of the world and its ways. On the contrary, 'it took those very men who had grown rotten here and who had become softer than mud; it told them to travel on the straight and narrow, the rough road of austerity. And it won them over to this way of life.'[29] 'Not only the meek and the mild and the good', he reminds us, 'would form the Church. The wild, the inhuman, and men whose ways were like those of wolves and lions and bulls would flock together with them and form one Church.'[30] Elsewhere, John, in a very beautiful image, describes the Church as an inn located along the road of life. She receives those travellers who are worn out from their journey who bring with them the baggage of their past sins. Here travellers can be freed from the weight of sin so that they may rest and take nourishment to enable them to continue on their way.[31]

There is, clearly, in Chrysostom's description of the nascent Church, a great pride in the apostolic zeal of those men and women who attracted converts by the thousand. But, above all, the conversion of the Roman empire expresses vividly for him the power of Christ's grace working through fragile human beings.[32] The more the Church was persecuted, the more it grew in numbers and apostolic zeal. The power of Christ's prediction was seen particularly in the days of persecution by the pagan emperors. How did the Church overcome so many obstacles? How did it arrive at the point, in the time of Chrysostom, when it had spread practically to the whole known world? Only through the invincible power of Christ who foretold it and then brought it about:

28 Ibid., p. 240. **29** Ibid. **30** Ibid., p. 214. **31** *Catena Aurea*, p. 519. **32** Chrysostom was very conscious of the great variety of backgrounds of those early converts: 'Aquila wrought at a craft. The woman who sold purple dye-stuffs supervised a busy workshop. Another was a prison governor and another a centurion like Cornelius. Yet another was in ill health, like Timothy. Another was a runaway from slavery, like Onesimus. Nothing proved a hindrance to any of these, but all were joyously welcomed and accepted, both men and women, both young and old, both slaves and freemen, both soldiers and civilian citizens alike' (*Homilies on St Matthew*, 43, 7).

> It was the result of an ineffable power that the fisherman, the publican, and the tentmaker, at their mere commands, raised the dead to life, drove out demons, drove off death, stopped the tongues of philosophers, stitched shut the mouths of rhetoricians, overcame kings and rulers, and were victorious over pagans, barbarians and every nation.[33]

The persecutions produced many martyrs, but they left the Church 'treasures that will never perish, columns that will always stand, towers that no force can take by storm. In death as in life, these martyrs have become a source of strength and assistance to those of a later age.'[34] These men founded many churches all over the world and at the same time they and their disciples were being slain, hunted down, imprisoned or exiled. Their persecutors scourged them, burned them or drowned them in the sea. And yet 'they did a far more difficult thing than build a church from stones. They built all these churches out of souls and principles, and not with stones.'[35] All this they did because of the power of him who said 'upon this rock I will build my Church and the gates of hell shall not prevail against it'.

DISCOURSE AGAINST THE GREEKS

Chrysostom had also to defend the Church against accusations that apostolic miracles were fictions perpetrated by the Church to gain acceptance for Christianity. In his discourse on Blessed Babylas he wanted to show that the martyrs and their relics were worthy of the highest veneration. It is a fine example of Chrysostom's directness and courage and his unwillingness to fudge things when the teaching of the Church was at stake. In his account of the death of Babylas, a former bishop of Antioch martyred under Emperor Decius, he concluded that Babylas demonstrated 'that one appointed to the priesthood is a more responsible guardian of the earth and what transpires upon it than one who wears the purple'.[36] Babylas had expelled the emperor from the Church because of his involvement in the murder of a young hostage.

John considers the question of truth in relation to the accusations of the pagans and says that it is so powerful that it has the capacity to survive and eventually be made manifest. Even if many try to extinguish it, not only is it not suppressed but it overcomes the attempt to destroy it with added lustre and stature.

> Our doctrine, which you say is fiction, has been assailed by tyrants, kings, orators of invincible eloquence, as well as by philosophers, sor-

33 *Pagans*, p. 214. 34 Ibid., p. 249. 35 Ibid., p. 248. 36 *Babylas*, p. 51.

> cerers, magicians and demons, and 'their tongues against them are made weak', according to the prophetic saying ... Emperors benefitted from their attack upon us only insofar as they gained a reputation for savagery worldwide. They were carried away by their anger against the martyrs into inhuman cruelty, and did not realize that they were incurring untold disgrace.[37]

Babylas had taken those who rejected Christianity to task, demonstrating that the philosophers they had chosen as their guide were 'characterized by vainglory, impudence and puerility'.[38] Chrysostom takes up this point and ridicules what he perceives as the inanity of some of their ascetical practices.[39] Reflecting on the emperor's sins, first that of the murder of the boy hostage and then the sacrilegious execution of Babylas, he goes on in an eloquent passage to describe the progressively deleterious effects of a sinful life:

> For a soul which once has tasted sin and becomes unfeeling, intensifies the malady more and more. Just as a spark falls into a huge forest and immediately ignites what it meets, and does not stop at that alone but extends to all the rest; and the more it captures with its flame, the more strength it acquires for the destruction of the remainder, and the multitude of stricken trees becomes a danger to the trees about to be vanquished, since the flame always arms itself against the trees that remain by what it has already captured – such is also the nature of sin: when it captures the mind and there is no one to extinguish the evil, it becomes more serious and intractable, as it gains ground. This is why the subsequent wrongdoings very often are more serious than the initial ones, because by additional sins the soul is continually aroused to greater madness and presumption, which weaken its own power and foster that of sin. In this way, to be sure, many fall into every kind of sin inadvertently, because they do not extinguish the incipient flame. Whence also that miserable man added to his earlier sins other worse ones.[40]

Attracted by the fame of sanctity of the martyr bishop, many visited his tomb in the grove of Daphne. Chrysostom describes 'the miraculous effect the

37 Ibid., p. 81. **38** Ibid., p. 100. **39** Now well into his stride he continues: 'I could also recount the absurdity, futility, and turpitude of the rest. Tell me, what is the use of eating human seed, as the Stagirite did? What profit to have intercourse with mothers and sisters, as the philosopher in charge of the Stoa legislated. As for the director of the Academy and his teacher and those whom they admire still more, I would expose their still greater depravity and, stripping off all the allegory, I would unveil pederasty, which they consider respectable and a part of philosophy, if my discourse were not so lengthy ... and had not amply convicted all by deriding one' (ibid.). **40** Ibid., pp 105–6.

consideration of the life of Babylas had even on those who went there with negative dispositions, and how those who were dissolute and licentious became temperate'.[41] He describes the change of fortune which occurred after Emperor Gallus died and was succeeded by Julian the Apostate. Gallus had shown that Christian respect due to the martyr bishop, but Julian, who initially played the role of the Christian emperor, was soon seen for what he really was. After the death of Constantius (361) he ordered the restoration of the pagan cults. John describes what happened, not as something new, but as recording what many people still living in Antioch had witnessed twenty years before.

Chrysostom wrote this apology about the year 382, that is, twenty years after the events he is describing. His criticism of Julian's behaviour is devastating:

> And the emperor dismissed generals and governors with contempt, but male and female prostitutes he made rise from the brothels in which they were prostituting themselves and form a cortege which he himself led around the streets of the entire city. And the royal cavalry and all the bodyguards followed behind at a great distance, while brothel-keepers, procuresses, and the entire company of prostitutes formed a circle with the emperor in the middle, promenading through the agora and speaking and laughing in the manner of people of this occupation. We know that to those who come after us these things will seem unbelievable because of their excessive irregularity: no ordinary person who leads a servile and ignominious existence would choose to act so unseemly in public. But I need not address myself to those who are still alive: they were present and observed these events taking place and now hear them also in narrative form. For this reason I am writing while there are still witnesses who survive; so that no one thinks that I am free to lie because I am recounting events of the past to people who are unfamiliar with them. For among the spectators of these events there still remain old men and youths, all of whom I request to come forward and prove that I have added anything. But they cannot convict me of adding but only of omitting some details, since it is impossible to represent in discourse the totality of the excess of his indecorum.[42]

WOMEN IN THE PREACHING OF JOHN CHRYSOSTOM

In fourth-century Antioch the primary role of women was seen as that of being mothers and homemakers. Chrysostom was of the opinion that woman was

41 Ibid., p. 117. **42** *Babylas*, p. 121.

better able to live a truly Christian life than man because she lived in the relative quiet of the home, while the husband was preoccupied with the affairs of the marketplace and the law courts. As regards the position of women, he follows the Pauline idea that while man is the image of the glory of God, the woman is man's glory (cf. 1 Cor 11:7). 'One is in command', he says, 'the other is subordinate, just as God had also said to woman from the beginning, "your yearning shall be for your husband, and he will be your master" (Gen 3:16)'.[43] Woman was created for the consolation of man, not man for woman (cf. 1 Cor 11:9).[44] At the same time he has a clear conception of the equal dignity of man and woman before God. In his commentary on the creation of Eve ('Let us make him a helpmate like himself' [Gen 2:20]) he says that Adam's companion was of the same kind as himself, with the same properties, of equal esteem, in no way inferior to him.[45]

He had a very high estimation of the influence of women especially on their husbands. When he returns home she can soothe his cares, help him to get rid of useless or angry thoughts, and send him off the next day cleansed of the aggression of the marketplace. 'Indeed nothing – nothing I repeat – is more potent than a good and prudent woman in moulding a man and shaping his soul in whatever way she desires.'[46] Because of his love for her a man will take advice from his wife when he will take it from nobody else.

> She shares with him his table and his couch, the procreating of his children, his spoken words and secret thoughts, his comings and goings, and a great many other things as well. She is devoted to him in all things and as closely bound to him as the body is fastened to the head.[47]

A prudent and diligent wife can, in Chrysostom's experience, transform a husband from being harsh and stubborn into a refined and civilized human being. She is the most important influence in the formation of the children.

At the same time he also encouraged husbands to show due honour and affection towards their wives: 'Show your wife you appreciate her company a lot and that you prefer to be at home rather than outside, because she is there. Show her a preference among all your friends and even above the children she has given you; love them because of her.'[48]

After outlining the influence women like Deborah, Judith and Esther exercised on men in Old Testament times, and how Persis, Mary and Priscilla shared effectively the apostolate of St Paul (Rom 16; 1 Cor 16:19), he encourages the

43 *Homily no. 8 on Genesis*, p. 111, in *St John Chrysostom, Homilies on Genesis*, vol. I (nos. 1–17), vol. II (nos. 18–45), vol. III (nos. 46–67), (Washington, DC, 1986). Subsequently this reference will be abbreviated after the style *Genesis no. 8*, p. 111. 44 *Genesis no. 15*, p. 200. 45 Ibid., p. 197. 46 *John no. 8*, p. 161. 47 Ibid. 48 *Homily no. 20*, on *Ephesians*.

women in his congregation: 'You also ought to imitate these women, and mould the character of your husbands, not only by your words but also by your example.'[49] In reply to an imaginary question from a woman in the congregation as to how to do this, he replies: 'When your husband sees that you are not an evil woman, or a busybody and a fashion plate, and that you do not demand an extravagant expenditure of money, but are content with what you have, then, then indeed, he will bear with you even when you give him advice.'[50]

Obviously the question of extravagant expenditure by women on personal adornment was no insignificant issue for some husbands in fourth-century Antioch. Wives are advised that they will be more immediately listened to if, instead of looking for golden trinkets, pearls, and extensive wardrobes, they cut down on their personal budgets and concentrate on modest and decorous behaviour. Adornment of the soul, Chrysostom reminds them, expressed in tenderness and decorum, will make them much more attractive to their husbands than the decking out of their bodies with expensive apparel. Physical beauty palls as it becomes more familiar, whereas the soul can grow more beautiful every day by the adornment of the virtues, and enkindle a still greater flame of love. 'So', he concludes, 'if you wish to please your husband, adorn your soul with chastity, piety, and the careful management of your household.'[51] For such a woman, he says, the praise of men will be hers in abundance; in addition the reward in store for her from God will be a generous one. Not only has John of the Golden Mouth great moral insight; it is clear that he has a deep knowledge of feminine psychology as well.

Chrysostom had a particular devotion to women martyrs. 'I greatly love the commemoration of the martyrs', he says, 'but especially when it is of a woman, for the weaker the vessel the greater the grace, the more noble the trophy the grander the victory – not because the sex of the heroine is frail but because the Enemy is overcome by the very things that once served his triumph. He overcame by a woman, but now he is overcome by a woman; a woman was once his instrument but now she is the instrument of his defeat, and he finds that this vessel cannot be broken; the first woman sinned and died, and now a woman dies rather than sin … What excuse can weak and cowardly men have when women bear themselves so bravely and manfully?'[52]

Chrysostom can at times be quite severe on the fair sex. He denounces the tendency some women of his time had to make a show of lamentation and grief on the death of loved ones, 'bareing their arms, tearing their hair, making scratches down their cheeks'. What is even worse, some do these things to attract the attention of men. At the thought of this disorder, the preacher of Antioch really gets worked up:

49 *John no. 8*, p. 161. **50** Ibid., p. 162. **51** Ibid., pp 162–3. **52** Attwater, pp 53–4.

> What are you doing, O women? Tell me, do you who are a member of Christ, shamelessly strip yourself in the middle of the market-place, when men are present there? Do you tear your hair and rend your garments, and utter loud cries, and gather a chorus around you, and act like a mad woman, and do you think you are not offensive to God? What great insanity is this?[53]

His point is that for Christians to behave in this way is a source of scandal to pagans, and will confirm them in their unbelief about the resurrection. Honouring the dead does not consist in mourning and lamentation, he says, but is best achieved by giving alms, performing good works, and taking part in divine service.

In the context of his commentary on Christ's words addressed to his Mother at the foot of the Cross, Chrysostom has generous praise for mothers, especially those who do not impose obstacles to the vocational commitments of their children:

> We must give them everything that is their due, and place them ahead of all others, in return for bringing us into existence, in return for their care of us, in return for the numberless ways in which they have helped us.[54]

In his treatise *On the priesthood* he tells us how much he owed to the care and self-sacrifice of his own mother; it was she who drew from one of John's pagan teachers the admiring remark, 'What splendid women there are among the Christians!'[55] In the same vein, when reflecting on Mary Magdalen's love for Christ and her weeping at the empty tomb (cf. Jn 20:11), he remarks: 'How tender-hearted and inclined to sympathy is womankind.'[56] All of which adds up to saying that, while some of his attitudes to women were unyielding, he had a real appreciation of those feminine qualities which represented the uniqueness and the best in womanhood.

In passing it is of interest to hear Chrysostom's opinion about the possibility of women priests, which is not irrelevant to the current debate on this topic. 'The divine law has excluded them from this ministry,' he says uncompromisingly. And still, he continues, 'they strive to force their way into it', and since they cannot succeed they work through others. Their influence is such, he claims, that 'they appoint to the priesthood and depose from it whomsoever they please', to the extent that the words of Scripture, 'subjects govern their rulers' (Eccles 10:7) are fulfilled. Indeed, he concludes, 'I have heard it stated

53 *John no. 62*, p. 174. 54 *John no. 85*, p. 433. 55 Attwater, p. 10. 56 *John no. 86*, p. 446.

that they have assumed such licence as to rebuke bishops of the Church more severely than masters do their slaves.'[57] Chrysostom would hardly be a popular figure among contemporary feminists pressing for the ordination of women.

And yet these comments would give an unfair impression of John's attitude to women. There are over 200 of his letters extant from the time of his exile (404–7), chief among these being seventeen he wrote to Olympias, a widow and a great servant of the church in Constantinople, who was one of the most devoted of his friends. He writes to her with affection, interest and concern for her spiritual welfare. In one of these letters he tells her, 'Give me some account from time to time of your own health; and also tell me that the cloud of despondency has passed away from you. If I were assured of this from yourself, I should write more frequently to you, under a feeling that my letters might be of service.'[58] Or again, writing to the same correspondent from his exile, and encouraging her in a particular sorrow she had to endure, he tells her:

> Greater also will be your reward, if you persevere under it with thanksgiving and becoming fortitude, as you do. You know this well, my religious lady; therefore beware of surrendering yourself to the tyranny of sorrow. You can command yourself; the tempest is not beyond your skill. And send me a letter to tell me this; that, though I live in a strange land, I may enjoy much cheerfulness from the assurance that you bear your trials with the understanding and wisdom which becomes you.[59]

CHASTITY

It is not surprising that in cities like Antioch and Constantinople, where immoral living was commonplace, Chrysostom frequently preached about chastity. He is realistic about the human condition, but is convinced of the transforming power of grace: 'We have by nature a desire for sexual intercourse but when we practise chastity we weaken the power of this urge. God has implanted in us, the desire for carnal intercourse for the sake of perpetuating our race by the generation of children, but without forbidding us to follow the higher way of continence.'[60]

Soon after becoming patriarch of Constantinople (397), he issued two pastoral letters dealing with the rather irregular situation of consecrated virgins in that city. The first was addressed to clerics, and in it he condemns the

57 *On the priesthood*, p. 50. 58 Letter no. 10, as quoted by John Henry Newman in his study of Chrysostom, in *Historical sketches*, vol. II (London, 1876), p. 242. 59 Letter no. 9, ibid., p. 252. 60 *John no. 85*, p. 432.

custom followed by some priests of having 'spiritual sisters', who were often consecrated virgins, in their homes to keep house for them, contrary to the express prohibition of the Council of Nicea (325). The second insisted that women religious should not have men residing permanently with them under the same roof. He pointed out that there had been no great amount of wrong-doing, but that such a situation inevitably gave rise to scandal. Though he writes with great pastoral zeal, the language is often sharp, comparing, as he does, such houses to brothels. Naturally these pastoral letters caused great indignation among the worldly-minded clergy.[61]

In his preaching he encouraged his audience to have great esteem for Christian virginity as something 'surpassing human nature and requiring assistance from on high', because those 'who have followed the vocation to virginity for the love of Christ imitate the life of angels though treading the earth and being clad in a body'.[62] This is perhaps an over-spiritualized view of virginity. We do not have an angelic but a human nature, and thus the beauty of virginity is grounded in the fact that it is a quality of both body and soul. Christian virginity, according to Chrysostom, found its highest expression in the virgin motherhood of Mary.[63] On the other hand, in his treatise *On virginity*, he denounces the pestilential errors of the Manichaeans and others who regarded marriage as sinful. While initially, in his zeal to defend the excellence of celibacy, he expresses some jaundiced views about marriage, as he grew in years and experience his appreciation of the marriage vocation developed and matured. Recalling Sarah and Abraham, the mother of the Maccabees, Aquila and Priscilla, he outlines the ideal and the reality of marriage very beautifully.[64]

On one occasion his context for preaching about chastity is a commentary on the idea that orthodoxy of doctrine is of no value if it is not accompanied by an upright life. He goes on to develop the point that if a man is unfaithful to his wife, he will be lost even if he has innumerable good works to his credit, 'because it is impossible to enter the kingdom of heaven if one is guilty of fornication, something which is even more true of adultery'.[65] Indeed he says a man is unpardonable if, though he has a wife and enjoys consolation in her, he brazenly has an affair with another: 'If cohabitation makes husband and wife one body, the man who lives with a harlot must become one body with her. How then', he asks, 'can a chaste woman accept him, since she is a member of Christ? Or how can she join to herself the member of a harlot?'[66] He admonishes his congregation that sexual immorality gives rise to innumerable evil consequences in this life, and one that brings everlasting punishment in the next.

61 Cf. *Adversus eos qui apud se habent virgines subintroductas* and *Quod regulares feminae viris cohibitare non debeant*, PG 47: 495–532. **62** *Genesis no. 18*, p. 11. **63** Ibid., *no. 49*, p. 46. **64** Cf. Attwater, pp 26–7. **65** *John no. 63*, p. 187. **66** Ibid., p. 189.

Chrysosdom warns those who are not prepared to get rid of the disease of impurity not to set foot inside the door of the church, since like a sheep with mange they would infect the other members of the flock. As they have become members of Christ, he urges them not to

> become members of a harlot. This place is not a house of ill-fame, but a church. And if you have the members of a harlot, do not stand in the church lest you offer insult to the place. Indeed [he warns] even if there were no hell, even if there were no punishment, how do you dare to cleave to another woman after the marriage vows made there, and the bridal torches, after that lawful couch, after the begetting of your children, after such intimate companionship?[67]

He leaves them in no doubt about the punishment merited by such deeds. However, as in all his sermons, he finishes on a positive note: 'May no one here present be subject to that penalty. On the contrary, by practising sanctity may we all deserve to behold Christ and to attain the blessings promised.'[68]

PRISONS AND PRISONERS

Chrysostom, we have seen, was acutely conscious of the condition of the more deprived members of society. In his sermons he often promoted the corporal works of mercy. In particular, in reference to the judgement (Mt 25:36 and 43), he speaks about the salutary effects of visiting prisons where, in fourth-century Antioch, conditions were atrocious. Men were bound with fetters, unkempt and clad in rags; some had their flesh torn by lashes, others were wasting away through hunger. The experience of such deprivation, he tells us, has the effect of focusing a man's mind on the consequences of the judgement and turning him away from sinful pursuits, especially carnal pleasures. 'Even', he says, ' if a licentious prostitute should meet a man as he is on his way from visiting the prison, it would do the latter no harm. For as one who has finally become immune, he will not thus be caught in the snare of that sight, since the fear of the judgement is at that moment before his eyes, rather than that wanton face.'[69]

We might be unable to bring in food to the prisoner or help by giving money. However, we can still cheer them with our company, and by doing what we can assist them in other ways such as by our conversation with the gaolers, and by making the guards more kindly disposed. Clearly, John is

67 Ibid., p. 190. **68** Ibid. **69** *John no. 59*, p. 145.

speaking here from personal experience. Elsewhere, in words put on our Lord's lips, he develops the spiritual consequences of this work of mercy:

> I am in prison. I do not ask you to free me. I only wish, that for your own good, you pay me a visit. That will be enough for me, and in return I will make you a gift of heaven. I have freed you from a prison a thousand times more harsh. But I am happy if you come and visit me from time to time.[70]

Although a person might object that prisons are filled with despicable types such as murderers, grave-robbers, purse-snatchers, adulterers and the like, Chrysostom retorts that precisely because he speaks in such terms about the prisoners, the objector clearly demonstrates his need to visit a prison. In this way, not only will he acquire a deeper appreciation of the misfortune of others and become less judgemental in outlook. He will also begin to realize that he himself has committed many offences which are deserving of punishment whether through calling his brother a fool, looking at a woman with unchaste glances, or partaking unworthily of the Eucharist. Consequently, we should not be harsh judges of others, after the example of Joseph in the prisons of Egypt. In addition, we will often find some admirable people in prison, and if we visit these institutions frequently, we will not fail to come across such men.

To emphasize this point Chrysostom said that Christ did not just speak to the just and flee the impure. On the contrary he dined with publicans and sinners. He received the Canaanite woman kindly, 'and also the Samaritan woman who was under a cloud, and impure besides. Further, He received and restored to spiritual health another harlot, because of whom even the Jews reproached Him, and He allowed his feet to be washed by the tears of an impure woman, to teach us to show a kindly attitude to those who are in sin.'[71] He goes on to point out that there are a lot of people walking free whose lifestyle merits imprisonment, such as those who carry on fraudulent business of different kinds, and that consequently we shouldn't overlook our own faults and sit in judgement on others, because it is 'difficult to find a man who is innocent of unjust dealing'.[72] Clearly the Antiochenes had quite a reputation for sharp practice in business affairs! He finishes up this particular homily by encouraging his congregation to visit prisons frequently, and to redirect into such good works their enthusiasm for the theatre and time wasted formerly in the marketplace and profitless pursuits. These works will be instrumental in obtaining many blessings for themselves as well as for those in prison.

70 *Homilies on Romans*, no. 15. 71 *John no. 59*, p. 147. 72 Ibid., p. 148.

THEATRE

One of the difficulties which the preacher had to contend with in Chrysostom's time was that many of the faithful, influenced by secular debate, tended to adopt the attitude of spectators at theatrical displays when they came to church. Thus they took sides, and listened to some preachers indulgently while others they treated with dislike. Consequently, St John says, they tended to listen more for pleasure than for profit. This propensity obviously made life difficult for preachers in fourth-century Antioch. They were quick to detect any plagiarism in the discourse of the preacher and as a consequence he was 'subjected to reproaches greater than if he had been guilty of theft'.[73] And so Chrysostom advises that the preacher should be able to check the inordinate passions of the people and to direct their attention to more profitable objects without, however, becoming their slave. To be a good preacher the first aim should be to please God.

The theatre, as we have seen, was a frequent topic of stricture in the homilies of Chrysostom. The Antiochenes had a passion for games and the theatre. If there is a renowned musician in town, the same spectators who flocked to see the athletes now fill the theatre: 'Having put aside all immediate occupations, necessary and urgent though these often are, they go up and take their seats, and most eagerly listen to the songs and accompaniments, criticizing the harmony of both. Indeed, this is the practice of the majority of men'.[74] As Chrysostom saw it, the theatre was essentially a pagan pursuit, inimical to Christian values and a constant danger to morals. The pagan performances, he says, are really festivals of evil spirits, not human shows. He chides his listeners about getting bored if his sermon is too long, yet they can happily spend from midday to nightfall at the theatre. He admonishes them that going to these spectacles is incompatible with sharing the table of the Lord.

Why this harsh rejection of the theatre? Basically because of its frivolity and indecency: 'In truth everything there is ridicule, everything is dishonour, everything is scurrility – both railings and gibes; everything is licence, everything is corruption.'[75] He castigates his listeners who know everything about dancers, charioteers and fighters, and can win arguments about their favourite performers, yet they give no thought or effort to defending the teaching of Christ and his marvellous deeds by which he attracted the whole world to himself.[76] They can talk endlessly about fighters and dancers, yet they are unable to put two sentences together about the things of God.[77] He reminds his congregation that it would be much more meritorious to give their money to the

73 *On the priesthood*, p. 108. 74 *John no. 1*, p. 3. 75 Ibid., p. 11. 76 Cf. *John no. 17*, p. 171. 77 Cf. ibid., *no. 18*, p. 185.

poor than to squander it to watch dancers. Not only are they wasting their money but, through their continued, ill-advised sponsorship of the performers, they will cause the latter to lose their souls.[78]

One aspect of the theatre which provokes the full wrath of Chrysostom's criticism is the effect the women performers have on men. For when they leave the theatre,

> they are on fire, burning with sinful desire. Indeed, when they have seen those lavishly decked out women on the stage, and have received innumerable moral injuries from the sight, they will be no more at peace than a billowy sea, as the impression of the faces, the clothing, the words, the gait, and all the other things, rises before their eyes and lays siege to their souls.[79]

However, Chrysostom has a soft heart and, despite his strictures, he again tries to end on a positive note. 'I should like to make these remarks frequently', he says in relation to the theatre, 'but I fear that I should be making myself unpleasant to you in vain and without profit ... Do my words prick you? I want them to do so; I want to place a restraint on you by means of the compunction aroused by my words, that you may reform your bad conduct in these matters.'[80]

FASTING

As we have already seen, fasting was an integral part of fourth-century Christian practice in Antioch. It should perhaps be pointed out that in the Eastern Church the laws of fasting are still quite rigorous, and have not been mitigated to the extent they have been in the Western Church. The many benefits of this practice are alluded to by Chrysostom. Fasting teaches us to keep anger in check, acquire mildness and kindness, develop a contrite heart, and banish a flood of unworthy passions.[81] Fasting will have this salutary effect on the soul if it is complemented by a prayerful reading of Scripture. For what is the good of it, he asks, if, at the same time, you waste your time on brainless nonsense like dice-throwing, and the shouting and brawls which it gives rise to? Fasting will lead to 'generous alms-giving, fervent prayers, and a heightened enthusiasm for listening to the divine sayings'. It will promote reconciliation with enemies and eradicate vindictiveness of soul. 'It holds the body

78 Cf. ibid., *no. 42*, p. 434. **79** *John no. 60*, p. 145. **80** *John no. 58*, p. 117. **81** *Genesis no. 8*, p. 113.

under restraint, checks its unruly movements, and, on the other hand, renders the soul transparent, gives it wings, makes it light and raises it on high'.[82] Indeed, sobriety in food leads to good health and avoids the disorders stemming from laden tables and immoderate eating, causing gout, migraine and countless other ailments.[83]

The Lenten fast in Antioch was relaxed on two days of the week. Chrysostom explained that just in the same way there are stopping places along the highways to enable the travellers rest from their weariness, so the Lord granted a short rest of two days each week 'so that we should rest the body a little from the rigours of fasting and comfort the soul', and thus be able to resume fasting again with enthusiasm.[84]

USE OF SCRIPTURE

Chrysostom had a great love and reverence for the Scriptures because in them he sees God speaking to us in human language. *Dei verbum*, the Vatican II constitution on Divine Revelation, repeats the words of Chrysostom about the *condescension* of divine wisdom in the inspired text so 'that we may come to know the ineffable loving-kindness of God and see for ourselves how far he has gone in adapting his language with thoughtful concern for our nature'.[85] Both *Dei verbum*, and before it Pius XII's encyclical *Divino Afflante Spiritu*,[86] refer to the writings of Chrysostom as a means for probing more deeply into the incarnational aspects of the Scriptures, drawing particularly on his distinctive notion of *synkatabasis* or divine considerateness. In his homilies on the book of Genesis, John frequently refers to God's gracious acceptance of the limitations of the human condition. In a manner analogous to that in which the divine is hidden in the Incarnate Word, so also the glory of God is veiled in human thought and discourse.[87]

His respect and veneration for the inspired text comes through in a constant way. Scripture, he tells us, 'says nothing idly or by chance; every single sound and syllable has a treasure contained in it.'[88] There is nothing superfluous in Scripture. In the same way that in working gold mines, an expert in metallurgy doesn't allow the smallest vein to be bypassed since it could produce great wealth, so in the study of the Bible not a single jot or flourish should be overlooked, because 'all are uttered by the Holy Spirit and there is nothing unimportant in them.'[89] The meaning of Scripture is not on the surface of the text,

82 Cf. *Genesis no. 10*, p. 129. **83** Cf. ibid., p. 130. **84** *Genesis no. 11*, pp 143–4. **85** *In Gen* 3:8; hom. 17,1, quoted in *Dei verbum* 13; see A. Flannery (ed.), *Vatican II: the conciliar and post conciliar documents* (Dublin, 1981), p. 758. **86** AAS 35 (1943) 316. **87** Cf. *Homilies on Genesis*, vol. I, Introduction, p. 17, by R. Hill. **88** *Genesis no. 18*, p. 13. **89** *John no. 36*, p. 351.

nor in the literal sense only, 'but, like a treasure, lies buried at a great depth'. To discover this treasure requires a careful and painstaking search.[90] Thus in the same way that if an inexperienced person were to try to dig a mine, he would not produce gold, but engage in fruitless work, so also those who are unacquainted with the sequence of Holy Scripture, its distinctive forms and laws, but merely perused all of it in the same way, would mix gold with earth and would not be able to discover the hidden treasure buried there.[91] Consequently the Bible should not be read casually or superficially, 'but with all care, so that one may not be confused.'[92] Vigilance, much study and earnest prayer are necessary to penetrate even a little into the mysteries contained therein.[93]

In particular he encouraged his congregation to focus on the Passion narrative: 'We should read our Lord's Passion constantly; what great benefit we will gain by doing so. Even if you are as hard as stone, when you contemplate that he was sarcastically adorned, then ridiculed, beaten and subjected to the final agonies, you will be moved to cast all pride from your soul.'[94]

Chrysostom had an encyclopaedic knowledge of the Scriptures. One commentator says that 'he had the Bible at his fingertips, and he expects his congregation to resonate to his wide-ranging scriptural references, which are not always explicit.'[95] What are the uses of Scripture? In one of his homilies John summarizes the good effects to be expected from listening to commentaries on it in church or from private reading at home: they are

> a treasury containing every sort of remedy, so that, whether one needs to put down senseless pride, or to quench the fire of concupiscence, or to trample on the love of riches, or to despise pain, or to cultivate cheerfulness and acquire patience – in them one may find in abundance the means to do so.[96]

Many blessings come from reading Scripture. It gives an appreciation of wisdom, raises the soul to heavenly things, and prevents us getting too excited about earthly realities. It fortifies our knowledge if we are assiduous in applying ourselves to its contents. And even if we weren't lucky enough to have a human teacher to explain it to us, 'the Lord himself would come from on high to enlighten our minds, shed light on our thinking, bring our attention to what had slipped our notice, and act as our instructor in what we have no knowledge of – provided we are prepared to contribute what lies in our power.'[97]

90 Cf. *John no. 41*, p. 415. **91** Cf. *John no. 40*, p. 403. Elsewhere he says, in the same vein, that 'Scripture has certain modes of speaking peculiar to it and it is necessary to observe its rules' (*John no. 68*, p. 239). **92** *John no. 58*, p. 116. **93** *John no. 21*, p. 202. **94** *Homilies on the Gospel of St Matthew*, 87,1. **95** *Homilies on Genesis*, vol. I, Introduction, p. 16. **96** *John no. 37*, p. 359. **97** *Genesis no. 35*, p. 305.

Chrysostom tells the Christians of Antioch that they will be able to silence the critics of the faith if they 'pay attention to the Scriptures and do not listen merely cursorily to them'. After a year of listening to the sacred text being read and commented on in church, even without reading them at home, if they pay attention to what is said, they will become quite familiar with them. He complains, however, that they are so apathetic, that even after such reading, they hardly know the names of the books. And they are not in the slightest ashamed about this. On the other hand, if a musician, or a dancer or anyone else connected with the theatre is in town, they will hurry off and spend an entire half-day with their attention fixed exclusively on the performer. 'Yet', he berates his audience, 'when God addresses us through Prophets and Apostles, we yawn, are bored, become drowsy.'[98]

HOME STUDY OF SCRIPTURE

Apart from coming to church to hear the word of God, John also encouraged his audience to study Scripture at home at least one day a week, and to read in advance the passages that will be commented on in church. In this way his work of preaching will be made easier because they will be familiar with the general tone of the words. As a consequence they will become more discerning and more eager to teach others.[99] He is familiar with the excuses people make for not reading Scripture – demanding business routine, hectic social life, or time given to the theatre or horse racing 'in which they often spend entire days'.[1] Another excuse the Antiochenes make is that they can't get books. For the rich he says this is a ridiculous argument. But even the poorer in his congregation don't get off lightly with this pretext. And besides, if they made a real effort to learn from his preaching in church, they would be well instructed in Scripture.[2]

As an example of commitment to Bible reading he lauds the efforts of the Ethiopian government official reading the Scriptures in his chariot on his way home from Jerusalem (cf. Acts 8:26–40). Chrysostom assures his audience that it is no easy matter to read while riding in a chariot (obviously having tried something similar himself). Yet this man was seriously attempting to do so, even though he didn't understand very much of what he was reading and was a pagan to boot. 'Let this be heeded by those people who don't even deign to do it at home', he expostulates, 'but rather think reading the Scriptures is a waste of time: claiming as an excuse their living with a wife, conscription in

98 *John no. 58*, p. 116. **99** See *John no. 11*, p. 104. **1** Ibid., p. 105. Elsewhere he berates them for having games and dice at home but never books (see *John no. 32*, p. 319). **2** Ibid., p. 106.

military service, caring for children, attending to domestics, and looking after other concerns, they don't think it necessary for them to show any interest in reading the Holy Scriptures'.[3] On the contrary, this barbarian doesn't neglect spiritual reading even on a journey, and 'is capable of proving a teacher of us all, those living a private life, those enlisted in military service, those who happen to be surrounded with pomp and circumstance, people in general, not only men – also women as well, as much those who live in the monastic life as those who spend their time at home'.[4] Chrysostom says that we can learn from this financial minister of the Kandake of Ethiopia that no job or time is an obstacle to Scripture reading. 'Rather, it is possible not only at home but also moving about in public, making a journey, being in the company of a crowd and involved in business affairs, to give oneself earnestly to these sayings'.[5]

While he encourages study of the inspired text, he puts the matter into context by telling his congregation that he is asking for less effort from them than they impose on their own children to learn at school. He expects them to come two days a week to church and explains the purpose of his progressive commentaries on the sacred text:

> We hope that it may be possible for you to receive them with ease, and store them in the treasury of your mind, and thus strive to remember them all, so that you may be able to repeat them accurately; unless, that is (here follows another of his typical chiding remarks), 'you should be very sluggish and slothful and lazier than a small boy'.[6]

Yet he also has high expectations in relation to children's familiarity with the Bible. 'Do you want your child to be obedient?' he asks.

> Then from the beginning bring him up in the discipline and instruction of the Lord. Don't think that it isn't necessary for a child to listen to the Scriptures; don't say, 'Bible-reading is for monks; am I turning my child into a monk?' No, it isn't necessary for him to be a monk. Make him into a Christian! Why are you afraid of something so good? ... We are so concerned with our children's schooling; if only we were equally zealous in bringing them up in the discipline and instruction of the Lord! (And then we wonder why we reap such bitter fruit when we have raised our children to be insolent, licentious, impious, and vulgar.) Let us heed the blessed Paul's admonition to bring them up in the discipline and instruction of the Lord. Let us give them a pattern to imitate; from their earliest years let us teach them to study the Bible ... Don't surround

3 *Genesis no. 35*, p. 305. 4 Ibid., p. 308. 5 Ibid. 6 *John no. 25*, p. 242.

> them with the external safeguards of wealth and fame, for when these fail – and they will fail – our children will stand naked and defenceless, having gained no profit from their former prosperity, but only injury, since when these artificial protections that shielded them from the winds are removed, they will be blown to the ground in a moment. Therefore wealth is a hindrance, because it leaves us unprepared for the hardships of life. So, let us raise our children in such a way that they can face any trouble, and not be surprised when difficulties come: let us bring them up in the discipline and instruction of the Lord.[7]

Careful and systematic study of the Bible will, according to Chrysostom, lead us to salvation, teach us sound doctrine, and an upright way of life. However, reading the Scriptures frequently does not produce the effects in the soul that it should. Why is this? Because 'we do not read them carefully, with compunction and contrition and remorse, but merely casually whenever we have time. Therefore since a great deal of debris accumulates from worldly affairs, it buries everything and, if there is any gain, destroys it'. So Chrysostom proposes as a remedy that people would study Scripture with presence of God, and then visit the tombs of the dead to be appropriately reminded of where their future lies also.[8]

POVERTY AND RICHES

One of the recurring themes in the preaching of Chrysostom is his concern for the poor. From the opposite perspective he speaks very harshly against greed, love of money, and constantly recommends alms-giving because of its salutary effects for the soul. In this context he points again and again to the importance of the Christian virtue of poverty for all, as expressed in a spirit of detachment from wealth and material well-being. There was clearly a stark contrast between the luxurious living of some and the plight of the many poor in fourth-century Antioch.

The debilitating effects of wealth on Christian living is reiterated by Chrysostom. 'In truth', he says, 'nothing so clouds the mind as clinging to present things', and unless we let go of them we will not 'be able truly to attain to heavenly things'.[9] He asks his listeners to learn from what they often see happening to others – at their last gasp they unwillingly leave their possessions to those around them and suffer much as a consequence. To avoid this trauma,

7 *Homily on Ephesians* 6:1–4, 'On marriage and the family', trans. Catherine P. Roth and David Anderson (Crestwood, NY, 1986). 8 *John no. 84*, p. 426. 9 *John no. 8*, p. 85.

while still in possession of good health he recommends that they bestow their wealth on projects for the benefit of souls. In this way not only will they enjoy the use of their resources, but they will win merits for themselves in heaven. One of the best ways of giving over our possessions to God is through alms-giving. Indeed Chrysostom goes so far as to say that 'it is impossible, even if we perform countless good works, to enter the portals of the kingdom without alms-giving'.[10]

John uses different images and analogies to impress on the Antiochenes the importance of this virtue of detachment. 'If you are wealthy', he tells them, 'you will not rejoice in your wealth because you have heard that she who was the wife of the carpenter and born of a humble family became mother of your Lord. Moreover, if you are poor, you will not be ashamed of your poverty, because you have learned that the Creator of the world was not ashamed of a very poor dwelling.'[11] If Christians reflect on these facts they will not be covetous, nor rob, nor steal; rather they will be desirous of poverty and despise wealth. 'And', he assures them, 'if this happens you will banish all evil.' Looking at the Child in the manger they will see the futility of wasting superfluous money adorning their own children.[12]

He repeats these things constantly and he 'will not cease from them, not so much from solicitude for the poor as for your salvation'.[13] To do this he frequently refers to the parable of the rich man and Lazarus. As an antidote to the desire for wealth he asks them to think about the day of judgement and what happened to the rich man in the parable: 'Let us say both to others and to ourselves as well: "There is a resurrection, and a fearful judgement awaits us"'.[14] Wealth, he warns, is a very ephemeral thing:

> shadow without substance, smoke that vanishes, flower of the field – nay, rather more worthless than a flower. Why then do you boast of grass? Does not wealth belong to thieves, and effeminates, and harlots, and grave robbers? Do you, then, vaunt yourself on this: that you have such as these as sharers in your wealth?[15]

So if pleading does not work, he tries to shame them into living virtuous lives.

Avarice, he warns his congregation, is the root of all evils. And by all accounts it would seem to have been a fairly widespread vice in Antioch. 'Let us, then, dread it', he implores, 'let us flee from this sin.'

> Give to the needy [he encourages those who frequent the theatre], let us refrain from this profitless expenditure; let us learn for what and

10 *John no. 23*, p. 231. 11 *John no. 53*, p. 63. 12 Ibid. 13 *John no. 27*, p. 267. 14 *John no. 45*, p. 458. 15 *John no. 33*, p. 330.

> when we ought to dispense our wealth. Let us not incur the anger of God by reason of the two extremes: both if we amass wealth from a source from whence we ought not, and if we spend it lavishly on what we ought not. Indeed, how much wrath would you not deserve if, while giving to a harlot, you ignore a poor man? Even if you are dispensing the fruits of honest toil, would it not be blameworthy to furnish the means of paying for evil, and to show esteem for things which deserve only punishment? If ever you support licentiousness by stripping orphans and dealing unjustly with widows, think what sort of punishment is in store for those who dare to do these deeds?[16]

The desire for money, in Chrysostom's book, is more bitter than any tyranny, because it brings no pleasure but only 'cares and envy and scheming, and hatred and slander, and countless hindrances to virtue: laxity, licentiousness, greed, drunkenness. These make even free men slaves and worse than slaves bought with silver; slaves, not of men but of the most serious of the passions and of the diseases of the soul'.[17] Surely man has a higher destiny than that? he wonders aloud to his congregation. He is saddened by the thought that all they will say is that he is harping on this topic every day. His response to this complaint is typical of the man: 'Would that it were possible to speak about it every night also!' And he continues in the same vein in a memorable passage,

> Would that I might follow you in the marketplace and at table. Would that wives and friends and children and servants and husbandmen and neighbours, and the very pavement and walls might be able to shout forth this word that we might then cease for at least a little while. This contagion has seized upon the whole world, and the great tyranny of mammon possesses the souls of all men. We have been redeemed by Christ and become the slaves of gold. We proclaim the rule of one Master and obey another'.[18]

He warns the Antiochenes against creating extra needs for themselves, because by doing so they circumscribe their own freedom. 'Complete freedom', he tells them, 'is to be in need of nothing at all'.[19] Love of wealth will be a cause of punishment if we do not take care, whereas living Christian poverty will be a source of peace and refreshment. Love of poverty means that we do not look for security in this life but in the next, that we do away with the superfluous and spend our possessions generously on the needy.[20] Perhaps his

16 *John no. 42*, p. 434. **17** *John no. 59*, p. 130. **18** *John no. 76*, p. 322. **19** *John no. 80*, p. 376. **20** The reason for the disparity in the distribution of wealth he explains as follows: 'Do you not

strongest rebuke for the Christians of Antioch is to tell them that he is ashamed to see some of the pagans despising wealth 'while all of us have a frenzied desire for it'.[21]

HOMILIES ON ST JOHN'S GOSPEL

We will already have gleaned much about Chrysostom's preaching style. However, it will be useful to examine it a little more closely in relation to his commentaries on St John's Gospel. The eighty-eight homilies making up this text were preached at Antioch about the year 390, usually in a church and in the early morning. The structure of the homilies followed a definite pattern. Each begins with a brief, rather informal introduction. This is followed by the explanation of or commentary upon one or more Gospel verses. The commentary is often rambling in style, leading the preacher down several byroads as he develops his theme. He draws his audience into the Gospel scene and, by the skilful use of imagery and dialogue, graphically unfolds the deeper meaning of the inspired text. Afterwards there is a moral exhortation, usually centred on a particular virtue, or its corresponding vice, often suggested by the text of the day. The diversity of life in the thriving city of Antioch provided him with abundant material on which to make penetrating moral comment and to drive home the salutary lesson. As one commentator points out, 'all the capital sins are castigated in turn in the form in which they are most prevalent'.[22] But, as already noted, covetousness in its multiple forms comes in for particular mention.

The eternal truths are never far from the mind of Chrysostom in his preaching, and thus the rewards of heaven and the pains of damnation are frequently referred to as an incitement to virtue and the avoidance of sin. Although the homilies are addressed to a fourth-century congregation, they have a perennial character and relevance. Every aspect of human morality is dealt with: bearing wrongs patiently, the evil of adultery, avoiding bad companionship, imitating the gentleness of Christ, the good influence of the mother in the home. We learn much too about the social and cultural history of the times through his comments on the theatre, dance, horse racing, the extravagance of women on self-adornment and the conditions in prisons. There is no facet of human life on which he did not discourse.

see how God has apportioned all things to us in common? In fact he has permitted some to be poor in the world's goods. He has also permitted this for the consolation of the wealthy, that they may be able to be rid of their sins by giving alms to the poor' (*John no.* 77, p. 337). **21** *John no. 84*, p. 426. **22** St John Chrysostom, *Commentary on St John's Gospel*, vol. II, Introduction, p. ix, by Sr Thomas Aquinas Goggin, SCH.

The Johannine homilies are more controversial in tone then those on Matthew, Acts or Romans. This is because in his exegesis of texts that have been misused by Arians, Manichaeans and other heretics, he includes their arguments, placing them in the mouth of an imaginary heckler, and then proceeds to demolish them skilfully. Let us hear how he approaches the task of preaching in his own words:

> Now, my preaching is addressed to all and provides a remedy in common for those who need one, but it is the duty of each one of my listeners to take what is suited for his affliction. I do not know who are the sick, who are the healthy. Therefore, I discuss subjects of every sort and suited to every ill: now censuring greed, and again delicate living; at another time, attacking licentiousness; now praising and encouraging alms-giving, then again each of the other good works. I fear that if my words are concerned about one thing only, I may, all unaware, be treating one illness, while you are struggling with others. If but one person were present here, I should not think it very necessary to make my sermon so many-sided. But, since in such a large crowd it is likely that there are many ills, it is not unreasonable for me to vary my teaching, for the sermon which includes all will surely find its own usefulness. In fact, this is the reason why Scripture itself also is many-sided, and speaks to us of numberless matters, since it is addressed to the common nature of mankind. Indeed, in such a great crowd as this all the diseases of the soul must be represented, even if all are not in every man.[23]

Many of his audience, it must be said, who were familiar with the eloquence of the sophists who exercised popular appeal at the time, were attracted more by the rhetorical brilliance of his speech than by the finer points of doctrine which he elaborated. But John's eloquence was in striking contrast to that of contemporary secular orators because of its clarity of exposition, and the sincerity and depth of its meaning. There is none of the exaggerated attention to form at the expense of content, characteristic of so much of the oratory of his day. It was the impact of these qualities on his listeners which gained him the title of Chrysostom, or John of the Golden Mouth. Nevertheless, above and beyond his oratorical brilliance, he was pre-eminently the teacher and the good shepherd who tried to enlighten, to encourage and to bring about the conversion of souls.

John's homilies varied considerably in length, some requiring as long as an hour for delivery; even the shorter ones would probably be considered exces-

23 *John no. 23*, pp 222–3.

sive by a modern audience. The very fact that he frequently refers to the inattentiveness or the obvious boredom of his listeners suggests that no less effort was required then to capture the attention of the congregation. He frequently notes with regret, as he looks down on a thin congregation, that attendance at the theatre is preferred to listening to sermons in church.

His commentary on the encounter of Christ with the Samaritan woman at the well of Sychar (Jn 4:4–54) is a brilliant example of his progressive exposition of the text. He devotes five homilies to it and it accounts for over fifty pages of text in his thousand pages of commentary on the fourth Gospel. The content of the dialogue between Jesus and the woman is drawn out in all its richness – theological, psychological, anthropological and historical. He brings his listeners into the very core of the scene, instructs them in the doctrine, and helps them to apply the moral conclusions from the conversion of the wayward Samaritan to their own lives. Among other things he praises the humility of the woman and draws out an object lesson about human respect.

> Let us, accordingly, imitate the woman ourselves, and let us not cater to human respect with regard to our sins, but let us fear God as we ought, since he both sees what is happening now and punishes hereafter those who do not repent now. At present, however, we are doing the very opposite of this, for we do not fear him who is going to judge us, while we shudder with fear for those who have no power to harm us and dread disgrace at their hands. Therefore, in the degree in which we have had this fear, in that degree we shall pay the penalty. He who now looks only to human respect and is not ashamed to do any disgraceful deed in the sight of God, if he is unwilling to repent and mend his ways, in that day will be put to shame, not in the presence of one or two only, but with the whole world looking on.[24]

His eloquence as a preacher is evident and his homilies contain many literary gems such as his commentary on John 1:14 ('And we saw his glory, glory as of the only-begotten Son of the Father, full of grace and truth') describing the works and miracles wrought by the Incarnate Word:

> The tax collector became Apostle; the persecutor and blasphemer and insulter was transformed into the world's herald; the magi became teachers of the Jews; a thief was proclaimed a citizen of paradise; a harlot shone by reason of the greatness of her faith; the Canaanite woman and the Samaritan – the latter also another harlot – one became

24 *John no. 34*, p. 338.

> the herald of her people, and having caught the entire city in her net, so brought them to Christ; the other contrived by her faith and perseverance to drive out an evil spirit from the soul of her daughter.[25]

He is constantly exhorting his audience to do better, to live more Christian lives, to fight against the temptations to vanity, greed, and the attraction of indecent spectacles at the theatre and the games. He encourages them to use the resources of prayer, self-denial, confession and the reading of Scripture as their support in the ongoing struggle. Sometimes, as we have seen, he complains a little saying that preaching is hard work. What makes it a light or heavy burden is the response of the people:

> If you despise my words or, though you do not despise them, do not embody them in your deeds, my toil will be heavy, because I am labouring fruitlessly and in vain. But if you pay attention and make my words manifest in your deeds, I shall not even be aware of the perspiration, for the fruit produced by my work will not permit me to feel the laboriousness of the toil. And so, if you wish to spur on my zeal and not to extinguish it or make it weaker, show me the fruit of it, I beseech you, in order that, viewing the leafy crops, sustained by hopes of a rich harvest and calculating my wealth, I may not be sluggish in engaging in this promising task.[26]

HUMANITY OF CHRYSOSTOM

John is always understanding with the limitations of his audience. At times he cuts short his preaching because he sees that the congregation has 'become weary and listless because of the length of my sermon'.[27] He is quick to encourage and even to flatter at times if it will attract the attention of his audience.[28] If he feels he has been too sharp in his correction he is eager to apolo-

25 *John no. 12*, p. 115. Commenting on the same passage he says: 'It was possible to see limbs repaired and made whole when they had been paralyzed and crippled, withered hands moving, paralyzed feet suddenly leaping, blocked-up ears made open, and the tongue, which previously had been kept silent by muteness, now speaking aloud. Even as some skilled architect who restores a house fallen to decay with age, so He restored our common human nature. Like the architect he supplied parts that had been broken off, fastened together the separated and disjointed portions, and raised up again that which had completely fallen down' (ibid., p. 114). **26** *John no. 22*, p. 212. **27** *John no. 2*, p. 23. **28** 'Your coming here, your attentive posture, your crowding on one another – pushing together to secure a closer position where my voice may be more clearly heard – and your unwillingness to leave, though closely packed together, until this spiritual theatre is dismissed, your clamorous applause and all such things may be thought indica-

gize the next day.[29] He is keenly alive to his own shortcomings, especially his tendency to give way to irritability and indignation. He is saddened when he finds that, though they have definite times for food and bathing and banqueting, they are reluctant to go to church once or twice a week. He is aware that at times he is not being listened to, but that will not prevent him speaking, because in doing so he will be justified before God 'even if there be no one listening to me'.[30]

John was not just a great preacher. After his appointment as archbishop of Constantinople he also showed himself to be an effective administrator of the Church. The presence of the emperor's court in that city had produced a spirit of worldliness and ambition among the clergy which he proceeded to uproot. He reformed community life for consecrated virgins and restored monasticism to its original austerity. He denounced the lax morals of the laity and didn't hesitate to confront the empress Eudoxia with her errors. As in Antioch, he continued to espouse the cause of the poor, and to attack greed and selfishness among the wealthy. However, in spite of the fact that he made life much less comfortable for many, he was loved and revered by the great bulk of the people of Constantinople. This mutual affection is reflected in the homilies he preached in this metropolitan see. In one of these he would say: 'Nothing is so dear to me as you. I would desire a thousand times to be anathema if by that means I could convert your souls, so much dearer to me than life is your salvation. I am filled with joy when I hear anything good of you.'[31] Again he tells them, 'You have never been wanting to me in anything. Were it possible you would have given me your eyes; and on my part I was desirous to give you even my life together with the Gospel. Our love is mutual.'[32]

John Henry Newman wrote much about the Fathers of the Church and was immensely attracted by them. Eventually they were to lead him to the fullness of the faith, and for this grace he frequently recognized his great debt to them. He read and studied them all but he does not deny that Chrysostom has first claim on his affections. There is a special flavour in his writing about John of Antioch:

tive of the fervour in your soul and of your earnest desire to listen. Therefore, it is actually unnecessary to urge you on in this regard' (*John no. 3*, p. 27). **29** 'Perhaps it seemed to you last time that we were more bothersome and tiresome than was necessary, and that we were employing a somewhat sharp manner of speaking, and drawing out at too great length our indictment of the indifference of most of you. Now, if we had done this only through a desire to annoy you, each one of you would have reason to be indignant. But if, because we were thinking only of the help we could give you, we disregarded in our words what might gain your favour, even though you are unwilling to approve us for our forethought, at least you are bound to pardon such great affection as ours' (*John no. 12*, p. 110). **30** *John no. 30*, p. 295. **31** *Homily no. 3 on Acts*. **32** *Homily no. 44 on Acts*.

> A bright, cheerful, gentle soul; a sensitive heart, a temperament open to emotion and impulse; and all this elevated, refined, transformed by the touch of heaven, – such was John Chrysostom; winning followers, riveting affections, by his sweetness, frankness, and neglect of self.[33]

I don't think it is forcing the argument too much to suggest that Newman found in this great Father of the East a reflection of many aspects of his own rich personality and, consequently, an inspiration for his life and work. Why, he asks, has he so much empathy with Chrysostom when so many other great saints, although they command his veneration, yet 'exert no claim' upon his heart? After comparing him with a number of other Fathers, Newman's considered response is that Chrysostom's charm lies

> in his intimate sympathy and compassionatness for the whole world, not only in its strength but also in its weakness; in the lively regard with which he views everything that comes before him, taken in the concrete ... I speak of the discriminating affectionateness with which he accepts every one for what is personal in him and unlike others. I speak of his versatile recognition of men, one by one ... I speak of the kindly spirit and genial temper with which he looks around at all things which this wonderful world contains; of the graphic fidelity with which he notes them down upon the tablets of his mind, and of the promptitude and propriety with which he calls them up as arguments or illustrations in the course of his teaching as the occasion requires.[34]

Newman is particularly taken by Chrysostom's approach to the Bible, the 'observant benevolence which gives to his exposition of Scripture its chief characteristic.' It is his capacity

> of throwing himself into the minds of others, of imagining with exactness and with sympathy circumstances or scenes which were not before him, and of bringing out what he apprehended in words as direct and vivid as the apprehension which epitomizes his biblical commentaries.[35]

We are here reminded of what the then Cardinal Ratzinger said in his Erasmus lecture in New York in 1988 about the current crisis in the historico-critical method of biblical exegesis. If this hermeneutical approach is to be effective, he said, an essential precondition is that there should be 'sym-pathia' between the exegete and the biblical text.[36] This is precisely the quality which

33 *Historical sketches*, vol. II (London, 1876), p. 234. **34** Ibid., p. 288. **35** Ibid., p. 289. **36** Cardinal

Newman picks out as fundamental in the exegesis of St John Chrysostom.[37] John of Antioch writes penetratingly not only about matters theological. One can glean from his homilies a clear perception of the ecclesiastical, social, and cultural conditions of his time. It is this human richness of his teaching which constitutes one of the most attractive dimensions of his writing.

FROM ANTIOCH TO CONSTANTINOPLE

As we have seen, it was during his years as a priest in Antioch (386–97) that Chrysostom wrote most of his homilies and commentaries, his book on the martyr Babylas, his treatise on virginity, etc. He is among the most prolific of the Fathers: 17 treatises, more than 700 homilies, including 67 on the Book of Genesis, 59 on the Psalms, 90 on St Matthew, 88 on St John, 55 on Acts, and homilies on all the epistles of St Paul. There are 241 letters extant. He was not a speculative theologian, yet there are great theological treasures hidden in his writings. He passed on the Church's tradition and reliable doctrine in an age of theological controversies, as sparked above all by Arianism. He is therefore a trustworthy witness of the dogmatic development achieved by the Church from the fourth to the fifth centuries. He has left us a great body of pastoral theology in his catechesis to prepare catechumens for baptism.[38] From the very first he was considered by Greeks and Latins as a most important witness to the faith. In 421 St Augustine claimed Chrysostom's authority in his battle against Pelagianism. His authority was also invoked at the Council of Ephesus in 431.

Particular incidents which happened in Antioch were the occasion for John to focus his homilies in a special way, as for example in the case of the *Homilies on the statues*. A serious disturbance took place in the city in 387 when the populace rose in revolt against the emperor, Theodosius, provoked by the imposition of a special tax. They destroyed a number of statues of the emperor and his family. The fragments were drawn through the streets while other acts of violence were committed. The emperor threatened to destroy the whole city, but Bishop Flavian in his old age travelled to Constantinople to plead with Theodosius. In the interim Chrysostom delivered a series of twenty vigorous sermons – consoling, calming, admonishing – and ingeniously making use of the episode as a point of departure from which to develop the theme of repentance. When Flavian finally returned with the emperor's pardon, John's efforts

Joseph Ratzinger, 'Biblical interpretation in crisis: on the question of the foundations and approaches of exegesis today', Erasmus lecture given in New York, 27 January 1988. **37** Cf. *Historical sketches*, vol. II, p. 289. **38** See the addresses by Benedict XVI on St John Chrysostom, *Osservatore Romano* (English language edition), 26 September and 3 October 2007.

had resulted not only in keeping his troubled flock in check, but also in giving a tremendous impetus to his own prestige. He seems, besides, to have become fully awakened to his own powers as an orator and the most fruitful period of his preaching followed.

After the death of Nectarius, patriarch of Constantinople, in 397, John was chosen to succeed him. Since he didn't show any willingness to accept, he was brought to the capital under military escort at the command of the emperor, Arcadius. In February 398 he was consecrated by his enemy Theophilus, patriarch of Alexandria.

Initially called Byzantium, it received its new name of Constantinople as early as 324, when the Roman court and government settled there permanently in its new capital. It was soon filled with beautiful edifices like those of Rome – senate house, forums, a capitol, circuses, and many churches. The most beautiful statues of antiquity were gathered from various parts of the empire to adorn its public places. In general the other cities of the Roman world were stripped to embellish the 'New Rome', destined subsequently to surpass them all in greatness and magnificence. Its first historically-known bishop dates from 306. In 381, at the Second Ecumenical Council held in the city, the bishop of Constantinople was given first place after the bishop of Rome.

Constantine had chosen this city as the new capital of the Roman empire, but due to wars and the needs of state, he rarely stayed there. The decision to build Constantinople would have profound implications for the development of the Church, apart from underlining the divisions between the Greek-speaking East and the Latin West. The rise of Constantinople and the Eastern court would establish a rivalry between the secular and papal thrones. After the fall of the Western Roman empire, the papacy would fill the void of secular leadership. It would assert papal supremacy over secular law. In the East the rise of Constantinople would inaugurate the beginning of caesaropapism, of imperial supremacy over the Church

It was only under Theodosius the Great (379–95) that Constantinople assumed definitive rank as the capital of the Eastern Roman empire. But the city and its inhabitants suffered much under the Arian controversy; the Arian heretics held possession of the Church for forty years. St Gregory Nazianzen restored religious peace to the Church of Constantinople early in the reign of Theodosius. This was the historical context of John's appointment. This metropolis, with its scarcely assimilated Western and Oriental elements, and saddled with a court noted for its luxury and intrigue, was a far cry from Antioch, however turbulent and confused the latter might at times have seemed.

Chrysostom now had complete authority to effect reform where he saw fit. He first set about a reform of the clergy who had become corrupt under his predecessor. The courage and directness of his attack won him eventually the lasting enmity of those in high places. The clergy were especially antagonized when he stripped the episcopal residence of all expression of luxurious living. He combated the dangerous abuse practised by some clerics of keeping 'spiritual sisters' in their houses contrary to the express prohibition of the Council of Nicea. He organized ecclestiastical charity so as to preclude waste or misdirection of funds. In his first year he built a great hospital for the poor with the money he had saved in his episcopal residence.

Though he could not preach as regularly or as often as he did in Antioch, he was able to continue to espouse the cause of the poor and to attack greed and selfishness where it existed among the wealthy. As in Antioch, he condemned the vanity and extravagance of women and the preoccupation of so many with vicious and degrading forms of entertainment. As a result, some of his flock, both rich and poor, felt a passionate devotion to their bishop, but many others viewed his efforts with ill-disguised hostility.

At first he had only esteem and admiration for Empress Eudoxia, but this changed when he had the courage to admonish the empress for an act of injustice to a poor widow (depriving her of a vineyard), so that he began to fall from favour at a time when Eudoxia was at the height of her power. The situation was aggravated when she was told that in a sermon against the extravagance of women the bishop was pointing his finger deliberately at her.

There was also ecclesiastical intrigue, fomented by Theophilus of Alexandria. In 403 Theophilus travelled to Constantinople and organized a secret council of 36 bishops, which procured the deposition, and banishment of Chrysostom, on false charges of immorality and high treason. This was the so-called Synod of the Oak, and when Chrysostom refused three times to appear before it, he was declared deposed in August 403. Emperor Arcadius accepted the synod's decision and exiled Chrysostom to Bythania.[39] This first expulsion did not last long as he was recalled the following day. When the news reached the people about Chrysostom's banishment, they besieged the palace and demanded the restoration of their bishop. Eudoxia implored the emperor to recall Chrysostom. A whole fleet went out to greet him, and the Bosphorous blazed with torches as they welcomed home their beloved archbishop. He re-entered the capital in a triumphant procession and delivered in the Church of the Apostles a jubilant address which is still preserved.

Good relations were soon re-established with Eudoxia but they were not to last for very long. Eudoxia aspired to semi-divine honours, and a column of porphyry with her silver statue for public adoration was erected in September 403 not far from the cathedral. Chrysostom complained about the noisy and

39 *Homilies on John*, Introduction, pp x–xv.

indecent public amusements and dances that marked the dedication of the statue. Chrysostom's enemies suggested to Eudoxia that this reprimand was meant for her.

On the feast of John the Baptist, Chrysostom preached a homily which was to have fatal consequences. He began with the words: 'Again Herodias raves; again she rages; again she dances; again she asks for the head of John on a platter.' John's enemies represented it to Eudoxia as drawing a parallel between herself and Herodias, and between Chrysostom and the Baptist. Once again she set in motion the machinery necessary to manoeuvre his deposition and exile.

The emperor ordered Chrysostom to cease performing ecclesiastical functions, which he refused to do. Thereupon he was forbidden the use of any church. When he assisted at the Easter Vigil of 404, the ceremonies were interrupted by an armed intervention, the faithful driven from the place, and the baptismal water stained with blood.

FINAL EXILE AND DEATH

On 5 June 404 Arcadius signed the edict of banishment. Chrysostom was conveyed under the scorching heat of July and August over Galatia and Cappadocia, to Caucusus in the Taurus Mountains, in the remotest corner of Armenia – a desolate and hostile landscape which was one of the last outposts of the Roman empire. Here he remained for three years. Even there he found ways to be active in promoting the evangelization of Scythia, Persia and Phoenicia.

Soon members of his former congregation from Antioch went on pilgrimage to visit their beloved preacher. From there he wrote many letters to friends and others, 238 of which are still extant. They are exemplary in their apostolic zeal and, at the same time, very human in their expression of interest and affection, and concern for every detail of the lives of his correspondents. Many are written in reply to those anxious to know about his health; others are in response to friends concerned about the condition of the Church in Constantinople. He is always ready with a word of encouragement for those who miss his spiritual leadership very much. John's optimism and magnanimity come through in all his letters; he never complains about his very difficult situation or the grievous wrong done to him. He is much too concerned with the needs of his correspondents to allow any selfish considerations intrude. Even Gibbon, who had some unfavourable things to say of Chrysostom's character, would write of John's last years:

> The three years which he spent at Cucusus and the neighbouring town of Arabissus were the last and most glorious of his life. His character

> was consecrated by absence and persecution; the faults of his administration were no longer remembered; but every tongue repeated the praises of his genius and virtue, and the respectful attention of the Christian world was fixed on a desert spot among the mountains of Taurus. [40]

Because of the large number of his faithful friends, John's enemies felt that he still was not far enough away from Constantinople, and so in the summer of 407 his guards were directed to set out with all speed for Pityus near the Caucasus mountains, at the eastern end of the Black Sea. Broken in health, this forced march caused John great hardship, and after 400 miles, fatigued and exhausted, he collapsed at Comana. He was carried into the nearby chapel of the martyr St Basiliscus where, after receiving Communion, he died on the morning of 14 September.

Almost from the time of his death Chrysostom was regarded in both the East and West as an outstanding preacher and exegete. Although not given to speculative theology in the same way as his brilliant contemporaries, Basil the Great and Gregory of Nyssa, he became a great authority on the *content* of the faith. At the Council of Chalcedon in 451 he was proclaimed a Doctor of the Universal Church.[41]

The heroic quality of his life, his banishment and exile which he brought on himself because of his fortitude in preaching and giving witness to the faith, all add to the attraction of his personality. He harboured no resentment for any of the injustices he suffered. He was an outstanding priest and preacher whose life and work have a perennial value for the Church. Indefatigable in his zeal for souls, he never allowed human respect to inhibit him in his teaching the truth revealed by God. He was no respecter of persons when error had to be uprooted, or the moral law proclaimed. Yet he combined these qualities with an immense charity and a human warmth which endeared him to all who sincerely searched for Christ.

In 438 his remains were returned to Constantinople, where he was buried with full honours in the Church of the Apostles with the deceased emperors and patriarchs. Emperor Theodosius II, a son of Eudoxia, went out to meet the funeral train, and prayed that his parents might be forgiven for their ill-advised persecution of the bishop. In 1204 his remains were translated to the first Constantinian basilica in Rome, and now rest in the chapel of the Choir of the Canons in St Peter's basilica. On 24 August 2004 Pope John Paul II gave a large part of the saint's relics to Patriarch Bartholemew I of

40 Edward Gibbon, *Decline and fall*, vol. V, ch. 31, as quoted in Attwater, p. 159. 41 Cf. *Commentary on St John the Apostle and Evangelist*, vol. I, Introduction, pp x–xiv.

Constantinople. Blessed John XXIII proclaimed him patron of the Second Vatican Council. We keep his feast on 13 September, the vigil of the day of his death at Comana in Pontus, where his last words were 'Glory be to God for all things'.[42]

42 See Newman, *Historical sketches*, vol. II (London, 1876), p. 302.

CHAPTER TWO

St John Fisher (1469–1535)

IN THE SUMMER OF 1535 Bishop John Fisher and Sir Thomas More were executed within weeks of each other on Tower Hill in London. Both died in the same cause – the spiritual supremacy of the Pope and the sanctity of the marriage bond. Yet while the fame of St Thomas More has grown apace, particularly in the present century,[1] the saintly bishop of Rochester has, by comparison, received little public recognition. More and Fisher took a committed public stand in defence of Catholic teaching against the Lutheran doctrines. Both had exceptional literary talents, coupled with a profound knowledge of the Scriptures and the Church Fathers which they used in their many writings in defence of orthodoxy. They were the two most outstanding Englishmen of their day.

It has been suggested that the main reason for the contrast between More's fame and the relative obscurity of Fisher is that one was a bishop and the other a layman. Christian tradition does not see anything special in the fact that 'the good shepherd lays down his life for his sheep' (cf. Jn 10:11). But that the father of a family who was noted for his wit and learning, who was one of the greatest humanists of his day, a statesman who reached the highest level of civic responsibility in his country – that such a man would give his life for the faith has always attracted attention, if it didn't evoke sentiments of respect and affection from people of the most diverse backgrounds. While More's reputation as 'a man for all seasons' made it difficult for his detractors to undermine his reputation, it was much easier to portray the gaunt Fisher, immortalized in the Holbein portrait, as a hidebound conservative, an image perpetuated by Reformation historiography in England.

If little is heard about St John Fisher today, such was not the case during his own lifetime. He was known, not only throughout England, but to all

1 Cf., for example, the critical edition of *The complete works of St Thomas More*, in 20 volumes, published by Yale University Press (1963–93); *Moreana*, the quarterly journal of More scholarship, published since 1963 by the Catholic University of Angers, France, edited by the distinguished Morean scholar, Professor Germain Marc'hadour. Biographies of More include those by R.W. Chambers, E.E. Reynolds, R. Marius, L. Monti, J. Guy, Peter Ackroyd, and G. Wegemer.

Europe, as an outstanding theologian and as an example of a model bishop. In 1510 Erasmus described Fisher as 'a man with whom no one in our time can be compared, either for holiness of life or greatness of soul'.[2] Cardinal Reginald Pole, who as a young man was part of the court of Henry VIII, in his *Apology* addressed to Emperor Charles V expresses not just his own opinion but the general esteem in which Fisher is regarded. He writes from Rome:

> Nothing could be so reasonable a prejudice against the new supremacy as the integrity of the leaders who opposed it. If anyone had asked the king, before the violence of his passions had hurried him out of the reach of reason and reflection, whom of all the episcopal order he chiefly considered? on whose affection and fidelity he most relied? he would, without any hesitation, have answered, The Bishop of Rochester.[3]

CAREER

John Fisher (1469–1535) was born in Yorkshire, the eldest of nine children. When he was about fourteen he started to attend Cambridge university. After a distinguished academic career he was ordained priest at twenty-two, in 1491, with a papal dispensation, being four years under the canonical age. Although a bit on the lean side, he was tall and handsome with well defined facial features. He was by nature somewhat reserved in conversation, but when he did speak he did so with grace and precision.

The university soon discovered that he was not only a brilliant scholar but also a man of exceptional administrative ability. Lady Margaret Beaufort, the mother of Henry VII, a woman of deep piety and love for the Church, quickly sensed his worth and in 1497 made him her confessor, a responsibility he was to discharge until her death twelve years later.[4] She was a munificent benefactress of the Church and followed the advice of her confessor in the dispensation of patronage. In one of his books Fisher comments about the Lady Margaret that 'though she chose me as her director, to hear her confessions and to guide her life, yet I gladly confess that I learnt more from her great virtue than ever I could teach to her'[5] – a tribute both to his own humility and the sanctity of his penitent.

2 T.E. Bridgett, *Life of Blessed John Fisher* (London, 1890), p. 98. 3 *Apologia ad Carolum V*, no. 20, quoted by Bridgett, ibid., p. 54. St Thomas More's own appreciation of his fellow martyr is interesting: 'In my list the place of honour goes to the Reverend Father in Christ, John, Bishop of Rochester, distinguished for virtue as well as learning, qualities in which he has no superior among living men' (*Selected letters*, London, 1976, p. 125). 4 These biographical details are drawn primarily from Bridgett, ibid., and E.E. Reynolds, *Saint John Fisher* (London, 1972). 5 *De veri-*

He saw that two of the great needs of his time were to improve the theological training of priests and to raise the standard of preaching. To this end he persuaded Lady Margaret to institute readerships in theology at both Oxford and Cambridge in 1503. Fisher's concern for good preaching is demonstrated by the fact that in 1502, while vice chancellor of Cambridge, he obtained a papal bull which granted to the university the privilege of appointing twelve adequately qualified priests to preach throughout the whole of England, Scotland and Ireland.

In 1504, while still only thirty-five, he was appointed bishop of Rochester, much to the surprise of public opinion. As Hughes points out:

> Nothing better reveals what type of ecclesiastic was then considered *episcopabilis* than the general astonishment at John Fisher's nomination to Rochester in 1504, a man young in years, who had never held any office at the Court, and was, as yet, wholly unbeneficed. For this astonishment (and what moved it) we have the Saint's own word. And we have also the testimony of Henry VII, that, in appointing him, the King intended a kind of reparation for the many unsuitable men he had so far promoted.[6]

Rochester was the smallest and the poorest diocese in England; it was considered the first step on the ladder of episcopal preferment.

That same year, 1504, he became chancellor of Cambridge university, being re-elected to this post each year until 1514, when he was conferred with the unique distinction of appointment as chancellor for life, in recognition of his immense contribution to that famous centre of learning. He was responsible for the foundation of two new colleges. He enlarged the university library, encouraged young scholars, and succeeded in attracting academics of European renown, including Erasmus, to the staff of the university.

ST JOHN'S COLLEGE

One of his great achievements as chancellor was the foundation of St John's college with an endowment left to him by the Lady Margaret. The aims of the college, as laid down in the statutes drafted by Fisher himself, were stated to be: the worship of God, training in uprightness of life, and strengthening of the Christian faith. The emphasis of the studies programme was on theol-

tate corporis et sanguinis Christi in eucharistia (On the truth of the Body and Blood of Christ in the Eucharist) as translated in Bridgett, ibid., p. 26. 6 Philip Hughes, *The Reformation in England*, vol. I (London, 1952), p. 79.

ogy, but there was also to be training in Greek and Hebrew. His concern was to encourage the learning of these latter subjects as an aid to the better understanding of Sacred Scripture and thus provide a more solid foundation for the development of theology as a science. Fisher was well aware of the debilitating effects which a decadent scholasticism was having on the study of theology. His own extensive study of the Fathers and of Scripture suggested that a new approach was necessary, and this he put into effect in the new college. It would be true to say that Fisher regarded St John's more as a seminary for priests than as a centre for secular studies. His zeal had only one end in view – to provide a body of learned and virtuous Catholic priests. This foundation was a real pioneering effort, anticipating at several points the mind of the Council of Trent on the establishment of seminaries for the proper education of priests.

EPISCOPAL RESPONSIBILITIES

The registers of the diocese of Rochester for the years of Fisher's episcopate have been preserved and they confirm the reputation that he left of being a very conscientious pastor of the flock entrusted to his care.[7] He carried out regular visitations of parishes, dealt effectively with cases of simony and heresy, and paid particular attention to the needy and the poor. At the same time he took seriously his other multiple responsibilities in Cambridge, in the House of Lords, in Convocation, and as a member of the king's council. He could have allowed affairs of state and the prestige of court life to draw him increasingly away from the care of his diocese – nor would anyone have thought this surprising. Of the sixteen bishops constituting the English hierarchy in 1504, when John Fisher was appointed, two were non-resident Italians who had never visited their sees, and the majority were chiefly occupied with state duties as administrators or diplomats. His commitment to residency would, forty years later, serve as an inspiration to Charles Borromeo, the great Counter-Reformation archbishop who adopted Fisher as his episcopal model, and who, out of veneration for the bishop of Rochester, kept a portrait of him in his study in Milan.[8]

He was exceptional in that he never allowed secular matters to distract him from what was his first responsibility – the pastoral care of the priests and the people of the diocese of Rochester. A knowledgeable contemporary of Fisher

7 Cf. S. Thompson, 'The Bishop in his Diocese', in B. Bradshaw and E. Duffy, eds, *Humanism, reform and the Reformation: the career of Bishop John Fisher* (subsequently referred to as HRR), (Cambridge, 1989), pp 67–80. 8 Cf. E. Surtz, *The works and days of John Fisher* (Cambridge, MA, 1967), p. 386.

recorded the following opinion of him: 'He was in holiness, learning and diligence in his cure (care of souls) and in fulfilling his office of bishop such that of many hundred years England had not any bishop worthy to be compared with him'.[9]

PREACHER

Fisher was a diligent preacher all during his life, even to extreme old age when feebleness forced him to preach from a sitting position. In his sermons on the penitential psalms he had written that he was well persuaded that 'all fear of God, also the contempt of God cometh and is grounded on the clergy'. His first care was, therefore, the piety and the orthodoxy of his priests. He had complained in the same sermons that pastors, who ought to be 'the nearest neighbours of all', stand aloof either by bodily absence or by silence: 'Bishops be absent from their dioceses and parsons from their churches ... We use by-paths and circumlocutions in rebuking. We go nothing nigh to the matter, and so in the mean season the people perish with their sins'.[10]

Fisher was exceptional among his episcopal colleagues in his zeal for preaching. Not only did he give a high priority to forming priests who were competent preachers, but he established a reputation as the most illustrious preacher in the England of his day. His style is direct and simple, but never bland.[11] There is no unnecessary show of erudition – his words reflect the mind of a very devout priest desirous to speak to the hearts of his congregation. From his surviving sermons there is evidence of a powerful use of imagery. The themes which dominate his preaching – repentance for sin, the ephemeral nature of the present life, the passion of Christ, the four last things – reflect the concern of the good shepherd for the wayward flock.[12] He tempers fear with love and hope, and never loses sight of God's initiative and the priority of grace when he stresses man's responsibility and the freedom of his will.[13] He has an ever-present consciousness of the consequences of sin for man's eternal happiness, and his sense of responsibility is heightened in this regard because he finds that many among the clergy have lost the zeal to proclaim Christ's call to repentance.

9 N. Harpsfield, *The life and death of Sir Thomas More*, ed. by E.W. Hitchcock and R.W. Chambers, Early English Texts Society (London, 1932), p. 239 (Rastell fragments). **10** Bridgett, ibid., p. 65. **11** In the preface to his *Ecclesiastes, or, the art of preaching*, published in 1535 after Fisher's death, Erasmus, recalling all that his friend the bishop of Rochester did to train good preachers in Cambridge university, tells us that Fisher himself *singulari linguae gratia praeditus*, 'was gifted with a singular charm of utterance' (cf. Surtz, ibid., p. 61). **12** Cf. B. Bradshaw, 'Bishop John Fisher, 1469–1535: the man and his work', in HRR, p. 4. **13** Cf. G. Marc'hadour, 'Fisher and More: a note', in HRR, p. 105.

He has a detestation of heresy because of the immense damage it can do to souls, and preaches against it with all the rhetorical and imaginative resources he can lay claim to. We get some idea of the powerful thrust of his sermons against heterodoxy from the preface to the published text of a sermon preached in 1526 against Luther at St Paul's in London. On this occasion he says that 'heresy is a perilous weed, it is the seed of the devil, the inspiration of wicked spirits, the corruption of our hearts, the blinding of our sight, the quenching of our faith, the destruction of all good fruit, and finally the murder of men's souls'.[14] In preaching during the Lutheran controversy, his objective was to persuade those caught up in heresy to return to the fullness of the faith. His genuine concern is reflected in his open invitation to those who have been attracted by Lutheranism to come to speak to him privately and in confidence if they wish; he is ready to talk to them at length.

The duty of keeping the people loyal to the faith and of resisting heretics is primarily the bishops' responsibility. It is, Fisher affirms, their obligation to counteract perverse opinions as early as possible lest they grow stronger by delay or produce worse harm later, incapable of extirpation. In the prologue to one of his books against the reformers he declares that if those whose business it is 'to catch the little foxes that destroy the vines' (Can 2:15) had confronted the heretics at an early stage, Luther would not now be a large and wily fox, impossible to restrain. Fisher does not mince his words about episcopal responsibility. It is up to ecclesiastical superiors, who have been entrusted with the care of souls, either to destroy the wolves or with a foolish pity to allow them the cruel slaughter of the sheep.[15] Nevertheless, in the life and the writings of the bishop of Rochester there is relatively little stress on the coercive function of the bishop. The duty of the shepherd to feed his flock through preaching the Gospel of Christ receives much more attention than the condemnation of error.

POLEMICAL WORKS

Fisher's literary output between 1520 and 1534 is quite astonishing. There are at least fourteen separate works in Latin and two in English, amounting to some 800,000 words.[16] The period from 1520 to 1527 was devoted to defending the Church's teaching against the Lutheran doctrines. From 1527 until his incarceration in the Tower of London in 1534, he expended much of his considerable intellectual and spiritual energies to vindicate the validity of Queen

14 *The English works of John Fisher*, published by the Early English Text Society (London, 1935), p. 434, as quoted by H.C. Porter in 'Fisher and Erasmus', HRR, p. 93. **15** Cf. *Defensio regiae assertionis* (The defence of the king's assertions) as translated in Surtz, ibid., p. 49. **16** Cf. Bradshaw, ibid., p. 10.

Catherine's marriage to Henry. There was also an ambitious though unfinished commentary on the psalms, and a defence of the divine inspiration of the Septuagint version of the Old Testament.[17] What is astonishing is that he accomplished all of this with scrupulous commitment to his diocesan duties, and the fulfilment of his other responsibilities as university chancellor, in Convocation, and in the House of Lords.

At the end of 1520 Luther publicly burned the papal bull *Exurge Domine* which had condemned his writings, including the *De babylonica captivitate* (On the Babylonian captivity), a slanderous attack on the Church's sacramental system. These works were being introduced surreptitiously into England and causing such concern that, on 12 May 1521, Cardinal Wolsey as lord chancellor decreed the public burning of heretical books at Paul's Cross. Fisher was asked to preach and the main thrust of his sermon on this occasion was that the promise of the Spirit of Truth safeguards the universal Church of Christ from false teaching. His sermon showed a remarkable penetration of Luther's doctrine at such an early date. In it he isolates the three main tenets of Lutheran theology – the denial of papal primacy, the assertion of the doctrine of justification by faith alone, and the principle of *sola Scriptura* (Scripture alone) as the foundation of doctrinal authority, even though neither of the latter two doctrines appear among the forty-one articles condemned by *Exurge Domine*.[18]

Henry VIII's reply to Luther's *De babylonica captivitate* was his *Assertio septem sacramentorum* (Assertion of the seven sacraments), published in July 1521, which won for him the papal title *Defensor fidei*, a title still somewhat incongruously sported on English coins bearing the image of the Protestant monarch! At the same time Fisher was working on his own refutation of Luther which was published in January 1523 – *Assertionis lutheranae confutatio* (The confutation of Luther's assertions).[19] It is a comprehensive refutation of Lutheranism. Apart from the Blesssed Trinity and the Incarnation, there is hardly a dogma in Catholic theology on which he does not discourse.[20] It was first published in Antwerp and ran into several editions, being published also in Cologne, Augsburg, Paris and Venice. It was the most complete critique of Lutheran theology available in Europe during the 1520s.[21] Between 1523 and 1564 twenty editions were published. As one scholar has pointed out, it was, throughout the rest of the century, one of the standard references for Catholic

17 *Pro assertione septuaginta interpretum translationis* (In defence of the interpretation and translation of the Septuagint); this work was probably written in 1527 – see Richard Rex, *The theology of John Fisher* (Cambridge, 1991), p. 150. **18** Cf. Rex, ibid., p. 88. **19** After *Exurge Domine* was published in 1520, Luther defended himself against the Bull in his *Assertio omnium articulorum* (Assertion of all the articles), published in December of the same year. Fisher's *Assertionis lutheranae confutatio* is his reply to this latter work of Luther. **20** Cf. Surtz, ibid., pp 309–19. **21** Cf. Rex, ibid., p. 80.

apologists in their controversial writings and speeches. One of the main reasons for this was 'the framework of the book, which corresponded quite directly with both the content of the papal bull excommunicating Luther, as well as with one of Luther's earliest replies to this detailed condemnation. Hence the *Confutatio* provided a convenient compendium of Catholic theology relating directly to the main points of divergence, according to Rome, between Martin Luther and Roman Catholic orthodoxy'.[22]

The *Confutatio* is Fisher's answer to Luther's challenge to the Pope after he had burned the bull *Exurge Domine* and the books of canon law in Wittenberg as an act of public defiance to papal authority. His approach is first to give an exposition of ten basic theological propositions which form the core of his argumentation against Luther. He responds to each of Luther's arguments, making use of his vast knowledge of the Fathers to demolish his opponent's assertions.[23] He writes trenchantly in defence of the Pope, yet with undisguised sadness at the state of things in the Holy See: 'If the Roman Pontiffs, laying aside pomp and haughtiness, would but practice humility, you would not have a word left to utter against them', he tells Luther. 'Yes, would that they would reform the manners of their court, and drive from it ambition, avarice and luxury. Never otherwise will they impose silence on revilers such as you.'[24]

Another passage in this context is also of interest from the point of view of Fisher's style. Luther concluded one of his attacks on the papacy as follows: 'Who will bring the pope to order? Christ only with the brightness of his coming. "Lord, who has believed our hearing" (Isa 53,1)?' Fisher replies: 'There is no reason to believe your hearing, since you have heard what you say from no other than the devil. It is he who has whispered in your ears that the pope is Antichrist. I do not, however, say this as if I were unwilling that the pope or his court should be reformed, if there is anything in their life divergent from the teaching of Christ. The people speak much against them, I know not with what truth. Still it is constantly repeated that things are so. Would then that, if there is anything amiss, they would reform themselves, and remove the scandal from the souls of the weak. For it is greatly to be feared, unless they do so quickly, that divine vengeance will not long be delayed. It is not, however, fitting that the emperor or lay princes should attempt such a matter, and reduce them to a more frugal mode of life'.[25] When it is recalled that Rome was sacked four years later by the constable of Bourbon, not with-

22 B. Gogan, 'Fisher's View of the Church', in HRR, p. 131. **23** Cf. Reynolds, ibid., p. 98. The previous year, 1522, Fisher had already come to the defence of the papacy. The historical tradition of St Peter's association with the see of Rome had been attacked by a minor humanist called Valenus. Fisher, acutely conscious of the importance of this tradition for the validity of Catholic ecclesiology and its defence against the Lutherans, refuted this thesis in his *Convulsio calumniarum Ulrichi Valeni* (cf. Surtz, ibid., pp 74–6; Rex, HRR, p. 111). **24** Bridgett, ibid., p. 120. **25** Cf. ibid., pp 121–2.

out the connivance of the emperor, Fisher's words have a profoundly prophetic ring about them.

The cogency of Fisher's vindication of the papacy is evident from the effect his *Confutatio* against Luther had on Thomas More. In a letter to Cromwell (1534) More admitted that he had at one time thought the Pope's supremacy was of merely ecclesiastical and not of divine institution. Yet after reading Fisher's work he was able to write:

> As regards the Primacy of the Roman Pontiff, the bishop of Rochester has made the matter so clear from the Gospels, the Acts of the Apostles, and from the whole of the Old Testament, and from the consent of all the holy Fathers, not of the Latins only, but of the Greeks also (of whose opposition Luther is wont to boast), and from the definition of a general council ... that it would be utterly superfluous for me to write again on the subject.[26]

Both More and Fisher died rather than betray their loyalty to the papacy. The greatness of their sacrifice has to be assessed in light of the fact that both lived under the worst of the Renaissance popes – Alexander VI ruled and died within their lifetime. The papacy they knew was very different from the one we know and respect today. They died for a papacy that, as far as men could see, was little else than a small Italian princedom ruled by some of the least reputable of the Renaissance princes. This was the marvel of their faith.

Thomas More was not unaware of the papal scandals of the time, yet he writes about the papacy with exquisite charity and loyalty in his *Responsio ad Lutherum.* After affirming the spiritual supremacy of the Pope in spite of his personal limitations, against Luther's call for the abrogation of the papacy he goes on to say: 'It is far more to be wished that God may raise up such Popes as befit the Christian cause and the dignity of the apostolic office: men who despising riches and honours, will care only for heaven, will promote piety in people, will bring about peace, and exercise the authority they have been given by God ... With one or two such Popes the Christian world would soon perceive how much preferable it is that the papacy should be reformed rather than abrogated ... I doubt not', he says, 'that long ago Christ would have looked down on the pastor of his flock if the Christian people had chosen rather to pray for the welfare of their Father than to persecute him, to hide the shame of their Father than to laugh at it'.[27]

26 *Responsio ad Lutherum* (1523), as translated in Bridgett, ibid., pp 138–9. In proving the direct and immediate conferral of the primacy on Peter, Fisher, as to be expected, gives detailed attention to Luther's interpretation of Mt 16:18 and Jn 21:15–17. While he draws fully from the evidence of tradition, he is at his best when dealing with the scriptural arguments – cf. Surtz, pp 77–8. **27** T.E.

LUTHER AND HENRY VIII

Luther's reply to Henry's *Assertio* is perhaps one of the most scurrilous pieces of theological polemic on record.[28] He called the king, to mention a few of the less offensive epiteths, a louse, an ass, a mad fool with a whorish face, a Thomist pig![29] It was felt that it would be beneath the dignity of the monarch to engage in further debate with the ribald Luther, and so both Fisher and Sir Thomas More were persuaded to come to his rescue.[30] This resulted in Fisher's next work, the *Defensio regiae assertionis*. Its printing was delayed by reports of a possible reconversion of Luther but, when this proved to be unfounded, the book was finally published in Cologne in 1525.[31] The *Defensio* was a short book and concentrated on Luther's denial of the Church's doctrine on the Eucharist, defending the traditional teaching on transubstantiation and the sacrificial nature of the Mass. In it he affirms that Luther's objective of removing the Mass from the Church amounts to 'no less a calamity than if he tried to snatch the sun from the universe'.[32] He also answers other Lutheran errors such as the non-apostolicity of the Epistle of St James, the denial of free will, and the appeal to popular judgement in matters of dogma as against the unanimous consent of the Fathers.

Simultaneously with the *Defensio*, Fisher published his work on the Catholic priesthood, the *Sacri sacerdotii defensio contra Lutherum*.[33] This was in reply to Luther's *De abroganda missa privata* (1522) in which he denied the institution by Christ of a ministerial priesthood essentially different from that of the common priesthood of the laity. Fisher tells his readers that he will make three rejoinders to Luther's attacks with which he will 'try to sponge away all the filthy and blasphemous things that have proceeded from his mouth against priests', and then outlines the plan of his argument. Firstly he demonstrates the prescriptive right of existing truth drawn from Tradition. In his second argument he enunciates a series of axioms, drawn from Scripture and arranged in due order, which establishes the existence of a visible priesthood. His third argument is a clear and direct rebuttal of Luther's objections,

Bridgett, *Life and writings of Sir Thomas More* (London, 1891), p. 219. **28** This was entitled *Contra Henricum regem Angliae* (Against Henry King of England) and was published in Wittenberg in 1522. **29** Cf. Bridgett, ibid., p. 210. **30** Their separate publications give the impression that the authors agreed on a division of labour. More, as Rosseus, was to quote Luther's work verbatim and return abuse for abuse in polished Latin in his *Responsio ad Lutherum*, whereas Fisher, as he states explicitly, omits the insults and concentrates on the important theological arguments – particularly the primacy of the Pope, the interpretation of Scripture, the sacramentality of Orders and Matrimony, and, most extensively, the Eucharist as sacrament and sacrifice (cf. E. Surtz, 'More's friendship with Fisher', in *Essential articles for the study of Thomas More* (Hamden, CT, 1977), p. 138. **31** Cf. Reynolds, ibid., p. 106. **32** *Defensio*, VI. 9; cf. translation in Bridgett, ibid., p. 40. **33** Published in 1525. Quotations are taken from the English translation, *The defence of the priesthood*, by P.E. Hallett (London, 1935).

one by one. In developing his argument for the existence of a visible priesthood from Tradition, the bishop of Rochester shows an extraordinary familiarity with, and knowledge of, the writings of the Fathers of the Church, all the more remarkable in that he must have been working mostly from manuscript copies. After marshalling a striking array of patristic testimony he says that

> from the unanimity of so many Fathers we may conclude with fullest certainty that the priesthood was instituted not in recent times, but in the very cradle of the Church. Wherefore, since Luther can adduce no orthodox writer who in any book that has ever appeared gives the contrary witness, nor can quote a syllable of Holy Scripture in opposition to the assertions of the Fathers, we lay down with the utmost justice against Luther as a matter of prescriptive right the truth of the priesthood.[34]

'How can it be imagined,' Fisher asks, not without a certain irony, 'that at length for the first time has shone upon Luther the light of a truth that no one of the early Fathers should have so much as suspected, the contrary indeed, of which they have unitedly asserted from the very beginning?'[35]

At the same time Sir Thomas More was writing his reply to Luther's diatribe against the king under the pseudonym Gulielmus Rosseus. He had obviously read Fisher's work before he published his *Responsio ad Lutherum*. In this he writes:

> The Reverend Father John Fisher, Bishop of Rochester, a man illustrious not only by the vastness of his erudition, but much more so by the purity of his life, has so opened and so overthrown the assertions of Luther, that if he had any shame he would give a great deal to have burnt his assertions.[36]

REAL PRESENCE

Bishop Fisher's last book against the Lutherans was entitled *De veritate corporis et sanguinis Christi in eucharistia*, published in 1527. Joannes Oecolampadius, professor of theology at Basle, published a short work on the Eucharist in 1525, in which he argued that the words *This is my Body* are to be taken figuratively. Fisher responded to the different arguments presented, giving a detailed defence of the doctrine of the Real Presence.

34 Hallett, ibid., p. 17. **35** Ibid., p. 19. **36** Bridgett, ibid., p. 138.

De veritate is divided into five books, each with its own preface, which latter in themselves constitute treatises on different aspects of Eucharistic theology. The preface to the first book is a general introduction; the second develops the richness of the doctrine of the Eucharist from a consideration of the different names given to it by the Fathers of the Church; the third and fourth books deal with different arguments for the Real Presence, while the final book is a vindication of the Eucharistic character of chapter six of St John's Gospel.[37] It is his longest and, in the opinion of one of his biographers, the most important of all his works.[38] His great love for the Eucharist comes through on every page. For Fisher the Eucharist was primarily what built up the unity of the Church, and this perhaps explains why he wrote more pages in defence of this sacrament than on any other issue in the dispute.[39]

His work is a running commentary on Oecolampadius' book. The latter, although much more irenic in his approach, departed even farther than Luther from Catholic doctrine. His style is unctious and conceited, and he offers his supposed new theological insights into the doctrine of the Eucharist as the result of prayer and dedicated study. Fisher cuts through the cant and sophisms of Oecolampadius like a razor through butter.

> No, he replies, neither prayer nor study of Scripture, nor both united will avail you ought; for both must be joined to humility. Oecolampadius thinks that the Doorkeeper, the Holy Spirit, has been so long idle in the Church, that he has not opened to the prayers and searchings of the saints for so many centuries ... Do you think none of our forefathers has done these things? Did not Basil and Chrysostom, Athanasius, Cyril, Cyprian, Jerome, Ambrose, Augustine, and the rest exercise themselves frequently? Are you the only one who has called efficaciously, you the only one who has humbled his heart, the only one who has sought with diligence, and dug out with much toil the sense of God's words? Their prayers, foresooth, were nothing to yours! Their humility compared with yours was pride! Their diligence and labour of no account! Is it not the very height of pride and self-conceit to yield to such folly for a moment? ... And are we to think that he has hidden

37 Cf. R. Rex, 'The polemical theologian', in HRR, p. 112. It has been pointed out by the well-known Morean scholar, Professor Germain Marc'hadour, that Fisher's *De veritate* had a considerable influence on some of More's writings on the Eucharist. Specifically, this is most evident in his *Answer to the poisoned book* (1533) which relies heavily on the preface to Book V of *De veritate*, and in the *Treatise upon the Passion* (1534), where the essay on the names of the Eucharist in Book II of *De veritate* provide the substance of More's 'second lecture' in the *Treatise;* see G. Marc'hadour, 'Fisher and More', in HRR, p. 107. **38** Cf. Bridgett, ibid., p. 124. Surtz refers to it as 'undoubtedly his theological masterpiece' (ibid., p. 337). **39** Cf.

> from all these the true meaning of his principal sacrament, in order that you may have the glory of discovering it?[40]

Fisher rowed in heavily against the distortion, truncation, and mutilation of patristic texts by Oecolampadius to make them prove his thesis, demonstrating the deceit by a staggering display of patristic scholarship.[41]

Although he wrote penetratingly about the Eucharist, and was well acquainted with all the patristic and other writings on this subject, because of his intuition of the great depth of this *mysterium fidei*, he maintained that it was far beyond the capacity of the human mind to grasp its full implications.[42] Oecolampadius' fundamental difficulty, from Fisher's point of view, was that he was seeking to understand, not to believe, trying to learn by argument, not by faith.

THEOLOGY OF JOHN FISHER

A fairly recent study of Fisher gives a penetrating analysis of his theological approach and the originality of his thinking. It also demonstrates the profound influence the writings of the saintly bishop of Rochester had on bishops and theologians in mainland Europe and, through them, on the deliberations of the Council of Trent.[43] According to the contemporary Spanish theologian, Francisco Vitoria, Fisher was the only bishop, at the outset of the theological debate against Lutheranism, who was intellectually equipped to do battle with the reformers.[44]

Marc'hadour, ibid., p. 106. **40** Cf. Bridgett, pp 128–9. '*Abeas in malum crucem*' says Fisher to his theological opponent, the nearest approach to a curse, Bridgett tells us, that the venerable bishop ever permitted himself, which he roughly translates as 'High hanging to you'. **41** For example, in the fourth book he charges Oecolampadius with suppressing unfavourable passages in Ambrose, with leaving a sentence in Irenaeus incomplete, with neglecting to furnish the whole context on one occasion, and inserting his own words on another occasion in Tertullian, and with giving only a fragment from Chrysostom when what precedes and follows contradicts him (cf. Surtz, p. 344). **42** 'Quis non videt, quantum istud omnes humani ingenii vires transcendat?' (Who does not see how much this exceeds all the powers of human ingenuity?) (*De veritate*, Bk I, chap. 4, quoted by Rex, op. cit., in HRR, note 83, p. 130). This comment recalls something very similar written by Pope John Paul II in his first encyclical letter, *Redemptor hominis*, in 1979. Referring to the rich tradition of Eucharistic doctrine handed down in the Church's Magisterium 'from the most distant times down to our own day', he comments that, nevertheless, 'we can say with certainty that although this teaching is sustained by the acuteness of theologians, by men of deep faith and prayer, and by ascetics and mystics, in complete fidelity to the Eucharistic mystery, it still reaches no more than the threshold, since it is incapable of grasping and translating into words what the Eucharist is in all its fullness, what is expressed by it and what is achieved by it' (no. 20). **43** Cf. Rex, *The theology of John Fisher*, pp 87–92. **44** Cf. Surtz, ibid., p. 17, and note 101: '… multi insurgunt haereses, et quasi nullus episcopus hactenus inventus est qui eis obviam eat. Solus unus episcopus est modo in Ecclesia, puta Roffensis, vir magnae doctrinae, qui scribat

Scripture was very much the soul of Fisher's theology. He describes the inspired text as the spiritual food of the soul. For him the Scriptures were written down under the inspiration of the Holy Spirit and as such are free from all error. Where the difficulty arises is in determining the meaning or truth intended by the divine author. In his own exegesis, however, he always follows the rule of the analogy of faith, that is, he rejects every interpretation which would make the biblical authors seem to conflict with one another, or with the doctrine of the Church. The foundation for the interpretative principle of the analogy of faith (which is reaffirmed in the Vatican II dogmatic constitution on Divine Revelation, *Dei verbum*, 12) is spelled out by Fisher as follows: (a) there is no discord, no contradiction between one part of Scripture and another, and (b) 'though there be many books of Scripture, both in the Old Testament and in the New also, yet all these books be so fully agreed by the expositions and interpretations of the holy doctors that they make but one book, and one body of Scripture, and have in them but one spirit of life, that is to say, the Spirit of Christ Jesus.'[45] On the basis of this principle he is able to bring very damaging charges against Luther of making some passages of Scripture repugnant to others, not least in relation to the Letter of St James and the Gospel of St Luke.

From the start of his controversies Fisher saw the need to treat the books of Scripture not only as divinely inspired, but also as documents which were the result of human authorship. In this latter sense the inspired text reflected the literary characteristics of the hagiographer and the cultural environment to which he belonged, and thus it was necessary to take the human dimension of Scripture into account in arriving at an authentic interpretation. Because he worked from the Hebrew and Greek texts, in addition to the Latin, Fisher was able to identify more easily with the cultural context of the human authors of the Bible. He in no way underestimated the exegetical competence of the heretics. Nevertheless, his judgement was that 'for lack of the spirit of truth they misconstrued them, ... they turned the wrong side of the Scriptures outward'.[46]

While Scripture is the basis of his theology, Fisher knew well that, because of the obscurity of many passages, on its own it was insufficient to settle controversies. Against the *sola Scriptura* principle of the Lutherans, he affirmed the need to listen to the living voice of an infallible Church and the unanimous consent of the Fathers, as extrinsic principles of interpretation. Indeed, he goes

contra lutheranos' (Many heretics arise and practically no bishop can be found who will take them on. There is only one bishop in the Church who is ready to do this, the bishop of Rochester, a man of superb doctrine, who writes against the Lutherans) (In 2.2 de fide, q.2, a.8, *Comentarios a la secunda secundae de Santo Tomás*, ed. Vincente Beltrán de Heredia (Salamanca, 1932–5), I. 76). This was a comment made by Vitoria during a course of lectures at the University of Salamanca in 1534–5. **45** From the sermon preached on the abjuration of Robert Barnes in 1526, quoted in Surtz, p. 122. **46** Cf. Surtz, ibid., p. 124.

so far as to say: 'As for me, I indeed cry boldly with Augustine that I would not believe even the Gospel, were it not that I believe the Church and the Fathers'.[47] Fisher combined exegetical skill with a deep knowledge of Tradition as reflected in the writings of both Latin and Greek Fathers. Although Augustine and Chrysostom were his favourite sources, his library of the Fathers was one of the most complete in its day.[48]

However, in 1527, with the arrival centre-stage of Henry's concern about the validity of his marriage, authority in scriptural interpretation ceased to be academic and became a matter of urgent and practical import. Fisher's stand was unequivocal: the Pope had the necessary authority to remove the ambiguity about the interpretation of the Levitical prohibition (Lev 20:21)[49] by declaring it to be judicial and not a matter of natural law. As we shall see, it was a stand that would ultimately lead to his execution.

In an age which frequently demonstrated little restraint in theological polemic, Fisher's argumentation was characterized by its eirenic qualities in contrast to the invective of so many of the other contenders. This doesn't mean that his writing lacked theological bite. On the contrary, his intellectual acuity enabled him to penetrate to the basic principles at issue in the Lutheran debate more quickly than any other theologian in Europe.

To get an overview of the theological co-ordinates within which Fisher worked, the following passage from the *Sacra sacerdotii defensio* (Defence of the sacred priesthood), where he uses the argument from prescription in defence of the institution of the Catholic priesthood, gives us a good idea of his approach:

> But consider diligently Christ's care for us: consider the certain truths of the presence and the activity of the Holy Spirit in the Church: consider the numberless clear testimonies of the prelates of olden times, illustrious not only by their holiness, but also by their learning and miracles: consider the unanimous agreement of all the churches, with no single exception through so many centuries. How can it be imagined that at length for the first time has shone on Luther the light of a truth that no one of the early Fathers could so much as have suspected, the

47 *Defensio regiae assertionis*, chap. 10, as quoted in Surtz, ibid., p. 130. 48 For Fisher the Fathers are 'always the more distinguished part of the Church', who have shone like stars because of their learning and holiness, and whose status has been confirmed by miracles. In his introduction to the *Confutatio* he writes: 'The Holy Spirit hitherto has used, and always will use, the tongues of the orthodox Fathers for the extirpation of heresies and for the full instruction of the Church in doubtful matters' (cf. Surtz, ibid., p.105). When both the heretical and orthodox quote Scripture, Fisher resorts to tradition as expressed in the Fathers to determine the true meaning of Church doctrine. 49 'If a man takes his brother's wife, it is impurity; he has uncovered his brother's nakedness, they shall be childless' (Lev 20:21).

> contrary, indeed, of which they have unitedly asserted from the very beginning? For if for so long the truth has remained imprisoned in darkness, waiting during so many centuries for Luther, and him only, to set it free, then Christ's solicitude for our Fathers in the faith was in vain; in vain, too, the coming of the Holy Spirit to teach them all truth; in vain their prayers and devout search for the truth, if all along they were unanimously teaching to the churches so dangerous a lie. And if there was an error in a matter so vital to the faith, then in vain, if I may use the language of Tertullian, were so many millions of men baptized, in vain were wrought so many works of faith and miracles, in vain so many graces given, so many functions of the priesthood performed, in vain did so many martyrs suffer, if indeed they all died in a false faith. For without the true faith, no one of them could please God.[50]

Fisher's works were drawn on by, among others, Bellarmine, Colchaeus, Erasmus, and Murner. Besides helping to shape the Catholic approach to Luther's doctrine, he contributed a number of particular arguments to the general thrust of Counter-Reformation theology. Fisher was one of the few contemporary theologians to be cited in the debates on justification at the Council of Trent (1545–63). There are several references to him in the published records of that Council on Scripture and Tradition, on sacramental confession, on indulgences, holy orders and on purgatory. His authority at the Council was, doubtless, enhanced by his martyrdom and reputation for holiness. Even more influential was Fisher's *De veritate*. Half of the references made to him at Trent were to his Eucharistic writings, and it would appear that *De veritate* seems to have been a sort of reference book for the debates on the Real Presence in the contributions of theologians, especially for Lainez and Salmeron, the Pope's theologians, who played such an important role in the Council.

To rubbish the rising reputation of Fisher after his execution, and to vindicate his barbarous liquidation, Henry organized some venal theological lackeys to spread the libel that the bishop of Rochester had written only out of a desire for personal glory. Fisher had no natural propensity for theological controversy – most of what he wrote was at the request of others, and out of a sense of responsibility to souls. As he himself explained in one of his first polemical works:

> I intend to confirm the faith of the weaker brethern, whose faith has for too long now been poised on the knife edge between heresy and orthodoxy … It was for their sake that the order to which I belong was ever-

50 Hallett, ibid., pp 19–20.

> lastingly established ... if this flock should perish through our negligence, the blood shall be upon our heads.[51]

Fisher's writings against the heretics are inspired by the view that, as a consequence of its God-given authority, it is part of the teaching office of the Church to interpret Scripture in the light of Tradition, and in this way to hand on to us the fullness of the truth taught by Christ. He was concerned about the pastoral implications of doctrine, because he was convinced that unsound teaching leads to false devotion. Precisely because of the intimate relationship between doctrine and devotion in the Eucharist, and the centrality of this teaching for Catholic faith, he devoted his best efforts to its defence.

The devastating consequences of Luther's ecclesiology prompted Fisher to develop a rich theology of the Church. In his articulation of this doctrine he draws much from the metaphor of the 'spiritual house' and 'living stones' (1 Pet 2:5–8; cf. Eph 2:20–22), stones that have to be strong and steadfast in the faith and good works in order to spread the Gospel to all nations, with Peter as the foundation.

However, it is the perception of the Church as the Mystical Body of Christ that predominates in Fisher's writings. In the *Confutatio* he asserts,

> So great indeed is the unity of this Mystical Body (which is the Church) that all we Christians are called, and actually are, not only one Body but also one Spirit on account of the Holy Spirit dwelling in us.[52]

Of the four traditional notes of the Church the one that is dearest to Fisher is that of unity, not only of head but especially of mind and heart as manifested in the writings of St Paul. On the other hand, the heretics, like the builders of Babel, have fallen out among themselves – a clear sign of error and heterodoxy. The unity of the Mystical Body, in space and time, is effected by its soul, the Holy Spirit. This lofty conception did not, however, as we have already seen, blind Fisher to the sad condition of the historical Church. Nevertheless, in spite of all its imperfections, the Church is still the Spouse of Christ and the Mother of Christians, and as such is worthy of filial love and protection.

Surtz sums up the general thrust of Fisher's ecclesiological arguments:

> Divine in origin, international in scope, lasting to the end of time, fruitful in justice and holiness, and marvellously balancing hierarchy and obedience, authority and freedom – she has always been defended by

51 Cf. *Assertionis lutheranae confutatio*, 'Dedication to the reader', as quoted in R. Rex, 'The polemical theologian', in HRR, p. 114. 52 Cf. Surtz, ibid., p. 37.

> her free and loyal sons against her five great persecutors: Jew, gentile, philosopher, tyrant and heretic. The Bishop of Rochester undoubtedly feels it to be his personal destiny and duty to shield her to the death against two particular classes of contemporary persecutors: against the tyrannical government of Henry VIII, Cromwell and Parliament, and against the heretical hordes of Luther, Oecolampadius, and Protestants.[53]

PIETY

Fisher's fortitude in the service of the Church and truth was nourished by a life of deep piety. While he gave generously to the poor and was a bountiful host, he treated himself harshly with regular fasts and severe penances. His generous spirit of reparation caused him to wear a hair shirt next to his skin, and to punish his body with a whip of cords. After Fisher was imprisoned in 1534, the king sent commissioners to his residence to make an inventory of his possessions. This document is still extant and gives a striking picture of episcopal poverty. In his private oratory in Rochester, the commissioners came across a coffer, in which they expected to find the gold and silver that had so far eluded them in their search. Instead, to their surprise, they found only a hair shirt and two or three disciplines. When the bishop heard in prison of the opening of the coffer, he commented that if haste had not made him forget this and many other things, they would not have found those items. Fisher was not a man to broadcast his private penances, and his sensitivities were offended at this invasion of an intimate part of his spiritual life.[54]

The bishop of Rochester, as we have seen, wrote much during his lifetime but he was at his best when he was writing about his Eucharistic Lord. He had a great love for the Holy Mass such that frequently tears fell from his cheeks during its celebration. His defence of the Mass and the ministerial priesthood against Luther is a classic of scriptural and patristic scholarship.[55] Nothing caused him greater sorrow and grief than the reformers' effort to eliminate the Holy Sacrifice of the Mass. In his prologue to the *Defence of the priesthood* Fisher says he had perused many of the books which had come from Luther's printing press, but of all of them there was none, in his opinion,

> more pestilential, senseless and shameless than the one he entitled *The Abrogation of the Mass*, for in it he tries utterly to destroy the sacrifice of

53 Ibid., p. 99. **54** Cf. Reynolds, ibid., p. 281; Bridgett, ibid., p. 286. **55** *Sacri sacerdotii defensio contra Lutherum* (1525).

> the Body and Blood of Christ which the Church had ever held to be the most salutary, and the chief object of devotion for all the faithful of Christ ...
>
> My God [he exclaims, after giving a sample of Luther's offensive and vitriolic diatribe against the Mass], how can one be calm when one hears such blasphemous lies uttered against the mysteries of Christ? How can one without resentment listen to such outrageous insults hurled against Christ's priests? Who can even read such blasphemies without weeping from sheer grief if he still retains in his heart even the smallest spark of Christian piety?[56]

It is while dealing with Luther's assertion that women have an equal right with men to preach in the name of the Church that John Fisher reveals to us something of his own tender devotion to the Mother of God:

> But as to the most Blessed Virgin, who bore for us the Lord Jesus, we need have no surprise if she, by a special privilege, still teaches the whole Church by her canticle. Can we wonder if she, the mother of the Word, proclaims the word to all? Sublime beyond all others is the prerogative of the Blessed Virgin, so singular in her perfections, who alone is the mother of God. What, then, was especially granted to her cannot be extended to others. Woe to those wretches who even in the smallest degree try to lessen the pre-eminence of this glorious Virgin, as I hear is a common practice of the Lutherans. Wherefore, unless they hasten to repent the divine vengeance will not fail to overtake them.[57]

DIVINE FILIATION

But if we are to get to the very core of the spiritual life of John Fisher we have to turn to the draft of a prayer in his own handwriting which has survived, and which was written while waiting for death in the Tower of London. Abandoned by all human support, he opens his heart to his Father God in this exquisite text which, in the opinion of one of his biographers, 'is the only truly intimate expression of his inner life'.[58] From this document we can measure something of the depth of Fisher's spirit of divine filiation, and can see revealed the tenderness of his love for God which he is more reserved about in his other writings. This confidence in a paternal, divine providence is the source of all his strength and consolation in his prison cell. 'Help me, most loving Father',

56 Hallett, ibid., p. 2. **57** Ibid., p.130. **58** Reynolds, ibid., p. 261.

he prays, 'help me with thy mighty grace. Rescue me from these manifold perils that I am in'. He is conscious that during his life he has not had that recourse to his Father God that he should have had. He is sorry for this negligence:

> Alas, woe is me! What shall I do? Whether may I turn? To whom shall I resort for help? Where shall I seek for any remedy against the worldly and earthly waywardness of my heart? Whither should I rather go than to my Father, to my most loving Father, to my most merciful Father, to him that of his infinite love and mercy hath given me boldness to call him Father?[59]

It is his son Jesus who teaches us how to see God as a Father, and because we can trust his words we can be certain of three things: that God is a Father; that he is a more kind and loving Father to us than are the human fathers of this world to their own children; that, to those who devoutly ask for it, he will give the gift of his most Holy Spirit.[60] The name of Father, he continues, is a name of love and tenderness, of delight and pleasure, a name which stirs the heart with hope and constancy, and many other delightful affections. What is clear is that Fisher had a deep, affectionate relationship with his own father, which subsequently allowed him to penetrate profoundly into the great mystery of divine sonship.

DEFENCE OF CATHERINE'S MARRIAGE

In May 1527 the first official act in what was to become known as the 'King's great matter' took place in Cardinal Wolsey's palace in Westminster. He and Archbishop Warham of Canterbury, as guardians of public morality, cited Henry to appear before them for having lived in sin for the previous eighteen years with his brother's widow. Being afraid to take the decision on themselves, the archbishops consulted other members of the hierarchy regarding the lawfulness of the marriage with a brother's widow. The replies didn't please Henry, most of them answering that such a marriage with a papal dispensation (granted by Julius II in this case) would be valid. Fisher, after careful study of the Fathers and Sacred Scripture, replied that he was thoroughly convinced there was no prohibition against such a marriage.

He said more. Knowing full well what Wolsey was capable of, and how he was likely to compromise the Pope by his advice in this matter, he tried to

59 Cf. ibid., Appendix C, p. 320. **60** Cf. ibid.

offset the possible scandal in a highly-charged emotional appeal to the two archbishops:

> With the greatest possible humility of soul, I beg the indulgence of the Most Reverend Lord Legates if I now reveal in these written words what I tearfully lament in the depths of my heart. For it makes me tremble even to think of the great inconsistency with which the Apostolic See hereafter will be charged if the Sovereign Pontiff Clement, for a cause which involves no difficulty arising from divine law, should break up a marriage which, in all kindness and all affection, at the solicitation of those most illustrious kings through their ambassadors, he had once confirmed by his authority. O for the misfortune of our times! O for the pitiable ruin hanging over the head of the Church, if there should be such an outcome to this affair – which God forbid![61]

From that time until Henry's attempted marriage to Anne Boleyn (January 1533), Fisher used every opportunity to defend Queen Catherine's cause in his preaching and in his writing.

By 1525 Catherine was forty years of age. She had presented Henry with one daughter, the future Queen Mary, but with no male heir. There had been several still-births and it now seemed unlikely that Henry could expect a son to succeed him. At some stage Henry became aware of the text of Leviticus: 'He that marries his brother's wife does an unlawful thing ... they shall be without children' (20:21), and thus felt he had grounds to question the validity of his marriage to Catherine, who had previously been married to Arthur, his elder brother. The king claimed that it was his concern for a legitimate male heir that first caused him to take the text seriously, but subsequent events were strongly to suggest that it was his passion for Anne Boleyn, one of Catherine's ladies-in-waiting, which was the determining factor in Henry's newly-acquired concern for biblical exegesis.

About September 1527 the king consulted Fisher personally about his 'great matter'. The bishop of Rochester told him that there wasn't the slightest doubt about the validity of his marriage, and that he was prepared to defend this view against all-comers. Seven years later, when he was imprisoned in the Tower of London, and interrogated about the number of books he had written concerning the king's marriage and divorce, he replied:

> I am not certain how many, but I can recall seven or eight that I have written. The matter was so serious both on account of the importance

61 *De causa matrimonii serenissimi regis Angliae liber*, Alcalá 1530, Second Axiom, translated by Surtz, ibid., p. 355.

> of the persons it concerned, and the express command of the king, that I gave more labour and diligence to seeking out the truth lest I should fail him and others, than I ever gave to any other matter.[62]

He fulfilled his responsibilities to his king, yet he never reneged on his support for Catherine. He consistently spoke out in her defence even though he knew well that such a stance was fraught with dangerous consequences.

THE ANGER OF THE PRINCE

Archbishop Warham of Canterbury was terrified of Henry. 'Indignatio principis mors est' was all he would say when Catherine asked for advice.[63] John Fisher, ignoring threats, sent Catherine word to be of good courage, that the dispensation granted by Julius II for her marriage to Henry was perfectly valid. After much negotiating Henry obtained from Pope Clement VII a commitment to set up a commission of inquiry into his marital status. Cardinal Campeggio, the absentee bishop of Salisbury, and cardinal protector of England, arrived in London in October 1528 as papal legate to study the matter with Wolsey.

Wolsey threw himself into the divorce issue with all his political acumen and administrative energy. Driven by personal ambition, he became the willing tool of Henry and espoused the dissimulation, fraud and intimidation employed by the king to obtain the divorce and rid himself of the defenceless Catherine. As Bridgett points out, from his study of all the documents involved, the most revolting aspect of the whole affair is the unmitigated hypocrisy practised by king and cardinal.

A prime example of this crass hypocrisy is the following. Before the opening of the legatine court in May 1529, news reached England of the Pope's illness and his likely approaching death. It occurred to Henry that if either Wolsey or Campeggio could be elected Pope, the divorce would be assured. Consequently in February 1529 he wrote as follows to his agents in Rome, giving them his full permission to use all his influence to determine the outcome of the election:

> If the cardinals present, having God and the Holy Spirit before them, consider what is best for the Church, they cannot fail to agree upon Wolsey; but as human fragility suffers not all things to be weighed in

62 Reynolds, ibid., pp 236–7. **63** 'The anger of the Prince means death' – cf. G. Mattingly, *Catherine of Aragon* (London, 1950), p. 191.

> just balance, the ambassadors are to make promises of spiritual promotions, offices, dignities, rewards of money and other things; they are also to show them what Wolsey will give up if he enters into this dangerous storm and troublesome tempest for the relief of the Church, all of which benefices will be given to the king's friends, besides other large rewards.[64]

Simony is proposed on a massive scale, and all with the sanction of Wolsey. Against the venality of Wolsey and Henry, and their subjugation of all the wealth and apparatus of state to force through the divorce issue, Fisher's directness and transparency in defence of Catherine stands out in stark contrast.

The legatine court eventually opened on the last day of May 1529. The king, playing out this legal charade, said to the judges that he could no longer remain in mortal sin, as he had done during the previous twenty years, and that he would never be at ease until the rights of his marriage were decided.

Before Henry started to take an interest in Anne Boleyn, her sister Mary had already been his mistress. With a view to the dissolution of his first marriage, the king had already drafted a bull of dispensation for a second marriage, into which he had a clause inserted affirming that such a relationship (his affinity with Mary) could not be an impediment to his marriage with Anne. What this demonstrated was that the question of affinity was the last thing that troubled Henry's conscience in relation to his marriage with Catherine. The hypocrisy of Henry's position was cogently underlined by Cardinal Pole, a relative and former courtier, in a document he wrote to the king shortly after Fisher's execution:

> Now what sort of person is it whom you have put in the place of your divorced wife? Is she not the sister of her whom first you violated, and for a long time after kept as your concubine? She certainly is. How is it, then, that you now tell us of the horror you have of illicit marriage? Are you ignorant of the law which certainly no less prohibits marriage with a sister of one with whom *you* have become one flesh, than with one with whom your brother was one flesh. If the one kind of marriage is detestable, so is the other. Were you ignorant of this law? Nay, you knew it better than others. How do I prove that? Because, at the very time you were rejecting the dispensation of the pope to marry your brother's widow, you were doing your very utmost to get leave from the pope to marry the sister of your former concubine.[65]

64 Bridgett, ibid., p. 146. **65** *De unitate Ecclesiae*, III, as translated in Bridgett, pp 148–9.

Everything seemed to be going in the king's favour until Fisher appeared at the fifth session of the legatine court to put the case in Catherine's defence. In his heart he knew the whole procedure was a farce and that, perhaps, was why he was so resolute and unyielding in putting the queen's case. No power, human or divine, he testified, could dissolve the marriage. And, he protested, he was ready to lay down his life in support of it's validity, as John the Baptist had done at another time.[66]

PARALLELISM WITH JOHN THE BAPTIST

In answer to Fisher, Henry replied to the legates in a manner which clearly showed how resentful he was at the bishop's protest, particularly his affirmation that he was ready to suffer like St John the Baptist, as it naturally suggested a comparison between Henry and Herod Antipas. However, the martyrdom of St John had long been a familiar subject of contemplation to Fisher, as is clear from his treatise in defence of Henry's book against Luther – the *Defensio regiae assertionis*.[67]

> One consideration, Fisher writes, that greatly affects me to believe in the sacrament of marriage is the martyrdom of St John the Baptist, who suffered death for his reproof of the violation of marriage. There were many crimes in appearance more grievous for rebuking which he might have suffered, but there was none more fitting than the crime of adultery to be the cause of the blood-shedding of the Friend of the Bridegroom, since the violation of marriage is no little insult to Him who is called the Bridegroom.[68]

Bridgett draws the striking parallel between the fate of the Baptist and John Fisher:

> At that time [when Fisher wrote the above in 1525] no thought of divorce had as yet, in all probability, entered the mind of Henry; Anne Boleyn, Fisher's Herodias, was then unknown. But the circumstances of Fisher's death bear so close a resemblance to those of the Baptist's, that

66 Campeggio's secretary wrote to Italy on 29 June 1529 describing how Fisher appeared on behalf of the queen: 'In order not to procure the damnation of his soul, and in order not to be unfaithful to the king, or to fail in doing the duty he owed to the truth, in a matter of such great importance, he presented himself … to declare, to affirm, and with forceable reasons to demonstrate to them that this marriage of the king and queen can be dissolved by no power human or divine, and for this opinion he declared he would lay down his life' (Bridgett, ibid., p. 170). **67** Cf. notes 30 and 31 above. **68** Bridgett, ibid., p. 175.

> it is strange even Henry did not observe and seek to avoid it. Both were cast into prison and left there to linger at the will of a tyrant; both at last were beheaded, and both by the revenge of impure women. But what Herod did reluctantly, Henry did with cruel deliberation.[69]

As we have seen, the bishop of Rochester wrote several books in defence of Catherine's cause. Some members of the English hierarchy were alarmed at Fisher's outspoken attitude. Warham, supported by others of his episcopal colleagues, urged Fisher to retract his writings. This he refused to do as he was not prepared to deny what he believed to be the truth. Wolsey and the king had created an atmosphere of terror and those who were near Henry knew full well that he was ruthless in pursuit of his own objectives. Sir Thomas More had no illusions about his friendship with the king, as he remarked on one occasion to his daughter Margaret's husband: 'Son Roper, if my head would win him a castle in France, it should not fail to go'.[70] It was little wonder then that people shrank from incurring the king's wrath. Most were terrified of him, including the bishops.

On 25 June 1529 Warham read out before the legatine court a list of bishops who had put their names to a document endorsing the king's position. At the mention of the bishop of Rochester's name, the tall, gaunt figure rose suddenly from the group of listening bishops. 'That is not my hand or seal', John Fisher snapped out, clarifying that Warham had tried to persuade him to put his seal to the document but that he had refused saying: 'I would never consent to no such act'. 'True', Warham admitted, but he insisted that Fisher had been eventually persuaded that he, Warham, should append Fisher's seal on the bishop of Rochester's behalf. Fisher retorted that this was totally untrue. Warham was highly embarrassed to have to admit his forgery, and Fisher went on to make a bold defence of the queen with a blunt assertion of the law: 'Whom God hath joined together, let no man put asunder'.[71] Fisher refused to allow himself to be pressurized by his episcopal colleagues to take the easy way out – the way of silence. On 23 July, much to the chagrin of Henry, the legatine court was suspended until October without coming to a decision. It never reconvened.

SUBMISSION OF THE CLERGY

In November 1529 Parliament met and a bill of complaints was passed against the clergy. The importance of the issue lay not so much in the complaints

69 Ibid. **70** William Roper, *The life of Sir Thomas More, Knight*, ed. E.V. Hitchcock, Early English Texts Society (London, 1935), p. 20. **71** Cf. Mattingly, ibid., p. 210.

themselves, but in the fact that the Commons were encroaching on what had hitherto been ecclesiastical territory. Fisher strongly defended the rights of the Church against this encroachment on its legislative powers. He saw that, if in the prevailing political atmosphere this first step were permitted, a greater intrusion would inevitably follow. However, he was outmanoeuvred by Henry and the bill became law.

Cardinal Wolsey's failure to carry through the divorce issue brought down upon him the ire of the king and his dismissal from office. He was prosecuted under the statute of *Praemunire*[72] on the trumped up charge that in exercising the office of cardinal-legate he had ignored the statute's provisions. Wolsey thought it safest to plead guilty and, after surrendering to the king the bulk of the wealth he had acquired while in office, he received a qualified pardon. The success of this process against Wolsey must have suggested to Henry the indictment of the whole of the English clergy under the same statute, on the grounds that they accepted Wolsey's legatine authority. It was a pure technicality, and, even more, everything had been done not only with the consent of the king, but with his authority and connivance. This was another example of the crass hypocrisy of Henry.

The writ was issued and, at the Canterbury Convocation (January 1531), the opposition of the clergy weakly and foolishly melted before this tyrannous charge. They offered to purchase a pardon for the sum of £40,000. Henry let it be known that the amount proposed was totally inadequate, so Convocation agreed to raise the then enormous sum of £100,000. But this still didn't satisfy the king. Feeling perhaps that he now had the clergy on the run, he followed up his request for more money with the preposterous demand that they would now recognize him as 'Protector and Supreme Head of the English Church and Clergy.'

Many of the bishops, out of fear of Henry, were ready to grant his request. However, John Fisher spoke out so strongly against the proposal that it was finally rejected unanimously. When Henry heard what had happened, and how influential the bishop of Rochester had been in bringing it about, he sent messengers to Convocation to remind the bishops of the perilous consequences of conviction on a charge of *praemunire* – forfeiture of all possessions and life imprisonment. Fisher again refused to accede to Henry's request, and earnestly encouraged the other bishops to do the same. He clearly foresaw the highly dangerous implications of granting Henry this recognition. He spoke out strongly against the measure and rebuked the bishops for their pusillanimity when he saw that they were likely to give way under pressure. Perceiving that

72 The term *Praemunire* was a convenient label for statutes passed in the fourteenth century to check the direct exercise of papal authority in England by prohibiting appeals to Rome. The penalty in case of conviction was forfeiture of all possessions and life imprisonment.

they lacked the fortitude to follow him all the way, Fisher then insisted that the conditional phrase *quantum per legem Dei licet* (as far as the law of God allows) should be inserted after the title. There was a further demand from the king to have the grant passed absolutely but, led by the courage of Fisher, Convocation insisted on the retention of the qualifying clause. Chapuys, the imperial ambassador in London, writing to Charles V about the incident says: 'The Bishop of Rochester is very ill with disappointment at it. He opposes it as much as he can; but being threatened that he and his adherents should be thrown into the river, he was forced to consent to the king's will'.[73]

HENRY AS SUPREME HEAD

In May of 1532 Henry made further demands on Convocation requiring that all future legislation passed by the bishops should have royal approval. It now became abundantly clear what the king meant by 'Supreme Head' of the Church. Fisher lay ill in bed at his house in Lambeth and took no part in the proceedings of Convocation. But the bishops, at a loss to know what to do, sent a deputation to him asking for advice about the best course of action to follow. In spite of what Fisher may have said to them, the bishops gave way to Henry's demand and promised not to legislate for the future without royal consent. On 15 May 1532 they surrendered the Church's divine right to legislate for the spiritual welfare of their people, an event which has become notorious in history as the 'Submission of the Clergy'. The very next day Sir Thomas More resigned as lord chancellor of England. He realized that he could no longer exercise any effective influence for good on affairs of state, and rather than acquiesce, he withdrew from public life. As soon as Fisher recovered from the illness which had kept him from attending Convocation, he publicly denounced in a sermon the evil which was now imminent, and continued to preach in favour of the queen despite the danger of imprisonment.

The year 1533 was an eventful one. In January Henry was secretly married to Anne Boleyn. Since Anne was pregnant it became necessary to expedite matters so that the expected offspring would be rendered legitimate. In March, at Henry's request, despite the opposition of John Fisher, Convocation passed two propositions:

a) that the Pope had no power to grant a dispensation for a man to marry his childless brother's widow, and
b) that the marriage between Catherine and Arthur had been consummated (Catherine had always claimed the contrary).

73 Bridgett, ibid., p. 209.

It must have greatly saddened the bishop of Rochester to see how the monarch had reduced episcopal authority to a level of servility without precedent in the history of the English church. Fisher was imprisoned on 6 April 1533 and not released until 13 June.

In the interim, Cranmer, Henry's creature as archbishop of Canterbury,[74] gave sentence against the validity of Catherine's marriage (23 May), and declared valid the marriage between Henry and Anne (28 May). On 1 June he crowned her queen of England in Westminster Abbey. Fisher, who was the most outspoken man in England in defence of Catherine and the rights of the Church, was, by his imprisonment, conveniently kept out of the way while Cranmer danced a canonical jig to Henry's tune. On 11 July the Pope declared the king's marriage with Anne to be null and void, and on 8 August a brief of censure was issued against Cranmer, as well as against Henry and Anne.[75] In September, Anne gave birth to the future Elizabeth I.

As Fisher observed the development of Henry's menacing approach to the Church and to Catherine, and the tyrannous imposition on England of a religious regime totally foreign to a millennium of Catholic tradition, in desperation he sent secret messages to the emperor, Charles V, Queen Catherine's nephew, to try to persuade him to send an invasionary force to England to help depose the king and to reverse the train of events. However, since Charles was preoccupied with other more immediate political concerns, and as Catherine would have none of it, Fisher's overtures never came to anything. It was an extreme and highly dangerous initiative, but at the time schism within the Church was seen as an evil that must be prevented at all costs, not excluding armed intervention.

The logic of the events of 1533 made it necessary to set aside the Princess Mary as illegitimate and to fix the succession on the king's offspring by Anne Boleyn. This was achieved by the passing of the Succession Act in Parliament on 30 March 1534. The preamble to the act recites the illegality and invalidity of the marriage between Henry and Catherine, the validity of the divorce pronounced by Cranmer, and confirms the lawfulness of the marriage between Henry and Anne. The act goes on to make it high treason to oppose the succession, and misprision of treason to speak against it.[76] The act required that all subjects of the realm would be obliged to take an oath to observe and maintain all the effects and contents of the act.

74 Archbishop Warham died in August 1532; Thomas Cranmer, a protégé of the Boleyn family, was consecrated as his successor on 30 March 1533. 75 Cf. Reynolds, ibid., p. 196. 76 'Misprison of treason', from the French *mepris*, contempt, means the bare knowledge and concealment of treason without any degree of consent to it – see Bridgett, ibid., p. 237.

TAKING THE OATH

The tyrant in Henry had now reached its full flowering, no doubt well tutored by Master Secretary Thomas Cromwell, an ardent devotee of the Machiavellian school of politics. Not content with the usurpation of all religious authority, the purpose of this new act was to eliminate totally the expression of any opinion contrary to the king's wishes. Taking the oath had very clear religious and moral consequences. It implied the repudiation of the spiritual authority of the Pope who in July 1533 had annulled the proceedings of Cranmer, and in March 1534 had finally confirmed the validity of Henry's marriage to Catherine. During this parliamentary session Fisher was confined to bed through illness and was unable to play his accustomed role in defence of the rights of the Church and the papacy. All the bishops took the oath at the end of March. On 13 April Fisher was summoned to appear at Lambeth Palace to do likewise.

When the bishop of Rochester was presented with the text of the oath he asked for time to consider it. Four days later he again refused it and was sent to the Tower of London, out of which he was not to come again until the time of his trial and execution in June of the following year. The Act of Supremacy, passed by parliament on 18 November 1534, made it high treason maliciously to deny to the king the title of Supreme Head of the Church. Henry had now closed off all possible escape routes to the opposition. To try to put extra pressure on him, Fisher was falsely informed that Thomas More had taken the oath – More had been imprisoned in the Tower around the same time as Fisher and had also refused the oath. Nevertheless Fisher stood firm and, as a consequence, the see of Rochester was declared vacant on 2 January 1535.

Fisher suffered considerably during his period of imprisonment. He was in very poor health. His cell in the Tower was cold and damp. In a very moving letter to Cromwell, dated 22 December 1534, he describes his condition:

> I beseech you to be good master unto me in my necessity; for I have neither shirt nor suit, nor yet other clothes, that are necessary for me to wear, but that be ragged and rent so shamefully. Notwithstanding, I might easily suffer that, if they would keep my body warm.[77]

He made two further requests – for a priest to hear his confession in preparation for the feast of Christmas, and for some books of spiritual reading 'to stir my devotion more effectively these holy days for the comfort of my soul'.[78]

One can only imagine the deprivation Fisher must have suffered during those dark months of imprisonment. Clothed in rags, suffering considerably

77 Bridgett, ibid., p. 291. 78 Ibid., p. 292.

from cold and ill-health he may have been, yet his trust in God never wavered, nor his loyalty to the Pope and Queen Catherine. It says much for his spiritual vitality that in spite of the appalling material conditions of the Tower, he managed to write three treatises during his sojourn in prison – two in English: *A spiritual consolation*[79] and *The ways of perfect religion*,[80] both written for his sister, a Dominican nun. The third was a discourse in Latin on the *Necessity of prayer*.[81]

It was while Fisher and More were incarcerated in the Tower (April 1534 – June 1535) that Henry pushed ahead in earnest with the task of setting up a national Church independent of Rome. This was accompanied by an insolent campaign of preaching against the Pope, orchestrated by the monarch himself, to vilify his person and repudiate his authority.[82] The king made several attempts to win over Fisher through the other bishops. When he was visited on one occasion by several bishops together, he let them know that he was greatly grieved to meet them under such circumstances. He told them, according to an early biographer, that they should be united in 'repressing the violent and unlawful intrusions and injuries daily offered to our common mother the Church of Christ', rather than trying to promote them. It was the occasion of that historic judgement made by Fisher on his fellow bishops: 'The fort is betrayed even by them that should have defended it'.[83] The fortitude and perspicacity of Fisher contrast with the pusillanimity and confusion of the rest of the English hierarchy. Henry, afraid of the negative influence Fisher's writings could have for the setting up of the new ecclesiastical order, at the beginning of 1535 ordered all his books to be suppressed.

THE RED HAT

On 7 May 1535 Henry sent one of his councillors, Richard Rich, to try to force Fisher into making a treasonable statement. Unaware of the trap being set for him, Fisher told the messenger 'that the king was not, nor could he be, by the law of God, Supreme Head of the Church in England'.[84] Henry now had the evidence he needed to bring about a conviction. Shortly afterwards news reached England that Fisher had been created a cardinal by Pope Paul

79 This text urges the reader to look to his own repentance and to beware of relying on others – no doubt influenced by the experience of finding himself totally on his own in defence of the papacy. **80** This treatise compares the quest of the seeker after holiness to that of the hunter after game. **81** *De necessitate orandi* – cf. Bridgett, p. 303. **82** In March 1534 Chapuys, the imperial ambassador, reports on the sermons preached in the king's presence: 'The invectives of the German Lutherans against the Pope are literally nothing in comparison with the daily abuse of these preachers' (Spanish Calendars, V, 26, as quoted in Bridgett, ibid., p. 319). **83** Bridgett, ibid., p. 336. **84** Cf. Harpsfield, ibid., pp 232–5.

III. The king's reaction was that the Pope could send Fisher the red hat whenever he liked, but he would make sure by the time it arrived that he would have to wear it on his shoulder, 'for head he shall not have to set it on'.[85] Fisher's execution had been decided on long before the trial which was scheduled to begin on 17 June. Because both he and More had such an unrivalled reputation in England, Henry, in an effort to undermine their prestige and moral authority, arranged that sermons would be preached against the two in practically all the churches in the country.

In reply to the charge of denying to Henry the title of Supreme Head of the Church in England, Fisher in his defence said that on his side he had the testimony of all the bishops of Christendom against the rest of the bishops of England. As such he was certain of his position and refused to give way. The intimidated jury found Fisher guilty of treason and he was condemned to be hanged, drawn and quartered, the most brutal of all possible deaths. With great equanimity he accepted the judgement handed down to him, but, before being led away, expressed the desire to speak his mind about the king's claim to the supremacy. He said it had always been his conviction, and he would affirm it again, that the king, as a temporal prince, could not claim any supremacy over the Church of God. However, if Henry were to pursue this ambition, he would incur God's deep displeasure to the great danger of his soul and that of many others. William Rastell, a lawyer nephew of Sir Thomas More who was present at the Fisher trial, leaves us the following account of the bishop's valedictory statement:

> He showed himself excellently and profoundly learned, of great constancy and of a marvellous godly courage, and declared the whole matter so learnedly and therewith so godly, that it made many of those present, and some of their judges also, so inwardly to lament, that their eyes burst out with tears to see such a great famous cleric and virtuous bishop to be condemned to so cruel a death by such impious laws and by such an unlawful and detestable witness (Richard Rich), contrary to all human honesty and fidelity.[86]

AWAITING EXECUTION

The execution was set for Thursday 22 June. Chapuys, the imperial ambassador, wrote to Charles V on 30 June 1535:

85 Bridgett, ibid., p. 359. **86** Harpsfield, ibid., p. 240.

> They gave him (Fisher) as a confessor a sworn enemy of his, and the staunchest Lutheran in the world, as well as the originator of all the devilish acts practised here; who, however, was so much edified by the Bishop's countenance and noble behaviour on the scaffold that he ceases not to say, that one of the best and holiest men in the world has been executed.[87]

As Fisher prepared himself in prayer for death there was an unusual cheerfulness and freedom of spirit in his attitude. When he was wakened by the Tower lieutenant early on the morning of 22 June, he enquired what time the execution was planned for. He was informed that it would take place at 9 a.m. Since it was still only 5 a.m. Fisher made a last request – that he be allowed to sleep for another hour or two. He told the lieutenant that he had slept little that night, not for any fear of death, but because of his illness. A contemporary biographer tells us that 'the prisoner slept soundly for two hours and more'.[88] He gave his servant his hair shirt and asked him to convey it privately out of the Tower. A fortnight later Sir Thomas More was to ask his daughter Margaret to do a similar service – they had both the same reserve in trying to keep from prying eyes the secret of their very personal and severe penances which were eloquent testimony of their love for their crucified Redeemer.

From the scaffold Fisher addressed the crowd which had gathered at Tower Hill to witness his execution: 'Christian people, I am come hither to die for the faith of Christ's Holy Catholic Church'. He asked them to pray for him so that his courage would not fail him at the instant of death, and that he would remain steadfast in every part of the Catholic faith: he was not in any way presumptuous about his ability to stand firm. He was very conscious that all his strength was on loan, and thus he begged the onlookers to pray for him to remain faithful in his final encounter.[89] On his knees he recited the *Te Deum* before surrendering his soul to God.

Because of his very poor health the sentence was commuted to a mere beheading, as it was thought Fisher would not survive being drawn on a hurdle to Tyburn, two miles away, thus depriving Henry of the satisfaction of his execution. However, that did not prevent the monarch ordering several outrages to be perpetrated against the decapitated body of the bishop of Rochester. The corpse was stripped by the executioner and left naked on the scaffold where, by command of the king, it remained uncovered for the greater part of the day. Because of the strong guard surrounding the scaffold nobody dared approach it.

About eight in the evening the naked body was carried by two of the soldiers and literally dumped into a shallow grave, without shroud to cover it or

87 Cf. Surtz, ibid., p. 114, note 1, quoting Spanish Calendars, V, pt. I, no.178, pp 504–5. **88** Cf. Bridgett, ibid., p. 393. **89** Cf. Bridgett, ibid., p. 396.

any other token of Christian burial. Henry's unrelenting rage and brutality were fully exacted on the body of the cardinal protomartyr – Fisher was the first cardinal in the history of the Church to suffer martyrdom. The following day Fisher's head was spiked on London Bridge as a warning to all of the dire consequences of refusing to acquiesce in the king's demands. On 25 June, three days after the execution, and before Thomas More's trial had even begun (1 July), Henry sent a circular around England in which, among other things, those addressed were commanded 'to set forth the treasons of the late Bishop of Rochester and Sir Thomas More' (as if the latter had already been found guilty).

As one historian has described it, 'the barbarous act of executing "the saintliest bishop in Christendom", already at death's door in any case, provided John Fisher with the opportunity of finally vindicating his conscience, and contributed in no small way to settling the reputation of Henry VIII as the most contemptible human specimen ever to sit upon the throne of England'.[90] Fisher was willing to accept the royal succession as decreed by parliament irrespective of how offensive he might personally have found it. What he was not prepared to do was to take an oath assenting to the validity to Henry's marriage to Anne Boleyn, effectively repudiating the authority of the Pope who had declared the marriage invalid. He died a martyr in defence of papal supremacy and the sanctity of the marriage bond.

The judicial murder of Fisher and More caused horror and dismay in Europe. The cardinals, in a special consistory in Rome, expressed their revulsion at the execution of one of their members. The Pope wrote to several monarchs imploring that justice be exacted on Henry, giving vent to his feelings in no uncertain manner. That an innocent man, famous throughout the world for his learning and holiness, endowed with the dignity of bishop and cardinal, should be given the death of a criminal, cried to heaven for vengeance. He had lain down his life for God, for the Catholic religion, and for the truth preserved by the universal Church.[91]

Cardinal Pole, although writing at a safe distance from the relative security of Rome, showed courage in the way he tackled Henry after the executions of Fisher and More. 'Is it possible?', he asks. 'Could you slay men like these, who by your own judgement in former days, and by the judgement of all, were held in the highest esteem for innocence, virtue and learning, and that for no other reason than that they would not violate their consciences by assenting to

90 Bradshaw, ibid., p. 15. **91** Cf. Reynolds, ibid., p. 300. Pope Paul III, writing to King Ferdinand of Hungary, brother of the Emperor Charles V and thus a nephew of Queen Catherine, refers to Henry in uncompromising terms. He is a schismatic, a notorious adulterer, a public murderer, a sacrilegious rebel guilty of high treason against the Church. For three whole years he had borne patiently with Henry's impiety hoping for a change of heart but, how fruitlessly, his recent deeds had amply shown (cf. Bridgett, p. 416).

your impious laws? Had you no care for your own judgement, no care for the judgement of other men, to say nothing of the judgement of God, though you knew that their memory would be loved and venerated by all good men for ever?' Nero and Domitian, if they had known Fisher and More, he tells Henry, would not have been as cruel to them as he was. When first he got news of their slaughter he was stupefied at its unheard-of cruelty and was almost afraid to speak about it; but now he was resolved to preach it from the rooftops.[92] Although urged by friends to modify his reproaches, after long deliberation he couldn't find it in his conscience to do so. Henry, unable to take his revenge on the author, since he was out of the tyrant's reach, turned his blood-thirst on Pole's aged mother, the countess of Salisbury, and in due course found reason to have her beheaded.

And what of the long suffering Queen Catherine? She must have found the execution of her faithful champion inexpressibly painful. Yet it didn't intimidate her. On the contrary, the example of Fisher and the others who died for the faith raised her aspirations to a new level. Writing to her nephew, Emperor Charles V, in October 1535, she tells him that she finds great consolation in the prospect that she too might have to follow so many blessed martyrs in the manner of her death. Her only regret is that she could not imitate them in life. In December she was encouraging the Pope to execute the decree of excommunication against Henry. 'For, should there be the least hesitation or delay', wrote this dauntless woman to her agent in Rome, 'it will be tantamount to letting the devil, who hitherto hath been only half bound, entirely loose and at liberty to do mischief. I cannot, indeed dare not, write to you in clearer terms'.[93] In less than a month, this brave lady had passed on to share the reward of her friend and guide in paradise. She died on 7 January 1536.

CONCLUSION

As Fisher meditated in the Tower of London on the condition of the Church in England, on the incredible change which had taken place over a period of ten short years, it brought great sorrow to his heart.

> Woe to us who have been born in this wretched age [he wrote in his book about the need for prayer], an age – I say it weeping – in which anyone who has any zeal whatever for the glory of God, and casts his eyes on the men and women who now live, will be moved to tears to see everything turned upside down, the beautiful order of virtue over-

92 *De Unitate Ecclesiae*, III, as translated in Bridgett, ibid., pp 423–4. **93** Bridgett, ibid., p. 427.

> thrown, the bright light of life quenched, and scarce anything left in the Church but open iniquity and feigned sanctity. The light of good example is extinguished in those who ought to shine as luminaries to the whole world like watchtowers and beacons on the mountains. No light, alas! comes from them, but horrid darkness and pestilent mischief, by which innumerable souls are falling into destruction.[94]

These words are primarily an indictment of his fellow bishops who had failed in their duty to be true pastors. Instead of supporting their flocks by their fidelity and their preaching against the tyranny of Henry, they were leading them to destruction by their silence and perfidy.

Yet, while the bishop of Rochester perceived more clearly than any other man in England the tragedy of the situation, he was not without hope. He knew that the Holy Spirit was always active in the Church and he believed in the power of prayer. The example of his own life and death would stand out like a shining star for hundreds of fellow English men and women who would later have the courage to face imprisonment and death rather than betray the old faith.

St Thomas More has, with a certain justification, become popularly known as 'a man for all seasons'. His lively wit, his love for family and friends, his capacity to be simultaneously outstanding as a statesman and writer, humanist and lawyer – all conjoin to give him such a magnetic personality that few have failed to be attracted by it. St John Fisher, on the other hand, does not have the same human attractiveness, yet the example of his life and work is no less valid for the Church today. A theologian of towering intellect which he used magnificently and unselfishly in the exposition and defence of Catholic doctrine, a bishop with an intense loyalty to the see of Peter, a pastor who nourished his flock with the bread of good doctrine and the example of a saintly life – these are surely qualities which make St John Fisher, if not a 'man for all seasons', certainly very much an inspiration and a challenge for the Catholic Church of the present day.

94 Bridgett, ibid., p. 435.

CHAPTER THREE

St Oliver Plunkett (1625–1681)

HISTORICAL BACKGROUND

To appreciate the significance of the life and death of St Oliver Plunkett, it is necessary to review briefly the historical background of his times. The seventeenth century in Ireland was one of religious persecution, the eviction of Catholics from traditional lands, and their plantation with English Protestants and Scottish Presbyterians. When James I (1603–25) succeeded Elizabeth in England, it was thought by Irish Catholics that the son of Mary, Queen of Scots, would adopt a more tolerant attitude than his predecessor. However, they were doomed to disappointment from an early stage. Religious persecution continued as it had been under Elizabeth. Proclamations were issued ordering the clergy to quit the country. Those who remained behind were hunted down: Cornelius O'Devaney, bishop of Down and Connor, and others, were pursued and executed.

The Acts of Supremacy and Uniformity were rigorously enforced. The earls of Tyrone and Tyrconnel fled the country (1607), believing that their lives were in danger. Their characters were slandered and their lands confiscated. Thus James I was able to plant the confiscated territories of Ulster with non-Catholics from England and Scotland. Under the new king, Charles I (1625–49), the policy of persecution and plantation was continued. Through the influence of venal judges and unscrupulous juries, good titles were declared bad and lands seized from Catholics, and the Adventurers† were made sharers in the spoil. All over the country there was anxiety, unrest, and disaffection; Irish and Anglo-Irish were equally menaced. Seeing the futility of appealing to a despotic viceroy or a perfidious king, the nation took to arms in the rising of 1641.

The plan of the rebel leaders was to capture the garrison towns by simultaneous attack. But they failed to take Dublin Castle. In Ulster the whole open country and the main towns fell to the rebels, and Munster and Connaught

†Adventurers were English-based financial backers of the Cromwellian army in Ireland.

joined the rebellion. The Catholic bishops declared the rebellion just, and the Catholics formed a confederation which, from its meeting place, was called the Confederation of Kilkenny. Composed of clergy and laity, its members swore to be loyal to the king, and to strive for the free exercise of religion. The Supreme Council exercised all the powers of government: administration of justice, levying of taxes, raising of armies, etc. Cardinal Rinuccini was appointed papal legate to the Confederation. For the years 1642 to 1649 the Church was able to reorganize. However, the seeds of discord were sown deeply in the Confederation, not least by the marquis of Ormond, who was a Protestant with intensely held prejudices against the Catholics, a friend of the king who returned to Ireland as his viceroy.

CROMWELL IN IRELAND

At this time a civil war raged in England between parliament and king. The royalists were beaten, the king executed, and the monarchy replaced by a commonwealth. In August 1649, Oliver Cromwell came to Ireland with 10,000 men. This Puritan army routed Ormond in Dublin, and, with Cromwell at the helm, slaughtered the garrison and the citizens of Drogheda. A month later the same fate awaited Wexford. Waterford, Clonmel and Kilkenny offered stout resistance, but other towns were easily captured or voluntarily surrendered. Clergy were hunted down mercilessly and executed without trial.

By the time Cromwell left Ireland in May 1650, Munster and Leinster were in his hands. His successors, Ireton and Ludlow, brought the other provinces to heel. The Catholic bishops repudiated Ormond who then left Ireland. The long war was ended in which a high proportion of the inhabitants of the country lost their lives. With the end of the military campaign a more systematic persecution began. In 1652 an order was issued that all priests should leave the country. However, priests in the country were so loyally shielded by the people that it was impossible to capture them. An Oath of Abjuration became law in 1657 which no Catholic could take as it contained a clause foreswearing papal jurisdiction and the doctrine of transubstantiation. Catholics refused to take it, showing how devoted they were to their faith.

The Cromwellian Settlement refers to the eviction of the traditional owners of lands east of the Shannon and their banishment to Connaught, followed by their replacement by the so-called English Adventurers and Cromwellian soldiers. The settlement was completed by 1658. The amount of suffering it inflicted and the massive injustice entailed far exceeded that of the plantation of Ulster. But it failed to make Ireland either English or Protestant, and in setting up a system of alien landlords and native tenants, it established a social structure which was to last for the next 250 years.

In January 1653 an edict banishing all 'Jesuits, seminary priests and persons in Popish orders' was published. As a conservative estimate, it is reckoned that a thousand clerics went into exile between 1650 and 1654, to Flanders, France, Italy, Spain, Portugal. In the city of Nantes alone, we find sixty Irish priests in July 1653.[1] This was the era of the Mass-rock. It was customary for priests to celebrate Mass and administer sacraments at night. They heard confessions until midnight and then offered the Mass on an improvised altar in a cave, under the protective eyes of scouts. The faithful came to these Masses at great personal risk from the nearby hamlets, villages or towns. To avoid capture, the clergy never remained long in the same locality.

From 1654 until 1659, there was only one bishop in the country, Eugene McSweeney of Kilmore, who was allowed to stay because of sickness and old age, and the fact that he was permanently bedridden. Three bishops had been executed by the Cromwellians and eleven were in exile. It was left to vicars appointed by the exiled bishops to shepherd the persecuted clergy and laity.

The restoration of the Stuart king, Charles II (1660–85), was welcome news for the Irish who had suffered so much on his behalf. However, they soon learned that Stuart gratitude meant little. Ormond, who as we said hated the Catholics, was Charles' principal advisor. The Cromwellians, who had murdered his father, were left in secure possession of their lands, and the Catholics were abandoned to their fate. Before the 1641 rebellion, two thirds of the lands of the country were in the hands of the Catholics; after 1665, scarcely a third was left to them.

Many secular priests and religious were executed during these years. Concentration camps for priests were set up on the Aran Islands and Inisboffin, drawing on priests in mainland prisons. Priest hunting was officially encouraged by the government, with a promise of a reward of £5 to anyone who would lodge a priest in jail. Bishop Patrick Plunkett of Ardagh, Oliver's tutor and cousin, ordained 250 priests between 1664 and 1669 from the various provinces in the kingdom; during this period he was one of only two bishops in Ireland, the rest were in exile.[2] However, these men had little or no theological formation before ordination and left Oliver Plunkett with the difficult task of coping with an all-too-large number of poorly trained and badly disciplined priests.

Rome was inundated with letters, reports and petitions stressing the urgency of the problem of vacant sees. But Rome's procrastination was based

1 Benigus Millett OFM, *A history of Irish Catholicism: survival and reorganization, 1650–1695* (Dublin, 1968), p. 5. 2 Patrick Francis Moran, *Life of the Most Rev. Oliver Plunkett* (Dublin, 1870), p. 54.

on reasons of diplomacy – Alexander VII had no wish to give any cause for offence to Charles II. Meanwhile clerical disputes were on the increase and clerical discipline was on the wane.

The persecution of the Catholics continued. To satisfy the Protestant ascendancy every effort was made to keep them in subjection and to restrict the activity of priests. Between 1661 and 1665 we read of priests seized while saying Mass, of raids on chapels in Dublin, and of the imprisonment of priests in Carrickfergus, Galway, Kilkenny, Wexford and Limerick.[3]

On 11 January 1669, Bishop Patrick Plunkett was transferred from Ardagh to Meath, and bishops were appointed to Ossory, and the metropolitan sees of Dublin, Cashel and Tuam. Oliver Plunkett was appointed to Armagh in succession to Edmond O'Reilly on 9 July 1669. The year 1671 saw a series of fresh appointments: Down and Connor, Clogher, Waterford and Lismore, Killaloe, Clonfert and Elphin were given new bishops, and vicars apostolic were named for Derry, Dromore, Kildare, Killala and Kilmacduagh. Of the newly appointed bishops only three appear to have had previous experience of pastoral care in Ireland. These returned exiles had indeed escaped the sufferings and the hardships of the Puritan persecution, but they came to their flocks as shepherds who were independent of local cliques and factions and therefore much more likely to settle disputes impartially. Hopes ran high in Rome that the new pastors would safeguard the Church in Ireland against the enemy, and nurse it back to health and strength.

EARLY YEARS

This is the Ireland in which Oliver Plunkett was born on 1 November 1625, a scion of a respected aristocratic family from Loughcrew, near Oldcastle, Co. Meath. His father was John Plunkett, baron of Loughcrew; his mother Thomasina Dillon, granddaughter of Sir Luke Dillon. He was connected with several noble families – a result from intermarriage over the generations. Oliver was one of a family of five, with an elder brother Edward, and three younger sisters, Catherine, Anne, and Mary. He was proud of his noble lineage, and would find his aristocratic connections very useful in the cause of the Church. His boyhood was an untroubled one, and his family connections protected him both against religious discrimination and the poverty which most of his countrymen suffered. Oliver himself says that as a boy he was reared by his cousin Sir Nicholas Plunkett.[4]

3 Cf. Millett, ibid., pp 12–22. 4 John Hanly, ed., *The letters of St Oliver Plunkett, 1625–1681* (Dublin, 1979), Letter no. 41, p. 77.

Dr Patrick Plunkett, a Carmelite and first cousin of Oliver's mother, took responsibility for Oliver's education until he was sixteen. He was then acting parish priest of Kilcloon in Co. Meath and would later be, successively, bishop of Ardagh and bishop of Meath. We do not know what sort of programme Oliver followed in his studies, but the Gaelic language became his first tongue. In later years Oliver always spoke of his cousin with great respect and affection. It was on his advice that Oliver decided to go to Rome and to study for the priesthood.

At this time, the 1641 rebellion in Ulster for constitutional rights for Catholics put an end to the peace of the country, and, as we have seen, led on the following year to the Confederation of Kilkenny, a parliament which had the support not only of the native Irish but also of the Anglo-Irish gentry. The wider Plunkett family was represented by several members in the Kilkenny Confederation. Given the unsettled conditions in Ireland, there was no way Oliver could complete his education there, and so he was sent to the Irish College in Rome.

We have little information about Oliver's reasons for choosing the priesthood. The fact that his parents had a strong faith would have been a factor, as well as the example of his tutor, Dr Patrick Plunkett. In addition, many of the wider Plunkett family had given priests to the Church, such that it was a tradition down through the generations. As the younger son, he had no rights or responsibilities as regards the family estates and was left to his own judgement. In any event, his choice was the priesthood, which he followed with a tenacity and singleness of purpose that were to be so characteristic of him in later life. Years later, writing to the secretary of Propaganda in Rome, Dr Patrick Plunkett would add an expression of gratitude

> for the affection displayed by you to Dr Oliver who is closely united to me by birth. Having educated him from his infancy until his sixteenth year, I sent him to Rome to pursue his studies at the fountain head of truth, and I now take pride in his having merited your patronage; neither do I believe that my judgement is led astray by flesh and blood, when I assert that he burns with ardent zeal for the Apostolic See, and for the spiritual progress of our country.[5]

Travelling to Rome was at the best of times a formidable undertaking. To the normal hazards there was added the complication that Ireland was now in a war zone, and England was a battlefield between Royalists and Puritans. Northern Europe was still in the grip of the Thirty Years War. It was not until 1647 that an

5 Moran, ibid., pp 9, 10.

opportunity presented itself for travel to Rome. Father Peter Scarampi had arrived in Ireland in 1643 as a special representative of Pope Urban VIII to the Confederation of Kilkenny, bringing with him arms and ammunition, as well as money (to the value of 30,000 dollars) collected by Fr Luke Wadding, OFM.

Among others, Fr Scampari made close friends with the Plunkett family. When he had finished his assignment, he chartered a ship to return to Rome from Waterford. He offered to take some students for the Irish College, and a group of five embarked with him in December 1646. Oliver Plunkett was one of these, as was John Brennan, later archbishop of Cashel, who was to become Oliver's constant companion and closest friend to the end of his life. Oliver was twenty-one when he set out on his European adventure.

However, it was not until February 1647 that weather permitted the ship to sail, and within a few days they found that two enemy cruisers were chasing them. Escape seemed impossible. But Fr Scampari went on his knees and made a solemn vow that if they were saved they would go on a pilgrimage to the tomb of St Francis of Assisi. Immediately afterwards a great tempest blew up and separated the cruisers from the Waterford boat. After three days the storm blew out. On 4 March they arrived at Ostend, where they were robbed by thieves; then they set out for Paris, eventually reaching Assisi at the beginning of May. There Fr Scampari fulfilled his promise before the travellers headed for Rome, which they reached well into the month of May.

ROME

Like many other Irish students before and after him, Oliver got to love Rome and was very much at home there. After the turmoil of his native country, the peace and order of the city were all the more striking to him. The contrast between the splendour of the Church in Rome and its poverty in Ireland were especially noticeable. In the recently completed St Peter's basilica, the Pope presided at solemn ceremonies in beautiful vestments. The finest artists of the day were employed to give greater magnificence to the liturgy. Bernini, the greatest of all the baroque architects, was at the height of his powers. Those days he was at work on one of his masterpieces, the Fountain of the Obelisk, in the Piazza Navona, and it is possible that Oliver and John Brennan were present at its inauguration. Oliver would never forget the impression Rome's buildings made on his young and receptive mind. He was to have the great happiness, and the good fortune, to spend in Rome the most vital years of his life (those from twenty-two to forty-four), of seeing the Eternal City acquire a new architectural splendour, the genius of great artists, and of living in association with some of the most distinguished men in Europe.

Oliver lived in a house in the Via degli Ibernesi with John Brennan and half a dozen other students. Both Oliver and Brennan, who were intelligent and industrious, were soon ranked among the foremost in talent, diligence and by the commitment with which they devoted themselves to their studies in philosophy, theology and mathematics.[6] Oliver was provided with a bursary by Fr Scarampi for his first three years in Rome. Thus he entered the Irish College with his companion John Brennan in 1650. The news that came to Oliver from Ireland must have been a great source of sadness for him. By 1649 the Confederation of Kilkenny had collapsed and Cromwell and his army had landed in Ireland to eliminate any remaining resistance. Bishops and priests were killed, exiled or imprisoned. Among those who lost all their property was Oliver's elder brother.

ORDINATION

In December 1653 Oliver and his companion John Brennan were ordained subdeacons in St John Latern. On 1 January 1654 Oliver was ordained to the priesthood by Dr Mageoghegan, bishop of Meath, who was in exile in Rome at the time. Oliver had been an excellent student, and the rector of the Irish College described him as 'a model of gentleness, integrity and piety'.[7] In accordance with the vow taken by all students of the college, he was to return to Ireland.

The joy of Oliver's ordination would have been dimmed by the dreadful news coming from Ireland. The last strongholds of the Irish had fallen to the Cromwellians. It was made high treason for any priest not only to exercise his priestly duties, but to exist at all! A similar sanction was imposed on those who harboured a priest, or who failed to denounce his presence. Children of noble families were sold as slaves to tobacco planters in the Barbadoes or in the swamps of Savannah.[8] His cousin, Dr Patrick Plunkett, now bishop of Ardagh, had to take refuge in France. Apart from Oliver's brother, a number of other members of his wider family were robbed of their property and driven to the continent. In the circumstances it was out of the question for Oliver to return to Ireland.

On 14 June he wrote to the Jesuit General asking to be dispensed from his vow. The letter was written in Latin and it is the earliest of his writings available to us:

> I, Oliver Plunkett, most humble petitioner, student of the Irish College, have completed my philosophical and theological studies; considering

6 Cf. Moran, ibid., p. 23. **7** Cf. Moran, ibid., p. 23. **8** Cf. Moran, ibid., pp 23–4.

> the impossibility of returning to Ireland (of which Your Reverence is well aware) according to the purpose and constitutions of this college as well as the oath taken in this regard by me, I humbly beg your Reverence that I be permitted to remain in Rome and take up residence with the fathers of San Gerolamo della Carità. I declare and promise that I shall be ready at a future date to go to Ireland whenever this will be commanded to me by Your Reverence or my superiors.
>
> Rome, 14 June 1654.[9]

His friend John Brennan also remained in Rome; nor is there any evidence that any other of his fellow students returned to Ireland at that time. The chances of arriving safely in Ireland were slim so Oliver decided to stay.[10] He continued his studies in canon and civil law at the Sapienza university, having taken up residence at San Gerolamo della Carità, a residence for priests run by the Oratorian fathers. He obtained his doctorate *in utroque jure* (in both civil and canon law) with great distinction.

But he combined several spiritual and pastoral commitments with his studies. His brother priests of San Gerolamo remembered him as a very zealous priest. He frequently visited the churches of the martyrs in Rome, and often expressed his desire to sacrifice himself for his countrymen. He was a regular visitor to the Santo Spirito hospital, serving the poor and the infirm. From the time he arrived in Rome with Fr Scampari in 1647, the latter took a keen interest in Oliver's welfare. It was he, we can imagine, an Oratorian himself, who made it possible for Oliver to stay with the Oratorians at San Gerolamo.

In 1656 the plague broke out in Rome, and Fr Scampari, who was generous in attending the sick on Tiber Island, succumbed to the disease. Before he died, and conscious that he had not long to live, he wrote to Oliver telling him the measures he had taken to secure influential patrons for his young Irish protégé. When Oliver heard of his death, he wrote to the superior general of the Oratorians (25 October 1656):

> With the passing of Fr Peter Scarampi Ireland has lost a tireless champion and a genuine benefactor. I myself in particular have lost a father more dear to me than my natural father, because he brought me from Ireland, braving in the course of a long journey many dangers from pirates and robbers; he conducted me to Rome at his own expense, he

9 Hanly, ibid., Letter no. 3, p. 4. 10 I do not agree with Desmond Forristal's suggestion that Oliver decided to stay on in Rome because he was attracted by the prospect of a successful academic career there and also because of his fear of what his return to Ireland at that time might involve. At no stage during his years as archbishop did Oliver show the slightest fear of dangers, not even of the barbarous death which he had to suffer; cf. Desmond Forristal, *Oliver Plunkett in his own words* (Dublin, 1975), pp 17–18.

> supported me for three continuous years both within and without our college, and when my studies were finished his assistance was never wanting to me, whether temporal or spiritual. God knows how I regret his death, especially at these times when Ireland has suffered almost total destruction at the hands of the anti-Catholic enemy. My relatives have been put to death or sent into exile and the whole Irish people live in extreme misery. I am afflicted with an unspeakable sadness seeing myself deprived of father and friends, and I should die of sorrow were I not relieved by the thought that I have not completely lost Father Scarampi: I can say that in part he is still with me since the good Lord has preserved Your Reverence alive and well. There is nobody who does not know how closely joined to him you were in friendship, in charity and in the sharing of the same inclination.[11]

THEOLOGY PROFESSOR

Shortly afterwards Oliver was appointed to the chair of Theology and Apologetics in the College of Propaganda Fide. He held these academic posts with distinction for twelve years (1657–69). He was also appointed consultor to the Congregation for the Index. His friend John Brennan was made a professor at Propaganda around the same time. The prestige of the Irish stood high in Rome during those years.

It was Oliver's good fortune to live in Rome during the years when two particularly enlightened and cultured popes, Alexander VII (1655–67) and Clement IX (1667–9), were busy making it the beautiful city which attracted visitors and pilgrims from all over the world. At this time Bernini built the great colonnade around St Peter's Square, the Scala Regia in the Vatican, and several other architectural projects. Apart from his academic work Oliver found time to do a great deal of charitable work. In the course of a letter written from Armagh (11 August 1677), he tells us that:

> While I was professor of theology and apologetics for many years at Propaganda college I had first-hand experience of the saintly life led by His Holiness and the high reputation for wisdom, prudence and piety which all had of him. I also rendered special service with Don Mercantonio Odescalchi (subsequently Innocent XI), often assisting him when he served the wretched beggars, needy and full of vermin, whom he gathered together in a house with all expenses paid by him,

11 Hanly, ibid., Letter no. 4, p. 5.

> even to their clothing – often he cleaned and fed them with his own hands etc.[12]

About three years after Oliver's appointment to the professorship in Propaganda (1660), the restoration of the Stuarts in the person of Charles II raised the hopes of the Irish Catholics at home and abroad that a period of toleration was in the offing. Charles II's wife was a Catholic, as was his brother the duke of York. Encouraged by this event, Dr Mageoghegan, bishop of Meath, left Rome and stole back in disguise to Ireland. In 1660 he wrote from Ireland to Rome *ex loco nostri refugii, Hibernia* (from my place of refuge in Ireland):

> We are beginning to hope for better times in consequence of the restoration of our king who, it is expected will heal the wound of our country, and at some future time will cause our property to be restored.

Then follows a sentence which says much about the condition of the clergy in Ireland: 'I live still in the caverns of the earth, and so do all the other members of the clergy'.[13]

Though the Stuart king, for whom the Irish had fought and endured much, was back on the throne of his father, the Cromwellians were still the rulers of Ireland. Things were not much better there – indeed from the point of view of danger to the Catholic faith they were much worse. The terrible damage done to Church organization in Ireland by the Cromwellian regime is very well reflected in the situation of the Irish hierarchy. In 1649 there were in Ireland four archbishops and twenty-three bishops. About five years later, after the establishment of the Cromwellian regime, there wasn't a single bishop in the country except the aged bishop of Kilmore. Three of the bishops had been hanged by the Puritan troops – those of Clogher, Emly, and Ross. A number of others had died of hardship including the archbishops of Armagh and Dublin. The others were scattered through Europe, in whatever country was willing to give them asylum such as France, Belgium, Spain.

In 1657 the see of Armagh, left vacant by the death of Dr Hugh O'Reilly, was filled by the appointment of Dr Edmond O'Reilly, vicar general of Dublin. He was consecrated in Brussels and with great courage, having already spent several years in English jails, he started back to his archdiocese. Like his comrade Dr Macgeoghegan he was obliged to live in woods and caves. Nevertheless he managed to hold a provincial synod and to ordain twenty-nine priests.

These were the two bishops, then, in Ireland when Charles II was restored to the throne and, as we have seen, there was a sense of expectation that mat-

12 Ibid., Letter no. 187, p. 492. **13** Helena Concannon, *Blessed Oliver Plunkett* (Dublin, 1937), p. 70.

ters would improve. However, the king's first Irish parliament was sufficient to demonstrate that the hopes of the Irish were based on a very insecure foundation. The Act of Settlement, passed by parliament, divided among the Cromwellians nearly three million acres, the ancestral property of the Catholic gentry, which had loyally served the king in exile. Not content with depriving the rightful owners of their property, the new owners spread calumnies about the Catholics – that their religious principles were incompatible with the safety of the crown, that they entered into solemn treaties but broke them at their leisure; etc.

ARCHBISHOP OF ARMAGH

In March Dr Edmond O'Reilly, the archbishop of Armagh, who was living in exile, died at Saumur in France. Although appointed in 1657, he was exiled twice and spent less than two complete years in his diocese. The clergy of Armagh let it be known that they did not want an outsider, and particularly a Meath man, to rule over them. The meeting of the Congregation of Propaganda to make the appointment was held on 9 July 1669. The Pope, Clement IX, was present. After an initial discussion proved indecisive, the Pope cut short the proceedings and said:

> There is no reason to consult longer about uncertainties, when we have a certainty before us. Here we have a man of well proved worth, of consummate doctrine, of long experience, conspicuous by every gift and quality: Oliver Plunkett. Him do I constitute Archbishop of Armagh by Apostolic Authority, him do I constitute Primate.[14]

His appointment came as a surprise, but in general there was satisfaction all round. The bishop of Ferns, an exile in Ghent, wrote to Rome, to return thanks to the Holy Father:

> that such a prelate of noble birth, and adorned with exalted talents, benevolence and virtue, and yet of no proud conceit, should be raised to the government of the primatial church, … in which office he will be a light to all who hope in the Lord.[15]

Dr John Maloney, the future bishop of Killaloe, wrote to Propaganda thanking the secretary for the recent episcopal appointments, and went on to say that the appointment of Oliver Plunkett

14 Ibid., p. 93. 15 Moran, ibid., p. 48.

> provided a pastor for the pastors themselves ... For it is not of the diocese of Armagh alone that he has the administration, to whom the primacy and guardianship of all Ireland is entrusted. One therefore in a thousand had to be chosen suited to bear so great a burden. That one you have found: one than whom none more pleasing or better could be found.[16]

After twenty-two years in Rome, Oliver had become very attached to the Eternal City, so it was only natural that he asked for the favour to be consecrated a bishop there. However, for reasons of prudence, probably due to the delicate relations of the Vatican with the English Court, it was decided that he would be consecrated a bishop in Belgium. Oliver bade his farewells to Rome. He didn't have much by way of worldly possessions – what income he had from Propaganda he generously shared with others, including the provision of a bursary for an impecunious Irish student at the Irish College. His estate consisted of a small vineyard on the slopes of Castelgandolfo, a few pictures and some books. All these he left to the Irish College.

We have one interesting record of his leave taking. A priest living in San Gerolamo tells us that when Oliver paid his farewells at the Santo Spirito hospital, a place where he had often visited the sick, he was embraced by Fr Jerome Mieskow, a Polish priest of extraordinary holiness of life, and as if prophesying said to him: 'My Lord, you are now going to shed your blood for the Catholic faith'. Oliver, replying said, 'I am unworthy of such a fate; nevertheless help me with your prayers that my desire for it may be fulfilled'.[17]

RETURN TO IRELAND

Oliver's journey from Rome to Armagh was an eventful one. He set out from Rome in August 1669. Because of an outbreak of the plague he had to avoid particular cities. He travelled via Innsbrück, Munich, Nuremberg, Mainz and Cologne. He went by boat down the Rhine from Cologne to Holland. Eventually he arrived in Brussels where he stayed with the internuncio, Msgr Arnoldi.

Oliver's consecration was arranged to take place in the private chapel of the bishop of Ghent. While in Brussels he made a brief visit to Louvain to call at St Anthony's, the celebrated college of the Irish Franciscans. Here he also met Nicholas French, the bishop of Ferns, in exile. The last time they had met was when Oliver was a young student in Rome. Oliver impressed Msgr Arnoldi very favourably:

16 Ibid., p. 50. **17** Moran, ibid., p. 35.

> I have found in Monsignor Plunkett the most excellent qualities, and his zeal to labour for the glory of God gives ground for the greatest hopes. I am consoled and rejoice that the favours of the Holy Father are so well conferred.[18]

Oliver's episcopal consecration took place on 30 November 1669, the first Sunday of Advent. For motives of prudence it was carried out in great secrecy in the private chapel of the episcopal palace.

Hardly had Oliver set his foot in Ireland after twenty-three years absence than he began a memorable series of letters to Rome, Brussels, etc., which have come down to us and which tell us the most that we know about the Primate. They not only provide us with a detailed account of the life and work of the archbishop of Armagh, but also give us a comprehensive description of the history of the Church in Ireland between 1670 and 1681.[19] That Oliver was a man of wide culture is confirmed by the many references to Latin classical sources we find in his letters. Most of the letters were written under strain and in an attitude of self-defence and explanation – hence the difficulty of deriving a rounded picture of Oliver from these same letters. It is only from the letters written from his condemned cell in Newgate that we get the more complete picture of the generous, great-hearted Christian gentleman and saint that Oliver Plunkett was. More than 190 letters are preserved today in the archives of the Sacred Congregation for the Evangelization of Peoples, formerly Propaganda Fidei.

It was a difficult journey from London to Holyhead – strong winds, snow, heavy rain; three times, he writes, he was up to his knees in water in his carriage the rivers were so high. At Holyhead there was an irksome wait of twelve days for a favourable wind.[20] All his relations were gathered at Sir Nicholas Plunkett's home in Dublin to welcome him back.[21] These included the earl of Fingal, and the baron of Louth. Above all he was overjoyed to meet his guardian and tutor of his youth, Dr Patrick Plunkett: 'Another consolation which I had was to find the bishop of Meath, although sixty-eight years of age, so robust and fresh looking that he seems a man of only fifty: he has hardly a grey hair in his head.'[22] It would appear that information about Oliver had arrived in Dublin, and in the troubled circumstances of the time it was necessary for one of his kinsmen, the earl of Roscommon, to go bail for him.

18 Moran, ibid., p. 62. **19** John Hanly, ed., *The letters of St Oliver Plunkett, 1625–1681* (Dublin, 1979). **20** Cf. ibid., Letter no. 36, p. 64 (12 March 1670). **21** Sir Nicholas Plunkett, an exceedingly able lawyer, had been championing the Catholic cause in Ireland over the previous fifty years. He was the outstanding legal figure in Ireland to whom persecuted Catholics could look to for advice in the solution of their problems in law. Cf. Alice Curtayne, *The trial of Oliver Plunkett* (London, 1953), p. 23. **22** Hanly, Letter no. 36, p. 65.

Oliver was keen to be with his flock before Lent was ended so that he might take formal possession of his see, and consecrate the oils during Holy Week. A letter dated 18 April 1670 gives a vivid account of his first impressions:

> Since my arrival in my diocese I have taken possession of my church and have carried out a visitation of the diocese. I found here Dr Daly who has been vicar-general of Armagh for many years, a learned man who is very highly thought of by the people, and I appointed him my vicar. Not only the vicar-general and clergy of Armagh, but all the other vicar-generals and clergy of the whole province have offered their perfect obedience to me,[23] and both they and the laity of my diocese are so deferent to me that they almost make me forget the delights of Rome; I for my part will take care to correspond with this to the full.
>
> Here there is a greater plenty of provisions than money. But it is possible to manage: the clergy have promised to support me by means of a respectable contribution. But what consoles me more is that I have found in the people such devotion, such piety and such constancy in the faith for the sake of which they have been reduced to great sufferings, that one could not ask for anything more in this world. So although my relatives outside this diocese would like me to come and live with them, I have resolved not to leave my diocesans, from whom I receive every sort of satisfaction. In holy week I consecrated the holy oils and ordained some priests… I have announced my intention of holding a provincial synod.[24]

Oliver was now metropolitan of the nine dioceses of the northern province. At that time the native Irish and the Anglo-Irish formed two distinct groups who were often at loggerheads. The Confederation of Kilkenny, which was supposed to unite them, made no real impact on the differences in the long run. The Anglo-Irish were almost all staunch Catholics and opponents of the Reformation; but at the same time they were equally staunch supporters of the English King and the English connection. By birth Oliver came from a long line of Anglo-Irish ancestors. As is clear from his letters, he was very much at home with the members of the gentry. He accepted without question that the English king was his lawful sovereign. He spoke English as fluently as he did Irish.

The great majority of priests in the Armagh diocese, and in all the province apart from Meath, were native Irish. They spoke English with diffi-

23 At this date, apart from Armagh, there were no other bishops in the northern ecclesiastical province. **24** Hanly, Letter no. 39, p. 69.

culty if they spoke it all. They were drawn mainly from the peasantry, since most of the Gaelic landowners had been dispossessed and driven into exile. Their allegiance to the English king was, to say the least, tenuous. That Oliver should have won over so many of the native clergy in so short a time says much for his tact, his spirit of total dedication, and the impact of his personal holiness.

About two months after his arrival, Lord Roberts was replaced as viceroy by Lord Berkeley (May 1670), who was married to a Catholic and had many Catholic friends. The new viceroy brought such a liberal attitude to affairs that by comparison with what went before it seemed like religious liberty. Oliver availed himself of this new freedom to the full. His next letter to Rome (6 May 1670) tells how he already had held two synods in different parts of the diocese, in which measures were taken to reform some irregularities. And he continues:

> At present I am compiling a report on all the priests of my province and all other matters of interest, in order to send to Monsignor Baldeschi as soon as possible a complete report. Apart from the ordination which I carried out this Easter, I have confirmed over ten thousand persons since coming to my diocese, so much so that at times I was unable to stand up.[25]

Since the diocese of Armagh had been almost wholly deprived of its bishop for many years, the Church in Armagh was torn by dissension, and the germs of many scandals had appeared in some parts of the diocese when Oliver arrived.

A report on the archdiocese of Armagh followed soon afterwards. It reflects the deep sense of Oliver's pastoral care for clergy and people, and the writer's concern for the ignorance of the younger priests, whom the difficulties of the time had prevented from enjoying the necessary education.[26] It also laments the condition of the sons of the Catholic gentry, deprived of their lands, and forced to drop to the condition of ploughmen, or to seek education at the hands of heretics.

Meanwhile the indefatigable Primate had found time to travel to Dublin to pay his respects to the new viceroy. In a letter to the Pope, Clement X (dated 20 June 1670), he gives a glowing account of the viceroy's benevolence towards Catholics:

> We in this country, Most Holy Father, experience the benign influence of our king of Great Britain in favour of the Catholics – we live in considerable freedom and the clergy themselves are publicly known and yet

25 Ibid., Letter no. 42, p. 81. **26** The decrees of the Council of Trent (1545–63) on seminary training for priests had not yet been introduced to Ireland because of religious persecution.

> are allowed to carry out their functions without the least disturbance.
>
> Our viceroy is a gentleman of great moderation and fair-mindedness. He readily receives Catholics and even treats privately with some of the clergy, exhorting them to attend to their own affairs discreetly. With this in view he has secretly called me to his presence on more than one occasion, and he has promised me his help in punishing those of the clergy who are found living scandalous lives. I perceive in him a certain spark of religion, and I find that several of the leading men of his administration are secretly Catholics. Those noblemen whose true origin is in this country are all Catholics, except three or four, and reckoning Catholics against non-Catholics throughout the whole country, there are some twenty of the former for every one of the latter; in Dublin however, the capital city, where the viceroy resides, the non-Catholics are in greater numbers.[27]

Given the favourable circumstances, Oliver decided to hold a meeting in Dublin (17–20 June) of the six bishops then in Ireland: the four archbishops and the bishops of Meath and Ossory. The business of the meeting covered three areas:

1) To remedy some irregularities which had crept in during the dreadful years of the Cromwellian persecution. The Litanies were to be said before or after Mass on Sundays, for the King, Queen, and Viceroy, and for the good government of England, Ireland and Scotland.
2) To draw up an address of loyalty to the King.
3) To petition the Holy See to appoint new bishops to the vacant sees, for which they submitted suitable names.

Dr John Brennan was named agent for the Irish bishops in Rome.

SCHOOLS

One of the benefits Oliver gained from the liberal viceroy was the promise of a government subsidy towards the schools he was proposing to build to cater especially for the education of the young clergy and the sons of the dispossessed nobility, something which he now saw to be an urgent necessity. Oliver himself says that the young priests ordained in the previous seven years in

27 Hanley, ibid., Letter no. 55, p. 106.

order to fill the vacancies left by the deaths of older priests were very backward in learning as they had no proper masters to teach them.

It was a measure of the organizational ability of the Primate that the first of these schools took shape in July of this very crowded year of 1670 in Drogheda. It was run by the Jesuits and in a short time they had 150 boys of whom no less than forty were Protestant, attracted by the excellence of the teaching. There was also a second school for twenty-five young priests. The promised subsidy didn't arrive very punctually, and the schools might have had to close down had not Propaganda come to the Primate's aid.

Having founded the schools, Oliver then undertook a visitation of the other dioceses in the northern province: Kilmore, Clogher, Derry, Down and Connor, and Dromore. Considering the difficulties of transport in Ireland at that time, the physical labours involved in these apostolic journeys must have been very demanding. This he did in addition to the administering of the sacrament of confirmation to thousands in woods and mountains, heedless of the rain and wind. We can only conclude that he must have had remarkable physical stamina to keep up the pace he set for himself. It was at such reunions of the people that the archbishop came very close to them:

> Barefooted, half starved and in rags though they were, 'they swarm to the Confirmations like flies', he (Oliver) had said. They thought nothing of walking twelve miles in any weather for the sacrament, and they went to extraordinary lengths to bring the infirm, the sick and their cripples to receive it. They were too poor to provide themselves with transport even of the most primitive kind, so they carried their invalids on their backs over mountains and across bogs. People of all ages and both sexes, from little boys and girls to men and women of thirty, forty and even up to sixty years of age, they would crowd before him, wave after wave of them, as if famishing for the Pentecostal grace. When the Archbishop moved among them he would find himself sharing their emotion, becoming increasingly aware of the terrific power of faith that charged the atmosphere. 'Better', he said, 'could not be found in the whole world'.[28]

Most of the dioceses of Ireland hadn't had a resident bishop for twenty years and as a result many people, adults as well as children, had never been confirmed. It was Oliver's custom during his visitation of the dioceses to administer the sacrament to the people of each district and to keep careful record of the numbers involved. Since there were few Catholic churches in the

28 Curtayne, *The trial of Oliver Plunkett*, pp 110–11.

country and most of them were very small, the confirmation ceremony was usually held in the open air.

PROVINCIAL COUNCIL

In August 1670 Oliver assembled a Provincial Council at Clones at which various decrees were issued. These were directed to the removal of liturgical deficiencies, the sanctification of the faithful, and the celebration of Holy Mass with due decorum. Parish priests were commanded to have a fixed place of residence; vicars general were prohibited from being absent from their dioceses for more than two months without leave from the metropolitan. All clergy were prohibited from frequenting taverns, and attending markets and fairs. It was further commanded that in each diocese there should be synodal examiners and two masters of ceremonies, the approval of one of whom would be required before any priest could be allowed to celebrate the Holy Sacrifice. All drinking at wakes was prohibited. The decrees of the Council of Trent were declared to be received in all the dioceses.[29] These measures show how Oliver, just after six months into his appointment, had already identified a number of deficiencies in the Christian life of the clergy and of the faithful, and was legislating for the process of bringing about a true reform of the Church in Ireland.

TORIES AND RAPPAREES

The following month saw the Primate in the saddle once more. This time he was on a commission from Viceroy Berkeley to the leaders of the numerous bands of 'Tories', many of them sons of the dispossessed Irish landowners, who had been driven by the Cromwellians into the glens and woods of Ulster. These were men who led a kind of guerrilla warfare against the new planters around the borders of Armagh and Tyrone.

> It would break your heart, Oliver wrote, to see the great families of the house of O'Neill, O'Donnell, Maguire, MacMahon, Maginnis, O'Kane, O'Kelly, and O'Farrell, who were great princes till the time of Elizabeth and King James, something which was fresh in the memory of my father and of men who are alive today. It is painful, I say, to see them and their children deprived of their property and the means of supporting their children or of giving them an education.[30]

29 Cf. Concannon, ibid., pp 131–2. **30** Hanly, ibid., Letter no. 104, p. 262.

It was in this sympathetic spirit that Oliver accepted the commission of the viceroy to persuade the leaders of the Tories to seek pardon from the government and transport themselves to France. At considerable danger to himself, he met them on the border of Co. Tyrone and spent an hour talking to them about the dangers to body and soul which they were bringing on themselves and their fellow-Catholics. He found these unfortunate men at the end of their tether and ready to grasp at any way out of their predicament. Eventually he succeeded in securing pardons for them, and the opportunity to go into exile in France.

At first, Rome, considering that negotiating with bandits was a task unbecoming an archbishop, wrote Oliver a critical letter of rebuke. However, when Propaganda became better informed, it wrote directly to the archbishop supporting his action.[31] In his letters Oliver often made the point that his only objective was to do what the Holy See asked of him. In response to one letter from Rome he said:

> I shall not neglect to work with pen, with tongue and with all my poor resources, and this for three motives: firstly to serve the divine majesty, secondly out of gratitude and duty towards the Apostolic See for education received, and the honours conferred on me by it, thirdly, because God commands that I obey and serve it, this service being inseparable from that of Christ.[32]

A few months before he had written to Propaganda: 'I can tell Your Lordship that I labour night and day in the affairs of my calling, and I neither give rest to my brain nor sleep to my eyes, and may it all be to the greater glory of God and the service of the Holy See, which is the spreading and preserving of the faith'.[33]

SOLVING DISPUTES

Oliver sent a stream of reports to Propaganda about his visitations in the northern province. He made lists of the names of all secular priests in the northern dioceses with a short character sketch of each. Most of them were men of blameless lives but occasional exceptions are noted: 'given somewhat to drink', 'weak in doctrine', 'frequents taverns and is under suspicion regarding observance of chastity but has promised reform', 'fathered children as a young man; sent concubine away but is somewhat addicted to drink'.[34]

31 Cf. Curtayne, ibid., p. 75. **32** Hanly, ibid., Letter no. 101, p. 254. **33** Ibid., Letter no. 85, p. 202. **34** Cf. ibid., Letter no. 67, p. 146.

There were irregularities too among the regular clergy, that is the religious orders. Of these the Franciscans were by far the most numerous and, it was only to be expected, most of his troubles with religious involved Franciscans. The friars had shown great heroism during the Cromwellian persecution and had stuck to their posts; for this they were held in universal esteem by the people. But the hard times had taken their toll, and discipline had grown lax in some of the smaller communities. Oliver's attempts at reform where inhibited by the fact that the Franciscans were to a large extent exempt from the authority of the local bishop. He asked Rome, without much success, for additional powers to deal with them. He complained that they had too many small, badly run novitiates – there were twelve alone in the Armagh province. He protested that Irish Franciscan communities on the continent used Ireland as a dumping place for misfits and malcontents. The friars, on their side, complained about the interfering archbishop and accused him of everything from simony to judicial murder.[35]

One of the most famous disputes on which Oliver had to give a decision was that between the Franciscans and the Dominicans about the ownership of three friaries, and the right to quest for alms in these areas. Although the dispute had become a public scandal, the Primate was reluctant to intervene.[36] On instructions from Rome, however, he investigated the affair and after a long and careful inquiry judged in favour of the Dominicans. His report to Rome on the issue, dated 8 September 1672, shows his ordered mind – calm, juridical, and impartial, cutting away inessentials and marshalling the essential facts in clear and logical order.[37] He did not rely entirely on his own judgement in the matter – he submitted his assessment of the evidence to the bishop of Meath, the vicar general of Kilmore, and the vicar general of Meath, all of whom agreed with his decision to give right to the Dominicans. However, this did not end the affair. As Oliver anticipated, his decision caused endless trouble for him. In his report to Rome, Oliver says that during the investigation he suffered a severe bout of illness. Obviously his health was beginning to deteriorate under his heavy workload.

DISPUTE ABOUT THE PRIMACY

Before the June 1670 meeting of the bishops broke up, a serious difference arose between the Primate and Dr Talbot, the archbishop of Dublin, about who should convey the address of loyalty to the viceroy. The Primate proposed his cousin, Sir Nicholas Plunkett, a man with much experience of public busi-

35 Cf. Forristal, ibid., pp 47–8. **36** Cf. ibid., pp 49–50. **37** Hanly, ibid., Letter no. 122, pp 326–8.

ness; but Talbot proposed himself, asserting that he was the proper person to discharge this role on the grounds that he was 'Primate of All Ireland'. Oliver refused to acknowledge this claim, pressing the historical claims of Armagh to the primacy of the Irish Church, adding that his bull of appointment gave him the title of 'Primate' whereas Talbot's did not.

The dispute was not conducted on very decorous lines. Throughout 1671 there were claims and counter claims. Both parties wrote to Rome complaining about the activities of the other. Oliver was worried that Talbot's continuing political intrigues were threatening the peace of the Church in Ireland; he had already antagonized the tolerant Viceroy Berkeley and was in danger of being banished. On 22 March 1671 Oliver wrote:

> Having little affection in any case for the archbishop of Dublin and all his family, for this and many other lapses he [the viceroy] wanted to exile him from the country. I strongly opposed this resolution of the viceroy, begging his Excellency to desist, assuring him that the archbishop of Dublin and I were on good terms, notwithstanding a certain difference of opinion in the matter of jurisdiction. His Excellency acquiesced, being very edified by my initiative on behalf of the archbishop of Dublin.[38]

Talbot and his supporters gave their own version of events to Rome. They told Propaganda that Oliver was imprudent and autocratic, that he had acted rashly in setting up schools and becoming involved with the Tories, that he was over friendly with the Protestants and particularly with the duke of Ormond (an old enemy of the Talbot family). These must have seemed mere peccadilloes when the further accusation was made that the Primate's relations with women were causing scandal, and that he had been guilty of sexual misconduct on a number of occasions.[39]

Oliver reacted energetically and indignantly to this latter allegation. His response (2 April 1672), however, must surely have caused raised eyebrows in the offices of Propaganda. He denies the charge explicitly and challenges his detractors to specify the charge. He outlines candidly the only possible grounds for accusing him in relation to his dealings with women:

> I predicted some time ago that after the decree issued in favour of the Dominicans there would be against me so many tongues, so many pens, so many calumnies. These things were written after the decree: there was no mention of them beforehand. Please write to me the list of all

38 Ibid., Letter no. 76, p. 178. **39** Cf. Forristal, ibid., pp 58–9.

> those things which have been written to you against me, so that I may be able to defend myself. Those who write or say that I practise unlawful relationships will have written when I had them, where the person with whom I had them lives, if I keep her at present, and whether she is married, or a widow or a spinster. Monsignor, I declare in the presence of God that I have no such relationship, nor ever had, not even in Piazza di Spagna when I was young, and had an odd doubloon in my pocket. If they write that I have such at present, it is evident and manifest to all that I have not, and that I live in my own house in the country for the past year and more, and that there is not another house as well regulated and as modest as mine ... Monsignor, when they write such things, if they do not state the circumstances of time and place, regard the informer as suspect ...
>
> In the time of Roberts, the other viceroy, who was my enemy and persecuted me, I went under the name of Captain Brown, with my sword, my wig and my pistols, a situation which lasted only two or three months. In the houses which I entered and in the inns, I used to kiss the women, I used to sing, and once when I was in the company of certain non-Catholics who showed some doubt about my identity, I took upon my horse with me the wife of the gentleman of the house where I was living at the time, and we rode for a mile in the company of the brother of the lady who was a Catholic. And this took place two years ago: so I beg you to note what is written and if the writer speaks in general terms, hold him suspect.[40]

In the same letter Oliver is quite frank about his assessment of his relationship with the archbishop of Dublin:

> The archbishop of Dublin writes letters to Rome about me, but they are nothing more than a pasquinade. He shows them to everybody before sending them. Despite all this I shall try every means to win him over, and I will not give up; to tell the truth he is a restless person and difficult to please – if you inform yourself of how he behaved among the Jesuits and at the court of the queen, you will have a better idea of him. He sees how the viceroy and the grand chancellor respect me. He also raises an outcry that the king has assigned me a pension. I hold public schools in my diocese and the governors of the cities of Ulster have never interfered with them. I unhesitatingly call to task wayward priests and vicars. All my undertakings have so far been successful. These

40 Hanly, ibid., Letter no. 115, pp 300, 301.

> things are the cause of his anger. He is moved by these things. In short, he explodes with envy because we are loved and approved of. I shall, however, take care to remove all occasions and, as Your Lordship commands me, I shall pretend not to notice, and shall be prepared to swallow many bitter pills for the sake of peace and to avoid scandalizing the little ones.[41]

Oliver, in support of his claim to the primacy, published *Ius Primatiale* in 1672, which had the happy effect of turning his attention to the ecclesiastical history of Ireland, which was of use to him in subsequent disputes. This is a small volume of seventy-five pages which gathers in all Oliver's arguments in favour of the primacy of Armagh, which had been maintained for more than a thousand years, and which he saw as his bounden duty to maintain. Dr Talbot complained of Oliver's 'imprudence and inconsistency'. Even Dr John Brennan, who could be considered an impartial observer, if not someone likely to take Oliver's side, sent Rome an account of what he called a 'noisy and scandalous dispute':

> While I was in Dublin I tried discreetly but persistently to reconcile them, and I tried to do the same by writing from here. All I succeeded in getting was fair promises and a superficial patching up of differences. I will keep on doing everything in my power but without much hope since both of them are hot-tempered and the dispute has now become public in England as well as in Ireland. As a result most of the Catholics are divided in favour of one or the other. I have also been told by an important person that in Dublin the Protestants are talking with great delight about this controversy, even from the pulpits.[42]

In claiming for Armagh the primacy of the Irish Church, Oliver did not intend to assert a merely nominal precedence. He looked on it as involving questions of jurisdiction, and held it carried with it the right to hear appeals from the other archdioceses. It was as primate that he heard marriage appeals, held visitations of some of the Connaught dioceses in 1674, and in those subject to Cashel in 1676.

FURTHER COMPLAINTS AGAINST OLIVER

As part of the dispute about the primacy, several complaints were made to Rome about Oliver. One of these was that he was spending too much time at

41 Ibid., p. 301. **42** Concannon, ibid., p. 63.

the court of the viceroy in Dublin. Oliver asked his correspondent in Propaganda not to condemn him until he had informed himself of the true situation through one of the other bishops. He makes a strong defence of himself in response to the accusations made against him:

> In the first place I am accused of leaving my duty to follow the court in a frivolous manner. But this can only be judged from its effects. I have now been in this native land of mine these six months only. I consecrated the holy oils, I held two synods in my diocese according to the custom, I carried out a visitation and sent a report of the same visitation; I have confirmed over ten thousand souls in it. I have held three ordinations, being obliged to do this because the old priests who are physically too weak to be responsible for the care of all entrusted to them; then I held a provincial synod where many decrees for the reformation of the clergy were made ... and this synod decreed that I should visit the whole province; I visited the dioceses of Kilmore, Clogher, Derry, Connor, Dromore and Down, all very large dioceses, and I settled all the clerical disputes in them; and indeed I found the diocese of Kilmore torn apart with factions; the diocese of Derry was upside down in its opposition to its vicar, Terence O'Kelly, who is a solemn simoniac; Down and Connor was also in turmoil, the Downmen being unwilling to obey the vicar of Connor even though the dioceses are united; in my own diocese, too, there were factional ... Now I leave your Lordship to consider if these are the actions of a man who passes his time at court ... Besides I have confirmed in these dioceses thousands and thousands and, thanks be to God, the whole province enjoys a deep peace as far as the secular clergy is concerned.[43]

Clearly Oliver had no time to be dancing attendance at the viceroy's court. His response to Rome showed how ludicrous this accusation was.

However, accusations against Oliver's good name were something he had to confront for most of the duration of his primacy, accusations which he heard of through Propaganda. Oliver roundly rejects the accusation that he was politically involved, saying to his Roman interlocutor, 'I have never spoken of political affairs or matters of state'.[44] He had already made that point clear a few months earlier: 'I am resolved not to meddle all the days of my life with civil or temporal affairs and to command my clergy the same, which if we do surely our affairs will go well.'[45]

43 Hanly, ibid., Letter no. 65, pp 137–8. **44** Ibid., Letter no. 70, p. 156. **45** Ibid., Letter no. 49, p. 94.

REACTION OF CLERGY

That Oliver had made a good impression on the clergy of his province is proven by the fact that the vicars general of the northern dioceses had a meeting in Armagh on 8 October 1670 and sent the following report to Propaganda:

> We have not written sooner to your Excellency regarding our most illustrious Primate, for we waited till his merits should be known to us by experience. And now that we have had this experience, we render exceeding thanks to the Apostolic See for having placed over us such a pastor and teacher. Since his arrival in the province of Armagh he is unceasing in his labours. To the great utility of the province he convoked diocesan synods, and instructed the clergy by word and example; and in the ordinations which he held he promoted none but such as were worthy, and only after they had passed a rigorous examination. He celebrated a provincial council in Clones, in which many salutary decrees were made; and to the joy of the whole clergy, and all the Catholics, the jurisdiction of Terence Kelly (see below), vicar of Derry was suspended, which many hitherto had attempted to accomplish, but always without success ... Truly he is assiduous in good works, his life and conduct are so exemplary that he has won for himself and clergy the love and reverence of even those who hate our faith, and since his arrival among us the clergy have not been subjected to persecution.[46]

This surely is a remarkable letter in its judgement on Oliver's performance in the first six months of his episcopacy. The indefatigable archbishop of Armagh seems to have been constantly on the move, but at the same time he was leaving his mark on the clergy and people of his province that was leading them to a deeper love of God and a more assiduous attachment to the discipline of the Catholic faith.

'PRAEMUNIRE'

There were laws on the statute book called *Praemunire*, the Latin name for some old statutes which made it an offence for anyone to exercise any authority derived from a foreign power including the Pope. This meant, for example, that if a bishop were to remove a parish priest or discipline him in some way,

46 Concannon, ibid., pp 135–6.

he was guilty of *Praemunire*, since his authority as bishop came from the Pope. He could be taken to law by the parish priest, found guilty and imprisoned, while the priest could continue undisturbed in his benefice.

One of the first warnings the archbishop received on coming to Ireland concerned the very Act of *Praemunire*. This caution came for his cousin, Sir Nicholas Plunkett, who told him to go very slowly in disciplinary measures, no matter how necessary they might appear. Sir Nicholas, an expert lawyer, did well to warn the archbishop, who before he was a year in office, was accused no less than nine times before the viceroy under the Act of *Praemunire*. Only the fact that Lord Berkeley looked benevolently on Oliver saved him from exile or worse. The effect of the Act on the Irish bishops was that they were compelled to conciliate the civil authorities, both local and central in order to administer their dioceses.[47]

One of the most notorious practitioners of this tactic was the vicar apostolic of Derry, one Terence O'Kelly. He had taken a mistress and lived publicly with her and their children for twenty years, defying all attempts to depose him. He had got more than one of those sent against him imprisoned. Two previous archbishops had trembled before him but not Oliver. He was a Plunkett and he knew that no court would bring in a verdict of guilty on such a trumped-up charge against a personal friend of the governor of Ulster. Oliver describes this event and other issues in one of his letters (23 February 1671):

> I went in person to the diocese of Derry, called together the clergy, suspended his (O'Kelly's) jurisdiction, and instituted in his place Dr Conwell, a good and learned man. He accused me before the civil tribunal, but the wretched man found the passes occupied both at the tribunal of the viceroy and at that of the governor of Ulster, the earl of Charlemont, and then he cried out at the top of his voice: 'The Italian Primate, the Roman Primate, has unhorsed me!'
>
> This earl of Charlemont had not molested a single cleric since my arrival; he is very friendly towards me; indeed on one occasion he said to me, seeing that I was somewhat afraid, 'don't be afraid, no man will lay a finger on you; and when you want to give Confirmation, do not go to the mountains, come here to the courtyard of my palace'. He gave me a garden and a fine orchard with two fields, and a fine house for my lifetime – it is in a lovely situation. And again it is a well known fact that the viceroy is very well disposed towards me and has, in fact, put me in the favour of the king himself; Doctor Brennan ... can tell Your Lordship more about this. Let it be enough to say that he granted me

47 Curtayne, ibid., pp 135, 136.

> the lives of three men tried and condemned to death in the city of Enniskillen. And then the earl of Drogheda ... allows me a public church with bells etc. in his estates, which are exempt from the jurisdiction of the royal ministers. Nine times I was accused before the viceroy's court because of the schools and for the exercise of foreign jurisdiction. But this benign gentleman has always reserved the cases to himself, and they faded out.[48]

The viceroy referred to was Lord Berkeley, who had been appointed to Dublin in May 1670, just two months after Oliver's arrival. It would, then, be a mistake to imagine that Oliver spent all his time in Ireland as a hunted man. There were plenty of anti-Catholic laws on the statute book but they were not enforced in a systematic way. It depended on the political climate – a tolerant viceroy or a friendly local lord could make a big difference. Lord Berkeley, who was viceroy for the period 1670–2 treated Oliver with benevolence. Oliver had many friends in high places and it was his objective to make the most of such opportunities. As he wrote:

> This is the time to do good. While the present viceroy remains with us we must be like those who go to sea: when the wind is favourable and astern, they hoist full sail and plough the waves at great speed, but when the wind is contrary they lower the sails and retire to the first available port or creek. While we have the present viceroy we must set sail: I shall do everything possible to advance our spiritual affairs, to reform the clergy and promote knowledge of doctrine among them.[49]

SKIMMING SWIFTLY ACROSS THE SEA

The years 1670, 1671, 1672 and 1673, the first four of Oliver's primacy, were years when he had the freedom to reorganize the church in the northern province, to improve the formation of his priests, and to deepen the sacramental life of the people. He visited all the main centres of population in 1670, and during 1671 he continued into the remoter areas, including the mountains of Donegal. When a new vicar general, Dr Luke Plunkett, was appointed for Raphoe (Donegal), Oliver himself led him through the mountain passes of this somewhat inhospitable area. In a letter written to Rome soon after, the vicar general described his impressions:

48 Hanly, ibid., Letter no. 73, p. 166. **49** Ibid., Letter no. 103, p. 259.

> In order that I might obtain peaceful possession, the Primate himself accompanied me through these rugged paths, truly like those of the Alps or Apennines …
>
> I confess, too, that the exhortations of the illustrious Primate, confirmed by his own example, moved me very much. For often has he confirmed children in these mountains and woods, and often has had no other food than oaten bread, salt butter, and stirabout, with only milk to drink. We are all amazed how a man of such delicate constitution, and, as I know, accustomed to the ease and comforts of his life in Rome, should be able to undergo so many labours, so many journeys, face such hardships and difficulties. Assuredly unless he make some change in his regime, he will lose his health and become useless to himself and others.[50]

As we have already seen, Oliver was also conscious from an early stage of the educational deficiencies of his young priests, for which he set up the school in Drogheda and invited two Jesuit priests to take charge of their formation. In 1673 he refers to fifty young priests as having benefited from the Jesuit teachers. He rightly felt that raising the standard of the clergy was one of the best services he could give to the Irish Church. What Ireland needed was not more priests but better priests; indeed from the point of view of mere quantity, the country had too many. In August 1673 he wrote:

> There are too many secular priests here. Every gentleman wants to have his own chaplain and to have Mass said under his own roof, under the pretext of being afraid of the government. They force the bishops to ordain priests and afterwards they move heaven and earth to obtain a parish for this priest, their dependent. The remedy for this would be to withdraw from me and from all the archbishops and bishops of this kingdom permission to ordain outside the specified times.[51]

The letter goes on to ask for six places in the Irish College for students from three of the northern dioceses. No one knew better than Oliver the advantages of a Roman education for the priesthood, specifically in the college of Propaganda, where they did a rigorous course in dogmatic and moral theology. They learned to preach and to master Hebrew and Greek, they were trained in Gregorian chant. They were better acquainted with the wishes of the Holy See, they knew its thinking. He speaks of scenes of Rome with great affection, the great variety of peoples one can meet there.

50 Letter, 1 November 1671, Concannon, ibid., pp 146–7. 51 Hanly, ibid., Letter no. 139, p. 373.

> Therefore I anxiously implore that I may be allowed to send half a dozen of the most talented young priests that I can find to be educated in that college ...
>
> If you don't grant me this favour, we shall be without leaders, without shepherds, and the wolves will devour our flocks. The Roman – that is, the man educated in Rome – has the knowledge and the ability to govern.[52]

In 1671, the year after Oliver's arrival in Ireland, four other bishops were consecrated. Among them was his old friend of Roman days, John Brennan, who was appointed bishop of Waterford and Lismore. This event must have brought great joy to Oliver's heart. Ordinations were held fairly regularly and usually in the house of the bishop – if he had such a thing, or at the mansion where he received hospitality. The Primate held ordinations in 1670, '71, '72, '73, '74, '75, '76, '78, and '79. The priests had to live on the offerings of the people at Easter and Christmas together with stole fees for baptisms, marriages and funerals. The churches built and enriched by their forefathers had been taken from the Catholics; and although the clergy of the Established Church had enormous revenues, they would not spend a penny to keep them in repair. When there was a question of repairing bells, organs or similar items, they compelled Catholics to contribute. Besides, they insisted that what was given to the parish priest for baptisms, marriages and funerals had to be paid to the Protestant minister so that he would permit the parish priest to perform these functions.[53] The Catholics from whom the churches had been stolen had to build Mass houses to replace them – poor, mud-walled edifices roofed with thatch.

We learn from Bishop Brennan that the priests, when they had no relatives or friends to put them up, had houses 'so miserable that sometimes when visiting them I have to go on my knees to enter the door'.[54] Yet they are a most zealous and exemplary body of men, 'indefatigable in promoting the salvation of souls, traversing the mountains and rough ways whenever they are called on occasion of sickness and other mishap'. In their little mud-walled, thatched Mass houses they strove to have decorous vestments, and a chalice and ciborium of silver. Bishop Brennan tells us that:

> the heretics enjoyed all the public offices, the land and the wealth. Out of the Catholics who lost their possessions in Cromwell's time, hardly six have recovered them. Thus the gentry are reduced to a poor condition, and all are excluded from public office for refusal to take the Oath

52 Hanly, ibid., Letter no. 100, p. 248. **53** Cf. letter Bishop Brennan, in Concannon, ibid., p. 154. **54** Ibid., p. 153.

> of Supremacy ... It is a remarkable thing, that in so many years, among so many noble inhabitants of these dioceses, only three have been perverted through a desire to recover their estates, or to attain to public position. One of these has already been reconciled to the Church by my ministry, and I will not fail to endeavour to win each of the others.[55]

ON THE RUN

The period of peace and toleration was broken in 1673 by a sudden storm. Charles II was obliged by the political situation in England to command the Irish government to issue an edict banishing all bishops and regulars. The revelation that the duke of York, the king's brother and heir to the throne, had been secretly a Catholic for many years, caused an anti-Catholic outburst in parliament.

The viceroy, Lord Berkeley, was replaced by the less sympathetic Lord Essex. He renewed the persecution that Berkeley had suspended. All Catholic schools and religious houses were closed. All bishops and vicars general were banished. The archbishops of Dublin and Tuam, together with the bishop of Killaloe had to flee the country. The other bishops, including Oliver and Dr Brennan, had to go 'on the run'. This was a courageous decision for Oliver, as it was the first time he openly flouted the law. He wrote to Propaganda in November 1673:

> The powers-that-be here do not dare to moderate in any way the edict of our exile, or to allow any time beyond 1 December for fear of parliament which is so rigorously anti-Catholic. I am exhorting the brethren to constancy, and not to abandon their flocks, but to imitate the pastors of the first three centuries and withdraw to some corner of their districts until the storm passes. I shall retire to a hut in some wood or mountain in my diocese with some candles and books. Nevertheless you may continue to favour me with your letters, and I shall continue to inconvenience you.[56]

Oliver informed Propaganda that Dr John Brennan would join him in hiding. By mid December, when both had established their hiding place, the worst news the Primate heard was that of the closing down of the schools in Drogheda. This must have come as a big disappointment to him because of the great expectations he had for these institutions. He wrote to Propaganda in mid December 1673:

55 Ibid., pp 154–5. **56** Hanly, Letter no. 143, p. 386.

> Things have become very difficult for us here, and all the more so because the date of the resumption of parliament draws near – 7 January. I have gone into hiding and Dr Brennan is with me. The Catholic laity are so much afraid of losing their property that nobody who has anything to lose gives lodging to either ordinary or religious; and although the secular priests have toleration and may remain on, the Catholic faithful are somewhat afraid to admit them to say Mass in their houses, and the priests give nothing to bishops or ordinaries, nor will they even approach them. I count myself fortunate now and again to obtain a little barley bread, and the house where Bishop Brennan and I are is made of straw and is roofed in such a way that from the bed we can see the stars, and at the head of the bed every small shower of rain refreshes us; but we would rather die of hunger and cold than abandon our flocks. It would be a shame if spiritual soldiers reared and trained in Rome should become hirelings. We shall do nothing unless commanded by our superiors.
>
> There is nothing which gives me greater interior pain, however, than to see the schools established by me here thrown down after such great expense. O what will the Catholic youth do now, so numerous and so talented![57]

The following month Oliver wrote to the internuncio in Brussels, updating him on the situation (27 January 1674):

> A further edict is expected, a more severe one, i.e., an order to all magistrates and lieutenants to send out the police around the houses in the cities and in the country to seek out bishops and religious: having been forewarned about this my companion and I on the 18th of this month (old style) after vespers – it was a Sunday, the feast of St Peter's chair – were obliged to take to the road. Snow mixed with big hard hailstones was falling, a cutting wind was blowing into our faces, and the snow and hail blew so fiercely into our eyes, and affected them so much that we are hardly able to use them even yet. Finally, after frequent danger of being suffocated by the snow in the valleys, we arrived at the house of a poor gentleman who had nothing to lose, but through bad fortune he had a stranger in the house, by whom we did not wish to be recognized, and so he put us in a fine big room under the roof where we have remained without chimney or fire for eight days now: may it be for the greater glory of God and the good of our souls and of the flock commit-

57 Hanly, Letter no. 144, p. 389.

> ted to us. The cold and hailstones were so rigorous that up to now the eyes of my companion and myself have been trickling water, and I think I shall lose more that one tooth because they are giving me severe pain. My companion has several ulcers on his arm and can barely use it. In fine, it can be truly said that our flight was in the winter and on the sabbath (Mt 24: 20), i.e. on Sunday and on the feast of St Peter's chair. God be praised that He gave us the grace to suffer for the chair of Peter and on the day dedicated to the chair founded upon the rock which, I hope, will in the long run break the violence of these tempestuous waves.[58]

We can see here Oliver's devotion to the Holy Father, and his willingness to suffer for him. Oliver must have experienced intense cold and hunger, but he was true to his commitment to remain with the flock. He was not a hireling; he was ready to lay down his life for the sheep. The following month he sent another letter to Rome:

> These times are like those of the early Church, and I hope they will be made glorious and rich by the sufferings and martyrdoms of the northern peoples, humble and devoted servants and imitators of Christ and the apostles, and that the storm will be more advantageous than the fine weather.
>
> These edicts and proclamations and decrees of theirs do not at present include Ireland, because it is not named by the king in them but I am sure that, as usual, we shall not be forgotten. If they come to me, praised be God, may they be welcome, either we shall suffer or we shall die, certainly we shall not be hirelings: with the halter around our throats they will drag us to the ship, otherwise we shall not abandon either the lambs or sheep. I beg you to procure for us the prayers of the servants of God that He may protect us from the 'plans of malefactors' (Ps 63:2) and give us the gift of holy patience and perseverance.[59]

The whole of 1674 and the first quarter of 1675 were likewise spent in hiding. However, the storm blew over. The government edicts caused great consternation in the beginning. All the regulars closed down their houses and the bishops moved about through the country by day and by night. As we have seen, three of the bishops fled into exile, but none of the others were arrested or imprisoned. The tempest had moderated, but there was a general impression that a far fiercer storm was in the offing.

58 Hanly, Letter no. 146, pp 398–9. **59** Hanly, Letter no. 147, pp 401, 402.

RESIDENCE

For a number of years the primate lived in a thatched cottage called 'Ballybarrack', situated near Dundalk; it was there that he held many of his ordinations. Nevertheless, by comparison with the other Irish bishops, he was much better off. None of the others had a house of their own. Because of their abject poverty, Oliver wrote to Propaganda,

> Bishops here have to carry on in a manner which brings shame on the mitre and the crozier ... Besides, no bishop has his own house, and to obtain his board he goes to-day to the house of this gentleman, to morrow to the house of another, not without embarrassment and already the gentlemen are tired of these visits. I leave it to your Lordship to judge if this is not a belittling of the crozier. From it arises the fact that the poor prelates are the slaves of the gentlemen, and if they do not confer parishes according to the wishes of the gentlemen, even to priests of little merit, they will not be very well received. [Poverty] is the reason why bishops do things which are not in keeping with their state: in reality all the bishops of this country are simoniacal, but since simony has become a custom and a habit here, nobody notices it.[60]

Letters like these from Oliver, looking for a minimum of financial support for the bishops from Propaganda, were quite common. Handicapped as he was by lack of financial resources and bodily strength, the energy and self-sacrifice he brought to his work never slackened during the eight arduous years of freedom that still remained to him after he took up his abode at Ballybarrack.

Oliver kept up an unceasing correspondence with the secretary of Propaganda, with the internuncio in Brussels, and with the prelates of the Irish Church, all of which took a heavy toll on his strength and energy, as well as on his financial resources. Occasionally Propaganda, in response to Oliver's many requests for money, sent him some financial assistance. However, he had to rely more on his relatives and friends to help him pay the bills.

REVIEW OF OLIVER'S ADMINISTRATION

In deciding some of the cases appealed to him, reports to Rome complained that the Primate acted rather hastily, or that he was somewhat lacking in judgement and knowledge of character. So many complaints reached Rome that the

60 Ibid., Letter no. 190, p. 498.

internuncio in Brussels asked Dr Brennan to make a confidential report on the Primate's administration. The immediate occasion for Propaganda requesting Dr Brennan's report was the difference of opinion which had developed between the archbishop of Armagh and Dr Thomas Fitzsimons whom the Primate had deposed from office as vicar general of Kilmore, a dispute which lingered on from 1676 to 1678.[61]

When Fitzsimons disobeyed a decree of the archbishop and persisted in his contumacy, the Primate deposed him, a judgement which was subsequently confirmed by Rome. After that Fitzsimons organized opposition to the archbishop, but not in relation to his deposition. Rather, he started to rake over the embers of the dispute between the Franciscans and Dominicans of five years previously, which the Primate had decided in favour of the Dominicans. As a consequence a number of people started to speak badly of Plunkett, 'injuring his character in every way, both at home and abroad; so much so that they induced several, as well among the priests as the laity, to take their part. All this said with probability but without evidence'[62]

The defeated faction sent the usual stream of complaints and accusations to Rome: Oliver was considered dictatorial, he favoured the Anglo-Irish at the expense of the native Irish, he used his political influence to have some priests arrested, he was too friendly with Protestant ministers. The Primate knew a few of the latter in so far as it was advantageous to him in the administration of his diocese. Brennan also rejected the accusation that the Primate showed himself hostile to the native clerics of the province of Armagh by giving preference to strangers in matters of promotion. It was Brennan's opinion that Plunkett had devoted himself more assiduously to the administration of his province than any of his predecessors for many years. He admitted it was true that some were envious of Plunkett because of his influence with the viceroy and other members of the government.[63] This letter of the archbishop of Cashel gives us a very clear idea of the sort of charges that were constantly being made to Rome against the Primate.

As another commentator points out, the real reason for clerical disputes with Plunkett was that Oliver was still a Palesman, a speaker of English, a bearer of Norman blood, with an entry to the corridors of power that none of the Old Irish could any longer command. For some of the Old Irish this would always be Oliver's unforgivable sin. They did not want this man to rule over them.[64]

About the time that Archbishop John Brennan was sending his confidential report to Rome on Oliver's administration, Lord Essex, the viceroy, was

61 Cf. Hanly, ibid., Letter no. 180, p. 478; Letter no. 181, pp 481–2. **62** Bishop John Brennan, Letter, 5 August 1677, in Concannon, ibid., p. 185. **63** Concannon, ibid., pp 184–8. **64** Forristal, ibid., p. 88.

replaced by Ormond. The new viceroy was not in a mood to stir up trouble and treated Oliver with a certain benevolence. The archbishop of Dublin, Peter Talbot, who was exiled by proclamation in 1673 and had lived in France for three years, asked Ormond for leave to return to Ireland. In 1676 he received permission to return to England where he resided until 1678. At this stage he was in very poor health and was permitted to return to Ireland in May 1678. He was arrested in September 1678, and spent the next two years in prison in Dublin Castle where he died in October 1680.

TITUS OATES

While an uneasy peace continued in Ireland, there were constant rumours of intrigue in London. Tension grew between the king and parliament, and the king's opponents found an able and unscrupulous leader in the earl of Shaftesbury. While Shaftesbury wasn't particularly anti-Catholic, he was willing to use any weapon, however dishonourable, to break the power of the monarchy. The king's wife and brother (the duke of York) were Catholic and the king was only waiting a favourable opportunity for becoming a Catholic himself; so it was plain enough to Shaftesbury, that by playing on the anti-Catholic suspicions of the mob, he could easily arouse them against the royal family. A variety of fantastic rumours were put into circulation, and anti-Popery demonstrations were organized.

Sometime in 1676 an impecunious clergyman by the name of Titus Oates arrived in London. Though still in his twenties, he already had various brushes with the law for crimes ranging from perjury to sodomy. He was befriended by some of London's poor Catholics and expressed a desire to enter the Catholic Church; he was received in March 1677. He tried out his vocation in the Jesuits for six months from December 1677 to June 1678 but was expelled as unfit. However, this period gave him all the Catholic contacts he needed. He sat down and in cold blood fabricated the entire 'Popish Plot'. It was to make his name immortal.

He skilfully blended fact with fiction in a long narrative, punctuated with people and places and dates, and succeeded in getting the document brought before the king's privy council. On 28 September 1678 he was summoned to appear before the council and there he reaffirmed all the lies written in the narrative. The council listened in amazement as he detailed the frightful conspiracy for them. The king was to be murdered and his brother put on the throne. The Protestant religion was to be proscribed and leading Protestants put to death. In Ireland a Popish army of 20,000 horse and 20,000 foot was ready to rise in rebellion and a French army would be sent to help them.

Immediate and dramatic action was needed if England was not to be reduced to a helpless vassal of Rome.[65]

The time Titus Oates spent in concocting the Popish Plot were years of quiet consolidation for Oliver Plunkett. His diocese, he reported to the internuncio, was now 'completely at peace, except for two priests who are refractory'. He continued his work of visitation and administered the sacraments of confirmation and ordination. According to the careful lists he had kept, he had confirmed 48,655 people up to the outbreak of the persecution of 1673, some in places that had not seen a bishop for forty years.[66] Now the crowds presenting themselves for confirmation were smaller. In 1676 he even allowed himself the luxury of a holiday and went to spend a few weeks with his friend, Bishop John Brennan of Waterford.

Oliver held a provincial synod in August 1678 at Ardpatrick, Co. Louth.[67] This gave a certain feeling of security despite what was happening in London. The synod wanted to demonstrate to Rome how ill-founded were the charges made against the archbishop of Armagh, so a letter giving the highest praise to his administration, signed by the bishops and vicars general present, accompanied the transmission of the decrees of the synod to Rome.[68]

In August 1678 no one had heard of the name Titus Oates. By the end of September he was on everybody's lips. The Popish Plot had been an unbelievable success. Frenzy gripped England for the next three years, partly due to the skilful stage management of events by Lord Shaftesbury, who took Oates under his wing and used him for his own ends. In London and in many parts of England, Catholic priests and laymen were hunted down and imprisoned. A series of trials began which was to lead to the execution of many completely innocent people. Hectoring and corrupt judges, packed juries, and a mob of shouting and jeering spectators made any kind of defence impossible. The verdict 'Guilty' was a foregone conclusion.

The king, though he knew he was the ultimate objective of the whole attack, felt himself powerless to deal with the situation; he signed the death warrants of his most loyal supporters and granted pensions and rewards to their false accusers. Only one thing was wanting to the full success of the plot – none of the victims confessed to the crimes of which they were found guilty. This was a blow to the credibility of Oates. They made every effort to extract a confession from condemned men, even offering them their lives, but it was to no avail.

From Ireland Oliver Plunkett followed events in England with anxiety. Ormond, who was viceroy, had no love for Catholics, but he knew as did

65 Cf. Forristal, ibid., pp 84–7. **66** Hanly, ibid., Letter no. 144, p. 390. **67** Ibid., Letter no. 198, pp 516–19. **68** Cf. Concannon, ibid., p. 191.

everybody else in Ireland, that the Irish part of the plot with its popish army of 40,000 men was completely without foundation. In addition he had many links by blood and marriage with the Plunketts: he was unlikely to take action against Oliver of his own free will. But to protect his own position he had to be seen to take some action. He ordered the arrest of the archbishop of Dublin who had recently returned from exile a dying man, and who had the misfortune of being named in Oates' narrative; and he followed this with a new edict of banishment. Again Oliver prepared to go underground and he wrote from Dublin to inform the internuncio of the situation on 27 October 1678:

> With the knowledge and approval of the provincial synod I undertook a visitation of the province, beginning with the diocese of Meath, and the principal suffragan sees, and going on to Clonmacnoise. I had hardly finished in the latter when there arrived to me in the post the news that the Archbishop Talbot of Dublin had been imprisoned in the tower or castle of this city. This news reached me on the 21st of last month, and after it a decree was published banishing all the archbishops, bishops and vicars-general as well as all religious, ordering them to have left the country by 20 November, and threatening fines and other penalties to any lay person who would give them food or drink, or assistance of any kind.
>
> It is not clear what precisely is the charge against the archbishop of Dublin – he is in close confinement and there is no communication with him ... Neither in this edict nor in the other of four years ago am I included or named, and so I shall stay here although withdrawn with some friend in the country, and I think that Dr Brennan and I shall be together.[69]

We don't know how Oliver spent the winter of 1678–9, as the next news we have of him is a letter to the internuncio dated 15 May 1679:

> Matters are going from bad to worse because of a public edict. Forty scudi are promised to whoever captures a prelate or a Jesuit, and twenty to whoever brings in a vicar general or a friar. Police, spies and soldiers go hunting night and day. The secular clergy have been given a certain amount of toleration up to now, but in many places, and especially around Armagh, they are considerably harassed, and many of them do not appear by day ... as well as this, the heaviest penalties have been published by edict against the Catholic laity who give lodging to prelate

69 Hanly, ibid., Letter no. 202, p. 528

> or religious. The wealthiest are afraid to lose their property, and the poor have nothing to give.

He then speaks about the poverty he is experiencing in a truly Pauline manner:

> I should be ashamed to say this if necessity did not compel me: I have achieved more, I have written more, I have laboured more during these past ten years than all the prelates of this country together. Now I find myself without any income from my diocese, deprived of my benefactor (Colonel Fitzpatrick), deprived of my house, and I have no money beyond fifty three scudi: this is how it is as God is my witness and I speak no lie … If necessity did not compel me I should never importune my superiors in this way.[70]

None of the Irish bishops left the country in consequence of the proclamation, but they all went 'on the run'. For a whole year Plunkett went about in secular disguise and under an assumed name, keeping in touch with his flock and even holding ordinations.

ARREST AND TRIAL

Up to this Ormond had closed his eyes to Plunkett's existence. However, once again his hand was forced. On 21 October 1679 he received orders from the privy council in London to arrest the archbishop of Armagh. Ormond entrusted the capture of Plunkett to Sir Hans Hamilton and hinted that money would not be wanting to secure the success of the enterprise. Before long Hamilton had some definite information. He had ascertained that Oliver had been staying at Naul, a village a few miles north of Dublin, under the assumed name of Mr Meleady. He had cut off his beard and moustache and was wearing a wig. He was probably visiting his old friend and tutor Bishop Patrick Plunkett who was dying. On 30 November Oliver was still at liberty. On that day he wrote to Rome to inform them that the aged bishop had gone to his reward:

> Now I must inform you of something which is grievous to me, namely the death of Bishop Patrick Plunkett of Meath, a prelate outstanding by birth as well as for his sincerity and integrity of character and his skill and experience of Church affairs. For thirty-three long years he exercised the pastoral care of souls with great concern for his flock, and

70 Hanly, ibid., Letter no. 203, p. 530.

> although he was the son of one of the foremost peers of this country he never gave himself to unlawful worldly pleasures in any way … For many years there was no other bishop in Ireland since all the others had fled because of the fierce persecution of Cromwell; because of birth and moderation he always enjoyed the protection or, at least, the toleration of the state … He died a poor man, because being a wealthy man in his lifetime he gave alms freely – his right hand did not know what his left hand did, and he never denied alms to any poor person – he frequently gave secret help to poor, ashamed gentlemen and widows, of whom we have many since the extermination carried out by Cromwell.[71]

One John Hetherington, who in early summer 1679 made his escape from Dundalk jail, let the Protestant bishop of Meath know that he had the means of procuring all the information required to implicate the Primate in the Popish Plot. The plan to include the Primate of Ireland in the Popish Plot had been concocted by Lord Shaftesbury and his friend in Ireland, the Protestant bishop of Meath, Henry Jones, both of these being old Cromwellian colleagues.[72] Hetherington got two renegade priests, Edmond Murphy, a suspended priest of the Armagh diocese, and John McMoyer, a disaffected Franciscan friar, to travel to London to give evidence about the proposed plot to Lord Shaftesbury. They were examined before the king and Council. McMoyer said that in Ireland there was a universal conspiracy of which the head and promoter was the archbishop of Armagh. It was in consequence of this information that Ormond received instructions to track down and arrest the Primate.[73]

On 6 December 1679 Oliver was arrested somewhere around Dublin. He was taken to Dublin Castle where he was lodged in a cell next door to Peter Talbot, archbishop of Dublin. For six weeks he was held incommunicado in solitary confinement while his papers were rigorously examined. Since nothing even remotely treasonable was found in them, he was given a greater degree of freedom and allowed to see some friends, including his faithful servant John McKenna. On 17 January he was given the opportunity to write to Rome and give some news about his situation.[74] The letter is a point by point refutation of accusations made against him by Anthony Daly, an apostate Franciscan friar. For the previous year Daly had been bombarding Rome and Brussels with allegations about the Primate's misdeeds, manifestly absurd. There is almost a tone of despair about Oliver's letter, as if he had given up on ever catching up with the slanders against him. It is saddening to read his attempts to clear his name with Rome, a prisoner already marked down for death.

71 Hanly, ibid., Letter no. 205, p. 536. **72** Cf. Alice Curtayne, ibid., p. 26. **73** Cf. Concannon, ibid., pp 201–2. **74** Cf. Hanly, Letter no. 206, p. 542.

Lord Shaftesbury, the 'manager' of the Popish Plot, let it be known that there was a profitable market in England for any information that would connect the Catholic bishops in Ireland with the alleged conspiracy. It was only gradually that Oliver came to realize that he was being set up as prime mover of the Irish branch of the Plot. He remained in prison in Dublin Castle during the spring and summer of 1680 while the case was being built up against him. Shaftesbury, seeing the credit of the English Plot waning daily, was determined to work up in the popular mind a scare as to its development in Ireland. Hetherington was sent over to Ireland, with unlimited money, to procure evidence proving Oliver's involvement in the Plot.

The indictment was at last prepared and the trial fixed for Dundalk on 23 and 24 July 1680. Though precautions had been taken to pack the jury with Protestants, the character of the Primate was so well known, and that of the witnesses against him so notorious, and there was such an array of evidence on the accused's side to disprove the charges, that the principal crown witnesses, Murphy and McMoyer, funked the ordeal of appearing in court to sustain their written depositions. The Primate, son of a family of great lawyers, found much that was strange and offensive in the procedure for criminal cases then obtaining in Ireland. He continues in his letter to the internuncio:

> The mode of procedure in criminal cases here is strange to me. The accused knows nothing of the accusation until the day of his trial, and he is not granted a lawyer to defend himself, nor is the oath given to the witnesses for the accused, and one witness alone is enough on the side of the king or the exchequer. Nevertheless they listen to what the witnesses for the accused have to say, even if they do not give them the oath.[75]

The letter goes on to tell of what happened after the aborted proceedings. He was brought back to Dublin Castle, after spending a lot of money on bringing witnesses to Dundalk for four days from different parts of the country. He was now 500 crowns in debt.

One issue of great consolation to Oliver in these dark days was his reconciliation with Peter Talbot, the archbishop of Dublin. Talbot was in prison in Dublin Castle, suffering terribly from ulcers and gallstones. His groans of agony reached Oliver in his cell, and hearing that Talbot was in danger of death, Oliver burst through his own guards and those posted at Talbot's door, and administered the dying prelate with the last sacraments. The old feuds and bitterness were cast aside, and the two archbishops were reconciled. October

75 Ibid., Letter no. 211, p. 555.

of 1680 saw both men depart Dublin Castle: Peter Talbot through death, and Oliver by the ship that was to take him to London, and Newgate prison, and ultimately to his death.

NEWGATE AND THE KING'S BENCH

Overriding Ormond's wishes, Shaftesbury had Oliver's trial transferred to London. Ormond maintained the elementary legal principle that a man should not be tried in England for an offence committed in Ireland. However, Oliver was cited to appear before the king and parliament in London on 21 October. At the beginning of November he was lodged in Newgate prison, where he was kept incommunicado for six months. Newgate had no sanitation and the prisoners had no facilities for washing themselves. The filth of the prison made it a public danger; typhus epidemics were frequent there.[76]

On 4 November 1680 he appeared before the committee of examinations. One observer says:

> he told his tale with modesty and confidence, and without any manner of hesitation and consternation ... In fine he told his tale with such plainness and simplicity that he left an impression with the Lords to his advantage.[77]

In the meantime, agents of Shaftesbury were scouring Ireland for witnesses to concoct a case against Plunkett. When they arrived in London these gentlemen were taken in hand by Hetherington and others and told what they were expected to swear. At last a bill accusing Oliver of high treason was offered to the Westminster grand jury in February 1681, but as the witnesses contradicted each other so evidently, the jury threw it out. They were taken in hand again and having learned the storyline more successfully, the Primate was arraigned once more before King's Bench on 3 May 1681.

He had been kept in close confinement all the time, and thus had been deprived of all opportunity of preparing a defence. When he was led to court, he protested that he could not proceed with a defence without his witnesses and the necessary documents which were in Ireland. He therefore asked that the trial be postponed until the Michaelmas term. All that the judges would allow was to put it back until 8 June. In the meantime his servant James McKenna travelled to different parts of Ireland enlisting witnesses to give testimony in Oliver's favour and bring them to London. He also looked for

76 Cf. Curtayne, ibid., pp 18, 20. **77** Concannon, ibid., p. 215.

friends to pay the expenses of the witnesses. However, there were only five witnesses willing to travel to London, and these were delayed in port for so many days due to contrary winds that they failed to arrive in time for the trial.

On 8 June Plunkett was brought under guard to Westminster Hall, where most of the state trials of the period took place. The lord chief justice refused to have the case postponed until the arrival of the archbishop's witnesses. This left Plunkett 'with his hands tied before his persecutors', since in this he was denied the most elementary sense of justice. Archbishop John Brennan, Oliver's great friend and colleague, describes the court scene:

> The Judges vied with each other in their partisanship, insolence and brutality. The very first question the prisoner asked about the jury was rudely repelled by the Lord Chief Justice, and when he attempted to cross examine the witnesses who appeared against him, he was interrupted and bullied, not only by the attorney and the solicitor-general, by the two serjeants-at-law and several other counsel, but by the three judges, who did not permit the witnesses to answer his questions, but answered themselves in their place. Sometimes when he pressed a question which might make a witness betray himself, or contradict another, he was told by the court not to waste his time lest he should not be allowed any to make his own defence, and when one of the witnesses for the crown began to retract his former evidence against the prisoner, he was interrupted and clapped into jail. It must be remembered, also, that the barbarous policy of the law at this period did not allow him the assistance of any counsel.[78]

And thus he was forced to fight single-handed against an array of the best lawyers of England,[79] weakened in body as he was by a year of rigid confinement in prison, which had prematurely turned him into an old man with many infirmities. But Plunkett was a consummate lawyer with the blood of great lawyers in his veins. Point by point, through the long hours of that June day, he fought his case, and he would have won had not justice been rigorously banned and barred from this perverted and disreputable court.

The specific charges on which Oliver was tried were:

1) that he had sent letters soliciting foreign powers to invade Ireland to defeat the Protestants.
2) that he had asked the French king for help.
3) that he exacted money from the clergy of Ireland for introducing 70,000 men from France.

78 Archbishop John Brennan, in Concannon, ibid., p. 221. **79** Cf. Curtayne, ibid., pp 41–54.

4) that he was preparing an army of 40,000 in Ireland.
5) that he had surveyed all the forts and harbours of Ireland, and that he had fixed on Carlingford as a fit harbour for the invasion.
6) that he had held several meetings where money was collected for this purpose.
7) that at a meeting in Co. Monaghan he had exhorted three hundred gentlemen to take up arms for the recovery of their estates.[80]

It was not the testimony of the witnesses but the fears and bigotry of the jury, and the scandalous abuse of their judicial functions by the judges, that procured a conviction. Despite all the coaching of the witnesses, they made a sorry showing.

As we have seen, from October 1680 to May 1681 Oliver was kept in solitary confinement in Newgate prison. During that time he never saw a friendly face or heard a friendly voice. His faithful servant James McKenna accompanied him to London in hope of being able to attend to him as he had done in Dublin, but when he tried to bring him some clean linen in the prison, he was himself arrested and locked up in another part of the jail. The filth of the prison was beyond words, the food was inedible, and the prisoners had to wear irons on their ankles, joined together by a heavy chain.

Oliver's health was now failing rapidly. That winter, one of the worst on record, was the dark night of the soul for the archbishop of Armagh. It was a time of trial from which he emerged with a new strength and clarity. Those months of pain and isolation prepared him to reach his full stature.[81] The full richness of his spirituality was now seen for the first time because of the way the circumstances of his life unfolded. But he also showed a serenity, a simplicity, a humility, a renouncing of his own will, and a submission to that of others which had not been there before. As Forrestal writes,

> In that foetid cell, in those days and weeks when he prayed without ceasing, and to the rigours of his prison added penances of his own, he came at last to a complete understanding and complete mastery of himself.[82]

When the chief justice addressed the jury, he told them, 'you must find him guilty ... It is pretty strong evidence'. Oliver replied, 'I can say nothing to it, but give my protestation that there is not one word of this said against me true ... I never had any communication with any French minister, Cardinal nor other'.[83] The jury took only a quarter of an hour to consider their

80 Cf. Concannon, ibid., pp 222–3. **81** Cf. Forrestal, ibid., pp 104–5. **82** Ibid., p. 106. **83** Curtayne, ibid., p. 178.

response, when they returned giving a guilty verdict. Oliver was heard say, *Deo Gratias*, thanks be to God.

A week later, 15 June, he was brought back to the court in Westminster Hall to hear his sentence. He was asked if he had anything to say against his execution. His reply was a powerful pleading against the iniquity of the trial and the guilty verdict. He pointed out how all his requests were denied him. He affirmed 'I am not guilty of one point of treason they have sworn against me, no more than a child that was born but yesterday'.[84] He said he had attestations for good behaviour from two viceroys – Lord Essex and Lord Berkeley. If his petition for time had been granted, he would have proved his innocence.[85]

The Lord Chief Justice Pemberton was not moved in the slightest by Plunkett's appeal for mercy. He said he had been indicted of the great crime of high treason – treason against God, against the king, and against the country where he lived. He continued:

> You have done as much as you could to dishonour God in this case, for the bottom of your treason was the setting up of your false religion, than which there is nothing more displeasing to God, or more pernicious to mankind in the world. A religion that is ten times worse than all the heathenish superstitions; the most dishonourable, and derogatory to God and his glory.[86]

It was clear that for the chief justice, independently of the counts on which Oliver was found guilty, the great crime the Primate committed was the propagation of the Catholic faith, and that there was no greater crime he could commit.

Pemberton was then about to pronounce judgement when Oliver asked to speak again. He had a startling revelation to make:

> If I were a man that had no care of my conscience in this matter and did not think of Almighty God, or conscience, or heaven or hell, I might have saved my life. For I was offered it by divers people here so I would but confess my own guilt and accuse others. But, my lord, I had rather die ten thousand deaths than wrongfully accuse anybody. And the time will come when your lordship will see what those witnesses were that have come in against me. I do assure your lordship, if I were a man that had not good principles, I might easily have saved my life; but I had rather die ten thousand deaths than wrongfully to take away one far-

84 Curtayne, ibid., p. 191. **85** Ibid. **86** Ibid., p. 192.

> thing of any man's goods, one day of his liberty, one moment of his life.[87]

With a gesture of contempt, Pemberton dismissed what Oliver said, and went on to pronounce judgement:

> You must go from hence to the place from which you came, that is to Newgate, and from thence you will be drawn through the city of London to Tyburn. There you will be hanged by the neck, but cut down before you are dead; your bowels shall be taken out and burnt before your face, your head shall be cut off, and your body divided into four quarters to be disposed of as his Majesty pleases – and I pray God to have mercy on your soul.[88]

The result of the trial caused revulsion not only in Ireland but in many European countries as well. The Pope urged the Catholic monarchs to do everything in their power to help the Primate. Strong pressure was brought to bear on Charles from foreign courts to exercise his royal prerogative of mercy, but he was afraid to grant a reprieve. Lord Essex, who had been viceroy in Ireland from 1672 to 1677, motivated by belated remorse, told the king that the matters sworn against Plunkett were so absurd in themselves that it was impossible for them to be true. The king criticized Essex for not saying something at the time of the trial, but said that he couldn't pardon anybody. As parliament had been dissolved the previous March and the king ruled as absolute monarch, there was nothing to prevent him exercising his prerogative and saving the life of the Primate.

A contemporary narrative of the martyred prelate's last hours provides us with some details of how this brave and generous man met his death. While awaiting sentence, as well as when it was being passed, and after it, Oliver

> displayed such a frankness of soul and heart – such a serene and joyous countenance, and was so composed in all his actions and deportment, that all were able to perceive not only his perfect innocence, but moreover his singular virtue, which was master and superior to every emotion of passion. And concerning this, the Catholics who were present wrote endless praises attesting that none could wish for a deportment more noble, more amiable, more worthy of Him, whom he there represented. Having heard the sentence, he asked as a favour from the judge to be allowed to treat of spiritual matters with a Catholic priest.

87 Ibid., p. 194. **88** Ibid., p. 195.

> 'You will have,' replied the judge, 'a minister of the Church of England'. But he replied: 'I am obliged for your good intentions, but such a favour would be wholly useless to me'.[89]

The feeling of honest resentment against the crying injustices of the trial brought many generous Protestants to the door of his cell in Newgate, amid the crowds of Catholics who came to offer their service, to provide some little comfort for him, and to beg his blessing for themselves and their children. And the letters that reached Rome in those days spoke of the crowds of Protestants as well as Catholics who visited the saintly prisoner.

During the final hours that were left to him Oliver was engaged in writing his last speech which would carry his voice from the foot of the scaffold at Tyburn to listening ears in every Catholic country in Europe. It seems that it was translated into several languages. He also engaged in a moving and edifying correspondence with his fellow prisoner, the Benedictine, Fr Maurus Corker, who became his spiritual director when his request for such was eventually granted him.

On 22 June he wrote to his former secretary Fr Michael Plunkett, now in Rome, and made what testamentary arrangements and provisions for his dependent nieces and nephews which his limited circumstances would allow. He speaks familiarly and with affection of his nephews Jemmy and Joseph, and his nieces Catty and Tomasina. He puts on record his gratitude to the noble English Catholics who had contributed so generously to a fund to bring over from Ireland witnesses for his defence. He refers again to the great generosity of the English Catholics – 'they are rare Catholics and most constant sufferers'.[90] He continues:

> Sentence of death was passed against me on the 15th, which did not terrify me in the least, nor take from me even a quarter of an hour's sleep. I am as innocent of all treason as the child born yesterday. As for my character, profession and function, I did own it publicly, and that being a motive of my death, I die most willingly, and being the first among the Irish, with the grace of God I shall give good example to the others not to fear death. But how am I a poor creature so strong, seeing that my Redeemer began to be afraid, and to be weary and to be sad, and drops of his blood ran down to the ground? I have considered that Christ by his fears and passion merited for me to be free of fear… I expect daily to be brought to the place of execution, where my bowels are to be cut out , and burned before my face, and then my head to be cut off, which death I embrace willingly. *Cupio dissolvi* (I long for the end).[91]

89 Ascribed to Fr Teeling, SJ, in Concannon, ibid., p. 241. **90** Curtayne, ibid., p. 201. **91** Hanly,

And he adds:

> I salute all my friends there as if I had named them and I recommend myself to their prayers. None of them ought to be grieved for my death, being as innocent of what is laid to my charge as a child unborn as to matter of treason … I did expect yesterday to be brought to execution, but finding I am not to be brought to it till Friday or Saturday I thought fit to write to you these few lines.[92]

EXECUTION AND BURIAL

An English lady, a Mrs Elizabeth Sheldon, was present at the execution, and placed the remains of the Primate in a coffin, and had receptacles prepared to enclose the holy head and the arms and hands. It was to her that Fr Maurus Corker wrote an account of the last days and death of the archbishop of Armagh. Oliver spent his time in almost continual prayer and fasted usually three or four times a week taking nothing but bread. He was unusually cheerful, 'without any anguish or concern at his danger or strict confinement'. By his attractive demeanour he caused those who came near him to have esteem and reverence for him.

Fr Corker had regular correspondence with the Primate after the trial was over and could perceive 'those lovely fruits of the Holy Spirit: charity, joy, peace, patience, etc., transparent in his soul'. And not just Fr Corker but many other Catholics who came to receive his blessing and were eye-witnesses, could testify to these things.

On 24 June Oliver wrote a letter where he speaks with pride of his brother bishops:

> They might have saved their lives by going overseas, but the Irish prelates are resolved rather to die than forsake their flocks … For if the captains will fly it is vain to exhort the single soldiers to stand in battle … By our deaths the number of Catholics will not be diminished but rather augmented, when they see we willingly die and contemn life, which is the only idol of our adversaries.[93]

That same day he was told that the execution was postponed by a week until 1 July. By bribing the gaoler, Fr Corker was able to ensure that the Primate was able to say Mass in his cell during all that week, his last on earth,

Letter no. 226, pp 572, 574; Curtayne, ibid., pp 200–1. **92** Hanly, Letter no. 226, pp 574 –5; Curtayne, ibid., p. 201. **93** Hanly, Letter no. 226, p.577.

and at 4.00 a.m. on the day of his execution. We can imagine the great love of God which filled his heart as he renewed the sacrifice of Calvary during these difficult days. Its effects can be seen in the letters he wrote those last days. He continues later in the same letter contemplating the sufferings of Christ:

> Jesus suffered cold, frost, hunger, prison, stripes, thorns, and the most painful death on the Cross for others' sins, and compared to the death of the Cross, Tyburn, as I hear the description, is but a flea biting. I ought therefore cheerfully to desire it, heartily covet it and joyfully embrace it, it being a sure way, a smooth path by which I may in a very short time pass from sorrow to joy, from toil to rest and from a momentary time or duration to never ending eternity.[94]

He wrote to Fr Corker on the eve of his death:

> I do most earnestly recommend myself to your prayers and to the most holy sacrifices of all the noble confessors who are in this prison, and to such priests as you are acquainted with; and I hope soon to be able to requite all your and their kindness…
>
> I desire that you be pleased to tell all my benefactors that for all eternity I will be mindful of them, and that I will pray for them until they will come where I hope to come soon, and then also will thank them *in conspectu supremi Domini* (before the Supreme Lord). They deserve all praise in this and, by God's grace, a crown of glory in the next.[95]

The very night before he died, he was perfectly at ease; he went to bed at 11.00 p.m. and slept soundly until four in the morning when he was awakened by his servant James McKenna on the morning of 1 July.

When he was carried out to the Priests' Yard on his way to execution, he turned around towards the windows of the priests' cells, with a cheerful face and raised his hand in blessing – there were nine other priests in jail in Newgate at this time. A moment later he stretched himself, face uppermost, on the rough wooden sledge. He was tied to it by ropes and was then dragged and jolted by the horses through the thronged streets of London to Tyburn, a distance of about two miles.

It was a hundred years since a Catholic bishop had been executed at Tyburn. Consequently there was a great curiosity to see a man of such dignity, one already famed for his noble deportment. An immense multitude of spec-

94 Ibid., Letter no. 226, p. 579; Curtayne, ibid., pp 204, 205, 206. **95** Hanly, ibid., Letter no. 229, pp 581, 582.

tators awaited his arrival, partly along the route, partly at the place of execution. On the scaffold he delivered a short discourse in which, protesting his innocence as to the charges of conspiracy made against him, he prayed for the life and health of the king and all the royal family, and gave a complete pardon to all his enemies and adversaries. He asked God to be merciful to him through the merits of Christ, the intercession of the Blessed Virgin, and of all the holy angels and saints in Paradise. He revealed that he had been offered his life if he would but falsely accuse others, which offer he of course rejected. He then said the *Miserere* psalm. A priest attached to the Spanish embassy followed Oliver from Newgate to Tyburn, and pronounced the absolution as the martyr was being hanged.

Among the English Catholics Oliver befriended in prison was the Sheldon family. They had obtained from the king – at whose disposition the body of the martyr had been put by law – leave to bring the dismembered quarters of the martyr to St Giles graveyard for burial. This place had been chosen by Oliver himself. Elizabeth Sheldon, however, felt so strongly that the day would come when the archbishop of Armagh would be venerated as a martyr, that she had special arrangements made for the preservation of the parts of the body. When she received possession of the body, she put the head in a special box which she had prepared for it, and the hands and arms from the elbows downwards in another. The other remains of the martyred body were interred beside the Jesuit victims of the Popish Plot in the graveyard of St Giles in the Fields. On the stone placed over the grave was a brass plate, which is now preserved in the Dominican convent in Drogheda, with an inscription which attests to the belief of those who buried him that Oliver had suffered death in *odium Fidei* (out of hatred of the faith), and that he was a martyr. This belief was widespread among Catholics at the time.

In his condemned cell at Newgate, Oliver had promised to remember the Catholics of England in heaven. He kept his word, for their persecution ceased with his death.

After the execution, the lives of those who gave perjured evidence against the Primate – four priests and four laymen – all ended up in a sorry condition, some of them remaining impenitent to the end. One of them, Fr Hugh Duffy, threw in his lot with the Rapparees, living with them on the hills. Instructions were sent from Rome to the head of the Franciscan order in Ireland that he was to be considered excommunicated and an apostate friar. Forty years after the archbishop's death, in 1721, when he was an old man, Duffy called one day on Dr Hugh McMahon, who was then archbishop of Armagh, and asked to receive the sacraments. Dr McMahon did not know him and was astonished when the visitor revealed his identity. Duffy threw himself at the Archbishop's feet, crying: 'Is there to be no mercy for me? Am I never to make my peace with God?' Dr

McMahon did not reply but opened the door of a shrine in his room. It contained the head of Oliver Plunkett, which had only a short while previously been brought back to Ireland as a precious relic. Duffy recognized it and as he had already suffered considerably from remorse of conscience, he fainted in the excess of his emotions. He was pardoned and died a sincere penitent.[96]

In 1683, when the memory of the Plot was looked on as a tragic nightmare, Fr Corker and his fellow Benedictines were released from Newgate and allowed to retire to the Continent. Loth to leave the remains of his martyred penitent in St Giles graveyard, Fr Corker had them exhumed, and brought them with him to a monastery of the Benedictine order in Lambspring in Germany. Here he had them interred in the crypt of the church.

Fr Corker was anxious to obtain leave to show certain honours to the martyr's remains if Propaganda would allow it. To get this permission it seems that Fr Corker travelled to Rome in 1684 and brought with him the head of St Oliver which thus came into the custody of Cardinal Howard, brother of the duke of Norfolk, who was then living in the Eternal City. When Cardinal Howard died, the precious relic was left under the care of his brother Dominicans at Santa Sabina in Rome. Here it was often visited by a young Irish student of the Ludovisi College, called Hugh McMahon, who frequently visited the places made venerable by the passage of the martyr, and who as a consequence developed a deep affection and devotion for the Archbishop. In 1700 McMahon returned to Ireland as bishop of Clogher, from which he was translated to Armagh in 1713. In 1722, when the first signs of religious toleration were faintly discerned on the horizon, Archbishop McMahon applied to the master general of the Dominican Order to have a convent of nuns founded in Drogheda where Dr McMahon usually had his residence. The first prioress was Mother Catherine Plunkett, a near relative of Oliver's. In what year Archbishop McMahon obtained possession of the head of St Oliver cannot be affirmed positively, but he had acquired it by 1721. When Dr McMahon made his will in 1735, the head was in the custody of the Dominican nuns in Drogheda. It is now enshrined in St Peter's church in Drogheda.

Oliver's friend, John Brennan, archbishop of Cashel, sent his report to Rome on the death of the martyr:

> In truth, his holy life merited for him this glorious death; for during twelve years of his residence here, he showed himself vigilant, zealous, and indefatigable above his predecessors, nor do we find within the memory of any of the present century that any Primate or Metropolitan visited his diocese and province with such solicitude and pastoral zeal as

96 Cf. Curtayne, ibid., p. 235.

> he did, reforming depraved morals amongst the people, and the scandalous lives of some of the clergy, chastising the guilty, rewarding the meritorious, consoling all, and benefiting, as far as was in his power, and succouring the needy: wherefore he was applauded and honoured by the clergy and the people, with the exception of some wicked enemies of virtue and religious observance.[97]

The cause of beatification of Oliver Plunkett was first opened in 1874 in the diocese of Westminster in London (the location of the martyrdom) and was approved by Rome in 1886. The remains of the Primate were transferred from Lambspring to Downside Abbey in England in 1883. In 1886, at the request of the Irish hierarchy, Pope Leo XIII ruled that Oliver's cause should be followed through from Armagh rather than from Westminster.

In 1918 the Declaration of Martyrdom was signed and Oliver was beatified on 23 May 1920. He was canonized on 12 October 1975, the first new Irish saint for almost 700 years, and the first of the Irish martyrs to be beatified. In his canonization homily, Pope Paul VI said, among other things:

> Today the Church rejoices with a great joy, because the sacrificial love of Jesus Christ, the Good Shepherd, is reflected and manifested in a new Saint. And this new Saint is Oliver Plunkett, Bishop and Martyr – successor of Saint Patrick in the See of Armagh. And on our part we bow down today to venerate his sacred relics, just as on former occasions we have personally knelt in prayer and admiration at his shrine in Drogheda.
>
> We praise God – Father, Son, and Holy Spirit – who gave the glorious gift of supernatural faith to Oliver Plunkett – a faith so strong that it filled him with the fortitude and courage necessary to face martyrdom with serenity, with joy, and with forgiveness. There was no rancour in his heart. In his pastoral activities, his exhortation had been one of pardon and peace. In his speech on the scaffold, his words of pardon were in fact: 'I do forgive all who had a hand directly or indirectly in my death and in my innocent blood'.
>
> Oliver Plunkett was, above all, a Bishop of the Church of God, serving as Primate of Ireland for twelve years. He was a vigilant preacher of the Catholic faith and champion of that pastoral charity which is fostered in prayer and manifested in solicitude for his brethren in the clergy – that pastoral charity which is expressed in zeal for the Christian instruction of the young, for the promotion of Catholic edu-

97 Concannon, ibid., p. 266.

> cation, for the consolation of all God's people. He infused into his flock new strength and fresh hope in time of trial and need.
>
> And the Church raises her voice in solemn affirmation, to authenticate and consecrate this testimony, and to reaffirm for this generation and for all time the true hierarchy of evangelical values in the world. The message of Oliver Plunkett offers a hope that is greater than the present life; it shows a love that is stronger than death. Through the action of the Holy Spirit may the whole Church experience his insights and his wisdom, and with him be able to hear the challenge that comes from Peter: 'Put your trust in nothing but the grace that will be given you when the grace of Jesus Christ is revealed' (1 Pet 1:13). May the Church understand this as yet another call to renewal and holiness of life, knowing as she does that, by reason of the power of God, there is no limit to love's forbearance (cf. I Cor 13:7).

These words of the Holy Father summarize in an eloquent way the meaning of the life and death of St Oliver Plunkett and his relevance for our times.

One of St Oliver's dominant characteristics was his fortitude in the face of adversity. This comes across very clearly in his letters and in his response to the demands of his episcopal office. He had many difficult assignments, especially in the area of the reform of abuses, but he never shied away from his responsibility, even when he knew that at times his efforts would generate criticism and calumny.

As Msgr John Hanly points out in his introduction to *The letters of Saint Oliver Plunkett*, perhaps the most striking characteristic of the life of the Primate of Armagh was his love for and obedience to the Holy See. Clearly those twenty-two years he spent in the Eternal City (1647–69), close to the Vicar of Christ, gave him a deep understanding of the role of the see of Peter in the government of the Church. But it was not only a deep understanding; it was above all a profound supernatural love for the Holy Father and his close collaborators, something which would remain with him all during his life. From his letters we see how grateful he was for all the advice he got from Rome as well as his spirit of humble obedience in everything that was asked of him. It was this spirit of docile response to God's will which caused him to lay down his life for the Church, and for the Pope.

CHAPTER FOUR

The Curé of Ars (1786–1859)

IN 1986, THE BICENTENARY of the birth of the Curé of Ars, John Paul II devoted his Holy Thursday letter that year to a consideration of the life of this exceptional priest. Now more that ever, he said, we need the example and intercession of St Jean-Marie Vianney's priesthood

> in order to face the situations of our times when, in spite of a number of hopeful signs, evangelization is being contradicted by a growing secularization, when spiritual discipline is being neglected, when many are losing sight of the kingdom of God, when often, even in the pastoral ministry, there is a too exclusive concern for the social aspect, for temporal aims.[1]

The Abbé Vianney, a model of priestly zeal for all pastors, showed by his love for souls the truth of one of his own sayings: 'The priesthood is the love of the heart of Jesus'. Because he was so deeply conscious of his pastoral responsibilities, he poured himself our through prayer, penance and preaching to win back the people of Ars from the ways of sin and lukewarmness to a vibrant Christian commitment in their daily lives. John Paul II, pointing out how the Curé sanctified himself through the dedicated exercise of his pastoral mission, encourages priests today to find holiness in and through their pastoral activities.

Essentially Fr Vianney dedicated himself to teaching the faith and purifying consciences, and these two ministries were directed towards the building up of a Eucharistic community. Should we not see here, today also, the three principal objectives of the priest's pastoral service? Do not all authentic pastoral activities centre on, or lead to, catechesis, the ministry of conversion, and the building up of a Eucharistic community?

The Curé's untiring devotion to the sacrament of reconciliation reveals to us his principal charism. At the present time when there has been such a considerable fall-off in attendance at this sacrament, the example of Fr Vianney is

1 John Paul II, *Holy Thursday letter for 1986*, no. 2.

a challenge to priests. 'It is', John Paul II reminds us, 'a sign of the urgent need to develop a whole pastoral strategy of the Sacrament of Reconciliation', because without a return to this sacrament 'the much desired renewal will remain superficial and illusory'.[2] Basically what the Holy Father is saying is that people will discover the value and the consolation of confession if priests give it the priority it deserves. In the first place this means regular preaching about the sense of sin, and the need to be constantly converted through frequent recourse to this sacrament. It also implies generous availability on the part of priests for this ministry of forgiveness, a ministry that should have priority over other pastoral activities.

In order to appreciate the charism of the Curé of Ars, we need to reflect on the life of this saintly parish priest. In doing so we will see how a man of very limited abilities allowed himself to be so transformed by grace that he became a most effective instrument in God's hands.

BIRTH AND YOUTH

Jean-Marie Vianney was born in 1786 in the village of Dardilly, in the neighbourhood of Lyon, the fourth of six children. He came from a farming background. Jean-Marie was a bright and cheerful boy with a vivacious character. As a youth he was impetuous by nature, so his subsequent calm and serenity suggest a committed effort in later life to curb this aspect of his character. He was brought up in a deeply Christian home, acquiring a precocious piety beyond his years, primarily through the influence of his mother.

The terrible events in Paris associated with the French Revolution in 1789 had little immediate effect on life in Dardilly. It was not until the Civil Constitution of the Clergy began to be enforced in 1791 that the influence of the Revolution began to take effect. The people of the parish began to notice that the sermons of the new parish priest were larded with words like citizen, civic, constitution, etc. It wasn't long before they realized they were listening to a schismatic priest.[3] Then began for the Vianneys and other families a period of secret religious practice: Mass in the woods, in a barn, sometimes in their own house, with priests in disguise coming from Lyon, all with a price on their heads and the danger of deportation or worse. The experience must have been very similar to what Irish priests and people experienced during the Elizabethan and Cromwellian persecutions, followed by the penal laws of the eighteenth century.

2 Cf. ibid., no. 7. 3 Priests were required to take an oath of fidelity to the constitution, which implied a separation from Rome. If they refused, they had to be prepared to suffer for their convictions, in many cases with their lives. 130 of the 134 bishops refused, but only 46,000 of the 70,000 priests did so.

Vianney was seven years old when the Reign of Terror came to Lyon in 1793, where the guillotine was busy all day. However, it is unlikely that this massacre at far-away Lyon impinged very much on the consciousness of a boy of seven. What had much more impact was the fact that the village church bells were silent and the door closed.

As a young boy Jean-Marie helped to look after the cattle in the nearby fields, absorbing the strong work ethic of the Vianney family from an early age. As a result of the Revolution an increasing number of beggars and displaced persons passed through the village who benefited from the traditional Vianney hospitality. Though Jean-Marie never experienced poverty in his own life, he saw enough of it as a child to realize what it was, observing the flotsam of society which passed through Dardilly during those years.

Jean-Marie had been taught the first elements of reading at home by his elder sister Catherine before he began his formal education at the age of nine. It seems that the three winters of 1795, 1796, and 1797 were all the schooling he received until very much later when as a young man he had to renew his studies. From all accounts, in those early years he was diligent and endowed with a good memory.

One day in 1797, when Jean-Marie was eleven, a priest called at the farm. He asked the boy how long it was since his last confession. 'I have never been to confession', Jean-Marie replied. 'Very well', concluded the priest, 'we can remedy that at once'. There and then he made his first confession, an event which he was to remember with affection and gratitude for the rest of his life. 'I remember it well', he told people many years later. 'It was under our old clock'. The priest, M. Groboz, decided the boy should be prepared for his First Communion, and so, in May 1798, arrangements were made for him to stay with his aunt Marguerite at Ecully (three miles away) where two nuns, turned out of their convent by the Revolution, carried out a secret work of catechesis. Jean-Marie made his First Communion a year later, during the Second Terror when Catholics were persecuted and hundreds of priests died through execution or brutal internment. Thus the circumstances of the time required that the ceremony be a clandestine affair in a manor-house at Ecully. In later years Jean-Marie could never speak about his First Communion without shedding tears. After a lapse of fifty years he would still show the children of Ars the plain Rosary beads he received on that occasion, exhorting them to preserve theirs also with jealous care. That same day, in the company of his parents, he returned to Dardilly. He was now a strong boy of thirteen ready for work on the family farm. His days were occupied with the hard physical work of ploughing, tending to the vineyard, and other farming duties. He was naturally devout and gave what time he could to prayer. He made a practice of offering his work to God each day. He read the lives of the saints, the *Imitation of Christ*, and the Gospels.

With the advent of Bonaparte and the ratification of the concordat with Rome in 1802, churches were opened again for celebration of the liturgical feasts. Jean-Marie was very happy that he could once again pray before the Blessed Sacrament in the church in Dardilly at early morning on his way to work. On Sundays he spent most of the day in church.

VOCATION TO THE PRIESTHOOD

By this time he felt sure he had a call to the priesthood, but he was not blind to the fact that there were great obstacles to be overcome to fulfil his ambition. He was nearly seventeen years of age, his elementary studies were sorely inadequate, and he had no knowledge of Latin. He knew his mother would support his desire but that he was likely to face a lot of opposition from his father, and this for different reasons. His brother François was about to be conscripted into Napoleon's army unless he was bought out, and his sister Catherine was engaged to be married and had to be provided with a dowry. Given such circumstances, his father would be in no position to pay seminary fees. Encouraged by his mother, Jean-Marie broached the subject of his vocation with his father. Matthieu Vianney was inflexible in his refusal.

About this time the Abbé Charles Balley became parish priest of Ecully. He was a man of great pastoral zeal. Among other things he sought out young men as likely recruits to fill the depleted ranks of the clergy. To ensure their preliminary education he established in his presbytery a small school where boys could obtain the elementary knowledge of Latin and other subjects needed for entrance to the seminary.

Jean-Marie's hopes revived when he heard this news. His mother explained to her husband that it would not mean great expense to send the boy to Ecully as he could stay with her sister Marguerite and go to the Abbé Balley for his classes. In light of this new proposal, and having become convinced of the piety of his son, Matthieu Vianney after two years of opposition finally withdrew his objections. The next thing was to convince Fr Balley to take Jean-Marie as a pupil. The austere parish priest of Ecully closely scrutinized the nineteen-year-old and found him to be well informed on religious topics, with an open and frank personality. He decided to admit him as one of his pupils.

Jean-Marie was in his twentieth year when he went back to school, hoping to learn what most boys, if they are to know it at all, should acquire by the age of ten. It was a challenging and demanding situation. He found Latin grammar and syntax very difficult, and his memory was of little help to him in this area. In addition, he gave no evidence of being bright intellectually. He prayed constantly and did penance to win grace from heaven for help with his studies. Even at this early age he fasted regularly and helped the poor from his meagre resources.

Despite his efforts lasting over several months he made practically no progress, and the signs of his penances began to show in his by now haggard face. Abbé Balley spoke to him, counselling moderation in penance, while at the same time encouraging him in his holy ambition to be a priest. Jean-Marie felt his efforts were useless and that he would do better to return to his father's farm. But Fr Balley, by now fully convinced of Jean-Marie's vocation, encouraged him to do a pilgrimage to the shrine of St Francis Regis at Louvesc. His protegé took up the idea with enthusiasm. It was the summer of 1806. He would travel the sixty-five miles on foot, begging for his bread en route. At Louvesc he prayed at the saint's tomb asking that, in imitation of St Francis Regis, he would become a priest and save souls in the countryside of the Lyonnais. On his return to Ecully his progress in Latin was sufficient to give him at least the hope that he would acquire enough to begin philosophy and theology.

SOLDIER BOY

However, one further difficulty loomed ahead of him. Jean-Marie had now reached the age of conscription, and Napoleon was desperately short of young men to fuel his military ambitions. His call-up papers were served on him at Dardilly. This despite the fact that Cardinal Fesch, the archbishop of Lyon and uncle to Napoleon, had managed to obtain exemption for his seminarians, among whom the Abbé Balley had included Jean-Marie Vianney. His father did not have the money to pay for a substitute so Jean-Marie had no option but to report for duty. The long years that he was likely to be away seemed to put paid to his cherished ambition to be a priest. However, events were to turn out very differently to what he expected.

In October 1809 Jean-Marie reported at the barracks in Lyon. He was profoundly shocked at what he saw and heard of army life. Two days after his arrival he was too ill to get up in the morning, and the doctor ordered that he be transferred to hospital. A fortnight later he was well enough to leave his bed, but too weak to march to Roanne for training before setting out for the campaign in Spain. He followed behind in a cart, but the journey was too much for him. On arrival he was sent to hospital where he remained for six weeks. On 5 January 1810 he was told that he must join a detachment setting out on the long march to the Spanish frontier. When he arrived at the adjutant's office in the afternoon for his marching orders he found it closed. The following day he learned that the contingent had left without him, and he was told in no uncertain terms what was the official view of his conduct. He was given his route and told to catch up with the rearguard.

He started off on the long road to Clermont. Along the way he revealed his plight to a young man who caught up with him. Seeing how Jean-Marie was so exhausted he offered to carry his pack for him. His companion turned out to be a deserter and informed Jean-Marie that there were many others like them in the surrounding woods. Eventually they came to the village of Noës where the mayor found a place for Jean-Marie to stay in safety. The mayor assured him that it was too late now to think of rejoining the regiment. Under the assumed name of Jerome Vincent, Jean-Marie spent the next two years in the village taking on, paradoxically, the job of school-master, giving children and some youths lessons in reading, writing , and the catechism. This unusual incident in the life of the Curé of Ars was explained during the process of his beatification by a witness who was well acquainted with the facts of the situation. He said that Jean-Marie's disobedience was more apparent than real, and the fact that he did not rejoin his regiment was due to unforeseen circumstances rather than to a preconceived plan.

STEPS TO THE PRIESTHOOD

At the beginning of 1811 Jean-Marie returned to the homestead in Dardilly. His joy at being reunited with his family was tempered by the death of his mother a few weeks later. To the end of his life her memory remained fresh in his mind, such that he could never speak about her without tears coming to his eyes. In a very special way he owed his vocation to her.

His father put no obstacle to Jean-Marie continuing his studies for the priesthood. So he returned to Ecully, this time residing in the presbytery with M. Balley. Apart from relaunching his study of Latin, he combined the role of sacristan and altar-boy, as well as accompanying the Abbé Balley on his parish rounds. In this way he spent a year of practical apprenticeship for the priesthood. Jean-Marie was now twenty-five years of age and Fr Balley felt a certain urgency about seeing his pupil ordained. He had him placed on the same footing as the students of rhetoric in the Petit Seminaire of Lyon, and so was able to present him for tonsure on 28 May 1811.

Fr Balley, who was sixty at the time, was a man of deep piety, true apostolic zeal, and generous in his spirit of penance. His student was much more perceptive in assimilating ideas about the spiritual life from him than he was about absorbing the specifics of Latin syntax and grammar. After completing a year with Fr Balley, Jean-Marie entered the minor seminary at Verrières to begin his three-year course for the priesthood consisting of one year of philosophy and two of theology. By normal standards this was a very inadequate course, but because of the shortage of priests caused by the ravages of the Revolution and the Reign of Terror, priests were needed quickly and so were given a three-year crash course to meet the urgency of the situation.

The year at Verrières was a very difficult one for Jean-Marie, both as regards his studies and in relation to his fellow students. He was ten years older than his classmates who were on average about fourteen years of age. The psychological difference was proportionately much greater than the gap in years. He found it difficult to grasp the elements of philosophy, primarily because of his poor knowledge of Latin. He felt humiliated before the other students and was frequently the butt of their jokes. 'At Verrières', he confessed later, in masterly understatement, 'I had somewhat to suffer'.

In July of 1813 he returned to Ecully where Fr Balley took him in hand once again to prepare him for this two-year theology course in the major seminary of St Irenaeus in Lyon. The whole course of dogma, scripture, liturgy, canon law and moral theology had to be crammed into two years. The classes were in Latin, but Jean-Marie found the dictated notes and the exchanges in the same language beyond him. To help him along, the professor appointed one of the brighter students to be Vianney's private tutor. When things were explained to him in French, he was able to follow them and to answer questions intelligently. Jean-Marie was not, as he is sometimes portrayed, a stupid dullard. It was simply that he had acquired no real grounding in Latin due to his late start and his poor memory. He took the end of year exams in the obligatory Latin, which he failed miserably since he didn't even understand the questions. The seminary authorities told him that it would be pointless for him to return the following year.

Jean-Marie was, naturally, very disappointed and poured out his tale of woe to the Abbé Balley. The latter took him in hand and covered the theological ground with him through French. After three months he again faced the board of examiners, but again his lack of Latin was his undoing. As a last resort M. Balley invited the vicar general of the diocese to come to Ecully and question Jean-Marie in French. This he agreed to, bringing the rector of the seminary with him.

In the presence of his tutor, and fielding questions in a language he could understand, Vianney made a good impression, giving satisfactory answers to all the points raised by the examiners. As a result, on 2 July 1814, in Lyon, he received all the minor orders and the subdiaconate, having prepared for them by doing a month's retreat, and after receiving the appropriate instruction on the powers he was to receive. Afterwards he returned to Ecully to receive his last year of theological preparation (1814–15) under his dedicated tutor. Vianney returned to the seminary in Lyon at the end of May 1815 to prepare for the diaconate which he received on 23 June. Returning to Ecully, Jean-Marie prepared for his final exam before the priesthood. Again the vicar general, M. Bochard, was persuaded to examine the candidate through French in Ecully. For more than an hour the Abbé Bochard questioned Jean-Marie on the most thorny questions in moral theology. Fr Bochard was very satisfied with his responses, expressing surprise at their clarity and precision. At last the final hurdle to his being ordained was overcome.

Dimissorial letters were issued for his ordination, which was to take place in Grenoble since his own bishop was an exile in Rome at this time. After walking the sixty-five miles from Lyon, he was ordained in the Grenoble seminary chapel on 13 August 1815, without the company of any family or friend. Thus at the age of twenty-nine, after many uncertainties, failures and tears, Jean-Marie was now a priest of Jesus Christ. Later on, in his catechetical instruction, when he spoke about the sublime dignity of the priesthood (as he often did), he must have relived with emotion the memory of that day in August 1815. 'Oh, how great is the dignity of the priest. The priest will only be understood in heaven. Were he understood on earth, people would die, not of fear, but of love.'[4] He said his first Mass in the seminary chapel the next day, 14 August, the vigil of the Assumption, setting out for Ecully on foot on the 16th. On arrival he was given a joyous reception by his tutor and confidant Fr Balley who knelt to receive his blessing. He was able to give Jean-Marie the good news that he had been appointed curate in the parish of Ecully, so they would continue to soldier together.

CURATE AT ECULLY

The Abbé Vianney set to work immediately. There was plenty to do as Fr Balley was in poor health and unable to fulfil his responsibilities with the same vigour as before. The two priests lived in the same presbytery and learned from each other the path to priestly holiness. The young curate visited the sick, preached, catechized and baptized. However, his testimonial letters for ordination specified that he should undergo a probationary period before he would be allowed to hear confessions, because it was felt that the priest who was to become famous for the apostolate of the confessional, should not be entrusted with this task immediately. When after some months he received faculties to hear confessions, the Abbé Balley was his first penitent.

As soon as it was known that Fr Vianney could hear confessions, the parishioners began to flock to him. People were attracted by his reserve, his

4 Francis Trochu, *The Curé of Ars: St Jean-Marie-Baptiste Vianney* (Rockford, IL, 1977), p. 91.

simplicity, and his kindness. He was a man of pleasant personality, with a sense of humour which came out more clearly as the years went by. Although not very bright intellectually, he was endowed with the deep common sense of his peasant background and a sharpness of mind which enabled him to deal with any situation. Gradually he began to take over the work of the parish as Fr Balley's health deteriorated, eventually passing to his eternal reward in December 1817. Jean-Marie wept for Abbé Balley as for a father. From him he had learned what it was to be a dedicated priest. 'I have encountered some beautiful souls in my time', he would recount later, 'but none so fine as his'. Every morning, for the rest of his life, he remembered his name at the *memento* in his Mass.

APPOINTMENT TO ARS

A few weeks later a new parish priest was appointed to Ecully, and in February 1818 Jean-Marie received word of his own appointment as parish priest of Ars.[5] The vicar general, as he handed him his letter of appointment, said: 'There is not much love of God in that parish; you will bring some into it'. As he set off for his new parish, he went there with the determination to make it the best parish in the diocese, not out of vainglory, but solely for the glory of God.

On 9 February 1818 he left Ecully to walk the twenty miles to Ars, followed by an ox-cart which carried some clothes, a few bits of furniture, and the bed and books bequeathed to him by Fr Balley. He had some difficulty finding the place, and asked a young boy for directions. In response to the boy's information, the Curé said by way of thanking the lad, 'My young friend, you have shown me the way to Ars; I will show you the way to heaven'. The young shepherd added that the spot where they stood marked the boundary of the parish. On hearing this the new Curé knelt down to pray.

It was nearly dark when he arrived at the village which consisted of a group of straggling cottages with a small church occupying a central position. It was a very ordinary looking, yellowish building with plain windows, dating from the twelfth century, with a make-shift wooden bell-tower replacing the tower which had collapsed some years before. Next door was the presbytery, a dwelling of five rooms: dining-room and kitchen on the ground floor and three bedrooms upstairs.

The ringing of the bell for Mass the following morning was the first indication for the villagers that they had a new parish priest. The general religious

5 Initially, when the Abbé Vianney was appointed to Ars, it was only a chapel of ease of Misérieux. Later, during the incumbency of Fr Vianney, it became a parish in its own right.

condition of Ars was not very encouraging. Practice of the faith had seriously declined since the eighteenth century. People felt no scruple about missing Mass on Sundays, for the most trivial of reasons, and especially during the harvest period. To cater for the sixty houses in the village, Ars had four taverns where a lot of drinking took place, resulting in drunken rowdiness, especially at weekends. The young men and women of Ars were passionately attached to dancing. Above all there was a pervasive religious ignorance in the parish.

One of the Curé's first tasks was to call on the local château to persuade the lady of the manor, Mlle des Garets, to take back from the presbytery some of the furniture she had lent for the comfort of the priest. Mlle des Garets was a woman of deep piety who divided her time between care of her household and visits to the sick. Faithful to a practice she inherited form her mother, she daily recited the divine office. At the time of the Curé's appointment Mlle d'Ars was sixty-four years of age. She had been educated at Saint-Cyr and had retained the characteristically French manner of the *ancien régime*. The family must have enjoyed a real popularity in the district, otherwise it would not be easy to account for the fact that the Revolution failed to deprive Mlle des Garets of her estate. The poor loved her because she paid their rent and provided them with food and clothing.

The apostolic field entrusted to the Curé was a barren one. However, instead of wasting time with idle regrets he set to work immediately to convert the village. He had no intention of developing that wider pastoral activity which was subsequently to make him a household name in the Church. He preached primarily for the benefit of the people of Ars. He thundered against the abuses that were rampant in the village. He was not trying to invent new remedies, but contented himself with those means which were always the basis of pastoral success: prayer, penance, and apostolic zeal.

He visited all the houses in the parish, going out each day at noon when he knew people would be at home for the midday meal. Dressed in his cassock, and wearing heavy peasant boots, he would appear as the family were at table. He would chat about things that were familiar to all of them: the work of the fields, the crops, the price of wool, the quality of last year's Beaujolais maturing in the cellars of these small homesteads. Nearly everywhere he got a good reception. He used these visits to find out about each family, the number of children, the state of their religious instruction, the difficulties each had to face, etc. He discovered too that there were some good families in the parish. He came to the conclusion that ignorance rather than malice was the greatest obstacle and the hard core of the resistance he had to overcome in fulfilling his ambition to convert Ars.

The first Easter in the parish was a particular disappointment for him. Many of his parishioners, especially the men, hadn't been to the sacraments for fifteen to twenty years. He realized clearly that there was a lot of uphill work to be done. Although filled with a sense of his own insufficiency, he didn't lose courage. He saw clearly the steps he must take. Young and old had to be instructed in the faith. Sunday work had to cease. The feasts of the Church had to be kept religiously, and for this to happen the dancing which took place, even in the open air just outside the parish church, had to be stopped. The four taverns which were the subject of more than one sermon had to be closed, and so remove temptation from the men who went there rather than to Sunday Mass. That was the programme which he set about resolutely to put into practice.

The Abbé Vianney was well aware that the biggest obstacle facing him was the complacency of a congregation that didn't wish to have their lives complicated by facing up to the demands of their faith. Conscious of his responsibility to his flock, he determined to give them no peace until he had brought about a conversion of their lives.

PRAYER AND PENANCE

The Curé's daily routine began to take shape. It soon became known in the village that long before dawn he was up and about and on his way from the presbytery to the church, where he spent a considerable time in prayer before Mass. Gradually news went around about his spartan culinary tastes, and the sound of the discipline which could be heard at night. Prayer and penance were the essential means he used to merit the grace of conversion for his parishioners. 'My God', he pleaded, 'grant me the conversion of my parish; I am willing to suffer all my life whatsoever it may please you to lay upon me; yes, even for a hundred years I am prepared to endure the sharpest pains, only let my people be converted'.[6] In the afternoon, whether there were visits or not, he would go out into the open air for exercise. He used these walks to pray or say his breviary. He loved the open country and enjoyed the beauty of nature, but a time would come when he would no longer be able to indulge this pleasure due to becoming a prisoner of the confessional.

His penances, which he tried to hide from prying eyes, were frightening, especially during his early years in Ars. Armed with a discipline, the effectiveness of which had been increased by the insertion of sharp pieces of iron, he mercilessly struck his 'corpse', 'this old Adam', as he used to call his poor body. In later years the Curé admitted that he was imprudent in the way he punished his body in the early years of his priesthood. The first period of his ministry at

6 Trochu, ibid., p. 118.

Ars was the most austere of his whole life. At that time he lived practically alone, and took full advantage of his independence. Sometimes he would let two or even three days go by without touching any food. One Holy Week, probably his first in Ars, he only ate twice. He had learned as a young priest to mortify his body from the example of Fr Balley of Ecully. Apart from self-administered penances, he also suffered from a double hernia and incessant headaches.

PREACHING

In addition to prayer and penance, preaching constituted the third element of his spiritual strategy to bring about the conversion of his parish. His first sermons cost him an immense effort. He prepared them with care, writing out every word. Occasionally he would leave the sacristy, where he wrote on the vestments press, and go to kneel before the altar. In this way he would spend hours preparing his sermons. When he had it all down on paper, he set about learning it by heart, thirty or forty pages of it, penned in his scraggly writing. When he thought he had mastered his sermon he would try it out in the churchyard late on Saturday night, and passers-by sometimes caught him at it. Examples of these sermons of his early days are still extant.

Fr Vianney made no claim to eloquence and he had no interest in oratorical success. While he had little confidence in himself, he nonetheless attached the highest importance to his mission as preacher. With great conscientiousness he undertook the religious instruction of his flock from the beginning of his ministry. He did not aspire to originality but drew from the volumes of sermons in his bookshelves – whatever referred to his subject. Culled from a great variety of sources, the passages he selected were then amalgamated like fragments of a mosaic or patchwork. To maintain contact with his people he translated these extracts from bookish sermons into more popular language, rounding them off in his own way. He would then embark on pastoral and practical considerations, or ardent appeals for conversion, quite unaware that this was the best part of his sermon.

At the beginning the listening public for these sermons was scanty enough. And when people felt like going asleep he kept them awake by his loud delivery. In those first months he preached to his flock about the proper way to behave in church, about keeping Sunday holy, and the purpose of his work in Ars as their parish priest, which was, he told them, to lead them all to heaven. His instructions dealt more with moral than dogmatic topics. Dancing and frequentation of taverns were the targets of his severest reproaches.

Initially there were occasions when the Curé lost the thread of his sermon, stumbled over a phrase and, remembering no more, was obliged to leave the pulpit. However, a time came when, caught in the pulpit and remembering nothing of his carefully written sermon, he began to improvise and so found himself a preacher. What he said came from his heart and flowed eloquently from his lips. And so his whole style was changed. What was to a degree artificial became more natural, and so more effective. He had something to say and he said it simply. His preparation now, rather than hours of writing at the vestment table was exchanged for long periods of prayer before the Blessed Sacrament, by his fasting and penances.

After some years he stopped writing out his sermons because the pilgrims left him no time. Then after a novena to the Holy Spirit he gave up the idea of memorizing passages and gave his own imagination and intuition free play. In the long run the ministry of the word came easily to him. 'There are two places where I can rest' he said, 'at the altar and in the pulpit'.[7] He spoke to his people in their own language, simply and directly with no studied effects. However, he was a great teacher in that he constantly used similes borrowed from nature and the countryside, and from village and home life. Dealing with abstract ideas was not his strong suit. However, he was singularly gifted at the level of the imagination as he showed in his preaching. In a sermon on faith he told his listeners:

> We are in this world as in a fog. But faith is the wind that scatters the fog and makes a splendid sun shine over our soul ... See how gloomy and cold it is with the unbelievers. There a long winter prevails. With us everything is cheerful, full of joy and consolation. Pull a fish out of water and it will no longer live. So too a person without God. 'Why, my God, have you put me into this world?' – 'In order to redeem you' – 'And why do you wish to redeem me?' – 'Because I love you.'[8]

In speaking about charity he uses equally graphic similes:

> What would you say about a person who ploughed his neighbour's field and left his own life fallow? That's exactly what you do! You constantly push your way into the conscience of others and leave your own by the wayside. When death comes, you will be sorry that you have busied yourself so much with others and so little with yourself. For we shall have to give an account of ourselves and not of others ...[9]

He had an unusual lucidity of mind, which allowed him to see into the depths of souls.

7 René Fourrey, *The Curé d'Ars: a pictorial biography* (London, 1959), p. 49. **8** Christian Feldman, *God's gentle rebels: great saints of Christianity* (New York, 1995), p. 141. **9** Ibid., p. 139.

His sermons, delivered in pointed, not to say rough language at times, were geared to shake his parishioners and the pilgrims out of their complacency. While he had no inhibitions in preaching about the 'hard sayings' of the Gospel, he much preferred to proclaim the marvellous goodness of God:

> He constantly spoke of God's love, God's presence, the need to remain united to him in order to sanctify our actions, the happiness and joy of paradise, the beauty of the soul in a state of grace, the blessings of the Holy Spirit, the need for prayer, the desirability of crosses.[10]

KEEPING SUNDAY HOLY

His first objective was the sanctification of the Lord's day and the return of his parishioners to Sunday Mass. In parallel with his preaching campaign to get people back to Mass, he set about refurbishing his church which was in poor material condition. In doing so he was driven by his own deep faith in the Eucharist and his desire to make the liturgy more attractive to the parishioners. He first installed a beautiful new altar. He made the journey to Lyons to order new vestments and sacred vessels of the best quality. By contrast with his rigorous style of personal poverty, he insisted that for the house of God only materials of the highest distinction would do. Gradually he transformed the church until it became worthy of the great mysteries being celebrated there. He acquired a beautiful new tabernacle and a throne for exposition of the Blessed Sacrament.

A new bell-tower was erected to replace the temporary wooden structure, and a side chapel dedicated to our Lady was constructed in 1820. The metal heart of the gilded statue of the Immaculate Conception held a ribbon on which he had written his parishioners' names one by one. As an expression of his devotion to the Blessed Virgin, every Saturday for the next forty years he said his Mass in this chapel. The ceiling and walls of the church were decorated. His zeal in this area didn't go unnoticed. Little by little new faces began to appear at Sunday Mass.

While there was an encouraging attendance at Sunday Mass for the first few months after the Curé's arrival, as soon as the Spring farming work started the congregation dwindled considerably. Hearing the carts rumbling to the fields and the blacksmith's anvil resounding to the blows of the hammer on Sunday mornings was a painful experience for Fr Vianney. The ringing of the church bell had little effect in summoning people to pray. Returning from the

10 Fourrey, ibid., p. 54 (From evidence given in the process of beatification by Guillaume Villier).

fields they put on their Sunday best and headed for the taverns where many became completely intoxicated. Meanwhile, in the public square in front of the church, the younger people danced far into the night to the music of the fiddle. Immodest songs and coarse jokes were interspersed with loud guffaws and blasphemies, all within earshot of the poor Curé who wept for the state of his parishioners' souls.

CATECHETICAL INSTRUCTION

Because he saw that ignorance of the faith was the greatest obstacle he had to cope with, he launched out on a programme of catechetical instruction which was later to become a permanent feature of the pilgrimage to Ars. He started with the children, gathering them in the church on weekday mornings at 6.00 a.m. between 1 November and the day in early summer when they made their First Communion. They were not easy children to teach as few could read and none was accustomed to school discipline. He explained the day's lesson after he got them to recite the topics of the previous day. The children had to be word perfect in their answers.

In order to attract the children to the church, he used various pious stratagems, such as a holy picture for the child who arrived first. After the initial prayer he would begin with some reflections which grabbed the attention of his young charges. He got them to carry a Rosary beads with them, and always had several in his pocket for the benefit of those who had lost theirs. Although kind and gentle, he kept a strict discipline. On Sundays there was a catechism session before vespers at about 1.00 p.m. in the afternoon, to which everybody was invited. The Curé never tired of repeating the fundamentals of the faith in these classes. Thanks to his zeal the children of Ars came to know their faith better than any others in the diocese. This was the judgement of the bishop when he came to Ars to examine the children before administering the sacrament of confirmation. Later on, those who succeeded Fr Vianney as parish priest were frequently astonished and edified at how well these simple folk knew their religion.

We have already commented on how the Curé prepared his sermons. He spoke clearly and directly, sometimes sharply, without a shadow of flattery. At times his manner was calm, gentle and appealing, as he realized that there were people in front of him whose hearts sought comfort, or souls that needed encouragement. As well as being a demanding teacher, he was also a shepherd and a father. The congregation needed a lot of staying power as his sermons on Sundays were often up to an hour long. He preached a lot about heaven. There, where they would see God, how happy they would be. 'If the parish is converted', he used to say, 'we shall go there in procession with the parish priest at the head'. It was a deeply felt conviction of the Curé of Ars that his own salvation was inextricably bound up with the salvation of his parishioners. This thought was a constant spur to his pastoral zeal in bringing about the conversion of his parish.

At first the poor Curé had to put up with a lot of uncouth behaviour in church. There was an affected nonchalance about the congregation which clearly betrayed a lack of interest. There was a lot of whispering and much noisy yawning. Late-comers banged the door; people in a hurry left in the middle of Mass; young people looked around them in a distracted manner. Faced with this kind of behaviour in church, Vianney, taking St Paul literally, was unsparing in his denunciation of it.[11] 'You poor people', he would say, 'how wretched you are! Pursue your wonted way! go on! but all you may expect is hell'. His caustic and mocking temperament showed itself occasionally during these early years of his priesthood. But his whole objective was to instil in his congregation a love for the liturgy and the Real Presence.

DRUNKENESS AND THE TAVERNS

Ars, with a population of something over two hundred souls, was, as we have seen, serviced by four taverns. Two of these were situated quite near the church, while the others were further up the village. It would appear that a lot of drinking went on in these establishments especially at the weekends. Vianney would have had no complaint against the taverns if they were nothing else but places where people met for innocent amusement. What horrified him was that God was blasphemed there, that they were the cause of drunken rowdyism in the village, and contributed greatly to undermining the celebration of the Lord's day. He reproached drunkards for 'degrading themselves below the lowest of the animals'. He made his own the words of St John Climacus: 'The tavern is the devil's own workshop, the school where hell retails its dogmas, the market where souls are bartered, the place were families are broken up, where health is undermined, where quarrels are started and murders are committed'.

He had harsh words for the innkeepers too: 'If he wishes to escape eternal damnation a priest may not and cannot absolve innkeepers who either at night or during church hours, serve those drunkards with wine'. It is unlikely that the innkeepers or their patrons were present in church to hear these sermons. All the same, word got around since the number of those frequenting the local inns became increasingly smaller. After a time both of the taverns near the

11 Cf. Tit 3:13: 'Rebuke them sharply, that they may be sound in the faith'.

church closed down, one of the owners having been given money by Fr Vianney to do so.

Eventually the other two in the more remote part of the village also closed their doors. However, seven others opened in succession, but one after the other, due to the Curé's preaching, had to retire from business. Gradually the message got through: if the men wanted to drink Beaujolais they had to take it from their own barrel at home. Apart from the moral implications, one of the very positive consequences for Ars was that the plague of pauperism in the village was considerably reduced. Later on, when outsiders began to flock to Ars, modest hostelries were opened to which Fr Vianney was in no way opposed.

DANCING

At this remove, the Curé's well-known struggle against dancing strikes us as being very severe and somewhat exaggerated. However, it is worth remembering that the Abbé Vianney was a child of his time and was not alone in his attitude. The manuals of moral theology current for the period confirm this. Dancing, they say, is not of its nature sinful or wrong, but as it frequently becomes sinful by reason of the different circumstances almost always attending it, it is wise for a Christian to abstain from it. Around the same time, the first synod of Maynooth (in Ireland) warned the faithful 'against the improper dances which have been imported into our country from abroad to the incomparable detriment of morality and decency'.[12]

In preaching and campaigning against dancing in his parish, Vianney was not therefore without authority on his side. He used every means in his power to extirpate this custom, including the confessional, where he refused absolution to dancers. He was harsh in his rebuke of parents who allowed their children to go dancing:

> Go, reprobate fathers and mothers, go to hell where God's anger awaits you, you and the fine things you have done in letting your children go wild! Go, and they will not be long in joining you, since you have so clearly shown them the way … My God, can your eyes be so bewitched that you believe there is no harm in this dancing, while it is in truth the cord by which the devil drags most souls to hell.[13]

The Abbé Vianney campaigned outside the church as well, prevailing on the mayor to forbid public dances in the square in front of the church. In 1823 a

12 Lancelot Sheppard, *The Curé d'Ars: portrait of a parish priest* (London, 1963), p. 59. **13** Ibid., p. 60.

second chapel, dedicated to St John the Baptist, was installed. Those addicted to dancing were reminded of their parish priest's attitude to it by the inscription which, not without a sense of humour, he got painted over the entrance to the chapel: 'his head was the price of a dance'.

It should also be remembered that the Curé's moral theology was not untouched by the spirit of Jansenism which still influenced French Catholicism. Basically Vianney saw dancing as an occasion of sin and he felt that it was his duty to eliminate it. The custom was so deeply rooted that it took him ten years to get rid of it. On one occasion he went in search of the fiddler who provided the music at the dance and asked him how much he earned for his services. Fr Vianney gave him double the sum so that he failed to turn up and the dance didn't take place. Another one of his tactics was to promote a deep piety among some of the young women who were now regularly attending church. He got them to say the Rosary and read the lives of the saints to them. He cultivated this small group to become a leaven to influence the parish. By 1830, twelve years after the arrival of the Curé, dances had been completely suppressed.

TRIALS OF THE FIRST YEARS

By 1828 the church in Ars was filled on Sundays. There was also a goodly attendance at daily Mass and for evening prayers. But this result was not achieved without considerable personal suffering. In addition to his penances, we have to add the concerted opposition of those most affected by the Curé's reforms. The innkeepers, the dancers, the men who worked on Sundays – all grumbled against him. Taking his condemnation of their conduct as a personal affront, they began to vilify him, gossiping about him and slandering him. When a young woman living near the presbytery had a child out of wedlock, attempts were made to spread the rumour that Abbé Vianney was the father. The true character of the Curé was too well known for this to be believed, but the attempt to blacken his name caused him much pain. His front door was splashed with dirt and, for the space of eighteen months, people stood under his window, night after night, insulting and reproaching the Curé for leading a disorderly life. It was also rumoured that his extreme pallor and emaciated body were a sign of secret debauchery. The Abbé Vianney made no effort to defend his good name but suffered these insults in silence.

In 1823 Ars became part of the new diocese of Bellay which was hived off from the metropolitan diocese of Lyon. The bishop, Msgr Devie, had no knowledge of Vianney. Thus, when he received anonymous letters full of venom against this priest, he considered it his duty to make an investigation of these complaints. He deputed a senior priest to do this, who found absolutely nothing to substantiate the complaints against Fr Vianney. We can judge the extent of such painful experiences for the Curé when we hear that towards the end of his life he one day remarked: 'If on my arrival at Ars I had foreseen all that I was to suffer there, I should have died on the spot'.[14]

At one stage he was so upset by the wicked gossip which was circulated about him that he decided to quit the parish. He would certainly have carried out this plan if one of his intimate friends had not succeeded in convincing him that by capitulating to these slanders he would give a measure of plausibility to the rumours. He forgave the guilty parties, even to the extent of offering his friendship towards them. In February 1843 he made the following amazing statement in the presence of several people: 'I thought a time would come when people would rout me out of Ars with sticks, and the bishop would suspend me, and I would end my days in prison. I see, however, that I am not worthy of such a grace'.[15]

In his relations with girls and women generally, Fr Vianney practised a great delicacy and reserve. In all his illnesses he would only be nursed by men. The woman who looked after the presbytery had strict orders never to be there except when he was out of the house. He lived an exacting guard of sight, and only in the confessional did he deal with women on personal matters. But in spite of all this reserve he was in no way tainted by any form of unnaturalness or prudishness. In light of these facts it is no wonder that the gossip about him gained no credence among the vast majority of his parishioners. Once the flow of pilgrims had begun, no one ever dared to cast even a shadow of a doubt upon the perfect integrity of his life.

Apart from these external trials, the Curé went through a difficult period of five years when he doubted his own salvation and was tempted to despair. The obligations of a parish priest weighed heavily on him, and despite his success at Ars his duty appeared to him impossible to carry out as he ought. He was haunted by the idea of hell, and went through weeks and months when he felt himself abandoned by God. 'My God', he cried, 'make me suffer whatsoever you wish to inflict on me, but grant that I may not fall into hell'. He had to go through this crisis by means of which his soul was purified of the last vestiges of attachment to self, and he was shown how to abandon himself totally into God's hands.

> To suffer lovingly [he exclaimed] is to suffer no longer. To flee from the cross is to be crushed beneath its weight. We should pray for love of the cross – then it will become sweet. I experienced it myself during four or

14 Ibid., p. 173. 15 Ibid., p. 174.

> five years. I was grievously calumniated and contradicted. Oh! I did have crosses, almost more than I could bear. Then I started praying for a love of crosses and I felt happy. I said to myself: 'Verily there is no happiness but in the cross'.[16]

One day his curate, the Abbé Monnin, asked him whether his trials had ever caused him to lose his interior peace. 'What?', he exclaimed, 'the Cross makes us lose our inward peace? Surely it is the Cross that bestows it on our hearts. All our miseries come from our not loving it'. Not only did his unshakeable faith never allow him to yield to discouragement, it was rather the dynamic that caused him to undertake such ambitious projects for God which others more talented, but less supernatural than he, failed to carry out. His life demonstrates the moral greatness and the merits which can be won from the limitations of this life. Expecting neither recognition nor reward from men, he worked with extraordinary ambition, but only for the glory of God.

His patience might win splendid victories, but his physical strength was being undermined by his immoderate fasting and the harsh manner in which he treated his body. In the summer of 1827 his doctor took a serious view of his condition and prescribed a more substantial diet. Fr Vianney was just forty, yet he felt utterly exhausted. He was suffering from a fever that never left him. When he felt bad enough to ask the bishop for a change, he was offered a parish five times the size of Ars, but at the last minute changed his mind, deciding to stay where he was.

PASTORAL PLAN

As already intimated, Fr Vianney's plan was to form a group who were well educated in the faith and piety of life. They would be, as it were, the heart of the parish who would help him in the task of reaching and winning souls. He was more far-sighted than his contemporaries in seeing that devotion to the Eucharist was, and always will be, the most effective means in bringing about a regeneration of people in the faith.

He was conscious of the great influence Mlle des Garets had in the village. While she was a truly valiant woman of deep faith, her piety was austere and narrow. Now under the guidance of the Curé she developed by degrees the habit of more frequent Communion and a deeper, warmer piety, including daily Mass and a daily visit to the Blessed Sacrament. The example of Mlle des Garets was followed by more humble women in the parish. They were also

16 Ibid., p. 178.

joined by the girls whom Vianney had grouped together in the confraternity of the Rosary. Thus as early as 1825, even before the great rush of pilgrims, there were always people (exclusively women) praying in the church before the Blessed Sacrament.

But one man, a farmer, began to visit the church on his way to work as a result of the Curé's sermons. He spent such a good while before the Blessed Sacrament that Fr Vianney's curiosity was aroused and one day he asked the man what he was praying about. The farmer replied simply, 'I look at the good God and he looks at me', an answer which deeply impressed the Abbé Vianney.

The Curé, conscious that women are naturally more religious than men, was convinced that there could not be a real conversion of his parish until he had won over the youth and the men of the village to the serious practice of their faith. With a view to fostering among them devotion to the Eucharist, he tried to breathe new life into the existing guild of the Blessed Sacrament, which was moribund. Despite all his efforts, despite his intense prayer and sacrifice, the men of Ars were not going to be hurried along the road to a deeper spiritual life. However, he did get to the point where they all appeared regularly at Sunday Mass. In addition, at the conclusion of vespers on Sunday there were always some who remained behind to spend an hour before the Blessed Sacrament.

In his first year, 1818, the Corpus Christi procession passed off as in previous years. But the following year Fr Vianney added as much ceremony and solemnity as possible to this public liturgical event. He went to considerable expense to see that all the children in the parish were dressed in white. While the children were delighted to be involved, human respect kept back a number of the adults from carrying a taper in the procession.

When Jean-Marie Vianney arrived in Ars there was little practice of prayer either in the church or at home. So he decided to turn his private evening prayer into a public exercise. Little by little people started to join him. A time would eventually come when every evening throughout the whole year, the church bell would ring out a summons to prayer, and the entire parish would join the Curé in the saying of the Rosary and night prayers. Fr Vianney was still ambitious to do more. To all his people he recommended a daily examination of conscience, and at bed-time, at least during the winter months, a short period of spiritual reading so that the truths of faith might become more deeply engraved in their hearts. The Curé was not one to think that because people worked the land or exercised a particular craft they were incapable of a deep spiritual life. He taught the art of prayer and meditation to simple peasants.[17] To those among the villagers who could give more, he opened up wider vistas in the spiritual life.

17 Cf. John Paul II, Apostolic Letter, *Novo millennio ineunte*, 30–1 (6 January 2001).

Several of the surrounding parishes benefited from Fr Vianney's preaching and pastoral zeal. Owing to the Revolution many of these parishes had been without a priest for years and so the bishop organized missions to recover them for the practice of the faith. The Curé was eager to help out his brother priests and was always available during those early years of the 1820s. Wherever he preached large crowds came to him for confession. In this connection one particular incident occurred at the beginning of 1823 when he gave a mission in Trévoux. Often he was detained in the confessional until after midnight. The last night of the mission there was such a crush around his confession box that the crowd very nearly pushed over both the confessor and the confessional, an incident which he delighted in recalling subsequently. What he did not speak about was the enormous number of people who sought him out and the conversions which resulted from his zeal. As a consequence of this pastoral outreach, people started to come to Ars from the neighbouring parishes for confession. Very soon the Curé found himself in the confessional from early morning until noon.

By 1827, it was obvious to all, even to the Abbé Vianney himself, that the village had changed for the better. 'Ars is no longer Ars', he was able to say from the pulpit. This outcome had been achieved by prayer and penance, and by daring pastoral initiatives (*Duc in altum*). He had met with a lot of opposition and contradictions along the way, but after ten years Ars was, as we would say to day, truly a Eucharistic community.

'LA PROVIDENCE'

During the first years of his pastorate Fr Vianney had added to the work of the parish by founding an orphanage which was also a girls school. He arranged for two young local women to be trained as teachers and to take charge of the enterprise. The building which housed the school and the orphanage he called *La Providence*. Tuition was given free of charge. Girls from the age of eight were accepted, and all were trained for farm-work and housework, and taught sewing and cooking. It was not long before they were in demand from the larger houses in the vicinity. At one time there were as many as sixty crowded into this small building, but Catherine Lassagne, whom the Curé placed in charge of *La Providence*, was a very competent administrator and was able to give it a homely atmosphere.

The orphanage lived up to its name in that the Curé had to trust in providence to find the financial resources to keep it going. He had to rely on the donations of friends and pilgrims. At times he would walk the twenty-two miles to Lyon to beg for its upkeep. More than once he sold some of his furniture to raise the necessary funds.

It was in this connection that the incident about the granary occurred. Because of a bad harvest in 1829, the supply of wheat ran low and there was nothing to feed the children with. The Curé swept together the few grains of wheat which were scattered on the granary floor in his attic, hiding a relic of St Francis Regis among them – the saint who had helped him in his studies for the priesthood. Then after asking the orphans to unite with him in fervent prayer, he set himself to praying also with great confidence. Then he told Jeanne-Marie Chanay, the baker of *La Providence*, to go to the granary. Imagine her surprise to find that she could hardly open the door as the granary was so full of wheat.

The Abbé Vianney loved the orphanage and the orphans as a true father. He visited it every day to give a catechism lesson in the middle of the morning. This in fact was the origin of the familiar instruction which for many years was given by him in the church of Ars. In the early days he would come into the orphanage wearing his cassock and surplice, a copy of the catechism in his hands, and leaning against the bread-trough he would start off on the lesson immediately. One witness recalls attending one of these sessions in 1842. When the Curé came in he began by saying, 'My children yesterday we stopped at the lesson on marriage'. After this preamble he read the question 'What is the most important cause of unhappy marriages?' Then he gave the answer which he set himself to explain:

> Ah! my children, when two people have just been married, they never weary of looking at each other; they deem themselves so loveable, so well endowed; they admire each other and they pay each other a thousand compliments. But the honeymoon does not last forever, no, not forever. A moment comes when they forget the wonderful qualities they had discovered in each other, and defects show themselves which they had not hitherto suspected. That is the time when some people can no longer bear each other's company, and the husband calls his wife names such as lazy, peevish woman, good-for-nothing, and so forth.[18]

Gradually pilgrims started to attend the catechism sessions in the *Providence*, but after a while the place became so crowded with people eager to hear the Curé's catechetical instruction that from 1845 onwards, Fr Vianney felt obliged to transfer it the short distance to the church. In this way a much greater number of pilgrims were able to listen to the Curé who continued to teach the truths of the faith in the same familiar manner as before.

18 Ibid., p. 210.

PARISH VISITATION

Parish visitation was one of the principal ways which Fr Vianney used to form families in a deeper commitment to the faith and to foster the religious customs and practices he introduced. The better they got to know their Curé, the more the people loved him and welcomed his visits. He enquired about the health of the parents and the children, the work in hand, the state of the crops. Without changing his familiar tone, he alluded to the importance of prayer and the Sunday Mass. He encouraged the children to be obedient to their parents and to learn the catechism. He took a particular interest in the young domestics, youths from neighbouring villages whom he wished to see treated as members of the family. They too were to be taught their religion and sent to Mass and vespers on Sundays.

When the pilgrimage to Ars took up more and more of the Curé's time, these house-to-house visits became less and less frequent, until they ceased altogether. For the people of the village who began to look forward so much to having the Curé in their homes, this was a source of deep regret. Although Fr Vianney received his visitors with special kindness, he always gave priority to the needs of his own parishioners. He would leave the crowds in the church to visit the sick of the village.

Both in the pulpit and in the confessional he constantly proclaimed the strictness and the dignity of the laws of marriage. That he was heard and understood is attested to by the fact that the population of Ars more than doubled during his pastorate. Fr Vianney constantly encouraged more frequent reception of the sacraments, but in this he came up against a deeply ingrained Jansenism which in particular kept the men away from regular reception of Holy Communion. To the better disposed he would suggest that they receive Holy Communion to celebrate the big anniversaries in their lives such as birthdays, First Communion and wedding anniversaries. He would recommend that those who were to stand as godparents at a baptism receive beforehand. Throughout his priestly life one of his great joys was the distribution of Holy Communion.

The Eucharistic discourses of Fr Vianney give the lie to the suggestion that he was a poor theologian. In these meditations he reveals not only an extensive knowledge of Eucharistic theology but also a highly developed capacity to explain different aspects of this mystery with original similes and analogies.[19] He uses Scripture liberally to illustrate the doctrine on the Eucharist. He is familiar with the teaching of the Fathers like St Augustine and St John Chrysostom, and he draws on writers such as St Bernard, St Thomas

19 Cf. *The Eucharistic meditations of the Cure d'Ars* (Dublin, 1977).

Aquinas, St Francis de Sales and St Teresa of Avila. However, the most striking characteristic of these sermons is the faith and the love for the Blessed Sacrament which comes through on ever page of his discourses.

To draw people to the Eucharist he tried to communicate to his parishioners a love for the liturgy. He carried out the ceremonies with dignity and with the utmost care of detail such that the bishop held him up as an example to other priests as to how to perform the liturgy. As we have already seen, he acquired the best in vestments in terms of quality and beauty not only as an expression of faith in the Real Presence, but also as a means to educate his parishioners in their appreciation of the liturgy. No wonder, then, that the celebration of the feast of Corpus Christi was a unique occasion, not only in terms of splendour, but also as an expression of faith and love. For the Abbé Vianney it was one of the happiest days of the year. For once the confessional was deserted for a few hours. He encouraged the villagers to erect as many altars of repose as possible so as to multiply Benedictions in the parish. As well as his own parishioners, the procession was attended by a great crowd from the surrounding villages. When he was in the company of priests he always tried to fade into the background, but on Corpus Christi he claimed the honour of carrying the monstrance in the procession. Walking under the canopy and clad in beautiful vestments, he advanced with great decorum with his eyes fixed on the Sacred Host.

As noted above he was eager to respond to requests to help his brother priests in pastoral tasks. However, as the years went on and people crowded into Ars, he was hardly ever able to be absent from the confessional. With his long working hours, his short night and spare diet, he was left, one would have thought, with little surplus energy. Yet in 1852, at the height of the pilgrimage to Ars, and after carrying the Blessed Sacrament for two hours in the Corpus Christi procession, he walked the five miles to the village of Jassans to visit Abbé Beau, who was ill, and then made the return journey on foot again.

THE DEVIL UNDISGUISED

From 1827 until his death thirty-two years later, the Abbé Vianney was increasingly occupied with the many pilgrims who came to Ars not only from different parts of France but from many other countries as well. They made the journey not just to venerate a saint in a shrine, but to make contact with a man who was considered a living saint, whose fame as a confessor had spread throughout Europe and North America.

We have seen that he brought about the conversion of his parish as a result of long hours of prayer and a generous acceptance of the Cross. One of the trials which he had to undergo was regular persecution by the devil during the period 1824 to 1858. These assaults began when during the winter of 1824–5 he was considering the setting up of *La Providence*, and they took the form of strange noises in the presbytery at night. It seemed to the Curé as if the curtains of the bed were being torn. He put the noise down to rats and brought a pitchfork to his bedroom the following night to frighten them off. The noise went on despite his efforts to dislodge them, and in the morning he could see that the curtains had suffered no harm. This continued for some time. The second stage was reached when loud noises were made on the presbytery door and shouts resounded through the rooms. The Curé at first thought perhaps he was dealing with thieves who were after the church valuables he kept in a large cupboard in the attic.

The second night he asked André, a local man, to keep him company; this neighbour kept watch with a loaded gun. At about one in the morning André heard a noise at the presbytery door as if someone trying to get in was rattling the latch and banging the door with a piece of wood. When he opened the door he saw nothing. The house seemed to shake with blows for a period of fifteen minutes. André felt his legs shaking and thought the house was going to fall down. He had enough after one night, so Fr Vianney had to go to the mayor looking for help. Nothing was heard over the next fortnight.

One night when there was snow on the ground the Curé heard a great noise, like an 'army of cossacks', all talking a language which he did not understand. He rushed down and opened the door. There was no one there and no sign of foot-marks in the snow. As soon as the Curé realized he was being persecuted by the devil, he no longer asked the men of the parish for protection during the night. 'I believed it was the devil because I was afraid', he told his bishop, and added, 'the good God does not make people afraid'.[20]

Abbé Vianney grew accustomed to his disturbed nights. In time he became convinced that when he was especially troubled by the devil, a great sinner, a 'really big fish', as he put it, was thus flagged for his confessional next day. He nicknamed his disturbing nightly visitor as the *Grappin*. 'The *Grappin* is a bit of a fool', he exclaimed, 'he always lets me know when great sinners are coming'. So for many years the raps, the knockings and the noises continued. Sometimes he heard a voice crying out 'Vianney, Vianney, you potatoe-eater! Not dead yet? I'll have you all the same'. Several times in bed Fr Vianney felt something like a hand passing over his face or rats running over his body. On some nights there was a noise as if men were tramping overhead. At times the bedclothes were pulled off the bed or the bed was moved about the room. The evil spirit remained invisible but his presence could be plainly felt.

20 Sheppard, ibid., p. 83.

Despite persistent sleeplessness, as soon as the church clock struck twelve, the Abbé Vianney, thinking about his penitents, got up and went to the church. On one occasion his sister Marguerite visited him. She heard a tremendous noise beside the bed that night as if five or six men had been striking heavy blows on the table. She was terrified. When she told her brother after he returned from the church what had happened, he said: 'My child, you should not have been frightened: it is the *Grappin*. He can't hurt you. As for me he torments me in sundry ways. At times he seizes me by the feet and drags me about the room. It is because I convert souls to the good God.'[21]

On one occasion in 1858 while the Curé was hearing confessions, some of the pilgrims noticed a fire in his room in the presbytery. When he was told about it, he just handed the key to those who had brought him the news so that they might put out the flames. Without any excitement he simply said, 'The villainous *Grappin*! he could not catch the bird so he burns the cage'. He left the church, however, and passed into the courtyard where he met the men who at that very moment were carrying out of the house the smoking remains of his bed. What was remarkable was the fact that the flames had not spread to any other part of the room apart from consuming the Curé's bed. His only comment on the incident was, 'this is a good sign, we shall see many sinners'. As it happened, this event was followed by an extraordinary influx of people into Ars, which lasted for several days.

There were many incidents which showed how the Curé acquired a power over the devil, getting him to desist from his infernal activities. When news of this got around, people who showed signs of diabolical possession were brought to the Curé to be exorcised. As Fr Vianney advanced in years these diabolical vexations decreased both in frequency and in intensity. Having failed to disconcert or discourage the Curé, by degrees the Evil One gave up the contest. From 1845 until his death (1859), M. Vianney was hardly ever disturbed by the devil at night.

THE PILGRIMAGE

The miracle that was Ars happened gradually. It started simply enough with former parishioners from Ecully where Fr Vianney had been curate. As early as 1818 he attracted people. They also came from the village of Noés, where he had spent those two years in hiding, to see 'M. Jerome' as a priest, because already, before his ordination, they held him in veneration. As we have seen, when he went to help with missions in the surrounding villages, people flocked

21 Trochu, ibid., p. 243.

to his confessional, and soon many of them began to make the journey to Ars to obtain his counsel. By 1827 people were coming from greater distances, when Ars saw something like twenty pilgrims a day. They were impressed, not only by the Curé, but also by the obvious piety of the people of Ars. During the octave of Corpus Christi that year there were large congregations every night at Benediction, among them many strangers.

In 1828 the Abbé Vianney was busy all day. People came not only for confession but, at the beginning, also out of curiosity. The parish priest of Ars was known to be a saint and this was part of the attraction – they wanted to see this man in the flesh. Whether they made the journey out of curiosity or for confession, the great majority went away consoled and shriven. From 1827 until 1859 the church of Ars was never empty. It quickly became known that the Abbé Vianney could read people's consciences and was reputed to work miracles. The first prodigies, including the multiplication of the grain for the *Providence*, soon came to the knowledge of the parishioners and to strangers who already flocked to Ars in considerable numbers.

ST PHILOMENA AND MIRACLES AT ARS

At an early date the sick and the infirm mingled with the crowd. After they had asked the prayers of Fr Vianney some were completely cured. These happenings naturally got talked about. However, the Curé recommended silence, so people were afraid to offend him by proclaiming favours they had received. Then his attitude changed. He began to attribute to St Philomena all the marvels that were being accomplished. Thanks to him, devotion to the saint spread rapidly both in the surrounding districts and all over France. Fr Vianney had obtained a relic of St Philomena from Pauline Jaricot of Lyon.[22] It was the Curé's way of diverting attention from himself by attributing to St Philomena all the cures and miracles which people obtained at Ars.

In the life of the Curé, St Philomena played a double role. To the pilgrims he projected her as the miracle worker who responded to their prayers, thus taking the spotlight off himself. In his own interior life he had a deep devotion to this saint which he transmitted to the pilgrims. Several times a day in the pulpit, in the confessional, in the square in front of the church, he exhorted them to call on his 'dear little saint', his 'representative', and his 'agent with God'.

22 Pauline Jaricot, from a wealthy family of Lyon, founded the Apostleship of Prayer.

CONTRADICTIONS OF THE CLERGY

What was the reaction of his fellow priests to the arrival of increasing numbers of pilgrims at Ars, including people from their own parishes? In general even the most zealous priests considered it abnormal that so many people should go to consult an eccentric Curé of an obscure parish of 200 souls. His dishevelled personal appearance told against him in a diocese where priests were noted for their decorum of dress. Deliberately, from a motive of mortification and humility, he wore a shabby cassock, an old hat, and shoes which were patched and always innocent of polish. Even at clerical conferences he appeared poor and contemptible. On the other hand, as the evidence of *La Providence*'s laundress confirmed, Fr Vianney had a natural love of neatness and cleanliness and changed his personal linen frequently.

His confrères considered as oddities actions which were in reality expressions of his holiness. Some charged him with avarice, others with hypocrisy and a secret desire to attract attention. His slovenliness in matters of dress might have been overlooked had he been a learned priest, but the deficiencies of Fr Vianney's theological career in preparation for the priesthood were well remembered. And so as the numbers arriving at Ars increased, some of his colleagues considered it a scandal that a man so lacking in theological formation should be allowed to counsel so many souls. As a consequence some priests forbade their parishioners, under threat of refusal of absolution, to go to Ars. Others preached against him, while still others took up their pens to write to the bishop about the dangers threatening those souls who made their way to Ars.

If formal theological training was lacking, the Curé acquired that uncommon theological wisdom which comes from a deep sensitivity to the action of the Holy Spirit in his soul. This is evident from the homilies he has left us on the Eucharist, on the dignity of the priesthood, and on the mediation of Mary. Fr Vianney himself gives us the key to this paradox about his theological insight which he expressed in one of his catechetical sessions: 'Those who are lead by the Holy Spirit have true ideas. That is why there are so many ignorant people who know far more than the learned.' The Curé was nothing in his own eyes, and so allowed the Holy Spirit to work freely in his soul, filling him with love of God and souls.

Fr Vianney was pained by the clerical gossip circulated about him. 'Poor Curé of Ars', he groaned. 'What do they not make him say, what do they not make him do! At present it is on him they preach, and no longer on the Gospel!' He received anonymous letters of complaint from priests accusing him of misplaced zeal. One young priest, however, the Abbé Borjon, had the courage to sign his letter. He was parish priest of Ambérieux, about five miles from Ars, and was so annoyed at the constant exodus of his parishioners to Ars that he wrote a stinging letter to the poor Curé saying, 'M. le Curé, when a man knows as little theology as you do, he should not go into the confessional.' Fr Vianney, who was pained at the letter, wrote the following reply:

> Most dear and most venerated confrère, what good reasons I have for loving you! You are the only person who really knows me. Since you are so good and kind as to take an interest in my poor soul, do help me to obtain the favour for which I have been asking for so long a time, that being released from a post which I am not worthy to hold by reason of my ignorance, I may be allowed to retire into a little corner, there to weep over my poor life. What penances there are to be undertaken! how many expiations there are to be offered! how many tears to be shed.[23]

This response had an immediate effect on the Abbé Borjon. He went to Ars at the earliest opportunity and threw himself at the feet of the man he had so unjustly attacked. Fr Vianney, who had already forgotten about the incident, enveloped the young priest in his arms. Fr Borjon often returned to Ars to be edified by Fr Vianney's example and guided by his counsels. Each year he lead his First Communicants to Ars so that they might receive the blessing of its holy Curé. He was later one of the witnesses to give evidence in his favour in the process of his beatification.

Fr Vianney was not unaware of the fact that he had been denounced to his bishop. Friends encouraged him to speak out in his own defence, but he preferred to remain silent. In his simplicity and humility he admitted that, 'Among other priests I am like Bordin' – Bordin was the village idiot. On one occasion a circular letter of denunciation of Fr Vianney was sent to the bishop, accusing him of sensationalism, ignorance, and ostentatious poverty and austerities. It was signed by a number of priests, but found its way to the Curé by mistake. With a black sense of humour, he himself countersigned it and forwarded the letter to the bishop.

Msgr Devie, the bishop, to satisfy himself about the falsity of the gossip and rumours did two things. He sent his vicar general to Ars to interview Fr Vianney, who as a result gave a highly favourable report on the Curé. Secondly, he asked the Curé to submit the more difficult cases he had met with in his pastoral ministry, together with the solutions he offered. Fr Vianney willingly complied with this request so that within the space of a few years he supplied the bishop with details of more than two hundred cases. As a result of a searching examination of these cases Msgr Devie came to the conclusion that Fr Vianney's solutions were accurate and no fault could be found with them. When the

23 Trochu, ibid., p. 274.

bishop heard that some of his clergy had ridiculed the Curé and even referred to him as mad, at the next retreat he said to the assembled priests of the diocese, 'Gentlemen, I wish that all my clergy had a small grain of the same madness.' By 1834 the local priests themselves were going to Ars for confession.

THE CURÉ OF ARS AS CONFESSOR

For thirty years or more, crowds of people came to see the Curé of Ars. These pilgrims arrived all the year round without any appreciable diminution during the cold months of winter. From November to March, Fr Vianney spent at least eleven to twelve hours a day in the confessional, and fifteen to sixteen during the summer months. As we have seen, the pilgrims started to arrive in Ars in the 1820s. From the early 1830s people began to come in large numbers, as many as 3–400 a day at peak times, and over 100,000 a year during the last decade of his life. In Lyon a special booking office was opened at the railway station to cater for the crowds who wanted to get to Ars. These tickets were good for eight days, since it was generally known that it took all of that time before a pilgrim's turn came to see Fr Vianney for confession or a word of advice.

While the visitors included the curious, the sceptical, and the agnostic, the overwhelming majority of the crowds were attracted by faith, piety and a deep desire for pardon for sins. Some came looking for spiritual illumination, for consolation, for advice about their vocation. They included people of every age and condition, the vast majority lay people, but also priests, bishops and religious. They arrived from every part of France, from all over Europe and even further afield. The editor of a local newspaper gives the following evocative description of his own experience as a pilgrim:

> Strangers in great numbers were standing in the old cemetery [around the church], and even in lanes nearby, awaiting their turn ... They bought medals and rosaries which they intended to have blessed, or candles destined to burn before the altar of St Philomena. In order to while away the time of waiting, several of them were contemplating the portraits of the holy priest, or they conversed together about him as children might talk of their father, though they had not as yet seen him.[24]

No matter how long it might take to get a place in the church, the visitors, with rare exceptions, never gave in to weariness. They had come determined

24 Ibid., p. 282.

to have a personal conversation with the Curé in the confessional, which was the primary motivation for their journey.

Once in the church another period of waiting began. It should be noted that although Fr Vianney gave to penitents the time strictly necessary in each case, he still had to spend over sixteen hours a day in the confessional. Despite such marathon sessions, during the last ten years of his life the majority of pilgrims spent thirty, fifty, seventy hours waiting in the church before reaching the confessional, a church which was stifling hot in summer and piercing cold in winter. People who wanted to go outside, and yet not lose their place, had to make special arrangements with those next to them or with the guardians of the church. People numbered themselves so as not to miss their turn when the church was closed for the short few hours of the Curé's night. While Fr Vianney showed no favour to anyone – bishops and barons had to await their turn like the rest – he made special exceptions for the sick and the infirm, and also for his own parishioners of Ars: they were not asked to wait.

For many the road to Ars became their road to Damascus. Apart from his prayer and penance, Fr Vianney did not use any unusual means to bring about the conversion of sinners. They were first moved to repentance by the fire of his preaching and by the illumination of conscience which came from listening to his catechesis. Then, when they came to have personal contact with the Curé in the privacy of the confessional, a few words were sufficient to bring about a sincere confession of sins.

Except in a special case, such as a general confession, he was brisk in his dealings with penitents, and he expected them not to waste time either. He was demanding when it came to penitents avoiding occasions of sin in the future. At times he would refuse absolution if he detected a lack of real sorrow or purpose of amendment. Generally his counsels were short and specific words of encouragement. To his own bishop his advice was, 'Love your priests a lot.' What on the lips of another priest might have seemed a commonplace, acquired a special power and efficacy when spoken by the holy Curé of Ars. But more than words, what moved people to repentance were the tears of the Abbé Vianney. When asked by one penitent why he wept so much, Fr Vianney replied, 'Ah! my friend, I weep because you do not weep enough'. Small wonder then that many emerged from the confessional in tears, men as well as women. As his bishop remarked, 'The good Curé had received from God a special gift for converting men'.

At this point it is perhaps appropriate to recall the impact Ars had on John Paul II as a recently ordained priest:

> On my way back from Belgium to Rome, I was able to spend some time in Ars. It was the end of October 1947, the feast of Christ the King.

> With great emotion I visited the little old church where St John Vianney heard confessions, taught catechism, and gave his homilies. It was an unforgettable experience for me. From my seminary years I had been impressed by the figure of the Curé d'Ars, especially after reading his biography by Monsignor Trochu. Saint John Marie Vianney astonishes us because in him we can see the power of grace working through human limitations. It was his heroic service in the confessional which particularly struck me. That humble priest, who would hear confessions for more than ten hours a day, eating little and sleeping only a few hours, was able, at a difficult moment in history, to inspire a kind of spiritual revolution in France, and not only there. Thousands of people passed through Ars and knelt in his confessional. Against the background of attacks on the Church and the clergy in the nineteenth century, his witness was truly revolutionary.
>
> My encounter with this saintly figure confirmed me in *the conviction that a priest fulfils an essential part of his mission through the confessional* – by voluntarily 'making himself a prisoner of the confessional.' Many times as I heard confession in my first parish at Niegowic and then in Cracow, my thoughts would turn to this unforgettable experience.[25]

Fr Vianney gave little importance to the physical cures obtained by the pilgrims. For him the great miracles were the conversion of sinners, for whom he imposed on himself special fasts at the approach of great feasts, and especially during paschal time.

While he treated penitents with gentleness, up to 1840 he followed the rigorism learned from Fr Balley which was heir to the strict eighteenth-century code of moral theology. Absolution was not provided unless he was assured of the contrition and purpose of amendment of the penitent. Thus to numbers of penitents he only gave absolution after repeated confessions, as the girls who went dancing in spite of his interdict had reason to know. But in the long run mercy prevailed over strictness. From 1840 onward, after a study of the theology of St Alphonsus Liguori, he showed himself sensibly less strict. In addition, his long experience of penitents confirmed for him that, above all else, kindness was the virtue required to bring about a conversion from the misery of sin. He rejoiced when big sinners came along. He exhorted them with all the fervour at his command, finding very simple and brief phrases that touched them to the depths of their soul.

The Curé was also very gentle in the penances he imposed, an attitude for which he was reproached by other clergy. His response was that he couldn't be

25 John Paul II, *Gift and mystery: on the fiftieth anniversary of my priestly ordination* (London, 1997), pp 57–8 (italics in original).

hard on people who had come so far and who had made so many sacrifices in getting to Ars. To a brother priest he explained his approach: 'I give them a small penance, and the remainder I myself perform in their stead.'

DAILY SCHEDULE

In effect from 1830 Fr Vianney never left Ars.[26] He was to spend every day of the rest of his life, totally dedicated to the penitents who came in search of his priestly services in this non-descript village which he made famous in the whole of the Catholic Church. To get some idea of the magnanimity of Fr Vianney's priestly soul, let us examine his day in some detail. It seems difficult to conceive how the Curé managed to crowd into a day not only the many hours spent in the confessional, and all the various demands arising from the pilgrimage, but also his other priestly duties, the breviary and the Mass, as well as time to eat and sleep.

His day began at one in the morning. Shortly afterwards the church bell rang out to inform the pilgrims that the Curé was in the church waiting for penitents. After kneeling on the altar step for a few moments he went into the chapel of St John the Baptist to hear the women's confessions until six or seven in the morning, when he said Mass. Afterwards he did his thanksgiving which was followed by a cup of milk at the *Providence*. He was soon back again in the sacristy to hear the men's confessions. At ten he broke off confessions to say the Little Hours of the breviary in the sacristy, returning afterwards to hear the men's confessions until eleven, when he went down into the church to give his catechism session from a small pulpit specially reserved for that purpose. Here for a period of fifteen years (1845–59), every weekday of the year, he gave a simple catechism lesson to the most varied audience of pilgrims. He began by reading out one or two questions with the answers, after which he laid the catechism aside. He then outlined his explanation of the text. However, he soon lost sight of the topic in question and passed on to consider some of those ideas which were central to his own spiritual life, the fruit of his prayer and contemplation.

At twelve, kneeling before the altar, he said the Angelus, and then left the church to have his midday meal in the presbytery. It was prepared for him in the *Providence* and left ready for him on the table. His meagre ration consisted of some vegetables, two eggs or, very occasionally, a little meat if he were feel-

26 Up to 1835 he was only absent for a week to do his annual retreat. But that year Msgr Devie sent him home as soon as he arrived saying that the penitents had more need of him than he had of doing a retreat. He never afterwards did an annual retreat. In 1843 he spent a week with his family in Dardilly to recover from a severe illness.

ing particularly exhausted. This was supplemented by a jug of water, a bottle of red wine and a piece of bread. He managed to finish his meal in ten minutes, never sitting down to do so, and reading his correspondence at the same time. He drank a little water which he coloured with a drop of wine, and nibbled at his bread. But there was always a considerable amount of the meal left on the plate when he had finished. After a ten minute siesta he was off to visit the sick of the parish including the pilgrims confined to bed.

At one o'clock he was back in the church to finish the day's office by saying vespers and compline. He then went straight to the confessional to hear the women until five, when he returned to the sacristy to deal with the men until eight. This was the time for night prayers in the church with the parishioners and the pilgrims, which included the chaplet to the Immaculate Conception.

After a long day he made his way to the presbytery where further interviews awaited him with visiting priests, or his curate (given to him in 1845 to look after the Ars parishioners). He was so tired at the end of the day that he could hardly climb the stairs to his room. Even then his sense of humour showed through. Occasionally, alluding to some ill-natured comment made about him, he would say, 'Well, well! The old wizard has done good business today'. When he eventually got to his room he said lauds and matins for the next day and read a little of the lives of the saints. And then he could go to bed, often not to sleep very well due to the attentions of the *Grappin* or to an irritating chest cough.

The conversion of sinners was the Abbé Vianney's constant prayer and the intention behind all his mortification and hard work. Once when asked if he had the choice of remaining on earth to continue his work or of going to heaven, which would he choose, he replied, 'If I were given the choice, I would remain on earth until the end of the world'. No wonder the devil reproached him through the mouth of a possessed woman, 'If there were three men on earth like yourself, my kingdom would be destroyed.'

In the midst of this extraordinary pastoral activity, or rather because of it, the Curé felt a deep longing to look for isolation, to find a quiet place where he could do penance and weep for 'his poor life'. He tried to take flight from the parish on three different occasions, but ultimately these experiences showed him more clearly that God wanted him to remain riveted to the seat of the confessional. Each time on his return he immediately went to take up his accustomed place. 'What would have happened to all the poor sinners?' he murmured, settling down to work again.

In a special way he saw his life as being an instrument for the salvation of sinners. He offered up his sufferings on their behalf. He prayed for them and got others to pray for them. He wanted them to feel that they had the support of multiple intercessions at the time he received them in the confessional. He abandoned his confessional only five days before he died, and even then some men managed to break in on him as he lay on his death-bed, looking for a last absolution from him.

THE CURÉ AS SPIRITUAL DIRECTOR

Kindness and encouragement were two of the principal characteristics of Fr Vianney as a spiritual director. The holiness of his life inspired people to have an unbounded trust in his counsel. He was clear, precise and prompt in his instructions. However, he did not lack prudence. At times, when he felt it necessary, he would ask for time for personal reflection on the situation or problem posed to him, or the opportunity to take counsel with a brother priest.

When people came to confess about their struggle in regard to particular virtues, he sketched a line of action for them and encouraged them by saying that he had been tempted in that respect too. And he added 'Anyone who has not been tempted to sin against humility or chastity does not know what spiritual life is'. He was able to disentangle the secret motives, conscious or unconscious, of certain aspirations, and he helped souls find their own level. He could be very down to earth with generous souls who entertained dreams of an illusory perfection in the religious life, by telling them to remain in the world and sanctify themselves there. He counselled people against having too many private devotions but encouraged assistance at Mass, recitation of the Rosary, the Angelus, and ejaculatory prayers. He not only encouraged people to develop the habit of daily mental prayer but taught them how to go about it. He recommended frequent reception of the Eucharist as a way to achieving holiness. In his catechesis on the Eucharist he brought out the need for this sacrament for spiritual growth:

> My children, every creature in the universe requires food that it may live; for this purpose God has caused the trees and plants to grow. It is a well-appointed table to which all the animals come for the food that suits them. But the soul must also be fed. Where, then, is its food? … My children, when God resolved to provide food for the soul so as to sustain her on the pilgrimage of life, he examined the whole of creation, but found nothing that was worthy of her. So he looked at himself and resolved to give himself… O my soul, how great thou art! God alone can satisfy thee! The food of the soul! what is it but the body and blood of God! O beautiful food! God alone can be the food of the soul! God alone can suffice her! God alone is able to fill her! God alone can allay her hunger! She feels an imperative need of her God! How happy are

> pure souls that unite themselves to our Lord in Holy Communion! In heaven they will sparkle like beautiful diamonds because God will shine through them.[27]

In one of the villages of the Beaujolais there was a lady who communicated very infrequently. After much persuasion Fr Vianney prevailed on her to receive Holy Communion once a fortnight. This woman made several pilgrimages to Ars and each time Fr Vianney told her to receive more often. Although she obeyed, the woman objected that such practice was not common in her parish, and she did not like to stand out. 'You have a good many friends', the Curé said; 'choose the more virtuous from among them and bring them to me; then you will no longer be alone'. She returned with two companions. 'You will come back in six months', the Abbé said to each of them, 'but not alone; you must win over two or three others'. At the end of six months twelve women of the Beaujolais set out for Ars. All were taught by the saint to receive Holy Communion frequently. Their own parish priest began to wonder at the transformation of his parish, and wanted to ascertain the cause. When he was told the story, he too journeyed to Ars to thank his zealous brother priest.[28] Thus at a time when frequent Communion was almost unknown in France, he was one of the first promoters of this practice. But he demanded an adequate preparation in terms of piety and doctrine before admitting people to frequent reception of the Eucharist.

For a young mother who felt anxious and overburdened with her large family he had words of encouragement:

> Come now, my little one [he said with fatherly kindliness], do not be alarmed at your burden; our Lord carries it with you. The Good God does well all that he does: when he gives many children to a young mother it is that he deems her worthy to rear them. It is a mark of confidence on his part.[29]

How did he respond to his brother priests? He was demanding in charting out a path to holiness for them. To one parish priest who came to him lamenting the indifference of his people and the fruitlessness of his labours he responded:

> You have preached, you have prayed; but have you fasted? Have you taken the discipline? Have you slept on the bare floor? So long as you have done none of these things you have no right to complain.[30]

27 Trochu, ibid., p. 316. **28** Cf. Trochu, ibid., p. 317. **29** Ibid., p. 312. **30** Ibid., p. 313.

While a different style of mortification may be more appropriate to contemporary society, the need for a deep spirit of sacrifice is still necessary for the priest to be pastorally effective.

PERSONALITY

Although pilgrims came by the hundreds each day to seek out the Curé of Ars, his natural disposition, like his namesake John the Baptist, was to do and to disappear. This was also the motivation behind his cultivation of a dishevelled appearance. Those who were looking for an imposing personality were disappointed. Like that lady from Paris whom Fr Vianney overheard expressing her disappointment when he didn't measure up to her expectations: 'So this is the Curé of Ars' she commented. He responded with some humour: 'The Queen of Sheba came to see Solomon expecting too little. You Madame have come to Ars expecting too much'.

Those who came drawn by faith were not deceived by the externals. They saw how the beauty of his soul transfigured his outward appearance which otherwise would have been ordinary enough. His complexion was pallid as a result of spending those interminable hours in the confessional, and his face was deeply lined from the harsh treatment he gave to his body. However, the most striking aspect of his appearance was the brilliance of his eyes which seemed to penetrate to the centre of people's souls, which in fact was what happened as many penitents confirmed. His small figure moved briskly like a man who knows the value of time.

There was nothing in his manner which was either affected or just conventional. He greeted people of every rank with courtesy, charm and simplicity, without a trace of obsequiousness. When necessary the Curé knew how to call people to order. 'I never wait anywhere, not even at the Vatican', said a great lady, who thought she could dazzle the Curé with her titles and so get to his confession before her turn. 'Oh', replied Fr Vianney, with a certain archness, 'you will, nevertheless, have to wait at the confessional of the poor Curé d'Ars.' Shafts of wit peppered his conversation. To the good nun who with artless simplicity said to him, 'People in general believe you are ignorant, Father'; he replied, 'They are not mistaken, my daughter; but it is of no consequence; I shall always be able to teach you more than you can learn.' What was unexpected about the Curé d'Ars was his natural good humour and sense of fun. This man who was so near to God, never missed an opportunity for a smile or a laugh or a joke.[31]

31 The following are some of the recorded comments of Fr Vianney in relation to pilgrims. A lady of some distinction from Paris commented to the Curé, 'I came to hear a good sermon, but

He was highly sensitive, gifted with a deep sense of compassion which easily brought tears to his eyes when confronted with the pain or sorrows of others. He had an exceptional power of consolation for every form of human misery which transmitted a deep sense of serenity and fortitude to face difficulties. Despite the pressures of work and his very mortified life, at night he could relax in the company of his friends with ease and a gentle sense of humour. He would listen to the news of the day about France and the Church. His vivacity and fiery glance betrayed an ardent temperament which he must have seriously taken in hand to achieve the patience which was so universally admired.

LAST DAYS

As he approached the end of his life his infirmities increased. On the feast of Corpus Christi 1859 (which fell on 23 June) he was so weak that he didn't have the strength to carry the Blessed Sacrament from one altar of repose to another: it was placed in his hands only at the Benediction. The Curé had intimations that he was approaching the end of his life and throughout 1859 he commented at different times that his life was drawing to a close. Nevertheless he still kept up his heroic dedication to the sacrament of reconciliation, though his words in the confessional became increasingly difficult to distinguish due to his failing strength and almost complete absence of teeth. When he left the confessional at 11.00 a.m. to give his instruction in the church, it was seen how weak and frail he was. He could hardly articulate his words and his ideas were spoken in a series of exclamations, often addressed directly to the tabernacle.

On Friday 29 July he felt worse than usual but managed to make his way to the confessional. At 11.00 a.m. he gave his catechism instruction but was barely audible. When he returned to the presbytery that evening he fainted at the foot of the stairs. Eventually he reached his room and was assisted to bed. He gradually grew weaker and was given the last sacraments on 2 August. At

there are much better sermons to be heard elsewhere.' 'Quite true, Madam', he replied, 'I am not very learned, but if you will do all I tell you, God will still have mercy on you.'

'Father,' said one lady, 'I have been here three days and I have still not had a chance to speak to you.' – 'In paradise, my child, we'll talk in paradise'.

'Father', said another, 'I have come two hundred leagues to see you.' – 'It wasn't worth coming so far just for that.'

And again, 'Father, I still haven't been able to see you!' – 'You haven't missed much.' – 'Father, just one word!' – 'My child, you have already said a dozen words.'

To a lady who asked sweetly how one should go to God, his response was 'Quite straight, like a cannonball'.

He told another woman she gossiped less in February because it was three days shorter than other months!

2.00 a.m. on the morning of 4 August he gave up his generous soul to God as the prayers of the dying were being said. He had been parish priest of Ars for forty-one years.

As soon as word of his death was noised abroad the roads to Ars became black with crowds of pilgrims from the surrounding countryside and farther afield. For forty-eight hours there was an uninterrupted procession past his body laid out in a downstairs room in cassock, surplice and stole. During his lifetime no one had been able to persuade him to pose for a photograph. Now, however, a picture was taken of him in death.

The funeral was held on Saturday 6 August. The funeral procession traversed the streets of his beloved Ars and halted in the square where the bishop preached his panegyeric. He was buried in the nave of the church. The Curé may have died but the pilgrimage continued to his tomb. The diocesan authorities began the process of his canonization in 1862. In view of this impending beatification the remains of the Venerable Vianney were exhumed in 1904 when it was found that his body was incorrupt. It was then placed in a marble altar with glass surrounds where it can be seen to the present day.

APOTHEOSIS

There were many significant events during the pontificate of Pius X, but it is probably true to say that none gave him such joy and satisfaction as the beatification of Jean-Marie Vianney, on 8 January 1905. He had a deep personal devotion to the Curé of Ars, whose statue he always kept on the desk in his study. At the reading of the decree which declared the authenticity of the miracles submitted for the beatification of the Venerable Vianney (21 February 1904), Pius X responded that, since he himself worked for so many years in parish ministry, words couldn't convey the depth of his joy at seeing this humble parish priest raised to the honour of Blessed. He strongly encouraged all parish priests to take the Venerable Vianney as their model, learning from him how personal piety is the most effective means to draw souls to God. He asked priests to imitate his charity so that the faithful would be more easily attracted to the path of virtue.[32] Shortly after his beatification, Pius X proclaimed him patron of the parish priests of France.[33]

A French bishop, seeing the statue of the new Blessed on the Pope's desk, said to Pius X that the presence of such an image was a great honour for France. The Pope replied, '*Socius meus*' (he is my companion), and then asked

32 Cf. Pierre Veuillot (ed.), *The Catholic priesthood: papal documents from Pius X to Pius XII* (Dublin, 1957), pp 15–16. **33** Cf. ibid., p. 16.

the bishop to pray to God to work the miracles that would be necessary to canonize him. But God had other plans. The humble Curé was canonized by Pius XI on the feast of Pentecost, 31 May 1925, who proclaimed him patron of parish priests throughout the world.

CHAPTER FIVE

Venerable John Henry Newman (1801–1890)

JOHN HENRY NEWMAN was one of the dominant religious figures of nineteenth-century England. The centenary of his death (1990) and the bicentenary of his birth (2001) were occasions of renewed interest in the life of this great English cardinal. They gave rise to a number of studies and assessments of his influence during the past hundred years in areas as diverse as theology, education, Scripture, literature and philosophy. John Paul II recalled that at the present 'there is an area of Newman's thought which deserves special mention. I refer to that *unity* which he advocated between theology and science, between the *world of faith and the world of reason*.'[1]

Newman is best known because of his writings. He was a great defender of the faith, and the eloquence and force of his ecclesiastical writings have encouraged some scholars to suggest that in due course he will be recognized as a Doctor of the Church. In this context it is of interest to note that he is quoted on four different occasions in the *Catechism of the Catholic Church*,[2] and that John Paul II refers to him in his encyclicals *Veritatis splendor*[3] and *Fides et ratio*.[4]

Newman was very conscious that he had a particular mission, a personal vocation from God to do him some definite service. John Paul II reflecting on his long life and subsequent influence, affirms that the 'particular mission entrusted to him by God ensures that John Henry Newman belongs to every time and place and people'.[5] And he continues:

> Newman was born in troubled times which knew not only political and military upheaval but also turbulence of soul. Old certitudes were shaken, and believers were faced with the threat of rationalism on the

1 John Paul II, Address, 27 April 1990 (italics in original). 2 Cf. *Catechism of the Catholic Church*, 157, 1732, 1778, and 2144. 3 'As Cardinal John Henry Newman, that outstanding defender of the rights of conscience puts it, "Conscience has rights because it has duties"': Encyclical, *Veritatis splendor*, 34 (The splendour of truth), 6 August 1993. 4 Cf. John Paul II, Encyclical, *Fides et ratio*, 74 (Faith and reason), 14 September 1998. 5 Letter of John Paul II to the archbishop of Birmingham on the occasion of the second centenary of the birth of Cardinal Newman (22 January 2001).

> one hand and fideism on the other. Rationalism brought with it a rejection of both authority and transcendence, while fideism turned from the challenges of history and the tasks of this world to a distorted dependence upon authority and the supernatural. In such a world Newman came eventually to a remarkable synthesis of faith and reason which were for him 'like two wings on which the human spirit rises to the contemplation of truth' (*Fides et ratio*).[6]

For Newman Christian life included all noble secular values. His emphasis on the need for a well-formed laity anticipated the teaching of Vatican II.

Newman as well as being a gifted writer was also a man of action. He was the focal point of the Oxford Movement during the years 1833–43 which reasserted the Catholic elements of doctrine in the Anglican Church. After his conversion he established the oratory of St Philip Neri in Birmingham and London. At the request of the Irish hierarchy he set up the Catholic University of Ireland in Dublin and was its rector for four years. He was also the driving force behind the establishment of the Oratory School in Birmingham to provide a Christian education for the sons of the Catholic gentry in England.

NEWMAN – FIRST CONVERSION

John Henry Newman was born in 1801, the son of a London banker. Both his parents were practising members of the Church of England. As a child he learned to love the Bible which was read to him by his mother until such time as he was able to read it for himself. John was the eldest of six children who grew up in solid comfort, and whose literary, musical and artistic talents were given every encouragement.

In 1808 he went as a boarder to a private school at Ealing where the foundations of scholarship were laid. When he was fifteen, Newman had his first conversion. He writes in his *Apologia*: 'In the autumn of 1816 a great change of thought took place in me. I fell under the influence of a definite creed, and received into my intellect impressions of dogma, which, through God's mercy, have never been effaced or obscured.'[7]

At this time too he read Thomas Scott 'who made a deeper impression on my mind than any other, and to whom (humanly speaking) I almost owe my soul'. For years, Newman said, he used almost as proverbs two phrases from Scott: 'Holiness before peace', and 'Growth is the only evidence of life.'[8] However, these books also impressed on his mind the current Protestant interpretation of Scripture that the Pope was the anti-Christ.

6 Ibid. **7** John Henry Newman, *Apologia pro vita sua* (London, 1890), p. 4. **8** Ibid., p. 5.

Adversity paved the way for a great change of thought in Newman. In March 1816 his father's bank collapsed and the family were reduced to precarious financial circumstances. During the summer Newman suffered an illness which, he wrote long afterwards, 'made me a Christian'. He was allowed to stay at the school during the summer holidays to convalesce. And it was during this period that he came under the influence of Walter Meyers, one of the masters at the school, who gave him religious books to read. As a result the doctrines of the Blessed Trinity, the Incarnation and the Redemption became a reality for Newman. Before he was sixteen he drew up a series of texts in support of each verse of the Athanasian Creed.[9] During this time he was also introduced to Joseph Milner's *Church history*, 'and was nothing short of enamoured of the long extracts from St Augustine and the other Fathers which I found there.'[10] He was instantly attracted to this 'paradise of delight'. In them he found a fusion of intellect and imagination which answered the unusual balance of Newman's mind. His love of music, poetry and drama prevented him from being over-intellectual in an educational system that gave priority to reason.

This intellectual conviction about basic church doctrines led Newman to accept wholeheartedly the Gospel ideal of holiness. He began to live more fully in the presence of God and to 'rest in the thought of two and two only supreme and luminously self-evident beings, myself and my Creator.'[11] Newman was a man of strong feelings, which meant at times that he had to struggle to control them. In his youth his anger could be so passionate that the effort to control them made him tremble and faint, but it was gradually overcome, not by mere repression but by the steady expansion of other more loving feelings.

NEWMAN AND CELIBACY

Around this time also he became convinced that he should lead a celibate life as a response to the vision of the Christian vocation which had gripped his mind. It is universally recognized that intellectual honesty was one of the outstanding characteristics of John Henry Newman. But he was also possessed of a much rarer quality, a unique *emotional* honesty, which is instructive and revealing for what he has to say about celibacy and how it influenced his own affective life.[12]

At fifteen he had a first intimation that his vocation was to be a celibate one.[13] From 1816 to 1829 his attitude to celibacy was not so much a resolution

9 See ibid., p. 5. **10** Ibid., p. 7. **11** Ibid., p. 4. **12** Cf. Meriol Trevor, *Newman: the pillar of the cloud* (London, 1962), p. 95. **13** See *Apologia*, p. 7.

as an 'anticipation' of a commitment. In 1829 he made that commitment. His journal and diaries testify to his deep appreciation of the virtue of holy purity which he acquired as the result of daily effort. As a boy of fifteen he wrote: '*Fac me temperatum, sobrium, castum.*'[14] Later, at twenty-three, around the time he received Anglican orders, he would note in his diary: 'Pray for purity, sobriety – chastity – temperance – self-denial – simplicity – truth – openness.'[15] It should also be mentioned that he did not consider sins against purity lightly.

As is clear from his letters, Newman loved people and places with an extraordinary tenacity. Much of his energy was spent in loving and in delighting in being loved; gratitude for the love of others, and a continual surprise that they should expend it on him, was a constant reaction all his life. Newman's letters from his early days show how affectionate he was by nature, and how eager to do things to please those he loved. He often expressed his gratitude, in a tone of surprise, at God's goodness in sending him so many friends; he felt he did not deserve so much affection.[16]

The combination of high intellectual gifts with such an affectionate heart was unusual. He had the reason of a philosopher and the imagination of a poet. Because he was so wholeheartedly a priest he never threw the whole force of his personality into either ability.[17] While he was careful to distinguish affection from its overflow into unchastity, he always maintained that 'man is made for sympathy, for the interchange of love.'[18] The essence of celibacy for Newman was to forego the privilege of marriage in order to give himself entirely to God and through him to bring many to birth in the Spirit.[19]

As an Anglican, Newman understands celibacy in the context of Christ who was born of a virgin and who remained a virgin. But such a choice then, as now, was strongly counter-cultural: 'the way of the world at present', he commented, 'is to deny that there is such a gift.'[20] The single life was valuable not only for the sake of the Church, but also for the spiritual life of the individual. To Henry Wilberforce, whom he tutored at Oxford, Newman wrote that 'the celibate is a high state in life, to which the multitude of men cannot aspire. I do not say that they who adopt it are necessarily better than others, though the noblest ethos is situated in that state.'[21]

His appreciation of celibacy grew after he became a Catholic, as also did his esteem for marriage.[22] As an Anglican he had to justify celibacy in light of

14 'Make me temperate, sober, and chaste.' **15** Joseph Tolhurst, 'The interchange of love: John Henry Newman's teaching on celibacy', *Irish Theological Quarterly*, vol. 59, no. 3 (1993), p. 218. **16** Cf. Meriol Trevor, *Newman: light in winter* (London, 1962), p. 340. **17** Trevor, *Newman: the pillar of the cloud*, p. 10. **18** Placid Murray, *Newman the Oratorian* (Dublin, 1969), Paper no.18, p. 277. **19** Cf. Trevor, *The pillar of the cloud*, p. 95. **20** *Parochial and plain sermons* (London, 1886), vol. VI, p. 187. **21** Ibid., p. 274. **22** This is evident if, for example, we compare what he wrote on these topics after his severe illness in Sicily in 1833 with his homily of 1852 on the topic; see Ian Ker, *John Henry Newman: a biography* (Oxford, 1988), pp 196–7.

a particular dedication, but afterwards he felt free to speak about a 'nobler state of life'. This he did eloquently in a homily preached on virginity and celibacy in 1852, at a time in England when celibacy was under constant fire from non-Catholics.[23] Newman responds to these vulgar attacks with a calm and dignified statement of Christian virginity and celibacy, drawing on the wisdom of Scripture and the Fathers of the Church. It is this composure, combined with his deep appreciation of the role of human love in marriage, which gives particular relevance to his insights in the context of the present polarization of ideas about optional celibacy. In the *Apologia*, Newman recognizes the apostolic origin of celibacy.[24]

So Newman would affirm that it is not possible to understand celibacy except viewed from a supernatural perspective. Nor could it be a rule of life unless supported by grace. In a fine passage from his discourse on *The Glories of Mary* he shows how the Blessed Virgin is the 'pattern of purity' and reveals to us something of his own personal struggle in the quest for this virtue:

> Above all, let us imitate her purity ... What shall bring you forward in the narrow way, but the thought and patronage of Mary? What shall seal your senses, what shall tranquillise your heart, when sights and sounds of danger are around you, but Mary? What shall give you patience and endurance, when you are wearied out with the length of the conflict with evil, with the unceasing necessity of precautions, but a loving communion with her! She will comfort you in your discouragements, solace you in your fatigues, raise you after your falls, reward you for your successes. She will show you her Son, your God and your all. When your spirit within you is restless and wayward, when it is sick of what it has, and hankers after what it has not, when your eye is solicited with evil ... what will bring you to yourself, to peace and to health, but the cool breath of the Immaculate and the fragrance of the Rose of Sharon? It is the boast of the Catholic religion, that it has the gift of making the young heart chaste; and why is this, but that it gives us Jesus Christ for our food, and Mary for our nursing Mother?[25]

Newman's capacity for love can be measured by the love he inspired in others. In spite of his shyness, his sympathy with others did not narrow as he grew older but increased and deepened. This enlargement of heart came as a consequence of the successive crises of his personal development. The desire

23 See Murray, pp 270–81. This was a homily delivered at the religious profession of Mary Anne Bowden, daughter of his oldest friend, John Bowden, from Oxford undergraduate days. **24** See *Apologia*, p. 54. **25** John Henry Newman, *Discourses to mixed congregations* (London, 1886), pp 375–6.

to follow Christ closely wherever he went was the motive power of his commitment to live a celibate life and in so doing to be totally available for what God asked of him.[26]

When Charles Kingsley attacked Newman's personal integrity, he responded in the *Apologia* with that classic defence of himself and of the Catholic priesthood in general, vindicating also the discipline of priestly celibacy. For his efforts he received the universal gratitude of the priests of England. Priests today can also be grateful to Newman not only for his deep theological insights into celibacy, but especially for revealing to us how the practice of it was reflected in the intimacy of his own soul.

OXFORD

Newman entered Trinity College, Oxford in December 1816. He fell in love with the place from the beginning, a love that lasted a long lifetime. Although there was no faculty of theology at either Oxford or Cambridge, these two universities between them provided the vast majority of the clergymen of the established church.

At the beginning of the nineteenth century, the level of scholarship in Oxford was low, with the exception of a few colleges. The great majority of young men idled. Drunkenness was a pervasive disorder which Newman found pointless and disgusting. As a mere sixteen-year-old he showed extraordinary courage in refusing to get involved in the annual drunken orgy of the Gaudy on the Monday after Trinity Sunday, in spite of considerable moral pressure. Newman's first year ended very successfully with his winning a scholarship which was worth £60 a year for nine years. It was of course great news for his family given their stringent financial situation.

Coming up to his BA examinations, Newman so overworked himself that he did quite badly. This was a great disappointment to him and to his family – they had been expecting a much different result. Nevertheless, because of the college scholarship he won in 1818, he was able to stay on at the university. In 1821 his father was declared a bankrupt. The following year, when he was just twenty-one, Newman was elected a Fellow of Oriel College, then the centre of intellectual excellence in Oxford university. He had won the greatest prize that Oxford could offer a young man. In his diary for that day Newman wrote: 'I have this morning been elected Fellow of Oriel. Thank God. Thank God.'[27] This achievement, against very strong opposition, enabled him to have an aca-

26 Cf. Trevor, *The pillar of the cloud*, p. 96. **27** Maisie Ward, *Young Mr Newman* (London, 1952), p. 73.

demic career and a regular income, which was much needed as his father never recovered his position after his bankruptcy and died in 1824, leaving Newman responsible for finding a home for his mother and sisters, and for his brother Frank's education.

All this time Newman had kept up his habits of prayer and meditation, and in 1822 he decided to enter the ministry of the Church of England. He wrote to his brother Frank: 'God sanctifies my studies by breathing into me all the while thoughts of Him.'[28] His grasp of doctrine was deepening with his prayers, and after his exam he notes that he now had more time to give to devotion. On his solitary walks he prayed 'for all friends and for all mankind.'[29]

Having to provide for the upkeep of his mother and three sisters meant that Newman was constantly pressed for ready cash, in spite of the income from his fellowship and private classes. He was also writing articles on classical and historical topics for encyclopaedias and reference books, which paid well.

ORDINATION

In June 1824 he was ordained deacon by the bishop of Oxford and accepted the curacy of St Clement's, a poor parish on the edge of Oxford. He was deeply moved by the ceremony and wrote in his journal in this regard: 'I have the responsibility of souls on me to the day of my death.'[30] His rector was an octogenarian invalid. The parish had about 2,000 faithful, and a scheme was on foot for building a new church. Newman had now to take up the work of collecting the necessary money, and of winning back the great mass of the parishioners who – as result of the smallness of the existing church and the inactivity of the rector – had drifted away according to their various fancies. He instituted a Sunday afternoon sermon which soon became popular, and he began a systematic visitation of the whole parish, all of which he managed to complete.[31] He visited the sick regularly and despite an initial cool reception, his presence was much sought after by them.

Up to this time Newman's Protestantism had a distinctly evangelical hue. However, as a result of the influence of his colleagues in Oriel College, and his own personal experience of pastoral work, his theological outlook began to change. He now accepted the doctrine of baptismal regeneration over the idea of subjective conversion. His reading of Butler's *Analogy of religion* taught him the doctrine of the visible Church and the historical character of revelation. In addition he became convinced of the existence of the Church as a substantive

28 Ibid., p. 64. **29** Ibid., p. 73. **30** John Henry Newman, *Autobiographical writings* (London, 1956), pp 200–1. **31** Cf. Ward, p. 100.

body which teaches doctrine. Newman was ordained a priest of the Anglican Church on 29 May 1825.

TUTOR IN ORIEL

In January 1826 Newman became a tutor at Oriel College with an income of over £600 a year. His perception of the responsibilities of the tutor was quite different from the established appreciation of it. Some approached it in a very casual manner, but to Newman it seemed the office of a tutor was in itself sacred – that it should involve not merely supervision of the studies of his pupils but also a true pastoral office towards them. He wrote to his sister that he saw the tutorship as a spiritual undertaking and not 'merely a secular office'. After only a few weeks acting as tutor, he was concerned about the 'considerable profligacy' of the undergraduates, mostly 'men of family, in many cases, of fortune.' Since he considered himself a 'minister of Christ', he might be forced to resign if he found he could not exercise a 'spiritual' influence over his pupils.[32] He took it so seriously that he resigned his curacy at St Clement's to have the necessary time to devote to it. In relation to his responsibilities in Oriel as a whole, he wrote in his diary:

> May I engage in them, remembering that I am a minister of Christ, and have a commission to preach the Gospel, remembering the worth of souls, and that I shall have to answer for the opportunities given me of benefiting those who are under my care.[33]

The youngest of the four tutors, Newman took up his duties with an energy that disturbed the placid surface of the established routine of college life.[34] He objected to the undergraduates being compelled to go to Communion, but got a poor hearing when he complained of this profanation. With his own students he built up a relationship of friendship, as compared with the martinet manner then in fashion with college tutors, and found time to be with them on outdoor pursuits, and during holidays. When he became vicar of the university church of St Mary's in 1828, the hold he had acquired over the students led them to receive religious instruction directly from his sermons. But from the first, independently of St Mary's, he had set before himself in his tutorial work the aim of gaining souls for God.[35]

Early in 1829 Newman was able to boast to a friend of the reforms he and the other tutors had implemented at Oriel: 'We have gone through the year

32 Cf. Ker, pp 27, 28. 33 Ward, p. 113. 34 The others were Hurrell Froude, William Wilberforce, and Joseph Dornford. 35 Cf. Ker, pp 37, 38.

famously, packed off the lumber, parted with spoilt goods, washed and darned what we could, and imported several new articles of approved quality. Indeed the College is so altered that you would hardly know it again.'[36] However, the provost of Oriel had a disciplinarian view of the tutor's duties as opposed to the pastoral interpretation of Newman and some of his colleagues. In the end he received no more students for tutoring and thus ceased to occupy this office in June 1830, with considerable loss of income. When he realized that his career as a tutor was over, he turned all his teaching energy into his sermons at St Mary's.

In 1825 Hurrell Froude was elected a Fellow of Oriel. He not only became Newman's closest friend, but also a powerful influence in the growth and change of his opinions. From Froude he learned the doctrine of apostolic succession and the essentially supernatural and sacramental character of the Church. With the election of Froude as a Fellow, Oriel had gathered in the last of the four men who were to lead the movement for the restoration of full Catholic dogma of the Anglican Church – Newman, Keble, Froude and Pusey.

NEWMAN AND THE FATHERS OF THE CHURCH

It was at this time too that Newman rediscovered his interest in the Fathers:

> In proportion as I moved out of the shadow of liberalism which had hung over my course, my early devotion towards the Fathers returned; and in the long vacation of 1828 I set about to read them chronologically, beginning with St Ignatius and St Justin.[37]

In 1830 he was asked to prepare a study of the Council of Nicea, which eventually appeared under the title of *The Arians of the fourth century*. It was in the process of writing this book that he learned that

> antiquity was the true exponent of the doctrines of Christianity ... The course of reading which I pursued in the composition of my work was directly adapted to develop it in my mind. What principally attracted me in the ante-nicene period was the great church of Alexandria, the historical centre of teaching in those times. Of Rome for some centuries comparatively little is known. The battle of Arianism was fought in Alexandria; Athanasius the champion of the truth, was Bishop of Alexandria; and in his writings he refers to the great religious names of

36 Cf. p. 32. **37** Ibid.

> an earlier date, to Origen, Dionysius, and others who were the glory of its see, or of its school. The broad philosophy of Clement and Origen carried me away; the philosophy, not the theological doctrine; and I have drawn out some features of it in my volume, with zeal and freshness, but with the partiality of a neophyte. Some portions of their teaching, magnificent in themselves, came like music to my inward ear, as if the response to ideas, which, with little external to encourage them, I had cherished so long.[38]

Work on the *Arians* was one of the elements gradually converging towards the Oxford Movement. As a result of this study Newman had come to the conclusion that in the Church of England, 'there was need of a second Reformation.'[39]

As we have seen, at the time of his first conversion as a schoolboy, Newman read a volume of early Church history, with the result that he acquired a deeply-felt attraction for the Fathers, who were to be a constant source of nourishment for his spiritual life, as well as providing a solid doctrinal foundation for his immense output of theological writing all during his life.[40] One can see in Newman's writings the progressive influence of the teaching of the Fathers.[41] Men like 'Origen, Tertulian, Athanasius, Chrysostom, Augustine, Jerome and Leo' are for Newman, 'authors of powerful, original minds, engaged in the production of original works.'[42]

During the years of the Oxford Movement, Newman tried to justify the apostolicity of the Anglican Church from his study of the Fathers and thereby establish it as the *Via Media* between Rome and Protestantism. He saw that it had a certain validity as a theology, but no counterpart in reality. And so, many years later, he could write to a former colleague of the Oxford Movement who did not convert:

> I recollect well what an outcast I seemed to myself, when I took down from the shelves of my library the volumes of St Athanasius or St Basil, and set myself to study them; and how, on the contrary, when at length I was brought into the Catholic Communion, I kissed them with delight, with a feeling that in them I had more than all I had lost.[43]

38 *Apologia*, p. 26. **39** *Apologia*, p. 32. **40** Cf. John Henry Newman, *Difficulties felt by Anglicans in Catholic teaching* (subsequently referred to as *Difficulties*), (London, 1872), p. 324. **41** Cf. I. Ker, *Newman the theologian* (London, 1990). In his introductory essays to selected texts, Ker gives a fine analysis of Newman's theological development and his dependence on the Fathers. He also communicates vividly the patristic influence on the English cardinal in his biography of Newman. However, to appreciate fully the extent of this influence there is no substitute for reading some of Newman's own works such as *Select treatises of St Athanasius; The Arians of the fourth century; Historical sketches, vols. I and II; Essay on the development of Christian doctrine; Apologia pro vita sua;* etc. **42** John Henry Newman, *Historical sketches*, vol. II (London, 1876), p. 475. **43** *Difficulties*,

And again:

> I am not ashamed still to take my stand upon the Fathers, and do not mean to budge … The Fathers made me a Catholic.[44]

Newman's great discovery was that the Catholic Church of the nineteenth century was the same as the Church of the Fathers.[45] In September 1845 the Oxford don concluded his *Essay on the development of the Christian doctrine*, proving conclusively to himself that any doctrinal development which had taken place in the interim in the Catholic Church, was in homogeneous continuity with the teaching of the Fathers. He wrote the Foreword to the first edition on 6 October;[46] he was received into the Church three days later.

TRADITION AND SCRIPTURE

As his appreciation for the Fathers' contribution to the life of the Church deepened, Newman became more acutely aware of the inadequacy and insufficiency of the Lutheran *sola Scriptura* principle as the rule of faith, from several points of view: for teaching matters of discipline, for furnishing or transmitting the whole of the Faith, for a unanimous profession of the faith, etc.[47] Because of his great knowledge of the inspired text, he realized that it did not carry its own explanation with it. It is precisely because the Fathers are 'witnesses' to the living Tradition of the Church from apostolic times, that their commentaries on Scripture are, for Newman, sure guides to its correct interpretation. They are incomparable 'expositors of Scripture' because 'they do what no examination of the particular context can do satisfactorily, acquaint us with the *things* Scripture speaks of.'[48] The Fathers, instead of telling us the meaning of words in their etymological, philosophical, classical, or scholastic sense, communicate to us 'what they do mean actually, what they do mean in the Christian Church and in theology.'[49] It is from the Fathers we get the real, useful, intended meaning of the words of the Bible.

Newman consistently insists on the necessity of being led both by Scripture and Tradition in order to attain the whole of revealed truth. It was more than evident to him that Scripture cannot, and does not, 'force on us its full dogmatic meaning.'[50] Therefore, Scripture could never be used alone, that

p. 357. **44** Ibid., p. 376. **45** Cf. *Essay on the development of Christian doctrine* (London, 1920), pp 97–8. **46** Cf. ibid., p. x. **47** Cf. Philip Griffin, *Revelation and Scripture in the writings of John Henry Newman* (unpublished thesis), (Pamplona, 1985), pp 280–91. **48** *Lectures on the doctrine of justification* (London, 1874), p. 121. **49** Ibid. **50** *Essays critical and historical*, vol. I (London, 1901), p. 115.

is, without Tradition. But once this is accepted, then Scripture, the written word, serves as a powerful and clear indicator of the Truth. With Athanasius he considered Scripture, as interpreted by Tradition, to be 'a document of final appeal in inquiry.'[51]

THE FATHERS AND CULTURE

Because patristic literature is also distinguished for its great cultural, spiritual and pastoral values, after sacred Scripture the Fathers are one of the principal sources of priestly formation.[52] Their cultivation is recommended by Vatican II as ongoing spiritual nourishment for priests during their whole lives.[53] Many of the Fathers were men of immense human culture, totally conversant with the Graeco-Roman philosophical and literary heritage. As the *Instruction on the study of the Fathers* points out, 'by imprinting the Christian stamp on the ancient classical *humanitas*, they were the first to make a bridge between the Gospel and secular culture.'[54] To mention but one example of this influence we need look no further than St Augustine and the extraordinary impact he exerted on the Christian civilization of the West during the whole of the Middle Ages.

Newman responded to this very attractive characteristic of the Fathers with immense delight and with an enthusiasm which was to remain with him all during his life. This dimension of patristic literature struck a deep chord in Newman because his own intellectual interests, indeed the very cast of his mind, found a deep resonance in the writings of the Fathers. He is profoundly affected by them because they are saints who come alive in their writings and he is thus able to establish a very personal relationship with them. It is this very *humanitas* which makes him 'exult in the folios of the Fathers.'[55]

Newman nourished his soul, intellect and will, on all of these early Christian writers. Because he studied the Fathers in the original Greek and Latin languages, he had access to all the nuances of their literary and theolog-

51 *Select treatises of St Athanasius*, vol. II, p. 51. Newman gives us a wonderful description of Tradition from his Anglican days: 'It is latent, but it lives. It is silent like the rapids of a river, before the rocks intercept it. It is the Church's unconscious habit of opinion and sentiment; which she reflects upon, masters, and expresses, according to the emergency. We see then the mistake of asking for a complete collection of the Roman Traditions; as well might we ask for a full catalogue of a man's tastes and thoughts on a given subject. Tradition in its fullness is necessarily unwritten; it is the mode in which a society has felt or acted during a certain period, and it cannot be circumscribed any more than a man's countenance and manner can be conveyed to strangers in any set of propositions' (Ward, pp 263–4). 52 Cf. Congregation for Catholic Education, *Instruction on the study of the Fathers of the Church in the formation of priests* (Rome, 10 November 1989), no. 41. 53 Cf. *Decree on the ministry and life of priests*, 19 (*Presbyterorum ordinis*). 54 *Instruction on the study of the Fathers of the Church*, 43 b. 55 *Historical sketches*, vol. II, p. 221.

ical riches. Their sure doctrine brought him unerringly to the fullness of the Faith in the Catholic Church. By means of the light of grace, and as a result of his great fortitude in search of divine truth, Newman was ready to make all the sacrifices which intellectual honesty demanded in pursuit of his goal.

NEWMAN AND THE CHURCH

As John Paul II has pointed out, the mystery of the Church was always 'the great love of John Henry Newman's life. His experience of the weaknesses in the human fabric of the Church did not undermine in any way his deep supernatural vision of her origin, purpose and effectiveness in the world.'[56]

For a man of his intellectual genius and accomplishment, perseverance on his spiritual journey required a considerable degree of humility also. In this, as well as in his constant recourse to the theological well-springs of the Fathers, he is a sure guide and example for theologians of the present day. It is also worth noting that when he started his research into the heritage of the Fathers, patrology had not yet acquired any significant profile in Catholic theological formation. He had, in a very real sense, anticipated the mind of the Church in this regard. The Fathers were everything, and more, for Newman, which Vatican II and the *Instruction* recommend them to be for the mind and heart of every theologian, for the life and work of every priest.

FAMILY

Newman had a deep love for his mother and sisters and this was more than reciprocated by them. A note in his diary runs:

> O how I love them. So much I love them, that I cannot help thinking Thou wilt either take them hence, or take me from them, because I am so set on them. It is a shocking thought.[57]

The feeling long persisted with Newman that God directly sent bereavements or heavy sorrows for our correction. Yet this was linked with his belief in a special providence of God, a special fatherly care from God in the details of daily life. He believed that God was interested in the circumstances of every man's life: in giving good gifts to all his children, or in drawing out of life's evils material for yet richer good here or hereafter.

56 Cf. John Paul II, Address, 27 April 1990, in *L'Osservatore Romano*, 30 April 1990. **57** Ward, p. 118.

Newman had three sisters (Harriet, Jemima and Mary), and two brothers (Charles and Francis). Harriet, nearest to him in age, shares his thoughts more deeply than the others. Their education, formally speaking, was sketchy, but it was supplemented by John, who advised on their reading and sent them problems by post – mathematical for Jemima, grammatical for Mary. Mary, the youngest of Newman's sisters, had a very attractive personality and a vivid literary style. She was a lively correspondent and was adored by the entire family. She could write to her mother: 'How sorry I should be to have a mother I was afraid of. I can write *almost* as much nonsense, and as easily to you, as I can to Jemima'.

On 4 January 1828 Mary suffered a violent spasm. She died next day – she was barely nineteen. Her death was a great sorrow to Newman. The depth of his feeling is evident from what he wrote about her afterwards: 'She was gifted with that singular sweetness and affectionateness of temper that she lived in an ideal world of happiness, the very sight of which made others happy.' Indeed, for 'some time' he had had a 'presentiment' that Mary would not live long: 'I was led to this by her extreme loveliness of character, and by the circumstance of my great affection for her. I thought I loved her too well, and hardly ever dared to take my full swing of enjoyment in her dear society.'

Now he could only say, 'I cannot realize that I shall not see her again.' Yet while having a constant sense of her presence, he was more convinced than ever of the 'the transitory nature of this world'. Still, he always felt her loss. In 1877 he would write to a domestic servant on the death of her sister: 'I too know what it is to lose a sister. I lost her 49 years ago, and, though so many years have passed, I still feel the pain.' He could never speak about Mary without tears coming into his eyes.[58]

Once he had gained the Oriel fellowship he was confident that he could support them all. The family moved from Brighton to Iffley near Oxford because his mother and sisters couldn't bear to be so far from John, 'their guardian angel', as his mother called him. They went to the university to hear him give his lectures and his sermons. Through John, Harriet and Jemima met their future husbands, the brothers Tom and James Mozley, both Oxford graduates. Newman was by nature shy with strangers, but perfectly at ease with friends. In any event, the experience of the Oriel Common Room drew him out of himself.

ILLNESS

Newman had an extraordinary capacity for work, and could work a sixteen to twenty hour day without showing any negative consequences. He was driven

58 Cf. Ker, *A biography*, pp 30, 610, 714.

by his philosophy of work: 'the only way ultimately to succeed is to do things thoroughly.'[59]

At this time he writes: 'I was beginning to prefer intellectual excellence to moral: I was drifting in the direction of Liberalism. I was rudely awakened from my dream at the end of 1827 by two great blows – illness and bereavement.'[60] His illness was in the form of a nervous breakdown through overwork, but he recovered from it fairly quickly. The bereavement was the death of his beloved sister Mary who, as we have seen, died in January 1828.

Newman was tall among his contemporaries, with a strong frame. He was always thin with a wiry toughness. He had tremendous nervous energy which carried him through formidable undertakings, and after any shock, mental or physical, he would recover extraordinarily quickly.

As we have seen, one of the people at Oxford who had a profound effect on Newman was Hurrell Froude. Newman writes about him in the *Apologia* with deep affection and an elegance of style which is such a hallmark of his writing. He describes how much he owes to Froude's influence: 'He fixed deep in me the idea of devotion to the Blessed Virgin, and he led me gradually to believe in the Real Presence.'[61]

MEDITERRANEAN INTERLUDE

After finishing the *Arians*, Newman was feeling quite exhausted, and so in late 1832 he accepted Hurrell Froude's invitation to take a Mediterranean tour with himself and his father, an Anglican clergyman from Devonshire. During the trip Newman wrote a shoal of letters to family and friends, as well as writing a lot of poetry. To his mother he said that the purpose of the holiday was to 'be a preparation and strengthening-time for future toil.'[62]

The party sailed across the Bay of Biscay, down by the coast of Portugal, and reached Gibraltar on 15 December. They berthed at Malta on Christmas Day and then steamed to Corfu where Newman tried to find out about the Greek Orthodox Church. From Corfu they sailed to Malta and thence to Sicily. Newman was fascinated by the island, its classical remains, and all its cultural resonances. He lost his heart to Sicily and determined to return there for a longer stay. They left Sicily on 13 February and arrived in Rome via Naples on 2 March. Even before he reaches Rome, Newman's strange mixed feelings about the Catholic Church become apparent. 'Rome', he wrote home, 'is the city of the Apostles, and a place to rest one's foot in, whatever be the after-corruption.' [63] Newman was captivated by Rome – his first sight of it was overwhelming:

59 Ward, p. 98. **60** Ibid., p. 149. **61** *Apologia*, pp 23–4. **62** Cf. Ker, *A biography*, p. 54. **63** Cf.

> And now what can I say of Rome, but that it is the first of cities, and that all I ever saw are but as dust (even dear Oxford inclusive) compared with its majesty and glory? Is it possible that so serene and lofty a place is the cage of unclean creatures? I will not believe it till I have evidence of it.[64]

Later he would write to one of his friends with an ambivalence which characterized most of his correspondence about Rome:

> How shall I describe the sadness with which I left the tombs of the Apostles? Rome, not as a city, but as the scene of sacred history, has a part of my heart, and in going away from it I am as if tearing it in twain. I wandered about the place after the Froudes had gone. I went to the church of S. Maria in Cosmedin, which Dionysius founded in A.D. 260, and where Austin is said to have studied rhetoric. I mounted the height where St Peter was martyred, and for the last time went through the vast spaces of this wonderful basilica, and looked at his place of burial, and then prepared for my departure … I ought to tell you about the Miserere at Rome, my going up to St Peter's … my pilgrimage to the place of St Paul's martyrdom, the catacombs, and all the other sights which have stolen away half my heart, but I forbear till we meet. Oh, that Rome were not Rome! but I seem to see as clear as day that a union with her is *impossible*. She is the cruel Church asking of us impossibilities, excommunicating us for disobedience, and now watching and exulting over our approaching overthrow.[65]

Before leaving Rome, Hurrell Froude and Newman called to see Msgr Wiseman, rector of the English College, who received them very courteously. He invited them to make a return visit to the city, but Newman replied, 'We have a work to do in England.'[66] Froude and Newman had discussed and reflected on many things during the trip, and had come to the conclusion that union with Rome in the present circumstances was impossible. Their minds at this time were in fact giving birth to all the elements later to be drawn out as the doctrine of the *Via Media*.

RETURN TO SICILY

The Froudes returned directly to London, but Newman went back to Sicily, drawn by the beauty of the place. He spent a few days in Naples en route and

Ward, p. 197. **64** Ibid., pp 200–1. **65** Ward, p. 203. **66** *Apologia*, p. 34.

climbed Mt Vesuvius. 'I never knew that nature could be so beautiful,' he wrote after his arrival on the island. 'Oh happy I! It was worth coming all the way ... I felt for the first time in my life, that I should be a better and more religious man if I lived there ... Etna was magnificent.'[67]

However, after a few days Newman fell seriously ill with typhoid fever. He gradually recovered, but in retrospect he saw the episode as one of the three great illnesses which led to such a decisive development in his religious life. The experience led him to a deeper conviction about the appropriateness of celibacy for the task God had in store for him. During the delirium he began to see the deficiencies in his own character: 'my utter hollowness ... with little love, little self-denial.' Yet he kept repeating to himself: 'I have not sinned against the light,' or 'God has still work for me to do.' On the return journey he wrote his most famous poem, 'Lead Kindly Light.'[68]

In the *Apologia* Newman tells us that at Rome he began to think that he had a mission, and that this presentiment began to grow stronger when he went to Sicily. During his illness he often sobbed bitterly, and when his servant asked what was the matter, he could only say, 'I have a work to do in England'.[69]

OXFORD MOVEMENT

Newman returned from Sicily in July 1833, with health restored and in a buoyant mood. He had pledged himself to undertake the work of renewing and purifying the Church of England, no matter what the cost. It was his supreme confidence in the truth of his principles which carried him on.

Later that year with university friends Hurrell Froude and John Keble he began the Oxford Movement. Newman wrote the first of the *Tracts for the times*, and with unbounded energy set about their distribution through a network of clergy in different parts of the country. Initially the Tractarian Movement was a protest against state interference in Church affairs, but as time went on it became more focussed on the renewal of the doctrinal base of the Church of England. The Movement caused great excitement in the 1830s, especially among the younger clergy, stirring them up to consider the nature of the Church and its position vis-à-vis the state, with which it had been inextricably entwined since Henry VIII had declared himself head of the Church in England. Newman, who at that time had begun his pioneering studies on the Fathers, realized that the Church had always conceived itself to be an autonomous community and Catholic, that is universal, supra-national in its scope.

67 Ward, p. 217. **68** See ibid., p. 219. **69** *Apologia*, p. 35.

Although he regarded himself as merely one of a group of friends, Newman was undoubtedly the most dynamic leader of the Movement, and his influence grew not only from the *Tracts*, but also from his sermons, which because he published them in book form, reached a nationwide audience. Readers, expecting controversial Catholic views, were faced instead with a psychologically penetrating preaching of Christ the Lord, the Christ of the Gospels, his words, his works of healing, his mysterious self-sacrifice on the Cross, his resurrection from death and continuing presence in the communion of his followers – and the challenge he presents to all to change their lives in following him.[70]

The *Tracts* were as nothing compared to Newman's personal influence, extended through the printing of his sermons to thousands who never met him. And this influence, although it affected people's ecclesiastical views, was essentially personal. He communicated a tremendous energy of will directed towards the true following of Christ, a sense of the urgency of immediate personal combat with the forces of evil, in the world, but still more in the individual soul. His sermons were directions for the campaign. Manning[71] thought his sermons too stern and wrote to tell him so. But to Newman it seemed worse than useless to attempt to fight the father of lies with comforting generalizations, which, he said, were useless without an everyday discipline of prayer and self-control carried out faithfully, even in the absence of feeling and in the midst of distractions. His insistence on persevering action in the details of ordinary life and on the eternal issues which depend on the moral choices which mould the character, was the 'strictness' so often complained about. Speaking about preaching he commented, 'Holiness is the aim.'[72]

The first volume of the *Parochial sermons* was published in March 1834 and the second a year later. As a result Newman's name began to be known beyond university circles. While these constituted an effective weapon for the Tractarian Movement, they will always form an important resource of Christian spirituality.

Newman's preaching at St Mary's became legendary. These weekly sermons were by common consent the motive force of the Oxford Movement. Some few had attended the lectures, many had read the Tracts, but everybody listened to the sermons. Every man of note in the University attended. His sermons transformed the preaching of the Church of England.[73] The better students flocked to hear him at St Mary's where he spoke about holiness of life in a way which challenged his listeners as never before. He was not afraid to

70 Cf. Meriol Trevor and Léonie Caldecott, *John Henry Newman* (London, 2001), p. 13. **71** A contemporary of Newman at Oxford who subsequently converted, and in time became cardinal archbishop of Westminster. **72** Cf. Trevor, *The pillar of the cloud*, p. 201. **73** Cf. Ward, p. 317.

speak about sin and its punishment, and urged his hearers to live in the presence of God. Here was a new voice, presenting the truths of faith, not just as intellectual propositions, but as invitations to each one to respond to God's call to holiness in their personal lives. He reminded his listeners that the Paschal mystery was at the centre of Christianity and that the benefits of grace were applied through the sacraments. In his preaching he put across a deep sense of the Church as a visible society deriving from the apostolic succession.

His preaching is described by Matthew Arnold in a striking evocation of 'the charm of that spiritual apparition, gliding in the dim afternoon light through the aisles of St Mary's, rising into the pulpit, and then, in the most entrancing of voices, breaking the silence with words and thoughts which were a religious music – subtle, sweet, mournful'. The characteristic most often noted was the 'sweetness' of the 'musical' voice, low and soft but also 'piercing' and 'thrilling'.[74] The sermons stress the mystery of Christianity, but there is no mystery about the demands Newman makes on his listeners:

> We dwell in the full light of the Gospel, and the full grace of the sacraments. We ought to have the holiness of the Apostles. There is no reason except our own wilful corruption, that we are not by this time walking in the steps of St Paul or St John, and following them as they followed Christ.[75]

Or again, his recipe for daily sanctification:

> If we would aim at perfection, we must perform well the duties of the day. I do not know anything more difficult, more sobering, so strengthening than the constant aim to go through the ordinary day's work well.[76]

'VIA MEDIA'

Newman's objective with the Tractarian Movement was to recover the Catholic dimension of the Church of England, and this is clearly reflected in the doctrine of the *Tracts*. Also, as he read more of the Fathers, the more Catholic his doctrine became. If the Anglican Church was, as the Tractarians claimed, a branch of the Catholic Church, of which the Roman and the Orthodox were the other two branches, then the Church of England was not a Protestant Church. Newman's theological project was, then, to distinguish

74 Cf. Ker, *A biography*, p. 90. **75** Ibid., p. 93. **76** Ibid., p. 94.

Anglo-Catholicism from Protestantism. However, the Church of England saw itself as essentially a Protestant, state Church. But this, claimed Newman and his fellow Tractarians, was not her true self at all. However, the more Catholic they discovered the true self of their Church to be, the more imperative it became to show why the Church of England was justified in her separation from the Church of Rome.

For Newman the English Church was the *Via Media* between Luther and Rome, but it had fallen away from its principles and needed a second reformation. To clarify his ideas on the Church, Newman lectured on this subject in St Mary's from 1834 to 1836, which resulted in the volume *The prophetical office of the Church*, published in 1837. In 1834 he also published two *Tracts for the times* on the so-called *Via Media* to show that Anglicanism lay between Rome and the Protestantism of the Reformation. In doing this work Newman seemed to some to be spreading the teachings of the Church of Rome and was accused of popery. In view of the fact that he still considered Roman Catholicism as the antichrist, the accusation appeared to him to be quite gratuitous. Newman was surprised at the growth of the Tractarian Movement throughout England, and at the influence which increasingly accrued to his name. The *Tracts* were now selling at a rate of 60,000 copies a year.[77]

Through his lectures, his preaching, his publications, and the example of his personal life he induced many people to embark on real spiritual lives. He proposed Christian truths not like a theologian in a lecture hall, but as a pastor who wanted his hearers and readers to build their spiritual lives on a complete doctrine drawn from the New Testament and the Fathers of the Church. The ongoing publication of the volumes of the *Parochial and plain sermons* continued to be read eagerly, running into several editions. The Gospel idea of holiness, which Newman put before people, challenged and attracted.

Newman also became involved in the Tractarian project for a library of the Fathers, translating three volumes of the works of St Athanasius. In 1843 he published his *Sermons preached before the university of Oxford*, in which he examined the relationship between faith and reason, a topic which preoccupied him since his first conversion. Well before the Oxford Movement got under way, Newman was fully conscious that in taking his stand on the full implications of revelation his real battle was with liberalism in religion.

In 1839,while studying the Monophysite heresy of the fifth century, Newman came to realize that the *Via Media* which he proposed was no longer tenable:

> My stronghold was Antiquity; now here, in the middle of the fifth century, I found, as it seemed to me, Christendom of the sixteenth and

77 Cf. Ward, p. 334.

> nineteenth centuries reflected. I saw my face in that mirror, and I was a Monophysite. The church of the *Via Media* was in the position of the Oriental communion, Rome was where she now is; and the Protestants were the Eutychians.[78]

He saw that the Church of Rome occupied the same position in the fifth as in the nineteenth century and that the Protestants were the equivalent of the Monophysites. If he accepted the Council of Chalcedon (which condemned the Monophysites in 450), he felt he had little reason for not accepting the claims of Rome.

A few months later Newman received another shock. His attention had been drawn to an article on the Donatist schism and its relevance to Anglicanism. At first the intellectual force of the analogy did not impress Newman, the two situations seemed so different.

> But my friend pointed out the palmary words of St Augustine. 'Securus judicat orbis terrarum'[79] … they were words which went beyond the occasion of the Donatists: they applied to that of the Monophysites … They decided ecclesiastical questions on a simpler rule than that of Antiquity; nay, St Augustine was one of the prime oracles of Antiquity; here then Antiquity was deciding against itself. What a light was hereby thrown upon every controversy in the Church![80]

These words, which sounded so loudly in Newman's ears, stimulated a series of intellectual reflections, but they also cast a new light on Church history, placing new problems in a new perspective:

> Who can account for the impressions which are made on him? For a mere sentence, the words of St Augustine, struck me with a power which I never had felt from any words before. To take a familiar instance, they were like the 'Turn again Whittington' of the chime; or, to take a more serious one, they are like the 'Tolle, lege, – Tolle, lege,'[81] of the child, which converted St Augustine himself. 'Securus judicat orbis terrarum!' By these great words of the ancient Father, interpreting and summing up the long and varied course of ecclesiastical history, the theory of the *Via Media* was absolutely pulverized.[82]

It was, Newman said, the study of history that opened his eyes to the identity of the Church of the Fathers with the Roman Catholic Church. The histori-

78 *Apologia*, p. 114. 79 Newman's own translation was: 'The universal Church is in its judgements secure of truth.' 80 *Apologia*, p. 116. 81 Translation: 'Take and read'. 82 *Apologia*, p. 117.

cal analogy struck him with tremendous force. Thus his comment, 'to be deep in history is to cease to be a Protestant'.[83]

'TRACT 90'

The year 1841 had still another blow in store for Newman as the vindicator of the Catholic character of Anglicanism. Parliament, with the connivance of the archbishop of Canterbury, voted for the setting up of a bishopric in Jerusalem that was also to be a bishopric for the Lutheran church of Prussia, thus admitting them to communion with the Church of England. For Newman this was collusion with heresy – he protested formally but to no avail. The incident of the Jerusalem bishopric made a mockery of Newman's efforts for the previous eight years to show that the Church of England was a genuine branch of the Catholic Church.

However, the Tractarian movement provoked hostility from the establishment. The inevitable clash came with the publication in 1841 of *Tract* 90, written by Newman, which gives a Catholic interpretation to the *Thirty-nine articles*. This he judged to be essential if the Church of England was to be part of the Catholic Church. The *Thirty-nine articles* are a set of formulae drawn up in the sixteenth century to which undergraduates as well as clergymen had to subscribe. Newman had no difficulty signing them – the articles were the expression of the faith of the Church of England. They were, however, ambiguous, and, in places, self-contradictory, and had historically been intended to be ambiguous because they had been drawn up to win both Lutherans and Calvinists. If they had one fundamental principle, it was that of royal as against papal supremacy. Generally the articles were assumed to be purely Protestant.[84]

The reaction to *Tract* 90 was immediate and far-reaching. Newman was condemned by Oxford university for trying to reconcile the Articles with 'Roman Catholic Error'. His 'Catholic' interpretation came as a severe shock because the Articles had long been regarded as the bulwark of Protestantism. London newspapers proclaimed that popery had been unmasked at Oxford – this was the beginning of the legend of Newman as a dissimulating, secret papist. In obedience to the bishop of Oxford, Newman ceased publishing the *Tracts*. He was censured by most of the bishops of the Church of England.

He decided to retire to Littlemore,[85] a village just outside Oxford, to avoid being a leader of a party opposed to the bishops. He wanted to think out the

83 Newman, *Essay on the development of Christian doctrine*, p. 7. **84** Cf. Ward, p. 366. **85** Littlemore was part of the parish of St Mary's.

problems he faced in an atmosphere of prayer and peace. Near the church which he had built at Littlemore he took over a row of stables converted into rooms and he made one into an oratory. A larger room accommodated his patristic library which was to give him such solace over the next few years. As part of his charge of St Mary's, from 1836 Newman began to give more time to Littlemore, and started a school for the poorer children of the village. It is here that we see Newman's pastoral side coming to the fore. He personally taught the children their catechism, and how to sing the psalms. He kept a rigorous Lent each year, with severe fasting. He read the daily office of the Roman breviary.

The process of moving from the Church of England to the Catholic Church was painful for Newman, as his conscience seemed to be dragging him away from what he saw as his life's work, and away from his oldest friends towards the Catholic Church, which in England had long been suppressed under penal laws, and consequently was little known, few in numbers, and with few educational opportunities.

CONVERSION

Newman wrote *Tract* 90 to prevent Anglicans going over to Rome, and it was not until it was decisively rejected by the Church of England bishops that the conversions began. He himself resisted the suggestions and premonitions that kept coming to mind that Roman claims might be well founded. Yet he could say in the *Apologia*, 'From the end of 1841 I was on my deathbed, as regards my membership of the Anglican Church, though at the time I became aware of it only by degrees.'[86] During this period Newman received many letters accusing him of being a papist in disguise, and telling him that the decent thing would be for him to be reconciled with Rome. Yet at a time when many assumed that he was on the point of joining the Catholic Church, he was in fact still trying to hold others back. He went on doing so until near the end of 1843.[87]

Newman, by reading the books Dr Russell sent him from Maynooth, realized that he had made unfair and untrue attacks on Rome, relying on the views of the Anglican divines. In 1843 he made a formal retraction of these attacks against Rome.[88] When some of the young men living with him in Littlemore started going over to Rome, he resigned from St Mary's in September 1843. By then he had become convinced that the Roman Catholic communion was the Church of the Apostles. He preached his last sermon as an Anglican –*The parting of friends* – that same year.

86 *Apologia*, p. 147. **87** Cf. Ward, p. 396. **88** Cf. Trevor, *The pillar of the cloud*, p. 286.

For Newman, his conversion process was concerned with one fundamental issue – the identification of the Church of Christ. His upbringing and early impressions created in him a strong aversion to Rome. He was not attracted to her by what he knew of her at the outset. It was the testimony of the early Fathers which eventually brought him to accept the claims of Rome. He wrote to Manning that he had resigned from St Mary's because he was convinced that the Church of Rome was the Catholic Church, and that the Church of England was not part of the Catholic Church because it was not in communion with Rome, and that he could not honestly be a teacher in it any longer.[89] Yet he did not make his submission to Rome for another two years. He continued to live at Littlemore, wrestling with the growing conviction that it was his duty to join the Roman Church.

Links with Oxford were being broken. His oldest friend, John William Boden, died on 15 September 1844, and he tells us that he 'sobbed bitterly over his coffin to think that he had left me still in the dark as to what the way of truth was, and what I ought to do in order to please God and do his will.'[90] There were extremely kind letters from Manning, Gladstone and others encouraging him to stay. The one thing that weighed heavily on Newman's mind during these last months was his awareness of the pain to which he was putting others – family, friends, and well-wishers. Besides the pain of unsettling people, he felt the loss he was undergoing in the good opinion of his friends. In a letter to his sister Jemima he writes (24 November 1844):

> A clear conviction of the substantial identity of Christianity and the Roman system has now been on my mind for a full three years. It is more than five years since the conviction first came to me, though I struggled against it and overcame it. I believe all my feelings and wishes are against change. I have nothing to draw me elsewhere. I hardly ever was at a Roman service, even abroad – I know no Roman Catholics. I have no sympathy with them as a party. I am giving up everything. I am not conscious of any resentment, disgust, or the like, to repel me from my present position; and I have no dreams whatsoever, far from it, of what I could do in another position. Far from it – I seem to be throwing myself away.[91]

Suspicion of his motives, suspicion of Rome, appeals to his tenderness for his friends – these were the burdens he had to carry in his last months before his reception.

89 Cf. ibid., p. 426. **90** Ibid., pp 429–30. **91** Ibid., pp 434–5.

One of the questions Newman asked himself while at Littlemore was, how could he be certain that the conviction he now had about the Roman Catholic Church might not change in the future? It was to provide an answer to this question that he started to write his *Essay on the development of Christian doctrine* in early 1845. The writing of this major work took only nine months, although he had been collecting material for it for some years. In the *Essay* Newman first states what are authentic doctrinal developments. He then applies seven tests to be able to distinguish true developments from corruptions. Through writing the *Essay* Newman's mind became at peace and there only remained the anguish of heart as he bade farewell to his friends, his family, and the university.

In writing the *Essay*, Newman concluded that, although there had been some corruption in practice and doctrinal exaggerations, the changes in doctrine had been the result of the Church's meditation on the original revelation of Christ, and the Church in all ages had been guided by the Holy Spirit, as promised by Christ. He says that the Christianity of history is not Protestantism. He speaks of the Anglican view of history as an attempt to 'fit the Thirty-Nine Articles on the fervid Tertullian.'[92]

Before he finished the *Essay*, Newman decided that the time had come to make his submission to Rome – his difficulties had cleared away. On 9 October 1845 he was received into the Catholic Church by the Italian Passionist, Fr Dominic Barberi, after he had made a general confession. The evening before he had written to his closest friends to advise them that he would be taking the definitive step the following day. What comes across clearly from Newman's letters after his reception is the joy he felt at being able to love our Lady freely, to invoke her and the saints. After Newman's conversion several hundred university men followed his example, including many clergy of the Church of England.

LIFE AS A CATHOLIC

Newman left Littlemore in February 1846 to take up residence at Maryvale near Oscott College, Birmingham. There he gathered around him some of the converts who had lived with him at Littlemore. In September he left for Rome, with his closest colleague Ambrose St John, to study for the priesthood at the College of Propaganda. When he arrived in Rome he was surprised to find that theology was taught from second rate manuals; not only was St Augustine unknown, but even St Thomas Aquinas was not read.[93]

92 Ward, p. 445. **93** Cf. Trevor, *The pillar of the cloud*, p. 402.

Eventually Newman, after much thought and prayer, decided that membership of the Oratory of St Philip Neri would best suit his mission which he saw before him in England. His little band of followers from Littlemore would constitute a group of secular priests who would live in the same house without vows, but bonded together by a refined charity. Each would have his own work which he would pursue through personal influence. Pius IX gave Newman authority to set up the Oratory in England and allowed him adapt St Philip's rule for that purpose.

Newman was ordained priest on 30 May 1847 and was back in Maryvale for New Year's Day 1848. The first house of the Oratory was set up in Maryvale a month later. Early in 1849 the Oratory was moved to the centre of Birmingham where a church was established with a parish and schools. Here, almost at once, poor factory children came crowding in every evening. For the next few years Newman lived there, working extremely hard, and so short of money that he couldn't afford to buy a new pair of shoes. He devoted himself to pastoral work among the poor and the immigrant Irish, most of them poorly instructed in the faith. His first sermons preached there were published under the title, *Discourses to mixed congregations*.

During the summer of 1850 Newman gave a series of lectures entitled *Certain difficulties felt by Anglicans in submitting to the Catholic Church*. He felt strongly that he had a duty to win over those who had been part of the Oxford Movement, and he spoke directly to them through these lectures. The re-establishment of the Catholic hierarchy in England in 1850 aroused a lot of anti-Catholic feeling among Protestants. In response Newman gave a series of lectures under the title, *The present position of Catholics in England*, which was an exposé of the fanatical Protestant view of the Catholic Church, a view that resulted in many injustices for Catholics.

NEWMAN AND CONVERTS

In the light of the influence he exerted in the Anglican church, and in view of the prominence which he acquired as a Roman Catholic for the latter half of his life, there is no doubt that Newman is one of the most prominent converts of modern times.

Letters had a particular importance for Newman: 'The true life of a man is in his letters,' he said.[94] It is estimated he wrote about 60,000 letters during his lifetime, about half of which are extant and published in the thirty-one volumes of *The Letters and diaries of John Henry Newman*. What is striking about

94 Stanley L. Jaki, *Newman to converts:an existential ecclesiology* (Pinckney, MN, 2001), p. 6.

these volumes is the number of letters they contain written to prospective converts. He also dealt with conversion in several of his books – *Loss and gain*, the *Apologia*, *Difficulties of Anglicans*. Most of Newman's letters to prospective converts date from the first ten years of his life as a Catholic (1845–55). When we consider how occupied Newman was during this period with other time-consuming matters, we begin to realize something of the zeal he had to win new converts. He was in Rome for a year and a half to prepare for the priesthood, and then on his return he set up two houses of the Oratory of St Philip Neri. He had to endure the Achilli trial and launch the Catholic University of Dublin. But Newman used all these involvements to make converts out of Anglo-Catholics and, at a more general level, to vindicate conversion to Rome. In the midst of all these concerns he sought out prospective converts and kept in touch with them, at least by letter.

This zeal for converts was to remain with him to the end of his life. The letters continued as before, but they grew shorter as he grew older because of the increasing pain such writing caused in his fingers. In particular Newman was zealous to convert his close colleagues of the Tractarian or Oxford Movement who came under his influence. He felt a particular urgency about their conversion. In his opinion the Tractarians had become so imbued with Catholic principles that they could not easily claim invincible ignorance as to the identity of the One True Church. He felt that not only had they a grave obligation to move towards Rome, but that he had a grave responsibility to encourage them along this path so that they might save their souls. For him belonging to the True Church was a matter of eternal life or death. As a Catholic he always emphasized this point by constantly calling prospective converts' attention to the Roman Church as the 'One True Fold'.

As long as Newman remained in the Anglican Church he was a guiding star for those who had doubts about the validity of Anglo-Catholicism as a branch of the One True Church. However, as soon as they saw that Newman no longer found this position tenable, they too started to think about conversion. By December 1845, three months after Newman's conversion, more that fifty clergy of the Anglican church had embraced the Roman Church, along with many more lay people.

Newman converted because he saw that the Catholic Church was the One True Fold, and realized that he could not save his soul unless he followed up on that conviction. In his letters to converts he constantly insists that Catholicism and Anglicanism are two very different religions. Through his letters we see his zeal to win souls for Christ's Church, but especially those who were close to it intellectually but far from it psychologically. One of the main difficulties Newman faced was in making Anglo-Catholics understand that the grandeur of the true Church did not need the support of a nation's cultural and political greatness, much less to be identified with it. It is in his letters that Newman asserts most forcibly that there is but One True Fold and that it is the duty of all to join it if they wish to save their souls.

Newman's *Essay on the development of Christian doctrine* contains the fully-fledged rationale of why he converted to Rome. The twelve lectures that he delivered in London in 1850, that were published under the title *Difficulties of Anglicans*, are a direct call to Anglo-Catholics to convert. The other set of lectures he delivered at Birmingham a year later, *The present position of Catholics in England*, reflects on every page the perspective of a convert so as to be of greatest use to those thinking about conversion. The *Apologia* is not only a vindication of his own conversion but a powerful invitation to Anglo-Catholics to convert. His reiterated use of the phrase 'the One True Fold' was a cogent summary of his repeated appeals to his correspondents to convert.

Newman's letters are the core of his unremitting apostolic zeal to bring souls into the Church of Christ. This zeal was supported by his constant prayer for light for individuals. For Newman the Roman Church was the Church of the Fathers because the perennial newness of the Church was due to the living tradition which it carried forward and out of which it emerged. This was the reality which constantly nourished Newman's conviction about the Church.

Different events in Newman's life, or in the life of the Church, prompted people to write to him for guidance as they made their way towards the truth. Apart from the great event of his own conversion, other such events included the publication of the *Apologia* in 1864 and the *Grammar of assent* in 1870. Similarly his *Letter to the duke of Norfolk* on the Pope's infallibility (1875) and his being made a cardinal (1879) prompted many letters from prospective converts.

For Newman the great reality of his life was the Church as manifested by its notes of One, Holy, Catholic and Apostolic. Everything he did after his own conversion in 1845 was to help people become more aware of this reality, to become part of it, and thus achieve salvation. The energy which Newman had previously put into the Catholic 'reform' of the Church of England he now channelled into showing Anglo-Catholics that the Roman Church was the true Church. Newman never felt ashamed about reminding those he had known from his Tractarian days of the sacramental nature of the Church whose destiny it was to bring about the salvation of souls.

On the first anniversary of his conversion Newman wrote to one of his correspondents:

> This day I have been a year in the Catholic Church – and every day I bless him who led me into it more and more. I have come from darkness into light, and cannot look back on my former state without the

> dreary feeling which one has on looking back on a wearisome miserable journey.[95]

Newman said much the same to all those who received his guidance in implementing the steps of their conversion. In dealing with the queries of converts, he adopts an essentially supernatural approach. He is uncompromising about the sacrifices they may have to endure to follow their consciences. They should be ready to suffer separation from family and friends, loss of employment or social position as a sharing in Christ's sufferings. In his letters Newman confides that he has experienced the same anxieties and suffered similar loses.

Throughout his correspondence Newman proclaims that the Catholic Church is a 'divine work'. To one correspondent he writes: 'I am now so convinced of the truth and divinity of the Catholic Church, that I am pained about persons who are external to it'. This is the kernel of his position. As he puts it in one letter, he is 'quite ready to go into the question of the exclusive divinity of the Roman Catholic Church, which is the basis of argument in my view of the controversy'. The point at issue is whether the Church Christ established continues in the Catholic Church.

For Newman the Church clearly possesses the four 'Notes' of the Creed – One, Holy, Catholic, and Apostolic. To one correspondent he confides that what prompted him to convert was the realization that the Catholic Church of his day did not differ from the Apostles' Church anymore than a photo of a man at forty differs from his photo at twenty – 'you know it is the same man'. In another letter he writes, 'I was converted by the manifest and intimate identity of the modern RC church with the ante-Nicean and Nicean Church'.

Newman, while he is not blind to the tares which have grown up among the wheat in the Church's history, affirms the broad view of the Church's unique contribution to civilization: 'Again, what Church but ours, in its principles, its structure, its large teachings, its consistence, its mode of acting, its vigour, its high courage, its grandeur in history, its saints, fulfils that idea of a "pillar and ground of the truth" which the Apostle makes the definition of the Bride of the Lamb?'

Newman often returns to the idea of there being a 'moment of grace' to which we must respond with 'prompt obedience'. What caused many of his converts to delay their decision was the desire for more certainty about controversial issues such as indulgences or papal infallibility. In his replies Newman says that whoever waits for utter certainty before acting waits in vain, because the Church's doctrines can never be fully proven by reason. They can

95 Jaki, p. 49.

only be perceived as excellent to a point. The basic question to be answered by the prospective convert is 'have I reason enough' to place my faith in the Church? The convert still has to act in the dark to some extent when he enters the One True Fold. His experience is that it is only after conversion that one receives full confidence in the doctrinal teaching of the Church, because one will then have the true gift of faith. Conversion is then to trust the word of Christ heard in the Church: 'is not our Lord worthy to be believed?'

In 1878 Newman heard that E.B. Pusey was seriously ill. He was one of those who had worked very closely with Newman during the Oxford Movement, but who had not converted. He wrote to a close friend of Pusey's:

> If his state admits of it, I should so very much wish to say to my dearest friend Pusey, whom I have loved and admired for over fifty years, that the Catholic Roman Church solemnly lays claim to him as her child, and to ask him in God's sight whether he does not acknowledge her right to do so.[96]

This is a good example of how clearly Newman confronted potential converts with their responsibilities.

UNIVERSITY IN DUBLIN

In 1851 Newman was invited by the Irish bishops to advise them on the setting up of a Catholic university in Dublin. He had many other responsibilities at this time but was eventually persuaded to come to Dublin to work on this unique educational project. Newman, looking to the future, saw it as the English-speaking university for the Catholic world which would promote an alternative to the Protestant Trinity College. In 1851 Cardinal Cullen, archbishop of Dublin, called twice to Birmingham to discuss the project with him, inviting Newman to become rector. When he first visited Dublin later in the year, Newman realized the magnitude of the task that lay ahead of him. The setting up of a Catholic university has to be seen against the background of the Queen's colleges established by the British government in Belfast, Cork, and Galway in 1847, which were completely undenominational. Rome condemned these colleges on account of their 'grievous and inherent dangers', and urged the bishops to establish a Catholic university.[97]

Newman was also asked by Cullen to give a series of public lectures on university education, the first of which was delivered on 10 May 1852, in the

96 Ker, *A biography*, p. 712. **97** Fergal McGrath SJ, *Newman in Dublin* (Dublin, 1969), p. 6.

Exhibition Rooms of the Rotunda in Dublin. After delivering five lectures, Newman returned to Birmingham for the Achilli trial (see below). He returned again to Ireland at the end of July to work on the remaining lectures. These were published in February 1853 under the title: *Discourses on the scope and nature of university education, addressed to the Catholics of Dublin*. This volume, which was to become the first half of the classic, *The idea of a university*, was considered by Newman to be one of the best of his works.[98] For Newman religion and knowledge were inextricably linked and this was why he made the claim: 'If the Catholic faith is true, a university cannot exist externally to the Catholic pale, for it cannot teach universal knowledge if it does not teach Catholic theology.'[99]

Newman found that the university project was a long time taking shape – two years had passed since Archbishop Cullen had first spoken to him about it, and little had happened. In fact he found Cullen a difficult man to deal with. He never answered Newman's letters, and to Newman they seemed at times to be working at cross-purposes. Important decisions were taken in relation to the university – for example, the acquisition of the site for the new campus – without Newman's knowledge. On the other hand Cullen was suspicious of Newman's concept of a university which provided a liberal education. Newman wanted a significant lay involvement on the board of management and in the different teaching posts. What effectively Cullen wanted was a seminary for lay people, which would be under the control of the bishops. Consequently it was inevitable that there would be tensions in bringing the project to birth.

Cardinal Wiseman, archbishop of Westminster, informed Newman of the proposal to appoint him a titular bishop to give him extra authority in his role as rector of the university. Cullen initially agreed with the proposal, but subsequently prevented the promotion for Newman because he considered it premature. In any event the papal brief setting up the university arrived in April 1854.

In May 1854 the bishops met in synod to approve the university statutes and to establish the university with five faculties: theology, law, medicine, philosophy, and letters. Newman was appointed rector, and solemnly installed in the Pro-cathedral on Whit Sunday, 3 June, after High Mass. He had now to find suitable staff to start the university. A number of these came from England as it was not possible to identify suitable candidates in Ireland for all the vacancies.

Newman was keen to have a church in Dublin for the university community and so requested John Hungerford Pollen, professor of Fine Arts at the

98 Cf. Ker, *A biography*, p. 382. **99** John Henry Newman, *The idea of a university*, ed. I. Ker (Oxford, 1976), p. 371.

university, to design it in the style of the early Roman basilicas. It was built in Stephen's Green on a piece of land Newman had acquired and financed out of the money left over from the Achilli trust fund for his legal expenses. The architect used a great variety of Irish marble in the decoration of the church, which was opened in remarkably short time on 1 May 1856.

During his second year as rector, the school of medicine was opened and received recognition from the various professional bodies in Ireland, Scotland and England, a development which Newman regarded as one of the crowning achievements of the university. At the June 1856 synod of the Irish bishops, with Newman himself in attendance, their lordships re-appointed Newman as rector for another three years. They had difficulty with the proposal to appoint laymen to the financial committee and with the degree of freedom which students were allowed.

In March 1857 Newman wrote to the bishops telling them of his proposed retirement. The reasons he gave were the fatigue arising from his frequent journeying between Birmingham and Dublin (he reckoned he had done all of fifty-six crossings of the Irish Sea for the university project), the need for a more active rector, and his responsibility to the Birmingham Oratory. Some of the bishops replied warmly, expressing their gratitude for all he had done for the university.

Cullen called to see Newman when he was back in Dublin at the beginning of the 1857–8 academic year and did everything possible to try to persuade him to stay for another three years. But Newman was determined that he was not for turning. Eventually a compromise was agreed whereby Newman would remain on as rector for a year, a vice-rector would be appointed to run the university, and Newman would come to Dublin but not for more than nine weeks a year. However, when he did not get confirmation of the arrangement for non-residence he returned to Birmingham. On 28 October 1858 Newman set out for Dublin for the last time. In the first days of November he gave three lectures which became part of the *Idea of a university*. On the evening of 4 November he returned to Birmingham. On 12 November he sent his formal resignation.

Newman and Cullen had their differences, but they had a great respect for each other. When in 1867 doubt was cast in Rome on some of Newman's writings, it was Cardinal Cullen's championship which established their orthodoxy. On Cullen's death in 1878, Newman wrote to Dr Russell, president of Maynooth: 'We were different men, but I always loved him and felt grateful to him – and highly reverenced him for his works' sake.'[1]

Many will claim that Newman's seven-year involvement with the Catholic University of Ireland would not have been wasted if it had only given to the

1 Cf. McGrath, p. 31.

English language one of its acknowledged classics – the *Discourses*, now known as *The idea of a university*. But he accomplished much more besides. He set up a university based on far-seeing principles, as the rector and senate of the Catholic University assured him in 1879 on his elevation to the cardinalate:

> We have always looked back with gratitude and admiration to your labours during the time you held office as first rector of this university, and we feel assured that the plan for higher education and the system of university government which you initiated and organized, will, centuries hence, be studied by all who may have to legislate for Catholic education, as among the most precious of the documents which they shall possess to inform and guide them.[2]

THE ACHILLI LEGAL CASE

After the restoration of the Catholic hierarchy in England in 1850, there were angry meetings of protest, mob attacks on convents, and pelting of suspected priests with mud and stones. Disturbances continued into 1851, and in the summer of that year Newman gave a series of lectures in Birmingham on *The present position of Catholics in England*, which was intended to calm the 'no-popery' passions. In the course of the lectures Newman made a serious attack on an ex-priest, the Italian Giacinto Achilli, who was touring the country courtesy of the Evangelical Alliance, posing as a victim of the Roman inquisition for conscience sake, inflaming passions with his tall tales of Catholic torture and clerical vice.

Cardinal Wiseman had exposed Achilli's real background in the *Dublin Review*, saying he had appeared in court in Rome for repeated seduction of young women, that he had been expelled from the Dominican order, and sentenced to detention in a monastery – from which he had escaped and turned Protestant. Newman had taken legal advice on whether he could safely use the material in Wiseman's indictment. He was advised that he could do so without much risk. However, the Evangelical Alliance persuaded Achilli to bring a libel case against Newman. Because Wiseman's documentary evidence was mislaid, Newman had to send two of the Oratorian priests to Italy to gather documents and evidence. In an affidavit Achilli denied on oath all the charges made against him. This allowed Achilli to institute criminal proceedings rather than a civil action against Newman's publishers, which forced Newman to accept personal responsibility for the alleged libel.[3]

2 Ibid., pp 31–2. **3** Cf. Ker, *A biography*, pp 372–7.

In the meantime Wiseman had been dilatory about obtaining alternative documents from Italy and the two Oratorians failed to come up with the evidence needed in time. The court refused to give Newman an extension of time to collect evidence and committed him to stand trial on a criminal charge. The anti-Catholic attitude of the court was obvious, but Newman knew that he had the whole Catholic body on his side. His lawyers advised him not to fight the case because of the difficulty of getting justice at this time of 'papal aggression', with the hope of avoiding punishment and legal expenses; otherwise there was the danger of a year's imprisonment. However, Newman was prepared to go to prison because he felt that failure to fight the case would 'betray a great Catholic interest'. He believed that in taking on Achilli he was taking on the devil, because since his conversion he had become the centre of attack for those who hated and despised what they felt he stood for, and who wanted to crush him.

The Achilli trial began on 21 and ended on 24 June 1852 when the jury gave their verdict that Newman had failed to prove his charges. Newman was not too put out by the verdict – he had lost legally but had won morally. A prejudiced jury refused to be moved by numerous testimonies in favour of Newman. Sentence was postponed until November. He was fined £100 with jail until it was paid. Newman received a severe lecture from the Protestant judge on his moral deterioration since his 'perversion to Rome'! Even *The Times*, no lover of papists, was shocked at the judge's bias. Such a trial, it said, would give substance to Catholic complaints that that they could not get justice in their own country. Although the Achilli trial reduced Newman's reputation among Protestants (so shocking to refer to seductions in a public lecture!), it raised it among Catholics, who regarded him as their champion. They subscribed to a fund for his expenses and he was cheered loudly 'by two hundred Paddies' as he left court. But it had been a gruelling experience.[4]

At this time Newman had been asked to preach at the first synod of the restored Catholic hierarchy in 1852. He called his sermon the 'Second Spring'. Most of the bishops and clergy present were in tears when he finished.

'APOLOGIA PRO VITA SUA'

In early 1864, Charles Kingsley, in a review of J.A. Froude's anti-Catholic *History of England*, gratuitously introduced Newman's name: 'Truth for its own sake, has never been a virtue with the Roman clergy. Fr Newman informs us that it need not, and on the whole, ought not to be.'[5] Kingsley was already a

4 Cf. Trevor, *The pillar of the cloud*, p. 629. 5 Trevor, *Newman: light in winter*, p. 314.

well-known novelist as well as being professor of modern history at Cambridge university.

After an initial exchange between the two, when Newman saw that Kingsley did not make a complete retraction of the charge of untruthfulness, he decided the time had come to vindicate his honesty and sincerity. The charge of untruthfulness was accepted by many in England who thought that, while still an Anglican, Newman had led a secret Catholic movement to undermine the Church of England. This imputation had lain on him for twenty years, and now he had an opportunity to remove it. 'I am bound now as a duty to myself, to the Catholic cause, to the Catholic priesthood, to give an account of myself without any delay, when I am so rudely and circumstantially charged with untruthfulness. I accept the challenge; I shall do my best to meet it, and I shall be content when I have done so.'[6] Newman was vindicating his personal honour and truthfulness in the years preceding his entry into the Church of Rome, but he was also defending the Catholic priesthood from Kingsley's violent accusations. The *Apologia pro vita sua* was an opportunity for him to vindicate his whole career before the English public from the accusation of insincerity.

Newman's approach to his self-defence was to tell the history of his religious opinions rather than developing an argument about the nature of truth. In telling his own story Newman was in a sense telling the religious history of England in its contemporary setting. 'Because it was cast in the form of history and not of argument, even the most hostile were ready to read it, if only to find further material for their hostility, or from mere curiosity.'[7]

The *Apologia* is by general agreement one of the great spiritual biographies of Christian history. Newman wrote it at speed during April and May of 1864, often putting in as many as sixteen hours a day to meet the weekly deadline for its initial publication in pamphlet form. He frequently had to rewrite sections several times to put things exactly right. Thus he completed his greatest literary and spiritual masterpiece in nine weeks. In it he used all his power of literary brilliance to engage public interest, establishing the strength and sincerity of his convictions which had led him into the Catholic Church. It was an astonishing feat.

Newman found that writing the *Apologia* was one of the most difficult things he had ever done. He was by nature reserved, especially in relation to the private details of his own spiritual life. Consequently, he found it very painful to have to reveal the intimacies of his soul in public in an autobiographical vein. The research and composition of the *Apologia* brought back vivid memories of matters which had caused him a lot of pain and so he was often in tears while he was writing.

6 *Apologia*, p. xvii. 7 Meriol Trevor, *Newman: light in winter*, p. 333.

The appearance of the *Apologia* was a triumph for Newman and the cause of truth. Public opinion which had either ignored or remained hostile to Newman since his conversion to Catholicism, now began to change in his favour. Many Anglicans renewed their friendship with him after holding aloof for twenty years. There was a wave of '*Apologia* converts', some of whom Newman received himself. Catholics regarded him once more as their champion and the vindicator of their clergy. Catholic priests rallied to his support and several addresses of congratulation signed by them came in gratitude for defending their sincerity along with his own. It won for Newman the heart of the country which he never subsequently lost. In addition to defending the Catholic Church against calumny, Newman in his *Apologia* was also vindicating the right of conversion to it of one 'who has given up much that he loved and prized and could have retained, but that he loved honesty better than name, and Truth better than dear friends.'[8]

The importance of the *Apologia* was not just its immediate and short-term purpose which it brilliantly achieved. Like St Augustine's *Confessions*, it has proved to be one of the great and enduring books, a classic of spiritual autobiography. From a literary point of view it is quite different from his other works of controversy. The emphasis is on facts and documentation rather than on polemical rhetoric. In the last section on the 'Present position of my mind since 1845', Newman intimates that he is perfectly happy in the Catholic Church, 'I never have had one doubt', he says: this is by way of response to those who were claiming that he had become disillusioned with the Catholic Church. However, he does not deny that the Christian Creed is beset with intellectual difficulties. But he immediately points out : 'Ten thousand difficulties do not make one doubt'.[9]

NEWMAN AND PAPAL INFALLIBILITY

During the 1860s the campaign for declaring papal infallibility in matters of faith and morals was aggressively pressed in English ultramontane circles. Manning was backed up by another Oxford convert, W.G. Ward, editor of the *Dublin Review*, where his intemperate dismissal of all other views but his own exaggerated infallibilism irritated Newman among many others. He was concerned that such extremism would have a disastrous effect on potential converts as well as on recent converts. His friends kept writing to beg him to 'speak out', especially when a Council of the Church was called which was to open in 1869. Papal infallibility was not at first on the agenda, but subsequently became a major issue for the First Vatican Council.

8 Ker, *A biography*, p. 548. **9** *Apologia*, pp 238–9.

Newman told one bewildered lady, who had felt drawn to Catholicism, that there had been a gradual development in the Church's understanding of the revelation made known to the Apostles. If the infallibility of the Pope were defined, then there would be reasons for its being done now rather than at another time: 'for instance, in the present state of the world, the Catholic body may require to be like an army in the field, under strict and immediate discipline'. True, he himself could see more reasons against a definition than for one, but if it were passed he would accept as an article of faith what at the moment he only held as a theological opinion.[10]

Newman did not see his way to making a public intervention himself, since he was not in a position of authority. However, his views did come out when a private letter he wrote to Bishop Ullathorne in Rome during the Council somehow became public. In it he refers to 'an aggressive and insolent faction' which was creating difficulties for everybody else. He would continue to pray that there would be no definition, but he would accept it if one was passed. However, although the letter became public knowledge, Newman was happy that his position became known before the vote rather than after it.[11] When in fact he saw the text of the proposal which had been passed by the Council, he was pleased with its moderation, although opposition to defining the dogma had led to eighty bishops leaving the Council before the vote was taken.

In an attack on papal infallibility Gladstone published a pamphlet in 1874 in which he said that no one could now become a convert to the Catholic Church 'without renouncing his moral and mental freedom, and placing his civil loyalty and duty at the mercy of another.'[12] The pamphlet became a best-seller, and Newman saw immediately that it would have to be answered. It revived all the old 'no-popery' bigotry, and an avalanche of letters descended on Newman calling on him to respond. He felt he could now write on infallibility, because he would be defending Catholics against the charge of disloyalty, by putting forward the moderate interpretation of the 'new' dogma in the context of the historical development of the doctrine of the Church.

It was the most strenuous work he had undertaken since the *Apologia*, and he wondered if his health would stand up to it. The pamphlet was to be in the form of a letter addressed to the leading Catholic layman, the young duke of Norfolk, who had been at the Oratory School. He finished it on 21 December after a month's continuous writing, and the 'pamphlet', which was actually 150 pages of close print, was published on 14 January 1875. In his exposition of papal infallibility Newman adopts a middle course between the ultramontanists who had hoped for a more comprehensive definition, and the 'inopportunists' or those who did not agree with the definition at all. He also dealt

10 Ker, ibid., p. 632. 11 Ibid., p. 652. 12 Kerr, p. 697.

with questions of religious and civil authority, all in his most telling and lucid style.

At the core of the *Letter to the duke of Norfolk* is the celebrated treatment of the sovereignty of conscience, which he discusses here in its relationship to legitimate ecclesiastical authority. He sees conscience as the law of God commanding obedience, and then gives us his famous definition:

> Conscience is the aboriginal Vicar of Christ, a prophet in its informations, a monarch in its peremptoriness, a priest in its blessings and anathemas, and, even though the eternal priesthood throughout the church could cease to be, in it the sacerdotal principle would remain and would have a sway.[13]

However, the dictate of conscience, in order to prevail against the voice of the Pope, must follow upon serious thought, prayer, and all available means of arriving at a right judgement on the matter in question. The onus of proof, then, lies on the individual conscience.

Newman's defence of papal infallibility was received with general enthusiasm by Catholics. At this stage the public had come to regard Newman as an English possession of which they were proud. Of all Newman's writings, except the *Apologia*, this was the most immediately successful. It completely reversed the public attitude. Misunderstandings were cleared up in every direction. The success of the *Letter* came as a surprise to Newman. He would have been very moved by the fact that extracts from it are quoted in the *Catechism of the Catholic Church* (1994).

BELATED RECOGNITION – NEWMAN CREATED CARDINAL

In December 1877 Newman received an invitation from the president of his old college in Oxford, Trinity, to become the college's first honorary fellow. He replied with a deep sense of gratitude and joy, saying that Trinity had always been 'in my habitual thoughts'. He asked for time to consult whether he could appropriately accept this honour. A few days later he wrote to Ullathorne who replied that it would be Newman who would be honouring the college, not the other way round. In his letter of acceptance to the president of Trinity, Newman said he had a lifelong affection for the place, and that he could not remember 'when he had been so much pleased.' It was another sign of the extraordinary change of feeling about Newman which had begun with the

13 Ibid., p. 688.

publication of the *Apologia*. At the end of February 1878 Newman spent a few nights at Oxford. He had lunch with the Fellows of Trinity and dinner with the president. He saw his old tutor and called on Pusey.[14]

In January 1879 Manning received a letter from the papal secretary of state asking him to find out how Newman would react to an invitation to become a cardinal. Manning sent the enquiry to Ullathorne, Newman's bishop, telling him that he had already forwarded to Rome a petition to this effect from the duke of Norfolk and other Catholic peers. Norfolk's objective was to obtain in this way the Holy See's confirmation of Newman's orthodoxy and loyalty. Leo XIII had just succeeded to the chair of Peter, but before that, as nuncio to Brussels, he had become familiar with the Oxford Movement. It was suggested that in fact the Pope had taken the initiative in promoting Newman.

Ullathorne strongly urged Newman to accept this exceptional favour. In his formal reply, Newman's only reservation was that he might be required to live in Rome as was customary for cardinals who were not diocesan bishops. However, when Manning forwarded Newman's reply to Rome, in his covering letter he incredibly interpreted it as a refusal. It took further correspondence between the duke of Norfolk, Rome and Manning to clarify that, of course, Newman would accept such a great honour, which was publicly announced in due course. The news caused a stream of congratulatory correspondence. Newman said he felt urged to accept, and gave his reasons to one correspondent for doing so:

> For 20 or 30 years ignorant or hot-headed Catholics had said almost that I was a heretic ... I knew and felt it was a miserable evil that the One True Apostolic Religion should be so slandered as to cause men to suppose that my portrait of it was not the true – and I knew that many would become Catholics, as they ought to be, if only I was pronounced by Authority to be a *good* Catholic. On the other hand, it had long riled me, that Protestants should condescendingly say that I was only half a Catholic, and too good to be what they were at Rome. I therefore felt myself constrained to accept.[15]

Newman set out for Rome in April 1879. He had chosen as his cardinal's motto, *Cor ad cor loquitur* (heart speaks to heart), which he had quoted from St Francis de Sales in *The idea of a university*.

On Sunday 27 April he had a long audience with Leo XIII who received him very affectionately. Newman arrived in Rome with a bad cold and at the beginning of May he retired to bed. He was, however, well enough on the 12th

14 Ibid., pp 710–12. **15** Ibid., pp 716–17

to receive from the secretary of state the *biglietto* informing him that at the consistory that morning the Pope had elevated him to the College of Cardinals. Newman's famous reply, called the *biglietto* speech, is an uncompromising attack on liberalism in religion:

> I rejoice to say, to one great mischief I have from the first opposed myself. For thirty, forty, fifty years I have resisted to the best of my powers the spirit of liberalism in religion. Never did Holy Church need champions against it more sorely than now when, alas! it is an error overspreading, as a snare, the whole earth ... Liberalism in religion is the doctrine that there is no positive truth in religion, but that one creed is as good as another, and this is the teaching that is gaining substance and force daily. It is inconsistent with any recognition of any religion, as *true*. It teaches that all are to be tolerated, for all are matters of opinion. Revealed religion is not a truth, but a sentiment and a taste; not an objective fact, not miraculous; and it is the right of each individual to make it say just what strikes his fancy ... As to Religion, it is a private luxury, which a man may have if he will; but which of course he must pay for, and which he must not obtrude upon others, or indulge in to their annoyance.[16]

The day after the *biglietto* speech Newman went to the Vatican to receive the cardinal's biretta from the Pope. Two days later there was the public consistory at which the cardinal's red hat was presented. Newman was deeply moved by the attentions of Leo XIII. He was the first cardinal appointed by him and the only one created at this particular consistory.

Newman arrived back at Birmingham in July to a great reception. During the weeks that followed he was presented with many congratulatory addresses. The duke of Norfolk hosted a number of celebratory dinners for him in London. Newman was concerned to see how he could use this unexpected position of authority to help the causes he believed in, and he made several contributions in writing to the question of the inspiration of Scripture and on his old subject of reason and faith in *The development of religious error*, published in 1885. Both these were in answer to attacks on Catholic teaching.

LAST YEARS

Newman spent the last decade of his life quietly at the Oratory in Birmingham. He now had the joy of seeing novices asking to join the Oratory,

16 Ibid., pp 720–1.

many of these former students of the Oratory school. However, from the latter half of 1886, his physical strength and his sight began to fail him. Nevertheless, despite the pain in his fingers, he still managed, to some extent, to keep up his vast correspondence. He said his last Mass at Christmas 1889. He died of pneumonia on 11 August 1890.

A crowd of 20,000 gathered to pay their respects as his funeral wended its way through Birmingham. He was praised and honoured by all the national newspapers which had once so bitterly attacked him. Cardinal Manning, who was to die only a few years later, was too frail to attend the funeral in Birmingham. But just a week later, in front of a huge crowd gathered from all over Britain and Europe, at a memorial service in Brompton Oratory, Manning gave a moving eulogy to the great churchman with whom he had sometimes differed:

> If any proof were needed of the immeasurable work he has wrought in England, the last week would be enough. Who could doubt that a great multitude of his personal friends in the first half of his life, and a still greater multitude of those who have been instructed, consoled and won to God by the unequalled beauty and irresistible persuasion of his writings – who could doubt that they, at such a time as this, would pour out the love and gratitude of their hearts? But that the public voice of England, political and religious, in all its diversities, should for once unite in love and veneration for a man who has broken through its sacred barriers and defied its religious prejudices, who could have believed it? He had committed the hitherto unpardonable sin in England. He had rejected the whole Tudor Settlement in religion. He had become Catholic as our fathers were. And yet for no one in our memory has such a heartfelt and loving veneration been poured out. Of this, one proof is enough. Someone has said, whether Rome canonizes him or not, he will be canonized in the thoughts of pious people of many creeds in England.[17]

DEVOTION TO OUR LADY

It is not surprising that the recent advance in the cause of beatification of John Henry Newman has generated interest in the spirituality of the great English cardinal.[18] While Newman's biographers have studied in detail many aspects of

17 Trevor and Caldecott, pp 52–3. 18 On 23 June 2009 the Vatican accepted a miracle as worked through the intercession of Newman. This clears the way for his beatification.

his personality and his intellectual qualities, only limited attention would seem to have been given to his reputation for holiness and to the devotional aspects of his life. John Paul II has emphasized Newman's great love for the Church.[19] One could also refer to his devotion to the Passion of Christ, to his love for the martyrs of the early Church, for the Fathers and the saints. In what follows I draw attention to some aspects of his devotion to our Lady as witnessed primarily by his own writings on this topic.

As we have already seen, it was from Hurrell Froude that Newman first learned to have devotion to the Blessed Virgin.[20] That this devotion progressed rapidly, and was based on a solid doctrinal foundation, is clear from a sermon he gave on the Feast of the Annunciation, 1832. The following extract from that sermon shows how much Newman the Anglican honoured the Mother of God:

> In her the destinies of the world were to be reversed, and the serpent's head bruised. On her was bestowed the greatest honour ever put upon any individual of our fallen race ... But further, she is doubtless to be accounted blessed and favoured in herself, as well as in the benefits she has done us. Who can estimate the holiness and perfection of her, who was chosen to be the Mother of Christ? If to him that hath, more is given, and holiness and divine favour go together (and this we are expressly told), what must have been the angelic purity of her, whom the Creator Spirit condescended to overshadow with His miraculous presence? What must have been her gifts, who was chosen to be the only near earthly relative of the Son of God, the only one whom he was bound by nature to revere and look up to; the one appointed to train and educate him, to instruct him day by day, as he grew in wisdom and in stature?[21]

After Froude's death in 1836, Newman was given his Roman breviary. He began to recite it daily, but omitted the prayers directly invoking our Lady as this practice was against the teaching of the Church of England.[22] Although he had often been accused of 'teaching popery' during the Oxford Movement in the 1830s, Newman's perception of the Catholic Church at that time was still a very defective one. In *Tract* 15 he wrote of Catholicism that 'their communion is infected with heresy; we are bound to flee it as a pestilence'. He complained of her 'lying wonders', including statues of our Lady.[23]

Professor C.W. Russell of Maynooth, who took a keen interest in Newman's progress towards the faith, wrote to him in 1841, after the publica-

19 John Paul II, Address, 27 April 1990. **20** C.S. Dessain, *John Henry Newman* (London, 1971), p. 9. **21** J.H. Newman, *Parochial and plain sermons*, vol. II (London, 1836), pp 143, 147–8, 151–2. **22** Cf. Dessain, p. 37. **23** Cf. ibid., p. 38.

tion of *Tract* 90 on the Thirty-Nine Articles. Newman replied graciously saying that, among other things, 'the extreme honours' paid to our Lady was still a big stumbling block to his acceptance of Catholic doctrine.[24] Russell assured Newman that if he had a fuller knowledge of Church teaching on the Blessed Virgin, his fears and reservations would disappear, pointing out to him how the Rosary was but 'a series of meditations on the Incarnation, Passion and Glory of our Redeemer',[25] and in no way derogated from the worship due to God alone. To assure him that there was no ground for the opinion which accused Rome of excessive devotion to Mary, in October 1842 Russell sent Newman a copy of St Alphonsus Liguori's book of homilies on our Lady, *The Glories of Mary*. The Maynooth professor commented that, although he could hardly think of anyone who spoke more strongly about the prerogatives of the Mother of God, he hoped Newman would see from a reading of these homilies how he had been misled by appearances into thinking that the Catholic Church gave too much honour to the Blessed Virgin at the expense of the Holy Trinity.[26]

It is interesting to note that when Newman came to write his celebrated *Apologia pro vita sua*, almost twenty years later, he recalled with gratitude the very significant part played by Dr Russell in his reception into the Church: 'He had, perhaps, more to do with my conversion than anyone else.'[27] One of the most important factors in Russell's contribution to Newman's conversion was his clarification of the Catholic position in relation to devotion to the Blessed Virgin.[28]

ESSAY ON DEVELOPMENT OF DOCTRINE

As Newman drew closer to Rome, he felt the need to justify rationally to himself the differences, as he saw it, between the doctrine of the primitive Church and that professed by the Catholic Church of his time. This was the origin of one of Newman's greatest theological works, *An essay on the development of Christian doctrine*. He finished it in September 1845, and was received into the Catholic Church a few days later, on 9 October.

The sixth of Newman's seven criteria, outlined in the *Essay*, for assessing the authenticity of a doctrinal development, reads as follows:

> A true development may be described as one which is conservative of the course of antecedent developments, being really those antecedents

24 Letter, Newman to Russell, 13 April 1841, in *Correspondence of John Henry Newman with John Keeble and others, 1839–1845*, edited at the Birmingham Oratory (London, 1917), pp 122–3. **25** Cf. A. Macauley, *Dr Russell of Maynooth* (London, 1983), pp 83–4. **26** Cf. ibid., p. 90. **27** *Apologia*, p. 194. **28** Cf. Macauley, p. 96.

> and something besides them: it is an addition which illustrates, not obscures, corroborates, not corrects, the body of thought from which it proceeds.[29]

This is the context in which Newman reflects on the question of Marian devotion shortly before he took the final step to enter the Church. He poses the question whether the honours paid to our Lady, which have grown out of devotion to her Son, do not in fact tend to weaken that devotion to Christ. A related question also presents itself: is it possible so to exalt a creature without withdrawing one's heart from the Creator?[30]

Newman replies that the question was to a large extent answered by the Fathers of Ephesus when they declared our Lady to be the *Theotokos*, or Mother of God, 'in order to protect the doctrine of the Incarnation, and to preserve the faith of Catholics from a specious humanitarianism'.[31] And he goes on to make the telling point that a survey of religious practice in Europe confirms 'that it is not those religious communions which are characterized by devotion to the Blessed Virgin that have ceased to adore her Eternal Son, but those very bodies which have renounced devotion to her'.[32] Is not, he asks, the character of much of Protestant devotion to our Lord no higher than that which Catholics pay to our Lady, differing from it, however, in that it is often familiar, rude and earthly?[33]

The seriousness with which Newman researched contemporary devotion to our Lady in the Catholic Church is shown by the fact that he did an analysis of about forty books of devotion in circulation among the laity in Rome at that time. He was surprised to discover how the person of Christ was so central to all of these devotions, and how relatively infrequent were the references to the Blessed Virgin. His Protestant prejudices about excessive cult of our Lady in Catholic piety were severely undermined. Newman was now satisfied that Marian devotion did not in any way detract from the divine worship due to the Three Persons of the Blessed Trinity. True, a special *cultus* is assigned to Mary, but this is always in virtue of the transcendent dignity of her Son.[34]

In the *Apologia* Newman explains how in the process of conversion he had gradually come to see how 'the Catholic Church allows no image of any sort, material or immaterial, no dogmatic symbol, no rite, no sacrament, no saint, not even the Blessed Virgin herself, to come between the soul and its Creator'.[35] And so in coming to the Church, he was able to state with full conviction: 'I had a true devotion to the Blessed Virgin, in whose college I lived,

29 *Essay*, p. 200. **30** Cf. ibid., p. 425. **31** Ibid., p. 426. The title *Theotokos*, or Mother of God, was familiar to Christians from primitive times and had been used by several of the early Fathers such as Origen, St Athanasius, St Ambrose, and St Gregory of Nyssa. **32** Ibid. **33** Cf. ibid., p. 428. **34** Cf. ibid., p. 436. **35** *Apologia*, p. 195.

whose altar I served, and whose immaculate purity I had in one of my earliest sermons made much of'.[36] Newman says that there is no honour too high to be given to our Lady.[37] There is nothing particularly new in this affirmation; it is simply another way of affirming the *De Maria numquam satis* (we can never speak sufficiently of Mary) of the early Church Fathers.[38]

CONCLUSION

The story of Newman's life is characterized above all by a great love for the truth and his willingness to suffer much to attain it. Providence led him to find its fullness in the Catholic Church which gave him a deep sense of inner peace irrespective of the challenges and controversies which his life as a Catholic involved.

As a writer and controversialist he had few equals. During his long life he generously used his many talents to promote an understanding of the Catholic Church as the unique instrument willed by God to bring about the salvation of souls. He did this especially through his writings and his voluminous correspondence. It is surely no small recognition of his theological orthodoxy that four of his volumes are quoted in the *Catechism of the Catholic Church*, and that John Paul II refers to his writings in his encyclicals, *Veritatis splendour* and *Fides et ratio.*

Newman lived his life as an exemplary priest. He had a deep devotion to the Mass and was assiduous in daily prayer. It was this deep piety which nourished his apostolic zeal, expressed especially in his constant efforts to win over converts to the Catholic Church. We have seen another side of this piety as it relates to his devotion to the Mother of God. There is nothing cerebral or merely intellectual in his approach. On the contrary, he writes about her with

36 Cf. ibid., p. 165. He is referring here to his 1832 sermon on the feast of the Annunciation – see footnote no. 22, p. 228 above. **37** Cf. *Discourses*, p. 363. **38** In this context the testimony of the former prefect of the Sacred Congregation for the Doctrine of the Faith is of particular interest. With refreshing frankness Cardinal Ratzinger tells us that 'As a young theologian in the time before (and also during) the Council, I had ... some reservations in regard to certain ancient formulas, as, for example, that famous *De Maria numquam satis*, "concerning Mary one can never say enough". It seemed exaggerated to me ... Now – in this confused period where truly every type of heretical aberration seems to be pressing upon the doors of the authentic faith – now I understand that it was not a matter of pious exaggerations, but of truths that today are more valid than ever'. He goes on to say that it is necessary to go back to Mary if we are to rediscover, in all its fullness, that triple truth proposed by John Paul II, at the beginning of his pontificate, as a programme for the whole of Christianity – the truth about Jesus Christ, the truth about the Church, and the truth about man. These are, obviously, not unconnected truths; on the contrary they constitute the very essence of God's self revelation to man; cf. *The Ratzinger report*, Interview with V. Messori (London, 1985), pp 105–6.

a warmth of feeling which is unusual for a man of his background and culture. Nevertheless, it is not surprising that this should be so in somebody who has been declared by the Church to have practised the Christian virtues to an heroic degree.

A central characteristic of Newman's life and work was his consistent effort to get to the real, to the truth of things. From this perspective we see the appropriateness of what he asked to have carved on his headstone – *Ex umbris et imaginibus in veritatem*: from shadows and images into the truth.

CHAPTER SIX

Archbishop John Baptist Lamy (1814–1888)

JEAN BAPTISTE LAMY was born on 11 October 1814, in the small village of Lampedes, about thirty-six miles from the city of Clermont-Ferrand, in the Auvergne district of France. His parents were well-to-do peasants who had eleven children, only four of whom survived into adulthood. Two sons – Louis and Jean Baptiste – became priests and a daughter Margaret entered a convent. The village of Lampedes grew up around a Romanesque church where an image of Our Lady of Good Tidings was venerated. From the time he was a five-year-old, Jean Baptiste began to pay her long and frequent visits, opening up vistas on a Marian devotion which was to become increasingly enriched all during his life.

The villagers of Lampades were staunchly Catholic, a place where vocation to the priesthood was seen as a natural expression of Christian faith. The French Revolution and the Civil Constitution of the Clergy seem to have made little impression on the traditional Catholicism of the village. As a child Lamy had the first inklings of his vocation, and was sent by his parents to the Jesuit college at Billom, a short distance from Clermont-Ferrand. He entered the diocesan seminary of Mont Ferrand in 1832 to complete a six-year course in philosophy and theology under the Sulpician fathers. It was here that he met Joseph Machebeuf, a seminarian in a class two years ahead of him, who was to become Lamy's closest friend for life.

Physically and psychologically the two were very different. Lamy was tall, well built, with a finely chiselled head, covered by a mop of black hair.

1 Paul Horgan, *Lamy of Santa Fe: his life and times* (New York, 1975), p. 30. This biography, which won the Pulitzer Prize, is my main source. Other bibliography: Rev. W.J. Howlett, *Life of the Right Reverend Joseph P. Machebeuf, DD, pioneer, priest of Ohio, of Colorado, and Utah and first bishop of Denver* (Pueblo, 1908); Most Rev. J.B. Salpointe, *Soldiers of the Cross: notes on the ecclesiastical history of New Mexico, Arizona, and Colorado* (Albuquerque, 1967); Louis H. Warner, *Archbishop Lamy, an epoch maker* (Santa Fe, 1936). Willa Cather's fictional account of Lamy's life, *Death comes for the archbishop* (New York, 1990), captures at several points the real spirit of the archbishop of Santa Fe. In particular she provides a deep insight into the loves that filled his heart as priest and bishop (cf. pp 253–5).

Photographs from his later life show him to be an exceptionally handsome man. Temperamentally he had an orderly mind; he was mild in expression, strong and patient after taking decisions. Gentleness was perhaps his most striking characteristic. 'He seemed all simplicity but he was woven of many strands – warm intelligence, charm, modesty, with a certain hardness veiled by habitual patience. Slow-moving, he went about his days with long strides at the pace of a countryman who thought in seasons rather than in days or hours'.[1] His friend Machebeuf had a totally different personality. He was small in size, with fair hair, and a lively and energetic character. His mind darted from one idea to another with a sense of gaiety and initiative, which kept him constantly on the move.

At Mont Ferrand, Lamy distinguished himself in his theological studies, but above all in his exemplary life. He spent much time reading about the lives of the missionary priests abroad and the heroic endeavours which at times were called for. Machebeuf was also thinking about missionary life, and it was North America in particular which attracted his attention. French priests who were now bishops in places like New Orleans and Kentucky occasionally returned to Mont Ferrand, their old alma mater, to try to persuade some of the seminarians to sign on for pastoral work in the New World. They had challenging tales to tell about building up the Church in the United States, which fired the imagination of the seminarians and their zeal to bring the Good News to this new uncultivated part of the Lord's vineyard.

In 1836 Machebeuf was ordained priest and Lamy two years afterwards. They were assigned to small parishes in the diocese of Clermont. In 1838 Bishop Purcell of Cincinnati, on his return from Rome, broke his journey at Mont Ferrand to recruit some young priests who would go to work with him in America. Lamy and Machebeuf were among the five who agreed to accompany him, four of whom subsequently became bishops. After making the necessary arrangements, on 21 May 1839 they set out for Paris where they were due to meet Bishop Purcell. Purcell was a man of generous nature with whom the new missionary recruits established life-long friendships. He was born in Ireland in 1800 and emigrated to the United States in 1818, where he began his theological studies. He was ordained in Paris in 1826 and at thirty-three was make bishop of Cincinnati.

On 7 July 1839 the group sailed from Le Havre for the New World; forty-three days later they disembarked at the port of New York. During the crossing Lamy and the others studied English assiduously. The next day they left for Cincinnati, travelling by canal boat as far as Baltimore. From there they completed the rest of the journey by stagecoach and steam-boat on the Ohio River as far as Cincinnati. The journey would have given the European travellers a first view of the spectacular American countryside.

CINCINNATI AND FIRST TASKS

But it was the rivers, with their great size and teeming currents, which would have supplied the newcomers with a real sense of the vastness of the continent. They arrived at Cincinnati on 10 September, and headed for the seminary which would be their temporary headquarters until they were assigned their new parishes. After three weeks, despite their inexperience and their lack of knowledge of English, they were assigned to mission parishes which had no regular pastors. Their assignment was to bring scattered settlers together to form parish groups and to build churches. Lamy was given an area called Danesville in the middle of Ohio, and Machebeuf was appointed to a district in the north of the same state.

It was still frontier territory. Rivers had not yet been bridged, the roads were still mud tracks, and the whole state was almost entirely covered by forest. Catholics were scattered in small settlements, but it was a time when they began to arrive in the state in great numbers. A number of settlements were grouped into a single parish. Wooden churches were built in the parish centre.

The parishioners accepted their new priest with great joy. Since he had no house of his own he stayed for periods with different families. He went by horseback to visit the different settlements. He performed his duties in halting English, but this did not prevent him mobilizing his parishioners to build a new brick church at Danesville. Bishop Purcell came from Cincinnati to perform the ceremony of dedication on 15 November. Protestant neighbours had helped in different ways to build the church. The new church was seen by the settlers not just as a place of worship but as an important stage in the development of the local civilization. By this stage Fr Lamy had won the reverence and affection of all those he led in the building of St Luke's church.

In 1840 he set about building a new church in Mt Vernon, a neighbouring parish. He showed his leadership and organizing ability in the way he got people to contribute in different ways to this project. Someone gave land, another provided timber; others worked the roads and canals to gather materials. In addition Lamy had to attend to eight other nascent parishes, so that usually he only spent two Sundays per month in Danesville.

In his travels he used a long leather bag to carry his vestments, Mass vessels, and other supplies, which was fixed to his saddle. The morning after he arrived, children would be sent in all directions to tell other remote Catholic settlers that the priest had come. Soon settlers from Germany, Ireland, France and the eastern states would arrive and the priest would be busy administering baptism and confession, followed by Mass and sermon. It was then on to the next cluster of settlements to provide the necessary pastoral care. He took time off too to visit the Irish canal workers on the Maumee river.

During his seminary days Lamy fell ill from time to time, revealing that he lacked a robust constitution. In Ohio, although he was dangerously ill for a few days, he responded very well to the physical demands of his pastoral mission. In 1841 he wrote to his bishop that there was a great deal to be done. In addition, life was made difficult by a national financial crisis which caused most of the banks to fail. It was nearly impossible to get bank credit in those which survived. Yet in 1841 Lamy finished his rectory at Danesville and continued work on his new church in Mt Vernon. It was almost finished when in March 1844 it was burned down due to some unverified cause. The bishop came to see the charred remains and preached to a large crowd, disconsolate at the loss of the church they had put so much effort into raising up for the glory of God. But that very day they provided 600 dollars to rebuild it. At the same time Lamy was supervising the building of a church at Newark about twenty-four miles from Mt Vernon.

Bishop Purcell was not only Lamy's superior; he was also his confidant. In 1841 Lamy wrote to him, 'I beseech you that you pray God that he may enable me to be a good priest, and to persevere in that state, that I may procure the glory of God and the salvation of souls which he has redeemed at so great a price.'

Lamy at this stage had four churches and was involved in building two others, a strong statement of his pastoral zeal. But with this development came the endless quest for money to pay for these works. His parishioners were generous, but means were limited and he turned to Purcell: 'If you give me permission I will go on a begging expedition, though I am not very bold … I am willing to go and beg, but before, could you not send me a little help to settle some of the more urging [sic] affairs.' He went to St Louis and thought of going to New Orleans from there, saying that a letter from the bishop would be helpful. 'I hope that difficulties will only enlarge my courage …'

He was constantly on horseback visiting his churches, but never complained of the work or the fatigue. The parishes were flourishing, but there were constant needs – vestments, sacred vessels, etc. Even in its first year there were over a thousand present at Danesville for the feast of the Resurrection, most of whom were not even Catholics. In four years Lamy had created an increasing pastoral network and was still a young priest of twenty-eight.

In 1845 the burned-out church at Mt Vernon was re-roofed. To complete the job took a considerable effort on the part of the parishioners. Yet in all his concerns Lamy felt the freedom and comfort of being able to open his mind to Purcell. As he said in one of his letters: 'It is to you Rev Bishop that I must open my heart. You have always been a father to me, and I bless the divine providence that I am in this diocese … I have the honour to be your devoted child.'

Lamy came up against opposition from some non-Catholics, especially the 'Know-Nothing' movement which tried to discredit Catholicism. Nevertheless, he received many converts, including the young son of his housekeeper, whom he later took to Rome to be educated for the priesthood, and who years afterwards would become pastor of Danesville. Writing on New Year's Day 1847 to Bishop Purcell, Lamy reported a big crowd at the first Mass on Christmas Day which he said at 5.00 a.m. People came from many miles, on very poor roads, in one the wettest winters in living memory. To visit his flock, Lamy had often to swim his horse across swollen rivers.

The rapid growth of the towns in northern Ohio resulted in the new diocese of Cleveland being established in 1846 in an area separated from the mother diocese of Cincinnati. Fr Reppe, one of the French missionary priests was appointed bishop. Initially Lamy was to change parish and become part of the new diocese, transferring to a city parish, but Purcell assigned him to the parish of Covington in Kentucky, an appointment for which Lamy was very grateful. On the other hand his departure from Danesville and the other forest parishes was not easy. He had established deep attachments to these people and in turn was greatly missed by them. His name lived on for generations in the affections of the people. A diarist in Danesville parish wrote that Lamy's 'name is held in benediction by all the old residents of the county, irrespective of creed'. For Lamy, he said, was a man 'so good that everybody loved him. I was a young boy when he was pastor here, but had such a high esteem for him I thought that God would not let him die but take him to heaven a live body and soul'.

LAMY TO FRANCE

In his new parish of St Mary's in Covington, Lamy set to work on the same tasks which he had so often undertaken before – acquiring land, forming communities, building churches, etc. The fact that his new parish was located just across the river Ohio from Cincinnati meant that he had more easy access to supplies of building materials.

It was now that Fr Lamy felt it appropriate to make his first return visit to Europe to settle some family matters which had arisen since the death of his father in 1846. In May of 1848 he set off, calling to see his friend Machebeuf on the way. He reached home in July, making many visits. He sorted out the details of his father's estate with his brother Etienne. He was happy that he could now repay Bishop Purcell some of the loans which he had advanced him for church building and other parish initiatives.

Unfortunately the seminarians of Mt Ferrand were on holidays, so he could get no commitments for the American mission. He did, however, persuade some older priests to travel with him. In addition, he brought his sister, an Ursuline nun, and his niece, Marie, to work with him in the New World. He crossed to England to visit the family of one of his seminarians who was studying in Europe, and then sailed from Liverpool for New York. He was home in Covington by September. Growing emigration had rapidly increased his parish work, especially the influx of Irish emigration after the Famine.

Fr Machebeuf had asked Lamy to do a number of errands for him in France, including the purchase of a lace alb, a pair of white dalmatics trimmed with gold, six beautiful gilded candlesticks, and a chalice of gold-plated bronze, so as to celebrate the liturgical ceremonies with 'pomp and solemnity'. As soon as he could, Lamy visited Machebeuf, and brought all the liturgical items to Machebeuf's great delight.

BISHOP OF SANTA FE

After the Mexican war in 1846, the US acquired the territories of Texas and California and all lands in between, which embraced New Mexico, Colorado, and Arizona. All the territories which had been ceded were administered ecclesiastically by bishops of Mexico who consulted Rome about exercising jurisdiction in the new US territories. Surprisingly Rome replied that the Mexican bishops should continue to exercise their episcopal authority north of the Rio Grande. This decision was to create intractable problems of jurisdiction for years ahead.

A synod of the American bishops was held at Baltimore in May 1849. One of the more urgent questions on their agenda was the question of the Mexican territories which were recently acquired by the US. The synod was well aware that the condition of the Church in these lands was deplorable. The behaviour of the Mexican priests was reprehensible, many of them openly living with concubines. The bishop of Durango in Mexico who was responsible for the whole of New Mexico, lived at a distance of 1,500 miles from Santa Fe and had only visited the territory three times in the twenty-year period 1826–46. The churches were for the most part in ruins. There were no schools, and there were only nine active priests to serve a territory of over 200,000 square miles. There was a high level of catechetical illiteracy, and many were left unbaptized and unshriven.

One of the decisions of the synod, in light of the situation, was to request the Holy Father for a vicar apostolic be appointed for the territory of New Mexico, and for its see be established in Santa Fe. Fr John Baptist Lamy was ranked first on the list of candidates for the vicariate of Santa Fe. His nomination was supported by a statement that he was '35 years old, for many years already working in the diocese of Cincinnati, well known for his piety, honesty, prudence and other virtues'. In July 1850 Pius IX established by decree the vicariate of New Mexico, and appointed John Baptist Lamy its first vicar apostolic.

Given the lamentable situation of the church in New Mexico, the inevitable confrontations which would arise with the native Mexican clergy, the need to rebuild practically all the churches in the territory, and the effort required to learn another language (Spanish) to be pastorally effective, Lamy's appointment to Santa Fe was an extraordinary vote of confidence in the young priest from Cincinnati. When Lamy got the news he was amazed at his new appointment. Santa Fe was so far away, so little was known about it, and even that was not encouraging. For all these reasons Lamy decided that he could not go alone. So he asked his great friend Machebeuf if he would volunteer to accompany him on this new adventure for the faith. Initially Machebeuf was reluctant to go, but after much prayer, and having consulted his bishop and other priest colleagues, he decided he would go with Lamy to Santa Fe. The episcopal ordination was set for November in Cincinnati cathedral.

In the interim Lamy was considering what route he would take to Santa Fe. There were basically two options. One was to travel to St Louis and then west across the prairies, along the Santa Fe trail, which could take up to ninety days. However, this was to travel through Indian country, with the hazards of Indian attack. The other way was more complicated and much longer. It would entail a long river trip south to New Orleans on the Ohio and Mississippi rivers, followed by a sea journey west from New Orleans to Galveston, across the Gulf of Mexico. The final stage was a land journey which passed through San Antonio, and then north to Santa Fe. In all it would take about six months, or twice as long as the prairie route. In the end Lamy decided to take the longer route via New Orleans, even though others had advised him to take the prairie route.

On 24 November 1850 Lamy was consecrated bishop in a three-hour ceremony, according to the rites of the ancient liturgy. Before a huge congregation and in the presence of many of his peers, he was subjected to an examination of his faith. This was followed by his consecration and investiture with the regalia of his office – pectoral cross, mitre, crozier, gloves and episcopal ring.

TO SANTA FE

The day after his consecration, Bishop Lamy went by river from Cincinnati on the first stage of his long journey to Santa Fe. Machebeuf would travel later and meet him in New Orleans. Lamy now had pastoral responsibility for the vast area of New Mexico. With the discovery of gold in California in 1848 travel to the West had vastly increased, but still very little was known about this huge area.

Lamy used the trip to start learning Spanish, the language of the people of New Mexico. Lamy's sister Margaret and niece Marie travelled with him, but by the time they reached New Orleans, Margaret was so very ill that she had to be hospitalized. There she remained, and when she was sufficiently recovered the plan was that she would sail back to France, as she was no longer able to cope with the demands of the American mission. Marie, however, went to school with the Ursulines of New Orleans.

Lamy spent some time with the bishop of New Orleans to plan his next steps westward. He purchased the necessary supplies for the land journey to Santa Fe. He called to see his sister who, as we have seen, was very ill in hospital, and made his farewells in early January 1851. He took ship from New Orleans to Galveston, arriving there on 8 January.

He stayed with Bishop Olim of Galveston who encouraged him to follow a different plan as regards his arrival in Santa Fe. Olim told Lamy that he would find a scandalous native clergy there and that rather than proceeding to his episcopal see immediately, he should first go to France to recruit a dozen zealous priests with whom he could, from the very first day, reorganize the vicariate of Santa Fe. Olim also suggested to Lamy that his passage to Europe would give him an opportunity to study Spanish, so that he could speak the language adequately when he arrived at his mission. Even more, he could purchase new vestments to replace the old rubbish which he would find in all the New Mexican churches. Olim himself had been shocked, on his journeys up the Rio Grande, at the filth of the churches in which he had officiated. Olim was very reluctant to see Lamy depart for his new mission without strong reinforcements. Nevertheless, Lamy was determined to reach Santa Fe as soon as possible, and took a steamer, the *Palmetto*, the following day for Port Lavaca and the overland trail to San Antonio and Santa Fe.

However, what the passengers did not know was that the *Palmetto* had been condemned as unseaworthy, but the shipping line continued her scheduled voyages. A violent storm blew up and the ship started to take water through the weakened hull. The captain ran her aground on a sandy beach. A line was taken ashore and secured and all the passengers – about 100 – were saved. The ship began to disintegrate and the passengers' luggage was sighted and some of it saved. Night was coming down and the passengers began to freeze in their wet clothes. Among the cargo were baskets of champagne and kegs of brandy. These were hauled ashore and before long most of the survivors were riotously drunk. Among the debris washed ashore was Lamy's trunk containing his books and vestments. However, he lost all the other equipment he had procured for starting his new mission in Santa Fe.

After availing of some local hospitality Lamy set out on the road to San Antonio, which was the largest military outpost in Texas. When he arrived, he assessed his losses and asked the Society for the Propagation of the Faith for a loan of 10,000 francs to cover his losses and continuing expenses. At San Antonio he was invited to join one of the regular army supply trains to New Mexico. For this purpose Lamy purchased a carriage and a mule train.

Meanwhile Machebeuf had arrived at New Orleans on 21 January where he read about the wreck of Lamy's steamer a few weeks before. There was a letter from Lamy awaiting him in New Orleans, urging him to follow Lamy to San Antonio. Machebeuf followed on with the sad news for Lamy that his sister Margaret had died in the hospital of the Sisters of Charity in New Orleans just after Lamy left.

At the beginning of February Machebeuf eventually caught up with Lamy in San Antonio. He found that Lamy had a badly sprained leg as a result of a serious accident and would not be able to travel for at least another six to eight weeks. However, further delay was signalled by the information that grass on the plains was very meagre; the army would have to wait for more fodder before setting out across a country which even at the best of times only provided sparse grazing.

While convalescing in San Antonio, Lamy wrote to Bishop Zubiría of Durango in Mexico, whose ecclesiastical jurisdiction up to now had included all of New Mexico. Lamy wanted to inform Zubiría that he had been appointed vicar apostolic of New Mexico and that in due course he would assume his responsibilities in Santa Fe. He also informed him that he would soon be travelling to Rome where his new assignment would naturally be recognized. At the time Lamy had no knowledge of the sensibilities involved, but it was an issue that was to haunt him for the next twenty years.

By May, Lamy was sufficiently recovered to join the army caravan heading for El Paso and the upper Rio Grande. They had 600 miles to go through Comanche territory before reaching El Paso. The journey was for Lamy and Machebeuf the first experience of the type of country which would be theirs for the rest of their lives.

TO THE RIO GRANDE

After leaving the grassy landscape of Texas, they passed through harsh scrubland as the caravan moved further west. They slept in the open air using their saddles as pillows, as the weather for the most part was fine. Lamy or

Machebeuf said Mass every day in a tent provided by the officer in charge of the army caravan. They were invited to eat in the officers' mess.

The caravan now turned in a north-westerly direction towards El Paso. They passed the foothills of the Guadalupe mountains which the Comanche Indians used as a sanctuary from which to raid passing caravans. They followed the Rio Grande to El Paso. News had gone ahead of the arrival of the new bishop, and people lined the roads for miles to greet him. Lamy was well received in El Paso and well provisioned for the final stage of his journey to Santa Fe. By the time Lamy arrived, the vast northern lands of the bishop of Durango's diocese (New Mexico and Colorado) had been transferred by the Holy See to the jurisdiction of the United States hierarchy.

Lamy stopped long enough at El Paso to get a feel for the religious commitment and the customs of the people. He could see that they were well disposed to him and had a strong attachment to their religion. However, he also learned that violence and vice of every kind were an integral part of the society. Lamy wrote to an episcopal friend: 'from the little I have seen here, no doubt I may expect to meet serious difficulties and obstacles'. As he travelled the last 300 miles north to Santa Fe by the banks of the Rio Grande, he passed through a number of the New Mexican villages which were part of his jurisdiction. Great crowds of people came out to meet him and escort him in procession to their local church. But the more they advanced towards Santa Fe, the more Lamy and Machebeuf saw that their first impressions had deceived them. The piety of the people was only a surface commitment; there was little or no sacramental life. But this was due to the lack of zeal of the clergy.

To look after the pastoral care of 70,000 Catholics scattered over a huge area, Lamy had only fifteen priests, six of whom were inactive due to old age. As for the other nine, he would discover that either they had little pastoral zeal or were leading such a scandalous lifestyle that the condition of his new diocese could not be worse. Lamy saw that to reform these Mexican clergy would require a lot of prudence, fortitude, and much prayer.

TRIUMPHAL ENTRY

On 9 August 1851 Lamy and Machebeuf entered Santa Fe. Thousands lined the route for five to six miles out from the city. The territorial governor greeted the bishop warmly. The resident Mexican rural dean, Msgr Juan Felipe Ortiz, came forward to meet Lamy. All the civil and military authorities took part in the reception. As the procession entered the city, the American artillery fired off a twenty-one gun salute. The bishop entered the sacristy of St Francis church to change from his dusty travel clothes. The church was filled with women kneeling on the earth floor, with black shawls on their heads. The men stood at the rear. Lamy saw that the church was in poor repair. As he entered the church, a Mexican string orchestra, together with the available clergy, sang the *Te Deum*. The bishop was now robed in a purple cassock, surplice, mozzeta, and a richly embroidered heavy white stole.

Looking at their new bishop who stood before them, the people saw a young man of thirty-seven, gaunt and sparsely built, weathered by his travels and ten years of hard work. He was mild mannered with sparkling eyes. He had a broad head with deep-set eyes, and long dark, curly hair. The bones of his face were well defined, giving him a handsome appearance. After the liturgical reception of Lamy, he was brought to the adjacent rector's house which became his episcopal residence. This was followed by a special dinner to which all the leading citizens – Mexicans, Americans, Protestants and Catholics – were invited.

New Mexico had been suffering from a drought for months. All the land was scorched, with cattle and sheep dying of starvation. The prospect of the threatened disaster was on everybody's mind. But the very day of the bishop's arrival clouds appeared from behind the mountains, and emptied themselves in such torrents of rain that the streets ran like rivers.

DEFIANCE

Although he took a leading role in the welcome given to Lamy, Juan Felipe Ortiz, the rural dean, together with the clergy over whom he presided, suddenly maintained that Lamy was not the bishop of Santa Fe and refused to recognize him as such. Ortiz argued that his own bishop, Zubiría of Durango, when present in Santa Fe just a few months previously, had told him that Rome had given a ruling that Mexican bishops should continue their episcopal authority north of the border. Lamy responded by referring to the papal bulls which set forth his faculties and authority in relation to Santa Fe and New Mexico. Ortiz replied that he had had no communication from Durango about the transfer of episcopal power, and until such time as this was done, he and the other clergy would continue to regard Zubiría as their lawful authority. As rural dean since 1832, Ortiz had been responsible for the entire administration of the church in New Mexico, but he had shown no zeal in the execution of his responsibilities, nor did the other clergy under his authority.

Lamy, naturally, was astonished at the attitude of Ortiz. He conferred with his vicar general, Machebeuf, and wrote to Zubiría in Durango, asking for a quick confirmation by letter of Rome's new appointment. Durango, as we have seen, was about 1,500 miles to the south in Mexico. A letter from there could take months. In the meantime, however, Lamy did not stay idle. His documents of appointment gave him the legal right to all church properties in New Mexico. He moved swiftly and took possession of church buildings, chapels, and other properties.

When, after a reasonable time there had been no word from Zubiría, Lamy decided that he would have to travel to Durango to show his documents of appointment to the old bishop and get him to agree to withdraw his claim to episcopal jurisdiction over Santa Fe. What was at stake was his authority over a diocese larger in area than the whole of France. New Mexico still loosely included all of present-day Arizona and other areas which were part of the Mexican cession after its war with the United States in 1846.

SANTA FE

Santa Fe had a population of about 4,000 souls. The language, the customs and the architecture were alien to Lamy when compared with his experience in Ohio. They were untouched by any of the modern developments which came with the building of canals and railways. There was little formal education in Santa Fe – what education the people had was received at home. Nearly ninety per cent of the population were illiterate. The greatest concern of the society in Santa Fe was the constant threat of raids by Indians – Apaches, Navajos, and Comanches. On their incursions they stole horses, mules, cattle and sheep, often murdering their owners and destroying property.

Nevertheless, among the Mexican families the seeds of faith were implanted in the minds and habits of children in the home. The culture of Christianity was transmitted from parent to child. They became familiar with the invisible company of Christ, the Holy Family, and the saints. Prayers and catechism were taught orally to young people and repeated until the lesson remained in the memory of the hearers. This was a great help to the priest who had to explain the chief mysteries of the faith to them.

FIRST NEEDS

In his first weeks in Santa Fe, Lamy became familiar with the religious situation of the people, which gave him a good idea of what he would have to do in the years ahead. He wrote to the Society for the Propagation of the Faith in Paris that 'the state of immorality in matters of sex is so deplorable that the most urgent need is to open a school for girls under the direction of the Sisters of Charity'. Already he was looking out for a site for a convent. He also wrote about the need for a boys school in each parish, and asked for 13,000 francs.

According to Lamy's own census there were in his diocese 68,000 Catholics, 18 missions, 12 native priests, 26 churches, and 40 chapels. He reckoned there were 8–9,000 Catholic Indians, and perhaps 30,000 who were amenable to conversion. But what he really needed were some zealous priests.

He was appalled at the condition of the local clergy, a concern which would cause him heartbreak for many years. There was hardly a priest who had not reared a family of illegitimate children. A Fr Lujan had a succession of mistresses, and when the last one died, he gave her a solemn funeral ceremony, to which he invited all the civic and army dignitaries. The pastor in Albuquerque, Jose Manuel Gallegos, had for his partner a married Mexican woman who had been the mistress of two Mexican officers in turn, by whom she had three children. Together they ran a general store which was open all day Sunday. Many of the local residents were appalled by Gallegos's conduct.

MEXICAN JOURNEY

In September 1851 Lamy wrote to his long-time friend and confident, Archbishop Purcell of Cincinnati, to help him in his search for teaching nuns who would be willing to come to Santa Fe, with all their expenses paid and a good house provided near the church. He was satisfied that the citizens of Santa Fe would give every support to the establishment of new schools.

Having taken the first steps to solve his educational needs, and having left the diocese in the care of Machebuef, his vicar general, Lamy set out on horseback to travel the 1,500 miles to Durango in Mexico. He would have to traverse unknown mountains and deserts, to confront Bishop Zubiría about the burning problem of territorial jurisdiction. Lamy headed south towards Albuquerque with an attendant who knew the long road to Durango. The scenery in New Mexico was spectacular and for a man who loved the open country, this aspect of the journey must have enthralled him. There were villages along part of the route where he might find hospitality for the night, but more often than not he would spend the night in a blanket on the ground, under the stars. Many people in Santa Fe thought the bishop was imprudent for setting out through country that had been terrorized for generations by Apaches who preyed on travellers. However it was essential for Lamy to establish his right to rule his own diocese.

He crossed over the Rio Grande and reached the boundary between New Mexico and the Mexican state of Chihuahua. Now he had to trek through desert country for miles, and as he rode south he encountered in rhythmic sequence, mountains, desert, and river courses. He passed through the city of Chihuahua which then had a population in the region of 10,000, having covered about 1,000 miles since his journey began. Eventually, after a five-week journey, Lamy arrived at the bishop's palace in Durango. Bishop Zubiría promptly received his visitor and they got down quickly to business. Zubiría had not heard anything from Rome about Lamy's appointment as bishop of New Mexico. He had heard rumours about the appointment which were confirmed by Lamy's letter to him from San Antonio in April 1851. Nevertheless, after the United States victory in the 1846 war and the cession to the US of the Mexican territories of New Mexico, Colorado and Arizona, Zubiría informed his visitor that he had been expressly ordered by Rome to continue to exercise episcopal jurisdiction over the full extent of his original diocesan limit, despite the new political boundary. Lamy showed Zubiría the papal bull appointing him bishop of New Mexico; Zubiría accepted the authority of the document and Lamy's right to govern that territory. This was what Lamy had travelled 1,500 miles to hear. They also discussed the disputed jurisdiction over some villages on the New Mexico border with Mexico. This arose because the maps of the area were inaccurate.

RETURN TO SANTA FE

Lamy arrived home to Santa Fe on 10 January 1852. The experience of the 3,000 mile round trip would harden him for all the travelling he would do in the years ahead, through the vast stretches of mountain and desert which characterized his diocese.

On his return, Lamy circularized all his priests to the effect that Zubiría recognized his jurisdiction in New Mexico and asked that they would in future give their obedience to him. They formally submitted but with such mental reservations that they would continue to create problems for Lamy in the future. While Lamy was away in Durango, most of the priests tried to convince the people that Lamy had no real authority, and that he would probably never return from Mexico. Very quickly Lamy saw that they were not going to submit to his authority by good will, and would have to be coerced into doing so. Rather than comply, some priests preferred to leave New Mexico. Lamy would have been happy to see them all leave, but this begged the question, where was he to get new priests?

Still, despite the scandalous behaviour of the priests, religion played a great part in the life of the people, even if it had its own local peculiarities. There was, for instance, the practice of the *penitentes* in northern New Mexico, deriving from the days of the Spanish colonists in 1598. During Holy Week the villagers indulged in rituals of flagellation upon each other and upon themselves, together with rites of initiation by mutilation. On Good Friday it was believed that the actual crucifixion of a chosen victim as the Christ would bring him and his family to heaven without passing through Purgatory. It was said that he was tied rather than nailed to the cross.

Bishop Zubiría, after his first pastoral visit to New Mexico in 1833, forbade the practices of the *penitentes* in a letter to his priests. But his orders never took full effect. The rituals which took place within the church buildings were now transferred to non-sanctified chapels and the people involved now operated as secret societies. Lamy was unsuccessful in eradicating these practices.

One of his first pastoral visits took him to Pecos, where the large mission church of the seventeenth century served eighteen villages in the upper Pecos valley. The pastor, an old man of sixty-five, was an inveterate gambler and an adulterer. Some months earlier, mounting his horse while drunk, he was thrown and broke his leg in three places. On this visit, Lamy suspended the pastor from all his functions but allowed him to keep one third of the parish revenues. Lamy was conscious that disciplining the old pastor had its risks – he was a powerful member of the territorial legislature; but he hoped this would be seen as a warning by the other delinquent priests.

In 1852 Lamy travelled north to visit some of the pueblos and towns he had not yet seen. He felt the need to get to know the people and the local circumstances of the church. He found crumbling earthen chapels, but also stations, and paintings, and wall decorations done by native artists.

The people were called on by the local pastor to bring him tithes of their produce: seed, animals, whatever commodities they had. There was no money of course, as hardly any was circulated in the territory outside the major towns. Much of such tribute stayed in the hands of the local parish priest, the remainder (up to 1851) was sent through bills of exchange to the bishop of Durango. These demands on the people amounted to extortion. As Lamy came across this situation in every parish, he decided that he would have to devise a more equitable system for levying dues. Parish priests were charging exorbitant fees for marriages, baptisms, and burials, much greater than the people could afford.

In the interim Ortiz had travelled to Durango to plead his case with Zubiría against Lamy's authority in New Mexico. Because Zubiría stood by Lamy, Ortiz returned a resentful man. Three parish priests received gentle admonitions from Lamy because of their scandalous behaviour. He was reluctant to discipline any other priests for the simple reason that he had too few priests available.

EDUCATION

He very soon realized that the greatest need in his diocese was education. This meant teachers and schools. He first thought of the Loretto sisters in

Kentucky. Since there was a meeting of the US bishops scheduled for Baltimore in April 1852, Lamy planned to take in a visit to the nuns on his way. In his absence he asked Machebeuf to find and prepare a house in which to install whatever teaching nuns he could recruit, with both residence and classroom facilities.

On 1 April he set out eastwards from Santa Fe to cross the Great Plains for the first time. The journey was then quite an adventure. The stage coach took two weeks to travel from Santa Fe to the Missouri river at Independence, Missouri. There were armed outriders to keep watch for Indians. The prairies consisted of hundreds of miles of rolling plains, which provided grazing for the immense herds of buffalo. Here, too, tribes of Indians lived who offered a real threat to travellers.

Lamy arrived at Baltimore in time for the opening of the first plenary council of US bishops on 9 May 1852. He reported to the council on the conditions in his vicariate, and on his trip to Durango to clarify his jurisdiction with bishop Zubiría. The plenary council decided to petition Pius IX to elevate the vicariate of New Mexico to an episcopal see, which would be subject to the metropolitan see of St Louis, and to appoint Lamy as bishop.

After the council finished its work on 20 May 1852, Lamy travelled to New York from where he wrote to the Society of the Propagation of the Faith in Paris and Lyon asking for funds to start the new school in Santa Fe. He also outlined his financial needs to refurbish churches and to replace vestments, sacred vessels, and candlesticks which were now in a sorry state.

Lamy next headed to Kentucky to persuade the Loretto sisters to open a school for girls in Santa Fe. He got a positive reception and a promise of teaching nuns. He made a quick trip by steamer to New Orleans to see his niece Marie at her convent school. After a few days he returned to St Louis to prepare for his trip west to Santa Fe, and to meet with the Loretto sisters as planned. He was already impressed by their willingness to make the dangerous plains crossing to Santa Fe. On 10 July Lamy's party took the steamer from St Louis to Kansas City, along the Missouri River, a journey of ten days mainly through flat country. Lamy used the journey to teach Spanish to the nuns.

St Louis was suffering from a cholera outbreak as they left the city, but within a few days the disease had spread on board to epidemic proportions. After six days on the river, one of the Loretto sisters died and three others were attacked by the disease. Because of fear of contagion, Lamy and his party were asked to leave the ship. They camped out in the woods for some days and towards the end of July Lamy's party began to organize themselves for the westward journey. The other nuns, victims of the cholera, slowly recovered, but one was too weak to go on to Santa Fe, and had to be returned to St Louis. Lamy was saddened by the loss of two of the six nuns who had originally set out with him, especially as it would affect progress on his school project in Santa Fe.

The group set out again but within a few miles an axle broke on one the wagons which took a day to repair. The wagons moved across the prairie, and at one stage they were trailed by a band of about 300 Indians who kept their distance. Lamy ordered the caravan to rest by daytime and travel by night as the Indians did not usually attack after dark. About six weeks after starting out they reached Las Vegas where Lamy said Mass for the group and the local Mexican population. He was delighted to see Machebeuf and some people from Santa Fe arrive to welcome him and the group. On 26 September they entered Santa Fe to a great reception. Over 1,000 turned out to meet them, and Lamy's party was led through a series of triumphal arches as far as the cathedral where the bells rang out in celebration. Msgr Ortiz met Lamy on the steps of the cathedral; all processed to the altar where Lamy intoned the *Te Deum* to a packed congregation.

OPPOSITION FROM PRIESTS

As we have seen, one of the clerical abuses which Lamy set out to eradicate was the enormous fees demanded by the priests for baptisms, weddings, burying the dead, etc. Most of this revenue was kept for themselves by the native priests. People who did not, or could not, pay had severe spiritual penalties imposed on them. Lamy was aware that even with the best of systems the financing of the diocese was going to be a difficult one. He could rely on Paris to make a significant contribution, but the people would have to pay according to their resources. Lamy put his thoughts about diocesan finances in a pastoral letter which was published on 1 January 1853. He first alluded to the new schools he had established – one for boys and the convent school for girls. He hoped the faithful would take advantage of the opportunity to give their children a good secular and religious education. Every expenditure he had undertaken was for the spiritual and temporal good of the faithful, and for the enhancement of divine worship. He then dealt with the question of stole fees. The cost of church services would be reduced by two thirds. For those who could not afford to pay in full, they could pay half at the time, the rest later.

The pastoral letter then went on to deal with the situation of priests. Each pastor was asked to say Mass once a month, on any convenient day of the week, in every chapel which was more than three miles from the parish church and which had a neighbourhood of thirty families. This was a totally new arrangement which had never been observed before. The priests' share of parish revenues was reduced drastically – to one fourth, which would still provide adequate sustenance for the clergy. Lamy allocated another fourth to the refurbishing of churches, which in general were in a deplorable condition.

He hoped that the faithful would approve his use of church revenues for the maintenance of the bishop and the clergy, the proper observance of divine service, and the establishment of schools, all of which were to be supported by the system of tithes, a system long established by Vatican decree. He pointed out that there was a serious obligation on Catholics to support the church, and anybody who didn't would be denied the sacraments. This was said not in an authoritarian way, but with his usual spirit of kindness and humility.

In the letter he moved on to deal with other matters which were a scandal in the diocese. He told his flock that he felt responsible before God for the state of their souls, and consequently he had to outlaw divorce, dancing and gambling. He used Christ's teaching on divorce (see Mt 19:6) to emphasize the divine origin of the law about conjugal fidelity. People, he said, who were not faithful to their marriage vows couldn't hope for a happy life.

In relation to the local type of dances, which caused scandal to all visitors, Lamy said they were conducive to evil, occasions of sin, and provided opportunity for illicit affinities. How many who frequented this pagan diversion lost their fear of God, their innocence and their honour? He used the same unrelenting language when he described gambling, saying it was absolutely and essentially evil and reprehensible. For these reasons it was prohibited by both church and civil law.

REBELLION

As was to be expected, there was strong reaction to the pastoral letter. But the most immediate and high-handed was the reaction from Dean Ortiz. He ordered Lamy out of the bishop's house saying that he had bought it years ago from Bishop Zubiría, and that he had a deed to prove it. Simultaneously Lamy had made known his decision to divide the parish of Santa Fe, keeping one half for himself to administer including the cathedral church of St Francis. He offered Ortiz the other half of the divided parish.

Ortiz refused to accept this decision, saying that canonically he was the life pastor of the whole parish, and that no one had a right to deprive him of his status. Ortiz organized a mob, including all the disciplined priests, which came to Lamy's house threatening to chase him out of town. Lamy tried to reason with them but made little headway. At last the crowd dispersed and the rebellious priests spent the next week composing elaborate and fallacious complaints against Lamy, for forwarding to Pius IX. There were further confrontations with Ortiz about the parish issue and in the end Lamy decided to rely on patience rather than on a legal battle. He restored the church of St Francis to Ortiz, but the parish division came firmly into effect.

Because the native clergy saw that Lamy, in his letter, had attacked outright their habits and privileges, giving notice of the strict reform which he was proposing for the diocese, they were ready to oppose him, and Ortiz was on hand to lead them. Immediately on receiving it, Ortiz refused to exercise his pastoral responsibilities in Santa Fe and departed to Durango to see what support or satisfaction he could get from Zubiría. Some priests refused to read the letter to their parishioners; others resigned immediately on receiving it. Some of them were already disposed to challenge the bishop – those he had suspended from their duties after earnest warnings about their life-style. One of these, the Santa Fe priest José de Jesús Lujan, had previously received censure from Zubiría. Lamy, in his early months in Santa Fe, learned that Lujan was 'living in a most scandalous manner, keeping a very young and beautiful married woman in his house'. Her husband would come and plead with her to come home, and even went to the bishop for help, but Lujan refused to send her back where she belonged, even when Lamy ordered him to do so. Lujan sneered at Lamy as a hypocrite and worse. And the bishop suspended him for two years. But the great need of curates soon obliged Lamy to send him off to another parish whose pastor had died. Yet he was no sooner there than Lujan sent for his mistress again – though this time he took the precaution of lodging her next door to his own house. When the pastoral letter reached him, Lujan refused to read it to his people. Lamy ordered him directly to do so, sending Machebeuf to hand it to him. But Machebeuf only met with insults, and Lamy promptly suspended Lujan.

Opposition to Lamy now came from an unexpected source. His vicar general, Machebeuf, during Lamy's long absence in 1852, had carried out an extensive pastoral work in Albuquerque and the villages of the middle Rio Grande valley. But now, in January 1853, these activities of Machebeuf became a weapon with which to attack Lamy. In a letter to Lamy some leading ranchers in the area accused Machebeuf of all kinds of pastoral delinquency, crowned by the accusation that he had revealed the secrets of the confessional. Lamy replied immediately to the leader of the group, Francisco Tomás Baca of Peña Blanca. Because of the gravity of the complaints, he refused to accept them without judicial proof. He said that until such time as he was given proof, he would consider the complaints as a calumny of the most malicious kind that could ever be made against the character of a priest. Accordingly, he said that he considered it his duty to punish those who made the accusations against Machebeuf. There was a further exchange of letters, with Baca threatening to write to Rome about Lamy.

EDUCATION

The schools set up by Lamy in Santa Fe were making progress. The convent school opened in January 1853 under the guidance of the Loretto nuns with ten boarders and twenty-two day students. Religion was an integral part of the curriculum. From the boys' school he expected vocations in the long term. In the interim he had to beg and borrow priests from whatever likely source he could identify, as his need was made more acute due to the suspension of a number of native priests or their defection to Durango.

At Easter 1853 six or seven of the remaining clergy in Santa Fe held a meeting against the bishop and sent him a letter which four of them signed. They announced that in future they would refuse to act on any of his instructions, and that, further, they would appeal to higher authority. Lamy wrote to Zubiría as the recalcitrant priests had returned to the latter's jurisdiction. He also wrote to his friend the archbishop of Cincinnati asking him to write to Rome on his behalf to counter what stories the rebellious priests might report about him. He also asked Purcell for the loan of two priests, given his great need of clergy at present in Santa Fe. He wrote to Cardinal Barnabo, prefect of the Propaganda Fide Congregation, in Rome, alerting him to the sort of communication to expect from the dissident Mexican priests.

One of Lamy's regulations which continued to cause trouble in the diocese was the system of tithing of the faithful for parish and diocesan support. In his pastoral letter Lamy had written about clergy abuse of this system, but now the opposition came from a small section of the laity led by Lamy's old opponent, Baca of Peña Blanca.

The state of morality in Santa Fe was often commented on by visitors from the Atlantic Coast or Americans living there. The US territorial secretary commented that the people had no moral training in the American sense of the word. They had been allowed to grow up without being taught that it was wrong to indulge in vicious habits. The standard of female chastity was deplorably low – prostitution was widespread. Sometimes parents sold their daughters to gratify the lust of the purchaser. This catalogue of moral depravity supported Lamy's findings.

The Mexicans of Santa Fe took a great delight in spectacles of whatever kind, and so when Lamy introduced the solemn Corpus Christi procession in 1853, there was a phenomenal response to it. Every house and shop where the procession was to pass was decorated with ornaments of every kind. Seven altar shrines were erected along the route. There was a choir and harmonium, and plenty of banners. The local commanding officer arranged for several rounds of cannon to be fired off during the procession, The bishop, vested in mitre and cope, carried the Blessed Sacrament at the rear. Great crowds of spectators lined the streets and the rooftops to get the best view. A great number turned out for the High Mass and Solemn Benediction during the octave of Corpus Christi. Nevertheless, Lamy had things more important than processions on his mind at this time. He had to get more priests and more financial aid so he started to plan a trip to Europe in January 1854.

INDIANS

The different tribes of Indians were threatening and dangerous. They swept down from the mountains and stole the horses of the Mexicans who looked on helplessly. At other times they plundered sheep and cattle and left behind the murdered shepherds to prevent them carrying back information. Lamy records how in 1853 the Indians had killed five Mexican shepherds and took away 10,000 sheep. However, there were about 10,000 Catholic Indians to be looked after in their pueblo churches, which had been empty of resident pastors since the withdrawal of the Franciscans in the 1820s.

On 6 January 1854 Lamy published a pastoral letter announcing the new status of the diocese and of himself – it had been elevated by Rome from an apostolic vicariate to that of a full diocese. A formal reception was held to celebrate the event to which the leading civil and military personalities were invited.

Lamy's plans for his European trip were finalized. He was going to take with him two promising Mexican youths to study classics and theology in Rome. He took with him his secretary, Fr Eulógio Ortiz, the old vicar's brother. Two days before he departed – 14 January – he published another pastoral letter admonishing pastors and people about proper preparation for the sacraments, matrimonial conduct, observance of the system of tithes, and a firm command that not a peso of parish funds was to be spent on theatrical comedies, dances, and other profane pastimes.

TROUBLE AT ALBUQUERQUE

Machebeuf remained in charge of the diocese during Lamy's absence, having particular responsibility for the parish of Albuquerque. Back in 1851 Lamy had received complaints against Fr Gallegos, the pastor of the city, where his irregular domestic life, his love of gambling, his involvement in private business affairs to the detriment of his pastoral duties, were publicly known. Lamy warned him about his behaviour, an admonition which had no long-term effect. In late summer of 1852, as Lamy was returning from Baltimore,

Gallegos, who was a prosperous trader, was completing plans to take seven wagon loads of merchandise to Mexico. He delegated his parish responsibilities to Fr Lujan, whose scandalous situation we have already taken note of. Gallegos let it be known that he had Machebeuf's permission for the trip, and was just about to depart when he heard that Lamy had returned to Santa Fe. However, he persevered in his endeavour. It turned out that Gallegos had nobody's permission to travel to Mexico and Lamy, when he heard about it, sent Machebeuf to take charge of Albuquerque and to publish a decree of suspension against Gallegos. Machebeuf told Lujan to absent himself from parish affairs which he, Machebeuf, would in future administer.

There was an immediate outcry against these actions from clergy and laity. A petition was sent to Lamy from 950 citizens of Albuquerque in defence of Gallegos. But on 1 March 1853 Gallegos returned, so they asked Lamy to restore their pastor to them and to withdraw Machebeuf. Lamy replied that the rehabilitation of Fr Gallegos would be very difficult for now, since he had disobeyed Machebeuf's orders during his absence. He also dismissed complaints against Machebeuf declaring that the vast majority of the people gave him their support.

But Gallegos and his supporters were not yet ready to give up the fight. There was a verbal confrontation between Gallegos and Machebeuf at Mass one Sunday before a congregation of Gallegos's supporters. Machebeuf carried it off with his usual aplomb, leaving Gallegos without a word to say in self-defence. Gallegos may have been defeated by the Church, but he now launched himself into another venture – politics – and managed, through every kind of fraud and intrigue, to get himself elected as a delegate from New Mexico to the Congress of the United States. He was a man of no mean ability.

Despite what had happened in his confrontation with Machebeuf and the fact that politics demanded considerable time in Washington, Gallegos refused to leave the priest's residence in Albuquerque. He claimed that it had been given to him personally by deed by Zubiría. Machebeuf wrote to Zubiría to check if this was true, and received a categorical reply saying that he had done nothing of the sort. Lamy made an out-of-court settlement with Gallegos to reimburse him for the improvements he had made to the parochial house.

ANOTHER TRIP

Lamy set off on the first stage of his trip to Europe in January 1854. He had stops at St Louis and Cincinnati, and called to the Loretto mother-house in Kentucky. After reporting to the nuns what their sisters had achieved in Santa Fe, he now made a request for further nuns to expand the great work of teaching still to be done there. After a sea journey of nine days from Boston, he disembarked first in England and made a trip to Birmingham to see if he could meet Fr John Henry Newman. Unfortunately Newman was out of town, but bishop Ullathorne showed him around Birmingham to see some of the developments in his diocese.

In March he proceeded to Boulogne, thence to Paris where he requested funds for his poverty-stricken diocese. Lamy arrived in Rome to make his first *ad limina* visit. The bulk of his official dealings were transacted in the great building of the Sacred Congregation of the Propagation of the Faith, which directed world-wide Catholic mission activities in dioceses which still were not self-supporting materially, or were not sufficiently mature to be able to separate from Rome in routine administration (US dioceses became independent of the Congregation in 1908).

Lamy was introduced to Cardinal Barnabo, prefect of the Congregation, with whom he would have voluminous correspondence in the years ahead. He had several meetings with him during his stay in Rome. One thing in particular came up for consideration – the dispute between Lamy and Zubiría about jurisdictional boundaries at the southern edge of the diocese of Santa Fe. Lamy used the opportunity of being in Rome to shop for church furnishings and to acquire some paintings for same. He also managed to persuade a Spanish Dominican, Fr Damaso Taladrid, to go to New Mexico with him to stay.

As with all *ad limina* visits, Lamy had an audience with the reigning Pope, Pius IX. He found him affable and generous, and detected his great devotion to our Lady. Later that year he would proclaim as a dogma of faith the doctrine of the Immaculate Conception. The Pope presented Lamy with a beautiful sixteenth-century chalice.

On 30 June Lamy embarked from Civitavécchia for France. Once again he was back in his old seminary of Clermont. He remembered how fourteen years before he had responded to the appeal of a visiting bishop to spend his life on the American mission. Now he was going to make the same appeal himself. He was very pleased with the response – three priests, a deacon, and two sub-deacons volunteered to go to Santa Fe. In addition two laymen would travel who would do their ecclesiastical studies in the seminary to be founded by Lamy.

Lamy called to see his brother Etienne, the father of young Marie being educated in New Orleans. Etienne agreed to lend his brother 25,000 francs repayable over four years. Afterwards Lamy called to the Society for the Propagation of the Faith in Lyon. He needed funds, priests, and religious to set his diocese in order. The schools were a constant drain on his resources, and now he was about to set up a preparatory seminary. He obviously put his case very well as he was told that he could rely on extraordinary help. He returned to Paris where he met up with Fr Taladrid.

Lamy and his party left for New York from Le Havre on 1 August, arriving twelve days later. They travelled by rail, coach and river to Kansas, and camped at Willow Springs, where Lamy had arranged to meet the Loretto sisters from Kentucky, promised to him on the outward journey. However, when by late September the nuns hadn't arrived, Lamy decided not to wait any longer.

There were twenty-eight people in his party, serviced by ten covered wagons with mule teams. The journey across the plains would take five weeks. They often saw Indian camp fires in the distance at night and were always on the alert for an attack, but luckily none came. Sometimes they saw immense herds of buffalo. On Sundays and great feast-days the bishop said Mass for his party in his tent to pray for a safe journey west. When the mountains of New Mexico came into view, they saw a reception party representative of all the civil and military authorities and a great crowd of Santa Fe citizens coming out to meet them. Lamy was given a rousing welcome home. It was mid November 1854. The night of his arrival Lamy's new sub-deacon died of cholera. It was a great cross for Lamy who had expected so much from his young seminarian.

In March of the following year, 1855, Machebeuf left for the east to collect the three Loretto nuns who had failed to turn up at Willow Springs the previous fall. By July he had linked up with a trading caravan on the edge of the plains which headed west. Just a few days started into the homeward journey they saw a party of Indians painted for war. A circle was made of the parked wagons and the nuns were hurried to their particular wagon. The Indians came quietly and were given gifts of some of the merchandise which was part of the wagon train. At last all the Indians had gone, so the caravan moved on to find an encampment for the night. The poor nuns were totally cramped from a day of forced confinement and prayer. Machebeuf's party arrived in Santa Fe at the end of July.

THE OLD DEAN

In the summer of 1855 Ortiz returned from Durango after an absence of two years. Lamy was away at the time, making pastoral visits to the parishes along the Rio Grande to administer the sacrament of confirmation. As soon as he returned Ortiz made him a call. Lamy was distressed that because of his suspension the old dean was unable to exercise his priestly functions, and restored to him the faculty of saying Mass. When he offered Ortiz a parish outside Santa Fe, Ortiz refused to accept it, saying that he wanted to be based in Santa Fe. Ortiz seized a number of sacred vessels which belonged to his old parish and wrote Zubiría to receive him once again in the Durango diocese. He explained to Zubiría that the items he had taken from the cathedral parish in Santa Fe were his in the sense that they had been given to the church by his relatives. He also implied that other liturgical items had gone missing due to lack of care of the cathedral authorities. Since Ortiz's impudence gave some comfort to the other suspended priests in the diocese, Lamy suspended him once more.

Despite these annoyances, he kept pushing ahead with his ambition to transform the diocese. In the fall of 1855 he issued a pastoral letter touching on a number of topics. He ordered the feast of the Immaculate Conception to be celebrated in December with the greatest solemnity as the Catholic world had unanimously and gratefully received the dogma of the Immaculate Conception defined by Pius IX the previous December. Everyone should therefore receive the sacraments in honour of our Lady. He reminded the faithful of their duty to support the church, pointing out that failure to do so took away the right to receive the sacraments. He also threatened to remove faculties to say Mass and administer the sacraments from all pastors who siphoned off funds and failed to support diocesan, educational, and charitable needs. The primary school for boys, the convent school for girls, and the pre-seminary school for older boys were thriving. The long-neglected outlying churches and chapels needed renewal and liturgical refurbishing in every area.

The cost of communications and travel, especially the annual crossing of the plains, was for Lamy a very big part of his budget. His diocese was the size of France and he had yet to visit the territories of Colorado and Arizona to the north and west of New Mexico.

MARTINEZ RAMPANT

One of Lamy's suspended priests, Fr Antonio José Martinez, pastor of Taos, was potentially his most formidable adversary. He had spent twenty-five years working in Taos. He had tried, before Lamy, to find native youths who could be trained for the priesthood. He was very intelligent and, high up in the mountains of Taos, he kept up a lively intellectual life. Now after the disputes with Lamy over the division of Santa Fe parish, and with Machebeuf about breaking the confessional seal had subsided, he seemed to have adopted a more pacific mood. He now wrote to Lamy saying that he was beginning to feel the limitations of old age and that he was troubled with rheumatism which gave rise to great suffering in his legs, especially when he was riding.

Lamy didn't reply immediately to Martinez – he had other concerns on his mind. He had evidence that the legislators of New Mexico, under the sponsorship of Gallegos and Ortiz were preparing a huge bill of complaints against him, to be addressed to Pio Nono. Lamy wrote to Barnabo at Propaganda Fide alerting him to what was afoot, and informing him that all the opposition to him was slyly plotted by two or three Mexican priests. Machebeuf was just about to leave for Rome to bring Lamy's documents to Barnabo, so it wasn't surprising that he didn't write by return to Martinez.

Among Lamy's papers to Rome was a letter to Pius IX requesting permission for his travelling priests to say two Masses in one day – keeping the fast – at far separated missions during the pre-Christmas novenas to our Lady, for he feared that without this privilege certain places would be deprived of the devotions and cause the feast-day to lapse into a merely secular celebration. Machebeuf had been assigned the task of looking for priests, seminarians, nuns, and religious in Rome to satisfy Santa Fe's needs. He set off to cross the plains in bitter, snowy weather. His itinerary was Paris, Clermont, Rome.

Meanwhile at home things were progressing. Repairs of the cathedral and some of the churches were well advanced. People were coming back to the sacraments; children were being catechized; new churches were being built; schools were improving; the priests he brought two years ago from France were doing great good. The fact that everything had to be transported across the plains added a very high cost to all materials with the consequent need to insist on raising money through the parish churches.

Dean Ortiz was still creating problems for Lamy. He it was who had induced the members of the New Mexico legislature to make a petition to Rome against Lamy, and now, in a bizarre turn, had the insolence to suggest himself to Rome as a replacement for Lamy. Another opponent, Fr Martinez of Taos, wrote to Lamy asking that, because of his poor health, a replacement be appointed. Martinez proposed that a Mexican priest be appointed to Taos, as the natives did not like European priests. Lamy was not at all happy with this proposal and within a fortnight wrote to Martinez saying that his resignation had been accepted and that the Spanish priest, Fr Damaso Taladrid, had been appointed his successor.

Machebeuf arrived at Mount Ferrand seminary by the end of May 1856 and succeeded in persuading six seminarians to sign up for the Santa Fe diocese. By the time Machebeuf reached Rome, Pius IX had already commissioned a report from Propaganda Fide about the voluminous documentation addressed to him by Gallegos with very serious charges directed against Lamy and Machebeuf. All the accusations were laid before Machebeuf who was asked to comment on them. He gave his detailed comments on each issue and wrote a spirited defence of Lamy and himself.

MARTINEZ, GALLEGOS, POLITICS

Fr Taladrid moved to Taos after Lamy had informed Fr Martinez that his resignation had been accepted. Taladrid had a streak of arrogance which caused him to judge the New Mexicans as an inferior breed. He regarded himself as a man of education and intellectually their superior. Martinez had asked for a younger priest as his successor, a man he could mould in his own independent attitudes. But when Taladrid appeared, Martinez found that he had to deal with a mature, sophisticated and unmannerly priest.

Martinez bided his time and then together with a priest colleague in a parish twelve miles north of Taos, they both spoke against Taladrid and did everything possible to undermine his authority. There were some bitter exchanges between Martinez and Taladrid, to such an extent that in the end Martinez wrote an open letter to the Santa Fe daily newspaper to give his side of the story. Lamy, angered by this turn of events, set out for Taos to try to bring about a reconciliation between the two priests. This first trip, and a second one later during the summer, were unsuccessful in making peace between Taladrid and Martinez. Lamy learned from his visits that Martinez had remodelled his residence to contain a private oratory, and there officiated as an independent pastor. His native following, including a large section of his relations, provided him with a regular congregation. Martinez refused to cease operating as an independent pastor, and eventually Lamy issued a decree of suspension from all his priestly duties in October 1856. He refused to obey his bishop and thus entered a state of open schism.

RETURN OF MACHEBEUF

In early August Machebeuf sailed from Le Havre with a party of thirteen in all. These included the six seminarians. On arrival in New York he wrote to Lamy with details of his planned return schedule to Santa Fe, and arranging for the bishop to meet them with wagons in Kansas City. They started the crossing of the plains on 4 October and completed their journey with little incident, arriving on 10 November. The six seminarians were a great source of hope for Lamy in his plan for reforming the diocese. After a month they were ordained to the priesthood by Lamy and assigned to different posts in the diocese. Machebeuf had also brought the good news from Rome that Barnabo had listened sympathetically to his defence of Lamy against all the charges laid against him.

THE EXCOMMUNICATIONS

The Martinez affair continued smouldering. He continued to write letters to Lamy. In November 1856 he declined to withdraw the hostile assertions he had made against Lamy in the public press. He instructed Lamy about the canonical requirements for a valid suspension, and in general proceeded to lecture him about how he should properly administer his diocese. There were further letters from Martinez without Lamy giving a reply. Even though suspended, Martinez quoted St Thomas Aquinas to prove that he could still administer the rites of penance and of burial.

In March 1857 Lamy wrote to his long time friend Archbishop Purcell to share his troubles with him. He told him that the difficult issues he had to cope with on arrival in the diocese in 1851 were far from being settled. The native clergy were his crown of thorns, and he names Gallegos, Ortiz and Martinez (all suspended) as the most obstreperous. They were constantly working to get the people withdraw their support of the church through tithings. However, he now had a number of young, zealous priests who were making good progress in the parishes.

Martinez found Lamy's silence unbearable, and in April 1857 sent him another voluminous letter, complaining about Lamy's failure to respond to his previous missives, and insisting once again that his suspension was uncanonical. When Lamy still refused to reply, Martinez wrote to Machebeuf attacking the bishop for his pastoral innovations and his own suspension.

At this time Lamy decided it was time to act definitively. In June 1857 he set in motion formal proceedings of excommunication against Fr Martinez and his principal supporter Fr Lucero. When Machebeuf arrived to publish, on three consecutive Sundays, the canonical admonitions demanding for the last time the submission of the two clerics concerned, there was great excitement and the situation threatened to explode into violence. The situation polarized into two camps – those for Lamy, and those supporting Martinez. One of those supporting Lamy was General Kit Carson. On the final Sunday, Machebeuf appeared in the Taos parish church to celebrate High Mass and pronounce the decree of excommunication. During the sermon Machebeuf explained the meaning of the excommunication. He read the decree to a hushed congregation. After Mass there was no disturbance and people dispersed quietly. Taos was left with two churches, one licit under Lamy, the other illicit under Martinez, who kept his followers and never gave up his independent parish while he lived.

SCHISM

Machebeuf went to Louisville in June 1857 to meet Lamy's fourteen-year-old niece, Marie, and another girl her age, to bring them to Santa Fe where they entered the Loretto convent, first as students and then as postulants. For Marie, joining her uncle in the West was the great adventure of her life. Lamy visited the missions in the various pueblos, travelling for four months alone, from mission to mission, even though he was in constant danger from Indian attack. He was planning to educate free the families of those who couldn't afford it.

Martinez wrote again to Lamy saying that he had come to an agreement with the pastor, Fr Ortiz, about dividing the parish duties of Taos, as if such a preposterous proposal from an excommunicated cleric was in his gift. Martinez had recourse again to the public prints, and pursued Lamy for years in tracts issued from Taos. His old charges against the bishop were regurgitated again and again – his love for money, his fanatical approach to religion, that he was a ravening wolf, etc.

But in summer 1857 Lamy was thinking more about the future than about delinquent priests. He needed more priests from abroad, but he was thinking particularly about the seminary which came before every other requirement, so that he could produce priests of his own. He had already harvested a number of suitable candidates who offered great hopes. He was also thinking about the territories of Colorado and Arizona which saw little of him as yet.

THE POISONED CHALICE

In mid summer 1858 Lamy attended a provincial council held under Archbishop Kenrick of St Louis. He planned to fit in another visit to Kentucky to petition for more Loretto nuns to staff his ever-expanding school. On 12 June he left to travel east across the plains and was given a great send-off by the nuns and pupils. He reached Kentucky by the middle of July, where he found Loretto nuns ready to go West with him for the rest of their lives. In September he was in St Louis for the second provincial council.

When he returned home he was to hear the tragic news that one of his young priests, Fr Antoine Avel, who had come with Lamy from France in 1854, had been poisoned at the altar. He had served on the cathedral staff for four years, and was then assigned to the village of Mora, to replace the parish priest, Fr Munnecom, who gave scandal and was suspended. The case involved a woman who lived with a man outside of marriage. She fell ill and needed the last sacraments, but Fr Munnecom refused to give her the sacraments until she had renounced her lover – which she did. Although she received the sacraments and died shortly afterwards, her lover wanted to get revenge on Fr Munnecom and poisoned the chalice before the 9.00 a.m. Mass one Sunday which he habitually said. However, Munnecom had just been suspended and Fr Avel was substituting for him at that particular Sunday Mass. On swallowing some of the *sanguis* at Communion, he knew that it had been polluted. He was barely able to complete Mass; by now he knew he was poisoned. He died a short time later, forgiving his murderer.

A Vatican decree of that same year, 1858, placed the immense, empty lands of Arizona under Lamy's jurisdiction. He sent Machebeuf to visit the Mexican bishop of Sonora, who up to then exercised the jurisdiction for this territory, to get him to concur in the transfer of authority and to obtain his agreement to the papal separation of his diocese according to the civil boundary between Mexico and the United States. Machebeuf had travelled 500 miles from Santa Fe when he reached Fort Buchannan. He moved on to Tucson. From there he travelled south into Mexico passing through Hermosillo during the winter of 1858/59, until he arrived at Alamos to await Bishop Loza of Sonora. The next day he was able to meet him, and he immediately agreed to write the necessary documents.

He returned the way he had come, arriving at Tucson. He stayed some time there looking after the spiritual needs of the people. In the neighbourhood mission town of San Xavier there was a magnificent church from colonial days (1781) which Machebeuf was particularly keen on. The Papago Indians living close to the mission had kept alive by oral tradition the prayers and even some of melodies of the liturgy. One of the tribal elders revealed to Machebeuf a treasury of five silver chalices, a gold-plated monstrance, two gold cruets and lavabo, a pair of silver candlesticks, two silver incensors, and the old sanctuary carpet which he had kept to protect them from theft. Machebeuf left for Santa Fe in early March, arriving home after an exciting and incident packed journey at the end of the month.

AGAIN TO AUVERGNE

Although by January 1859 Lamy had established eighteen parishes with the young priests he had brought from France, he knew this was only the beginning of the plan he envisaged for New Mexico. He sent his present vicar general, Fr Peter Eguillon, to France to enlist more priests and more teachers for the boys' schools. He also had seventeen possible candidates for seminary training. He wrote to the Society for the Propagation of the Faith in Paris asking for financial help to make these plans a reality, and to form young people solidly in the faith, so as to be able to cope with the 'incredible efforts' of the Protestant proselytizers.

Like Lamy before him, Eguillon went first to the seminary of Clermont-Ferrand where he had received his theological formation, and began to make a personal appeal to the seminarians based on his own experience of the great need for priests in New Mexico. As a result of his efforts two young priests and three seminarians volunteered to go West for the glory of God. Eguillon also managed to enlist four members of the Clermont Brothers of the Christian

Schools as teachers for Lamy's schools in Santa Fe. With four pre-seminary young men and Fr John Raverdy from Reims, Fr Eguillon's party totalled fifteen, one of whom was to become the second archbishop of Santa Fe. They had crossed the plains unaware that there were many massacres by Indians during these months. They had according to Lamy, been protected by Providence in a special way.

The new arrivals were impressed by the affable simplicity of Bishop Lamy, who invited them to sit at his table for their first meal in Santa Fe. He encouraged them to learn Spanish (which was spoken generally by the people) and English, which was the language of government.

GOLD RUSH

When in the 1850s gold was discovered in Colorado, there was a rapid increase in the population. The diocese of Kansas, which included the plains and the Indian Territory, as well as Colorado, was now stretched far beyond capacity. The archbishop of St Louis notified Lamy that he had petitioned Rome to give him an extra assignment – to take over the jurisdiction of Colorado which was much nearer to Santa Fe than to Kansas.

Lamy wasn't at all happy about this new development. He felt he was barely able to manage what he had already responsibility for. He wrote to Barnabo at Propaganda Fide saying that he had no desire to extend the jurisdiction of Santa Fe. Barnabo replied in the blandest terms, encouraging him to send a priest to Colorado. Rome wrote to Bishop Miège of Kansas approving the transfer. Miège wrote in turn to Lamy giving him jurisdiction of the Colorado territory. Denver, the largest mining town in the area, was in the process of building a church. However, he reckoned there were 100,000 people in the area; more towns were going up; pastoral needs were severe. The problems didn't bear thinking about: the size of the new territory; the distance from Santa Fe (400 miles); who to send to the territory; etc. It didn't take long for Lamy to realize that Machebuef was the man for Colorado. He had all the energy, initiative, and apostolic zeal required of a man in this pastoral situation. With him he sent the young Fr John Raverdy who had come from Clermont as a deacon in 1858 and had just recently been ordained. Machebeuf started to put together all the equipment he needed for his new assignment: liturgical items for a few chapels, personal effects, blankets for their bedding, and provisions for their journey. Once again Lamy, sacrificing his strongest friend and helper to the wants of others, would be left to govern New Mexico, Arizona, and now Colorado, from Santa Fe, with only one or two priests in the capital.

On 27 September 1860 Lamy made out two documents for Machebeuf and Raverdy giving them full faculties for their new pastoral assignment. The highest mountains of the Rockies, with their great ranges and vast interior parks, now awaited Machebeuf and his assistant. On the lower slopes of these great peaks were the rude, fast-growing settlements, which they had to evangelize for Christ. They said their first Mass in Colorado at a place called Eldorado City in the foothills of Pike's Peak. When Machebeuf arrived in Denver he found that a small congregation, impatient for his arrival, had obtained a gift of two sites on the outskirts of town for the erection of a church.

In 1858 gold was found in the Platte River and the next year there was a rush of people to Denver. The energy of the whole nation seemed to be behind the movement westwards. It was a rough and tumble society where thieves and criminals were treated to mob justice. Many were attracted by the thought of making a quick fortune and then returning home to their families. By the time Machebeuf arrived in Denver it was buzzing with commerce and ongoing development. The gold-rush had, however, created a very materialistic community and Machebeuf felt the need to bring the religious dimension of life to the fore once more. He crossed the highest range of the Rockies several times in his first year to visit the poor Catholics close to the deepest mines. He was constantly on the move.

MARIE, THE CONVENT

Marie Lamy, the bishop's niece, at fourteen went to board with the Loretto nuns in 1857, and two years later she asked to be admitted to the order. Lamy officiated at the reception of his niece. She took the name Sister Mary Francesca, and with her arrival, the number of nuns reached twenty-six. There were many among them who eventually came to think of Sister Francesca as a saint.

In 1859 Lamy was happy to confirm that there were over 200 pupils between the boys' and the girls' schools. By 1861 the number had reached 300, and it was plain to see that the Christian formation of the children was having its effects on the parents. During these years Lamy put a lot of effort into the physical development of the schools, but the seminary still remained a top priority.

In 1861 a smallpox epidemic reminded Lamy of the need for a hospital. He seemed to ignore his own somewhat fragile health. In 1859 he had fainted at the altar when saying Mass on the feast of Sts Peter and Paul. He recovered consciousness after a short while and was back to his normal routine that same day. His life continued in Spartan simplicity. But he knew how to celebrate as well. After school term in 1860 he invited the nuns to a picnic at his ranchito about four miles outside Santa Fe. He loved the country and from time to time would spend a few days in his little retreat to rest and enjoy rural life. He spent a good deal of time at his desk dealing with Rome, the needs of the Santa Fe diocese, and, now, the requirements of Colorado. The raising of loans and their repayment absorbed an increasing proportion of Lamy's time. On a pastoral visit about this time he saw eight new churches being built.

CIVIL WAR AND SANTA FE

Archbishop Kenrick called a provincial council of his bishops for May 1861. Lamy took the opportunity to travel by way of Denver to see for himself the different pastoral activities being promoted by Machebeuf in Colorado. He spent two weeks there with his friend and was amazed at how rapidly the population was growing. After Easter Machebeuf took Lamy to see the mines. The most impressive was a place called Gregory about forty-five miles from Denver. Mines were still being discovered daily. He visited some of the mills at work, where some of the miners made as much as 500 dollars a day. Lamy saw that a lot of farms had already been fenced in. Machebeuf and Raverdy, one or the other, were generally out visiting mountain chapels. As a result of his visit Lamy decided to include a significant portion of south Colorado in the New Mexico parish of Mora.

He continued on to St Louis only to discover that his journey was in vain. The southern states had seceded from the Union and the country was in the opening weeks of the Civil War. He stayed in St Louis for a few days, but wanted to get home as he had heard that there had been great troubles in New Mexico. In addition there was a party of six priests and three Christian Brothers awaiting him at Kansas City to be taken across the plains to Santa Fe. They began their journey on 21 May at a driving pace. They often travelled thirty miles without pause. Under the bishop's directions each had a job to do at each camping site so that there were no unnecessary delays. They made the whole crossing in eighteen days, for a passage which often took six weeks.

When he arrived home Lamy found that the predominant sentiment among the citizens was not to take any part in the Civil War. But Texas had other ideas. Its plan was to use New Mexico as the access road to the Colorado gold mines, and then to turn west and capture California with its great gold deposits. With these acquisitions they would pay for the Confederate war. The southern area of New Mexico, even before the declaration of war, had voted to ally itself with the Confederate cause. A small Confederate force entered the southern part of the diocese. The territorial governor proclaimed New Mexico loyal to the Union and ordered conscription of all males from eighteen to forty-five. New Mexico had no pro-slavery laws. Apart from the Civil War issues, Apaches and Navajos were on the rampage and reports came in every week of their latest atrocities.

But fortunately Colorado was quiet, and when Lamy heard in late 1861 that Machebeuf was dangerously ill in Denver, he sent Fr Ussel, the pastor of Taos to bring Machebeuf to Santa Fe for proper care. Ussel found him partially recovered. Machebeuf had fallen ill to mountain fever and for two months hadn't been able to say Mass. He kept Ussel for two weeks, until he was able for the journey to Santa Fe. After a long reunion with Lamy, he travelled to Albuquerque to spend most of December with his old parishioners.

The Texans moved up to Santa Fe and on to Fort Union. There they were met by a Union battalion from Colorado at Apache Canyon which ended in a total rout for the Texans who trailed back to Texas never to return.

Lamy resumed his visits to the northern parishes of the diocese. He blessed two new churches, and inspected seven under construction – the total of new churches since 1851 was now close to thirty. Machebeuf appealed to Lamy for two new priests in order to cope with the growth in the Catholic population in Denver and in the new settlements. But there was no one to send him.

Lamy was planning two long journeys – one to Arizona and the West in this year of 1863, and the other to Rome in 1864 on his *ad limina* visit. In mid summer he had received a letter to say that Fr Machebeuf had been the victim of a terrible accident. He was in the mountains when his carriage fell from the narrow road to the rocks far below. The letter gave few details, but Machebeuf's condition was clearly life-threatening. Lamy left for Denver within the hour. He took little provisions with him and was well known to be able to survive on one meal a day, a cup of black coffee and a piece of bread morning and evening.

When eventually he arrived at Denver, Machebeuf opened the door for him, on crutches. He was, naturally, surprised and happy at the meeting. He told Lamy about the accident. When he was returning in his buggy from Central City, on a narrow rocky road cut out of the mountain side, he met a train of supply wagons. When he drove close to the outer edge to let them pass, he miscalculated, the buggy slipped, and he was thrown down the slopes to the rocks below. His right leg was broken at the hip. A doctor was called who inexpertly set the leg, but for many months he would not be able to say Mass. Machebeuf would in fact be a cripple for life: he could never ride again, and would have to go about all his work by carriage.

Lamy spent five days with him, visited some of the local congregations, and blessed the new church in Denver. As he returned home in late summer, the civil government was taking very strong action against the Navajos and

Apaches, and proceeded to implement a plan to enclose them in reservations, to prevent their constantly increasing warfare against the Mexican and Anglo-American citizens and the peaceful Pueblo Indians. Lamy was among those who most deplored the savageries of the Indians. A short time earlier one of his own priests had been murdered by the Navajos.

ACROSS ARIZONA

On 27 October 1863 Lamy set out to visit the new third of his diocese – the territory of Arizona. He resolved to go as far as San Francisco to meet the Jesuit superior to seek to persuade some of his men to undertake pastoral activities in his diocese. He was accompanied by Fr Conderet as his secretary and companion. They went down the Rio Grande to Albuquerque, where they turned west across the desert into Arizona. Lamy was very well received in the pueblos where he said Mass and administered the sacraments.

He arrived at Granite Creek on Christmas Eve. One of miners put his cabin at the bishop's disposal where snow blew through the cracks. On Christmas Day he said Mass for about twenty-five miners kneeling on the night-time's snow. The altar was improvised from old planks set up within the cabin. Only a few men could kneel inside the cabin – the rest were outside in the cold. It was so cold that a fire was lit in the cabin, and several times Lamy had to bring the chalice with its frozen wine and water to be thawed out by the stove. The snow was falling so heavily that so much came through the cabin walls, to fall on the altar, that it had to be continually brushed away.

It was soon time to move on again. He distributed mail entrusted to him in Santa Fe to bring to some of the miners. He continued on his journey, crossing the Colorado river and going west towards California. They crossed mountain after mountain until finally they were able to see a plain stretching out before them and the Californian city of San Bernardino beyond. There Lamy met by accident an old parishioner from his Ohio days, an Irishman called Quinn who had gone to settle in California. He gave Lamy every hospitality and set him off on a stagecoach for Los Angeles. In Los Angeles Bishop Amat was glad to see Lamy. He had come all the way to ask Amat about priests for Arizona. The bishop of Los Angeles was able to tell Lamy that two had already gone to Tucson. This was good news for Lamy. He spent some days with Amat who showed him the sights of California, visiting some of the mission stations on the way.

Lamy set out for Tucson and arrived there on 19 March 1864. It was a badly run-down habitation, and so hot during the day that people closed their windows and doors between eleven in the morning and four in the afternoon and slept. The mission was run by two Jesuits, Fr Osco and Fr Massea. Lamy remained there almost a month, administering baptism and confirmation to hundreds of people, both in Tucson and in a local village, San Xavier del Bac, where there were 4,000 Catholic Indians. Then he set out for home, having now completed his physical review of all the territories included within his jurisdiction.

However, on this last tract of journey, Lamy got weak in the saddle and lapsed into a semi-coma. It seemed certain that he couldn't travel any farther. Nevertheless, as on a previous occasion, he recovered consciousness and was ready to ride again. On 24 April 1864 he rode into Santa Fe. The bishop with his secretary had been absent for six months. He was within a few months of turning fifty. Welcoming him home, the *New Mexican* newspaper said: 'The Bishop is an energetic, hard-working, and faithful steward. Favoured are the spiritual flocks, who have so thoroughly upright, just and wise a shepherd ... Much good, we trust, will result from his labours ... Though sometimes weather-beaten, he appears in full health and spirits. His friends, and the members of his church, rejoice to see him again.'

All the harder, then, when he learned in August that one of the two priests at Tucson, Fr Osco, in failing health had returned to California, and since he could not safely cross the desert alone, nor could one alone tend the whole mission, Fr Osco had taken Fr Massea with him. Arizona, after all, was once again abandoned.

HOSPITAL AND SCHOOLS

There was habitually a lot of administrative work piled up awaiting Lamy's return from his pastoral journeys. He was obliged once again to alert Barnabo in Rome that six or seven miserable priests, whom he had suspended, were sending a petition against him. He reported to the Society at Paris about the progress in erecting new churches, saying that some of the buildings could accommodate as many as 1,000 people.

Although the building of a new cathedral was one of his long-term projects, there was an immediate urgency about setting up a hospital. The big question was where to find hospital staff. He had a particular building in mind to house this initiative, and wrote Mother Josephine of the Sisters of Charity in Cincinnati, asking if she could spare some of her sisters for Santa Fe. He was also making preparations for setting up an orphanage. In August 1864 Lamy got permission from Rome to delay his *ad limina* visit which was due that year – it was an exceptionally busy time in his diocese, and in any case he didn't have the money to pay for such an expensive trip.

At this time, in an effort to curtail murder and pillage, the Navajo and Apache Indians were being forced into reservations by the American army. The military authorities asked Lamy to help in civilizing the Indians by exposing them to the teachings of Christianity. Lamy's response was to open a school in one of the reservations.

The Loretto nuns at Santa Fe were not only expanding the school, but were also getting vocations to their order. As a consequence they were able to open new schools at Mora, Taos and Denver. With the arrival of extra Christian Brothers, the schools for boys were also advancing. Lamy was particularly encouraged when Fr Ussel, the pastor of Taos, arrived in Santa Fe, bringing with him twelve seminarians from Lyon. They had come by way of Denver after an exciting crossing of the plains. In the Atlantic they had met a fearful storm lasting four days and nights. Crossing the plains they had been attacked twice by Indians, and had skirted peril in a snowstorm. But all were in good health, and what was more, four Christian Brothers came with the party. Lamy could not adequately tell his gratitude to the Paris Society for their help in paying the passage for such invaluable additions to his human resources.

Another concern of Lamy was the restoration of the Arizona mission. Having seen the situation there at first hand, he was reluctant to assign anybody; so he left it to volunteers. In the spring of 1865, three proposed themselves. One could not be spared – he was building two schools at Mora. But two others, Frs Lassaigne and Bernal, offered themselves, and were sent off down the Rio Grande to Las Cruces, there to find an expedition westward, which they could join, since to go alone would be the utmost folly. In Las Cruces, they found no organized trains willing to face the Apaches. All travel had been stopped, and after three weeks of trying to find a way westward, they returned to Santa Fe and their old duties. Arizona had to wait its turn again.

HOSPITAL

A little over a year after negotiations begun, four Sisters of Charity arrived in Santa Fe in September 1865, to make Lamy's dream of a hospital in the diocese become a reality. He gave up his own house to accommodate the sisters. It was frontier country for them, but with great generosity of spirit they adapted to what were really primitive conditions. The city of Santa Fe responded generously to the financial needs of setting up the hospital under the direction of the nuns, two of who have been nurses in the Civil War. Lamy felt he could open the hospital in January 1866.

On Christmas Eve 1865 an incident occurred which left Lamy shook. It was a bitterly cold night. Midnight Mass was over by 2.00 a.m. when Lamy went to sleep in his room at one end of the hospital. In the cold and quiet of the night a man entered Lamy's room and, showing a revolver, said, 'Give me fifty dollars or I will kill you.' Lamy recognized his voice – he was one of his own servants, perhaps somewhat inebriated. Almost immediately Lamy's chief houseman arrived, and Lamy said, 'Take him out and give him fifty dollars.' The houseman took the intruder outside and sent him away, refusing him the fifty dollars. But the servant then broke into a room nearby where two priests were sleeping, one of who was seriously ill. One of the priests awoke and the stranger said, 'If you don't give me something to eat, I will kill you,' and not waiting for a reply, fired his revolver at him, hitting him in the neck. Then going to the bed were the sick man lay, he shot him in the head and in the leg. The shots roused others and the man was arrested and taken off to jail. However, the two priests, due to the expert care of the Sisters of Charity, recovered fully.

As the New Year opened, a new start in Arizona seemed promising. Fr Salpointe, whom Lamy had enlisted from Clermont in 1859, volunteered to go. Lamy sent three others with him – two priests and a young Mr Vincent as schoolteacher. The dangers of the trip to Arizona had not abated, especially from marauding bands of Indians. Hardly a week went by without reports of atrocities on travellers' paths everywhere in Lamy's enlarged diocese.

However, they set out on 6 January 1866, heading for Tucson, as Lamy had done three years before, arriving there exactly a month later. Tucson was as poor as ever, with its 600 inhabitants, its lawless life, and its unfinished church still unroofed. Salpointe was happily received and set to work in conditions far less promising than even those in Santa Fe in 1851, and Denver in 1860. It was a very difficult assignment, with most of his initial pastoral and educational efforts ending up in failure. But following Lamy's example, he gradually established the foundations for evangelization: missions first, schools next, charitable activities afterwards, and in due time, as a combination of all these, a slow emergence of the Christian life at different levels.

During May of 1866 Lamy went to Denver on a pastoral visit. He was amazed at the development of the city in the intervening years. Machebeuf brought him to Central City to lay the foundation stone for a new church, to administer confirmation, and to dismiss an Irish priest who was making trouble. Lamy gave confirmation in a number of mission centres in Colorado.

The Colorado mines were attracting people and capital from the East, especially investment in railways to reach the foot of the Rocky mountains. As the states were developing, Lamy could see the very real difference in character between New Mexico and Colorado; New Mexico remained largely Mexican, whereas Colorado was flooded with an Anglo-American population of a wholly different style, energy and values. Lamy saw that it was inevitable that a change in jurisdiction would soon come about – Colorado would become an independent vicariate apostolic. He had no doubt that Machebeuf would be its first vicar apostolic.

ROME, 'AD LIMINA' VISIT

Lamy attended the second plenary council of the American bishops, convened in Baltimore on 7 October 1866. His plan was to go on from there to Rome to make his postponed *ad limina* visit. The council agreed to petition Rome to create apostolic vicariates for Colorado and Arizona. Lamy spoke several times on these and other subjects, and was entrusted with bringing to Rome the decisions of the council. Lamy set sail from New York on 27 November, arriving in Brest nine days later. He spent three days in Paris in negotiations with the Society for the Propagation of the Faith about contributions for his return journey and the expenses of his expanding diocese.

He arrived in Rome on 16 December and stayed in the North American College. He met Pius IX in an informal way after a beatification in St Peter's. A few days later he had his private audience with the Pope during which he presented him with a richly bound copy of the Baltimore decrees. On a later date Lamy had the honour of serving the Holy Father's Mass. Lamy would have been impressed by the splendour of the Church in Rome, but would not have been scandalized by comparing it with the rather primitive condition of his own mission and desert diocese.

He reported that his diocese had a total of 135 churches and chapels. The Loretto sisters maintained five schools. Their first novitiate for postulants had good numbers, and many of the novices belonged to the first families. The boys' schools of the Christian Brothers were thriving. There were the beginnings of a seminary in Santa Fe under the direction of a priest. The number of students had never surpassed six and so far only four had been ordained priests.

The chief difficulty of the mission lay in maintaining connections with the outside world, in particular the challenge of crossing the great plains which isolated his diocese from the rest of the United States. Crossing the plains meant a journey of 900 miles without seeing as much as a hut on the way, and the constant threat of Indian attack. The journey usually took about two-and-a-half months. The three different territories of his diocese had, together, a Catholic population of approximately 140,000, divided between New Mexico (125,000), Colorado (8,000), and Arizona (7,000). He had 51 active priests; 11 were retired or suspended. Of the active priests 14 were Mexican, and 37 were European. On his current trip he expected to take another 8 or 10 back to Santa Fe.

He had made three pastoral visits to Colorado and one to Arizona. During the latter, he had travelled over 3,000 miles on horseback. In many cases he and his companions had to sleep under the stars. Through all his report there seemed to show a love of the desert and the mountainous southwest which had gradually cast its spell on him. In his final audience with Pius IX, the Holy Father gave him permission to leave Rome. Using Cardinal Barnabo's influence, Lamy was able to persuade the general of the Jesuits in Rome to send five men (three priests and two brothers) from the province of Naples to Santa Fe. In addition he managed to enlist an Italian priest and deacon. In January 1867 Lamy set sail for France from Civitavécchia.

He spent three active months in France. He enlisted six seminarians from Clermont and two more Christian Brothers. In all, Lamy would have a party of twenty-one when he disembarked from Le Havre on 9 May 1867. In America he would add several more Loretto nuns from Kentucky to the group. This was a significant increment to his diocesan resources. They arrived in New York on 23 May and two days later were at Baltimore where Lamy left the seminarians, including his nephew Anthony Lamy, who was Marie's brother, for further study with the Sulpicians. They then boarded the train for St Louis, where three Loretto nuns and two Christian Brothers joined the party. Here Lamy prepared for the plains trip west. He had twenty mules, two small wagons, and two saddle horses.

There were disturbing reports of constant Indian attacks on the prairies. However, despite the dangers, Lamy set off with his party on 14 June. While encamped some days later, four mounted Indians suddenly appeared, who scrutinized everything with immense curiosity. After asking for coffee and tobacco, they went away as quietly as they had come. Eventually they overtook a large caravan of eighty wagons heading for Santa Fe. It had well-armed protection, so Lamy decided to join it and avail of the protection it offered his people and supplies. On Sunday 14 July Lamy said Mass and preached on two topics: the need to bear with fortitude the evils of the world, and the absolute requirement that all had to give strict obedience to orders. For soon they began so see little detachments of Indians reconnoitring and retreating over and over again.

But now another trial came to afflict the wagon train: cholera was endemic to the plains and had now affected some of Lamy's wagoners. A priest who travelled part way with Lamy saw how he 'was always the same, affable, in good spirits, stout-hearted, passing his courage along to his missioners'. Such steadfastness was needed in an atmosphere of uncertainty and in the face of obstacles that the party encountered. Scouting parties had found evidence that a great number of Indians – as many as a thousand – were coming together for an attack.

As darkness was falling on 17 July, Lamy's train halted and prepared to camp for the night. Suddenly a group of Indians appeared and attacked the camp with showers of bullets. However, the Mexican drivers returned the Indian fire and the raiders disappeared into the night. The next day the bishop's train crossed paths with trains coming from Santa Fe. The same Indian party had attacked these latter the previous day, which resulted in the death of two men and several others wounded.

Lamy's train now reached the point for fording the Arizona river. The wagons were formed in a semicircle, with the passenger wagons and the animals in the centre. The news from the other wagon trains was that the Indians were in belligerent mood and no chances could be taken. A group of fifteen were sent out to survey the land above the camp. In double quick time they returned pursued by hundreds of Indians. The men in the camp fired at them and they retreated. But they kept coming back, riding with great skill, hidden behind their horses' bodies as they galloped past.

The battle continued unabated with volley after volley. The din of arrows and bullets and war cries was almost unbearable for those huddling in the wagons. One of nuns – the youngest, Sr Mary Alphonse – a Loretto nun of eighteen, was terrified out of her mind. They heard the drumming hooves advance and retreat, hoping every retreat would be the last, but the sustained onslaught lasted for three hours. Finally the main body of the Indians retreated.

The battle had gone on most of the day. Early next morning the entire train crossed the river, and marched until late. The success in the battle was in no small way due to Lamy's leadership. There was no sign of the enemy. As they came to halt that night Sr Mary Alphonse had lost all her strength. She was in fact dying. Lamy gave her the last rites. As the caravan was moving off next morning she asked that her body not be left behind but be taken to Santa Fe for burial, because she was mortally afraid that the Indians would desecrate her grave if they found it. She died at 10.00 a.m. on the morning of 24 July. Lamy wrote of her 'that she was a girl beautifully educated, and a true model of piety and all the virtues.' Her last wish couldn't be fulfilled – there was always the chance of contamination by the cholera. Towards evening Lamy, assisted by one of the priests, buried her by the trail, in a rude coffin made out of some planks taken from a wagon. A wooden cross was put on the head of her grave (In all, ten people died of cholera on the journey and were buried on the plains).

Lamy and his party arrived in Santa Fe on the feast of the Assumption. People came out to meet him, and as he entered the city he was greeted by all the bells of Santa Fe. He had been absent for almost a year, and his plains crossing, with all its encounters had taken sixty-two days. As one of his party commented about Lamy: 'his whole caravan was saved through his foresight, nerve and kindness'.

A QUIET CONSCIENCE

Just a few weeks before Lamy's return, Fr Martinez died in Taos. In his will Martinez revealed himself as one of the richest natives of New Mexico, and also confided to this same testament that his conscience was 'quiet and happy'.

Lamy wrote to the Society for the Propagation of the Faith in Paris about developments in Santa Fe. He reported that he was opening two new schools for boys with the four Christian Brothers he had come home with. In Santa Fe and elsewhere, the Loretto nuns had opened five schools. He felt the need to inform Paris about the extraordinary expenses of his year-long trip to Rome which left him practically insolvent – he would need an advance of 12,000 francs out the Society's allotment for next year. He wrote to Barnabo asking if any decision had been made about the proposed separate establishment of Colorado and Arizona. News of this came sooner than expected, given the sixteen year wait for a decision about the jurisdiction of some Mexican enclaves in US territory.

Machebeuf heard from Barnabo of his designation as vicar apostolic of Colorado and Utah. Before the Roman bulls reached him with his official appointment, he could only think of reasons for not accepting it. As a consequence of his accident, he was often in great pain, especially at Mass. In addition the Irish in his parish were actively hostile to him because Lamy had dismissed an Irish priest some years previously. As well, he had, on the orders of the archbishop of St Louis, opposed the Fenian Brotherhood, an Irish-American secret society devoted to political agitation for the independence of Ireland from England. This was a costly position for Machebeuf to take, for it meant that the Fenians – and the Irish immigration to the mines had been large – refused to contribute to the upkeep of the Church.

In any event he was persuaded to accept the appointment, and in a short while was off to Montreal to look for a priest who could be his vicar general. Machebeuf was consecrated bishop in Cincinnati by Archbishop Purcell, with as co-consecrators two priests who had come with Lamy to the US thirty years before. Lamy was relieved that he was now able to pass on to Machebeuf the jurisdiction of Colorado which he formally did in a document dated 28 September 1868. In November of the same year Lamy received the documents from Rome setting up Arizona separate from New Mexico, with Fr Salpointe as the new vicar apostolic.

Now Lamy could turn his mind to other things, such as the building of a decent cathedral in Santa Fe. He wanted a building of Romanesque design which could be constructed around and over the old earthen church. As the new stone walls would rise, they would gradually hide the adobe elevations; there would for years be a complete church within one on the outside, unfinished.

VATICAN COUNCIL

Fr Salpointe, named as the new apostolic vicar of Arizona, decided to return to Clermont to be consecrated a bishop there. Lamy entrusted to him the job of finding an architect for the cathedral and some stone masons. He then set off for Rome to attend the first Vatican Council, which was scheduled to open on 8 December 1869, the feast of the Immaculate Conception. It was attended by 600 bishops in white mitres and copes. We do not know what was Lamy's view of papal infallibility, the main issue to be decided by the Council. In any event, he got permission to leave Rome early, and arrived at Auvergne in the spring of 1870. For Machebeuf he brought back a loan of 12,000 francs which Machebeuf had raised from his brother, to cover the cost of building a church and the travel expenses of three Irish priests who were heading for Colorado.

In 1871 Lamy had the happy experience of ordaining his nephew Anthony to the priesthood. During these years he was committed largely to consolidating works begun for some time. He travelled to Baltimore to raise funds for his cathedral. He brought three more Loretto sisters from Kentucky on his return. The schools, hospital, and orphanage were making continuous progress. Lamy took his meals with the orphans. He often took his midday meal with the workers on the cathedral, serving them himself. It continued to make slow progress. Still he could report in 1872 that, including those under construction, he now had 180 churches, and that he had forty private schools under the Loretto nuns and the Christian Brothers.

FOR THE PUEBLOS

In the mid 1870s the question of the education of the Indian pueblos became a live issue. These people who were Catholic still, had a remnant of the Franciscan education brought to them in the previous century. Now the Federal government was appointing agents for Indian affairs who took charge of education in the pueblos. Resident teachers were appointed who were not Catholic, with the total neglect of religious education.

Lamy wrote a detailed account of the history of the Indian pueblos and sent it to the proper authority at Washington. What he proposed was that the government give him a modest subsidy to set up a system of education in the pueblos – a total of 6,000 dollars. This would be enough to pay a teacher in each village, and also to procure some benches, tables, stationery, books, etc. The priests' residences could serve as school-rooms. For another 6,000 dollars he would be able to bring another thirty or forty boys and girls a year to the Sisters' and the Brothers' schools at Santa Fe and elsewhere, and pay their room, board, clothing, and supplies. In the end, Lamy's proposal for the Indian schools came to nothing. For one thing, he did not have any deep experience of the American tradition of the separation of Church and state. But although he failed in his plan, he once again revealed his compassion for the needs of those entrusted to his care.

HARD TIMES

In 1874 a meeting of the provincial council of St Louis proposed, against Lamy's advice, that Santa Fe should become a metropolitan see, with Lamy as its first archbishop, with Colorado and Arizona as suffragan sees. The proposal was approved by Pius IX in February 1875. A Roman official brought the pallium for Lamy, the badge of his new office and a symbol of his participation in a special way in the Pope's pastoral office. The event was celebrated on 16 June 1875. At daybreak nine cannon guns fired off in salute. At 9.00 a.m. crowds were gathering in the street for a procession. The two suffragan bishops and twenty of the clergy of Santa Fe were assembling at the cathedral. But because the cathedral was too small for the large crowd expected, the investiture took place in an open courtyard.

There was pontifical High Mass during which the pallium was placed on his shoulders. Afterwards Lamy spoke to the crowd about his appreciation of the honour done to him by the Holy Father. The ceremony finished with the singing of the *Te Deum*. There were many forms of celebration organized by the ordinary citizens of Santa Fe, which involved not only Catholics, but also Protestants and Jews as well. This was a reflection of the universal respect and affection with which Lamy was regarded.

In November 1875, Lamy reached his silver jubilee as a bishop, an event which was celebrated with great pomp and rejoicing in Santa Fe.

ANTHONY LAMY

Fr Anthony Lamy, the archbishop's nephew, was unable to go to Santa Fe to see his uncle receive the pallium. In fact he hadn't heard about it until the archbishop mentioned it to him in a letter afterwards. He wrote to his sister

Marie in the Santa Fe convent about the poor communication with his desert parish of Manzano, and asked her to send him a detailed description of the great ceremony. Marie, or Sister Francesca as she was known in the convent, kept her brother happy by writing to him often for they had a deep affection for each other. She never forgot how she would play him a musical treat in his earlier visits to the convent. Late in 1875 he wrote her that he had visited a man in a prison cell condemned to death. He stayed with him for over an hour giving him all the spiritual consolation he could. He had done this against advice, for there was fever about, and he himself was not feeling well. But he continued to visit the condemned man and, at the end, rode in the same cart with his body to bring it for burial. Already ill, Anthony was open to contagion, caught the fever, and died on 7 February 1876, at the age of twenty-nine. As none of the Sisters could face the task, Lamy had to tell his niece that her brother was dead. 'Marie', he said, 'the bells are tolling. They are tolling for your brother.' The nuns said that she never again touched her piano. We can only imagine the immense grief and sadness that welled up in the hearts of uncle and sister as they buried Anthony. He had come to the West to give his life as a priest of God, but by an inscrutable design of Providence, the Lord took him in the full bloom of his youth.

DIOCESAN CARES

Because of the immense size of his diocese and his long experience of the difficulties of travelling by horseback to the scattered outposts of New Mexico, it is not surprising that Lamy was one of the great supporters of the development of the railroad within his jurisdiction. His was gratified to see the arrival of the railway in 1880. He could now travel in comfort to see his colleagues in Denver and Arizona.

Despite his poverty and that of the diocese, Lamy always invested in vestments of quality, especially those for big feasts and ceremonial occasions. The building of the cathedral was a constant drain on his resources. Fundraising for the project was a permanent pressure on his time. At various times he raffled off his horses, and his carriage, to raise a little money for the building. He got generous contributions from the citizens of Santa Fe – Catholic, Protestant, and Jewish.

Lamy, drawing on his experience and knowledge of the Romanesque architecture of his home country, exercised considerable influence on the design of the cathedral, mixing Romanesque with Mexican themes. In 1884 the new nave was closed over by the vaultings of the roof. And now the citizens came, on a volunteer basis, to take down, brick by brick and timber by timber, the old church, until nothing was left of the original nave, revealing the new columns and arches.

At this time the Loretto nuns and the Christian Brothers were completing new buildings for educational purposes which were very ambitious in their scope and in their style, effectively putting down markers for the future development of Santa Fe as a modern city. Mother Magdalen, who had accepted the post of superior of the Loretto sisters on the banks of the Missouri in 1852, was obliged to resign because of ill health. She was succeeded by Marie Lamy, who became Mother Francesca. She had grown into a capable maturity, and her appointment was popular with her sisters. She and her uncle remained as close as ever in affection and temperament, and their sense of family was sustained by the nearness of Marie's surviving brother Jean and his wife, who lived in Santa Fe for some years.

In 1876, when Lamy was sixty-two, he asked for a coadjutor for reasons of health, to carry out diocesan visitations with the necessary frequency; and to deal with all the extra work arising from the planning and constitution of new parishes. He proposed as coadjutor the rector of the cathedral. However, his petition was lost sight of for years in the Vatican bureaucracy without a response. Lamy made his last visit to Rome in 1878, with the appointment of a coadjutor as top of his agenda. He felt himself gradually losing the energy which he used to have, and he wanted to ensure the succession in Santa Fe, and the continuation of what he had begun. Rome asked him for the usual nominations which he forwarded after his return home.

In mid winter 1880 the city was alarmed that the archbishop was suddenly taken seriously ill. For five weeks he was close to death. The last sacraments were given him. Mother Francesca stayed with him as often as possible – during one period of five days and five nights when he was most seriously ill she scarcely left him. Lamy's strength slowly recovered, but if it did, it was now evident that he would never again be as confident and effective as before. The following year he was sick for several months, needing rest and repose to recover his spirits again.

As soon as he could write, he pressed Rome again for a coadjutor. His renewed arguments were both touching and powerful. He had difficulty applying himself to work. When he tried to go out on pastoral visits he became ill. He referred again to the immensity of his diocese, and recalled the experiences of desert and plains and Indian hazards.

One concern lay heavily upon Lamy in his choice of successor: the future of the Mexican people. He could see that very few of them would be able to follow modern progress, and he deemed it necessary that his successor should be a bishop who knew the Mexicans and who could empathize with them. Lamy really loved the native people in spite of their limitations, and wanted to make sure that they would be cared for with a fatherly affection in the new, modern society which was beginning to develop in New Mexico. He was in favour of the new developments which would bring a minimum of economic well-being to his people. However, he never became attached to things. 'I have always been poor,' he wrote, 'and I hope to die poor.'

In April 1882 he went out to administer confirmation in Red River Valley, to the north-east of Santa Fe. Travelling, as he still often did, on horseback he arrived so ill with fever that he was unable to say Mass, and only with a lot of determination was he able to administer confirmation to a large class of children. He went to bed and suffered great pain for two days. On the third day he returned to Santa Fe, having cancelled another confirmation appointment.

The question of the appointment of Lamy's coadjutor dragged out over the next two years. The archbishop's health deteriorated; his mental faculties were less responsive; his physical condition deteriorated. In the end, to Lamy's delight, Bishop Salpointe of Tucson was appointed as his coadjutor on 7 April 1884. Salpointe was one of the French priests whom Lamy had enlisted in Clermont so many years ago for the Santa Fe mission. The new appointment relieved the burden on Lamy's mind and seemed to give him a new lease of life.

THE GARDEN

One of the archbishop's pleasures was the cultivation of his garden, which he developed over the years. There was no culture of fruit trees in New Mexico, so every time Lamy crossed the plains or travelled to Europe he brought back cuttings of fruit trees, and shade trees, and grape vines, bringing them all the way in a water container, to be planted on his arrival home. The garden was laid out by the first French architects who came to build the cathedral. Formal walks reached from one end of the garden to the other. At one end was a spring which fed into a pond covering half an acre. He chose varieties of plants which would keep new blooms coming up all during the year. He loved to bring wildflowers in from the country and plant them with the other flowers. Many of the trees bore fruit and he worked season by season to improve their size and the flavour. From cuttings of California vines he grew grapes whose bunches finally measured fifteen inches long. Among his shade trees he cultivated elm, maple, and weeping willow.

Within his garden walls he delighted to see visitors – the garden was a famous sight of Santa Fe. Everybody saw that Lamy loved the work of the garden, but it was clear that he did not follow it for personal pleasure alone. He would say that the purpose of it all was to demonstrate what could be done to bring the graces and comforts of the earth to a land largely barren, rocky and dry. At a deeper level, it was a metaphor of how the soul, if cared for properly, could reach the striking fruitfulness of holiness.

One of the Loretto sisters served as the chapel sacristan. It was her duty to summon the archbishop for early Mass. When she rang the rising bell she would see his light instantly come on. At the altar he was never hurried, every motion was exact, careful and devout. The nuns saw how he kept as much time as possible for prayer and spiritual reading. His library gave evidence of much use – theological and devotional works in French, Latin, and Spanish.

Lamy was praised by others for his kindness, his affability. He was a realist, and when he believed himself to be right, he could be as firm as a rock. He was a great letter writer, and left a prodigious correspondence in the archives of Rome, Cincinnati, Paris, and Lyon. There were daily challenges for the archbishop of Santa Fe, but he lived and worked without doubts, confident that what he was doing was sharing in the providence of God. He drew his strength from love of God expressed through the long labours he pursued calmly during his life. His spiritual dedication was very moving, the result of an abiding innocence which animated all his life.

THE APOSTLE

With Salpointe installed as coadjutor, Lamy was lighter in spirit and more energetic than he had been for some time. His main local concern was to see the cathedral completed. He directed a lot of his energies to raising funds and in July 1884, to the astonishment of all in Santa Fe, he set off on a trip of several months to Mexico to raise money by donation, loan, and the little fees that would come to him for administering confirmation.

He was very impressed by the beauty of the churches he saw in Mexico. He wrote to Mother Francesca frequently during the tour, dealing with administration and business affairs that had to be attended to. He preached each time he administered confirmation. Crowds came out to meet him, and in one place he confirmed 4–5,000 people. Invitations kept arriving from other places asking him to come. He spent at least two months in the diocese of Puebla. He planed to be back in Santa Fe by early November, where he would have a few days to prepare for a meeting of the Plenary Council of the US bishops in Baltimore later that month. When he reached home in late October, he had travelled about 10,000 miles, and confirmed 35,000 people – a remarkable feat for a man in his seventy-second year.

Lamy travelled by rail to Baltimore, to the Plenary Council presided over by Archbishop Gibbons. His voice was heard in the debates, but not so strong as many remembered it. He was more than gaunt – almost emaciated now. His robes hung loosely about him. The long Mexican ordeal coming after his illnesses, and beyond these the lifetime of extraordinary exertion demanded of his so often vulnerable health, had hurried the reckoning which he was ready to meet. On his return to Santa Fe he wrote to Leo XIII, submitting his resignation with explanations as to why he should so do. Now that the succession was ensured, Lamy wrote to Cardinal Simeoni, the new head of Propaganda Fide, in January 1885, asking him to press for the Pope's acceptance of his petition.

Lamy's deepest wish was still to do something for the Indians, so he asked Salpointe to visit a number of the pueblos to see what their reactions would be to the establishment of schools. They were unanimously in favour of them.

Six months after he had offered it, Lamy's resignation was accepted by Leo XIII. On 18 July 1885 the Vatican wrote to Lamy that 'the Holy Father, with saddened heart, saw the Archdiocese of Santa Fe being widowed by the departure of its good and most worthy pastor. However, after a close examination of the reasons revealed by Your Excellency, His Holiness has accepted your resignation', thanking him for all the pastoral work he had done over the years in Santa Fe. Lamy now wrote his letter of farewell to the clergy and faithful of his diocese. He explained that the reason for his resignation was his inability to fulfil his mission due to ill health. He would use the time left to him to prepare his soul to appear before God. He recommended himself to the prayers of his people but especially to the prayers of his priests, who together with him had borne the heat of the day. He reminded them that their holy ministry would be effective to the extent that their good example accompanied their instruction. He congratulated 'most of the clergy' for their zeal and labours, a suggestion perhaps that there were still some who had not measured up to Lamy's high standard of personal dedication.

He commended himself to the prayers of the faithful, especially those whose lively faith had edified him on many occasions. He encouraged them to frequent the sacraments and to maintain their devotion to our Lady. Finally having asked forgiveness for the faults he might have committed in the exercise of his pastoral ministry, he said he would not forget to offer to God his humble prayers for all the souls that the Lord has entrusted to him during so many years. The letter was dated 26 August 1885.

The 1885 end-of-the year report of the Santa Fe diocese to the Society for the Propagation of the Faith, which bore so great a share of the expenses of the mission districts all over the world, provides a summary of Lamy's life work. It recorded 238 churches and chapels, where Lamy in 1851 found 61; 54 priests instead of 12; 2 colleges, 8 schools, many parish schools, Indian schools; a hospital and an orphanage. This was, however, only the physical plant. Lamy's great achievement was the transformation of the people through catechesis and sacramental participation, and the effect which this in turn had on society. He gave himself to his people with total generosity – there was no sacrifice which he spared himself to bring about the evangelization of the diocese of Santa Fe. This he did in a territory which at its greatest covered one tenth of the size of the United States. Lamy's last liturgical service in favour of Santa Fe was on 7 March 1886 – the blessing of the bells which had been newly hung in the new stone tower of the cathedral.

In his retirement he stayed much of his time at the Villa Pintoresca, his little country house about four miles from Santa Fe. There he had his books and his telescope, and his far view of the Rio Grande valley. Salpointe kept an eye on the old man's health and reported of it to Machebeuf. During his retirement he had the satisfaction of hearing that the government in Washington would provide financial support for the setting up of day schools in eight of the Indian pueblos. Visitors called and saw in him what an army captain saw when he called at his residence in town: 'a venerable gentleman, whose finely shaped head, clean-cut features, clear, bright eyes, discover him to be a man of acute intellect and whose gentle smile and modest, courteous manner conceal the great scholar and man of wonderful executive ability he is known to be'.

In February 1888 he developed pneumonia. Initially the doctor thought there was no need for worry, but a few days later his condition grew worse. Lamy sent for Salpointe and asked him to administer the last rites. Two nuns kept watch over him day and night – one of them was his niece Marie, Mother Francesca. During the night of 12 February Lamy coughed considerably and towards morning he was restless. One of the priests came and saw what he had to do at once – he began the prayers for the dying. Within half an hour the archbishop came to himself and looked with recognition on all in the room. His niece said he smiled as though he had seen a heavenly light. He died without pain or stress. It was 13 February 1888, and soon all the bells of Santa Fe began to toll.

After the embalming, the body was brought to the Loretto chapel to lie on a bier in the sanctuary while the community kept vigil all night. He was vested in a red chasuble with purple gloves on his hands. The pallium lay on his shoulders and breast. A white mitre emblazoned with the Holy Spirit was on his head. His hands held a crucifix. His large amethyst ring gleamed on his right hand. His feet were encased in purple slippers. The altar was fronted in black and silver.

In the morning Lamy's body was carried on a bier by six priests, led by Salpointe, through the city and the thousands of mourners to the cathedral, which it was never to leave again. He lay in state for twenty-four hours during which 6,000 people passed by to get a last glimpse of their beloved archbishop. Many kissed his purple slipper.

On Thursday 16 February, at 9.00 a.m., the obsequies began with a solemn Requiem Mass celebrated by Archbishop Salpointe, assisted by Bishop

Machebeuf and Msgr Eguillon, the vicar general. When Mass was over, Salpointe gave a eulogy in English, Eguillon in Spanish. At noon the congregation was dismissed. The ring and the crucifix were taken from Lamy's hands, the one to be kept by his niece, the other to be given to a friend.

On the evening of the funeral the corpse was enclosed in a plain wooden coffin; four days later it was removed to a metallic casket, and then lowered into the narrow crypt before the high altar of the church. The next day when his niece, Marie, started to lead the sisters in the *De Profundis*, she began to cry and could not proceed.

He died in his seventy-fifth year, having been a priest for fifty years, and a bishop for thirty-eight. Archbishop Salpointe wrote to Europe, saying how Lamy had lived so long, and was so identified with the desert and the mountain West, that all its people, regardless of their religious beliefs, were attached to him, and prided themselves on belonging to him.

A year later, Bishop Joseph Machebeuf, his life-long friend, died in Denver.

CHAPTER SEVEN

St Pius X
(1835–1914)

THE TITLE OF St Pius X's apostolic exhortation on priestly holiness, *Haerent animo*, recalls a seminal document and the memory of a great pope.[1] Giuseppe Sarto was about to celebrate the golden jubilee of his ordination to the priesthood (September 1908) and he took that opportunity to open his heart to all the priests of the Church, to share with them his great love for the priesthood, and to exhort them to have a deeper appreciation of the dignity and sanctity of their vocation. The many pastoral offices which he had exercised with such zeal and effectiveness during the fifty years of his priesthood made it easy for him to speak with authority on a subject very dear to his heart. In his first encyclical letter he urged bishops that their first concern had to be the formation of their priests in sanctity. 'All other preoccupations', he insisted, 'must yield to this.'[2] It was obvious that he would have much more to say on this topic in the future. In fact, during his eleven year pontificate, apart from *Haerent animo*, Pius X was to touch on the theme of priestly holiness in fourteen other documents to a greater or lesser degree.[3]

Before considering *Haerent animo*, and to appreciate more clearly the idea of priestly holiness as understood by Pius X, it will be instructive to consider how Giuseppe Sarto arrived to the priesthood and how he fulfilled his ministry in the many different pastoral and ecclesiastical responsibilities with which he was entrusted. When Cardinal Sarto was elected Pope in 1903, the conclave had departed from tradition by selecting, not a Curia cardinal, but a man who had come up through all the pastoral ranks of the diocesan clergy.

SEMINARY

Giuseppe Sarto was the second of ten children born to a poor family of peasant stock in 1835, in Riese, a rural town in the Veneto region of north-east

1 Apostolic Exhortation, *Haerent animo*, 4 August 1908. The English translation is taken from *The Catholic priesthood*, ed. P. Veuillot, vol. I (Dublin, 1962), pp 52–78 (subsequently abbreviated to CP, I). 2 Encyclical Letter, *E supremi apostolatus* (1903); cf. CP, I, p. 10. 3 See CP, I, pp 7–89, for the English translation of these writings.

Italy.[4] His father combined the role of village secretary with that of small farmer. His mother, who trained as a seamstress, was a woman of great gentleness with an exceptional capacity for work. He was nurtured in a home where deep faith and mutual affection were the staple environment of his youth. As a child he early demonstrated a keen intelligence, and also a capacity for initiative and organization which were to mature and flower in later years. The parish priest of Riese cultivated this particularly cheerful and pious altar boy, and in 1846 arranged for him to attend the classical course at the secondary school in Castelfranco, about seven kilometres from Riese. During the next four years he would travel on foot each day to and from the school. He was an exceptional student, always top of his class.

Beppi[5] Sarto never had any doubts that his vocation was the priesthood. Yet he realized that, since he was the eldest[6], this would involve great sacrifices for his parents. The family were in such poor straits that there was no way they could pay the seminary expenses. However, they prayed earnestly for a way around the difficulty and, as a result of the initiative of the parish priest, a scholarship was obtained from the patriarch of Venice. In the autumn of 1850 he entered the seminary in Padua. Although the scholarship paid for his keep there, a village collection was needed to pay for his books and clothes. He had just turned sixteen. Of medium height, he was thin and bony but enjoyed excellent health. He was reflective rather than extrovert, but always affable and good humoured. Very soon professors and colleagues realized that he was a student of outstanding intellectual and moral qualities. Yet because of his affability and naturalness, and his total lack of any kind of affectation, he was very popular among the seminarians. He became expert in Latin and Greek, and at the end of the first year he was ranked by the faculty *prima con eminenza* in a class of fifty-six.[7] He also acquired a keen interest in Gregorian chant, eventually becoming director of the seminary choir.

Padua, situated about twenty-five miles south of Riese, was a whole new experience for Giuseppe Sarto. An ancient university city, he came to love the architectural beauty of its churches and civic buildings. Here he could see the

4 For biographical details see the following: R. Bazin, *Pius X* (London, 1928); B. Pierami, *The life of the servant of God, Pius X* (London, 1929); Cardinal Rafael Merry del Val, *Memories of Pope Pius X* (London, 1939); K. Burton, *The great mantle* (Dublin, 1950); B. Giordani, *St Pius X: a country priest* (Dublin, 1955); H. Leonard von Matt and Nello Vian, *St Pius X: a pictorial biography* (London, 1957); H. Dal-Gal, *St Pius X* (Dublin, 1959); Gianpaolo Romanato, *Pio X: la vita di Papa Sarto* (Milan, 1992). **5** *Beppi*, the diminutive for Giuseppe, was the name by which he was affectionately called at home. **6** The first child died shortly after birth. **7** His report at the end of the first year read as follows: 'Disciplinae nemini secundus – ingenii maximi – memoriae summae – spei maximae' ['In discipline second to none, of star ability, endowed with a powerful memory, and offering the highest promise] (See Dal-Gal, p. 8). This style of report was invariably repeated at the end of each year of his stay in the seminary.

work of Michelangelo, Donatello and Giotto, and develop an appreciation for the great Italian artistic heritage. The seminary itself was a complex of fine buildings which included a printing press and a rich library. In this splendid environment he spent eight very formative years – two of humanities, two of philosophy, and four of theology. Blessed with a speculative cast of mind and a clear and ordered judgement, he applied himself with diligence to the study of Scripture and St Thomas Aquinas. He became a devoted and convinced admirer of the Angelic Doctor who led him to the Fathers of the Church. The latter he studied with uncommon avidity and never neglected them during the rest of his life. His pastoral letters and other papal documents give ample proof of this.

In his second year at the seminary his father died (March 1852). It was a particularly poignant situation as his mother gave birth to her youngest child the same day. She was left a widow at thirty-nine with nine children to rear. But Margharita Sanson, a woman of strong and deep piety, took on this daunting task with immense faith in God. Her eldest son would later sum up her life as follows: 'She worked so hard and suffered so much that she should have a permanent place in the thoughts of everyone who knows the meaning of work and of suffering.'[8] The grim financial prospect for the family weighed heavily on Beppi, especially as he was the eldest and was the only one who could do something about it. The obvious thing was for him to give up his studies and take his father's place at home. However, his mother and her good neighbours in Riese would hear none of this, and the parish priest made sure that Beppi could continue at the seminary and that the financial needs of the family were looked after.

In his last year in Padua he began to collect books for a small library. In January 1858 he writes enthusiastically to his mentor, Don Jacuzzi (the former curate at Riese), that, in a shop in Padua, the best works of St Cyprian and St John Chrysostom, in 'a fairly correct edition', were to be had at a moderate price. These, in twenty-four volumes, he had managed to procure 'by going without other things', and he offered to get a set for his friend.[9] He received the diaconate in June 1858, and was ordained priest in the cathedral of Castlefranco on 18 September of the same year.

FIRST APPOINTMENT

His first appointment was that of assistant pastor in Tombolo, a town of some 1500 inhabitants about five miles from Riese, in his own diocese of Treviso. Its

8 von Matt and Vian, p. 1. **9** Bazin, p. 34.

chief business was cattle raising and trading. The peasants were strong and sunburned but good-hearted and pious, even though given to swearing and over-indulgence in wine. Fr Sarto lived first with an elderly couple, but after a few months he managed to rent a small house and got his sister Rosa to look after it. His pastor, Don Antonio Costantini, was a man of piety and culture and quickly recognized the exceptional potential of his new curate. He was a real father to the young priest, and a deep bond of friendship was established between them. He shared Fr Sarto's interest in study, music, prayer, and pastoral zeal. Shortly afterwards Don Antonio would write to a friend:

> They sent to me as curate, a young priest, with orders to mould him to the duties of a pastor; in fact however, the contrary is true. He is so zealous, so full of good sense, and other precious gifts, that I can learn much from him; some day or other he will wear the mitre, of that I am sure. Afterwards! Who knows?[10]

The Tombolese quickly took a liking to their new curate, who was thin but strongly built, of middle height with an attractive face. He mixed easily with young and old, joining them at times in their games of bowls or cards to win their confidence. One day during his first year as curate he heard one of the younger men lamenting the fact that he could neither read nor write. As a result he decided to set up an evening school with two streams. Those with some rudiments of knowledge were taken by a local teacher; the totally illiterate he taught himself. In addition he gave extra classes to boys from Tombolo and nearby towns who expressed a desire to become priests, to prepare them for the secondary school entrance exams.

Confessions, catechism classes, choir practices, as well as visitation of the sick kept him constantly on the move. He was singularly attentive to the dying, preparing them to receive the last sacraments, encouraging and consoling them with the hope of the reward to come. He settled disputes, called people to their duties, made peace among families. The young priest was always busy – 'in a state of perpetual motion', as his sister Rosa described him. His excessive workload was due to some extent to the fact that the parish priest was a very sick man for most of Fr Sarto's nine years in Tombolo. His concept of adequate sleep was four to five hours a night. When Rosa complained about all the candles he was burning up, he replied truthfully that the night hours were the only time he had for study and reading. During these years he deepened his knowledge of Sacred Scripture, canon law, and the *Summa* of St Thomas.

Don Constantini passed on to his young curate all his knowledge and experience as a preacher. He had a good student, and very shortly Fr Sarto's

10 Pierami, p. 19.

fame as a preacher so spread that he was invited to speak from the pulpits in neighbouring towns. He had a fine, sonorous voice and a great command of language. His ideas were clear and well ordered. But it was his ability to speak from the heart, and make the Gospels come alive, that won for him a reputation as a preacher. People knew that he practised what he preached.

There was poverty aplenty in Tombolo. Fr Sarto was moved by compassion for the plight of poor families, and he responded to every request as long as he had anything to give away or something to pawn. His personal experience of poverty gave him a penetrating insight into the needs of the poor. Their humiliations found a deep echo in the soul of the priest who as a seminarian had to beg from door to door in Riese to find the money to pay for his books and clothes for the seminary. The people soon knew when he would be in funds and were on hand when he returned from a preaching assignment in another town to provide him with an immediate opportunity of parting with the stipend he had just received. Yet in no way did he confuse the Christian virtue of poverty with misery or mere absence of material possessions. In 1862 he was asked to preach the funeral sermon in the neighbouring town of Galliera for a rich lady who had spent her money generously for the benefit of the Church and the poor. He took as his text the phrase 'Blessed are the poor' from the Sermon on the Mount, saying that it applied, as well, to those 'who though abounding in riches, are detached in their hearts and wills from all the possessions that earth can offer them ... Truly poor she was, even though a rich woman, with a poverty which has its roots in the example of Jesus'.[11]

The Tombolese saw that he was totally dedicated to them, a true priest after the manner of Christ. He understood them because he loved them. The people reciprocated that love and, as a consequence, they came to respect the Church and to change their lives. The Eucharist was the centre of his day. A great deal of his time was taken up in preparing children for their First Holy Communion, and inculcating a deep devotion to the Real Presence in the Tombolese faithful. He encouraged people to come to Communion frequently. He realized very quickly, however, that the greatest obstacle to his mission as a priest was the religious ignorance which he encountered among his parishioners, and so he set about an enthusiastic programme of catechesis. This aspect of his priestly responsibility was to occupy an important part of his ministry for the rest of his life, whether as bishop of Mantua, patriarch of Venice, or Vicar of Christ.

11 Burton, p. 44. He continued, 'Neither do I look upon those as truly poor who wander from place to place dressed in rags, because for the most part under the appearance of poverty is hidden the desire of possession' (Bazin, p. 43).

PARISH PRIEST

At thirty-two he became parish priest of Salzano, a town of about four thousand inhabitants, one of the largest parishes in the diocese. That was July 1867. While the Tombolese were heartbroken at the news that they were losing their beloved curate, the parishioners of Salzano were surprised that one so young would be appointed to a position normally reserved for seminary professors, monsignori or experienced parish priests. They didn't display much enthusiasm for the new arrival, but the atmosphere in the town changed radically after they heard him preach on the day of his induction. They were soon asking why did the bishop allow such a zealous and competent priest be buried for so long among the poplars of Tombolo!

He threw himself into his new responsibilities with the same commitment and generosity which characterized his previous appointment. There was an orphanage, elementary schools, and a poor house to be attended to. Every family was visited. He gave special attention to the youth of the parish, organizing classes and activities for them, gradually drawing them to the sacraments and regular participation in the religious life of the parish. He taught them Gregorian chant, and so communicated his own enthusiasm for it that they learned to love the Mass through this medium. However, he saw that much work remained to be done to bring about a deep conversion of his parish.

As before, he was convinced that the most effective weapon for the eradication of vice and sowing the seeds of virtue was the constant, thorough and enthusiastic teaching of the catechism. Fully persuaded of the direct correlation between sin and ignorance of the things of God, he exhorted his parishioners at every opportunity to attend the parish catechetical instruction. Those who came were deeply impressed by the profound conviction and the originality with which he explained the fundamentals of the faith. They found him easy to listen to. He introduced a system of dialogue instruction with the assistance of a young priest from a neighbouring parish. Large crowds were attracted every Sunday evening, not only from the outlying districts of his own parish, but from other parishes as well. When the neighbouring parish priests found themselves preaching to diminishing congregations they complained to the bishop. However, his lordship, who was following with increasing interest the prodigious activity of the youthful pastor of Salzano, gave them little satisfaction and simply told these disgruntled priests to go and do likewise.

EUCHARISTIC FORMATION

Development of Eucharistic devotion was at the centre of his pastoral strategy for the parish. He prepared the children to receive their First Holy

Communion at an age notably earlier than was customary at the time. It was here that the seeds were sown of that great Eucharistic renewal in the Church which, years later, would earn for its chief architect and promoter the title of 'the Pope of the Eucharist'. Only two years after his election to the chair of Peter, he issued a decree encouraging daily Communion.[12] Because of the plague of Jansenism and unnecessary rigor about the required dispositions to receive Communion, he was very conscious that the recommendations of Trent about frequent Communion[13] had effectively become a dead letter. Pius X taught in this decree that since Christ compared the Eucharist to the manna, the daily food of the Israelites in the desert (cf. Jn 6:59), the Christian soul should be daily nourished by the Eucharistic bread and thus have access to the supernatural resources to grow in virtue and avoid sin. His own pastoral experience revealed to him the deleterious effects of infrequent reception of the Eucharist. Drawing on the example of the early Christians (cf. Acts 2:42), he proposed frequent and daily Communion as a practice earnestly desired by Christ for all who are in the state of grace and who approach the Table of the Lord with a devout intention.

All during his priestly ministry Giuseppe Sarto prepared children to receive Holy Communion at seven or eight years of age. This was a daring innovation, since the normal age for making First Communion then was twelve or older. But the priest from Riese had frequently meditated on the import of Christ's words: 'Let the children come to me, do not hinder them; for to such belongs the kingdom of God' (Mk 10:14). He also realized how highly Jesus regarded the innocence and simplicity of children, as for example on the occasion when he reminded his disciples that unless they became like little children they would not enter the kingdom of heaven (cf. Mt 18:3–5). Down through the centuries many errors and abuses had crept into the matter of determining the age of discretion, such that frequently children were fourteen and over before they received. Pius X was painfully conscious of the grave damage caused to the souls of the young by depriving them of the nourishment of the Eucharist at a critical time in their lives, a time when they were surrounded by temptations and often in danger of falling into bad habits. This erroneous attitude to early First Communion was also the result of Jansenism which saw the Eucharist as a reward rather than a remedy for human frailty. Hence, after his election to the papacy, he clarified that the historic mind of the Western Church was that children could and should approach the Eucharist when they reached the use of reason.[14]

12 Decree, Congregation for the Council, *Sacra tridentina synodus*, 20 December 1905. For a very accessible source for the principal doctrinal writings of St Pius X, see *My words will not pass away: doctrinal writings of St Pius X* (Manila, 1974). **13** Council of Trent, 22nd Session, chapter 6. **14** Decree, Congregation for the Discipline of the Sacraments, *Quam singulari*, 8 August 1910.

DEVOTION TO OUR LADY

In Salzano he introduced May devotions in honour of our Lady. Devotion to the Mother of God was a characteristic mark of the piety of Giuseppe Sarto from the days when, as a schoolboy, he went on pilgrimage to the shrine of the Madonna of Cendrole, just outside Riese. We get some idea of the depth of his Marian piety from a pastoral letter he wrote in September 1885, a few months after his arrival as bishop of Mantua:

> Say the Rosary, my dear children, for, if in our times intellectual pride, which scoffs at submission, corrupts the heart and undermines Christian morality, lamentably prevails, there is no more secure means for the triumph of faith than meditation on the mysteries of the most holy Rosary. Say the Rosary, because if piety is becoming tepid and is extinguished in the hearts of many, nothing can rekindle its flame better than the prayer which Jesus taught, the one with which the angel saluted Mary and the one which is continually chanted around the throne of God in heaven. Say the Rosary, for it is an exercise of piety which unites the faithful in prayer and cannot fail to inspire sentiments of concord which bring unity to families and peace to society. Say the Rosary; this will be the spring of untold blessings, the safeguard of the city and its people, for it is impossible that God should turn a deaf ear to the invocation of so many of his children and that Mary should not answer the prayer with which the Church implores her patronage.[15]

In 1873 a cholera plague hit the whole of the Veneto region, bringing with it many casualties. In spite of the highly contagious nature of the disease, Fr Sarto tried to get to the bedside of every stricken person, especially the poor, comforting them and administering the sacraments. Indeed, because of the deplorable sanitary and hygienic conditions in the poorer quarters of the town, he acted not only as pastor but, in conjunction with the one overworked medical doctor in the region, as infirmarian and sanitary inspector also. He had learned much about how to deal with this disease from his experience of a similar outbreak in Riese while he was still a seminarian. During the epidemic, as a hygienic precaution, the bodies of the dead were buried at night. Don Sarto, however, was always in attendance, not only to perform the burial ceremony, but also to ensure that in these emergency circumstances the bodies of his dead parishioners would be treated with respect. By the time the epidemic was over the parish priest was just skin and bone. His health had deteriorated seriously,

15 Dal-Gal, p. 87.

and he became so weak that even the very sight of food nauseated him. The bishop came from Treviso to urge him to rest and he finally consented to a brief vacation, financed by a local Jewish industrialist who had become a close friend of Fr Sarto. After a few months he was back to his normal pristine health.

It is not surprising that the people of Salzano acquired a deep affection and veneration for their pastor. His concern for their welfare was not limited to the purely spiritual. He had an extraordinary grasp of practical affairs as well. He set up a hospital in the town, and promoted rural savings banks to solve the difficult social problems of the time. The working classes, impressed by the practical concern of their pastor to improve their often squalid material conditions, were attracted back to the practice of the faith. His reputation for holiness was also growing apace.

SPIRIT OF POVERTY

He was prodigal in his relief of the poor, as usual spending beyond his means. The remonstrances of his sisters Rosa and Anna were of no avail – the only answer they received was: 'God's providence will never fail us'. At one point, when his clothes and shoes had become the worse for wear, his sister Rosa conspired with the other priests to buy new clothes to bring his wardrobe up to scratch.

At every stage of ecclesiastical preferment he practised a deep spirit of detachment and of personal poverty. The last thing he would do was to live at the expense of others, nor would he allow anyone use the Church for material advantage. This is illustrated particularly in the case of his own sisters, Rosa and Anna, who kept house for him in Tombolo, Salzano, Mantua and Venice, and Maria who joined them when he took over episcopal responsibilities in Mantua and Venice. They were happy to serve the Church through serving their brother, to whom they were devoted and for whom they had a deep affection. Apart from their minimal expenses they didn't expect, nor did they ever receive, a regular wage. When their brother was elected Pope, they never hoped for any recognition and were happy to return to Riese. On the day of his election he was asked by a representative of the papal aristocracy what title he would give to his three unmarried sisters who had looked after his needs over so many years. 'What title?', he repeated; 'call them the sisters of the Pope; could there be a more honourable title than that?'[16] However, he still wanted to have them close to him. Although it would have been expected that

16 Dal-Gal, p. 199.

they would live with him in the Vatican – and the Pope had every right to so arrange – he established his sisters in a modest apartment in a neighbouring piazza, and they came to visit him on Wednesdays and Saturdays, and to eat with him occasionally. Their greatest privilege, and they asked for none other, was to be present in his private chapel for Mass on the great feast days of the year. They gave their time to charity and good works, most of it at the request of the Pope.

We are told by Cardinal Merry del Val, Pius X's secretary of state, that when Rosa, the eldest, to whom he was particularly attached, fell ill and died (1912), the fact of not being able to attend to her at the last, because of protocol requirements, cost him dearly. Her Requiem Mass was celebrated by the Pope's chaplain in St Peter's. It was attended by all the cardinals living in Rome, members of the diplomatic corps and many others who came to honour the person who, apart from his mother, had first claim on the affections of the Holy Father. In his last will Pius X expressed the wish that a small allowance would be made to his sisters during their lifetime:

> Having to provide for my sisters, Rosa, Maria and Anna, who have always lived with me and served me without the slightest remuneration, I recommend them to the generosity of the Holy See, that so long as one of them lives a monthly allowance of three hundred lire be allotted to them.[17]

As Merry del Val points out, this minimal request for his sisters contrasted with the regal generosity he showed whenever the opportunity arose of offering assistance to those in need.

CHURCH MUSIC

From an early age Beppi Sarto acquired a great love for music through the encouragement of the curate in Riese. He had an opportunity to develop this interest in the seminary in Padua and, as we have seen, became so proficient that he was entrusted with the task of directing the seminary choir. He developed a deep interest and affection for Gregorian chant and taught it to the youth of the parishes in which he served as a means to help them acquire a deeper love for the liturgy and the Mass. In Salzano, as soon as the organ was repaired, he got together a fine choir of men and boys. He was pleasantly surprised at the response of these young people to plain chant, but even more

17 Merry del Val, p. 68.

pleased at the evidence of the deeper piety which it inculcated. Consequently, it is not to be wondered at that he took exception to the presence of music in churches which he considered more appropriate to the theatre or the concert hall. In Venice he published specific instructions as regards church music, excluding secular music and restoring Gregorian chant to pride of place, encouraging its use in liturgical functions.

He had a natural talent for music. The fact that he managed to acquire a considerable knowledge of the technicalities of the art, despite his constantly absorbing pastoral duties, confirms this. He appreciated good music of every kind, but sacred music interested him most. He wanted for the liturgy of the Church music which was truly sacred and eminently in keeping with the sentiments of the faith. His guiding principle in the selection of music was that it should be an aid to devotion and lead us to God. When it became excessively prominent in liturgical ceremonies and ceased to be subsidiary to divine worship, he rejected it.

Although he did much to reform and embellish Church music, he didn't impose a particular taste because there was no narrowness in his conception of sacred music. His tastes were not confined to Gregorian chant: he welcomed polyphonic music provided the principles of its religious character and gravity were maintained.[18] Merry del Val, as secretary of state, was the Pope's closest confident and friend. The cardinal with the quintessential aristocratic background became the greatest admirer of the peasant Pope from Riese, acquiring a profound appreciation of Giuseppe Sarto's many natural talents, as well as learning much from his sanctity. He too had a great love of music and so was in a privileged position to assess this aspect of the Holy Father's culture.

> I recollect, he tells us, how intensely he enjoyed listening to Persosi's great oratorio, *The Last Judgement*, which by his own wish was executed under the personal direction of the author in the Sala Regia. How he commented on the inspired rendering of the Scriptural texts, the richness of the orchestral parts, without failing to point out the qualities or deficiencies he had noted here or there either in the composition itself or in the singers. He experienced even more pleasure in the glorious chant of several hundred voices during the solemn Pontifical Mass which he sung in St Peter's for the centenary of the great St Gregory.[19]

As Cardinal Ratzinger points out, 'insisting on chant as the truly liturgical music was for him part of a larger reform programme that was concerned with restoring to worship its purity and dignity and shaping it according to its own inner claim.'[20]

18 See Merry del Val, pp 50–3. **19** Ibid., pp 50–1. **20** Joseph Cardinal Ratzinger, *A new song for*

CANON OF TREVISO

The talent and pastoral zeal of the young pastor of Salzano had not gone unnoticed by his bishop. In 1875, when Fr Sarto was just forty, he was summoned to the diocesan office in Treviso. There he was informed by his bishop, Dr Zanelli, that he had been appointed spiritual director of the seminary and chancellor of the diocese. He did everything possible to persuade the bishop to choose somebody more suitable for these tasks, but to no avail. These were responsibilities which called for intelligence, sound judgement and prudence, and Dr Zenelli well knew that in Fr Sarto he had his man. He returned to Salzano with sorrow in his heart at the prospect of leaving the people to whom he was now attached by bonds of deep affection. He would also have to live in the seminary which meant that he would have to dispense with the generous care and attention of his sisters Rosa and Anna.

One of the joys of his new appointment was that it brought him back into close contact with his old and well-loved friend of Riese days, Don Jacuzzi, who was now rector of the seminary which had over 200 students and a fine staff. His first talk to the seminarians startled them somewhat. He said they probably expected him to be a man of great learning with much experience in ascetical theology. However, he had to tell them that he was really only a country parish priest, and that they would have to be indulgent with him. Yet, after listening to that first conference, with its exceptional clarity and order of ideas, and observing his patent humility and love of God, the students were in no doubt that this was a somewhat different 'country parish priest'. By his natural charm he very quickly won the hearts of the seminarians, and most of them wanted him as their confessor even though they had the freedom to choose other priests.

He encouraged learning but never at the expense of piety. He preached to them and directed their monthly days of recollection and annual retreats. In his formation of the students he insisted on the dignity of the priestly vocation, the importance of apostolic zeal, and the need for a deep and unostentatious piety if they were to be effective pastors of souls. He encouraged love for study and obedience to superiors but, above all, he emphasized detachment from the things of the world and a readiness to sacrifice everything to carry out one's duty as another Christ.

He did not neglect the human side of their formation. He encouraged order, cleanliness, and refinement. Indeed it soon became well know that Monsignor Sarto had a passion for cleanliness, which was another attractive aspect of his positive spirit of poverty. He taught the seminarians the impor-

the Lord (New York, 1997), p. 131.

tance of politeness and good manners. Although always very understanding and approachable, he would not tolerate slothfulness or carelessness, and only became annoyed when he saw evidence of softness or self-indulgence. He knew how to reprimand but, no matter how stern his corrections might have been, no one ever felt hurt or bore a personal grudge against him on account of it. They knew he would never withdraw his friendship from them.

Apart from his work in the seminary, his main responsibility was that of chancellor of a diocese with 210 parishes and 350,000 souls. In 1878, three years after his arrival in Treviso, he was appointed vicar general of the diocese at the relatively young age of forty-three. The bishop was now in failing health, so an increasing proportion of the work of diocesan administration fell on the broad shoulders of Monsignor Sarto. He continued his old habit of working late and rising early. However, at his own request, he still found time to do what for him was a labour of love – the preparation of the children in the school for their First Communion.

When the bishop died in 1879, the cathedral chapter unanimously elected their youngest member, Monsignor Sarto, to be diocesan administrator. He exercised this task with the competence and zeal to be expected of a man of his track record until the new bishop was appointed seven months later. He continued as chancellor under the new ordinary and, to his great delight, he was able to return to the seminary to the work he loved. He would have been happy to spend the rest of his life there training young men for the priesthood. However, he was only given a temporary respite. In 1884 he was informed that Leo XIII had appointed him bishop of Mantua.

BISHOP OF MANTUA

When shown the official document of his appointment, his first reaction was that there must have been a mistake. That very day he wrote a letter to Rome listing the reasons why he considered himself unfit to fill such a position. Given the recent history of this diocese, he had some justification on his side.

Mantua was a suffragan see of the Milan archdiocese, about a 120 kilometres south west of Treviso. It had a population of a quarter of a million spread over 150 parishes. When Mantua was under Austrian control there had been a struggle between Rome and Vienna over the appointment of bishops, which had left the diocese vacant at various times for several years. In 1866, after the integration of the province of Lombardy under Italian rule, the new anti-Catholic government closed all monasteries, took on itself the management of religious foundations, and loaded Church properties with heavy taxes. In 1871, when Bishop Rota was appointed, he was not only refused the official recognition to carry out his duties, but was forbidden to live in Mantua. Political differences had caused a deep cleft between the bishop and a large number of the clergy and laity who were enthusiastic supporters of the New Italia. The see remained vacant for most of the years intervening before the appointment of Monsignor Sarto in 1884. His immediate predecessor had effectively to be withdrawn because of his inability to make any impression on what was a very difficult situation.

Many parishes were without priests, and there was a history of discord between priests and people. Preaching and the teaching of catechism were neglected because there were few zealous priests. It did not help matters that, after the transfer from Austrian rule, the social condition of the clergy was at a low ebb; the majority were badly provided for. The seminary had been closed for years and, although it had been reopened for a short while by Bishop Sarto's predecessor, it remained closed because of lack of funds and the fact that there were few aspirants to the priesthood.

The educated elite were strongly influenced by freemasonry and liberalism of the virulent, continental anti-Catholic stripe. During this period also anti-religious socialism was gaining powerful support among the working classes. For all these reasons, as can be imagined, many of the faithful had become estranged from the Church and religious indifference prevailed. Civil marriages were common and attendance at Easter duties was dwindling rapidly. In a word, the diocese of Mantua was in a state of religious and ecclesiastical disarray when Leo XIII requested Monsignor Sarto to take it over and turn it around. The Pope had kept himself well informed about the talents and performance of the indefatigable parish priest of Salzano and vicar general of the diocese of Treviso, and when he had to make this difficult appointment he was convinced that Giuseppe Sarto was the right choice.

He took over his new responsibility in April 1885. While he applied himself with his exceptional energy and initiative to the difficult tasks facing him, what he needed most, and what he possessed in abundance to restore unity and discipline, was a deep supernatural outlook and the capacity to lead by way of example and authority. He saw very clearly that, if the diocese was to be recovered, the first thing he needed was a new generation of zealous, hard-working priests. Just a month after taking over his new responsibilities, reflecting on the impossible state of the diocese, he wrote to a friend: 'On the first Sunday of August I shall ordain the one and only priest for the diocese this year – the only fruit of the seminary! – only one when I need at least forty!'[21] Consequently his first priority was the restoration of the seminary and the promotion of vocations to the priesthood.

21 Dal-Gal, p. 57.

PROMOTION OF SEMINARY

Within weeks of his arrival in Mantua he addressed his first pastoral letter to the whole of the diocese on the matter of the seminary. It was a passionate appeal to the people to pray for vocations and for financial support. His great anxiety, he told them, was the lamentable condition of the seminary. He spoke to them about the evils which afflicted society as a consequence of the lack of priests:

> Have you yourselves not witnessed the unused church, the abandoned altar, the empty confessional? Have you not seen young men growing up ignorant of the things essential for their salvation, the sick and the dying without the consolations of religion, the mystic Sion now solitary? Love the seminary! This is the desire of your bishop. Let no one allege the scantiness of his income or the poverty of his parish, for there is no one who cannot give a centime, a fruit, a vegetable. Nothing is impossible to him who loves. Love the seminary! This is most necessary for the diocese of Mantua at the moment. Your small offerings will renew for you the prodigy of the widow of Sarepta, who, for the morsel she gave to the prophet Elias, received the promise that the pot of meal should not waste nor the cruse of oil be diminished. Love the seminary! In this you will fulfil the great desire of your bishop and you will merit to see this dear family, the apple of my eye, growing to its fullness.[22]

His clear message was that the people of Mantua had to do all in their power to make the seminary flourish again to provide for the priestly needs of the diocese. In talks to priests and laity, while on parish visitations, Monsignor Sarto used to repeat constantly, 'I want you to love your seminary at Mantua! Support it by your prayers and alms! Ask that vocations may increase among the young, for the life of souls depends on it.'[23]

The response to such ardent appeals was immediate and generous. Within a few years, as a result of his vigorous apostolic zeal and his fortitude in overcoming the financial and academic problems associated with the restructuring of the seminary, the number of seminarians rose to over 150. By the time he was to leave to become patriarch of Venice, nine years later, he would have ordained sixty men to the priesthood with many more in formation. By any standard this was surely a remarkable achievement.[24]

This development did not, however, happen automatically. The personal input of the bishop to the seminary during this period was immense, including

22 Ibid., p. 58. **23** Bazin, p. 82. **24** Dal-Gal, p. 60; also Pierami, p. 57.

taking on the responsibility of rector during the first difficult years. He visited it each evening when he wasn't absent on parish visitation, and took an interest in everything – academic staff, studies programme, examinations, the material needs of the students, etc. He impressed on the superiors the need to exercise great vigilance in accepting candidates, and he worked out with them a programme of spiritual formation to ensure that the seminarians were solidly grounded in the spiritual life. His primary concern was to form the students with a true priestly spirit, to make them zealous for the salvation of souls, and unstinting in their self-sacrifice.

Monsignor Sarto choose his professors carefully, making sure they were competent and orthodox. He increased the philosophy and theology courses, giving particular emphasis to the doctrine of St Thomas Aquinas, the importance of which he appreciated as few others did at that time. He added other courses to deal with current philosophical and theological errors. He went further. Despite his other multiple responsibilities, he took on the teaching of the more difficult subjects of the theology course, and often supplied for other professors when, for some unavoidable reason, they were unable to give their classes. He passed on to his future priests the benefit of all his own immense pastoral experience.

He got to know the students well, their family background, their strengths and weaknesses. They had to show that they were making a serious effort to grow in piety and be diligent in their studies – otherwise they had no future in the seminary. He was a strict disciplinarian, but because of his affable character they enjoyed being in his company. Monsignor Sarto, for his part, looked forward to relaxing with his seminarians in the summer villa which he acquired for them, and where he took his holiday breaks. After completing the seven year seminary course, the newly-ordained priest was allocated to a suitable parish under the vigilance of a zealous priest. However, his studies were not yet completed. Monsignor Sarto stipulated that during the subsequent four years the young priest had to present himself annually before a board of examiners to be questioned on a prescribed course. The bishop was always present at these examinations.

PRIESTS OF MANTUA

In his first report to Rome at the end of 1885, he informed the Vatican authorities that there were over 300 priests and 350 churches in his diocese. His first objective was to develop a spirit of unity and fraternity among the clergy. He worked indefatigably to eradicate the divisions which he had inherited, and he gradually won over the priests by his kindness and patience. He impressed on them the need to inculcate in the young men of their parishes esteem for the priestly life. Whenever they saw a possible candidate they were to leave nothing undone to encourage his vocation.

Some priests, however, brought him much sorrow as well. In Mantua, Protestantism had taken root and several of the priests had been infected by it. The bishop prayed constantly that the Lord would enlighten the minds of these men. So one can imagine what a bitter experience it must have been for him when the parish priest of Rovere publicly apostatized to Protestantism. Although deeply grieved, in order that the faith of the people might not be weakened by the scandal, he immediately announced a mission in the parish which he preached himself, even though it was midwinter. To make reparation, he decided to hold the Forty Hours devotion in the parish. When he went to look for the monstrance, he was dumbfounded to discover that it had been stolen by the curate who had also lost the faith!

His priests were always welcome at his table. Gradually he won them over to a deeper commitment to their priestly vocation, even the most reluctant. When amiability didn't achieve his purpose he could be more direct, as in the case of the priest in Mantua city who didn't respond to encouragement to arrive in time in the church for confessions before the early morning Mass. One morning, just before Mass was to begin, this priest saw a queue outside the confessional with people entering and leaving. When he pulled back the curtain to investigate who the uninvited confessor was, he found his own bishop smiling out at him. Needless to say, the recalcitrant priest didn't require any further encouragement about fulfilling his pastoral responsibilities.

In several pastoral letters, as well as in personal conversation, he encouraged his priests to live up to the dignity of their calling:

> Wherever he is, or in whatever work he engages, the priest must never cease to be a priest, accompanied by the dignity, gravity and decorum of a priest. He must therefore be holy; he must be saintly, so that his words and his works express his love, impress his authority and command respect.[25]

He expected them to work hard, to be generous and obedient, to be paragons of virtue. This would guarantee integrity of faith and the courage to profess and defend it. In a pastoral letter addressed to the clergy of Venice and Mantua in 1894 (just before he took possession of the see of Venice), a letter which is regarded as among the most important of his episcopate, he denounces the position of the so-called liberal Catholics, influenced by modernism, and the damage which they were doing to the Church:

25 Dal-Gal, p. 72.

> Let priests take care not to accept from the liberals any ideas which, under the mask of good, pretend to reconcile justice with iniquity. Liberal Catholics are wolves in sheep's clothing. The priest must unveil to the people their perfidious plot, their iniquitous design. You will be called Papist, clerical, retrograde, intolerant, but pay no heed to the derision and mockery of the wicked. Have courage, you must never yield, nor is there any need to yield. You must go into the attack wholeheartedly, not in secret but in public, not behind barred doors but in the open, in view of all.[26]

The sanctification of his priests was a concern dear to the bishop of Mantua's heart, as it would later be in Venice and in Rome.

In his dealings with his priests he preferred persuasion to compulsion, kindness to severity, and many remarked that it was the charm of his virtue rather than the strength of his authority (which he certainly didn't lack, and which he didn't neglect to use when necessary) which enabled him to hold his diocese in the palm of his hand. Respect and veneration for their bishop was enhanced by the knowledge that personal influence held no weight with him. Priests quickly became aware of the fact that recognition and promotions in the diocese were giving strictly according to merit. He particularly enjoyed the time spent with them doing his annual retreat. When he preached to them he did not give formal sermons, but spoke from the heart, with compassion and kindness, touching their souls with the love of Christ which shone so brightly in his own.

PARISH VISITATION

Three months after his arrival in Mantua he announced his intention of carrying out a canonical visitation of every parish in the diocese, starting with the city of Mantua. This he did primarily to get to know his priests and people, and to form an accurate idea of the needs of his diocese. Acutely aware of the poverty of his priests, he let it be known in advance that he did not want any formal dinners in the parishes as was the custom on such occasions.

He visited the church, inspected the parish registers, and then began house-to-house visitation of the parish on foot. He went to the confessional before Mass to help the priests prepare the faithful for Holy Communion. He preached as many as four times a day during these visitations. There were marriages to be regularized, children to be legitimated, priests to be reinstated, and all sorts of abuses to be wiped out. He administered the sacrament of confir-

26 Dal-Gal, p. 74.

mation, visited the sick, taught catechism to children, and relieved poverty. He faced up to every difficulty squarely and uncompromisingly, yet always seasoning his approach with the compassion of the good shepherd. One of the gravest faults he had to correct was the neglect by priests of their preaching duties and the teaching of catechism. By his example, encouragement and, where necessary, severe reprimand, he gradually won them over to a deeper commitment to these responsibilities.

Very soon the people and priests of Mantua began to appreciate that their new bishop was a gift from God. He quickly won their esteem and affection. As time passed people could only be amazed at his phenomenal pastoral activity, his ability as an organizer, and the kindness and amiability with which he treated people of every social rank, especially the poor. The more educated began to realize that he was a man of immense culture as well.

DIOCESAN SYNOD

About mid way through his first parish visitation, on the basis of the direct information derived from this task, he formed a clear idea of what his next step should be. He now felt that it would be timely to hold a diocesan synod to provide remedies for the many pastoral problems he had to cope with. And so, in February 1887, he wrote to his priests to tell them that he planned to hold a diocesan synod in the autumn of the following year. The purpose of the synod was to draw up a compendium of statutes and laws appropriate to the needs of the diocese.

In his letter he explained that the purpose of the synod was not to find out who among his priests were learned or eloquent preachers. Rather he wanted them to come prepared to discuss their work from the point of view of their success in teaching the faith, and with proposals about how to overcome the difficulties. He assigned a theme to each parish priest, which he was to investigate carefully with a view to finding remedies in the shape of laws which could easily be obeyed in practice. The regulations of the Council of Trent recommended that such meetings be held annually, and while this had proved difficult to implement, in most Italian dioceses these meetings had taken place with reasonable regularity. Mantua, however, hadn't held a synod for 230 years!

In September 1888 over 200 priests processed into Mantua cathedral for the opening Mass of the three-day synod celebrated by Bishop Sarto. He addressed the synod each day, speaking to his clergy about priestly unity and fraternity, zeal for souls, and the importance of daily meditation. Many subjects were discussed in the general sessions, the most important referring to discipline, questions of faith and morals, liturgy, celebration of marriages, First Communion of children, the rights of the Church, the negative influence of particular books and newspapers, attitudes of Catholics to Jews (a third of the population of Mantua was Jewish), workers unions, Church music, etc.

We have to remember that the Church did not yet have a universal code of canon law and thus a number of points of church discipline were still undefined. The code of diocesan regulations drawn up by Bishop Sarto was regarded at the time as a model of episcopal legislation, which contributed in no small way to the moral and religious restoration of the diocese of Mantua. It involved a considerable work of research, collation and conflation of sundry existing laws, as well as legislative advances in different areas such as religious instruction, prompt preparation of children for First Communion, the obligations of the clergy to give religious instruction, the catechesis of children, Catholic youth associations, confraternities, relations between ecclesiastical and civil authorities, marriages and social problems. The experience of this legislative endeavour in the diocese of Mantua would later inspire the future Pius X to set about the much greater task of codifying, for the first time in its history, the canon law of the universal Church.

CATECHETICAL TEACHING

In his second report to Rome at the end of 1888 he had much progress to report. He concluded by stating that he planned a second visitation of the diocese the following spring in order to see the effects of the synod on the priests and their work. He was urged by his close advisers not to take on such a wearying task so soon again. However, his response, as always, was that to be a priest and to work meant the same:

> Our first duty is to work. We have to clear the field of tares and to sow the word of God; to build the holy house even higher; to fight the holy fight against the enemies of the faith; to build and fence and tend the vineyard. There is no time for us to rest. To put it plainly: to be a priest and to be vowed to toil – these are one and the same thing.[27]

In this second visitation he particularly wanted to see how catechetical teaching was progressing. He never tired of driving home the point to his priests about the importance of giving the people a thorough grounding in the truths of the faith. For Monsignor Sarto the greatest obstacle to progress in virtue was ignorance of the basics of the faith, and he now wanted to see how

27 Burton, p. 81.

the synod regulations on this topic were being implemented. He was also very conscious that a superficial knowledge of the faith was a particular danger for those who were exposed to the new currents of philosophy which were invading religion at the time.

In a pastoral letter written in 1887 he referred to those who called on the Church to adapt her doctrine to the needs of the times:

> In this modern Christianity the folly of the Cross is forgotten and the dogmas of the faith are twisted to fit in with the ideas of a new philosophy. The moral code, now considered too severe, must adapt itself to the self-indulgence of the times, and all forms of discipline which run counter to human nature must be abolished, so as to assist the glorious progress of the laws of liberty.[28]

What is of interest here is that fully twenty years before he would write his encyclical *Pascendi dominici gregis* (1907) on modernism, he had identified its philosophical roots and was perfectly conscious of its doctrines and intentions.

In a pastoral letter, written a few months after his arrival in Mantua (1885), he laid down that in all parishes a school for teaching Christian doctrine should be set up, and that on all Sundays and major feast days the parish priest should explain the catechism to both children and adults. Parents who habitually prevented their children from attending these instructions were to be refused absolution – a measure of the extraordinary importance he gave to this activity. Now, in May 1889, announcing his second visitation, he came back to the same topic:

> It will be my greatest consolation to enter a parish and find the teaching of Christian doctrine regular and systematic. I have already recommended this to you very strongly, and in this visitation it will be the point on which I shall most insist.[29]

He had a special affection for those who helped out in the organization of teaching catechism. To encourage his priests to take a lively interest in the task, he offered generous financial rewards to those who suggested methods which he considered simple, effective and suited to the circumstances. He was happiest when he was surrounded by large groups of children or adults for the purpose of explaining some point of doctrine to them. He himself was willing to walk miles to a parish where there was no priest available to carry out this task. If there was a priestly fault which caused him anger it was the neglect of

28 Dal-Gal, p. 84. **29** Dal-Gal, p. 68.

this responsibility. He reminded one parish priest, who was not fulfilling this task properly, that a pastor who, in spite of the grave deliberations of the synod on this matter, neglected his obligation of giving his people regular instruction in Christian doctrine could not consider himself free from mortal sin. He saw it primarily as a question of the salvation of souls and as such would accept no excuses.

To ensure that the catechetical instruction would not be omitted, he issued a prohibition against the giving of sermons by priests in neighbouring parishes on Sundays during Lent and Advent, as had heretofore been the custom. When some objected that this would make it difficult to procure Lenten preachers, with sure practical sense he replied: 'I would much prefer to see the Lenten sermons omitted, for very often they prove absolutely fruitless, whereas people who are unable to absorb oratorical outpourings benefit much more from the simple explanation of the catechism'.[30] To others who suggested that the explanation of the Gospel text would be more beneficial than the catechism, Monsignor Sarto answered with deep conviction:

> No! The explanation of the Gospel and the teaching of the catechism are two entirely distinct obligations. The explanation of, or commentary on, the Gospel narrative always presupposes that the people are thoroughly grounded in the rudiments of their faith, whereas in explaining Christian doctrine your object is to move the heart and to make it conform to the spirit of Christ, which you demonstrate with a few well chosen examples from Sacred Scripture. This is in keeping with the spirit of Trent, which tells us to explain doctrine 'with brevity and simplicity of speech'. With brevity because as St Francis de Sales tells us, 'when there is too much leaf on the vine there is less fruit', and with simplicity, in imitation of the apostles, who, as St Gregory the Great tells us, 'took the greatest care of the unlearned' and so avoided all high-flown speech.[31]

The first National Catechetical Congress was held in Italy in September 1889. Because Bishop Sarto was busy with his second visitation of the diocese, he couldn't attend. However, he did make a written contribution which was regarded as one of the most significant documents of the Congress. In his submission, referring to the disadvantages of having a variety of catechetical texts, many of which were defective not only from the point of view of presentation but also in dogmatic precision, he proposed that a standard catechism be adopted for the whole country. While respecting the right of each bishop to

30 Ibid., p. 70. **31** Ibid.

decide the form of catechism appropriate to the needs of his own diocese, he proposed that the Holy See be asked to prepare and introduce a popular catechism, with brief questions and answers. The proposal was accepted unanimously, but how many of those present at the Congress could have imagined that the actual putting into effect of this petition would be the work of the very man who proposed it, when he later became Pius X?[32]

In his very first encyclical he affirmed that the surest way to restore God's rule in the mind of man was through effective and ongoing religious instruction. Many people, he said, hated Christ and shrunk from the Church through ignorance rather than from malice, an ignorance which led to widespread loss of faith.[33] In his encyclical on catechetical instruction, he would reaffirm the grave responsibility for pastors of souls to protect men's minds from the dangers of religious ignorance, quoting from Jeremias: 'I will give you good shepherds according to my own heart, and they shall feed you with knowledge and doctrine' (Jer 3:15). The priest, he said, has no more important obligation than to provide religious instruction; his first duty is to instruct the Christian people.[34] As Pope he will repeat the regulations he had already laid down for his priests in Mantua and Venice about the instruction of children and adults on Sundays and feast days, but now in the context of the universal Church. The depth of his concern about the religious ignorance of many of the faithful finds heartfelt expression in his encyclical, *Acerbo nimis*, coupled with severe words for pastors who are negligent in this duty:

> How many alas! there are, we are not speaking merely of children, who in their adult years or in advanced age are completely ignorant of the mysteries of faith; ... it is vain to hope for crops from land where the seed has not been sown; how can one expect right moral conduct from a generation which has not received timely instruction in Christian doctrine? We are entitled to conclude that, if the faith in our own day has languished and is at the point of death in many, the explanation is that the duty of catechetical instruction is being discharged negligently, or completely disregarded.[35]

32 In his submission he said, 'As the Holy See has in fact already unified the catechism for parish priests it is my wish that there should be introduced without delay a popular catechism of history, dogma and morals, with brief questions and answers, and that it should be taught in all schools and translated into all languages. It would be a great advantage, in these times of easy communication, when so many leave not only their diocese, but also their fatherland, to have the text so unified that in all places the teaching of the Church could be heard in the same words in which they were learnt at our mothers' knees' (Dal-Gal, p. 71). **33** Encyclical *E supremi apostolatus* (1903), in CP, I, pp 12–13. **34** Encyclical *Acerbo nimis* (15 April 1905), in CP, I, pp 33–7. **35** Ibid., p. 36.

CARDINAL PATRIARCH

The happenings at Mantua did not go unnoticed in Rome. Tombolo, Salzano and Treviso had admired the prodigious pastoral energy of Don Sarto, but it was Mantua that witnessed the full flowering of his virtues and talents. This was true not only in the pastoral area, but also in his abilities to restore concord at the civic level and gain the trust of government authorities. There was no doubt that the difficulties of Mantua were the biggest challenge Giuseppe Sarto had so far faced. But the very demands of the situation evinced a depth of virtue, both human and supernatural, which was universally acclaimed.

On 12 June 1893, while still bishop of Mantua, he was named a cardinal by Leo XIII. Although he would be appointed patriarch of Venice a few days later, the Pope wanted to make it clear that the cardinalate had been conferred on Bishop Sarto for his personal merits rather than because of the importance of his new diocese. The former parish priest of Salzano pleaded with Leo XIII to be dispensed from accepting such an eminent position. However, the Pope would hear none of it. Given the difficult relationship between the civil authorities of Venice and the Holy See, Leo XIII was sure that Giuseppe Sarto was the best choice for this demanding task. There was stiff opposition to the new appointment from the government of the city which would not allow Cardinal Sarto enter Venice for a period of several months.

In his new role, which he took up on 24 November 1894, he continued to apply all his human and supernatural talents in the service of God and the Church. He did not allow his additional responsibilities to withdraw him from contact with people. On the contrary, he soon let it be known that anybody could have an appointment with him between 10.00 a.m. and 2.00 p.m. any day except feast days. He was even more prodigal in his generosity with the poor and the needy. He climbed the stairs of the most squalid apartments to administer confirmation to sick children. He frequently visited hospitals and prisons, and in 1900 he spent long hours hearing confessions during a mission in the Giudecca penitentiary to prepare the prisoners to gain the Jubilee indulgence.

As in Mantua, he took a special interest in the seminary of Venice, reforming it and implementing a new rule of discipline. He visited it frequently, getting to know all the seminarians personally. Among other things he cultivated in the students a deep devotion for the Holy Father and encouraged celebrations on papal feast days. He made a point of always being present for the big days in the seminary, whether liturgical or academic. He gave a new orientation to the philosophy and theology studies. This concern for orthodoxy and relevance in ecclesiastical studies, together with his intimate experience of seminary life in Treviso and Mantua, would later crystallize into specific guidance for the seminaries of the whole Church from the chair of St Peter. In his very first encyclical he would encourage bishops:

> It should be a matter of paramount concern to make provision for the proper organization and direction of the seminary, so that sound doctrine together with holiness of life may flourish within it.[36]

Why this ongoing deep interest in the seminary? Because for Giuseppe Sarto, whether as bishop or Pope, his primary concern was always the sanctity of his priests; and for him the success of this enterprise depended largely on the foundations laid in the seminary. Some years later, after the experience of the modernist crisis, in his Motu Proprio *Sacrorum antistitum*,[37] he ordered that the basic principles of Thomistic metaphysics be taught in seminaries. Only on this solid foundation, he affirmed, could a sound theology be built up, drawing on Sacred Scripture, Tradition and the Magisterium. He would return again to this topic. In June 1914, just a few weeks before his death, he published the document *Doctoris angelici*,[38] on the study of Thomistic philosophy, to clarify the import and the reach of the instructions already laid down in *Sacrorum antistitum*.

VENICE

In Venice he quickly realized that the teaching of the faith was in a lamentable state. At the same time he found that some of his priests were more concerned with style and eloquence in preaching than with the instruction of the people. And so in January 1895, barely two months after his arrival at the see of St Mark, he sent a circular letter to the clergy of the archdiocese, expressed in his usual direct style:

> We have far too much preaching and far too little real instruction, he commented. Have done with these flowers of eloquence; preach to the people with simplicity and piety, give them the truths of the faith and the precepts of the Church; tell them the meaning of virtue and the danger of vice ... The people thirst to know the truth; give it to them; give them what they need for the salvation of their souls.[39]

Repeating the experience of Mantua, he carried out a canonical visitation of every parish in the archdiocese in 1895. There was no church or chapel in

36 Cf. Encyclical *E supremi apostolatus* (1903), in CP, I, p. 10 37 Published on 1 September 1910.
38 Published 29 June 1914, the last great document of his pontificate. 39 Dal-Gal, p. 109.

the city, or surrounding countryside, that he did not visit. There was no religious or Catholic institution which did not hold interest for him. After completing his programme of parish visitation, and based on this intimate knowledge of the Church in Venice, he held a synod for the archdiocese in 1897. Many of the points discussed were very similar to those dealt with in the synod of Mantua ten years previously. Statutes were drafted to cover all the pastoral and disciplinary needs of the archdiocese which the archbishop took particular care to see were observed. The synod and its consequences were perhaps Cardinal Sarto's greatest legacy to the church in the city of the lagoons.

In Venice, as in Mantua, his first concern was the holiness of his priests. This was the solid foundation on which he built his whole pastoral enterprise there. To promote the sanctity of his priests he insisted that they did a yearly retreat, and that they attended a day of recollection on the last Thursday of each month. He looked forward to joining his priests on these occasions, and spoke to them during exposition of the Blessed Sacrament about fidelity, holiness of life, and zeal for souls. In dealing with his priests he knew how to combine straight talking with a paternal concern for each one of them. As in Mantua, they came to love and revere their patriarch who, though ruthless with regard to abuses, was prodigal in his kindness and generosity when they came to consult him about personal problems or pastoral difficulties. He was absolutely fair and impartial in his appointments to offices and benefices, never showing the slightest favouritism. He would not tolerate any of his priests intriguing by means of a third party to obtain favours.

This attitude is amply demonstrated by the following incident. The pastor of a particular parish in Venice died. Because of his negligence, and that of his assistant, the condition of the parish had deteriorated considerably. To bring about its reform the Cardinal was planning to appoint as parish priest a man of exceptional ability and pastoral zeal. However, the delinquent curate aspired to succeed his pastor and had already approached Rome, through ecclesiastics of influence, to obtain through the Vatican what he knew the Cardinal would not give. A badly advised Leo XIII wrote to the patriarch on behalf of the priest. Cardinal Sarto replied, with due respect, telling the Holy Father that he was ready to do the will of His Holiness, but that he declined all responsibility in the case. The Pope commended the cardinal's attitude and he was immediately allowed to go ahead with the appointment he had originally planned.[40] Not even in relation to his own family did he allow any concessions in this respect.

One of the negative hangovers from the clerical style of government associated with the Papal States was the expectation of preferential treatment because of influence in high places. By contrast, what we might call the 'lay

40 Cf. Pierami, p. 92.

mentality' of Giuseppe Sarto is well illustrated by the following incidents. He had a nephew, Monsignor Giovanni Battista Parolin, who was a priest of the diocese of Treviso, and for whom, as Cardinal Merry del Val affirms, the Pope had a warm affection. It was expected that Pius X would use his services in the Vatican and thus have the pleasure of his attendance and his company, not least because at that time the Pope was effectively a prisoner of the Vatican. Indeed, many cardinals who knew that his nephew's presence would be a real joy for Pius X, tried to persuade him to do this. However, all efforts failed in this respect, being met with the inevitable response: 'Yes, Don Battista is a good priest, but he is young and he must work in the ministry. He has a parish and he is better there than in a palace.'[41] Benedict XV, the successor to Pius X, on the very day of his election, appointed Monsignor Parolin a canon of St Peter's in Rome.

Another example in this context is recalled by Cardinal Merry del Val, which illustrates the family traditions of his own home in Riese and throws light on the environment which shaped his character. When the Venetian provinces were invaded during the First World War in 1917, three years after the death of Pius X, people fled by the thousand from these areas. The refugees included several nieces and nephews of the Pope with their families, who eventually arrived in Rome with little or no belongings, and made their way to the small apartment of the late Pope's sisters. Anna and Maria willingly provided them with the limited shelter and comfort they could offer for the unexpected group of twenty-three visitors. Cardinal Merry del Val visited them the next day, and was profoundly impressed by their dignity and simplicity, and the total absence of any lamentation or complaint about the hardships they had endured. When he asked what they most needed, the reply invariably was: 'We should like to find work, in order not to be a burden to others; if your Eminence can assist us in this way, we shall be deeply grateful.' The group included a sculptor, three were teachers, others were tradesmen. The former confidant of Pius X continues:

> But that which impressed me more than aught else was, that neither then, nor later on, nor at any time, did a single one of them ever mention or even indirectly refer to their close relationship with the late Pontiff, nor appear to consider that this exceptional circumstance gave them any title for special consideration in the eyes of others or afforded the least claim on the generosity of the Holy See. This point of view did not seem to have entered their minds.[42]

41 Merry del Val, p. 67. **42** Ibid., p. 79.

CHAIR OF PETER

In his very first encyclical,[43] published within a few weeks of his election as Pope, Pius X is very frank in his admission that he had tried to evade the burden of the papacy. He felt he was totally unworthy to occupy such a position when he compared himself with the lofty qualities of mind and soul of his predecessor. Certainly the twenty-five-year pontificate of Leo XIII was a hard act to follow, and nobody appreciated that more than Cardinal Giuseppe Sarto who had developed a profound veneration for the towering intellect and pastoral zeal of the author of such groundbreaking encyclicals as *Aeterni Patris* (on the renewal of Christian philosophy), *Rerum novarum* (the first major statement of the Church's social teaching), and *Providentissimus Deus* (on the study of Scripture). In addition he felt totally inadequate to deal with the difficult condition of human society as he found it at the beginning of the twentieth century, brought about by a progressive apostasy from God.

Yet those who worked closely with Pius X give testimony to qualities of character and virtues of soul which were to make him one of the outstanding popes in the Church's history. Not only did he leave an indelible imprint as a result of his great encyclicals on modernism, and the teaching of Christian doctrine, but also his cogent statement of the rights of the Church against the predatory aims of the French government on her liberties was a remarkable expression of fortitude and faith. Between 1882 and 1904 the French parliament passed a series of hostile and repressive laws against the Church. The French government flaunted its aggressive secularism which led to a confrontation with Pius X. It broke off diplomatic relations with the Holy See and abrogated its concordat (1905). Religious were expelled and Church property confiscated, with the result that priests and bishops were reduced to a state of penury. While some Curia cardinals were in favour of a compromise solution, Pius X replied to the actions of the French government in two encyclicals in 1906 demonstrating the injustice of the legislation in uncompromising language. Addressing the bishops and people of France, he tells them:

> You have seen the sanctity and indissolubility of Christian marriage violated by laws in direct opposition to them; the secularization of schools and hospitals; clerics torn from their studies and ecclesiastical discipline, and forced into military service; religious congregations dispersed and despoiled, and most of their members reduced to utter destitution. These legal measures have been followed by others, as you well know: abolishing the law prescribing public prayers at the opening of parlia-

43 *E supremi apostolatus* (1903).

> ment and the law courts; suppressing the traditional signs of mourning on board vessels on Good Friday; deleting from the legal oath everything that gave it a stamp of religion; banishing from the courts, from schools, the army, navy, and all other public institutions, every act and emblem which served in any way as a reminder of religion.[44]

His instructions on frequent Communion,[45] the early reception of First Communion,[46] biblical studies,[47] church music[48] and the study of the doctrine of St Thomas Aquinas[49] established markers for piety and doctrine which are still relevant today. In addition, the initiative, energy, and inspiration he put into the immense task of codifying, for the first time, the vast accumulation of centuries of ecclesiastical law marks him out as one of the greatest legislators in the history of the Church.[50] He was very innovative in relation to biblical studies. He established the Pontifical Biblical Commission to which he gave exceptional doctrinal authority. He also set up the Biblical Institute to teach Sacred Scripture at the higher levels, which he wanted endowed with all the resources of modern scientific progress. Its creation was a decisive step in the biblical revival in the Church. He entrusted to the Benedictines the work of revising the Latin Vulgate edition of the Bible.

St Pius X applied his exceptional administrative ability to a complete reorganization of the central government of the Church. He introduced the most far-ranging changes in the organization of the Roman Curia since those of Sixtus V in the sixteenth century, reducing the number of congregations from twenty to eleven.

During his eleven-year pontificate, Pius X, as we have seen, had to deal with many difficult problems to protect what he called 'the interests of God'.

44 Encyclical, *Vehementer* (1906). 45 Decree, *Sacra tridentina synodus* (1905). 46 Decree, *Quam singulari* (1910). 47 Apostolic Letter, *Quoniam in re biblica* (1906), on the study of Scripture in seminaries; Motu Proprio, *Praestantia sacrae Scripturae* (1907), on the decisions of the Pontifical Biblical Commission. 48 Motu Proprio (1903). In 1904 he commissioned the Benedictine monks of Solesmes to prepare an official edition of the liturgical chant of the Church. 49 Motu Proprio, *Doctoris angelici* (1914), on the study of Thomistic philosophy. 50 The Church had, of course, collections of canon law, official and non-official, but since an ever-increasing number of these provisions were replaced over time by new laws, these collections were becoming obsolete and unmanageable. Several Fathers at Vatican I had expressed a desire that a codification of the laws of the Church be put in hand. Some limited work was done under Pius IX and Leo XIII, but it was Pius X who undertook the colossal task of revising the whole body of canon law. In the very first year of his pontificate he set up a commission under Cardinal Gasparri and gave it precise instructions for the project of codification. He imbued it with a sense of urgency and followed all the subsequent stages of its work with a direct personal interest. By 1912 the first draft of a universal code was available and by the time of his death the revisions were almost complete. Benedict XV, who promulgated the new code in 1917, declared that Pius X was primarily responsible for this unique legislative achievement, and that his name would be celebrated in Church history alongside such eminent legislators as Innocent III, Honorious III and Gregory IX.

One of the most difficult issues he had to confront was the rise of modernism, a grave doctrinal error that disputed the very foundations of the Christian faith. Modernism was a humanist doctrine undermining the spiritual substance of the faith. Out of the maelstrom of secularist philosophies, nineteenth-century scientism and liberal Protestantism, modernism began to take shape in the Church. Many had hoped that this new way of looking at the faith would reconcile Catholicism with the modern mind and bridge the perceived gap between faith and science. But, as Pius X had seen from as far back as his days in Mantua, the threat of modernism was its capacity to empty Catholicism of its supernatural content. Modernism tried to rationalize the faith so as to bring it into line with what were thought to be advances in historical and philosophical studies and biblical exegesis. Immanentism was the philosophical principle at the core of modernism, which set up 'religious consciousness' as the supreme norm of religious life. The inherent ambiguity of the modernist creed, emphasizing 'spirit' at the expense of dogma, was perfectly clear to Pius X. Because he had no doubts about its capacity to devastate the faith, he moved energetically against it and laid bare all its potential danger in the encyclical *Pascendi dominici gregis* (1907), and condemned its doctrine in the decree *Lamentabili* published in the same year.

Was there a change in Giuseppe Sarto's personality after he was elected successor of Peter? Did the burden of the papacy withdraw him from people? While undoubtedly the demands of Vatican protocol considerably restricted his freedom, his attitude and personality remained totally consistent with the man people knew as parish priest of Salzano or bishop of Mantua. Those who met him for the first time as Pope were deeply impressed by his goodness, gentleness and charity. His charm, his good humour and his prodigal generosity were also a frequent cause of comment. However, to suggest that these attractive qualities summed up the whole of his character as Pope would, Cardinal Merry del Val tells us, be a complete misrepresentation of the truth.[51] Coupled with this kindness and refinement was

> an indomitable strength of character and an energy of will to which all must testify who really knew him, but which not infrequently surprised or even startled those who had only experienced the constant proofs of his habitual gentleness and restraint.[52]

He was quick to give way in matters which were not essential and to accept the opinion of others where no principle was at stake. However, when the rights and liberties of the Church required to be stated and upheld, when the purity and

51 Cf. Merry del Val, p. 24. 52 Ibid.

integrity of Catholic doctrine needed to be asserted and defended, or ecclesiastical discipline had to be maintained in the face of laxity or worldly influence,

> then Pius X would reveal the full strength and energy of his character and the fearless vigour of a great ruler conscious of the responsibility of his sacred office and of the duties he felt called upon to fulfil at any cost.[53]

Here we are listening to the judgement of the man who, as secretary of state, was the closest collaborator of Pius X during his eleven-year pontificate. His daily audiences with the Holy Father during all of that period gave him a privileged insight into the mind and heart of Giuseppe Sarto. He tells us that Pius X had a very affectionate temperament, but never lost control of his feelings. Gifted with a refined, artistic sensibility, 'he loved beautiful things and he had seen many in the course of his life in Mantua, Padua and Venice'.[54] However, underlying all of these qualities – gentleness, charity, sense of humour, fortitude, indomitable will, etc. – was a virtue which gives the key to his whole personality, to the sanctity of his life, and to the effectiveness of his pontificate. Quoting St Augustine, *ubi humilitas, ibi maiestas* (Where there is humility, there is majesty), (Sermon 14), Merry del Val affirms that this axiom was manifest to an extraordinary degree in the life of Pius X. An authentic, profound and unaffected humility was, he considered, so prominent a characteristic, so entirely the outstanding feature of his whole temperament as to have become second nature to him.[55] There was nothing here of the shallow, false attitude of mind which is only indicative of weakness or a craven form of self-consciousness, and which is in fact a caricature of true humility. Because of the low estimation he had of himself, and his deep conviction that all human talents are gifts from God, it cost him no effort to be humble and to readily admire good qualities in others rather than discover them in himself. Adulation or praise was totally repugnant to him. In his presence people sensed this immediately and words of admiration died on their lips. Although simple of habits, and fatherly and homely in private, there was a quiet and unassuming dignity and nobility in his bearing which never failed to impress those who attended his official receptions, or were present at his public functions. Not many people, Merry del Val tells us, had occasion to realize fully how gifted the Holy Father was, or to appreciate the wide reach of his cultural and intellectual attainments, for the very simple reason that he made a point of concealing them whenever possible. However, those who lived in close intimacy with him were constantly discovering the richness of his knowledge and experience.[56] There is ample evidence of this wide intellectual and cultural per-

53 Ibid. **54** Ibid., p. 43. **55** Cf. ibid., p. 62. **56** Cf. ibid., pp 62–8.

spective in the weighty encyclicals and the other official enactments of his pontificate.

Although a man of deep humility, he could also affirm, 'when we recall the spot on which we stand and on which this Pontifical See has been established, we feel perfectly secure on the rock of Holy Church'.[57] Why? Because down through the centuries the supernatural power of God was never lacking in the Church, nor did the promises of Christ ever fail. Looking back over the sweep of history he saw how so may philosophical systems had fought against the Church claiming victory, boasting that they had destroyed her teaching or demolished her dogmas by proving their absurdity. One after another all these philosophical systems had passed into oblivion, but all the while the light of truth shone out undimmed from the rock of Peter.[58]

Trusting in the grace of God who called him to such high office, he set himself the ambitious programme 'of re-establishing all things in Christ' (Eph 1:10). Although faced with the challenge of those who were perverting religion and rejecting the truths of faith, he had no doubt about the outcome, that ultimately the victory would be God's. Pius X saw priests as the principal agents in bringing about this rebirth in Christ. But if they were to be truly effective in this regard, priests themselves must first be clothed with Christ and have clearly stamped on them the image of the Master.

EXHORTATION ON PRIESTLY HOLINESS

When he came to write *Haerent animo* in 1908, barely a year had passed since the publication of his encyclical *Pascendi* against modernism. While few priests espoused the principles of modernism, Pius X saw that its spirit of criticism of the Church influenced many. He well knew that the programme he had set himself of renewing all things in Christ (cf. Eph 1:10), could only become a reality by inculcating in priests a great love for the Church and a deep awareness of the dignity of their own vocation. *Haerent animo*, written after fifty years of an immensely fruitful ministry, is in many ways simply a description of Giuseppe Sarto's own priesthood and of the virtues which he strove to develop all during his priestly life. Pius X would, however, have been the last person to claim this. He speaks from the heart rather than expound a blueprint for the ministry and life of the priest. Indeed one has the clear impression that he is recounting the history of his own spiritual life. This is confirmed by his Secretary of State, the man on whom Pius X relied most during his pontificate. The Pope penned *Haerent animo* whilst audiences and work of all kinds

57 Encyclical *Iucunda sane*, on the thirteenth centenary of the death of Pope St Gregory the Great, 12 March 1904, in *My words will not pass away*, p. 77. 58 Cf. ibid., p. 79.

crowded in on him, writing it page by page, during intervals of spare time, in little over a fortnight. 'It was', Cardinal Merry del Val tells us, 'exclusively his own personal effort, and it was truly a labour of love.'[59]

PURSUING SANCTITY IS A DUTY

The first part of *Haerent animo* deals with the obligation of the priest to strive for holiness, which is demanded in a special way of the priest by reason of the dignity of his vocation.[60] This dignity derives from the fact that in his hands Christ has placed all his treasures, his sacraments, his very self. He has entrusted him with the destiny of souls and the power to open the gates of heaven to them. At no stage in Giuseppe Sarto's priestly career is there the slightest hint of that identity crisis which seems to have afflicted so many priests of our present generation. He had a deep conviction of his calling by God, of his divine vocation. Christ, the Eternal High Priest, was for him a model who stood out with luminous clarity all during his life. For St Pius X the priest was, in a special way, the friend of Christ. He saw those words of our Lord at the Last Supper, 'I have called you friends ... I chose you and appointed you that you should go out and bear fruit, and that your fruit should abide' (Jn 15:15–16), as applying in a special way to God's ordained ministers. The priest is the friend, representative and minister of Christ. 'Priests', he tells us, 'must have the same affections, the same sentiments, the same mind as Jesus Christ'. The mission of the priest is to form Christ in others after the manner of St Paul, experiencing, as it were, the same spiritual birth pangs (cf. Gal 4:19). However, if zeal in forming others is to yield the hoped-for fruits, it must be seasoned by charity expressed as patience, kindness, and gentleness. He well knew the effectiveness of this approach.

There was nothing eccentric or offbeat about the sanctity of Giuseppe Sarto. He was a man of rich human qualities with an immensely attractive personality. As bishop of Mantua, his seminarians looked forward to the extra time he would spend with them during the summer holidays. They loved him because they saw the image of Christ so clearly etched there, not only in what he said, but more particularly in what he did. He had a quick sense of humour coupled with a brilliant intellect.

59 Merry del Val, p. 38. **60** Summarizing the teaching of the Fathers and Doctors of the Church, Pius X says that 'there should be as much difference between the priest and any other upright man as there is between heaven and earth; consequently, the priest must see to it that his life is free not merely from grave faults but even from the slightest faults' (CP, I, p. 58). While Pius X had an exalted view of the priesthood, clearly the idea of the universal call to holiness was not yet recovered for the Church. This development had to await the Magisterium of Vatican II.

In speaking about the nature of priestly holiness, Pius X gives a warning which is as valid today as it was a hundred years ago:

> There are some who think and even declare openly that the true measure of the merits of a priest is his dedication to the service of others; consequently, with an almost complete disregard for the cultivation of the virtues which lead to the personal sanctification of the priest, they assert that all his energies and fervour should be directed to the development and practice of what they call the 'active' virtues. One can only be astonished by this gravely erroneous and pernicious teaching.[61]

This point is cogently reaffirmed in the 1994 *Directory on the ministry and life of priests*:

> Due to numerous duties stemming in large part from pastoral activity, the priest's life is linked, now more than ever, to a series of requests which could lead to a growing exterior activism, submitting that life to a frenetic and disordered pace. In light of such a 'temptation', one must not forget that the initial intention of Jesus in convoking the Apostles around him was above all that they 'remain with him' (Mk 3:14). The Son of God himself has wished to leave us a testimony of his prayer.[62]

The *Directory* then goes on to give several examples of Christ praying at all the different stages of his ministry, and concludes:

> Following the example of Christ, the priest must know how to maintain the vivacity and abundance of the moments of silence and prayer in which he cultivates and deepens his own essential relationship with the living figure of Jesus Christ.[63]

The holiness of the priest must be based on a life of self-denial, and on that humility which Christ invited us to learn from himself (see Mt 11:29). It is not just for his own sake that the priest has to strive for sanctity, but so that he may be an effective instrument of holiness for the souls entrusted to his care. Priestly holiness is of its nature essentially apostolic. Pius X goes as far as to say that:

> if this holiness ... is wanting in the priest, then everything is wanting. Without this, even the resources of profound learning, or exceptional

61 CP, I, p. 59. **62** Congregation for the Clergy, *Directory on the ministry and life of priests*, 31 January 1994, no. 40. **63** Ibid.

> competence in practical affairs, though they might bring some benefit to the Church or to individuals, are not infrequently the cause of lamentable damage to those who possess them.[64]

'On the other hand', he affirms, 'there is abundant evidence from every age that even the humblest priest, provided his life is adorned with overflowing sanctity, can undertake and accomplish marvellous works for the spiritual welfare of the People of God.'[65] Sanctity alone makes up for all the other limitations of the priest, as is clear from the outstanding example of the Curé of Ars.[66]

What, he asks, must the priest do to become an *alter Christus* (another Christ) among men? The means he suggests are those which served himself so well during the half century of his own priesthood, means which continue to have a perennial validity for the spiritual growth of every priest.[67] In the first place he points out the very close connection between holiness and prayer. A commitment to daily prayer is essential if the priest is to maintain the dignity of his vocation and fulfil his duty; prayer which is persevering, which is the overflow of a deep faith, which is sincere and humble in recognizing one's limitations, daily faults and failures. He goes on to specify that a fixed time for daily meditation is essential. 'No priest', he says, 'can neglect this practice without incurring a grave charge of negligence and without detriment to his soul.'[68]

These are strong words. Pius X will not accept the excuse of a busy schedule of activities for omitting daily meditation. Rather he says, 'Let those words of Christ, "Be watchful, be vigilant and pray" (Mk 13:33), be deeply engraved in your hearts.'[69] Prayer, as we all know, protects us from a spirit of routine or carelessness in our priestly duties, and ensures that we have a realistic sense of dependence on God's grace and providence.[70]

64 CP, I, p. 62. **65** Ibid. **66** Earlier in his pontificate Pius X had already outlined the level of sanctity he expected of priests: 'You have a duty to be holy, not simply in a mediocre degree but completely; ordinary holiness is not enough, your holiness must be outstanding; you must avoid not only mortal sins but also the smallest sins' (address to French seminarians, 23 February 1905, in CP, I, p. 31). **67** The *Directory on the ministry and life of priests* says the priest 'should give absolute pre-eminence' to his spiritual life, 'avoiding any neglect due to other activities' (no. 38). It then goes on to summarize the basic elements of what should constitute the structure of the priest's spiritual life: it should embrace 'the daily Eucharistic celebration, with adequate preparation and thanksgiving; frequent confession and spiritual direction already practised in the seminary; the complete and fervent celebration of the liturgy of the hours, on a daily basis; examination of conscience; mental prayer; divine readings; the prolonged moments of silence and prayer, above all in periodical Spiritual Exercises and Retreats; the affectionate expression of Marian devotions, like the Rosary; the *Via Crucis* and other pious exercises; and the fruitful reading on lives of the saints' (no. 39). **68** Cf. CP, I, p. 64. **69** Ibid., p. 68. **70** We find parallel ideas articulated in the *Directory on the ministry and life of priests*, 41: 'To remain faithful to the obliga-

SPIRITUAL READING

Pius X also recommends to priests the daily practice of spiritual reading as a complement to daily meditation – in the first place, the reading of sacred Scripture supplemented by books of sound theological and spiritual content. Familiarity with works of this sort provides a regular input of solid and rich ideas for the interior life. The Pope who gave us the encyclical *Pascendi dominici gregis* was very conscious of the immense damage done to many priests by imprudent reading of books of modernist inspiration. 'Be on your guard, beloved sons', he writes in *Haerent animo*, 'do not trust in your experience and mature years, do not be deluded by the vain hope that you can thus better serve the general good.'[71] This advice is equally relevant today, when one considers the veritable explosion which has occurred in the publication of theological literature of all kinds over the past forty years. Without a certain amount of prudent guidance, a priest runs the risk of wasting time on reading which, at best, is lightweight theologically speaking, but which could often be a real danger to his faith.[72]

EXAMINATION OF CONSCIENCE

It was not that Pius X ever felt that piety on its own was sufficient. The man who previously had devoted so much effort to the intellectual formation of seminarians was not withdrawing in any way from that commitment, as is clear from the very specific indications of his encyclical *Pascendi* on the philosophical and theological formation of students for the priesthood. To counteract the influence of modernism, Pius X laid down in *Pascendi* that scholastic philosophy, after the manner of St Thomas Aquinas, should be taught in all seminaries. In doing so he was only reaffirming the measures already proposed by Leo

tion of "being with Christ", it is necessary that the priest know how to imitate the Church in prayer' (*Directory*, no. 41). After reminding the priest of what was said to him by the bishop on the day of his ordination about finding Christ in the Scriptures and in the Eucharist, the *Directory* continues: 'Strengthened by the special bond with the Lord, the priest will know how to confront those moments in which he could feel alone among men; effectively renewing his being with Christ who in the Eucharist is his refuge and best repose. Like Christ, who was often alone with the Father (cf. Lk 3:21; Mk 1:35), the priest must also be the man who finds communion with God in solitude, so he can say with St Ambrose: "I am never less alone than as when I am alone". Beside the Lord, the priest will find the strength and the means to bring men back to God, to enlighten their faith, to inspire commitment and sharing' (ibid., no. 42). **71** Cf. CP, I, p. 70. **72** The *Directory* indicates the following priorities for the priest's spiritual reading: 'Among his reading material, the primary place must be given to Sacred Scripture; and then the writings of the Fathers, classical and modern spiritual Masters, and the documents of the Magisterium, which constitute the authoritative and updated source of permanent formation' (no. 87).

XIII. He clarified this point later in the Motu Proprio *Doctoris angelici*, the last important document he wrote before his death:

> When we appointed St Thomas as the chief guide in scholastic philosophy, it is obvious that we had in mind above all his principles, which are the very foundation upon which scholastic philosophy rests. It is for this reason that we have already sought to convey to those who teach philosophy and sacred theology the warning that departure from St Thomas, especially in metaphysics, involves grave loss. And now we go further and declare that those who wrongly interpret or completely despise the principles and major theses of the philosophy of St Thomas, are not only not following St Thomas, but have strayed far from him. Whenever we ourselves or our predecessors have specially commended the doctrine of some author or saint, and when that approval was supplemented by invitation or even command to spread and defend this doctrine, it can easily be understood that the doctrine was recommended insofar as it was in full accordance with the principles of St Thomas, or was in no way opposed to them.[73]

While Pius X was concerned to get the foundations right, as always he was innovative and forward looking. In *Pascendi*, in addition to scholastic theology, he recommended the study of positive theology. He also saw a definite role for the study of the natural sciences in priestly training. To be salt and light it was necessary to join learning to piety. Seminarians needed a profound grasp of Christian philosophy and theology to be able to answer people's difficulties.[74]

The former parish priest of Salzano also recommends daily examination of conscience as another important means to acquire priestly holiness. This he says will enable the priest to see whether he is seriously striving to put into practice the insights he has received through his meditation and spiritual reading. It will be an effective instrument to keep in clear focus the daily effort to achieve sanctity. Its fruitfulness, he tells us, has always been recommended by the great masters of the interior life. At this point in the exhortation he quotes from St Bernard as follows:

> As a searching investigator of the integrity of your own conduct, submit yourself to a daily examination. Consider carefully what progress you have made or what ground you have lost. Strive to know yourself. Place all your faults before your eyes. Come face to face with yourself, as though you were another person, and then weep for your faults.[75]

73 Motu Proprio, *Doctoris angelici*, 29 June 1914; CP, I, pp 46–7. **74** Address to French Seminary in Rome, 23 February 1905, CP, I, p. 30. **75** CP, I, p. 71, quoting St Bernard, *Meditationes*

He highlights its importance by contrasting the commitment of those who in business keep a tight control of income and expenditure and do a careful balance of their accounts. How much more necessary is it not, in the business of eternal life, to identify strengths and weaknesses, to detect incipient deviations from the path of sanctity, and to set the soul on course again with a clearly defined resolution for the morrow?

Daily examination has the extra bonus that it provides a deeper appreciation of the need for frequent confession as an antidote to our own weaknesses, as well as being a powerful means to progress in the interior life. Pius X has harsh words for priests who neglect regular confession because it demonstrated a carelessness and indifference to one's own spiritual welfare. There has, with good reason, been a lot of comment in recent years about the massive decline in numbers attending regular confession. It is a counter-sign of spiritual vitality and, at the same time, there are, clearly, real difficulties about reversing this trend. However, a priest will not be able to speak with conviction about the advantages of frequent confession if he is not a regular penitent himself. As Pope John Paul II remarked in this context, good penitents make the best confessors.[76] It is also worth noting the particular importance which the *Directory on the ministry and life of priests* gives to the frequent reception of this sacrament by the clergy.[77]

PRIESTLY VIRTUES

In the latter part of his exhortation, Pius X again encourages priests to strive after those virtues which are particularly appropriate to their condition as intermediaries between God and man – charity, obedience, apostolic zeal, chastity, and a spirit of sacrifice – virtues which will win veneration for them among their communities and which will yield an even greater harvest of holi-

piisimae, Ch. 5. **76** Cf. John Paul II, Apostolic Exhortation *Reconciliatio et paenitentia*, 31 (2 December 1984). **77** 'Like any good faithful, the priest also needs to confess his own sins and weaknesses. He is the first to realize that the practice of this sacrament reinforces his faith and charity towards God and his brothers. In order to effectively reveal the beauty of Penance, it is essential that the minister of the sacrament offer a personal testimony preceding the other faithful in living the experience of pardon. This constitutes the first condition for restoring the pastoral value of the Sacrament of Reconciliation. In this sense it is good for the faithful to see and know that their priests go to confession regularly: "the entire priestly existence falls into decay if there is lacking, through neglect or for any other motive, the periodic recourse, inspired by true faith and devotion, to the Sacrament of Penance. In a priest who no longer went to confession or did so poorly, his essence and action as priest would feel the effects very quickly, as would the community of which he is pastor" (*Reconciliatio et paenitentia*, no. 31)' (*Directory*, no. 53). John Paul II, in his Holy Thursday Letter for Priests for 2001, outlined in some detail the spiritual and ascetical advantages of regular confession for priests.

ness. These were the 'passive' virtues so stigmatized by the modernists, but which for Giuseppe Sarto constituted the foundation of authentic pastoral effectiveness. He encourages priests to be truly apostolic after the example of Christ:

> Strive eagerly not only by means of catechetical instruction which once more with even greater earnestness we commend to you – but by unsparing use of all the resources of wisdom and skill at your command, to deserve well of all. Whether your immediate task be to assist, to protect, to heal, to make peace, let your one aim and most ardent desire be to win or to secure souls for Christ. How unwearied, how industrious, how fearless are Christ's enemies in their activities, to the immeasurable loss of souls![78]

Personal experience in Treviso, Mantua and Venice, whether guiding seminarians or priests, convinced him of the need for, and the great benefits to be derived from, the yearly retreat and attendance at monthly recollections. In his exhortation he earnestly encourages priests to use these means of formation for growth in holiness. He had already recommended this practice in a letter to his cardinal vicar for Rome, and asked him to arrange for a number of such retreats to be organized for the secular clergy of the city.[79]

While there is no doubt but that *Haerent animo* is clearly influenced by the sad experience of the modernist crisis in matters of doctrine and discipline, it is no less marked by the unmistakable stamp of the Pope's personal holiness which gives to his words a striking warmth and refinement. He openly admitted in his first encyclical that he had a special predilection for priests who, while not neglecting theological or secular studies, were particularly devoted

78 CP, I, p. 75. **79** 'Sad experience has taught us only too clearly that man's nature is so inconstant that even those who are most devoted to their duties, unless they receive a timely and repeated stimulus, tend to become half-hearted in the pursuit of virtue and finally to grow weary of it and to fall away into sin. Priests are not exempt from this common failing; and so, to avoid the danger of falling short of their obligations through slackness, they must from time to time have recourse to appropriate means for the restoration of their strength and the renewal of their first fervour. It would appear to be clearly the will of God that the means to achieve this should be sought chiefly in the pious solitude of a retreat of some days devoted to the consideration of one's past life: "I have thought upon my ways, and turned my feet unto thy testimonies" (Ps 18:59)'. After describing how Christ, when the apostles returned from preaching, often invited them to retire with him into a place of solitude to rest and be refreshed spiritually, Pius X continues: 'This invitation of Christ was assuredly addressed not only to the Apostles to whom he was speaking, but to all those who were to have a share in the apostolic ministry; it was his will that those who, by the holiness of their ministry and the sanctity of their own lives, were to be the light of the world, the salt of the earth and almost divine beings on earth, should have recourse to the most effective means of preserving and increasing the sanctity of their lives' (Letter to cardinal vicar of Rome about retreats for priests, 27 December 1904, CP, I, p. 27).

to the welfare of souls.[80] With typical humility Pius X had begun his Exhortation thus:

> We have nothing to say which you have not already heard, no doctrine to propound which is new to anyone, but we treat of matters which it is necessary for everyone to bear in mind, and God inspires us with the hope that our message will not fail to bear abundant fruit.[81]

The means of sanctification which are recommended by Pius X have a permanent validity. The counsels of *Haerent animo* have been frequently repeated by his successors in the chair of Peter, who have invited generations of priests to meditate on the simple yet forceful words of their saintly predecessor.[82]

Not surprisingly Pius XII, the pope who beatified and canonized Pius X within the short space of three years, was blessed with a particular insight into the mind and heart of Giuseppe Sarto.[83] In his prodigious output of magisterial documents and addresses, he several times recommends and refers to the teaching of *Haerent animo*.[84] In his homily at the beatification ceremony, on 3 June 1951, Pius XII extolled the work of his predecessor for the priesthood. 'Who can read without emotion', he asked, 'his paternal exhortation *Haerent animo*, that shining reflection of his own priestly soul on the occasion of his priestly jubilee? Being wholly imbued with the thought of St Paul that the priest is appointed by men in all things that pertain to God (cf. Heb. 5:1), he overlooked nothing that contributed to the more efficacious exercise of this sublime office.'[85]

80 Cf. CP, I, p. 12. **81** Ibid., p. 54. **82** Benedict XV, writing in his first encyclical *Ad beatissimi* (1914), about the importance of priestly sanctity for the good of the Church, requested that 'the instructions given in … the Exhortation to the Clergy of Pius X may never be forgotten, but may be scrupulously observed'; cf. CP, I, p. 92. Pius XI, in his great encyclical on the Catholic priesthood, *Ad catholici sacerdotii* (1935), recommended to priests the frequent reading of *Haerent animo;* cf. CP, I, p. 243. **83** Pius X was beatified on 3 June 1951, and canonized on 29 May 1954. **84** Pius XII quotes *Haerent animo* in his instruction to Lenten confessors about the demands of prudence in hearing women's confessions (cf. CP, II, pp 74–5). He also refers to it in his Apostolic Exhortation *Menti nostrae*, on the sanctification of priestly life (1950); cf. CP, II, p. 157. In his address to students of the North American College on 14 October 1953, Pius XII quotes from *Haerent animo:* 'to be a priest and to be a man dedicated to work is one and the same thing' (CP, II, p. 256). In the encyclical *Sacra virginitas* (1954), in the context of developing the virtue of chastity in young clerics, Pius XII refers to that part of *Haerent animo* which outlines the means to acquire priestly holiness; cf. CP, II, p. 303, footnote no. 100. **85** In a letter to priests in 1956 about the need for interior life, Pius XII again recommended *Haerent animo*: 'They shall constantly meditate on, and regard as salutary nourishment what was taught on this subject by our predecessor of holy memory, Pius X, in the Apostolic Exhortation *Haerent animo* (1956), cf. CP, II, p. 127. In his last discourse, prepared for delivery on 19 October 1958, Pius XII speaks about priestly formation and priestly holiness. He recalls all the work done by his saintly predecessor, Pius X, for the formation of priests, and refers to *Haerent animo* as a document 'in which the saintly Pontiff expounded, as though depicting his own self, the ideal of the priest' (1958), cf. CP

GIANT BUT GENTLE

Some will remember how the announcement that Pius X would be canonized in May of the Marian year 1954, three short years after his beatification, was greeted with immense joy by the universal Church. After the ceremony Pius XII recalled with deep emotion 'the giant but gentle figure of the saintly Pontiff'. In the forty years which had elapsed since the death of Pius X, deeper reflection on his life and writings, and the abundant evidence of his intervention in the life of the Church in ways miraculous and otherwise, left no doubt about the sanctity and the stature of this man of God. 'As a humble parish priest, as bishop, Supreme Pontiff, he was always thoroughly convinced that the sanctity to which God called him was priestly sanctity.'[86] At the end of his homily on that splendid day in the history of the Church, Pius XII offered a prayer to the newly proclaimed saint:

> St Pius X, glory of the priesthood, you, in whose person humility appeared in union with greatness, simple piety with profound doctrine, you, Pontiff of the Eucharist and the catechism, of sound faith and unshaken firmness, turn your gaze upon holy Church which you loved so much and to which you gave the best of the treasures which divine goodness, with prodigal hand, had deposited in your soul; obtain for her integrity and constancy in the midst of the trials and persecutions of our time; come to the assistance of poor humanity, whose sorrows afflicted you so profoundly that finally they stopped the beating of your great heart.[87]

This is a moving petition which reflects many of the qualities of this great saint, the first Pope to be canonized since Pius V, who occupied the Chair of Peter almost 350 years before Giuseppe Sarto. It is a prayer for the Church and humanity which is as relevant today as it was when spoken for the first time on that May morning over fifty years ago.

PERENNIAL RELEVANCE

One might be tempted to think that St Pius X has somehow gone out of fashion in this post-conciliar age. Certainly in some theological circles the pope of *Pascendi dominici gregis* is not exactly a cult figure. However, it would be very wrong to assume that the teaching of St Pius X is now passé. When the Fathers of Vatican II came together to write the two decrees of the Council

II, p. 253. See CP II, p. 21, footnote no. 2. **86** CP, II, p. 6. **87** CP, II, p. 9.

which bear most directly on the formation, lifestyle and holiness of the Catholic priesthood, the teaching of Pius X was never very far from their minds. *Optatam totius*, the decree on the training of priests, gives particular prominence to *Haerent animo*, referring to it on three separate occasions.[88]

Similarly, in *Presbyterorum ordinis*, the decree on the ministry and life of priests, we come across two references to the same apostolic exhortation in the context of the bishop's responsibility for the sanctification of his priests, and the duty of the priest to seek holiness in and through his ministry.[89] Apart from these specific references, there is also a significant parallelism between the contents of Chapter III of this decree, dealing with the call to holiness of the priest, and the doctrine we find in *Haerent animo*.[90] Hence we can affirm that the substance of St Pius X's charter for priestly holiness will always be present in the living tradition of the Church. As part of the teaching of Vatican II, it will be available for the benefit of all future generations of priests. While Pius X is often seen today only as the anti-modernist pope, the then Cardinal Ratzinger affirmed that a recent critical biography of Giuseppe Sarto 'has clearly shown how much this pope of pastoral care was a pope of reform.'[91]

To put the life of Giuseppe Sarto in perspective, we can in fact draw some parallels with the ecclesiastical career of John Paul II. Both came to the see of Peter with immense pastoral experience derived from every level of diocesan responsibility. We see too in both men a profound concern for the formation and sanctity of priests. In very different circumstances, St Pius X and John Paul II displayed extraordinary fortitude and courage in defending Christ's teaching, and in affirming the rights of the Church against the tyranny of secular power. Both Popes produced catechisms for the use of the universal Church. While John Paul II had the freedom to carry out pastoral visits to every part of the world, existing protocol effectively made Pius X a prisoner of the Vatican. Nevertheless, this man of the people found a way around these restrictions by inviting people from the different parishes of Rome to come and visit him on Sunday afternoons in the Cortile San Damaso where he gave them a catechetical address in his usual vivid style.

88 *Optatam totius*; in A. Flannery (ed.), *Vatican II: the conciliar and post conciliar documents* (Dublin, 1981), pp 707–24. The first reference to *Haerent animo* is at the very beginning of the conciliar document (cf. footnote no.1) where it states: 'The Council is fully aware that the desired renewal of the whole Church depends in great part upon a priestly ministry animated by the spirit of Christ.' The second reference to Pius X's exhortation is in footnote no. 12, where the text affirms: 'Those who are to take on the likeness of Christ the priest by sacred ordination should form the habit of drawing close to him as friends in every detail of their life.' The third reference to *Haerent animo* is in footnote no. 41. **89** Decree, *Presbyterorum ordinis*, Flannery, pp 863–902. See footnote no. 39 of Chapter II and no. 7 of Chapter III. **90** The text of *Presbyterorum ordinis* reaffirms many of the same points made in this Apostolic Exhortation; see in particular nos. 15 to 19 of this conciliar decree. **91** Joseph Cardinal Ratzinger, *A new song for the Lord*, p. 131, referring to Gianpaolo Romanato, *Pio X: la vita di Papa Sarto* (Milan, 1992).

The last months of Pius X's life brought heavy crosses which contributed to a rapid deterioration in his health. In early 1914 he received reports from Mexico that the bishops had been forced to flee their country. On June 28 newspapers reported the assassination of the Archduke Ferdinand, heir to the Austro-Hungarian throne. Pius X, realizing more than anybody else the likely consequences of this tragic event, used all the authority of his office to beg the governing powers to avoid the horrors of war. He had for several years a premonition of the blood bath that would engulf Europe in August 1914. He offered his life to the Lord to suspend the scourge of war, which he clearly saw, taking effect. His last public act was to receive in audience seminarians who were leaving Rome for their respective countries to fight in a war which would see them pitted against each other: French, German, Belgian, Austrian, English, Slav. The Church was being torn apart before his very eyes. He asked them not to forget the great law of mercy, even in the fury of war. As he blessed them he did not disguise his tears.

On 2 August he sent a moving exhortation to the Catholics of the whole world to implore peace. On the afternoon of 15 August he felt extremely ill. Gradually his condition worsened until early on the morning of 20 August he breathed his last.

CHAPTER EIGHT

Blessed Clement von Galen (1878–1946)

DACHAU IS A SMALL rural town in southern Germany not very far from Munich. It looks no different from many other similar farming communities in that part of Bavaria, yet the mere mention of the name of Dachau evokes horror for anyone acquainted with the history of Nazi barbarities during World War II. After Hitler took control of Germany in 1933, the totalitarian nature of the Nazi regime soon began to show itself. Subsequently the number of offenders taken into 'protective custody' began to increase rapidly. At first the victims were socialists, communists, and other political opponents of National Socialism. However, not long after a decree was issued against the 'abuse of the pulpit for political purposes', which resulted in the imprisonment of many Catholic priests. It was to the concentration camp at Dachau that these priests were generally sent.[1] Hitler protested that the priests he arrested and eliminated were not being executed because of their religion, but because of their political crimes against the state.

From the beginning the Catholic Church was one of the main targets of Hitler's policy of annihilation – the totalitarian aims of National Socialism would not tolerate any opposition or allow any other organization compete for the loyalty of the German people. The Gestapo were active everywhere, even to the extent of intruding into confessionals to trap priests into making unguarded statements. Priests were kept under active surveillance. As a consequence, hundreds of clergy were arraigned before Nazi courts of summary jurisdiction and condemned to death or internment in concentration camps.[2]

In Dachau alone, no fewer than 2,700 priests were imprisoned, of whom at least 1,000 died from hunger, disease or ill-treatment.[3] Acts of brutality, torture and murder were commonplace in these camps, yet they were the context

1 Cf. G. Lewy, *The Catholic Church and Nazi Germany* (London, 1964), pp 170–2. 2 Cf. B. Hoffmann, *And who will kill you: the chronicle of the life and sufferings of priests in the concentration camps* (Preroc, Poland, 1994). 3 Cf. Robert Royal, *The Catholic martyrs of the twentieth century* (New York, 2000), pp 133–5.

of daily acts of heroism, as in the case of Maximilian Kolbe[4] in Auschwitz, or the secret and daring ordination in Dachau of Karl Leisner, the young seminarian from Münster.[5] At first priests could hear confessions in the camps but in 1934 it was prohibited. Subsequently the privilege of saying Mass was withdrawn. The majority of the priests interned in Dachau were of Polish origin, 1,780 in total. However, apart from German nationals, there were large numbers of French, Czechs, and Austrians. Dachau was host to priests from all over Nazi occupied Europe. Seminarians from these same countries were drafted in as part of forced labour gangs in Germany. No less than 4,000 priests were put to death during these years, either as 'political saboteurs', or, after incarceration in concentration camps, by hanging, starvation, mishandling, lack of medical aid, or as victims of medical experiments including euthanasia. It is a story of courageous and heroic resistance against the overwhelming power of a police state.[6] These are just some of the facts related to the Catholic resistance to Nazi terrorism during one of the most terrible periods in modern history. It is important to remember the sacrifices of these heroic men at a time when a revisionist rewriting of history would suggest that Catholic opposition to the totalitarian ambitions of Hitler was a mere token resistance.[7]

In this context also the memory of a great German ecclesiastic deserves to be recalled for his heroism at another level. Count Clement August von Galen was bishop of Münster, the ecclesiastical capital of the strongly Catholic region of Westphalia and the Lower Rhine in north-west Germany. He took a consistently courageous stand against the policies of Hitler and the Gestapo, and was unrelenting in his criticism of them. His immense prestige at home and abroad was what ultimately saved him from the extermination that many of his own priests suffered.

At that time one of the directors of propaganda in the British war office was Brigadier General R.L. Sedgwick, a convert to Catholicism. He recalls that the

4 Cf. André Frossard, *Forget not love: the passion of Maximilian Kolbe* (San Francisco, 1991). 5 On 12 January 1996 the decree of martyrdom of Fr Karl Leisner was promulgated by the Congregation for the Causes of Saints. He was beatified that same year. 6 Cf. J.C. Conway, *The Nazi persecution of the Churches, 1933–1945* (London, 1968), pp 298–99, and note 24, p. 447. An Austrian priest wrote a chilling account of his six-and-a-half years in Dachau – cf. John M. Lenz, *Christ in Dachau or Christ victorious*, trans. Countess Barbara Waldstein (Möliing bei Wien, Austria, 1960). Yet this courageous priest could sum up his experience as follows: 'What we priests were forced to endure under the Nazi regime, especially in Dachau concentration camp, is no more than a cup filled from the vast sea of human suffering in the world today. It is not this suffering as such which is important. The important thing is to show those who have crosses of their own to bear in life just what the grace of God can do for those who follow faithfully in the footsteps of Christ the Crucified' (p. 141). 7 There were about 21,000 priests in Germany in 1932, just prior to the Nazi rise to power. Royal points out that of these more than 8,000 clashed with the Reich, of whom several hundred perished at Nazi hands (See ibid., p. 132).

bishop's sermons provided the war office with the most powerful anti-Hitler propaganda.[8] During the war the BBC sent out transmissions specifically targeting the forty million German-speaking Catholics. Day after day the radio broadcasts from London drove home the point of Hitler's hatred for Catholicism. The bishop's sermons, Sedgewick says, were like manna from heaven in the propaganda war against the Nazis. The BBC transmissions, drawing on these sermons, also endeavoured to show that National Socialism constituted a grave threat to the family and the religious ideals which it enshrined. Sedgwick had met von Galen in Rome in 1939 before the war. After the cessation of hostilities in 1945 he was appointed controller general of religious affairs for the British zone in Germany. In this capacity he had occasion to get to know von Galen well and has left on record his impressions of the bishop of Münster.[9]

Von Galen's sheer size was impressive – six feet six inches tall and built accordingly – he was a colossus of a man. His features revealed his aristocratic background:

> The eyes, which inspired confidence, were of a soft grey above which lay long, bushy white eyebrows, carefully brushed, which beetled when he grew indignant. The whole head suggested a powerful mind well under control. Except when he smiled or laughed, and I was soon to learn that he had a fine sense of humour, his appearance could not be called happy. On the contrary his features bore the evidence of much sorrow and worry, of much strenuous labour wrought in this world.[10]

The war had brought him untold suffering; and his cathedral and episcopal palace had been destroyed by Allied bombing raids, which devastated the city of Münster.

> No one could fail to mark, Sedgwick recalls, the austerity and self discipline in his expression. When he spoke there was in his voice, which was only occasionally loud, a mingling of controlled quietness and animation which made him master of those around him. His laughter had the ring of a jovial mockery about it which was quite unforgettable … Here visible in the flesh was the legendary being, the defier of Hitler and all his works; the man whose sermons we had exploited by fair means and foul – the Lion of Münster himself who was just as ready to roar at us as he had been at the Nazi leaders.[11]

8 Cf. H. Portmann, *Cardinal von Galen* (London, 1957). This is a translation by R.L. Sedgwick of the original German biography entitled *Kardinal von Galen, Ein Gottesmann seiner Zeit*, published in 1953 in Münster. It is the main source of the biographical material used in this chapter. **9** Cf. Portman, *Introduction* by R.L. Sedgwick. **10** Ibid. **11** Ibid., p. 15.

He was a man of iron will, yet possessed of a deep humility and simplicity. Not only had he great prestige abroad and among Catholics in Germany; among the German bishops themselves he was regarded as the most important Church leader of their country.

FAMILY BACKGROUND

Clement August von Galen was born in 1878 in Oldenburg, in the Drinklage castle which had been the seat of the family for three centuries. The von Galens had a long tradition of deep loyalty and of practical service to the Church. August was later to look back with affection and gratitude to the family which prepared him so well for his vocation to the priesthood. One of thirteen children, he was reared in a family of deep Catholic piety. There was daily Mass in their private chapel, and in the evenings the family Rosary. During May they would go to the shrine of our Lady in the grounds of the castle, to pray and sing to the Mother of God.

At twelve he went to a boarding school in Feldkirch for four years, finishing the last two years of his secondary education in Oldenburg. Following studies at the seminaries of Innsbruck and Münster, he was ordained to the priesthood in Münster cathedral in 1904. Little did he realize that thirty years later he would become the acknowledged leader of Catholic Germany as a consequence of his courageous sermons from the pulpit of this same cathedral. One of his first appointments was as curate in the parish of St Matthias in Berlin which, according to an old tradition, was always served by priests from the diocese of Münster. There was a large proportion of poor in the parish and he carried out an extensive pastoral activity among them. He took a keen interest in the youth of the parish and became president of the Catholic Young Men's Association in Berlin. His preaching to them focused on four objectives: they were to be good Christians, good citizens, first-rate men at their work, and, above all, exemplary fathers of families.

His lifestyle as a priest was one of great sobriety, even frugality. When he later became parish priest of St Matthias, his curates noticed his self-denial at meals. He was a man of prayer and practical humility. He confessed every Saturday evening to his senior curate and, before going on his annual retreat, he came to the same priest with great simplicity, asking what defects he ought to be specially on guard against, and what faults he ought to correct. This younger priest was always very moved to see the efforts Fr von Galen made subsequently to overcome these faults. Out of devotion to the Holy Souls he had the habit of reading the breviary in the afternoon in the nearby cemetery. He was a constant visitor to the sick in his parish. Because of his aristocratic background, he frequently received invitations to lunch or dinner from people in the upper strata of society in Berlin; these he invariably refused. He wasn't, by all accounts, an inspiring preacher; his language was plain and direct, yet his words were always those of the good shepherd admonishing, beseeching, and calling to conversion.

In the years after the First World War the decline of authority in Germany was accompanied by a degeneration in moral values. Revolution was in the air. The old values which bonded society together were disappearing, and Christianity was more and more being excluded from public affairs. Years later, when he preached among the ruins of Münster cathedral in July of 1945, he lamented that it was in the period following 1918 that the ground was prepared for Hitler's godless state. If man believes that all authority proceeds from the people alone, the state rests on fragile foundations. The ballot-box alone cannot guarantee a democracy in accord with the demands of human dignity – it needs, he said, to be anchored in the Christian vision of man as well. And so in 1945 he would tell the Allied Powers that, if the German people were made a present of freedom from outside, there was no guarantee that, in the course of party conflicts, a particular party might not win over a majority of the people and set up a dictatorship again in the name of democracy. No one could accuse von Galen of lacking patriotism. However, his love for the German people didn't blind him to a recognition of the forces of evil threatening that society, which were especially dangerous in an environment of practical atheism.

RETURN TO WESTPHALIA

After twenty-three years ministering in Berlin, he was recalled to his own diocese in 1929 to become parish priest of St Lambert's in the city of Münster. He had given the German capital the best years of his life, yet his pastoral experience there was to be of immense advantage when later he would be appointed bishop of Münster.

In 1932 he published a work which attracted widespread attention; it was entitled *The pestilence of secularism and its different manifestations.*[12] It dealt with the secularization of human society, and the rejection of God and his laws. He traced how, over the years, there had been a gradual evolution leading men away from the supernatural. By this time the Nazi Party had made considerable electoral gains and Alfred Rosenberg, the chief ideologue of National Socialism, had published his *The myth of the twentieth century*, which was the handbook of the new 'positive Christianity' based on a theology of race, soil

12 The title in German was *Die Pest des Laizismus und ihre Erscheinungsformen.*

and nature. In Rosenberg's view, Christianity had been distorted throughout its whole history by the 'political Jew', St Paul, into a religion of submission, humility, and slavery. He skewed history to make it read that Jesus was not a Jew at all, and affirmed that the German people were not the subject of original sin but of original nobility. This heritage authorized them to move mercilessly against all who opposed their divine spirit, especially the lesser races whom God had intended to be ruled by the pure Aryans. These outrageous claims were of course, at the time, demolished by Catholic and Protestant scholars. But Rosenberg was appealing not to German intellects, but was exploiting their sense of resentment over the harsh Versailles Treaty which crippled Germany after World War I, leading to utter chaos, and which, according to Rosenberg, was the consequence of a Jewish conspiracy.[13]

Practising Catholics were drawn into the ranks of National Socialism for different reasons. The vision of national renewal and the hope of political stability which the Nazis seemed to offer made many believe that all sorts of new possibilities were open. Von Galen was concerned about the consequences of the rejection of the transcendent in the new religion, which resulted in man and nature being put at the centre of things with the rejection of God's claim on man. Only a year later events proved that his concerns were not without cause.

1933 was the key year in the growth of National Socialism. In January Hitler became chancellor of Germany. In February the Nazis took over the key positions in government and began to dominate the whole country. On 28 February, after the burning of the Reichstag, Hitler, under the plea of preventing communist terrorist activities, persuaded President Hindenburg to issue a decree effectively taking away the basic freedoms of every German citizen. This led to the passage of the Enabling Bill which abolished parliament and gave the cabinet total legislative power. On 23 March Hitler gave a policy statement in which he promised, among other things, to work for peaceful relations between Church and state. Five days afterwards the German bishops, in a joint statement, said that, though they maintained a negative attitude to Nazism in the past, in view of the public guarantee of Hitler in the Reichstag a few days earlier to respect Catholic doctrine and the rights of the Church, they now believed that the previous general warnings and prohibitions were no longer necessary.

The way was now prepared for the signing of the much desired concordat between Germany and the Vatican, with the prospect of substantially improved conditions for the Church. Hitler had no intention of honouring the concordat – he saw it merely as a political weapon to be used as appropriate to achieve other objectives. It was ratified on 10 September 1933, but it was no defence against the

13 Cf. Royal, pp 147–8. See also Nathaniel Micklem, *National Socialism and the Roman Catholic Church* (New York, 1939), p. 23.

Nazi determination to wipe out all Catholic influence outside the sacristy – in schools, in the press, in youth and professional organizations. The spirit and the letter of the concordat were violated by Hitler from the very first day.[14]

The Catholic episcopate was not alone in failing to perceive the totalitarian goals of the Nazi movement. The Protestant churches, most of the intellectuals, and many people abroad showed the same political naivety.[15] Hitler resented the influence of the Church, in particular its strong bonding with German Catholic youth. He would use the Church as long as it furthered his own political ends but, as history was to demonstrate, he hadn't the slightest scruple in using terror, suppression, murder and liquidation where the aims of the Church clashed in any way with his own. He hated and despised the Christian faith and his long-term plan was to bring about its extinction.

On 2 September of this fateful year of 1933, Clement August von Galen's nomination as bishop of Münster was announced. His appointment was well received by clergy and laity alike. It was already clear that a comprehensive attack on the faith was inevitable, and there was an intuitive awareness among the faithful of Münster that a man of von Galen's courage and fearlessness was needed to stand firm against the assault of National Socialism. Under the provisions of the recent concordat, he had to take the oath of allegiance before Göring, the president of the council of ministers. At a lunch afterwards, Göring emphasized the need to get the clergy on the side of National Socialism; von Galen replied, with his usual directness, that according to the concordat the clergy should not become involved in party politics.

BISHOP OF MÜNSTER

A decade before National Socialism came to power von Galen had read the signs of the times. He had no illusions, as he took charge of the diocese of Münster, about the confrontation that would ultimately ensue. However, the hostility of the movement towards Christianity did not become clear immediately. Hitler spoke in the Reichstag about the need for the loyal co-operation of the Christian Churches, and a number of Catholics were taken in. There was thus a period of hesitation in which it was felt that the new men should be given a chance to prove themselves. It was precisely during these years (1933–7) that National Socialism was able to get a hold on many key aspects of German society.

14 Twelve years later, looking back on the history of the Concordat which was ratified while he was still Secretary of State, Pius XII recalled that 'though often violated, it did give Catholics a legal ground of defence, a platform from which to resist as long as possible the tide of persecution' (AAS 37 [1945], p. 160). 15 Cf. Lewy, p. 98.

Von Galen paid close attention to the literature of National Socialism, and in his first Lenten pastoral (January 1934) he opposed the fundamental doctrine of the new politics, the worship of the race. The unity of men brought about by the redemption of Christ was, he taught, of a much higher order than any unity derived from race, because through Baptism, irrespective of race, we had all become children of God. He would return to this same idea in his powerful Lenten pastoral for 1939:

> Those who place the Race or the Nation or the State … as the supreme norm of all things, even of things religious, and deify them with a divine cultus, are distorting and falsifying the divinely created and divinely ordained order of things. Only superficial minds can fall into the error of speaking of a national God or of a national religion. The personal immortality of the human soul is being denied. As a substitute for this, they offer us in high-sounding phrases a so-called 'eternity' in the form of a chain of succession between forbears and offspring. Whoever uses the word immortality to mean only collective survival in the continuity of one's own people for an undetermined length of time in the future, perverts and falsifies one of the fundamental verities of the Christian faith. Those who dare to demand obedience to commands and ordinances that are in opposition to the holy will of God, misuse their power and forfeit the right to require obedience. In such cases it would be our duty to withstand the authority thus abused, in accordance with the example set by the holy Apostles. For this reason we cannot accept a totalitarian demand to follow other doctrines or pursue purely earthly aims.[16]

A few weeks after his 1934 Lenten pastoral, he sat down to write his Easter message. He was now much more certain of where National Socialism was leading – the systematic destruction of the faith in Germany. Consequently he saw that it was absolutely necessary to speak very clearly, and to use all the authority and resources of his episcopal office to open people's minds to what was happening. The pastoral was read in a solemn manner, in the presence of the bishop wearing his mitre, with crozier in hand. It was listened to by a crowded congregation in expectant silence. The pastoral was unambiguous:

16 *The persecution of the Catholic Church in the Third Reich: facts and documents* (London, 1942), p. 34 (subsequently referred to as *Facts and documents*). This book, translated from the German and published during the Second World War, brought to the attention of the Catholic world the ruthless persecution of the Church in Germany under the Nazi regime from 1933. It is a detailed chronicle of facts and events that speak for themselves. It draws particularly on the pastoral letters of the German bishops since, with the Catholic Press effectively muzzled, they were the only means of informing Catholics of the realities of the situation.

'Hell itself is let loose with its deceit,' the bishop warned, 'which may even mislead good men.'

In two churches the reading of the pastoral was interrupted by SS men in protest. It caused a widespread stir, not only in Westphalia but in many other parts of Germany as well; von Galen had publicly challenged the principles of National Socialism. After Easter 1934 he continued his defence of the Catholic position against the ideology of the movement in addresses to many gatherings of Catholics. While he took the initiative in co-ordinating the efforts of the bishops of north-western Germany against National Socialism, he nevertheless was very strongly of the view that, since each bishop is ultimately responsible for the defence of the Church in his own diocese, he had to be completely free to take any personal initiative he felt necessary.

THE STRUGGLE AGAINST NATIONAL SOCIALISM

In April 1934 a ban was imposed on dual membership of Catholic Workers organizations and the Nazi-sponsored German Labour Front; membership of the latter became in effect a condition of employment. Von Galen telegraphed Hitler on 1 May requesting him to withdraw the order to avoid excluding many Germans from the task of reconstruction of the country. He suggested to his fellow bishops that if Hitler did not change his policy, the Church should condemn the neo-pagan teachings that were jeopardizing the faith and morals of German Catholics, and prohibit membership of organizations that involved danger to the faith: 'Not all, but very many German Catholics are today fully prepared to listen to the word of the Church and to obey it even at the cost of sacrifices.'[17]

On 20 December 1934 the notorious Conspiracy Law was promulgated which gave the police almost unlimited powers of arrest and which was increasingly used against the clergy. Early in 1935 a campaign of vilification of the clergy and of members of religious orders was launched. Priests and nuns were accused of violating currency regulations on trumped up charges designed to stir up anti-clerical feeling among the population. The virulence and scurrility of these attacks failed to produce the desired results – the laity refused to desert their priests and rallied more strongly to their defence.

At the end of May 1935 von Galen wrote to the governor of Westphalia protesting against a proposed Nazi rally in Münster at which Rosenberg was scheduled to speak. 'The overwhelming Christian population of Westphalia', he said, 'could regard the appearance of Rosenberg only as an outright provo-

17 Cf. Lewy, pp 121 and 125.

cation, designed to pour contempt on their holiest and most cherished religious convictions.'[18] On 7 July the massive rally was held in Münster's main square, in front of the bishop's palace. Von Galen was denounced as a reactionary and as a leader of a political brand of Catholicism which refused to recognize that times had changed. Was Nazism intolerant?, asked Rosenberg. How could it be, given that the bishop was allowed to write such disgraceful letters against the leader of the Nazi movement without being gaoled as a consequence?[19] Catholic Münster replied the next day with a huge procession of thanksgiving, a traditional event which took place every year in July. Von Galen addressed the crowds and told them that he would never yield to the enemies of Christianity and the persecutors of the Church.

When the day for the big procession of 1936 arrived, the police, mindful of the huge crowds von Galen had drawn the previous year, roped off the cathedral square to prevent large numbers of people from assembling. Von Galen went to the pulpit of the cathedral and thundered his indignation: 'Can the shepherd be severed from his flock? Can the police divide Catholics from their own bishop by ropes and chains?' There were loud shouts of 'No'! from the crowd at this. 'The bonds between us can be destroyed or broken by no one as long as we continue together through life in the following of Christ,' he added.[20]

However, people were fascinated by the buoyancy of National Socialism. Unemployment disappeared, economic life was cranked up, and there was more money in circulation. All this has to be borne in mind to appreciate how difficult it was for the bishop to combat the pagan ideology which lay at the root of it all. Christianity and the Church were attacked in a subtle and not so subtle manner as being the basis of all Germany's ills. The ideas of the new paganism were instilled into German youth, making use of the whole apparatus of the state. All Catholic youth organizations were abolished. Von Galen protested vigorously against the dissolution of the Catholic Youth Association in a courageous sermon delivered in November 1937:

> If we are misunderstood and abused by our own fellow-countrymen, even by representatives of the secular power, if we are forced to submit to treatment which we feel is bitterly unfair – that was the lot of Christ, and let us say with Him: 'Father, forgive them, for they know not what they do' ... On October 29th the Münster Diocesan Organization of the Catholic Young Men's Association was dissolved. No intimation was first given of any illegalities. There was no possibility of defence or of going to court. According to the secret police order, not only is the Diocesan Organization itself suppressed but also, it would appear, all

18 Cf. Conway, p. 21. **19** Ibid., p. 127. **20** *Facts and documents*, p. 247.

> affiliated parish societies for youths, even the sodalities of our Lady, and their property, including the dedicated church banners, has been confiscated. A decree of February 28th 1933, designed to meet Communist activities, is invoked in order to destroy Catholic associations. It is a perverse and wanton insult to German Catholics and their priests and bishops. It is a flagrant injustice to the leaders and members of our Youth Associations, who with untiring selflessness have successfully aimed at one thing only: to lead the youth of Germany to fidelity to Christ and to love of their Fatherland, to a sense of duty and common endeavour for the well-being of our fellow countrymen.[21]

Catholic publications which could have resisted these ideas were suppressed. Only the pulpit remained.

Von Galen's Lenten pastoral of 1935 was directed against the pantheism which denied a personal God and asserted that the true God was embodied in the race of men of German blood. In a famous sermon, preached at Xanten on 9 Februaray 1936, he castigated not only the philosophy of National Socialism, but its crimes as well. He spoke of the arbitrary imprisonment of ecclesiastics, and of the graves of those whom Catholics regarded as martyrs for the faith, but the manner of whose death was a closely guarded secret:

> See how Holy Church, the Pope, the bishops, priests and religious, see how the loyal children of the Church today in Germany are insulted, reviled and derided with impunity. How many Catholics, priests and laymen, have been attacked and insulted in the papers and at public meetings, driven out of their professions and positions, and imprisoned and ill-treated without judicial sentence being passed! ... There are fresh graves in German soil in which are lying the ashes of those whom the Catholic people regard as martyrs for the Faith, since their lives gave witness to their most dutiful and loyal devotion to God and the Fatherland, to the nation and the Church, while the dark secrecy which surrounds their deaths is most carefully preserved.[22]

A few weeks later, on Sunday 22 March 1936, just days before the General Election, in a courageous sermon which confronted Hitler directly with the atrocities of Nazi persecution, he made known publicly what he would like to write to the Führer on his voting slip:

> Is the Führer and Chancellor of the Reich aware of the spiritual distress of countless men and women whose consciences are oppressed, whose

21 *Facts and documents*, pp 111–12. **22** Ibid., p.19.

> Faith is slandered, whose rights are encroached upon and whose honour is injured? Does he know of the insults and the base insinuations against Christianity and the Holy Catholic Church to which he himself belongs by baptism, against her divinely appointed head, the Pope, against bishops and priests, against Catholic organizations and societies, which are printed and propagated in Germany, and are forced and thrust upon audiences at meetings and training courses? I can scarcely believe that he knows all this, or is aware of the frightful danger of this fiery war against the Faith that has been set ablaze … Does the Führer know that men belonging to the Movement are themselves directing this war on Christianity and fanning the flames of conflict in speeches, and in publications issued and recommended by official quarters in the Party? Is he aware that this onslaught against Christianity and our most sacred religious convictions is even carried out by the agency of meetings, technical journals, and professional periodicals which are obligatory for the various professions concerned? Does he know that, even in the publications issued by the Supreme Command of the Hitler Youth, Christianity is made contemptible as being alien to the German nature and an enemy of the German race, so that our young people are actually given instruction in disloyalty to God, to Christ and to His Church? Does the Führer and Reich Chancellor know all that? How can Christian parents with a good conscience allow their children to take part in the Land Year, labour camps, Hitler Youth meetings and training courses, when they know that the religious guidance and instruction, which is so necessary for the young, is lacking; or when they even have good cause to fear, by repeated experience and reports, that perhaps mistrust, and indeed, hatred, of Christianity and the Church will be preached to those who take part in such gatherings![23]

But it was the literature of National Socialism which von Galen regarded as the most dangerous influence. He spoke against the calumnies directed against the Church which frequently appeared in its journals. As already remarked, Rosenberg's *Mythus* had become the manual of the new 'Christianity'. Von Galen courageously sponsored the publication of a critique of this document in the Münster diocesan gazette. It was a scholarly study but devastating in its criticism. The main errors were highlighted and the insults to the Pope and the Church were shown for what they were. Though the Gestapo confiscated the pamphlet, it nevertheless reached a wide audience.[24]

23 Ibid., pp 20–1. **24** Cf. Lewy, pp 153–5.

CAMPAIGN AGAINST THE CHURCH

It was in 1936–7 that the ideological campaign against the Church reached its peak before German efforts began to be concentrated primarily on the Nazi military objectives. The cult of Hitler as the future saviour became for many a substitute for Christian faith. An ersatz theology was built up on Nazi theories of race and soil, and a new pagan liturgy was created to substitute 'outdated' Christian ceremonies. The annihilation of Catholic education was one of the anchor points of the Nazi campaign against the Church. The attack was carried out in three stages: (i) the destruction of the Christian character of the denominational schools (stripping crucifixes from the classrooms, etc.); (ii) the removal of priests and nuns as teachers from the schools; (iii) the forcible conversion by law of denominational schools into National Socialist community schools.

From the beginning von Galen fought a courageous and unyielding battle to defend the system of Catholic education in his diocese. In October 1936 the German News Agency distributed an article in which it was maintained that the denominational schools (Catholic and Protestant) divided the community and destroyed the unity of the nation. The bishop of Münster was naturally highly indignant at the mendacity of such a claim and wrote a stinging reply in the diocesan gazette.

> Is this contention true? I address this question publicly to those official quarters which have forced our local newspapers to print this article and disseminate this contention. Is it true, then, that the German State, whose Führer at a solemn moment announced to the whole world that the National Government regards the two denominations as most important factors for the preservation of our national heritage … is it true that this same Germany today wishes to suppress and destroy the very foundation on which the maintenance of these factors depends – namely, the denominational schools?[25]

By means of propaganda, terror tactics, and intimidation of parents, the work of demolition of the well organized system of German Catholic education got under way. However, against all the odds, Catholics resisted bravely, especially in their efforts to retain the crucifixes in the classrooms.

In von Galen's own diocese a government order was issued on 4 November 1936 to the effect that all crucifixes and religious symbols were to be removed from the schools. Ten days later a letter was read in all churches

25 *Facts and documents*, p. 117.

urging Catholics to resist, and to stand firm for education in the faith of the Cross, the sign of their redemption. People rallied to the call and came by the thousand from every parish in the Oldenburg territory of the Münster diocese to protest in the streets of the city, demanding the rescinding of the government order. For once the authorities were unnerved by the scale of the demonstration, and offered the compromise solution of allowing crucifixes to be put up in classrooms during periods of religious instruction. However, the outrage of the brave people of Münster was so vehement that the order of 4 November was rescinded and the crucifixes were restored to the classrooms.

On Sunday 29 November the bishop, in a rousing pastoral letter, ordered a *Te Deum* to be sung in thanksgiving in all the churches of the diocese. He thanked his diocesans for their fortitude and commitment to the faith and, at the same time, was magnanimous enough to express his appreciation to the governor of Oldenburg for reversing the order about the crucifixes:

> It had been ordered that the Cross should be removed from all public buildings, and even from the schools in which Catholic children were taught by Catholic teachers. When you heard that, and when we heard it, a thrill of horror went through our hearts. Had it already come to this pitch? … My beloved diocesans! Let us thank God that he has opened our eyes, and enabled us to recognize what an unholy development was taking place here in our midst and what immeasurable evils stood before us. You did recognize it, and because you did so you poured out your tears before the Almighty in fervent prayer; day after day in overflowing churches and in your family devotions before the Crucified you have besought God to avert this dreadful evil. But not only have you prayed, you have bestirred yourselves in the matter as well. From nearly every parish your representatives, brave German men, tried and tested both in war and peace, have journeyed to Oldenburg, and, casting aside the fear of men, have given witness for you and for your loyalty to Christ, the Crucified one. Thank God for this manly Christian courage, which is indeed at all times a Christian duty, but is more than ever necessary today … 'The crosses shall remain in the schools.' Those are words which we hear with enthusiasm and gratitude. The Cross shall remain in our village streets and pathways. The Cross shall remain in our rooms and in our churches. The Cross shall remain – and that is the most important of all – in our hearts. Nothing ought, nothing must, nothing will separate us, our youth, our people or our homeland from the Cross. We will avoid all companionship with those who are enemies of the Cross of Christ. We will read no books that shame the Cross of Christ, we will not suffer them in our

> homes, in our show-cases, in our shop windows. And if it should be our lot for the sake of the Cross to suffer shame and persecution with Christ Crucified, than we shall neither fear nor shrink. For then we shall think of him who, himself dying on the Cross, yet won for us the victory of life eternal.[26]

Another tactic used by the Nazis was to undermine Catholic education from within. This they did by employing in the schools teachers who had fallen away from the faith or who had left the Church. In a pastoral letter read on 21 December 1936, von Galen protested vehemently against this direct violation of the concordat, and warned parents to be on their guard in face of this more subtle attack on the faith of their children.

> In spite of our protests, in Catholic elementary schools of our diocese teachers are employed who have fallen away from the faith or have left the Church, whose own children do not receive a Catholic education or have received an exemption from attendance at religious instruction. It is obvious that such teachers do not 'accord with the special needs of Catholic schools,' as is required by Article 24 of the Concordat. By the employment of such persons the remaining Catholic schools are being undermined from within. They are certainly undermined from within when teachers speak to children slightingly of bishops and priests, or when teachers speak disparagingly of the Bible stories of the Old Testament and hold them up to contempt. They are undermined from within when teachers lay regrettable cases of offences against the Catholic moral law to the charge of the whole Church, or even to the charge of the priesthood or religious state as such. They are undermined when teachers or other Youth leaders, in their hatred against the Church and her priests, incite the children to disorderly conduct during the hour of religious instruction, to ask impudent questions, to create disturbances, and to ridicule the priest who is giving the instruction. These deplorable cases must be publicly pilloried, so that parents may know what is happening and what is being tolerated in the Catholic schools that yet remain.[27]

In the same pastoral he protested against the unchristian character of some books being used in the schools:

> Parents are especially warned to exercise their vigilance in regard to the school books recently prescribed, particularly in the case of reading

26 *Facts and documents*, pp 124–5. **27** *Facts and documents*, p. 128.

> books and history textbooks. When we find that in such books our Christian heritage, Christian traditions, and Christian interpretation of world affairs and daily life receive little or no treatment or recognition, we at once realize how little authoritative circles are concerned to support and assist Christian parents in the Christian upbringing of their children by means of the school.[28]

A year later he returned to this concern, expressing his deep sorrow and anxiety that unbelieving teachers would misuse religious instruction to destroy the faith of Catholic children. 'Woe to the poor children who fall into the hands of such impostors', he lamented. 'Better no instruction in the school than one which offers poison in place of true nourishment.' He continued:

> Whoever denies the immortality of the individual human soul and tries to satisfy man's hope of eternity and his longing for life everlasting by prating of an 'eternal Germany' and of an eternal consciousness consisting only of an awareness of the past and the future of the People, such a one teaches no true religion, but destroys all religion; he offers the children a religious substitute which cannot instil any lasting sense of personal obligation, but can only destroy and corrupt it ... Christian parents, when teachers dare to forbid your children to relate to you at home what they have been taught in school, or to repeat the remarks that have been made with regard to religious truths, then know and be sure that something is happening in the school which they would keep secret from you, something which will alienate from you the hearts of your own children. This being so, you are justified, nay obliged, to protest to these Educational Authorities that employ such teachers, and through petitions and complaints and all lawful means to prevail upon them to remove people who are destroying both the children's trust in their parents and proper family life, to remove them from a position which they can worthily fill only by co-operating in all honour and loyalty with the parents of their pupils.[29]

The campaign of vilification of the clergy was intensified in the Nazi press. Readers were fed with sensational allegations of sexual immorality among priests and members of religious orders. 'Immorality trials' were staged in courts and, by ingenious spacing, were made to appear as an unbroken series of clerical offences. Priests were pilloried as idlers and criminal offenders. The bishop of Münster was a particular target of this invective. Groups of thugs, organized by

28 Ibid., p. 129. **29** *Facts and documents*, p. 183, from a sermon preached in November 1937.

the Gestapo, threw stones at the windows of his residence at night, singing obscene songs specially composed to ridicule von Galen, to the accompaniment of the noise of breaking glass. The degree of surveillance imposed on Catholic bishops, both over their private lives as well as their official activities, was unprecedented even by Nazi standards, especially during the war years.[30]

The Nazis gradually and effectively destroyed the independence of the Catholic daily press by a series of draconian laws. From April 1935 articles with a religious content had been banned. The Catholic weeklies were still published but the net began to tighten around these also. In 1936 the publication of pastoral letters was banned. The following year a diocesan weekly in Münster was ordered by the regional office of the Propaganda Ministry to publish an article about a secondary schoolboy accused of serious sexual offences as a leader of Catholic youth. Bishop von Galen refused to comply with these smear tactics. The Gestapo forbade the paper to appear until such time as the order from the Propaganda Ministry was obeyed. Von Galen would not yield. After three months the Gestapo suppressed the diocesan weekly for good.[31]

The question of whether to show the swastika flag on churches caused considerable tension. It became the national flag in 1935. Von Galen, even after it had become official, refused to have it hoisted on the church, maintaining that the house of God was dedicated to divine worship and therefore removed from the secular domain.[32]

PERSONAL LIFE

What were the sources of the bishop's courage and vision during these difficult years? We get some idea of this aspect of von Galen's life by a consideration of his personal piety. As we have already seen, he had a deeply supernatural outlook, an attitude impressed on his mind from early childhood. Life for him was an opportunity to learn to love God and to do his will, no matter what the cost. On the other hand, he was aware that God loved us to the extent of dying for us on the Cross, and that he would always support us with his grace. The great truths of God's intervention in human history were constantly before his mind, reinforced by daily reading of the Scriptures. On the other hand, he had a simple piety which expressed itself in love for the Blessed Eucharist, in devotion to the Rosary, to relics and pilgrimages. He was very conscious of the effects of original sin, and consequently he not only went to confession frequently as an antidote, but lived a deep spirit of self-denial with regard to food and creature comforts. He did the Stations of the Cross every Friday after-

30 See Conway, p. 243 **31** See Lewy, p. 140. **32** Cf. ibid., p. 222.

noon. He renewed the consecration of his diocese to the Sacred Heart every year, a devotion which grew and matured deeply in his soul, especially during the difficult war years.

He kept in close contact with his seminarians. There were 200 in the St Charles Borromeo seminary on the other side of the cathedral square from the bishop's palace. A different seminarian served his Mass each morning and was invited to have breakfast with him afterwards. The bishop encouraged the seminarians to talk over breakfast and give their views on all the different topics relevant to the life of a seminarian. In this way he got to know them well – their outlook, thinking, concerns, etc. Every First Friday he went to the seminary to say Mass for the students. He tried to keep in touch with developments in theology, but was not entirely sympathetic to some of the newer tendencies since by inclination and training he was a strong traditionalist. He had a firm, clear understanding of the fundamentals of the faith and, as a consequence, grasped more quickly than others the decline in the state of belief and the dismantling of moral values.

He encouraged his priests to teach the whole truth about God, because that was the only way to set man free from the bondage of sin and to give him real comfort in his loneliness and misery. The priests of his diocese appreciated the way their chief pastor preached against the new heathenism, and how he supported them in their personal trials. The Nazi campaign against his priests was unrelenting. Apart from those sent to the front, others were taken into 'protective custody' by the Gestapo, others were expelled or prohibited from giving religious instruction, others still were sent to that hell on earth, Dachau, from which they were never to return. Wherever hatred or craft could eliminate a priest, no opportunity was lost. Von Galen protested at every crime committed against his priests, and excoriated the brutality of the Gestapo with considerable risk to his own life. During the war years he had an enormous correspondence with his priests at the front, who wrote to him at length about their experiences, the joys of their priestly work, or the burden of the Cross in their lives. They wrote to him as they would to a father, and he replied to every one of those letters personally, even though it made considerable inroads on his time. On the occasion of big feasts of the Church, he used to send them a circular letter to tell them about the joys and sorrows of their home diocese.

Von Galen was a deeply patriotic German who loved the Church and who was devoted to the spiritual welfare of his countrymen. At the same time it was only natural that he shared to some extent the limitations in the outlook of the German people of his time at the psychological, cultural and nationalistic levels. This tended to a preference, at the political level, for strong authoritarian government, the desire for the recovery of that prestige lost through the humiliation of Versailles, and support of the German war effort and the country's expansionist ambitions. An example of this was von Galen's reaction to the crossing of the German army into the demilitarized zone of the Rhine in 1936. He cabled the Supreme Commander of the army: 'In the name of the staunchly Catholic Germans of the diocese of Münster, and especially of the Lower Rhine, I welcome the German armed forces which from today will again shield the German Rhine, as protection and symbol of German honour and German justice.'[33]

PIUS XI

Pius XI's encyclical, *Mit brennender Sorge* (With burning anxiety), was the Pope's response to the critical situation of the Church in Germany. It was secretly smuggled into the country and read from every Catholic pulpit in Germany on Palm Sunday, 21 March 1937. In it the Pope reaffirmed his concern at the growing oppression of the Church in Germany and the consistent violation of the 1933 concordat. He restated the teachings of the faith obscured by Nazi ideology. Belief in a natural God was a grave error – true belief in God, he said, was incompatible with the deification of earthly values. He reminded Catholics that they were not bound in conscience by human laws which were contrary to natural or divine law. Priests and laity were called upon to remain loyal to Christ, his Church and the primacy of Rome. He exposed the bad faith of the regime which considered 'violation (of the concordat) more or less official, as a normal policy'. Hitler was furious because the Catholic Church had dared to defy his authority publicly before the whole world. All copies of the encyclical were seized and it triggered off a whole series of repressive acts against the Church. In his 1937 Christmas address, Pius XI came out very strongly against the Nazis:

> In Germany there exists in very truth a religious persecution. For considerable time efforts have been made to make men believe that there was no persecution. But it is known that there is such a persecution and that it is a heavy one. Indeed, seldom has there been a persecution so heavy, so terrifying, so grievous and lamentable in its far-reaching effects.[34]

In May of 1938, when Hitler made his first official visit to Rome, Pius XI left the city, closed the Vatican Museum, and forbade Catholic buildings to show the Nazi flag although it was flying everywhere else in Rome. He publicly

33 Lewy, p. 202. **34** AAS, 30 (1938), p. 21.

expressed his grief 'that on the Feast of the Holy Cross (3 May) there is openly borne the badge of another cross which is not the Cross of Christ.'[35]

In the summer of 1937 von Galen preached a lengthy sermon defending the Pope, pointing out the frequent and extensive violations of the concordat. He referred to the illegal dissolution of Church organizations and the confiscation of their property; the suppression of denominational schools; the restrictions on religious instruction, etc. 'All that', he claimed, 'and much else that is in contradiction to the concordat with the Reich, is known to all of us ... And the Pope knows it too! Should he therefore remain silent?' He then went on to describe the brutal revenge tactics adopted by the government because of the distribution of the encyclical.[36] The weapons used were those of propaganda, police intimidation, economic pressure and personal defamation. Throughout 1937 and 1938 all Catholic lay organizations were one by one forced to close down; many had their property confiscated. Stringent limitations were imposed on Church processions and pilgrimages. By the summer of 1939 all private and denominational schools had been abolished. The campaign against the theology faculties in the universities was equally tyrannical and successful.

HIS GREATEST HOUR

For over 300 years, on the feast of the Visitation of our Lady, the faithful of the diocese of Münster went on pilgrimage to the shrine of our Lady of Telgte, some eight miles from the cathedral town. They did so again in early July of 1941, even though Allied bombing raids had already started in that area.

On Saturday 12 July the Gestapo confiscated two Jesuit houses in Münster. As soon as the bishop heard about it, he went at once to the premises and caught the Gestapo in the very act of driving the religious from their homes. He called them thieves and robbers to their faces. He returned home in a state of profound anger and indignation at the barefaced injustice of the Gestapo. That night he wrote the sermon which drew the bishop of Münster to the attention of the world. He was firmly convinced that his own life was in danger, but the interests of God had to be defended and National Socialism had to be shown up for what it truly was – the ally of the devil.

He read the sermon the following day in St Lambert's parish church, in that part of the city which had been most affected by the bombing raids of the previous week. He recounted how the previous day the Gestapo had seized the two Jesuit houses and forced the occupants to leave the city, as well as other

35 Cf. Michael O'Carroll, *Pius XII: greatness dishonoured* (Dublin, 1980), p. 45. 36 Cf. *Facts and documents*, p. 24.

cities in Westphalia and the Rhineland. The same fate had overtaken a convent of nuns. Thus what had been happening in southern Germany, in Austria and western Poland was now extended to Westphalia. He warned his listeners to be ready for a repetition of these crimes. Despite several protests to official authorities he could get no explanation. He threatened that, if these actions did not stop, he would continue to protest publicly at the suffering of the innocent. He referred to the fact that two canons of the cathedral chapter had recently been dragged from their residences by the Gestapo and exiled because he, their bishop, had displeased the government (he had confirmed their appointment to the cathedral chapter despite the fact that the government had taken exception to their nomination): 'Let them hale me before the courts if they think I have contravened the law,' he countered.

In his sermon he attacked the Gestapo mercilessly. No German citizen, he said, had any defence against their power; they had replaced the courts and were above the law. He continued:

> Not one of us is certain, though he be the most loyal, the most conscientious citizen, though he knows himself innocent, I say that not one of us is certain that he will not any day be dragged from his house and carried off to the cells of some concentration camp. I know full well that this may happen to me, perhaps now or on some future day. And it is because I shall then no longer be able to speak out publicly that I do so today. I openly warn them not to pursue these actions which I am firmly convinced will call down God's punishment and bring our people to misery and ruin.[37]

Von Galen was well aware that in saying what he said, he was not just going to be pilloried in the press. He knew he was playing with his life. Because of the extent of the Nazi tyranny, it is difficult for us today to appreciate the courage that was required to speak out as he did. It is a measure of the true greatness of the man. After recalling the recent crimes of the Gestapo he continued:

> The right to live and be free, the right to inviolability is an essential part of every moral social order. No one denies the State the authority to restrict the rights of its citizens by way of punishment, but this applies only to those who break the law, whose guilt must be proven by impartial juridical procedure. Any State which overrides this divinely imposed

37 The text of this sermon, and the two delivered on 20 July and 3 August, are given in the Appendix to Portmann's biography (see note 4), pp 231–46. They are also available in booklet form in English under the title, *Three sermons in dark times*, published by the office of the episcopal vicariate general of Münster, Postfach 1366, 48143 Münster, Germany.

> limit, and allows or causes the punishment of blameless men, undermines its own authority and the respect for its dignity in the conscience of its citizens.

He then went on to cite the case of the well-known Lutheran minister, Pastor Niemöller, who had been already imprisoned without trial for four years. He praised his religious faith, his courage and fortitude; he said the rights he was demanding transcended any religious affiliations. He reaffirmed that justice was the foundation for any state:

> We grieve to see today this foundation being shaken and we deplore that the natural and Christian virtue of justice, which is indispensable to the ordered condition of every human community, is not being dispensed and maintained unequivocally for all. We beg, we ask – nay we demand justice not only in defence of the rights of Holy Church, not only for the rights of the individual, but also because we love our people and are deeply anxious about our Fatherland.

He said that because he was bound by his oath as bishop to uphold the moral order, he had to speak out publicly against the acts of the Gestapo. He finished off with an uncompromising warning:

> We demand justice! If this plea is unheard and unheeded, if the rule of true justice is not brought back, our German nation will, notwithstanding the bravery of our soldiers and their splendid victories, collapse from internal corruption and uncleanness.

Von Galen's secretary, who was present at St Lambert's for the sermon, recalls the scene. The bishop prayed for several minutes before he mounted the steps of the pulpit. There was a quiver in the first few sentences; after that he spoke with a great strength and serenity. The tall pastoral figure left an impression of great dignity with his commanding presence. His voice had the sound of thunder as the challenging words fell on the expectant congregation, some trembling, some gazing at him with tears in their eyes. Protest, indignation, fiery enthusiasm followed each other in successive waves. The calm, the self-assurance, and latent power which characterized his delivery that morning in St Lambert's, and which was undoubtedly a gift of God in those unnerving circumstances – all this accompanied him during the rest of his struggle against the Nazi regime.[38]

38 Cf. Portmann, pp 103–4.

On the Monday morning after his sermon, the bishop despatched telegrams to the chancellery of the Reich, to Göring, to the ministers for public worship, justice and home affairs, and to the supreme command of the army, demanding that the Gestapo be put under proper control and made answerable to a recognized authority for its activities. His telegram to Göring shows something of the calibre of the man: 'With the power at your disposal, it will be a small matter for you to confer help and justice on those persecuted by the Gestapo' – if he could not appeal to his sense of justice, he felt he might get some change out of his vanity. However, all he got were evasive answers or none at all.

THE SECOND SERMON

A week after the first sermon (19 July 1941), von Galen preached in the parish church of Überwasser in the city. The Gestapo had persisted in confiscating religious houses, which the bishop listed off at the beginning of his sermon. 'We are now', he warned, 'contemplating the ruins of inner national unity'; recent atrocities could only stem from a hatred of the Christian religion and the Catholic Church. He outlined how he had contacted the different government and state departments about the Gestapo, but had got no satisfaction. He encouraged his listeners to continue to do their duty out of loyalty to God and for love of their country. He said they couldn't fight the enemy 'within our own gates' with weapons, but only 'by strong, prolonged and stubborn endurance'. He used the metaphor of the anvil to describe the resistance German Catholics should offer to the hammer-blows of the enemy:

> Obedience to God and conscience, he continued, may cost us life, liberty and home; but let us die rather than commit sin. May God's grace, without which we can do nothing, grant us and sustain in us this adamant resolution.

He finished his exhortation with the encouraging words of St Peter to the persecuted Christians of the early Church:

> Humble yourselves therefore under the mighty hand of God, that in due time he may exalt you. Cast all your anxieties on him, for he cares about you. Be sober, be watchful. Your adversary the devil prowls around like a roaring lion, seeking someone to devour. Resist him, firm in your faith, knowing that the same experience of suffering is required of your brotherhood throughout the world. And after you have suffered

> a little while, the God of all grace, who has called you to his eternal glory in Christ, will himself restore, establish, and strengthen you. To him be the dominion for ever and ever. Amen (1 Pet 5:6–11).

The Gestapo continued to confiscate religious houses until an order from the Führer on 30 July put an end to this practice. The echo of von Galen's words had reached the Reichstag and had their effect.

THE THIRD SERMON

However, around that same time, the end of July 1941, the chaplain at the mental asylum in Marienthal, in the diocese of Münster, called on the bishop to brief him about another sinister development in the Nazi litany of crimes. It had been decided to remove a number of the insane patients to kill them off because they were 'unproductive'. This was what triggered off the third of von Galen's historic sermons within a month, in which he attacked the Nazi practice of euthanasia and condemned the 'mercy killings' taking place in his own diocese. As early as 1935 Hitler had surreptitiously begun to implement this aspect of his eugenics policy. In September 1939 he issued a secret order that all persons with incurable diseases be killed. From the beginning of 1940 regular transport buses brought the unsuspecting patients to particular medical centres where they were speedily put to death, mostly by gas poisoning but sometimes by the injection of drugs.[39] From that time on the Catholic authorities protested to the government at the growing evidence of euthanasia. They were ignored but the matter came to a head with von Galen's intervention on 3 August 1941.[40]

This, however, was not the bishop of Münster's first involvement in the eugenics debate. A statute which provided for the compulsory sterilization of people affected by particular diseases or disabilities came into effect on 1 January 1934. Later that month von Galen attacked the government for subjecting the innocent inheritors of particular genetic traits to the violence of sterilization 'in violation of the inalienable right to the integrity of their bodies.'[41] Now he confronted a central element of government policy with a devastating attack which was to echo around the world.

Just a month previously, on 6 July 1941, a pastoral from the German bishops had been read in all the churches, which pointed out that it was never

39 Cf. Conway, p. 268. 40 In August 1940 the bishops conference appealed to Rome for help. On 28 November the Holy Office published a decree which stated that the direct killing by public authority of those who had committed no crime, but who, from mental or physical incapacity were unable to benefit the state, was against divine and natural law. 41 Cf. Lewy, p. 259.

lawful to take the life of an innocent person except in war and in lawful defence. Von Galen had added an addendum to the pastoral in his own name in which he condemned the practice whereby patients suffering from incurable diseases, on instructions from Berlin, were being forcibly removed from homes and clinics. Their relatives were later informed that the patient had died, that the body had been cremated, and that the ashes could be claimed, without giving any explanation as to the cause of death. Von Galen said that numerous cases of unexpected deaths in the case of the insane were deliberately caused.

Now again at St Lambert's, on Sunday 3 August, he condemned this ghastly doctrine which tried 'to justify the murder of blameless men', and which sought 'to give legal sanction to the forcible killing of invalids, cripples, the incurable and the incapacitated'. He had ascertained at the Health Ministry that no attempt was made to hide the fact that a great number of insane people had already been deliberately killed and that the process would continue. He called the perpetrators of these crimes murderers and demanded protection for the innocent.

> If, he said, the principle is established that unproductive human beings may be killed, then God help all those invalids who, in order to produce wealth, have given their all and sacrificed their strength of body. If all unproductive people may thus be violently eliminated, then woe betide our brave soldiers who return home wounded, maimed or sick. Once admit the right to kill unproductive persons, then none of us can be sure of his life. A curse on men and on the German people if we break the holy commandment 'Thou shalt not kill' ... Woe to us German people if we not only licence this heinous offence but allow it to be committed with impunity.

He pointed out how God, because of his love for us, had engraved the ten commandments on our hearts. With extraordinary frankness he went on to give specific examples of how the government establishment had broken, or encouraged the breaking of, each one them. Reverting to the Gospel theme of Jesus weeping over Jerusalem for its rejection of him, he finished by saying that what alone could bring peace, what alone could avert the divine wrath from Germany was a renewed commitment to the Catholic faith, and a willingness to die rather than disobey God's commandments. By prayer and penance the faithful could again bring down on their city and country the grace and forgiveness of God. His final words were a moving petition to the Sacred Heart of Jesus for mercy for all, for their country and their leader.

The impact of his sermon reached far beyond the crowded congregation that flocked to hear him. Copies were made by the thousand and distributed throughout the country. They were smuggled to soldiers at the front where his references to the threat of death hanging over invalids and seriously wounded soldiers spread like wildfire. Von Galen's words had a powerful effect. By the end of August the programme for euthanasia had been suspended, but not before 100,000 people had been killed in this manner.

Copies of the three sermons spread all over Germany; hundreds of thousands were printed in response to requests from many cities. These and other sermons were so important to the Allies that they were printed by the million and dropped by the RAF as anti-Nazi propaganda all over Germany and the occupied territories. A number of people in Leipzig were sent to concentration camps for distributing the sermons, and some met their death there. The Nazi party staged a campaign against von Galen up and down the country because of the extraordinary influence he wielded. The Gestapo tried various ruses to get him out of the country so that he could be arrested at the frontier and thus neutralized.

Official German documents, discovered after the war, contained records of discussions among Nazi leaders about how to get rid of him. In Berlin his sermons were regarded as 'the strongest attack against the German political leadership for decades'.[42] Hitler hated him but feared to put him in prison. Instead he planned to kill him when Germany was victorious. Bormann agreed that hanging would be an appropriate penalty. Walter Tiessler, head of propaganda, wanted him arrested and then killed. Goebbels, more cautious, turned this down but only because he felt the whole of Münster and Westphalia would be lost to the Nazis if so popular a figure as von Galen were to be treated with the severity he deserved. Hitler, though furious, was afraid to make a martyr of the bishop and decided to postpone his revenge. What is clear is that the High Command had lost its nerve in relation to von Galen – they were afraid to take direct action against him because of his extraordinary courage and prestige. Von Galen's challenge drew the following response from Hitler some months later:

> I am quite sure that a man like Bishop von Galen knows full well that I shall extract retribution to the last farthing. And, if he does not succeed in getting himself transferred meanwhile to the Collegium Germanicum in Rome, he may rest assured that in balancing our accounts, no 't' will remain uncrossed, no 'i' undotted.[43]

It was a great consolation for the bishop to know that by his words he had given courage and heart to those of his countrymen who repudiated everything Hitler stood for. Towards the end of August he received a letter from the

42 Cf. Conway, p. 281, note 57. **43** Cf. ibid., p. 283.

bishop of Innsbruck, telling him that the Holy Father had read his three homilies aloud to his closest associates in the Vatican, expressing the strongest possible approval of them. Shortly afterwards he received a letter of warm congratulation from Pius XII. Referring to the sermons he said:

> They have caused us also consolation and satisfaction such as we have not felt for a long time on the path of sorrows which we have followed with the Catholics of Germany.[44]

PIETY AND SPIRITUAL LIFE

Von Galen did not suddenly develop the virtues of courage and daring to an heroic degree in the summer of 1941. Only a few months after his appointment in 1933, he was already being praised as a fearless fighter against National Socialism. His episcopal motto – *nec laudibus, nec timore*[45] – was a very appropriate one. He possessed strong, natural leadership qualities from his youth and this, together with a capacity for fearlessness in any situation, gave that dimension of power and energy to his personality which grew with experience of the episcopal office. He had a positive sense of superiority in relation to his opponents which was based on the conviction of doing God's will. It was not a haughty superiority which is often associated with people of his aristocratic background; it was rather a dignity that sprang from strength of character fortified by the grace of God.

He could refer contemptuously to the members of the National Socialist party as 'that brown gang.' He could be withering in his comments where party ideology was concerned. At an educational conference in the early years of his episcopate, the chairman proffered the opinion that a wife and mother was of much more value as a teacher than a spinster. Von Galen immediately detected the National Socialist propaganda which underlay this comment. He struck the table in anger with his fist saying: 'I won't listen to talk like that; Germany is not a stud farm.' He preferred plain speaking to what might be described as diplomatic language, especially were National Socialism was concerned.

After the Allied victory in the spring of 1945, many regretted that he used the same outspokenness with the British and American authorities, when he felt that there had been a lack of justice in the treatment of Germans. Indeed,

44 *Actes et Documents du Saint Siège relatifs à la seconde guerre mondiale*, II, p. 230, published by Vatican City Press, 1965–75, 9 parts, 10 vols, eds. Blet, Martini, Schneider, and Graham. This gives the full documentation related to the pontificate of Pius XII and the Second World War. The translation of the letter is from O'Carroll, p. 118. 45 In translation, 'not to be influenced either by the praise or fear of men'.

when the point was made to him in July 1945 by a representative body of the clergy that he should tone down his language because of the negative effects it might have, he responded: 'I am grateful to you for your advice, but I shall go straight ahead in my own way, as I have done all these years. I look neither to the right nor to the left.' The combative side of the bishop's make-up, this harshness and rigidity of character was tempered by an unusual depth of tenderness. The pain and misfortune of others often brought tears to his eyes. He could be deeply moved by witnessing the religious devotion of others, or by expressions of appreciation and gratitude; at times he could cry like a child.

His secretary tells a story which is illustrative of the character of the man. In the spring of 1944, as he walked across from the episcopal palace to the seminary to ordain students to the diaconate, he saw workmen laying a new pathway across the courtyard of the palace. Angry that the municipal authority hadn't asked permission or given him notice, he went up to the workmen and protested in the strongest terms about lack of respect for private property. For the rest of the way to the seminary he fell silent; his secretary commented that one could feel he regretted that, as a bishop, he had attacked these simple workmen who were only carrying out orders. As he went into the seminary chapel he beckoned to a Capuchin priest, and went with him to the confessional before going to vest for Mass.

DESTRUCTION OF THE CATHEDRAL

On Sunday 10 October 1943 Allied air-raids began again on the city of Münster and the cathedral was hit by incendiary bombs. The fire started in the left tower and then spread to the roof of the building, which became a huge conflagration fanned by the rising wind. That evening foreign broadcasts carried news of the destruction of the cathedral – it was, naturally, suppressed on the home stations. This was followed by many anxious queries about the bishop himself – was he alive? was he safe? where was he? He had in fact survived miraculously, although the episcopal palace was practically destroyed in the bombing. It was naturally a cause of great sorrow to von Galen to see his cathedral in ruins.

After a relatively quiet period of a year the bombardment of the city began again in September 1944. Because of the damage to Münster the bishop and the diocesan administration had to move out to Sendenhorst, a small town about twelve miles to the south-east of the city. As the weeks wore on and the Allies advanced, the bombardment of the towns became more and more intense. Von Galen was saddened by the constant flow of bad news, of destruction and death. Yet his trust and faith in God held firm. He spent more time before the Blessed Sacrament, realizing that in the madness of the war God alone was his support. His diocesan staff noticed that through all this very trying time he never lacked serenity, and that he said his morning Mass with greater piety and intensity.

On Easter Sunday, 31 March 1945, American tanks rolled into Sendenhorst. On 12 April von Galen went to Münster for the first time since it had been occupied by the Americans. His purpose was to make a public protest against the excesses of the Russian and Polish workers. These were the thousands from the forced labour camps who had been released by the Allies after the retreat by the Germans. They had been very badly treated and now, unrestricted by the military, were taking their revenge on their former persecutors by plundering, torturing and murdering the inhabitants.

He also verbally communicated his concerns to the British commander in Westphalia. He said he had fought against the Nazis in the interests of truth, freedom and justice, and that now he was doing the same against the occupying forces. The German people, he said, were willing to obey the military authority, but it was a fundamental duty of that authority to maintain public safety and to protect life and property from unnecessary outrage, destruction and plunder. He then went on to list the crimes committed by the Russian and Polish workers, and the plunder and rape engaged in by some of the American forces themselves. He looked upon himself not only as a shepherd of souls, but now also, with the collapse of all civil authority, as the protector of the rights of his fellow countrymen. The Allied commanders had the height of respect for von Galen as they were aware of his courageous stand against Hitler.

On Sunday 1 July 1945 von Galen accompanied his flock in the annual pilgrimage to the shrine of our Lady in Telgte. As he had previously done in this same place against the crimes of the Nazis, he now indicted the new rulers for their supine attitude in dealing with the crimes being committed up and down the land. He had expressed his concern several times with complaints, petitions and in conference with the Allied commanders, but with no tangible results. Now as bishop of the diocese where Catholics entrusted to his care were undergoing terrible hardships, he felt it his bounden duty to speak out on their behalf. He listed the crimes which were being committed against the German faithful with the connivance, and under the very eyes of the occupying authorities. He pleaded for the same principles of justice now as heretofore he had demanded from the Nazis. Once again news of the sermon spread through Germany like wildfire. From all parts of the country letters of thanks flooded in on the bishop of Münster. However, communications between von Galen and the British military authorities were strained. They saw matters from very different points of view.

Von Galen had a mountain of correspondence to deal with from all parts of Germany. There were queues waiting for him at all hours of the day, with all the anxieties of a people devastated by the war and its terrible consequences. Reporters came from all parts of the world trying to get interviews with the bishop who had defied the Nazi regime, and who had lived to tell the tale.

CARDINAL

As the autumn of 1945 came around and the guns remained silent, the devastation of the war and its consequences gradually revealed itself in all its horror and suffering. People from the great industrial cities trekked into the countryside to try to find the barest necessities to keep body and soul together. Hordes of evacuees poured back into Westphalia from southern and central Germany. The bishop made regular visits to all the areas which had been badly affected by the war to encourage and console. Relations with the Allied commanders improved. Von Galen administered confirmation to nine American soldiers in September. They were impressed not only by the bishop's personality, but also by the piety with which he celebrated the Mass and rite of confirmation.

In December 1945 a document was discovered confirming that the Nazis wanted to hang von Galen but didn't dare to carry it out. The Sunday before Christmas it was announced on radio that Pius XII was going to create thirty new cardinals, among them von Galen. Some of his priests went to congratulate him; he refused to believe it: 'the radio has tricked us before, and it's not much better nowadays.' But the confirmation arrived; von Galen would be the first bishop of Münster ever to wear the purple. The announcement was greeted with enthusiasm all over Germany.[46]

The bishop's love and loyalty to the Holy See was well proven. In February 1939, on the death of Pius XI, he had preached the panegyric in the cathedral. This pope had been the subject of increasing insult and ridicule by the National Socialist party. Von Galen felt the shame of this treatment deeply. In his homily he said he had a duty to speak, a duty which was owed to the dead pontiff and to the honour of all Catholics, not only in Germany but throughout the world. It was a duty to protest at the abuse to which Pius XI had been subjected in official German quarters:

> We are no true German men but base wretches if we do not feel deeply, and utterly condemn such infamous derision which is aimed at our spiritual Father; to take advantage of the defencelessness of the Pope is a symptom of the vile disease which is ravaging our reputation, and is a renunciation of the best aspects of our German way of life.[47]

46 Two other German cardinals were appointed at the same consistory – Preysing of Berlin, and Frings of Cologne. **47** Portmann, p. 173.

Each year von Galen reported the events of his diocese to the Vatican, and on a number of occasions he was gladdened by the personal replies he received from the Pope during the war years, which were a great consolation to the bishop during those long years of persecution. He was well aware that Eugenio Pacelli (Pius XII), the former apostolic nuncio in Germany for many years, had a great love for his country, and was consequently very angered when the Pope was slandered in Germany. Among the slanders circulated by Nazi propaganda was the report that the Pope held shares in the Italian fleet, and had forbidden or hindered its attempts to rescue German soldiers fighting in Africa. Another was that he had financially supported the war effort of the Allies. In October 1943, the very morning of that sad day when his cathedral was destroyed, von Galen spoke out in defence of Pius XII:

> It is nothing short of disgraceful, and it reflects the greatest shame on us, that such wicked and nonsensical slanders should be hawked around the streets ... I urge you to counter these infamous lies. Ask for proof, real proof; despise and reject rumour and mere statement so often made by the enemy of the Church, whose sole delight it is to besmirch and denigrate it ... He who attacks the Pope attacks us, and impugns the honour of 40 million German Catholics and hundreds of thousands of Catholic soldiers.[48]

Von Galen was particularly grateful to Pius XII for his Christmas message of 1945. When his country lay devastated and prostrate, Pius XII's was the lone voice which asked for mercy for Germany: 'He who seeks to punish those who have committed crimes must take care that he has not done the same. He who demands reparations must do so on the foundations of moral principles, and not forget that natural rights are also valid for those who surrendered unconditionally'.

On the feast of the Epiphany 1946 the bishop read extracts from the Pope's Christmas message in the Church of the Holy Cross in Münster, adding: 'We rejoice that the Holy Father has acknowledged before the whole world the sanctity and inviolability of the rights of men on this earth – not forgetting the vanquished'. That very afternoon he wrote to the Holy Father to thank him for appointing him to the College of Cardinals:

> It is a solace to me if I may see in this nomination a recognition of the brave steadfastness shown by the majority of Catholics in my diocese of Münster, of their loyalty to Christ, His Holy Church, and to the Holy Father during those years of persecution and oppression, and of their

48 Ibid., p. 175.

> public witness to the rights of God and his Church, and for the stand which they made on behalf of the God-given rights of the human person. The unrestrained manifestations of joy shown in my diocese when the news of my appointment became known, and the countless congratulations from all parts of Germany which I have received, would seem to give me the right to accept this mark of Your Holiness' favour.[49]

Three days later he wrote to his sister-in-law, Countess Paula von Galen:

> It was also manifest that he (Pius XII) wished to reward my brave diocese for making it possible for me, by their support, to speak the truth openly however unpleasant it may have been. At the same time I must admit that this event distresses and embarrasses me… I beg you to pray that I may be worthy of this increased responsibility. I know only too well from the closest observation that many other German bishops have laboured more than I have. You will feel with me, I know, how much it worries me to have taken away the preferment from them.[50]

This is hardly the letter of a proud man who felt he had earned this honour. That he had earned it was the unanimous verdict of the Catholic world. After his famous 1941 sermons, letters arrived by the hundred at the episcopal palace to thank the bishop of Münster for his courageous stand. Now five years later, letters of congratulation poured in by the thousand, rejoicing in the honour conferred on von Galen. They were from people in every stratum of society and every walk of life – academics, soldiers, non-Catholics, non-believers, government representatives, etc.

ROME

After an adventurous journey Bishop von Galen arrived in Rome on Friday 15 February 1946, accompanied by the two other cardinals designate, Dr Frings of Cologne and Dr Preysing of Berlin. He had an audience with the Holy Father the following morning – they hadn't seen each other since May 1939. It was difficult to imagine all that had happened in the intervening years. The Holy Father was now able to thank the great German bishop personally for all he had done for the Church in the interim, not only in Germany, but also because of the example which he had given to the entire Catholic world.

Von Galen preached the following day in the Church of Santa Maria dell'Anima in Rome. Deeply moved, he thanked the Holy Father for the great

49 Ibid., p. 177. **50** Ibid., p. 178

love he had shown to Germany at a time when the world had declared the entire German nation guilty. He protested against the monstrous crimes then being perpetrated in East Germany, and the fact that the whole of the German people had been blamed collectively. He referred to the heroism of so many Christians in Germany during the period of satanic tyranny.

The press had a field day. The immense size of the German bishop was reported with a mixture of awe and admiration. The Americans took film of him. The Romans, already aware of his great moral stature, were now astonished to see that physically he was a colossus of a man – all of six feet six inches and built accordingly. It heightened their affection for him. He met the German community in Rome and had a very emotive encounter with sixty German military chaplains who were prisoners of war in Italy.

On Wednesday 20 February the new cardinals went to the Sistine chapel for the conferring of the biretta and the *cappa magna*. There was an unforgettable moment during this ceremony when the British and American cardinals went up to their German counterparts to congratulate them. Cardinal Spellman of New York, aware that the German mark was worthless in Rome, paid for the expenses of the impoverished German cardinals in the Eternal City and, with typical magnanimity, arranged for an American airforce plane to take them back to Frankfurt.

On the Thursday morning the cardinals received the red hat from Pius XII in St Peter's in the public consistory. The new cardinals processed from the Blessed Sacrament chapel, where they had taken the oath always to defend the rights of Holy Church, to the main altar, where the Holy Father was already enthroned. Each national group in the huge congregation greeted their cardinal with applause. When the towering figure of von Galen slowly mounted the steps to the papal throne there was a veritable explosion of applause from the whole congregation; *un applauso trionfale*, the newspapers described it. The Holy Father imposed the red hat and, as he leaned forward to embrace von Galen, whispered, 'God bless you, God bless Germany.' When he turned to face the vast crowd he was greeted with a storm of applause, led by the other cardinals, which lasted several minutes. The crowd in St Peter's that morning were conscious they were witnessing a unique event, the recognition of moral courage on a par with that of the Roman martyrs of the early Church.

A few days before, the German cardinals attended a reception for diplomats accredited to the Holy See. Von Galen made use of the opportunity to explain to the diplomats the situation in his country; who else could do it? – Germany had no civil representative to speak on its behalf. On the Sunday afternoon he was a guest at the Collegium Germanicum. From there he went to the nearby Capuchin church, where fifty Jewish converts recently received were waiting to hear a word from the new German cardinal.

PRISONER OF WAR CAMPS

On Tuesday 26 February he drove south from Rome to visit a prisoner of war camp at Taranto. Here he met 10,000 of his countrymen, looking tired and dejected in their worn-out uniforms. As he looked down on this motley-looking throng from the reception platform, he saw that many of them were mere youths of sixteen. He found it difficult to put his opening words of greeting together – his mind was filled with conflicting emotions. He consoled his fellow-countrymen. He told them they had been obedient to the call of duty, that they had fought and suffered for the Fatherland, and that now they had to undergo the bitter fate of the prisoner. He gave them news of Germany. At the end of his talk, the men from Westphalia and the Rhineland closed in around the cardinal. For them he was now the only man who had taken up their cause; he was in a very real way their only source of hope.

Von Galen repeated this routine, as many as seven times a day in different camps, over the next several days. In Bari, the prisoners were driven from the nearby camps to the biggest church in the city where the cardinal celebrated Mass for them. It was a moving occasion. The Mass was sung by a choir of thousands of soldiers in their ragged uniforms, with von Galen in full pontificals and served by two elderly men from Bavaria. He ended his sermon, as he had ended his talks in the camps, with the words, 'And now good-bye, my dear friends, until we meet in heaven.' Did he then have an intuition that somehow he had not long to live?

Afterwards, he visited the church of St Nicholas in Bari and had the opportunity to venerate the relics of the saint so honoured in Germany. In Foggia he visited another camp and dined with the prisoners. In Caserta he called on the American commander-in-chief to thank him for making his visits to the prisoner of war camps possible. It was however von Galen's immense prestige among the Allies that had opened all the doors. At the same time he used the opportunity vigorously to express his views on what he considered the illegal retention of the prisoners of war, and earnestly requested the general to set in motion the administrative machinery for their repatriation. All camps in southern and central Italy were disbanded a few weeks later and most of the inmates were sent home. On Saturday 2 March von Galen stood amidst the ruins of Monte Cassino. Not even in Germany had he seen such destruction and desolation. The next day he took possession of his titular church in Rome.

HOME TO DIE

The following Sunday the German cardinals arrived back in Cologne. Von Galen stayed a few days with his brother before returning to Münster. On

Saturday 16 March, his sixty-eighth birthday, he visited the shrine of our Lady at Telgte for the last time. That afternoon he arrived home in triumph to his episcopal city. Fifty thousand people had congregated around the great mountain of rubble which had once been his cathedral. He responded to all the addresses of welcome and congratulation with a simple dignity. Neither he nor the vast crowd who listened with pride and joy to his words realized that this was to be the great bishop's valedictory address. His fight, he told them, had been made possible by the unshakeable faith of the people of Münster; it was the steadfast spirit of his indomitable diocese that was the cause of his being alive that day. When he returned to his rooms after the fireworks display he didn't feel well.

The following day, Sunday the 17th, he said a pontifical High Mass. His last words to the faithful of Münster were an exhortation to papal loyalty, especially to the reigning Pope, Pius XII. The choir sang the *Te Deum* in celebration. There was a reception after the Mass, and at 1.15 p.m., after the last guest had gone, the cardinal suddenly grew faint and had to sit down. His colour was ashen and his hands trembled. Despite the misgivings of the vicar general, he attended an academic celebration that evening. Afterwards he complained of a stomach pain and took a little fruit juice. Next morning he celebrated Mass for the last time. He said he was drained of energy, but suggested he would recover by lying down for a while on a sofa. He could not be prevailed on to go to bed. Only a fortnight before in Rome he had jested, truthfully, that he hadn't spent a day in bed since 1890.

Unfortunately he wouldn't allow a doctor to be called until the Tuesday morning. The diagnosis was serious and he was told that he would be operated on that afternoon. He asked to receive the last sacraments and expressed a wish to do so in the presence of the entire cathedral chapter. The bishop said to those standing around his sick bed: 'Today is the anniversary of my baptism, and also the feast of St Joseph, the patron of the dying …' Then his voice faded.

The operation revealed a perforation of the appendix and intestinal paralysis. Only a miracle could save him. The news spread like wildfire around the diocese. The medical bulletins got worse by the hour. Fully conscious he thanked all those who had striven day and night to save his life. On Friday morning, 22 March, the doctors said he was unlikely to survive the day. At 4.30 the auxiliary bishop began the last prayers; the cardinal was breathing slowly and with difficulty. At 5.00 p.m. he breathed his last.

He lay in state for four days in the church of St Maurice during which an unending procession filed past the catafalque. It is not difficult to imagine the sense of loss which these people felt; the only man who could stand up for their rights was now dead. On 28 March the solemn burial took place. The same crowd which just a short week before had shouted their joy at the return of their cardinal in triumph from Rome, now stood silent and stunned in the ruined streets of Münster, as the huge coffin, drawn by four horses, passed on its way. The cardinal's last resting place was the von Galen chapel amid the ruins of his cathedral, where the remains of a former prince bishop, Christoph Bernard von Galen, had been interred in the seventeenth century. As his coffin was lowered into the ground, a mighty volume of sound rose up from the vast crowd as they sang the great Easter hymn, *Wahrer Gott wir glauben Dir* (True God we believe in you). It resounded through the ruins of the cathedral, as an expression of the unconquerable hope of the Catholics of Münster.

On 19 October 1956 Msgr Keller, his successor in the see of Münster, ordered the opening of the diocesan process for the beatification of Bishop von Galen. During his pastoral visit to Germany in May of 1987, John Paul II prayed at the tomb of Cardinal von Galen, where he warned that we should not be so sure of our immunity to committing similar crimes as those condemned by the intrepid bishop of Münster.

CONCLUSION

In historical retrospect the German hierarchy has often been criticized for not taking a stronger stand against the Nazi regime. The verdict of one German who fled the Nazi pesecution is not without interest.

> Being a lover of freedom [writes Albert Einstein in 1944], when the revolution came in Germany I looked to the universities to defend it, knowing that they already boasted of their devotion to the cause of truth: but no, the universities were immediately silenced. Then I looked to the great editors of the newspapers, whose flaring editorials in days gone by had proclaimed their love of freedom: but they like the universities were silenced in a few short weeks. Then I looked to the individual writers who, as literary guides of Germany, had written much and often concerning the place of freedom in modern life, but they too were mute. Only the Church stood squarely across the path of Hitler's campaign for suppressing truth. I never had any special interest in the Church before, but now I feel a great affection and admiration because the Church alone had the courage and persistence to stand for intellectual truth and moral freedom. I am forced, then, to confess that what I once despised I now praise unreservedly.[51]

51 Quoted in Coulton and Lunn, *Is the Catholic Church anti-social?* (London, 1947), pp 30–1, abstracted from *Hibbert Journal*, January 1944.

Certainly the bishops fought with heroic efforts to defend the interests of the Church and German Catholics against the embattled might of Nazism.[52] On the other hand they had to exercise a certain restraint in their protests so as not to aggravate Gestapo terrorist activities, in particular against their priests. It has been asserted that bishops like von Galen and Preysing (Berlin) felt hindered by their more conciliatory episcopal colleagues with whom they often disagreed on matters of tactics.[53] This is undoubtedly what the then Cardinal Ratzinger was referring to in his comment in *The Ratzinger report* (1985) where he says that 'the really powerful documents against National Socialism were those from individual courageous bishops. The documents of the [episcopal] conference, on the contrary, were often rather wan and too weak with respect to what the tragedy called for.'[54]

Cardinal von Galen was beatified in Rome on 9 October 2005. After the ceremony Pope Benedict XVI spoke with great joy to the many pilgrims who had come from the diocese of Münster and from many other parts of Germany to be present at the beatification ceremony. He said:

> All of us, and particularly we Germans, are grateful because the Lord has given us this great witness of faith who made the light of truth shine out in dark times and had the courage to oppose the power of tyranny.
>
> However, we must also ask ourselves: 'where did this insight come from in a period when intelligent people seemed as if they were blind? And where did he find the strength to oppose it at a time when even the strong proved weak and cowardly?' He drew his insight and courage from the faith that showed him the truth and opened his heart and his eyes.
>
> He feared God more than men, and it was God who granted him the courage to do and say what others did not dare to say and do. Thus, he gives us courage, he urges us to live the faith anew today, and he also shows us how this is possible in things that are simple and humble, yet great and profound.
>
> Let us remember that he often used to make pilgrimages on foot to the Mother of God in Telgte, that he introduced perpetual adoration at St Servatius and that he frequently asked for the grace of forgiveness in the Sacrament of Penance and obtained it.
>
> He therefore shows us this simple Catholicity in which the Lord meets us, in which he opens our hearts and gives us spiritual discern-

52 Cf. Annedore Leber (ed.), *The conscience in revolt: portraits of the German resistance, 1933–1945*, trans. Thomas S. McClymont (Speyer, Germany, 1994); Wolfgang Benz and Walter H. Pehle (eds), *Encyclopedia of German resistance to the Nazi movement*, trans. Lance W. Garmer (New York, 1997). 53 Cf. Lewy, pp 320–5. 54 Joseph Ratzinger, *An exclusive interview on the state of the Church* (London, 1985), p. 61.

> ment, the courage of faith and the joy of being saved. Let us give thanks to God for this great witness of faith and pray to him that he will enlighten and guide us.

The life of Blessed Clement von Galen of Münster is one which brought great honour to the Church and to his country.[55] Like many bishops before him, he demonstrated once again the apostolic effectiveness and the power for good of courageous spiritual leadership. His first concern always was to be faithful to the interests of God and the Church at whatever cost. He never allowed himself to be intimidated by human respect or the popular perception of his actions; he felt answerable only to God. It was precisely this single-mindedness in fulfilling his vocation in the episcopal office which confirmed so many Catholics in their loyalty to the faith, and gained for him the respect and allegiance of countless others far beyond the boundaries of his country and his faith.

55 When John Paul II visited Germany in November 1980, he addressed a large gathering of priests at Fu lda and asked them to consider the many outstanding bishops and priests which that country had produced, and to study their lives closely. Among those named by the Pope was Cardinal von Galen (see Address, 17 November 1980).

CHAPTER NINE

St Josemaría Escrivá (1902–1975)

IN ROME, ON 6 October 2002, more that 300,000 people packed St Peter's Square and environs to participate in the canonization ceremony of Josemaría Escrivá de Balaguer, founder of Opus Dei. The presence of 400 cardinals, archbishops and bishops, together with pilgrims from over eighty countries indicated the universal dimension of the apostolates of Opus Dei and the personal appeal of the new saint. The huge crowd overflowed St Peter's Square, stretching down the length of the Via della Conciliazione to the river Tiber. A striking feature of the event was the very large proportion of young people attending the ceremony, which was reckoned to be about forty per cent of those present.

In his homily, the Holy Father recalled that St Josemaría's vision for Opus Dei, which he founded in 1928, harmonized with the Vatican II's message that Christians should not shun the world but sanctify it from within. Even in the grind of 'apparently monotonous daily events, God comes close to us, and we can co-operate in his plan of salvation', the Pope said. The new saint 'continues to remind you of the need not to let yourselves be frightened by a materialist culture that threatens to dissolve the genuine identity of Christ's disciples ... Following in his footsteps, spread in society the consciousness that we are all called to holiness whatever our race, class, society or age'. John Paul II also reminded the pilgrims that to evangelize every human setting required 'constant interior growth nourished by prayer' and an 'intense and constant sacramental life' which was the secret of St Josemaría's apostolic fruitfulness.[1]

The day after the canonization, Bishop Javier Echevarría, prelate of Opus Dei, offered a Mass of thanksgiving in St Peter's Square for another record crowd of about 250,000 people. Addressing pilgrims in the Square after the Mass, John Paul II emphasized some of the core elements of the new saint's teaching:

> St Josemaría was chosen by the Lord to announce the universal call to holiness and to point out that daily life and ordinary activities are a path

1 Cf. John Paul II, Homily, 6 October 2002.

> to holiness. One could say that he was the saint of ordinary life. In fact he was convinced that for those who live with a perspective of faith, everything is an opportunity to meet God, everything can be an incentive for prayer. Seen in this light, daily life reveals an unexpected greatness. Holiness is truly within everyone's reach.[2]

He then went on to describe Escrivá de Balaguer as 'a very human saint'.

> All those who met him, he added, whatever their culture or social status, felt he was a father, totally devoted to serving others, for he was convinced that every soul is a marvellous treasure; indeed, every person is worth all of Christ's Blood.[3]

Among those present in Rome for the ceremony was Dr Manuel Nevado, a Spanish orthopaedic surgeon, who was miraculously cured of cancerous radiodermatitis through the intercession of Blessed Josemaría Escrivá, and which cleared the way for his canonization. This is a disease typical of doctors whose hands have been exposed to radiation from X-ray machines over a long period of time. Radiodermatitis has no cure – it is a progressive disease that leads to skin cancer. At present the only treatments available are surgical – skin grafts or amputation of the affected parts of the hand. Dr Nevado's is the only recorded case of a spontaneous cure from this disease.

Nevado, born in 1932, worked as an orthopaedic surgeon from 1956, frequently exposing his hands to X-rays. The first symptoms began to appear in 1962 and continued to worsen. By 1984 he could only do minor operations because his hands were so seriously affected, and in the summer of 1992 he had to stop work altogether. However, in November of that year he heard about Blessed Josemaría and began to pray to him that his hands would get better. In about a fortnight the lesions had disappeared completely, and in January 1993 he was able to return to work and carry out normal surgical operations without any problem.

Who is this priest whom the church has declared was instrumental in bringing about the cure of Dr Nevado? Apart from the miracles which paved the way for his beatification and canonization, over the past thirty years since Fr Josemaría's death in 1975, the postulator's office in Rome has received, from all over the world, tens of thousands of reports of favours granted through the new saint's intercession. Why has devotion to him spread so far afield? To answer these questions we need to look at some of the main events in the life of Josemaría Escrivá and to reflect on some aspects of the organization which he founded, Opus Dei.

2 John Paul II, Address, 7 October 2002. **3** Ibid.

He was born in 1902 in the town of Barbastro in the north of Spain where his father, José Escrivá, was a textile merchant. His parents were comfortably well off and had four daughters as well as Josemaría: Carmen who was three years older than him, and Asunción, Dolores, and Rosario who came after him. When Josemaría was two years old he fell seriously ill, such that the doctors gave up hope for his recovery. Because his parents had a deep faith they prayed insistently for his cure. His mother Dolores promised to bring the child on a pilgrimage to the shrine of our Lady of Torreciudad (about 12 miles distant) if Josemaría was cured. The child recovered miraculously.

The Escrivá children grew up in an atmosphere of deep Christian piety. His mother taught young Josemaría his childhood prayers which he was to recite with affection all during his life. At the age of six or seven he made his first confession. St Josemaría must certainly have recalled his own family's experience when, teaching the spirit of Opus Dei, he encouraged Christian parents to make their homes 'bright and cheerful'. Marriage, he said, is 'a divine pathway, a vocation, and this has consequences for personal holiness and apostolate.' The first and principal field of sanctification and apostolate is in fact the family itself. 'Christian couples should be aware that they are called to sanctify themselves and to sanctify others, that they are called to be apostles and that their first apostolate is in their home. They should understand that founding a family, educating their children, and exercising a Christian influence in society is a supernatural task. The effectiveness and the success of their life – their happiness – depends to a great extent on their awareness of their specific mission.'[4]

He was a cheerful, pleasant, normal boy who played with his schoolfriends. The joyful rhythm of his life was interrupted with the experience of the Cross at an early age. These were times of high infant mortality and in 1910 his baby sister Rosario died when she was just nine months old. Two years later Dolores died when she was five. And the following year Asunción died when she was eight. Seeing his sisters die one after another, from the youngest upwards, Josemaría took to saying with childlike naivety 'next year its my turn'. But he stopped when he realized it upset his mother. She would say to him, 'Don't worry, you have been offered to our Lady of Torreciudad.'

On 23 April 1912 Josemaría made his First Communion at the age of ten, which at the time was quite young as the indications of St Pius X about the age for receiving First Communion had not so far been implemented. Receiving our Lord for the first time was such an important event in Josemaría's life that subsequently he would celebrate its anniversary with affection for the rest of his life.

4 Josemaría Escrivá, *Conversations with Monsignor Escrivá de Balaguer*, no. 91 (Manila, 1977).

LOGROÑO

When Josemaría was twelve his father's business failed. It was not the fault of José Escrivá, but being a man of deep nobility of character, he insisted on paying off all the creditors himself, which left him bankrupt. As the Escrivá family were now reduced to poverty, José had to move to Logroño to take a job in a clothing store. Josemaría's sensitive soul felt deeply the sufferings of his parents and the straitened circumstances which resulted from the collapse of the family business. But God was using this cross and the experience of the deaths of his three sisters to prepare his soul for the task which awaited him. In 1915 the whole family moved to Logroño, the capital of the well-known Rioja wine-producing province.

Despite the hardships of those first years in Logroño, Josemaría always spoke in later years of his 'bright and cheerful home.' His parents gave him an example of Christian dignity and hidden heroism, always accompanied by a smile. Such was the environment he later sought to replicate in the centres of Opus Dei. Josemaría attended high school in Logroño where he did exceptionally well in his studies. He had considerable natural ability, and this was enhanced by his habitual diligence and concentration.

From his early teens Josemaría experienced a restlessness in his soul which led him to daily Mass and Communion and a deeper spirit of prayer. He had intimations that God was asking something of him without knowing what it was. Then one morning, in the winter of 1917–18, he saw a line of footprints in the snow left by the bare feet of a Discalced Carmelite. Deeply moved by the love of God which this implied, he now felt the call to put himself completely at the Lord's disposal. Up to this point Josemaría had intended studying architecture, but now he decided to become a priest.

In due course he talked to his father about it. For José Escrivá it was another test of his trust in God. In previous years he has seen his three youngest daughters die, one after another. He had accepted without complaint the collapse of his family business, which forced him to move with his wife and two remaining children to Logroño. At the age of forty-eight he had to start from scratch, and had not spared himself any humiliation or sacrifice to look after his family. Now when he had managed to restore his financial stability, when he was thinking that his son could lend him a hand in the not too distant future, the unexpected news from Josemaría brought tears to his eyes. 'It was the only time I ever saw him cry,' St Josemaría commented many years later. 'He had other plans but he did not object. He told me "My son, think it over carefully. A priest has to be a saint ... It is very hard to have no house, no home, to have no love on earth. Think about it a bit more, but I will not oppose your decision." And he took me to speak to a friend of his who was a priest.'

SEMINARY IN SARAGOSSA

His parents encouraged him in his vocation and so he began his philosophical studies at the seminary in Logroño in 1918. After two years he transferred to the seminary of San Carlos in Saragossa to study theology at the pontifical university in that city (1920–5). In parallel with his theological studies, on his father's advice, he attended lectures at the civil university with a view to taking a law degree.

His straightforwardness, his kindly smile and his openness to everyone impressed the seminary rector. He was a devout seminarian, with a constant and manly piety; he got on well with his fellow-seminarians. They remembered him afterwards as an excellent student with a warm personality, a ready sense of humour, and a very high standard of personal and social behaviour. The superiors of the seminary soon noticed his leadership qualities and in 1922, when just twenty years old, he was appointed prefect of the seminary, a task normally assigned to a priest or deacon. Josemaría carried out his job conscientiously and with kindness to the seminarians in his care.

On his way to lectures at the pontifical university, Josemaría found time each day to visit the shrine of our Lady of the Pillar and to entrust to her the future of his priestly vocation. At the seminary he often spent long hours before the Blessed Sacrament asking for light about God's will for him. He already had intimations that the Lord wanted something specific of him, and to discover it he frequently repeated phrases from the New Testament like 'Lord, that I may see' (Mk10:51), or 'Lord, what do you want me to do' (Acts 22:10). The record of his exam results shows that he had a brilliant academic career in theology and canon law in Saragossa.

Josemaría was in his last year in the seminary when in November 1924 he got news that his father had died of a stroke at the relatively early age of fifty-seven. He returned home for the funeral and had to borrow from a priest friend the money to pay for the funeral expenses.[5] Early in 1925, on Josemaría's initiative, his mother came to live in Saragossa with Carmen and Santiago,[6] since all of them now depended on him for their support. He was ordained priest on 28 March 1925 and offered his first Mass for the soul of his father who had died a few months before. From then on Mass became even more central in his life. Within the Mass he received some of the most important inspirations from God as regards the development of Opus Dei. The Holy Sacrifice became the centre of his interior life. He placed on the paten all his

5 Josemaría repaid the loan later. In gratitude he always remembered this priest in his Mass. **6** When Josemaría decided to become a priest in 1917, he prayed that his parents would have another son. He always felt it was in answer to his prayer that a year later his brother Santiago was born.

requests and petitions; from there he drew his strength to fulfil God's will. Thus he was able to counsel others:

> Keep struggling, so that the Holy Sacrifice of the Altar really becomes the centre and root of your interior life, and so your whole day will turn into an act of worship – an extension of the Mass you have attended and a preparation for the next. Your whole day will then be an act of worship that overflows in aspirations, visits to the Blessed Sacrament, and the offering up of your professional work and your family life.[7]

The following day he took up his first appointment as a supply in a country parish about fifteen miles from Saragossa where the parish priest had fallen ill. The villagers of Perdiguera gave the newly-ordained priest a warm welcome, and Fr Josemaría responded by spending long hours in the confessional and fulfilling his pastoral duties conscientiously. He took special care of the sick, visiting them often and doing his best to draw them all to the sacraments. He prepared the children for First Communion with great pastoral diligence. During his two month stay in Perdiguera he managed to visit all the families in the village, house by house.

FOUNDATION FOR THE SICK

Having worked for two years in different parishes, he got permission from his bishop to transfer to Madrid in 1927 with a view to doing a doctorate degree in civil law.[8] Shortly after his arrival there he became chaplain to the Foundation for the Sick. This was an institution run by nuns from which blossomed a variety of charitable and apostolic undertakings – care of the sick in their homes, schools, soup kitchens, catechetical programmes for children in the poorer areas of Madrid, clothes distribution centres, marriage preparation programmes, especially for those in irregular situations, etc. In 1928 these good nuns ran fifty-eight schools catering for 14,000 children in Madrid. While Fr Josemaría was involved in every pastoral aspect of the Foundation, his time was increasingly absorbed by the work of the confessional. This was especially so at the weekends when the children from the different schools came to him for confession and to receive final preparation for First Communion. He would always look back with affection on the thousands of hours he invested in this work, ministering to children, thanking God for all that he had learned about holiness from them.

7 Josemaría Escrivá, *The Forge*, no. 69 (London, 1988). 8 At that time a doctorate in civil law could only be done in Madrid.

We get some idea of the enormous pastoral activity of this twenty-six-year-old priest from the records of the Foundation for the year 1928. This included 4,251 sick people attended to; 3,168 confessions; 483 anointings of the sick; 1,251 weddings; 147 baptisms.[9] But beyond that, it took more than one meeting – and a lot of persuasion and prayer – to recover the many couples who had been living in irregular marriage situations for years, as well as getting people back to confession who had been away from the Church for long periods. Thus the bare statistics, even though they are staggering, don't fully reflect his enormous pastoral input.[10]

FOUNDATION OF OPUS DEI

In spite of this intense pastoral activity, Fr Josemaría always gave priority to his personal prayer-life. He never neglected his Mass, mental prayer, saying of the breviary, etc., which provided the spiritual structure and nourishment for his day. In his visits to the sick and the schools he covered great distances either by tram or walking, but made use of this time for saying several Rosaries, doing his spiritual reading, or his meditation. He had a deep unity of life in that his pastoral work gave him a constant presence of God, and also many lights and graces to prepare his soul for what the Lord was asking of him. It was in fact while he was caught up in this phenomenal pastoral activity that he saw God's plan for Opus Dei. This special light from God, which came to him on 2 October 1928, gave him a new focus for his apostolic work. He was doing a retreat at a house of the Vincentian Fathers in Madrid. There, in his room, as he read some notes of spiritual inspirations he had received over the previous few years, he saw with great clarity the mission God was entrusting to him: to open a path to holiness through daily work and one's ordinary duties. From that day he knew with utter certainty that this was the task to which he had to devote his entire life. He now saw clearly that this inspiration was what he had been praying for since his adolescent years. He saw Opus Dei as the Lord wanted it, and as it would be down through the centuries. That 2 October 1928 was the feast of the Guardian Angels. Fr Escrivá remembered that, as

9 Andrés Vázquez de Prada, *The founder of Opus Dei: the life of Josemaría Escrivá*, vol. I (Princeton, NJ, 2001), p. 208. Fr Josemaría was assisted at the Foundation by another priest, Fr Norberto Rodríguez, who was twenty years his senior. However, he had suffered a nervous breakdown some years previously which prevented him from carrying out regular ecclesiastical duties (cf. Vázquez de Prada, pp 233, and 571, note 148). Fr Josemaría developed a deep friendship with Fr Norberto and brought him on visits to the sick and the schools so that he would feel useful and appreciated; cf. ibid., p. 233. **10** These 1928 statistics were not exceptional – the figures for 1927 are similar: 4,396 sick people attended; 3,225 confessions; 486 anointings of the sick; 1,192 weddings; 161 baptisms (cf. Vázquez de Prada, p. 565, note 68).

background to the special grace he received about Opus Dei, he heard the sound of the bells of the nearby church of our Lady of the Angels pealing out in honour of their patron. Those bells would continue to resound in his ears for the rest of his life.

Prudence led him to enquire whether something like Opus Dei might not already exist in the Church. He contacted church entities throughout Europe, from Spain to Poland, eventually being convinced of the originality of the message he had received. God was asking him for something specific and new. He therefore began to gather together people, especially young people, to whom he could transmit this ideal.

Everything in his life up to then now fell into place. He understood how all Christians are called by God to be real, canonizable saints as a consequence of their baptism. Fr Escrivá saw that his own task was to teach people how to put this ideal into practice – Christians from every background dedicating themselves to reaching holiness and union with God in their daily work, by doing it well and offering it wholeheartedly to the Lord. He also saw that this dynamic of holiness, which would bring people close to Christ, would inspire them in turn to help those around them to find God in their work, friendships, and family life. On 2 October 1928 all this was a vision in the soul of one man. All the theology and all the practical apostolic methodology had still to be worked out.

When Fr Escrivá started to preach the idea of personal holiness and apostolic commitment for all Christians in the middle of the world, he was proposing an ideal which was virtually unheard of in the early part of the twentieth century. It would take another four decades for Vatican II to spell out in detail the nature of the lay vocation and the universal call to holiness:

> The laity, by their very vocation, seek the kingdom of God by engaging in temporal affairs and by ordering them according to the plan of God. They live in the world, that is, in each and in all the secular professions and occupations. They live in the ordinary circumstances of family and social life, from which the web of their existence is woven. They are called there by God so that by exercising their proper function and being led by the spirit of the Gospel, they can work for the sanctification of the world from within, in the manner of leaven.[11] ... All the faithful of Christ, of whatever rank or status, are called to the fullness of the Christian life and to the perfection of charity.[12]

Although his life now acquired a new apostolic focus, he continued his pastoral duties at the Foundation with the same intensity as before. While opening up

11 Second Vatican Council, Dogmatic Constitution *Lumen gentium*, 31. 12 Ibid., no. 40.

the call to holiness for lay people would absorb his best energies for the rest of his life, pastoral concern for the holiness of his brother priests would continue to be an integral part of his apostolic outreach.

WOMEN IN OPUS DEI

Initially Fr Escrivá did not envisage women members of Opus Dei. However, on 14 February 1930, while saying Mass, he got a special light to see that women should form an integral part of the Work. He drew his spiritual daughters to Opus Dei with the same spirit of prayer and self-sacrifice that attracted his sons. He formed them and looked after them with the same unstinting, fatherly approach. He set before them the whole gamut of women's professions, so that they might see them as fields in which to serve God and other people.

What did Fr Escrivá consider as the role of women in the Church? In a 1968 interview he responded as follows:

> Women are called to bring to the family, to society, and to the Church characteristics which are their own and which they alone can give: their gentle warmth and untiring generosity, their love for detail, their quick-wittedness and intuition, their simple and deep piety, their constancy … A woman's femininity is genuine only if she is aware of the beauty of this contribution for which there is no substitute – and if she incorporates it into her own life.[13]

Care and affection for her husband and children, the creation of a warm Christian family life – this would always be the primary task of women and would occupy a most important place in their life. But, he added, 'this is not in opposition to her participation in other aspects of social life – even of politics, for example. In those sectors too, women can make valuable contributions. And they will always do this by means of the special characteristics of their feminine nature.'[14] He had a particularly high regard for women's work in the home:

> Certainly there will always be many women whose only task is to run their homes. This is a wonderful job which is very worthwhile. Through this profession – because it is a profession, in a true and noble sense – they are an influence for good, not only in their family, but also among their many friends and acquaintances, among people with whom

13 Josemaría Escrivá, *Conversations*, no. 87. **14** Peter Berglar, *Opus Dei: life and work of its founder Josemaría Escrivá* (Princeton, NJ, 1994), p. 160.

> they come in contact in one way or another. Sometimes their impact is much greater than that of other professional people.[15]

HOSPITALS AND THE POOR

Fr Escrivá continued his work as before, but Opus Dei began to take shape slowly and silently in his soul. As he wrote in his spiritual journal on the third anniversary of the foundation of the Work:

> From that day onwards [2 October 1928], the mangy little donkey became aware of the beautiful and heavy burden which the Lord, in his inexplicable goodness, had placed on his shoulders. That day God founded his work. From that day on I began to guide souls, lay people – students or otherwise – but young people. And I began to form groups. And to pray and to get them to pray. And to suffer … without ever hesitating.[16]

He continued his care of the poor and the sick, as well as preparing his doctoral thesis and giving private classes to support his family who had come to live in Madrid. He gathered young people around him to give them a Christian formation and to open apostolic horizons for them. These young men were attracted by his optimism, his sense of humour, and his obvious holiness.

In the hospitals he not only brought the sacraments to the patients and helped them to offer their sufferings to God, but he also did many practical things for them which they could not do for themselves like washing them, cutting their nails, emptying the bed-pans, etc. He helped the patients to see that their sickness was a treasure if they united their sufferings to those of Christ on the Cross, and could be a powerhouse of grace for the whole Church. He himself relied on their prayers for the grace to establish the foundations of the Work and its apostolates. On Sunday afternoons he invited young men to go to the hospitals with him and to help him in his work there, teaching them to do it with loving care for the sick. These visits to the poorest patients made a deep impression on the young men, helping them to see how Christ is especially present in those who suffer.

In 1931 Escrivá gave up his chaplaincy at the Foundation for the Sick so that he could devote more time to laying the foundation for Opus Dei. He became chaplain to the King's Hospital, a large institution housing 2,500 patients suffering from infectious diseases like smallpox, typhus, and tuberculosis. In this dreary

15 *Conversations*, no. 88. **16** St Josemaría Escrivá, 'Intimate Notes 306', 2 October 1931.

institution men and women spent the last days of their lives without any hope of recovery. Opus Dei began to spread thanks to the grace that came from the patient sufferings of the poor, the sick and the dying. But that was not all. Its firm roots and remarkable fruitfulness in society called for the deaths of some of its first members after only a brief period of giving themselves to God.

Fr Josemaría was able to share his heavy work load at the King's Hospital with a young priest named José María Somoano. Soon they became close friends. Official membership of the Work was not yet possible for priests, but Somoano was one of the first to be in some real way associated with Opus Dei. He attended a weekly class of formation given by Fr Escrivá for a group of priest friends and he fully assimilated the spirituality of the Work. He was a priest filled with a glowing love for Christ and souls, and he understood how a secular priest could also follow a vocation to secular holiness in Opus Dei. For the short time granted to him, Somoano lived side by side with Escrivá. He died in July 1932, most likely poisoned by anticlerical fanatics. He was just thirty, and his death was a great blow to Fr Josemaría, because he had hoped that Fr Somoano would be a solid support in the gestation of his new apostolic enterprise.

In the same year Luis Gordon, one of the first laymen to join Fr Josemaría in Opus Die, died and ten months later the first woman, Maria Ignacia Escobar, who asked for admission to the Work, died of tuberculosis. She had joined Opus Dei when she was already ill and offered her intense sufferings for the future apostolate of the Work. St Josemaría could with justification repeat in later years that Opus Dei had been born 'among the poor and the sick in the hospitals of Madrid'.

CHRIST AT THE PINNACLE OF ALL HUMAN REALITIES

During this period Fr Josemaría received many foundational graces. On the feast of the Transfiguration 1931, as he said Mass, he heard the words of Scripture as an inner locution: 'And I, when I am lifted up from the earth, will draw all things to myself' (Jn 12:32). He understood it as meaning that Christ was to be placed at the pinnacle of all human activities by Christians who were dedicated to him in the middle of the world. It confirmed for Fr Josemaría that everyday work is not only an encounter with Christ dying triumphant on the Cross, but is also, in a special way for lay people, the means, the raw material as it were, for their sanctification in the world. Daily work as a means to holiness and apostolate was one of the core ideas of his teaching from the beginning. Jesus' thirty years of hidden life were for him a source of inspiration for this teaching and opened up many avenues for the rich theology of work which he developed. John Paul II took up this point in his canonization homily:

> Ever since 7 August 1931 when, during the celebration of holy Mass, the words of Jesus echoed in his soul: 'when I am lifted up from the earth, I will draw all to myself' (Jn 12:32), Josemaría Escrivá understood more clearly that the mission of the baptized consists in raising the Cross of Christ above all human reality and he felt burning within him the impassioned invitation to the Apostle Peter, *Duc in altum* (Put out into the deep). He transmitted it to his entire spiritual family so that they might offer the Church a valid contribution of communion and apostolic service. Today this invitation is extended to all of us: 'Put out into the deep', the divine Teacher says to us, 'and let down your nets for a catch' (Lk 5:4).[17]

SANCTIFICATION OF WORK

One of the original contributions of St Josemaría was not only to preach the universal call to holiness, but also to provide a particular spirituality as a means of putting this teaching of Vatican II into practice. Throughout his life, he constantly reminded people of the importance of work for the Christian. Daily work, he used to say, 'is the hinge on which our calling to holiness is fixed and turns'.[18] It is not only the context in which the majority of men should become holy, but he goes so far as to say, 'it is the raw material of their holiness'.[19] What God asks of the Christian is 'the miracle of turning the prose of each day into heroic verse by the love which you put into ordinary work. God waits for you there. He expects you to be a responsible person, with the zeal of an apostle and competence of a good worker'.[20]

Daily work acquires a particular importance for the Christian because it is the free, responsible activity of the human person, as one who is called by God to participate in both his creative and redemptive activity. It often involves effort and weariness. But it also bears witness to the dignity of man. It is an opportunity to develop one's personality. The experience of work bonds us to others and develops friendships. It is a means to support one's family, and allows us to contribute to the improvement of society. And, since the time Christ worked as a carpenter, work for us 'becomes a redeemed and redemptive reality… It is something to be sanctified and something which sanctifies'.[21]

St Josemaría saw holiness through work as a logical consequence of that unity of life, which all Christian are encouraged to cultivate.[22] In this way the grace drawn from the Mass, the sacraments, and daily prayer, provides the spiritual resources to sanctify family life, daily work and social commitments.

17 John Paul II, Homily, 6 October 2002. **18** Josemaría Escrivá, *Friends of God* (Dublin, 1981), no. 62. **19** *Conversations*, no. 70. **20** Josemaría Escrivá, *Christ is passing by* (Dublin, 1982), no. 50. **21** Ibid., no. 47. **22** Cf. John Paul II, Apostolic Exhortation, *Christifideles laici*, 59 and 60 (30 December 1988).

For St Josemaría this was the essence of the Christian vocation of the laity. It is in the context of these normal daily activities that we find the opportunities to live a spirit of service, to respect the rights of others, and to exercise a sense of responsibility. Here, by practising the virtues of industriousness, generosity, sobriety, cheerfulness, charity, etc., we can grow in personal holiness.

WORK WELL DONE – OBJECTIVE ASPECT OF WORK

St Josemaría said that we sanctify work by uniting it with the redemptive work of Jesus: by doing it with love, doing it out of service to others, to family and society. Our work has an effect on the material things of this world, on human culture, and civilization. Through our work God calls us to care for the earth and to humanize it. We can only sanctify work if we do it well, with attention to detail, overcoming tiredness, by keeping our word and also by respecting deadlines out of concern for the needs of others. Sloppy, careless work, according to Opus Dei's founder, cannot be sanctified because it is not appropriate raw material for sanctification. It cannot contribute to the 'humanization' and 'redemption' of the world in which we live.

In the light of the Paschal mystery we can see more clearly how everyday work, often demanding and exhausting, is a time of encounter with Christ dying and triumphant on the Cross. St Josemaría never considered holiness as something to be achieved in spite of the demands and challenges of work and family life. Rather, he regarded these situations as so many opportunities of grace in which the fatherly providence of God makes itself felt. Thus, what seem to be obstacles are converted into a means to holiness. Grace does not eliminate the difficulties but rather pervades them, transforming them in the process. By reason of our baptismal commitment to participate in Christ's redemptive mission, our own work has an apostolic character because, as St Josemaría reminds us, it is an opportunity to give ourselves to others, to reveal Christ to them, and to lead them to God the Father.[23] As we were reminded in John Paul II's pastoral programme for the New Millennium, Christians are called to co-operate in a new evangelization, which will imbue the home, the workplace, and public and private life with the values of the Gospel.[24]

DIVINE FILIATION

After 2 October 1928 God gave St Josemaría new graces to develop and complete what he had seen on that date. He was at the same time encountering many

23 Cf. *Christ is passing by*, no. 75. **24** Cf. John Paul II, Apostolic letter, *Novo millennio ineunte*, 40, 41, 51, 52 (6 January 2001).

obstacles to his specific apostolate, since with the coming of the Republic in April 1931 a full-scale campaign against the Church had begun in Spain. In addition, the financial situation of his family was a cause of concern since he was the sole breadwinner. It was in these circumstances that, as he often described it, he experienced one of the greatest graces of his life. On 17 October 1931, in the midst of the hustle and bustle of Madrid, while he was deep in prayer on a tram, the mystery of divine filiation was revealed to him in a profound way – that God is a Father who is close to us at all times, that he is interested in everything we do, that he loves us more than all the mothers in the world love their children. He felt that God himself was forming in his heart and on his lips, irresistibly, the tender invocation, 'Abba! Father'. This experience was so vivid that he remembered the exact time and place where it happened.[25] What occurred that day was not only to leave a deep mark on his soul for the rest of his life, but was also to be a constant theme of his preaching and writing in the years ahead. It was the theological prism through which he was to see everything that affected his own life and God's loving engagement with the world. He summarized the significance of this insight by saying that a person who was unaware that he was a child of God was ignorant of the deepest truth about his or her existence.[26] Fr Escriva explains:

> I understood that divine filiation had to be a fundamental characteristic of our spirituality: Abba, Father! And that by living from within their divine filiation, my children would find themselves filled with joy and peace, protected by an impregnable wall; and would know how to be apostles of this joy, and how to communicate their peace, even in the face of their own or another's suffering. Just because of that: because we are convinced that God is our Father.[27]

As a consequence, the conviction that he was a son of God became the cornerstone of his spiritual life, and this in due course was to become the foundation of the spirituality of Opus Dei.

For the founder of Opus Dei, recognizing that we are children of God has to be more than something theoretical: it should have direct consequences in our daily lives. Fr Josemaría explained it this way:

> We must try to be children who realize that the Lord, by loving us as his children, has taken us into his house, in the midst of the world, to be members of his family so that what is his is ours, and what is ours is his; and to develop that familiarity and confidence which prompts us to ask him, like children, for the moon.[28]

25 Cf. Vázquez de Prada, vol. I, p. 296. **26** Cf. Josemaría Escrivá, *Friends of God* (London, 1981), no. 26. **27** Vázquez de Prada, p. 296. **28** Escrivá, *Christ is passing by*, no. 64

THE DYA ACADEMY

As Fr Josemaría developed his apostolate with young people (mostly students) he saw the need to have a centre where these young men could come to study and to receive formation. So in 1933 the first corporate apostolate of Opus Dei was launched, the DYA academy in Madrid. At first it provided classes in a variety of subjects; subsequently it was expanded to become a hall of residence for university students. Fr Josemaría had to overcome many obstacles to set up the residence, particularly financial problems. However, he worked hard, and with the help of the young men who by this time had joined Opus Dei, he made sure that the environment of the residence was as welcoming and home-like as possible. The students who came to the academy were made realize that study was to be taken seriously, as it was the means by which they were to sanctify themselves and grow in their Christian vocation. Fr Josemaría would later write, 'An hour of study, for a modern apostle, is an hour of prayer.'[29]

The academy really came to life in the afternoon, with students coming to attend classes in architecture, and legal subjects, as well as mathematics, physics and chemistry (common entrance subjects for a number of special schools and for university). Fr Josemaría gave classes in Christian doctrine and was availabe for spiritual guidance for anyone who wanted to avail of his services. After a short while he was kept constantly busy.

The DYA academy was the first of a great variety of corporate apostolates which Opus Dei would set up all over the world in subsequent years. Today they comprise a wide variety of apostolic activities in many countries. Among them are universities, trade schools, student residences, farm schools, primary and secondary schools, dispensaries, medical centres, language institutes, and youth clubs. All of them have an exclusively apostolic goal: to prepare people of every social level to turn their family, work and social environment into a zone of Christian influence. The principles behind these works have not changed since the DYA academy was set up. They are not church-related, but secular activities established in accordance with civil law and their organization structure is completely lay.

CIVIL WAR

Midway through the 1930s the apostolate was expanding in Madrid and vocations of young men were beginning to come. Fr Josemaría was preparing to send some of them to Valentia and other cities in Spain to start the apostolate

29 Josemaría Escrivá, *The Way* (Dublin, 1968), no. 335.

of Opus Dei there. Paris also beckoned as the first location for expansion outside Spain. However, all these plans were changed abruptly by the outbreak of the Spanish civil war on 18 July 1936.

In the first months of that year the storm clouds loomed. Spain was divided in two. The Republican side, which supported the Popular Front government, was on the whole violently anti-Catholic. On the other side were the Nationalists, in general loyal to the Catholic Church. As election day (16 February) approached, demonstrations in the streets ended more and more frequently with the burning down or looting of churches and convents. The point was reached when the two sides could no longer negotiate and the result was civil war. Most of the army had risen in revolt against the government in support of the Nationalist side.

The fratricidal struggle covered Spain in blood and became a sombre landmark in the history of religious persecutions. On one day, 25 July, the feast of St James, patron of Spain, 95 churchmen up and down the country were put to death. In August this barbarous anti-clerical fury swept the cities and towns. Over 2,000 priests, religious and nuns were slain that month. Also, many lay people, men and women, were murdered for the simple fact of being Catholics.

Madrid was firmly in the Republican zone and, as a priest, Fr Josemaría's life was in constant danger. Militia groups were stopping people in the streets, and any priests or religious were usually shot or hanged on the spot. Fr Josemaría heard with great sorrow that a priest who was thought to be him was hanged in front of his mother's apartment. For the rest of his life he remembered the dead priest in his Masses. On the day of the army uprising Fr Josemaría had to leave the students' residence disguised in workman's overalls. He could not return there because sooner or later the militia would come looking for him. He spent the next three months on the run in Madrid, going from one place to another, never staying anywhere for long and in constant danger.

In October 1936 he had to take refuge in a psychiatric clinic where the medical director, a friend of Escrivá, concealed him among his patients where he feigned madness. He remained there until March 1937 when he was able to move to a slightly safer place, the Honduras legation in Madrid. There Fr Escrivá was joined by four young people of the Work, and by his younger brother Santiago. He was there for several months and had lost so much weight that when his mother went to visit him she did not recognize him until she heard him speak. For Fr Escrivá this was a time of intense prayer and penance, a time of interior suffering and spiritual growth.

In August 1937 he managed at last to get some faked identification papers which allowed him to go about Madrid with a certain freedom. He was able to resume his apostolic work. Given the circumstances, he had sometimes to hear confession while apparently just going for a walk with the person concerned.

He also administered baptism clandestinely. He even preached an itinerant retreat to five people, constantly changing house so as not to arouse suspicion. Those attending the retreat would meet in one place for a meditation, then disperse, and meet somewhere else for the next one to avoid being noticed.

Since no one knew how long the war was going to continue, Fr Escrivá decided to try to reach the Nationalist zone where he could continue to carry out his apostolate. In November 1937, with a small group of members of Opus Dei and some friends, he made his way to Barcelona and from there escaped from the Republican zone on foot over the Pyrenees mountains. It was a very harsh, dangerous journey, in which their lives were constantly threatened by the difficult conditions and by the border guards who would shoot suspected fugitives on sight. With a number of other refugees they were guided through the difficult terrain by a series of smugglers who undertook the task for financial gain.

At one stage on the journey Fr Josemaría said an open-air Mass on a rock in a sheltered valley. A student who was not part of the Escrivá group, wrote in his diary at the time:

> The most moving moment of the trip was the holy Mass: a priest in our company said Mass on a rock. He didn't say it like priests in the churches. His clear and heartfelt words penetrated to our souls. I've never heard Mass like today. I don't know whether its because of the circumstances or because the celebrant is a saint.[30]

After two gruelling weeks they reached Andorra on 2 December 1937. There for the first time in many months, Fr Josemaría was able to celebrate Mass in normal conditions. He prayed for his family and for those who had stayed behind in Madrid, and for those sons of his scattered about the different warfronts, some of whom would have the joy of seeing him soon.

From Andorra Fr Josmaría went to Lourdes to thank our Lady for having brought them safely out of the Republican zone. Then in January 1938, after a stop-over to do a retreat in Pamplona, he arrived in Burgos, the capital of the Nationalist zone, to take up the threads of the apostolate that had been interrupted by the war. Though worn out by all he had been through during his last months in Madrid and by the exhaustion of the crossing of the Pyrenees, after his retreat in Pamplona, he redoubled his prayer and mortification for the apostolate. He decided to reduce his hours of sleep and to spend a whole night each week in prayer.

30 Vázquez de Prada, vol II (Princeton, NJ, 2003), pp 154–5.

BURGOS

After his arrival in Burgos, Fr Josemaría spent the next fifteen months working intensely. He wrote letters to all the people of the Work he could locate, and to the young men who had been involved with his apostolate in Madrid. To keep people in touch with each other, he produced a newsletter which was circulated among all his contacts. Despite his precarious financial situation, he travelled tirelessly, visiting his spiritual sons wherever they were, getting as close as possible to the different battlefronts. He gave them spiritual guidance and encouragement in their vocation, and even material help in so far as he could. Whenever they got leave, he invited them to spend a few days with him in Burgos. They always went away strengthened and encouraged, with clear guidelines about how to maintain contact with God even in the demanding circumstances of a war situation.

Burgos had attracted many refugees from Republican dominated areas of Spain. This was an opportunity for Fr Josemaría to find new possible openings for his apostolate. He contacted families he knew, made new acquaintances, and spoke to several bishops about Opus Dei and the new spirituality it was bringing to the church. He also offered and gave his assistance to nuns, trying to adapt this to their particular spirituality, as well as to the Teresians, whose founder, his friend Padre Poveda, had been assassinated. Not content with the already exhausting amount of work he had taken on, he spent a certain amount of time working on his doctoral thesis.

RETURN TO MADRID

The civil war was coming to an end. With the fall of Madrid to the Nationalists, Fr Josemaría was the first priest to enter the city on 28 March 1939. The student residence which had cost so much effort to set up three years previously was in ruins. However, he was not discouraged and within a few months new centres were opened in Madrid as well as in Valencia. Thanks to the zeal and dedication of Fr Escrivá, Opus Dei grew rapidly from 1939, and centres of apostolate were set up in several Spanish cities. In 1941 the Work received its first, formal, written, Church approval from the bishop of Madrid.

At the same time, Fr Josemaría began to be much in demand among bishops all over Spain, and at their request he travelled from one city to another giving retreats to priests. These men had suffered greatly during the civil war, when over 4,000 of them, including thirteen bishops, were assassinated by Republican forces. Fr Josemaría saw the retreats as an opportunity to give the spirituality of these priests a fresh impetus. During the period 1939 to 1946 he gave retreats to as many as a thousand priests a year, such that by 1946 nearly half the priests of Spain had passed through his hands.

The constant apostolic work of Fr Josemaría was rewarded with a rapid rise in vocations, especially during the forties. These were, in general, young men and women from different backgrounds, who, energized by the spirituality of Opus Dei, had committed themselves fully to follow Christ in the world, seeking holiness through the sanctification of their daily work and through an apostolate of personal influence among their colleagues. To adequately look after the sacramental needs of these vocations, and to provide the necessary spiritual and theological formation for the many people who were attracted by this new spirituality, Fr Josemaría realized that he would need more priests. But it had also become clear to him that these priests would have to be drawn from among those who had already joined Opus Dei as laymen.[31] Enlightened by grace, he saw that this approach was necessary to guarantee the faithful transmission of the charism which he had received from God. This idea, however, gave rise to novel implications at the canonical, theological and practical levels. For a number of years the founder had been praying for a solution to this difficulty. With deep faith in God, he was already preparing the first three men for the priesthood, drawing on the services of a team of top theologians from Madrid.[32] He got many people to pray for this intention and sought advice from eminent canonists.

Then, on 14 February 1943, while saying Mass he received another foundational grace. After Mass he had a clear vision of how Opus Dei could provide priests from within its own ranks, even to the point of being able to write down the name of the entity to which these priests would belong – the Priestly Society of the Holy Cross. Later that year, the Vatican approved his proposal and, in June 1944, the bishop of Madrid ordained the first three priests of Opus Dei. From this small beginning, over the next thirty years Fr Josemaría would call nearly a thousand men to the priesthood. For Fr Josemaría this was a further development of his aim of serving the Church – Opus Dei was providing lay people with a path to holiness in ordinary life, and was also contributing priests to the church to serve all souls.

At the same time, in accordance with Fr Josemaría's vision of what Opus Dei should be like, priests did not form a separate group or class within the

31 After Opus Dei received definitive papal approval in 1950, married people could join, a development which the founder had envisaged from the beginning. Married members constitute 70% of the faithful of the prelature. 32 The outbreak of the Second World War in September 1939 took many of the professors from the Roman pontifical universities by surprise while on holidays at home in Spain. These were the men Fr Escrivá drew on to teach his spiritual sons in preparation for ordination.

apostolate of Opus Dei. Rather the apostolate of both complemented each other within an organic unity. As Pope John Paul II was to say many years later, addressing the Prelate and members of Opus Dei, 'You are here representing the components by which the Prelature is organically structured, that is priests and lay faithful, men and women, headed by their own Prelate.' And the Holy Father continued:

> It will be the direct witness of lay people … that will reveal how it is only in Christ that the highest human values attain their fullness. And their apostolic zeal, fraternal friendship and supportive charity will enable them to turn daily social relationships into opportunities for awakening in others that thirst for truth which is the first condition for the saving encounter with Christ. Priests, on their part, form an irreplaceable primary function: that of helping souls one by one, by means of the sacraments, preaching and spiritual guidance, to open up the gift of faith. A spirituality of communion, therefore, will enable the role of each one of these constitutive ecclesial elements to be appreciated to the full.[33]

In the context of priestly spirituality, Fr Josemaría often recalled the teaching of Vatican II on the unity that should exist between a priest's consecration and his mission – in other words, between his personal life of piety and the exercise of his priestly ministry, between his filial relationship with God and his pastoral relations with people. He did not believe that a priest could carry out an effective ministry unless he was a man of prayer.[34]

In keeping with a long tradition in the Church, he was an enthusiastic supporter of associations which helped the spiritual life of secular priests without in any way interfering with their ministerial responsibilities, as recommended by Vatican II.[35] It was very clear to him that by virtue of the sacramental and juridical bond, the diocesan priest depended on the bishop in everything that related to the assignment of his particular pastoral work, including the doctrinal and disciplinary instructions received for the exercise of his ministry, celebration of the liturgy, etc. While recognizing all this, Fr Josemaría also affirmed the freedom which priests, like other members of the faithful, enjoyed in organizing the spiritual, social and financial aspects of their lives at a personal level.[36]

Out of his long experience of giving retreats to priests and encouraging them individually through spiritual guidance, Fr Josemaría was totally commit-

33 John Paul II, Address, 17 March 2001. **34** Cf. *Presbyterorum ordinis*, 4–6. **35** Cf. ibid., no. 8. **36** Cf. *Conversations*, no. 8.

ted to helping them find personal holiness in the exercise of their ministry. For him personal sanctity was also the most effective way for priests to offset possible crises arising from isolation, indifference, routine, fatigue or, what was often the root cause of crises of obedience, lack of supernatural outlook in their relations with their own bishop, or even with their brothers in the priesthood.[37]

When Opus Dei received its final approval by the Vatican in 1950, the way was open for secular priests to join the Priestly Society of the Holy Cross in order to receive spiritual guidance and support without in any way modifying their diocesan vocation. In this way they could be formed in a spirituality which encouraged zeal in pastoral tasks, reaffirmed obedience to the bishop, and encouraged the promotion of vocations to the priesthood. At present about two thousand diocesan clergy belong to the Priestly Society of the Holy Cross world-wide.[38] Fr Josemaría was so committed to this work of formation of diocesan priests that he was ready to leave Opus Dei and found a separate entity when at first it did not seem possible to include it under the auspices of Opus Dei.

OPPOSITION

By 1946 there were centres of Opus Dei in eight cities of Spain and one in Portugal. In parallel with this expansion Fr Josemaría had to face a growing amount of opposition to, and misunderstanding of this work. Some Catholics at the time saw the clergy as being the essence of the Church, and thought that the only thing lay people could do was try to lead good lives, join in the apostolate organized by the clergy, but if they wished to aim for real holiness, they had either to become priests or religious. They tended to think that daily work in the world and ordinary social life were necessarily obstacles to holiness. The idea that lay men and women could aim for true holiness in their everyday working and married lives seemed madness, even heretical. A campaign against Fr Josemaría was organized from pulpits and confessionals, and the message went forth that a great danger to the church was threatening. Rumour then gave way to slander and this in turn to the wildest fantasies. Oddly enough some of these calumnies were spread by practising Catholics who thought they were fighting in a good cause, and many of them were convinced that what they were doing was pleasing to God. The persecution took on a particularly bitter tone in Barcelona where at the time there were no more than half a dozen members of Opus Dei. In the midst of all these difficulties Fr Josemaría could always count on the solid encouragement of the bishop of Madrid, who

37 Cf. *Conversations*, no. 16. 38 Cf. Peter Bristow, *Opus Dei: Christians in the midst of the world* (London, 2001), p. 60.

was a loyal and constant supporter of this new family in the church. Fr Josemaría's answer to these obstacles and slanders was always to forgive. He forgave and forgot, and taught the members of Opus Dei to do the same. No matter what might happen, or what people might say, they were to 'say nothing, pray, work, smile'.

ROME AND APPROVALS

When the Second World War ended in 1945, Fr Josemaría began to think about the expansion of the message of Opus Dei to other countries outside the Iberian peninsula. However, in order for the Work to take root and develop in other nations it needed to be recognized by the Church at a universal level to guarantee the secularity of its faithful and the unity and universality of its apostolates in all the dioceses where it would take root. To achieve this objective, Fr Josemaría went to Rome in June of 1946, and with a few other members of the Work settled in a flat in the Piazza della Cittá Leonina which overlooked the papal apartments. He always had a deep love for the Pope and his teaching. As he wrote:

> Your deepest love, your greatest esteem, your most heartfelt veneration, your most complete obedience and your warmest affection have also to be shown toward the Vicar of Christ on earth, towards the Pope. We Catholics should consider that after God and the most Holy Virgin, our Mother, the Holy Father comes next in the hierarchy of love and authority.[39]

He was so deeply moved by his physical proximity to the Vicar of Christ that, despite his tiredness, he stayed up the whole of his first night in Rome in a vigil of prayer for the Pope.

He had come to look for the juridical approval for the Work. The reception was mixed. Opus Dei's novel approach to apostolate and its distinctive spirituality met in part with admiration, notably from Msgr Montini, later Pope Paul VI. Others were sceptical about finding an adequate place for Opus Dei within the Church's structure. Indeed one ecclesiastic said that Opus Dei had been born a century too soon. However, Fr Josemaría couldn't afford to wait that long. A harvest of vocations was coming to Opus Dei and in view of the imminent expansion to many new countries, the Work needed a basic juridical recognition.

39 Josemaría Escrivá, *The Forge* (London, 1988), no.135.

On 16 July, a few weeks after Fr Josemaría's arrival in Rome, the Holy Father granted him a private audience which left him very moved. 'I cannot forget', he was to comment later, 'that it was His Holiness Pope Pius XII who approved Opus Dei, when this path of spirituality seemed, to more that one person, a heresy; nor will I forget that the first words of kindness and affection I received in Rome were spoken to me by the then Monsignor Montini'.

Fr Josemaría worked closely with Vatican officials over the next nine months, and on 2 February 1947 the document *Provida Mater Ecclesia* establishing the new form of secular institutes was promulgated. Opus Dei was given its first Vatican approval under this title, three weeks later, on 24 February 1947, and definitive papal approval on 16 June 1950. The legal mould of secular institutes was not entirely suitable as it did not take fully into account the secular nature of the members of Opus Dei as ordinary faithful striving for holiness in the middle of the world. Not until November 1982 did the Work receive its definitive legal status when it was erected by John Paul II as a personal prelature. This was a juridical configuration which fully and definitively recognized the characteristics of the Work and which fitted perfectly with the founder's charism. Fr Josemaría had foreseen from the beginning that the Work would require this type of legal framework.

PERSONAL PRELATURE

The concept of a personal prelature was recommended by the Second Vatican Council and then established by Paul VI in 1966. It was proposed as an answer to the search for more flexible structures to deal with the needs of the contemporary apostolate. The Council Fathers suggested that among other institutions, 'special dioceses, or personal prelatures' should be established 'to carry out special pastoral tasks for the benefit of different social groups in different regions or among any race in any part of the world'.[40]

A personal prelature is part of the jurisdictional/hierarchical structure of the Church. Most jurisdictions in the Church are territorial, as in the case of a diocese, where the faithful who belong to it are determined according to their territory or domicile. However, jurisdiction is not always linked to territory, but may depend on other criteria such as employment, religious rite, immigrant status, or agreement with the jurisdictional body in question. The last-mentioned applies in the case of military ordinates (military bishoprics) and personal prelatures.[41]

Personal prelatures, as envisaged by the Second Vatican Council, are made up of a prelate, a presbyterate of secular clergy, and men and women lay faith-

40 Vatican II (*Presbyterorum ordinis*), no. 10. **41** Cf. Bristow, pp 54–7.

ful. The prelate, who may be a bishop, is appointed by the Pope, and governs the prelature with power of governance and jurisdiction. One of the main purposes of personal prelatures is to carry out special pastoral enterprises or apostolic tasks.[42] In 1928 there was no provision in Church law for an institution that was international in character and that consisted of secular priests and laity – men and women, celibate and married – dedicating themselves completely to sanctity and apostolate in and through their everyday duties and responsibilities. Fr Josemaría had to find a formula that would safeguard the secular and international character of Opus Dei as well as the unity of priests and lay people. It was a task that was to last beyond his own lifetime. John Paul II set up Opus Dei as a personal prelature in 1982 after years of study and after hearing the views of bishops throughout the world, wherever Opus Dei was established.

The special pastoral task of Opus Dei is to proclaim the universal call to holiness and to apostolate through the commitments of ordinary life – work, family and social involvements. In order to achieve this aim, the prelature offers spiritual formation and pastoral care to its members as well as to many others.

Apart from setting up in Rome the central offices for the government of Opus Dei, on 29 June 1948, Fr Josemaría established the Roman College of the Holy Cross. This was an international centre of formation for young men of Opus Dei from all parts of the world who would study not only philosophy and theology, but would also learn the spirit of Opus Dei directly from the lips of the founder. This stay in the Eternal City was also a means used by Fr Josemaría to 'Romanize' Opus Dei, an opportunity for the founder to instil in his sons a deep love for the Church and the Pope. Since 1948 thousands of members of the Work from different parts of the world have been formed in the Roman College of the Holy Cross. Some have been ordained priests, and all have contributed to give the people of Opus Dei in their different countries of origin a universal spirit. The setting up of the Roman College of Our Lady in 1953, an international centre for the formation for women of Opus Dei, was inspired by a similar objective.

These early Roman years were a period of intense work for Escrivá, which he managed despite suffering from a very severe form of diabetes. He contracted the disease in 1944, but was miraculously cured in 1954.

FAMILY AND MARRIAGE

With the pontifical approvals of the Work in 1947 and 1950, the way was now clear for married people to become members of Opus Dei. As we have seen, the core of St Josemaría's preaching was that all Christians are called to holi-

42 Cf. Code of Canon Law, no. 294.

ness. And since marriage is the normal context for the life of most lay people, it was clear to him that if they were to achieve holiness, it had to be through the sanctification of married life and family responsibilities. Thus, from the very beginning of his apostolate, St Josemaría encouraged couples to strive for holiness within the context of their marriage and family life. Marriage, he reminded people, is a divine vocation, 'a real supernatural calling.'[43]

> It is important for married people to acquire a clear sense of the dignity of their vocation. They must know that they have been called by God not only to human love but also to a divine love through their human love. It is important for them to realize that they have been chosen from eternity to co-operate with the creative power of God by having and then bringing up children. Our Lord asks them to make their home and their entire family life a testimony to all the Christian virtues.[44]

God, as we know, is the author of marriage, which came into being with the creation of the first couple. Raised by Christ to the dignity of a sacrament, it participates in God's covenant of faith and love. St Paul reminds us that the marriage of a Christian couple not only exemplifies, but participates in the spousal love of Christ for his Bride, the Church (cf. Eph 5:31–33). This is why the sacrament of matrimony provides a special grace to spouses to cope with all the challenges and demands of marriage. Because it draws on Christ's redeeming power, spouses transmit his saving grace to their families, and to the larger family of the Church. In this way they reflect in their marriage the love that Christ has for his Church. St Josemaría offered married couples a practical programme for sanctifying daily life:

> The marriage union, the care and education of children, the effort to provide for the needs of the family as well as for its security and development, the relationships with other persons who make up the community, all these are among the ordinary human situations that Christian couples are called upon to sanctify.[45]

He saw the mutual love of husband and wife as something noble and sacred which our Lord blesses and sanctifies. Thus for him, human sexuality was 'a divine gift, ordered to life, to love and fruitfulness'.[46] But to accept it as a divine gift requires the virtue of chastity 'which leads a couple to respect the mystery of sex and ordain it to faithfulness and personal dedication'.[47] St

43 Escrivá, *Christ is passing by*, no. 23. 44 *Conversations*, no. 93. 45 *Christ is passing by*, no. 23. 46 Ibid., no. 24. 47 Ibid., no. 25.

Josemaría emphasized that authentic joy in married life was the result of generous co-operation with God in bringing children into the world.

OPUS DEI SPREADS TO THE FIVE CONTINENTS

The first vocations outside of Spain came in Italy and Portugal within a year of the end of the Second World War – Sr Lucia, the visionary of Fatima, had already asked Fr Josemaría in 1945 to have the Work start in Portugal as soon as possible. Apostolic work started in England in 1946, and in 1947 in Ireland and France. In 1949 the Work went to the United States and Mexico, and in 1950 to Argentina and Chile, followed by Columbia, Venezuela, Peru, and Ecuador. The Work took hardy root in these diverse areas.

Opus Dei began work in Africa in 1958 where it was first established in Kenya. Here the initial apostolic project was a secondary school, Strathmore college. At the time schools were run on racial lines, but Msgr Escrivá insisted that from the start Strathmore should be completely multi-racial, and open to all religions. This was a total innovation in Kenya and at the start encountered a fair amount of opposition. In 1965 the Work began in Nigeria and has since started to do apostolic work in the Republic of the Congo, the Ivory Coast, Cameroons, Uganda and South Africa.

In most cases Msgr Escrivá sent out his modern apostles as our Lord had sent his, without money or material possessions. He gave them a crucifix, an image of our Lady, and his blessing. He always followed their development closely, and while giving them full responsibility and the freedom to take whatever apostolic initiatives they deemed necessary, he supported them unfailingly with encouragement, advice and prayers. Sometimes he took the initiative in sending people to start in new countries; at other times he responded to invitations from bishops around the world to set up the activities of the Work in their dioceses.

The year after starting in Africa, he began sending his sons and daughters to Japan. They set up language schools and have since brought many converts to Christianity. By the beginning of the 1960s Opus Dei had taken root in almost every country in Western Europe and North and South America. In 1963 it began in Australia and in 1964 in the Philippines.

Msgr Escrivá was able to pass on his breadth of vision to his spiritual sons and daughters, so that they shared his concern to improve the conditions of life in the countries they went to. Like him they were not deterred by the fact that they often had to start off in a very small way. What was of supreme importance was their relationship with God through their prayer and daily work. Then, before any project was set in motion, came their personal apostolate, done through work and based on friendship and good example. With Msgr Escrivá's encouragement and guidance, they brought a Christian viewpoint to bear on problems of poverty, unemployment and lack of education which they came across. In due course, and with the help of many other people, they set up all sorts of social and educational projects, which although very different from one another, all focussed on enabling people to realize that all Christians as such are called by God to holiness through the faithful fulfilment of daily duties and responsibilities in their working lives.

As fruit of the personal apostolate of these men and women, a great variety of apostolic initiatives blossomed in different parts of the world: farm schools, medical dispensaries, youth clubs, technical schools, student residences, etc. These works were started with the idea of giving a response and a solution to specific needs and problems. They are, moreover eloquent testimony to the creative originality of Christians who respond fully to the demands of their vocation in the middle of the world.

Fr Josemaría always pointed out that these tasks – started and run by his sons and daughters in Opus Dei with the help of many others who share their desire to work for Christ and the good of mankind – were of limitless potential. He encouraged them to bring the light of Christ to all these human undertakings, putting into practice the same evangelizing spirit of the first Christians.

CATECHETICAL JOURNEYS

Msgr Escrivá took a keen interest in the progress of the Second Vatican Council. Among the many teachings of the Council which gave him special joy was the doctrine of the universal call to holiness, which confirmed in solemn fashion some fundamental aspects of his preaching and apostolate since 1928.[48] He was also very grateful for the Council's texts on the responsibility of the laity in the Church's mission to bring the values of the gospel into all secular activity.[49]

However, in the years after Vatican II when a number of doctrinal errors grew up in the Church provoked by an appeal to a spurious 'spirit of the Council', Pope Paul VI frequently felt the need to alert the pastors of the church to these errors and misrepresentations of Church teaching. In an address to the College of Cardinals on 23 June 1972, the Pope energetically denounced 'a false and abusive interpretation of the Council, which would wish for a rupture with tradition, to the point of rejecting the pre-conciliar

48 Cf. *Lumen gentium*, 31. **49** Cf. Vatican II Decree on the Lay Apostolate, *Apostolicam actuositatem*.

church and of adopting a libertine approach of conceiving a "new" church, almost "reinvented" from the inside, in its constitution, dogma, customs, and law'. A few days later, in his address for the feast of Sts Peter and Paul, the Pope said he sensed that 'the smoke of Satan had entered through some fissure into the temple of God.' St Josemaría felt very much united to the sentiments and prayer of the Pope, and suffered deeply at the thought of the damage which was being done to souls as a consequence of the doctrinal confusion. He had recourse to prayer and mortification as a way of making atonement to God and encouraged his spiritual sons and daughters to do the same. He consecrated Opus Dei to the Holy Spirit, asking the Paraclete to enlighten the Church. Without losing his optimism and trusting in the life-giving action of the Spirit, he took the measures necessary to ensure that Opus Dei remained faithful to the authentic teaching of Vatican II.

He also undertook a succession of pilgrimages to Marian shrines, asking the Mother of God to bring to a swift end the time of trial of the Church. His increasing petition for the Church led him in 1970 to pray at the feet of our Lady of Guadalupe in Mexico, accompanied spiritually by all his daughters and sons. On the fifth day of his novena to our Lady he addresses her as follows:

> O Lady, all I can offer you now – I have nothing else – are thorns, the thorns embedded in my heart; but I am sure that through you they will turn into roses ... Grant that in us, in our hearts, roses may blossom all through the year, little roses, the roses of daily life, ordinary roses but filled with the perfume of sacrifice and love. I deliberately say little roses, because they are what suit me best, because all through my life I have only dealt with ordinary, everyday things, and even then I often haven't been able to finish them; but I am sure that it is in this ordinary, daily activity, that your Son and you await me.

During his years in Rome from 1947, Fr Josemaría dedicated himself to the governance of Opus Dei worldwide and to promoting its apostolic work. He made a number of pastoral trips to different centres of Opus Dei in European countries, meeting with the members in small groups, encouraging them and sharing with them his immense human warmth and apostolic zeal.

In Mexico, however, he began to meet with larger crowds, carrying out a deep work of catechesis. His words moved his listeners to conversion, to improving their spiritual life, to decisions about following Christ. During the period 15 May to 23 June all kinds of people came to listen to him: mothers of families, craftsmen, professional men of the city, farm workers, etc. People would ask him questions about any aspect of the Christian faith or moral life, and he would reply with a great naturalness and spontaneity. He had the gift of being able to speak the language of the questioner such that he was always able to adapt his response to the personal needs of his listeners.

Two years later, inspired by the same apostolic desire, he carried out a long catechetical journey all over Spain and Portugal in October and November of 1972. During this trip he met tens of thousands of people in very large gatherings. He spoke about the Christian vocation, receiving the sacraments, sanctifying work, the meaning of marriage and family life, and the responsibility of Catholics to spread the faith and help one another to be loyal to it. He spoke out passionately in defence of the Church, and was not afraid to talk about sacrifice and the Cross. And always an insistent recommendation: he encouraged, almost begged people to go to the sacrament of confession, because, as he pointed out, without confession there can be no reconciliation with God, and if we are not reconciled with God it is pointless to speak of Christian living or real holiness.

In May 1974 he began a catechetical trip to South America where he visited Brazil, Argentina, Chile, Peru, Ecuador and Venezuela. Here he had the joy of meeting many of his sons and daughters for the first time, and to see for himself the fruitfulness of the apostolate of Opus Dei after twenty-five years of dedicated work.

A subject he never tired of speaking about was sincerity. He encouraged people to be, first of all, sincere with themselves in their personal examination of conscience, to acknowledge what they had done wrong and why. He emphasized the importance of being sincere in their relationship with God, so as to make prayer a genuine conversation with our Lord. He asked people to be very sincere in the sacrament of penance and spiritual guidance, to speak clearly and not allow themselves to be inhibited by human respect. Thus he would say that sincerity is the only solid basis for a real relationship with other people. In focussing on this point he was revealing his own approach to God and advising others to do what he found invaluable himself. His frankness and directness was one of the very attractive aspects of his personality.

Although these gatherings were attended by crowds of several thousand, his warm personality and, still more, his obvious love for God and for them as individuals, made everyone feel as if it was just a friendly, personal conversation. In the questions and answers which were exchanged, people could feel his constant good humour. His cheerfulness was one of the most noticeable characteristics of his personality and it had a contagious quality. In answer to a specific question, deep theological comments were spliced with simplicity and good humour. Because of the spirit of intimacy which was the hallmark of these gatherings, everybody felt drawn into the dialogue. His final catechetical journey was to Venezuela and Guatemala, in February 1975.

WRITINGS

In keeping with his name 'Escrivá', Fr Josemaría was a prolific writer. His published work includes *The Way* in 1939 (printed in 42 languages, totalling four and a half million copies), *Holy Rosary* in 1934, now published in 25 languages with a total of one million copies printed. He also published three books of homilies: *Christ is passing by* (1973), and *Friends of God* (1977). Posthumous works include *The Way of the Cross*, *Furrow*, *The Forge*, and *In Love with the Church*.

As early as 1930 he started to write foundational documents about the spirit and the nature of Opus Dei and its apostolates. He continued to write in this vein all through his life. A critical edition of these documents will be published in due course. The first volume (*The Way*) of this critical edition of all his works has been published and others are being worked on. His style is direct and stimulating. This is especially the case with *The Way*, *Furrow*, *The Forge*. These books are the fruit of St Josemaría's interior life and his experience with souls. They were written with the intention of encouraging personal prayer and making it easier. This is why in structure they are made up of short points of four or five lines, gathered together under headings that relate to different aspects of the Christian life – generosity, daring, sincerity, suffering, fishers of men, humility, prayer, work, truthfulness, purity, beyond death, etc.

St Josemaría's teaching brings together the divine and the human aspect of Christian holiness as exemplified in the Incarnate Word. In his writings he has given us a rich presentation of the life and work of the Christian in the middle of the world. Although *Furrow* and *The Forge* were published posthumously, they were begun in the 1930s. They come from notes written by the founder of Opus Dei in journals which he kept. In these personal jottings he recorded incidents that showed the action of God in his soul, so that he could meditate on them in his personal prayer. He also recorded events and anecdotes from everyday life from which he always tried to draw some supernatural lesson.

LAST MONTHS

During the last months of his life he could see very little with his right eye, due to a cataract which had been forming over the years. Then another cataract began to affect his left eye. He took these upsets so much in his stride that only those who worked closely with him everyday noticed his loss of vision. It was also during this time, perhaps with an inkling of his approaching death, he would say as he did on 19 March 1975: 'I'm no longer needed. I'll be able to help you better from heaven'. Together with this feeling there was growing in his heart a yearning 'to see the face of Christ'.

On 28 March he celebrated the golden jubilee of his ordination to the priesthood. It fell on Good Friday and he spent the day in recollection and prayer. On the eve of the anniversary he did his meditation out loud, opening his heart to God and to those sons who accompanied him in the oratory:

> Fifty years have passed, he prayed, and I am still like a babbling child. I am just beginning, beginning again, as I do each day in my interior life. And it will be so until the end of my days ... A glance backwards ... What an immense panorama, so many sorrows, so many joys. But now all is joy, all joy ... because experience teaches us that sorrow is the chiselling of the divine artist, who is eager to make each one of us, of this shapeless mass that we are, a crucifix, a Christ, that *alter Christus* each one of us is called to be.
>
> *Gratias tibi, Deus, gratias tibi!* The life of each one of us ought to be a hymn of thanksgiving: just look how Opus Dei has come about. You, Lord, have done it all, with a handful of good-for-nothings ... *Stulta mundi, infirma mundi, et ea quae non sunt.* Saint Paul's teaching has been fulfilled to the letter. You have laid hold of instruments who were utterly inadequate and in no way suitable, and you have spread the Work all over the world. People are thanking you all over Europe, and in places in Asia and Africa, and in the whole of America, and in Australia. Everywhere they are giving you thanks.[50]

At the beginning of May 1975 Fr Josemaría made his last trip, a visit to the Marian shrine of Torreciudad, about 13 miles from this home town of Barbastro in the north of Spain. In thanksgiving for his cure as a two-year-old child through the intercession of our Lady of Torreciudad, he had encouraged the erection of a shrine in her honour. He had followed the project closely from the design stage right through to its completion. He indicated that there would be forty confessionals there as he foresaw that the principal miracles that would occur there would be spiritual ones of conversion and renewed commitment to the Christian life. Now he could contemplate the magnificent reredos, a large altar sculpture with scenes from the life of the Blessed Virgin, and in the centre of it the tabernacle and the ancient, venerated image of our Lady which dates from the eleventh century.

On 26 June 1975, in the morning, he visited his daughters in the Roman College of our Lady in Castelgandolfo, near Rome. He said to them:

> I will tell you as I do whenever I come here that you, by the simple fact of being Christians, have priestly souls. Your brothers who are laymen

50 Cf. www.josemariaescriva.info/index; Founder of Opus Dei # I seek your face

> also have priestly souls. With your priestly soul and with God's grace, you can and you should help the priestly ministry which we priests carry out. Together, we shall work effectively.

After twenty minutes he began to feel unwell and the visit had to be brought to an end. After a brief rest he returned to Rome. When he arrived at Villa Tevere he greeted our Lord in the tabernacle and continued on to his office. As he entered he collapsed and died of a heart attack.

In the afternoon his body was laid out in the oratory of our Lady of Peace. From that time, right through the night, priests of the Work said Requiem Masses for Msgr Escrivá until the time of the burial Mass on the evening of 27 June. His remains were laid to rest in the crypt underneath the oratory of our Lady of Peace.

From the very first day people started to come to pray beside his tomb, asking for favours through his intercession, especially spiritual favours. Those who got to know Msgr Escrivá realized that he was a man of great holiness, something which everyone who met him as early as the 1930s became convinced of. This opinion was based not only on the man himself, but also on the fruit of his works: the lives of the members of Opus Dei bore eloquent witness to the holiness of their spiritual father. Pope Pius XII told an Australian bishop that he considered Fr Escrivá 'a true saint, a man sent by God for his time.' To Pope Paul VI he seemed 'a man who had been given more graces than others, but who had also given himself up to them with extraordinary devotion.'

One of the earliest testimonies comes from the bishop of Madrid who was familiar with every stage of the development of Opus Dei and one of Fr Josemaría's strongest supporters:

> Father Josemaría – and please don't let this reach his ears – is a good man, a real saint ... But above all, he is a holy man. We are accustomed to venerating the saints only when they are raised to the altars, and tend to forget that they are people who walked the earth, just as we do. Father Josemaría Escrivá – have no doubt about it – is a saint whom we are going to see canonized on the altars.[51]

In 1981 the process of beatification of Msgr Escrivá was introduced, and concluded with his beatification on 17 May 1992 by Pope John Paul II, on the basis of a miraculous cure in 1976 of a rare disease, lipomatosis, suffered by Sr Concepción Boullón Rubio, whose family had prayed to Fr Josemaría to intercede for her cure. A crowd of about 250,000 people, from all parts of the

51 Vázquez de Prada, p. 367.

world, thronged St Peter's Square for the ceremony. Pope John Paul II in his homily said:

> The spiritual and apostolic life of the new *Beatus* was based on knowing himself, through faith, to be a son of God in Christ. This faith nourished his love for the Lord, his evangelizing drive, his constant joy, even in the great trials and difficulties he had to overcome. 'To carry the cross is to find happiness and joy', he said in one of his Meditations, 'to carry the cross is to identify oneself with Christ, to be Christ, and therefore to be a son of God.'

After the beatification the body of St Josemaría was transferred from the crypt of the oratory of our Lady of Peace and placed under the main altar.

Subsequent to 1992, the prelature, with the prayerful intercession of Blessed Josemaría, began apostolic work in India, Israel, Lithuania, Estonia, Slovakia, Lebanon, Uganda, Kazakhstan, Croatia, Slovenia, and most recently in Russia.

In the meantime, a constant stream of reports of favours, obtained through the intercession of Blessed Josemaría, continued to reach the postulator's office in Rome. Among these was the report of the cure of Dr Nevado's cancerous radiodermatitis. As we have already noted, this was the miracle cure which paved the way for the canonization of Blessed Josemaría on 6 October 2002. On the occasion of the canonization, the then Cardinal Ratzinger commented in the *Osservatore Romano:*

> I have always been impressed by Josemaría Escrivá's explanation of the name 'Opus Dei': an explanation which we might call biographical and which gives us an idea of the founder's spiritual profile. Escrivá knew he had to found something, but he was also conscious that what he was founding was not his own work, that he himself did not invent anything and that the Lord was merely making use of him. So it was not his work, but Opus Dei (God's Work).
>
> All this helps us understand why Josemaría Escrivá did not claim to be the 'founder' of anything, but only someone who wanted to do God's will and second his action, his work, precisely, God's … This is how the name and the whole reality that we call Opus Dei is profoundly linked with the interior life of the founder who, while remaining very discreet on this point, gives us to understand that he was in permanent dialogue, a real contact with the One who created us and works for us and with us.[52]

52 Cardinal Joseph Ratzinger, *Osservatore Romano*, 9 October 2002.

In his canonization homily, Pope John Paul II described St Josemaría as a:

> master in the practice of prayer, which he considered to be an extraordinary weapon, to redeem the world … It is not a paradox but a perennial truth: the fruitfulness of the apostolate lies above all in prayer and in intense and constant sacramental life. This, in essence, is the secret of the holiness and the true success of the saints.[53]

In 2005 a large statue of St Josemaría was placed in one of the niches in the exterior wall of St Peter's basilica and blessed by Benedict XVI.

53 John Paul II, Homily, 6 October 2002.

CHAPTER TEN

Pope John Paul II

(1920–2005)

IT WAS EASTER WEEK 2005; Pope John Paul II lay dying in Rome. The news media of the world were focused on the Eternal City and relayed the latest medical bulletins, interspersed with commentary on different incidents from the Pope's long life. There were flashbacks to the halcyon days of his youth when he enjoyed skiing on the slopes of the Tatras mountains in Poland, and subsequently in the Dolomites after his election as Pope. However, the vigour of that youth began to decline in his later years due to a series of illnesses.[1]

In 1994 he was diagnosed with Parkinson's disease which at first caused a tremor in his left hand and arm. But as the years went on the disease was to take its toll, causing the muscles of his face to become rigid. He was finding it more and more difficult to articulate his words, the voice became slurred, his shoulders stooped. Yet he continued to push himself at a gruelling pace, whether it was the pastoral visits to the farthest corners of the world, the demanding celebrations of the Great Jubilee Year 2000, or his phenomenal literary output in encyclicals, apostolic letters, and other documents.

John Paul II appeared at the window of his study in the papal apartments on Sunday 10 January 2005 to release two symbolic doves. He spoke a few words to the pilgrims but was clearly a sick man. His schedule for the next day was cancelled due to flu. Over the next few days his breathing deteriorated, and he was admitted to the Gemelli hospital. On 11 February the Holy Father returned to the papal apartments, and sent out his World Day of the Sick message. However, the breathing difficulties continued and he was again taken to the Gemelli hospital on 24 February for a tracheotomy to ease his difficulties. He returned to the Vatican again on the evening of 13 March. For the first time in his twenty-six years papacy, John Paul II had to delegate the Holy Week ceremonies to some of the Curia cardinals. His Palm Sunday (20 March) message recalled the first World Youth Day held exactly twenty years before (1985), and he asked the youth of the world to gather in Cologne in August.

1 For a number of the details in this section I am indebted to George Weigel, *God's choice: Pope Benedict XVI and the future of the Catholic Church* (New York, 2005), pp 3–20.

On Easter Sunday he appeared briefly at the window of the papal apartments to bless the faithful, but was unable to speak.

On Wednesday of Easter Week (30 March), the medical bulletin said the Holy Father was running a high temperature. On Friday 1 April the news about the Pope's health was more serious. The press briefing described John Paul II's condition as very grave. He was still fully conscious, and asked that the Stations of the Cross be read to him. On TV, reports from around the world showed that a spontaneous prayer vigil had begun, with the thoughts and affections of the people focused on the man who was suffering his death agony in the papal apartments in Rome. These were days when the unity of the Church was palpable, as people felt intimately united to the Holy Father who was now going to meet his reward. They prayed that he would be released from his sufferings, but had no doubt that his great and generous soul would go directly to heaven. As his strength failed, he still had a message for the young people who had gathered below in St Peter's Square: 'I have sought you out. Now, you have come to me. I thank you.'

The Pope went into a coma at about 5.00 p.m. At 8.00 p.m. Archbishop Stanislaw Dziwisz, the Pope's personal secretary for nearly forty years, celebrated the vigil Mass for the Octave of Easter on an altar erected at the foot of the Holy Father's deathbed. John Paul II died shortly after the Mass had ended. The world had to come to terms with the death of the man who had been its most powerful moral leader for a quarter of a century. People had experienced in him consistency in moral values, the courageous defence of human life at all stages from conception to natural death, passionate preaching of the message of Jesus Christ, and an apostolic zeal which literally brought him to the ends of the earth.[2] Karol Wojtyla came to the papacy as a complete outsider. He was the first Slav Pope and the first non-Italian elected to the see

2 Commenting on some of the biographical efforts which had appeared about him up to the mid 1990s, John Paul II said, 'they try to understand me from the outside. But I can only be understood from the inside' (George Weigel, *Witness to hope: the biography of Pope John Paul II* [London, 2001] p. 7). There have been several biographies of John Paul II, but all of them have failed because they were unable to grasp the point that the true achievement of Karol Wojtyla is comprehensible only in the light of the spiritual and apostolic dynamic which animated his life. In everything he did, John Paul II was first and foremost a disciple of Jesus Christ. It is too early yet to give a definitive judgement on his place in history, but the range of his achievements, the scope of his writings, and the effects of his pastoral journeys, have already resulted in calls for him to be known as John Paul the Great, a title which has been bestowed on only two other Popes in the history of the Church.

George Weigel, in *Witness to hope*, has given us a masterly presentation of the life of John Paul II, and he succeeds in his efforts because he writes about Karol Wojtyla 'from the inside'. He was privileged to have many hours of personal conversation with the Pope, which enabled him to evaluate accurately the Holy Father's thinking and motivation in relation to many aspects of his life. In this study, although I draw freely from John Paul II's many published writings, it will also be clear that I rely on Weigel's interpretation of some of the events in the life of Karol Wojtyla.

of Peter for 450 years. He had extensive pastoral experience gained in the teeth of communist repression, and a richness of personal qualities and pastoral achievement which was without parallel in the Church.

YOUTH

Karol Wojtyla was born on 18 May 1920 in Wadowice, a small town about nineteen miles from the city of Krakow. His older brother Edmond, born in 1906, graduated in medicine in Krakow in 1930. Emilia, Karol's mother, gave birth to a daughter, Olga, some years after Edmond, but she died in infancy. In 1926 Karol began elementary school. From early on it was clear that he was a brilliant student. When he was nine his mother died in 1929 of heart and kidney failure. Karol's father, an uncommissioned army officer, passed on to his son a deep understanding of the Church and its message of interior conversion and promise of eternal life. John Paul II wrote with gratitude about his father:

> Day after day I was able to observe the austere way in which he lived. By profession he was a soldier and, after my mother's death, his life became one of constant prayer. Sometimes I would wake up during the night and find my father on his knees, just as I would always see him kneeling in the parish church ... *His example was in a way my first seminary*, a kind of domestic seminary.[3]

In 1930 he attended the state secondary school. Beforehand he often went to early morning Mass with his father at 7.00 a.m. He made good friends among his school colleagues and his teachers, and also with his confessor. This latter, when he was transferred to Krakow, invited Karol as a teenager to the cathedral to attend the Holy Week ceremonies there. John Paul II would later write how these ceremonies left a 'profound impression' on him as a young schoolboy.[4]

Karol was an avid sportsman, with particular interest in football and skiing, the latter in which he excelled. At school Latin and Greek were part of the curriculum, as well as Polish language and literature, history, and mathematics. Karol developed an interest in and love for the Latin language which was to last him all his life. When the archbishop of Krakow visited the school, it was Karol who was chosen to deliver the welcoming address in Latin. In his final years at school he had become absorbed in Polish literature and the theatre, so it was only logical that when he went to the university in Krakow he would pursue a career in the humanities.

3 John Paul II, *Gift and mystery: on the fiftieth anniversary of my priestly ordination* (London, 1996), p. 20 (italics in original). 4 Cf. *Gift and mystery*, p. 25.

In summer 1938 Wojtyla graduated from the secondary school and planned to begin his studies at the Jagellionan university in Krakow in October. His father went to Krakow with him and they lived in the basement flat of a house belonging to his mother's family. He became immersed in the study of the Polish language and took a leading part in the university theatre society. During the summer of 1939 storm clouds gathered on the horizon. The threat of a German attack became more and more likely. On 1 September German planes started to bomb Krakow. For the next six years Karol Wojtyla was to experience violence, cruelty, extreme poverty, and the death of colleagues and friends. There was the incessant bloodshed, the systematic execution of university staff, the banishment of Jews to the liquidation camps of Auschwitz and those further west. The Germans were working to a plan to destroy Polish culture and eventually to destroy the Polish nation. Priests and nuns were a prime target of Nazi brutality.

At the outbreak of the war Karol and his father fled eastwards with thousands of Poles, many of them Jews. When they reached the river San about 120 miles from Krakow, they learned that Russia had invaded Poland from the east. Since they knew they faced summary execution from the Russians, they decided to return to Krakow and take their chances under the Germans. It was important to have a job in Krakow, otherwise there was the danger of being shipped off as slave labour to work camps in Germany. Hence Karol got himself a work card and managed to get a job as a store man, which allowed him to spend time reading and studying French. In 1940 he got a job with the Solvay quarry, at first shovelling limestone into railway cars and then with the dynamiting crew. After his first year in the quarry, he was transferred to the Solvay chemical plant in another suburb of Krakow, where he worked in the plant's purification unit. Here he had good opportunities to read, and the other workers facilitated this. During these four years Karol Wojtyla learned much about work and workers. Years later he would incorporate the fruits of this experience in one of his first encyclicals, *Laborem exercens*, published in 1981.[5]

John Paul II remembers his time at the Solvay quarry (1940–1) and the Solvay chemical plant (1941–5), and describes it as a 'true seminary'.[6]

> No doubt I owe much to one single year at Poland's most ancient university, but I am not afraid to say that the following four years, in a working-class environment, were for me a blessing sent by Providence. The experience that I acquired in that period of my life was priceless. I

5 John Paul II, Encyclical Letter, *Laborem exercens* (On human work), 14 September 1981. 6 *Gift and mystery*, p. 21.

> have often said that I considered it possibly more valuable than a doctorate, which does not mean that I have a poor opinion of university degrees.[7]

He says that it was only later he realized how important his contact with the world of work was for his pastoral work. He came to know these men who were doing heavy work; their families, their interests, their human worth, and their dignity. He experienced many kindnesses from them. They knew he was a student and it did not bother them that he brought books to work. They would say: 'We'll keep watch: you go ahead and read.'[8] He made friends with the workers. Sometimes they invited him to their homes. Later as priest and bishop he baptized their children and grandchildren, blessed their marriages and officiated at many of their funerals. These contacts remained close, some of them even after his election as bishop of Rome through correspondence.

DEVOTION TO OUR LADY

It was during this period of physical work that Wojtyla met Jan Tyranowski, a man of deep interior life who was the leader of the 'Living Rosary' apostolate. Tyranowski, a tailor, was the man who inspired Karol and the other young men he had gathered around him by his example and obvious sanctity. He gave Karol responsibility for the spiritual tutoring of fifteen young men and introduced him to the writings of St John of the Cross, the sixteenth-century Spanish mystic and reformer of the Carmelite order. He also introduced him to Louis Marie Grignon de Montfort's *Treatise on the true devotion to our Lady*, which gave his devotion to Mary a rich theological framework.

During the time he was working in the Solvay chemical plant, he had decided to distance himself from his childhood Marian devotions in order to focus more on Christ. However, he came to understand, through a reading of de Montfort's book, that true devotion to the Mother of God is Christocentric, and is profoundly rooted in the mystery of the Blessed Trinity, and the mysteries of the Incarnation and Redemption. And so he rediscovered Marian piety with a deeper understanding. This mature form of Marian piety found expression in the encyclicals *Redemptoris Mater*,[9] and *Mulieris dignitatem*.[10] John Paul II makes the point that such devotion not only addresses a need of the heart, but that it also corresponds to the objective truth about the Mother of God. His Marian

7 *'Be not afraid!', André Frossard in conversation with Pope John Paul II* (London, 1984), p. 15. 8 *Gift and mystery*, p. 22. 9 John Paul II, Encyclical Letter, *Redemptoris Mater* (Mother of the Redeemer), 25 March 1987. 10 John Paul II, Apostolic Letter, *Mulieris dignitatem* (The dignity of women), 15 August 1988.

devotion was tied to practices of piety he developed in his youth – praying before the image of our Lady of Perpetual Help in the parish church of Wadowice, his use of the scapular of our Lady of Mount Carmel, and his visits to the shrine of our Lady of Kalwaria near Wadowice. Another chapter in his life was Jasna Gora with its icon of the Black Madonna.[11] It was as a result of these different Marian influences that his motto *Totus Tuus* (I am totally yours) crystallized. These Marian devotions were fundamental in leading him to the priesthood, and were a continuous guide for him for the rest of his life.[12]

VOCATION TO THE PRIESTHOOD

Paradoxically, while working in the Solvay chemical plant, and precisely as a protest against the Nazi banning of all cultural events, Karol became more intensely involved in clandestine theatre activities. He met with fellow students from the university to read Polish classical texts and to rehearse for productions. It is from this time too that we can date Karol's first efforts at play writing. It was also from this period that he learned his skills at articulation, his sense of timing, and his ability to connect with audiences, skills which he used very effectively with vast audiences after he was elected Pope.

Karol's father became bedridden at Christmas 1940 and died alone a few months later while Karol was at work in the Solvay quarry. He grieved for his father and every day would pray for him at his grave as he returned from work. At the same time, the horror of war was all around him in Krakow. Arrests, brutal deaths, and executions were everyday affairs. Jews were being rounded up and sent to the extermination camps. This experience of the war had an effect on his vocation. In the face of the spread of evil and the atrocities of the war, the meaning of the priesthood and its mission in the world became much clearer to him. The death of his father, the last remaining member of his immediate family,[13] brought about a progressive detachment in his life, all of which brought him to a clear realization that God wanted him to be a priest, a new light that brought him a great inner peace.

> My priestly vocation took shape in the midst of all that, like an inner fact of unquestionable and absolute clarity. The following year (1942), in the autumn, I knew that I was called. I could see clearly what I had to give up and the goal that I had to attain, 'without a backward glance'. I would be a priest.[14]

11 John Paul II, *Crossing the threshold of hope* (London, 1994), pp 212–14. **12** Cf. *Gift and mystery*, pp 28–30. **13** His brother Edmond (a medical doctor) died in 1932, having contracted typhus from one of his patients. **14** Frossard, p. 15.

He was always convinced that the grace of his vocation owed much to the great sacrifices of Polish priests in the Dachau concentration camp during the war years.

In autumn 1942 he went to the archbishop's residence and asked to be admitted as a candidate for the priesthood. He joined what was then a clandestine seminary at great risk to his life. On one occasion five seminarians were arrested – some of these were immediately executed and the others dispatched to Auschwitz. Karol continued his work in the chemical plant, he studied in his free time and presented himself to the professors for examinations at appropriate intervals. He also found time to study during the night shift at the chemical plant. It was here that he encountered the metaphysics of St Thomas Aquinas. Initially he found it a mind-blowing exercise, but later he would say that Thomistic metaphysics became the foundation of his philosophical thinking for the future. There were, he said, two stages in his intellectual journey. 'In the first place I moved from literature to metaphysics, while the second led me from metaphysics to phenomenology.'[15]

In 1944, as he was walking home from the chemical plant, he was knocked down by a Nazi truck and left unconscious. He was brought to a local hospital and woke up with his head wrapped in bandages and a broken shoulder in a plaster cast. He spent the next two weeks in hospital recovering from concussion.

After the Warsaw uprising in August 1944, the Gestapo carried out a sweep of Krakow, rounding up young men to forestall a similar exercise there. Karol had a close call, and he and all the clandestine seminarians were called by Archbishop Sapieha to stay in his residence so that they could live with a greater sense of security. In this way Karol got to know Archbishop Sapieha who was a bishop of aristocratic background, known as the 'Prince Archbishop'. He was a man of great natural authority and was effectively the moral leader of Poland during the war years. He did everything he could to protect his priests from being sent to concentration camps. He ordered baptismal certificates to be issued to Jews to save them from execution. He was the unshakeable foundation of Catholic resistance to the Nazi occupation. In the seminary Karol was able to observe the archbishop at close quarters and became deeply impressed by the human and spiritual calibre of the man. He would become Karol's model of what a good priest and bishop should be. As John Paul II wrote about him:

> A powerful influence on our whole period of formation for the priesthood was exercised by the towering figure of the Prince Metropolitan, the future Cardinal Adam Stefan Sapieha, whom I remember with

15 John Paul II, *Rise, let us be on our way* (London, 2004), p. 95.

> affection and gratitude. His influence on us was increased by the fact that, during the period of transition before the reopening the seminary, we lived in his residence and met him every day. The Metropolitan of Krakow was made a Cardinal immediately after the end of the War, when he was quite old. All the people welcomed this appointment as a worthy acknowledgement of the merits of a great man who throughout the German occupation had succeeded in holding high the honour of the nation, clearly displaying his own dignity before all.[16]

The Germans pulled out of Krakow in January 1945 as the Russians started to drive in from the east. Meanwhile life started to return to some semblance of normality in the Krakow seminary, and Karol completed his third year of theology at the Jagiellonian university as the war wound down in the west. However, what the seminarians did not know was that Poland was about to be subjected to a new totalitarianism as a result of the post-war share-out of Germany and eastern Europe by the victor nations.

Karol began his fourth year of theology in the fall of 1945. His intellectual brilliance did not go undetected by his teachers. They also noticed that he wrote a short aspiration such as 'To Jesus through Mary', 'Jesus, Mary, and Joseph', at the top of every page of each paper he submitted. This was a habit which he had formed some years before and which he would continue right through his writing life. One of the principal elements in the piety which Karol learned in the seminary, was the need for total self-giving to follow Christ closely. This was inculcated in the communal recitation of the 'Litany of our Lord Jesus Christ, Priest and Victim', based on ideas from the Letter to the Hebrews. This was a devotion which left a deep impression on John Paul II:

> The truth about Christ's priesthood has always struck me in an extraordinary eloquent way in the Litany which used to be recited in the seminary in Krakow, especially on the eve of priestly ordination ...What profound reflections it prompted! ... the invocations of the Litany call to mind the many aspects of this mystery [the sacrifice of the Cross]. They come back to me with all the rich symbolism of the biblical images with which they are interwoven. When I repeat them it is in Latin, the language in which I recited them in the seminary and then so often in later years.[17]

Towards the end of June 1946 Karol successfully passed his fourth year theology exams. On 1 November Cardinal Sapieha ordained him priest; he said his first

16 *Gift and mystery*, pp 17–18. **17** Ibid., pp 79–80.

Mass the following day in the crypt of Wawel cathedral in Krakow. He chose this location in order to express his spiritual bonds with the history of Poland, with those buried in the cathedral – kings, queens, cardinals, bishops, poets.[18]

DOCTORATE IN ROME

Immediately afterwards the archbishop sent him to Rome to study for a doctorate in theology at the Angelicum university. He came to Rome with a desire to get to know the Eternal City beginning with the catacombs. During his two years there he systematically explored the city under the guidance of those who knew its monuments and history. His priesthood and his theological and pastoral formation were part of his Roman experience from the beginning. During his two years there he made every effort to get to know Rome, and acquired a profound conviction of the universality of the Church and the essential role of the Vicar of Christ in its government. Here too he learned how much the priesthood is linked to the apostolate of the laity.[19]

During the summer of 1947 he visited the Netherlands and Belgium where he gave a month long mission to Polish Catholic miners near Charleroi. On the way back to Rome in October 1947 he stopped off at Ars. His visit to the church where St John Mary Vianney heard confessions for more than ten hours a day, taught catechism, and gave his homilies, was a very moving experience for the young Fr Wojtyla, who had read Francis Trochu's biography of Vianney and been profoundly impressed by it.[20] He was particularly moved by the Curé's apostolate of the confessional, which, he says, 'was able to inspire a kind of spiritual revolution in France, and not only there. Against a background of attacks on the Church and the clergy, his witness' Wojtyla affirms, 'was truly remarkable'.[21] This lead him to the conviction 'that a priest fulfils an essential part of his mission' by voluntarily 'making himself a prisoner of the confessional'. He always tried to maintain this link with the confessional all during his life, 'even in Rome, if only symbolically, when every year on Good Friday I sit in the confessional in St Peter's basilica'.[22]

Back in Rome Karol began work on his doctoral thesis under Fr Reginald Garrigou-Lagrange OP, which explored the act of faith in the writings of St John of the Cross. His defence of his dissertation in June 1948 received the highest possible marks. However, since he could not afford to pay for the printing of his thesis (a precondition for granting his degree), on his return to Poland he resubmitted his dissertation to the Faculty of Theology of the Jagiellonian university in Krakow which, after appropriate review, conferred

18 Ibid., p. 47. **19** Ibid., pp 53–4. **20** Cf. Frossard, p. 20. **21** *Gift and mystery*, pp 57–8. **22** Ibid., p. 58.

on him the degree of Doctor of Theology in December 1948. His two years in Rome gave him a more profound vision of the Church. He returned from Rome to Krakow 'with a sense of the universality of the priestly mission which found authoritative expression at the Second Vatican Council', and with a conviction that 'every priest must be personally concerned for the whole Church and in some way feel responsible for the whole Church.'[23]

BACK TO KRAKOW

Karol arrived back to a country in the grip of an atheistic communist regime. The communists not only dominated the economic and political life of Poland, but were intent on the destruction of Polish Catholicism and all that that meant for the cultural life of the country. Immediately after the war there were massive movements of population from eastern to western Poland, and then another two million Poles returned from the German forced labour camps. This was the world to which Fr Wojtyla returned.

Stefan Wyszynski, an underground chaplain during the war, was appointed as archbishop of Warsaw in November 1948 after spending two years as bishop of Lublin. As primate he would courageously lead the Polish Church over the next thirty years.

On his return from Rome, Fr Wojtyla was appointed curate in the village of Niegowic, about fifteen miles east of Krakow. His main pastoral responsibility was teaching catechism to young children in the five elementary schools in the parish. He also spent a lot of time in the confessional. That he was a man of big ideas soon became clear. The golden jubilee of the parish priest's ordination was approaching and people were suggesting different things that could be done to honour the pastor, like painting the church, etc. Fr Wojtyla shocked the parishioners by saying the best present they could give the parish priest was an entirely new church, which they could raise the money for and build. They took him at his word, and the brick church remains in use to this day.[24]

In March 1949, eight months after his arrival, Fr Wojtyla was transferred to St Florian's in Krakow, a parish that contained leading members of the city's Catholic intelligentsia. It was one of the liveliest parishes in the city and was serviced by four priests. Fr Wojtyla's brief was to head up a student chaplaincy to care for the students of the Jagiellonian university, and other institutions of higher education. He worked sixteen to eighteen hours a day promoting a series of intellectual, liturgical, cultural and pastoral innovations for the students, which at the same time rebutted the efforts of the communist regime to

23 Ibid., p. 60. **24** Cf. Weigel, ibid., p. 93.

undermine Poland's culture and history.[25] To generate pastoral business he visited all the student residences and boarding houses. Students were attracted by the quality of his preaching, as were also other parishioners. Very soon he began to find his way into intellectual circles outside the confines of St Florian's and the student chaplaincy.

While in Rome Fr Wojtyla had been influenced by the liturgical renewal movement, and now he decided to implement some of these ideas. He started a choir and taught the students Gregorian chant so that they could sing various parts of the Mass. He encouraged his students to use daily missals so that they could follow the Mass more intelligently, and he initiated dialogue Masses in which the students made the responses in Latin. This was quite a bold initiative at this time.[26]

THE FAMILY

One of the main points of attack by the communists on the Christian culture of Poland was the family. They knew that if they could undermine the love and the cohesion of the traditional Polish family, they would be able to manipulate it more freely. Work schedules and school hours were massaged so that children would be separated the maximum number of hours from their parents. Apartments were built which could only accommodate small families, so that children would be regarded as a problem. To respond to the threat on family life by the authorities, Fr Wojtyla launched at St Florian's in 1950, the first marriage preparation programme ever held in the archdiocese of Krakow. He covered a programme which systematically prepared young couples for Christian marriage and family life, comprising the theological, moral, and pastoral aspects, together with the practical questions of sexual intimacy and child rearing. He helped these couples to see that the sexual drive was a good thing, a gift from God, and wasn't afraid to speak about sexual relations as a means to holiness. In preparing these programmes, Wojtyla invited doctors, nurses and others to help present relevant parts of it. In two-and-a-half years at St Florian's he officiated at 160 weddings.

The experience of guiding couples towards a truly Christian marriage was to be an important stage in Fr Wojtyla's development of a theology of the body which would reach maturity in later years. It was during these years at St Florian's that some of his deepest friendships were made, friendships that were to endure to the end of his life. Throughout his papacy, John Paul II gave particular attention to the question of marriage and the family. As we have seen, he carried out an extensive apostolate as priest preparing young couples for marriage. Much of

25 Cf. ibid., pp 93–5. **26** Cf. ibid., p. 96.

this experience is captured in his 1960 publication, *Love and responsibility*,[27] where he draws on the resources of the phenomenological method to achieve profound insights into the nature of human sexuality, love and marriage.

The concerns of *Love and responsibility* are repeatedly echoed throughout his pontificate, starting with his extensive catechesis on the nuptial meaning of the body from 1979 to 1984, through his apostolic exhortation *Familiaris consortio*,[28] his *Letter to families*,[29] his many addresses on the topic to interest groups, and, always, during his pastoral visits. He sees the family as the nucleus of the 'communion of persons', as the place where this communion can be realized naturally in its most committed way. It is here that each one is first welcomed and appreciated for what he or she truly is – a unique person, and not in view of one's social or economic function. It is love that creates this community of persons. In *Redemptor hominis* John Paul II wrote:

> Man cannot live without love. He remains a being that is incomprehensible for himself, his life is senseless, if love is not revealed to him, if he does not encounter love, if he does not experience it and make it his own, if he does not participate intimately in it. This ... is why Christ the Redeemer 'fully reveals man to himself'.[30]

He repeats this refrain in *Familiaris consortio*, insisting that it applies primarily and especially within the family.[31] This is surely one of the Holy Father's deepest and most important anthropological convictions, expressing succinctly a whole programme for family formation at both the philosophical and theological levels. For John Paul II, the future of the Church and society hinge on the stability of the family. It is not surprising, then, that he invested so much of his immense intellectual and spiritual energy in the promotion and defence of the family. For him the family was the first and most important school of life and love, and this uniquely stabilizing influence was the principal service it offered to society and the Church:

> Faced with a society that is running the risk of becoming more and more depersonalized and standardized and therefore inhuman and dehumanizing, with the negative results of many forms of escapism – such as alcoholism, drugs and even terrorism – the family possesses and continues still to release formidable energies capable of taking man out of his anonymity, keeping him conscious of his personal dignity, enrich-

27 Karol Wojtyla, *Love and responsibility* (London, 1981). **28** John Paul II, Apostolic Exhortation, *Familiaris consortia*, The Christian family in the modern world, 22 November 1981. **29** John Paul II, *Letter to families*, 2 February 1994. **30** John Paul II, Encyclical Letter, *Redemptor hominis* (The Redeemer of man, 10), 25 March 1979. **31** Cf. *Familiaris consortio*, 18.

> ing him with deep humanity and actively placing him, in his uniqueness and unrepeatability, within the fabric of society.[32]

This is a powerful statement of the indispensable role of well-adjusted families for building up a healthy and stable society, in which divine and human rights are respected.

One of the questions André Frossard put to John Paul II was about human love. He responded very clearly:

> In this domain I have received more graces than battles to fight. A day came when I knew for certain that my life would not be fulfilled in the human love the beauty of which I have always felt deeply. As a pastor, I have had to prepare many young people for marriage. My status as priest has never separated me from them; on the contrary, it has brought me closer to them and has helped me to understand them better … The fact that my path differs from theirs did not make me a stranger; quite the contrary. I read once in the works of Max Scheler that virginity and celibacy have a particular importance for a better understanding of the value of marriage, of family life, of motherhood and fatherhood. I think that this view is an extremely just and pertinent one … Christ has asked us for purity of heart according to our station in life and our vocation. He demands it squarely. But what is more, he shows us the way to values, which are only revealed to the pure vision and the pure heart. We cannot acquire this purity without renunciation, without inner struggles against our weakness; but, once acquired, this maturity of heart and mind makes up a hundred fold for the efforts which it rewards. The result is a new spontaneity of feeling, of gesture and of behaviour which facilitates relations with people, especially with children … [33]

John Paul II was at the beginning of his papal career when he said these words. He was still to carry out his extensive catechesis on the theology of the body and to produce such original documents as *Familiaris consortio*[34] and his *Letter to families*.[35]

FRIENDS AND FRIENDSHIPS

Fr Karol developed a network of friends during his time in the university chaplaincy at St Florian's. There was also a group of young adults and young mar-

32 Ibid., 43. **33** Frossard, p. 16. **34** Cf. note 28. **35** John Paul II, *Letter to families*, 2 February 1994.

ried couples with whom he did apostolate and with whom he went on vacation. The students went to his 6.00 a.m. Mass on Wednesdays, and to his Thursday night lectures. They kept coming back despite Fr Karol's dense philosophical talks, because of the authentic friendships that were developing among the group, but above all because of the attractive personality of the priest. Fr Wojtyla encouraged them to visit the blind and the sick. He gave them days of recollection. He was present for their exam and birthday celebrations. He suggested to the students that they invite others to join the group. They attended his Mass regularly. As a result of their contact with Fr Wojtyla, the students felt a deep sense of inner freedom in spite of the totalitarian atmosphere imposed by the communist system.

Fr Wojtyla preached an annual retreat to them during the fourth week of Lent. As those who had first contact with Wojtyla as students graduated and started professional work, other groups began to form around him which discussed the relationship between philosophy and the hard sciences. Romances blossomed among the members of these groups, and Fr Wojtyla would organize a day of prayer and reflection for each couple before their wedding. He officiated at all their weddings. When children began to arrive he gave a day of recollection to each expectant mother before her delivery. He baptized the babies and came to bless their homes.

Fr Wojtyla was a great lover of nature. His young friends loved skiing and kayaking and so he joined them for holidays in the mountains or on the rivers. Every summer until 1978 there was a kayaking trip which included daily Mass. Soon the children were able to join the parents on the trip and Fr Wojtyla made a point of taking each meal with a different family group each day, so that eventually he got round to all the families. In the evenings they discussed books or papal encyclicals. These young people, who had regular contact with Fr Wojtyla, commented that the most striking characteristics of this priest who was their closest friend, were his openness and his ability to listen. He was interested in all their concerns. They respected him as a priest but saw that he had a truly lay mentality unencumbered by any kind of clericalism.

He never imposed his view on others but had the ability to ask the searching question which confronted his friends with their responsibilities. Their round-the-fire get-togethers in the camp were often about literature and other intellectual topics. At other times they simply exchanged jokes or sang songs. Fr Wojtyla saw his vocation as a priest as one of 'accompaniment' of the people around him, of helping them to face the difficulties they encountered, and sharing their problems. While Fr Wojtyla's priestly personality was always present in his multiple encounters with young people, his priestly style was most manifest in the confessional. His penitents bear witness to the fact that from their point of view he was a great confessor. He would spend as much time with each one as he thought necessary. Fr Wojtyla approached confession with the understanding that it was a sacrament which sanctified all of one's life.

During these early years of his priesthood, Fr Wojtyla published a number of articles on ethics, theology and other topics. He also wrote plays and poems, not as a literary hobby, but as another way of carrying out his apostolate of accompaniment, of being present to others. One of his best-known plays, *The jeweller's shop*, is a reflection on the mystery of marriage which owed something to his pastoral work with his young married friends. It focuses on self-giving love as the foundation of the unbreakable bond of marriage.

POVERTY

Fr Wojtyla never had a bank account, nor did he ever have any personal money. Material possessions had little meaning for him. When, as John Paul II, he made his first pastoral visit to Brazil (1980), he visited, among other places, the favela Vidigal, the poorest quarter of Rio de Janeiro. The people greeted him with a specially composed samba. The Holy Father, seeing the abject poverty of the people, took the ring from his finger and gave it to the local parish priest. He had earlier denounced the chasm between the wealthy and the majority living in poverty, and affirmed, against Marxism, that only Christian social justice could achieve a just distribution of wealth. He quoted the first beatitude to his listeners and said:

> Among you … the poor are numerous. The Church in Brazil wants to be a Church of the poor. She wants to bear witness to the first Beatitude. The poor in heart are those who are most open to God and to the 'wonders of God'. Poor, for they are always ready to accept this gift from on high which comes from God himself. Poor in heart, for, conscious of having received everything from God, they live in gratitude and think that 'everything is a favour'… [The Church] wishes to draw from the Beatitudes all that concerns man, every man, the poor man and the rich man; everyone has to hear in the first Beatitude what is addressed to him personally … The Church asks those who live in abundance to avoid spiritual blindness, to resist with all their strength the temptation of the power of money. The Beatitude about the poor should constantly nag them like a permanent demand and prevent them from barricading themselves in the fortress of egoism and sated sufficiency. If you have much, remember that you must give much! That you must think how to give, how to organize social and economic life so that it tends to more equality and does not dig abysses. If you are edu-

> cated and occupy a position at the top of the social hierarchy, do not forget for one minute that the more one has, the more one must serve. Serve others. Otherwise you risk departing from the Beatitudes, especially the first. One can be rich and poor in heart, when one never ceases to make a gift of what one has and of what one is, when one never stops serving[36]

This is a powerful exposition of Christian social teaching, of the implications of the first beatitude, and of the responsibilities of those who are endowed with a generous share of this world's goods. It was a theme he would return to many times during his pontificate.

Little by little the Polish communist state put increasing pressure on the Church. The government announced in 1953 that it would in future appoint and remove bishops and parish priests. But Cardinal Wyszynski rejected this move and Gomulka, the Polish leader, climbed down. It was in the Church in Krakow, which had to struggle for survival against two totalitarian regimes, that John Paul II learned to appreciate the importance of fundamental human rights. The Polish church, he said, 'is a church which has defended man, his dignity, and his fundamental rights; it is a church which has fought courageously for the right of believers to profess the faith'.[37] He got to know Nazism marked by the horrors of war and its concentration camps, and communism with its regime of oppression and terror, as it were, from the inside. With this background he says it was easy to understand his 'deep concern for the dignity of every human person and the need to respect human rights, beginning with the right to life'.[38]

PROFESSOR AT UNIVERSITY OF LUBLIN

In September 1951 the archbishop of Krakow gave Fr Wojtyla a two-year leave of absence to do a second doctorate, the 'habilitation' thesis which would allow him to teach at the university. Initially Fr Wojtyla disagreed with the plan but eventually he accepted the idea and moved to the Old Town district of Krakow. Although he was supposed to devote himself full-time to his thesis, he found ways to keep up contact with the students and the young professionals. The title of his dissertation was 'An Evaluation of the Possibility of Constructing a Christian Ethics on the Basis of the System of Max Scheler.' Writing this thesis was an important stage in the development of Karol Wojtyla's own philosophical system. He was awarded the doctoral degree by

36 Frossard, pp 142–5. **37** *Gift and mystery*, p. 66. **38** Ibid., p. 67.

the Jagiellonian in 1954. However, the government suppressed the Jagiellonian at this time and so Wojtyla turned to the university of Lublin, the only Catholic university in Poland and the only one behind the iron curtain to survive the cold war.[39]

Wojtyla was appointed professor of ethics at Lublin university. His appointment to the faculty of Lublin was approved by the archbishop of Krakow. In 1956 he was appointed to the chair of ethics there, a position he was to occupy until 1978. While continuing his student chaplaincy work in Krakow he went to Lublin every second week during the academic year. He took the overnight train from Krakow to save time, arriving at Lublin in the morning. Wojtyla was a very popular professor, who could be approached at any time. His ability to relate philosophical theory to issues of everyday life made his classes very attractive for students. While in residence in Lublin, he devoted a lot of time to confessions and spiritual guidance.

In the late 1950s he was writing his book, *Love and responsibility*, which dealt with sexual ethics, especially in relation to married life. He used his doctoral students as a sounding board for the ideas he developed in the book. Wojtyla's extensive pastoral experience in marriage preparation and as a confessor convinced him that the Church's teaching on sexual morality needed to be presented anew. Young men and women, he felt, needed affirmation in their vocation to sexual love in marriage.[40] Love had to show respect for the person and thus avoid 'using' the other person for selfish ends, without reducing them to objects. Love is the opposite of using. The true object of a sexual act is the other *person*, not the other body. Another way Wojtyla used to express this idea is what he refers to as the 'law of the gift', whereby the sexual act is seen as an expression of total self-giving to the other person. Chastity in this context is the virtue that makes it possible to love the other as a person. Chaste love involves putting oneself in the custody of the other.[41]

Love and responsibility was first published in 1960 when Wojtyla had been a bishop for two years. In it he reaffirms the Church's teaching that the only morally appropriate means to regulate births was the responsible use of the natural cycle.

THE BATTLE FOR NOWA HUTA

In August 1958 Karol Wojtyla was summoned to Warsaw by the primate, Cardinal Wyszynski, who told him that he had been appointed auxiliary bishop of Krakow. At thirty-eight he was the youngest bishop in Poland. Even though

39 Cf. Weigel, pp 123–6. **40** Cf. ibid., p. 141. **41** Cf. ibid., pp 142–4.

he spent every second week in Lublin, his pastoral work in Krakow expanded. His student chaplaincy work at St Florian's continued to develop and he carried out an extensive ministry with health care professionals. He continued lecturing in Lublin, but with a reduced lecture load because of the multiple pastoral responsibilities he had to undertake as auxiliary bishop.

In 1959 Bishop Wojtyla began the custom of saying midnight Mass on Christmas Eve, in an open field at Nowa Huta, the model workers' town outside Krakow, which had been deliberately built without a church. The neighbourhood was home to many thousands of people. The new town was filled with enormous apartment blocks, some of which contained as many as 450 flats. It was meant to be a workers paradise but was in reality a concrete jungle. Every year from 1959 until 1977 Archbishop Wojtyla said an open-air Mass there until the new church was consecrated in 1977.

According to the authorities, Nowa Huta was to be a perfect model of a socialist city with no link of any kind to the Church. Initially the communist authorities yielded to pressure and gave permission to build a church. However, the permission was later withdrawn. This was vehemently opposed by the people, resulting in a confrontation with the police in which some people were injured. This was the first in a series of incidents in a long battle for freedom and dignity. Finally permission to build a church was granted in 1967. Ten years of volunteer labour from all over Poland and throughout Europe contributed to the construction of the church. The parish priest suggested to his parishioners that each of them bring a stone that could be used for the foundations and the walls, so that everyone felt personally involved in the construction of the new church. The interior is dominated by a great steel figure of the crucified Christ, forged by the workers of the Nowa Huta Lenin steelworks, the largest in Europe, with 35,000 employees, mostly drawn from the uprooted, vulnerable, rural workers. Factory workers came after-hours to work without pay on the building.

Even after permission had been granted, the authorities created as many difficulties as they could for the building of the church. When the steel roof supports had to be welded, electric current was cut off until five in the afternoon. No cranes were allocated to the site until foreign currency was subscribed. Cement mixers were withheld so that all the cement was mixed by hand and carried in wheelbarrows. Meanwhile an immense movement of goodwill was generated. Students came from all over Poland to work on the church during holiday time. Despite every kind of delaying tactic the church was ready for consecration in 1977.

The church was dedicated by Cardinal Wojtyla in May 1977, ten years after the first sod was turned. In his homily he eloquently answered what the communists tried to do with Nowa Huta: 'This is not a city of people who belong to no one, of people to whom one may do whatever one wants, who may be manipulated according to the laws or rules of production and consumption. This is a city of the children of God. This temple was necessary so that this could be expressed, that it could be emphasized …'[42] A crowd of 50,000 attended the ceremony. There were delegations and gifts from many countries. Pope Paul VI, who took a special interest in the project, sent a stone from St Peter's tomb to be placed in the foundations of the church.

The church, dedicated to our Lady Queen of Poland, is the church of the largest parish in Poland; and is one of the best attended in the world. On Sundays, Masses begin before dawn, and go on all day on the hour. The building, of which the nave alone can hold 5,000 people, is crowded to the door, with overflowing attendance sometimes twenty deep. An estimated 10,000 attend each Mass.[43]

APOSTOLATE OF THE LAITY

Despite his crowded schedule, the archbishop did find time to relax. Each summer he would kayak for a fortnight with his young friends. He also found time to ski, a sport which he loved and at which he was very good. Through his pastoral work as priest and bishop with lay people from many different backgrounds, he was always aware of the urgent need for an apostolate of the laity in the Church. Thus he says, 'when the Second Vatican Council spoke of the vocation and mission of lay people in the Church and the world, I rejoiced: what the Council was teaching corresponded to the convictions which had grounded my activity ever since the first years of my priestly ministry'.[44]

As successor of Peter he would take up Vatican II teaching on the laity and spell it out in more detail in the apostolic exhortation, *Christifideles laici*, the lengthy document he gave the Church on 30 December 1988.[45] It is without doubt the magisterium's most comprehensive statement on the vocation and mission of the laity in the Church and the world. *Christifideles laici* articulated an exciting vision of a laity fully living its mission of bringing Gospel values into the family, society, culture and the world of work. In this way they exercise their common priesthood as an expression of the universal call to holiness. This call is 'intimately connected to the mission and to the responsibility entrusted to the lay faithful in the Church and in the world'.[46] Their task is to continue Christ's saving mission in the world 'which is the place and means for lay faithful to fulfil their Christian vocation'. The sanctification of the world –

42 Ibid., p. 190. **43** Michael O'Carroll, *Poland and John Paul II* (Dublin, 1979), pp 71–4. **44** *Gift and mystery*, p. 70. **45** John Paul II, Post-Synodal Apostolic Exhortation, *Christifideles laici*, 30 December 1988. **46** *Christifideles laici*, 17.

society, culture, work – is the distinctively 'secular' vocation of the laity.[47] There is little doubt that this document will prove to be an abiding influence in the Church, even though it may take some time to work out the full implications of its rich theological and apostolic content.

After the death of Archbishop Baziak in June 1962, Bishop Wojtyla, although the youngest of the auxiliaries, was elected vicar capitular to administer the diocese of Krakow until the new archbishop was appointed by Rome.

VATICAN II

A few months later the Second Vatican Council got under way in October 1962. Bishop Wojtyla attended every session of Vatican II and had often commented on how much he owed personally to the experience of the Council, which he called a great gift to the Church. It was, for John Paul II, essentially a religious experience in which the Holy Spirit was the chief protagonist. The Council was also for him a deep experience of the universality of the Church.

In 1959, in response to a request sent to all the bishops of the world by the Preparatory Commission, Bishop Wojtyla sent a proposal suggesting the Council should state what the Church had to say about the human person and the human condition in light of current philosophies – scientific, positivistic, materialistic. The Church, he said, needed to give an answer to the question, what is Christian humanism?, and to say how it was different from other humanisms. In his submission he spoke about the evangelization of modern culture, and the affirmation that all of life could be sanctified. He wanted the Council to affirm a rich Christian anthropology.[48]

He made contributions to all the four sessions of the Council. He asked that the vocation of the laity be given higher visibility in any document on the Church, so that men and women would feel a deeper sense of responsibility for the Church. He requested that a discussion of Mary's role in the Church would deal with her motherhood, which would conform all her sons and daughters to Christ. Later, in the third session, he presented a lengthy document on Mary's place in the proposed dogmatic constitution on the Church.

In the same session, in the discussion on the Decree on the Lay Apostolate, he welcomed the revised text because it identified the source of the lay apostolate as a responsibility stemming from the sacrament of baptism, and not from the fact of belonging to a specific apostolic movement. It is interesting to note that Bishop Wojtyla was the only Council Father to recognize the presence of women as auditors at the Council, beginning his remarks:

47 Cf. ibid., 15. 48 Cf. Weigel, p. 159.

Venerables Patres, Fratres, et Sorores.[49] He emphasized that a renewed apostolate of the laity shouldn't clericalize them, but should rather renew them as apostles in the world of culture and of work.

He had much to say on the Decree of Religious Freedom. One of his core points was that it was only by living in the truth that man could be really free. He made another detailed contribution on the subject of religious freedom at the beginning of the fourth session. However, his principal contribution was to the Pastoral Constitution on the Church in the Modern World (*Gaudium et spes*).[50] He said that such a schema was essential bearing in mind the situation of men and women in the world, who were waiting to hear what the Church had to say to them.[51] Having put so much effort into the drafting of *Gaudium et spes*, it is not surprising that this document would retain a prominent place in the thinking of Karol Wojtyla for the rest of his life. During his subsequent papacy he would quote paragraph 22 of *Gaudium et spes* more frequently than any other Council text, a paragraph which is at the core of the Church's teaching on a Christian anthropology.

ARCHBISHOP

The archbishop of Krakow died in June of 1962, and over the next eighteen months the Polish government would veto seven different candidates to replace him. At this stage the name of Karol Wojtyla was mentioned because the communists had completely misread the character of the young auxiliary bishop of Krakow. He was appointed archbishop of Krakow in 1964, and cardinal in 1967. His model as archbishop was the prince cardinal, Adam Sapieha, from whom he had learned so much as seminarian and priest.

He did most of his thinking at a desk facing the tabernacle of his private oratory. He went regularly to the shrine of Kalwaria Zebrzydowska when he had to consider important decisions, and every Friday he did the Stations of the Cross at the Franciscan church across the street from his residence. During his fourteen years as archbishop of Krakow, Karol Wojtyla pursued different priorities. He consistently fought for the minimum of religious freedom, exercised in a special way in the building of new churches, and in the public exercise of Christian worship symbolized by the annual Corpus Christi procession. His great victory in this regard was the winning, after several years struggle with the public authorities, of permission to erect the new church at Nowa Huta.

He had limited success with the Corpus Christi procession in that the communists severely curtailed the extent of the route. Nevertheless, the streets

49 Cf. ibid., p. 163. 50 Second Vatican Council, Pastoral Constitution on the Church in the Modern World, *Gaudium et spes*, 7 December 1965. 51 Cf. Weigel, pp 167–9.

were crowded with people and Cardinal Wojtyla spoke at the stations along the route in tones which were both patriotic and religious. His addresses at the Corpus Christi processions added to his stature and reputation as a speaker. In 1954 the government closed down the faculty of theology of the Jagiellonian university. This would have meant no theology classes for the seminarians. However, after the closure of the faculty the expelled professors established a faculty of theology within the Krakow archdiocesan seminary.

As archbishop of Krakow, John Paul II always paid close attention to his seminary. The seminary, he said, had to be the *pupillum occuli* of the bishop, the apple of his eye, his most cherished apostolate, because 'vocations are the future of the diocese and ultimately the future of the church.'[52] He said that no bishop should fail to challenge young people with the great ideal of priesthood:

> A young heart can understand the reckless love that is needed for total self-giving. There is no greater love than Love with a capital 'L'. On 3 May 2003, in Madrid, during my last pilgrimage to Spain, I confided in the young people: 'I was ordained a priest at the age of twenty-six. Fifty-six years have passed since then. Looking back, and remembering those years of my life I can assure you that it is worth dedicating yourselves to the service of others. It is worth giving your lives for the Gospel and for your brothers and sisters! The young people understood the message and echoed my words by chanting over and over again: "It's worth it! It's worth it!"'[53]

Wojtyla was interested not only in the formation of seminarians but also in the formation of his priests. He believed that the effectiveness of the pastor of souls had to be based on personal holiness and commitment to the care of people. He met his seminarians regularly, and got to know each of his future priests personally. He kept up contact with each class of newly-ordained priests through the early years of their ministry, often going for hikes with them or meeting them on the ski slopes. Whenever he got together with them he constantly encouraged them to have a deep prayer life.[54] During his time as archbishop the number of seminarians increased from 191 in 1962 to 250 in 1978, and that of priests from 771 to 956.[55] These were years when in the free world seminary recruitment was collapsing and men were leaving the priesthood by the thousand.

Following Christ's teaching on the Good Shepherd (cf. Jn 10), he made a point of getting to know as many people as possible in the local church, and so that they in turn would get to know him personally. He went beyond mere casual acquaintance, getting to know what brought joy into their lives and

52 *Rise, let us be on our way*, p. 125. 53 Ibid., pp 126–7. 54 Cf. Weigel, pp 188–93. 55 Cf. ibid., p. 194.

what saddened them. This, he said, 'comes from a genuine interest in what is happening in their lives regardless of age, social status, or nationality, whether they are close at hand or far away'.[56] He says he was greatly helped in relating to people by the study of personalism during the years he devoted to philosophy. He was always concerned to safeguard the personal quality of each relationship. Interest in others, he added, began with his prayer life. In this way he came to know others quite well, even though there was little time to spend with them. He prayed for everyone every day. As soon as he met people he prayed for them and this helped his relationship with them. He welcomed everyone as a person entrusted to him by Christ.[57]

SUFFERING

John Paul II tells us, with great candidness, how initially he didn't find visiting the sick an easy task. He freely admitted that as an adolescent he was intimidated by human suffering, that there was a time when he was afraid to approach those who were ill – he felt a sort of remorse when confronted with suffering which he had been spared. However, his pastoral duties enabled him to get rid of this timidity, and it was the sick themselves who helped him discover the great human and spiritual richness that can hide behind human suffering.[58] It was only when he grasped the profound meaning of human suffering and its contribution to the life of the Church that he felt at home with sick people. Through their prayers and sacrifices, he affirmed, the sick not only ask for mercy, but 'open up spaces for mercy'.[59] He entrusted the needs of the Church to the prayers of the sick, 'and the results were always positive'.[60]

In 1984 he wrote an eloquent letter (*Salvifici doloris*)[61] about suffering. It gathers up the basic scriptural insights on suffering from both the Old and the New Testaments. He was also able to write from his own experience of suffering, both moral and physical. By the time he was twenty he had lost all his close family relatives. He had suffered physically during the Nazi occupation of Krakow, and had to fight for his life after the assassination attempt on 13 May 1981. At one point he writes in *Salvifici doloris*:

> Suffering is present in the world in order to release love, in order to give birth to works of love towards neighbour, in order to transform the whole of human civilization into a 'civilization of love.'[62]

56 *Rise, let us be on our way*, p. 65. **57** Ibid. **58** Cf. Frossard, p. 83. **59** *Rise, let us be on our way*, p. 75. **60** Ibid., p. 76. **61** John Paul II, Apostolic Letter, *Salvifici doloris*, 11 February 1984. **62** Ibid., no. 30.

Cardinal Wojtyla also encouraged youth movements which organized retreats and formation sessions for teenagers. He gave particular emphasis to the catechetical activities organized for altar boys and their families. He urged students to take care of abandoned or neglected Jewish cemeteries. In his pastoral programme for the archdiocese he gave particular importance to family apostolate. During his time at St Florian's, and later, he acquired a lot of experience of this apostolate when he promoted marriage preparation courses. As archbishop, faced with a communist regime that relentlessly tried to undermine family life, he expanded this pastoral programme to reach every corner of the diocese, through a network of people he helped to train. He organized two-year courses for 250 students at a time, at the pontifical faculty of theology, to train people in family studies in areas related to the theology of marriage, human sexuality, child care, and healing post-abortion stress. These students were seminarians, priests, lay men and women who became instructors and facilitators in the parish-based marriage preparation programmes.[63]

Catholic charitable institutions were banned in Poland from 1950, but Archbishop Wojtyla created a whole new parish network to care for the sick and needy in the parish, providing food, medicine and clothing. The pastoral ministry of charity organized retreats for the sick, the elderly and for handicapped children. Pilgrimages were organized during the summer to local Marian shrines. Students and seminarians were recruited to help in the running of these pilgrimages. The archdiocese organized an annual 'Day of the Sick' from 1965, a celebration which was continued at a universal level, when Archbishop Wojtyla became Pope, through his letters for the 'World Day of the Sick.' He asked the sick to offer their sufferings for the intentions of the archdiocese and for the Church universal.[64]

He was very diligent about parish visitation because he saw it as the centre of the Church's life. Parish visitation usually lasted several days. It included administration of the sacrament of confirmation, a special Mass for married couples and a personal blessing for each couple. He met the parish religion teachers. He visited the local cemetery, prayed the rosary with the parishioners for the souls of the dead, and blessed new graves. People appreciated the time and care Cardinal Wojtyla put into parish visitation. For him it was at the very core of his episcopal ministry.

He rose every morning at 5.00 a.m. and spent the first hour of his day in prayer in his private oratory. This was followed by Mass with his secretary and personal staff. After breakfast he returned to the oratory from 9.00 a.m. to 11.00 a.m., to work on his writing at a desk facing the tabernacle. After 11.00 a.m. he was free to see visitors until 1.00 p.m. Those last seen were often

63 Cf. Weigel, ibid., p. 196. **64** Cf. ibid., p. 199.

invited to lunch. Afternoons and evenings were devoted to more meetings and to reading and study. He had no television but listened to Radio Free Europe's Polish service while shaving in the morning.[65] To optimize his use of travel time he had a desk top and lamp fitted in the back seat of his car so that he could read or write while being driven to his appointment. He had the ability to do two things simultaneously, for example, he could run a seminar and attend to his personal correspondence at the same time. He insisted on holidays to recover his energy – kayaking during the summer, and skiing in the winter. He lived a simple and frugal life by choice.

SYNOD OF KRAKOW

During Vatican II, Cardinal Wojtyla took several initiatives to keep his diocese informed about developments in Rome as the Council unfolded. In 1970, after writing *Sources of renewal*,[66] an introduction to the sixteen documents of Vatican II, he decided to hold a synod in Krakow to implement the Council's proposals. This would be an opportunity for the whole diocese to relive the experience of Vatican II. This was to be a pastoral synod which would begin its preparatory work in 1971. His aim for the synod was that it would turn the Church of Krakow into a vibrant, apostolic community. After a year of preparation the synod was solemnly convened on 8 May 1972 at Wawel cathedral, with representatives of the entire diocese attending. It met 117 times. Eventually it published 119 pages of documents covering every aspect of the life of the Church in Krakow. These documents were in turn organized under three headings, reflecting the three offices of Christ as priest, prophet, and king.

Five hundred study groups were formed to read through the texts of Vatican II, with the cardinal's *Sources of renewal* as a commentary. These study groups were the heart and soul of the synod, the vast majority of them being parish based. In them suggestions were made as regards the application of the Council's proposals to the different diocesan ministries. Through these study groups the synod built Christian community according to Vatican II's concept of the Church as communion. In this way the diocese of Krakow avoided many of the post-Vatican II tensions which were a common experience in other dioceses. Cardinal Wojtyla left Krakow for Rome before the synod completed its work, although he presided at its solemn closing as Pope John Paul II in June of 1979.

65 Cf. ibid., p. 201. 66 Karol Wojtyla, *Sources of renewal: the implementation of Vatican II* (San Francisco, 1980).

'HUMANAE VITAE' CONTROVERSY

Pope John XXIII established a commission to advise on problems of family, population, and birth rate, a commission which was reappointed by Paul VI. For the general public it became known as the Papal Birth Control Commission, and the only issue at stake was whether Catholics could use the contraceptive pill. In the highly charged political atmosphere of the post-Vatican II Church, birth control became the litmus test between theological 'progressives' and theological 'conservatives'. When we add to this the widespread challenge to all established authority in the sixties in the West, together with the spread of the sexual revolution, it was clear that a balanced public discussion of conjugal morality had little chance of success. When Paul VI issued *Humanae vitae*[67] in 1968, it immediately became the most controversial encyclical in history and caused serious problems in the Church, especially in Western Europe and North America. It seems that in the commission a majority opted for change, arguing that conjugal morality should be measured by 'the totality of married life', rather than by the openness of each act of intercourse to conception. In this view it was licit to use chemical or mechanical means to prevent conception as long as this was in the overall moral context of a couple's openness to children. The Minority Report reiterated traditional Catholic teaching, that the use of contraceptives violated natural moral law by separating the procreative and unitive dimensions of sexuality. For the minority view the only licit way to regulate births was through the use of the natural rhythms of fertility. *Humanae vitae* confirmed classical teaching that every marriage act had to be open to life. A storm of criticism followed with the most widespread public Catholic dissent.

Archbishop Wojtyla, well-known to Paul VI as the author of *Love and responsibility*, had been appointed to the papal commission but was unable to attend the June 1966 meeting, at which the majority took a negative position with regard to the traditional teaching – the Polish government had denied him a passport. Wojtyla, nevertheless, played an important role in the development of *Humanae vitae*.

In 1966 he established his own diocesan commission to study the problems being debated by the papal commission. The Krakow commission, in which Archbishop Wojtyla took an active part, sent a summary of its conclusions in French to Paul VI. The Krakow report included the moral analysis in *Love and responsibility*, and went on to say that nature had inscribed a moral language and grammar in the sexual structure of the human body. This grammar included the unitive and procreative aspect of human sexuality: sexual inter-

67 Pope Paul VI, Encyclical Letter, *Humanae vitae*, 28 July 1968.

course as both an expression of love and the means for transmitting new human life. Any act that denied one of these dimensions violated the grammar of the act and necessarily, if unwittingly, reduced one's spouse to an object of one's pleasure. The marriage act retained its truly human character by its openness to the possibility of new life.[68] The Krakow commission affirmed that living marital chastity this way required real sacrifice, but recommended education in chastity as self-mastery. It pointed out that the pastor should not just criticize promiscuity, but should give a positive teaching on Christian humanism for the church's teaching to ring true.

While *Humanae vitae* makes reference to Christian personalism, to the good of sexual love, and to the duty and responsibility of planning one's family, it did not adopt in full the rich personalist context suggested by the Krakow commission. While it came to the same conclusion as the encyclical on the question of how to legitimately regulate fertility, it offered a more compelling explanation of why this position was better fitted to the dignity of the human person and particularly to the dignity of women.[69]

WORLD STAGE

During the 1970s Karol Wojtyla became one of the best-known churchmen in the world to his peers in the higher echelons of the Church. Becoming cardinal in 1967 intensified his involvement in international Catholic affairs. It meant that he attended the synods of bishops held in Rome every few years, in which he took an active part. He was appointed *relator* of the 1971 synod which discussed evangelization, which meant he had to draft the final report on which the synod fathers would vote.

Cardinal Wojtyla travelled a lot as archbishop of Krakow – to Canada, USA, Australia. In 1976 Paul VI invited him to give the Lenten retreat to himself and the Roman Curia. The meditations of this retreat were subsequently published under the title, *Sign of contradiction*. He spoke to his audience, among other things, about the greatness of the sacrament of penance and what he had learned as a confessor:

> When a man goes down on his knees in the confessional because he has sinned, at that very moment he adds to his own dignity as a man. No matter how heavily his sins weigh on his conscience, no matter how seriously they have diminished his dignity, the very act of turning again to God is a manifestation of the special dignity of man, his spiritual

68 Cf. Weigel, ibid., p. 208. **69** Cf. ibid., pp 206–10.

> grandeur ... the grandeur of the personal meeting between man and God in the inner truth of his conscience.[70]

WAR AGAINST COMMUNISM

The great struggle which Cardinal Wojtyla was involved in as archbishop of Krakow was his battle with the communist regime in Poland. Because it tried to impose an atheistic belief system, Wojtyla fought it all the more because it denied people the freedom to believe. Traditionally the archbishop had always been the defender of the people of Krakow, and this was a responsibility that Wojtyla took seriously. His challenge to the communist regime was at the level of the faith and culture. It was often in fighting the system to obtain permission for new churches or religious processions that the battle was most strenuously fought, and were symbols of rising cultural resistance to the communist monopoly on political power.[71] Cardinal Wojtyla maintained solidarity with the church in Czechoslovakia, one of the most brutally suppressed churches in all of Eastern Europe. As an expression of this support he secretly ordained priests for service in that country.

John Paul II learned much from Polish history and the struggle of Poland to achieve freedom. Freedom, the Pope said, is not 'possessed'; it is 'conquered'. When he speaks of it's role in the life of the human being, he says: 'One's life as a person and a social being must be built out of it.'[72] From a spiritual perspective, the Holy Father adds:

> In my view, when Christ says to us, 'You will know the truth, and the truth will make you free', he is thinking of an organic link between freedom and responsibility as well as of the dynamic of freedom whereby man conquers himself and thus turns the kingdom of God into reality.[73]

ELECTION AS POPE

By 1978 Cardinal Wojtyla had become one of the most widely respected leaders in the Church, a man eager to engage contemporary culture. He had grappled with problems – pastoral, intellectual, and theological – which few other churchmen had engaged. He was a towering intellectual and yet a man whose soul was nourished by popular devotion. His seminary in Krakow was full of

70 Karol Wojtyla, *Sign of contradiction* (New York, 1976), pp 142–3. **71** Cf. Weigel, p. 233. **72** Frossard, p. 24. **73** Ibid., p. 101.

young men eager to serve the Church as other Christs. He had perhaps the most highly organized family apostolate in the world, in place in his diocese. Although he lived under the shadow of a brutal communist regime, he did battle against it with optimism, courage, and political savvy.

Pope Paul VI died at the papal summer residence at Castelgandolfo on 6 August 1978. The papal election began in the Sistine chapel on 25 August. Cardinal Albino Luciano was elected on the fourth count and took the name of John Paul I. Because of his winsome personality, he immediately engaged the affection and sympathy of the Catholic faithful and beyond. Yet his pontificate was only to last thirty-three days – he died from a heart attack on 29 September.

Cardinal Wojtyla arrived in Rome on 3 October and went with Cardinal Wyszynski to pray before the body of John Paul I in St Peter's basilica. On 14 October he entered the papal conclave for the second time within two months. Shortly before he went to the Gemelli hospital to visit his long-time Polish friend, Bishop Andrzej Deskur, who suffered a stroke the day before.[74]

According to the consensus view that has formed over the years, on the first day of the voting, 15 October, there was deadlock between Cardinal Siri of Genoa and Cardinal Benelli of Florence. On the second day, the votes started to transfer to Cardinal Wojtyla, who was voted Pope on the eighth count that evening, 16 October, the first non-Italian Pope in 455 years, and the first Slav Pope ever. In doing so the cardinal electors had done the unthinkable, but the sudden death of John Paul I had impressed them at a deeply spiritual level, preparing their minds to break traditional patterns of thought. After this barrier had been overcome, his well-known record as a diocesan bishop must have been a priority consideration.

Cardinal Wyszynski told John Paul II that he was the Pope to lead the Church into the third millennium. Certainly a Pope elected at the relatively young age of 58 was very likely to be on St Peter's chair in the year 2000. Thousands rushed into St Peter's Square when the news of the white smoke got around Rome. When he appeared at the loggia of St Peter's he immediately broke a long tradition: instead of just giving his blessing in Latin, he spoke directly to the crowd in Italian, establishing a rapport with them at once.

It took several hours for Polish TV to announce the news of Cardinal Wojtyla's election – a party position had to be worked out. In Krakow the city went into a spontaneous celebration, with the bells of all the churches ringing out their joy, and Polish flags flying. Swarms of journalists arrived in Krakow and Wadowice to learn more about this man whose background was so different from that of his predecessors in the chair of St Peter.[75] Catholics all over

74 Cf. Weigel, p. 251. **75** Cf. ibid., pp 254–5.

the world rejoiced that Poland, which had suffered so much for the faith, was now rewarded with the election of Karol Wojtyla as Vicar of Christ.

On 22 October, prior to the ceremony of his installation as Pope, John Paul II prayed at the tomb of St Peter. He was invested with the pallium, a symbol of the authority he had received at his election on 16 October. Then each of the cardinals processed up to his chair to pledge obedience to him.

At the end of the Gospel, John Paul II addressed the huge crowd in St Peter's Square, and an even bigger audience through radio and TV connections. Polish state television was broadcasting its first Mass ever. The first part of his homily was a reflection on St Peter's act of faith: 'You are the Christ, the Son of the living God' (Mt 16:16). It was Peter's mission to bear witness to the truth about Jesus, the Son of God, who redeemed mankind, and taught them the greatness of their vocation.[76] And then rang out those words which were to symbolize the pontificate of John Paul II:

- Be not afraid to welcome Christ and accept his power.
- Be not afraid. Open wide the doors for Christ. To his saving power open the boundaries of states, economic and political systems, the vast fields of culture, civilization and development.
- Be not afraid. Christ knows 'what is in man'. He alone knows it.[77]

Commenting on this theme of his homily, John Paul II said that the exhortation, 'Be not afraid', was in a certain sense addressed to all people, an exhortation to conquer fear in the present world situation. We should have no fear, he said, because man has been redeemed by God. The redemption pervades all of human history and so the power of Christ's Cross and Resurrection is greater that any evil which man could or should fear. In particular, he says, it was the confidence in our Lady which he brought to Rome from his native land which enabled him to say, 'Be not afraid'.[78] John Paul II came to have the conviction that if victory comes, and he was sure that it would, it would come through our Lady. 'Christ will conquer through her, because he wants the Church's victories now and in the future to be linked to her.'[79]

Karol Wojtyla did not see his papal responsibilities as a totally new task; rather he saw it as a job in continuity with his episcopal responsibilities in Krakow. For this reason he felt at home in the papacy from the beginning. He had his own vision for the way things should be done, and in pursuing this line he was not afraid to break with tradition. Indeed the very day after his election as Pope, he called to the Gemelli hospital to visit his friend Bishop Deskur, something which broke well-established papal protocol.

76 Cf. ibid., p. 261. **77** Cf. ibid., p. 262. **78** Cf. *Crossing the threshold of hope*, pp 218–22. **79** Cf. ibid., p. 221.

EARLY MONTHS OF PAPACY

A few days after his election he told the College of Cardinals that his first task was to complete the implementation of Vatican II. Recalling that each cardinal swears to be faithful to Christ, even to the extent of shedding his blood for him, he linked it with the countless unknown Christians around the world who had suffered prison and humiliation for Christ. This was the second explicit reference to the persecuted church in three days. He had a crowded programme of visits and meetings from the beginning, making his first Roman parish visit on Sunday 10 December. Over the next twenty-six years he would visit 316 of Rome's 333 parishes, something which no previous Pope had ever done.

On the thirtieth anniversary of the United Nations' Declaration of Human Rights, 11 December 1978, he urged freedom of religion for everybody. He took up this theme again in his Christmas Eve homily, and in his address to the diplomatic corps on 12 January. During the Christmas season he visited the Christmas crib set up by Roman street cleaners near the Vatican, where a street cleaner's daughter asked the Pope if he would officiate at her wedding ceremony. John Paul II smiled and agreed. A few days later he began leading the First Saturday Rosary, internationally broadcast over Vatican Radio, which up to then was led by Roman clergy.

Within months of his accession to the see of Peter, John Paul II had made it clear that evangelization and re-evangelization were his pastoral priorities, and that he intended to exercise his titles of 'bishop of Rome' and 'primate of Italy' much more directly than his Italian predecessors.

He kept a similar timetable to that in Krakow: he rose at 5.30 a.m. and after dressing he went directly to his private oratory, where he spent more that an hour in personal prayer, in which he included the hundreds of personal requests from all over the world which were typed up by his staff on sheets and placed on his pridieu each morning. He concelebrated Mass at 7.30 a.m. with his secretaries before a small congregation which included invited guests. At 8.30 a.m. he had breakfast. From 9.30 a.m. to 11.00 a.m. he did his writing, often before the Blessed Sacrament in his private oratory, and retained the life-long habit of putting a brief aspiration at the top of each manuscript page to help his presence of God. It was thus that he wrote his encyclicals, apostolic letters, and other documents. At 11.00 a.m. his official appointments began followed by lunch at 1.30 p.m. After lunch, while walking, he prayed one of the many Rosaries which he said during the day.

At 3.00 p.m. a locked briefcase came from the secretariat of state with documents from the different Vatican departments to be studied and signed by the Pope, or sent back for further study. In the late afternoon, official appointments began again. Dinner was served at 7.30 p.m., and afterwards another briefcase with more documents arrived from the secretariat of state. John Paul II spent what was left of the evening reading, writing, or checking the incoming faxes. Relaxation for John Paul II was catching up on reading in philosophy.[80]

His personal secretaries say that he was very easy to work with and that he promoted a family atmosphere among his personal staff.[81] His collaborators observed that his entire day was punctuated by prayer, not just by going to the oratory to recite the Liturgy of the Hours, but in between audiences, in the car, in a helicopter. He prayed the Stations of the Cross every Friday, and every day during Lent. He went to confession each week.

MEXICO

In January 1979, in his first pastoral trip abroad, John Paul II visited Mexico to open the General Assembly of CELAM, the council of Latin American bishops' conferences. He was given a very enthusiastic reception in Mexico when he arrived there on 26 January 1979. Two days later he addressed CELAM in Puebla, conscious of the intense debate about 'liberation theology' which was going on in South America. Liberation theology was impatient with the reform approach of Vatican II and was in favour of a more revolutionary strategy which fed on Marxist categories of social and economic analysis. The 'sinful social structures' of the established order were to be overthrown through class struggle. In this struggle, the Church, exercising a 'preferential option for the poor' would organize small Christian 'base communities', where the poor would be taught to recognize their own situation and take up the task of recreating society. The Church, by accepting the class struggle as the foundational dynamic of history, had to be a partisan player, favouring some people against others. These liberation theologies were picked up by South American priests in European universities and imported to South America.[82]

John Paul II had a delicate task in addressing the CELAM bishops' gathering. He told them that their chief duty as bishops was to teach the truth. He rejected the image of Jesus as a politically-motivated leader and affirmed the clear distinction between the things of God and those of Caesar. True liberation was to be found in the salvation offered by Christ expressed in his redeeming love. The kingdom of God could not be reduced to a mere changing of structures in society. Against the Marxist reduction of man to a materialist principle, the Church proposed the truth that man is made in God's image and can't be reduced to a pawn in materialistic economic analysis.[83] The next day in Cuilapan

80 Cf. Weigel, ibid., p. 275. **81** Cf. ibid., p. 276. **82** Cf. ibid., p. 283. **83** Cf. ibid., pp 283–5.

he spoke to more than half a million Indians. He told them that he wanted to be their voice, 'the voice of those who can't speak or who are silenced.'[84] He criticized those who neglected the poor and showed little respect for their dignity.

FIRST PASTORAL VISIT TO POLAND, JUNE 1979

Two month later John Paul II published his first encyclical, *Redemptor hominis*.[85] It was the first encyclical ever devoted to Christian anthropology. This was a topic which had exercised his mind from the first days of his priesthood. The ideas of *Redemptor hominis* had matured in the Pope's mind especially during his term as archbishop of Krakow: 'Everything I said in *Redemptor hominis*, I brought with me from Poland.'[86] He reaffirms the depth of God's love for man and announces that man is called by vocation to love, that this is what gives meaning to his life. Love, he affirms, is greater than sin, than alienation, than every human frailty. This love can only be encountered in freedom, and this is why the Church has to be a guardian of human freedom.[87]

John Paul II's pastoral visit to Poland in June of 1979 was his first trip to his native soil since his election as Pope eight months before. There was a great sense of expectation in Poland at the return of the country's most famous son. He would surely come with a message which would lift their hearts, and give them hope for a brighter future. As it turned out, their expectations would fall far short of what eventually the Pope's visit brought about. The return of John Paul II to his native land, caught in the grip of a harsh communist regime, was to have unimaginable consequences, not only for Poland, but also for all the east European countries influenced by the Soviet Union.

The city of Warsaw was transformed to welcome the Vicar of Christ. Hundreds of thousands of people lined the route from the airport to the city centre. On 2 June three million Poles, twice the city's normal population, had come to see their countryman who was now Pope John Paul II.

After the reading of the Gospel, a deep silence fell over the expectant crowd as they wondered what he was going to say. He opened with a prayer of gratitude to divine providence for the opportunity to fulfil a wish of Paul VI to visit the soil of Poland in 1966, but a desire in which his predecessor was thwarted. He said he came as a pilgrim to his native land to celebrate the ninth centenary of the martyrdom of St Stanislaw in 1079, who died in resistance to the tyranny of autocratic state power, and who had been a special sign of the pilgrimage all Poles were making through the history of the Church. Why had

84 Cf. ibid., p. 286. **85** Cf. note 30. **86** John Paul II, *Memory and identity: personal reflections* (London, 2005), p. 5. **87** Cf. Weigel, ibid., pp 288–9.

a son of Poland been called to the chair of Peter?, he asked. Was it not because the Poland of today had become, through the terrible trials of the twentieth century, 'the land of a particularly responsible witness?' Poles had a right to think that it was to their country one had to come 'to read again the witness of his Cross and Resurrection'. At this the crowd began to chant, 'We want God. We want God.'[88]

He went on to say that 'Christ cannot be kept out of the history of man in any part of the globe ... The exclusion of Christ from the history of man is an act against man ... Without Christ it is impossible to understand the history of Poland.' Anyone who denied this or tried to uproot it damaged the Polish nation. Throughout the Pope's sermon the crowd responded rhythmically, 'We want God, we want God in the family, we want God in the schools, we want God ...' John Paul II had come to his native land to reclaim the nation's history and its Christian culture, and, in doing so, to refute the culture of denial and mendacity imposed by the regime.[89]

As Weigel points out, the *Ostpolitik* and the character of papal diplomacy as a whole changed radically on 16 October 1978 with the election of Karol Wojtyla as Pope. Having brought to the papacy his own personal experience of living under two totalitarian regimes, he contributed a distinctive reading of the contemporary Church to the papacy and a new model of papal diplomacy. Since he was a native of east central Europe, John Paul II knew that there was something radically different about communist regimes, a point that did not seem fully appreciated by the Vatican diplomats who conceived and executed Paul VI's *Ostpolitik*. All states commit criminal acts sometimes, but communist regimes were criminal enterprises by their very nature. The 'rule of law' in a communist regime was a fiction:

> Communist regimes committed violent acts and maintained an enormous apparatus of repression on principle. Under a communist regime, terror was a routine way to maintain order, which could give communist regimes an air of invincibility. The Pope, however, had measured communism's weaknesses as well as its apparent strengths. And he knew that cultural resistance would be an effective antidote to the seemingly impregnable position of a criminal state. John Paul II adopted a far more assertive approach to the problems of the persecuted Church than was hitherto the case.[90]

Over one million Poles gathered at the shrine of our Lady of Czestochowa in Jasna Gora on 4 June to hear John Paul II speak, at times emotionally, about

88 Cf. Weigel, p. 293. **89** Cf. ibid., pp 305–7. **90** Ibid., p. 295.

the profound connection between our Lady of Czestochowa and the Polish nation. He met several groups there and had a meeting with the whole of the Polish episcopate. In his address to the Polish bishops he reminded them how at different times in the history of their country they had saved the nation in time of crisis, even at the price of their blood. It was clear that John Paul II was saying to the bishops that in the conditions then prevailing they also might have to give witness with their lives.

KRAKOW

The Pope arrived in Krakow on the evening of 6 June to an ecstatic welcome. That night, and for the next three nights, young people thronged the streets and the rooftops around the episcopal palace, where an impromptu get-together took place with John Paul II. He was in sparkling form and dialogued with the young people of Krakow and shared songs with them. The next morning he visited the shrine of Kalaria Zobrzydowoski, one of the great pilgrimage sites in Poland, which played a large part in Karol Wojtyla's spiritual life.

From Krakow he went to his birthplace, Wadowice. During his visit to Auschwitz (7 June) he said Mass for a crowd of over half a million people. He walked through this place of human degradation and reflected on all the nationalities buried there, victims of the Nazi extermination policy. His concelebrants were bishops and priests who had been imprisoned in Dachau and other concentration camps during the war. In his homily he said this was a place meant 'to trample radically not only on love but on all signs of human dignity, of humanity'. Remembering Auschwitz, he concluded, had to bring with it a commitment – to respect the rights of every human being as enshrined in the Universal Declaration of Human Rights, written in the shadow of Auschwitz, and to honour and respect them along with the legitimate rights of nations to their language, culture and freedom.[91] That evening he presided over the solemn closing of the synod of Krakow. Later he addressed the young people who had gathered outside the Wawel cathedral. He told them: 'Allow Christ to find you … Be afraid only of thoughtlessness and pusillanimity.'[92]

The next morning he visited the Cistercian abbey on the outskirts of Nowa Huta. Forbidden to visit the church that had cost him so much effort, John Paul II threw a bouquet of flowers over it from the window of a helicopter. The parishioners of Nowa Huta wanted John Paul II to crown a new statue of our Lady for the church, but now that the Pope was prohibited from

91 Cf. ibid., pp 314–15. **92** Cf. ibid., p. 317.

going there, they brought the statue to him at the Cistercian abbey. In his homily he said, in summary, 'You have built the church, now build your life on the Gospel.'

On Saturday 10 June, the last day of his Polish pilgrimage, John Paul II said Mass on Krakow Common for the biggest crowd in Polish history – between two and three million people – to mark the close of the St Stanislaw jubilee. He told the vast crowd that 'fulfilment in life and the human vocation was to be found in God'. They had to be strong with the strength of faith: 'Today more than in any other age you need this strength. You must be strong with the strength of hope, hope that brings the perfect joy of life ... You must be strong with love, which is stronger than death ... So I beg you: never lose your trust, do not be defeated, do not be discouraged ... I beg you: have trust.'[93]

It was as if John Paul II could see through the dark tunnel of communist domination to the bright light at the other end which promised religious and political freedom. He wanted to buoy up the hope of his people in his final meeting with them before he returned to Rome. Thirteen million Poles, over one third of the national population, had seen the Pope in person. Things the people had believed for decades, but could not say publicly, John Paul II had affirmed. He had given the Polish people a sense of their own dignity and a deeper hope for the future. However, he had left them in no doubt that personal moral renewal was necessary to offer a serious challenge to the regime.[94] He constantly encouraged people to see that the great obstacle was their own lethargy which permitted, by tacit consent, the continued imposition of an alien form of political control on their country.

THEOLOGY OF THE BODY

In September 1979, before he had concluded the first year of his pontificate, John Paul II began a series of addresses, which over the next five years would develop the idea of sexual love as an icon of the inner, Trinitarian life of God. When he was elected to the papacy, Karol Wojtyla knew that the Church's last effort to address the sexual revolution and its relationship to the moral life (Paul VI's 1968 encyclical *Humanae vitae*) had been a pastoral and catechetical failure, especially in countries of Western Europe and North America. *Humanae vitae*'s teaching on the regulation of human fertility had been rejected by great numbers of Catholics and even by some national hierarchies.[95] A situation developed in which anything the Church said subsequently about

93 Cf. ibid., p. 319. **94** Cf. ibid., p. 320. **95** Cf. Janet Smith, *Humanae vitae: a generation later* (Washington, 1991), pp 153, 154.

human sexuality was viewed with suspicion, and in some cases with hostility. The reaction related to a changing concept of 'freedom' which was making progress in the Church, the freedom to make a judgement of conscience without any reference to the teaching of the Church.

John Paul II obviously considered that a new approach was necessary. The result was 129 general audience addresses between 1979 and 1984, which make up John Paul II's theology of the body. Using Sacred Scripture as his foundation, he explored the nature of human sexuality from the perspective of humanity as male and female, dealing with topics such as marriage, divorce, chastity, celibacy, sexual relations and fertility within the context of marriage as a vocation to holiness. The addresses are not always easy reading, as scriptural insights were united with deep philosophical thinking in John Paul II's unfolding style.

John Paul II proposes that sexual love in marriage is in keeping with God's plan when it is an expression of total self-giving between spouses. All, he says, are called to responsible parenthood. There can be morally worthy reasons for limiting fertility, as there might be for having a bigger family. If every married couple is asked to be responsible as regards family size, how is fertility to be regulated so that the spouses' human dignity is protected, and the expression of married love as total self-donation is respected? John Paul II says it is dehumanizing to transfer mechanical and chemical methods to the realm of sexual love. Periodic abstinence from sexual activity, using the natural rhythms of the body as a means of regulating fertility, is a more humanistic method of exercising procreative responsibility and living marital love in chastity. He also says that periodic continence is more in keeping with the sacrament of marriage and becomes a vehicle of grace. What is 'natural', he argues, is what is best in keeping with human dignity, to the nature of the human person called to self-mastery. Contraception demeans our humanity and damages the communion of persons which sexual love is intended to foster.[96]

AT THE UNITED NATIONS

On 2 October 1979, during his first visit to the United States, John Paul II gave one of the most important public addresses of his pontificate to the General Assembly of the United Nations, at its headquarters in New York. What he said there about human rights was a direct challenge to the way most UN member states thought about international politics. He came to the UN at a time of increasing political anxiety about the nuclear arms race between East and West.

96 Cf. Weigel, ibid., pp 336–43.

He opened his speech by saying, that following Christ, his role was to bear witness to the truth. He had come not to address the delegates, not as another diplomat, but as a witness to the truth about 'man in his wholeness, in all the fullness and manifold riches of his spiritual and material existence.' Human progress had to be measured by a criterion worthy of human beings, and this meant assessing progress not only by science and technology but 'also and chiefly by the primacy given to spiritual values and by the progress of the moral life.'[97]

In 1995 John Paul II went back to the UN to address it on the occasion of its fiftieth anniversary. As in 1979, his theme was the universality of human rights. The global character of the human rights movement, he said, empirically confirmed that there is a universal human nature and a universal moral law.[98]

ABORTION

The battle against abortion was one of the great issues of John Paul II's papacy. In 1984 the world population conference in Mexico had stated flatly that abortion was not a legitimate means of family planning. However, UN officials, European politicians, and American-led NGOs that supported the Clinton administration were preparing to redress the Mexican decision at the World Conference on Population scheduled for Cairo in September 1994.

Vatican II described abortion as an 'abominable crime'[99] that not only kills the child but also does grave damage to the mother.[1] To declare this a 'right' not only debased language but threatened 'the legitimacy of international law'. John Paul II insisted that abortion was not an issue of sexual morality but of human rights. At Cairo, the Americans pushed for an internationally sanctioned right to abortion. The Cairo conference threatened to be another example of First World countries imposing their policies and understanding of morality on Third World countries, using the threat of decreasing foreign aid as a weapon.[2]

This was the crucial human rights issue of the 1990s. For John Paul II the abortion issue was not one issue, but *the* issue for the emerging world culture that would sustain or corrupt the free societies of the future. Once the premise was granted that some lives were expendable, the logic of this position inevitably led in due course to infanticide, euthanasia, and coercive reproduction policies. That was what was happening in advanced industrial democracies.

On 19 March 1994 John Paul II sent a personally signed letter to every head of state in the world and to the secretary general of the UN. It began by

97 Cf. ibid., p. 348. **98** Cf. ibid., pp 774–6. **99** *Vatican II*, Decree on the Church in the Modern World, *Gaudium et spes*, 51. **1** Cf. John Paul II, Encyclical letter, *Evangelium vitae* (The Gospel of life), 25 March 1995, 58–63. **2** Cf. Weigel, ibid., pp 715–18.

affirming the Holy See's support for the UN's current International Year of the Family, and referred to the duty of civil authorities to strive to promote harmonious growth of the family. That was why he had found the proposed draft document for the Cairo conference 'a disturbing surprise'. There was reason to fear that it could cause a moral decline resulting in a serious setback for humanity.

Economic development was in fact the issue of primary concern to most of the world, yet these issues had been almost entirely overlooked in the Cairo draft document, which seemed far more interested in promoting a completely individualistic idea of human sexuality, to the extent that marriage now seemed totally outmoded, with disastrous consequences for the family. The proposed general international recognition of a completely unrestricted right to abortion was, John Paul II affirmed in his letter, another grave moral issue raised by the Cairo draft document. It gave the troubling impression of imposing a lifestyle typical of certain fringes within developed societies, societies which were materially rich and secularized.

Finally John Paul II asked the heads of state to think abut the future. The draft document was holding up to young people the model of a society of things and not of persons. Self-mastery, self-giving, and a sense of responsibility were deemed 'notions belonging to another age.' The world's leaders were depriving the young of reasons for living because they were failing to teach the duties incumbent on persons endowed with intelligence and free will. Population and development were indeed serious issues, John Paul II concluded. But they could not be seriously addressed without a sense of the sacredness of life, and an understanding of the human capacity for love and self-sacrifice. This, in summary, was what was missing from the Cairo draft document.

The draft document for Cairo effectively ignored the Conference topic of 'Population and Development', devoting to it only six of its 112 pages. Nothing was said about the important role of the family rooted in marriage. Sexual activity after puberty was treated as a 'right' to be exercised at will, without reference to parents. There was no reference to marriage. States were mandated to override parental prerogatives in the education of adolescents.

An extraordinary consistory of the world's cardinals, held on 13–14 June, issued a statement expressing solidarity with the Pope's teaching on the nature and the rights of the family. A fortnight later John Paul II began a public campaign, aimed at rallying world public opinion against the destructive agenda which the American-led UN was proposing to unleash in Cairo. It consisted of ten twelve-minute audience addresses, at the Sunday Angelus audiences. In these addresses he pointed to the moral errors of the Cairo draft document, and offered ethical alternatives to the reductionist proposals which it contained. He spoke about the right to life as the basic human right. He reaffirmed the traditional view of the nature and responsibilities of marriage. He sketched the outlines of a Christian feminism. He rejected coercive family planning programmes. No just state, he affirmed, could authorize abortion. Sexuality apart from ethical references was inhuman and dehumanizing.[3]

On 5 September, in the first hours of the conference, Prime Minister Benazir Bhutto of Pakistan took the rostrum to defend the sanctity of life, and to condemn the Cairo draft document for trying to 'impose adultery, sex education … and abortion on all countries.' In the days of impasse which followed, the delegates tried to reach consensus on the final report. There was a volte-face about the imposition of abortion as a fundamental right. The document now said that 'in no case should abortion be promoted as a method of family planning'. Thus the Americans and their allies had abandoned the central plank of their agenda for Cairo. The revised final report now recognized the rights and responsibilities of parents towards their teenage children.

The defeat of the Clinton administration and its international allies wasn't due to the Holy See's efforts alone. Political leaders in South America, Africa, and Asia, realizing that they were to be the object of the UN agenda, were suspicious and sided with the Holy See. No one claims, either, that John Paul II was the most important influence on the outcome of Cairo, but his insistent campaign throughout the preceding months was of huge importance in obtaining the outcome that resulted.

It was in this same year of the Cairo Conference (1994) that John Paul II published his *Crossing the threshold of hope*. Here he summarized his attitude towards abortion:

> For man, the right to life is the fundamental right … The legalization of the termination of pregnancy is none other than the authorization given to an adult, with the approval of an established law, to take the lives of children yet unborn and thus incapable of defending themselves. It is difficult to imagine a more unjust situation, and it is very difficult to speak of obsession in a matter such as this, where we are dealing with a fundamental imperative of every good conscience – the defence of the right to life of an innocent and defenceless human being.[4]

He highlights the frequent lack of responsibility of the man in this issue,[5] and goes on to speak about the need to support the woman cast in this difficult situation:

3 Cf. ibid., pp 723–4. 4 *Crossing the threshold of hope*, pp 204–5. 5 'It is necessary to recognize that, in this context, we are witnessing true human tragedies. Often the woman is the victim of male selfishness, in the sense that the man, who has contributed to the conception of new life, does not want to be burdened with it and leaves the responsibility to the woman, as if it were "her

> In firmly rejecting 'pro-choice' it is necessary to become courageously pro-woman, promoting a choice that is truly in favour of women. It is precisely the woman, in fact, who pays the highest price, not only for her motherhood, but even more for its destruction, for the suppression of the life of the child who has been conceived. The only honest stance, in these cases, is that of radical solidarity with the woman. It is not right to leave her alone.[6]

In his encyclical on the Gospel of Life (*Evangelium vitae*), one of the most important documents of his twenty-six year papacy, he reiterated Vatican II's condemnation of murder, genocide, abortion, euthanasia, slavery, prostitution, the selling of women and children.[7] This situation, he commented, had not improved but was rather deteriorating. So he says that 'choices once unanimously considered criminal and rejected by the common moral sense are gradually becoming socially acceptable.'[8] 'Abortion and euthanasia are', he said, 'crimes which no human law can claim to legitimize. There is no obligation in conscience to obey such laws; instead there is a grave and clear obligation to oppose them by conscientious objection.'[9] Such laws, he says, are a lethal assault against the very idea of human rights, they destroy the moral foundation for democratic governance, and actively promote the culture of death. John Paul II affirms that these crimes are always gravely immoral and that this is the infallible teaching of the ordinary, universal magisterium of the Church.[10]

Other specifics addressed in the encyclical include embryo research, the rights of the physically and mentally handicapped, techniques of artificial reproduction, and the need for policies favouring adoption, the moral corruption of the medical profession, the temptation of eugenics, illegitimate means of population control, and capital punishment. In each instance, the Pope brings the argument back to the declaration, 'The direct and voluntary killing of an innocent human being is always gravely immoral.'[11]

PRIESTHOOD

John Paul II, while archbishop of Krakow, devoted considerable time to the care of his priests, to their spiritual and theological formation. He was convinced that the call to holiness of the laity depended largely on the level of

fault" alone. So, precisely when the woman most needs the man's support, he proves to be a cynical egotist, capable of exploiting her affection or weakness, yet stubbornly resistant to any sense of responsibility for his own action' (*Crossing the threshold of hope*, p. 206). **6** Ibid., pp 206–7. **7** Cf. *Gaudium et spes*, 27. **8** Cf. *Evangelium vitae*, 4. **9** Cf. ibid., 73. **10** Cf. ibid., 57, 62, 65. **11** Ibid., 57. Cf. Richard John Neuhaus's article, *Wall Street Journal*, 3 April 1995.

holiness of the priest, and hence his attention to the priests' spiritual life. It was therefore not surprising that when he went to Rome, he continued to give priority to the pastoral care of priests.

When John Paul II was elected in 1978 there had been a crisis in the priesthood since the end of Vatican II. This crisis was reflected in two areas in particular, the number of defections from the ministry, and the collapse in the number of vocations. The priesthood was suffering an identity crisis, and this was why, in October 1990, John Paul II summoned a synod of bishops to study the question of the ongoing formation of priests and seminarians. This resulted in the most comprehensive magisterial document to-date on the Catholic priesthood, the apostolic exhortation 'I will give you Shepherds' (*Pastores dabo vobis)*, issued by John Paul II on 25 March 1992. While the Pope uses several analogies to develop a theology of priesthood (the priest as servant and spouse, as icon of Christ, etc.), without doubt the dominant image running through the whole of *Pastores dabo vobis* is the priest's configuration to Christ as Head and Shepherd. This is the basic reference and background for the description of the nature and mission of the priest, and the context in which the theological foundations of the priest's spiritual life are discussed.

John Paul II had a deep scriptural and theological vision of the priesthood, as *Pastores dabo vobis* and *Gift and mystery* testify. Drawing on St Paul, he sees the priest as 'a steward of the mysteries of God' (1 Cor 4:1), as one to whom the owner entrusts his goods so that he will manage them justly and responsibly. And so 'in exactly the same way the priest receives from Christ the treasures of salvation, in order duly to distribute them among the people to whom he is sent. These treasures are those of faith.'[12] The priestly vocation is a mystery, John Paul II explains. It is the mystery of a wondrous exchange – *admirable commercium* – between God and man. So John Paul II writes:

> A man offers his humanity to Christ, so that Christ may use him as an instrument of salvation, making him as it were into another Christ. Unless we grasp the mystery of this 'exchange', we will not understand how it can be that a young man, hearing the words 'Follow me', can give up everything for Christ, in the certainty that if he follows this path he will find complete personal fulfilment. In our world is there no greater fulfilment of our humanity than to be able to re-present every day *in persona Christi* the redemptive sacrifice, the same sacrifice which Christ offered on the Cross?[13]

One of the very original ways in which John Paul II kept in contact with the world's priests was by writing a letter to them every Holy Thursday, which

12 *Gift and mystery*, p. 72. 13 Ibid., p. 73.

emphasized a particular aspect of priestly formation each year. He referred to Holy Thursday as 'the birthday of priests', frequently encouraging them to go back in thought to the events of that first Holy Thursday in the Upper Room, when Christ ordained his first priests. This was especially the theme of his letter for the Jubilee 2000, when he himself celebrated Mass in the Cenacle in Jerusalem as part of his pilgrimage to the Holy Land. On other occasions he wrote about priestly celibacy, the Eucharist, the prayer of Jesus, Mary in the life of the priest, priestly identity and the need for priests, the priest and women, the priest and the Holy Spirit. On every pastoral trip he made, he usually had a meeting with priests; the addresses he gave on these occasions constitute an immense treasury of priestly theology and pastoral orientation.

Like all his other writings these letters draw deeply from the Scriptures, and are more often than not written in the form of a prayerful reflection rather than the traditional doctrinal discourse. It is clear too that they bring the rich experience of his own priestly life to this annual communication with his brother priests. In summary, John Paul II can say: 'the celebration of the Eucharist must be the most important moment of the priest's day, the centre of his life.'[14] Speaking about the role of the priest in today's world, the Holy Father, summarizing fifty years of priesthood, emphasizes the primacy of holiness:

> While the Second Vatican Council speaks of the universal call to holiness, in the case of the priest we must speak of a special call to holiness. *Christ needs holy priests!* Today's world demands holy priests! Only a holy priest can become, in an increasingly secularized world, a resounding witness to Christ and his Gospel. And only thus can a priest become a guide for men and women and a teacher of holiness. People, especially the young, are looking for such guides. A priest can be a guide and teacher only to the extent that he becomes an authentic witness.[15]

'CROSSING THE THRESHOLD OF HOPE'

Crossing the threshold of hope,[16] published in 1994, was the response of John Paul II to a series of questions put to him by an Italian journalist, Vittorio Messori. In the interview John Paul responded to several questions covering a very wide field, including topics such as: The Pope: a scandal and a mystery; How does the Pope pray? Does God really exist? Is Jesus the Son of God? Why is there so much evil in the world? Was God at work in the fall of communism? Why does God tolerate suffering? What does 'to save' mean? Is there really hope for the young? The defence of every human life, etc.

14 Ibid., p. 75. **15** Ibid., p. 89. **16** John Paul II, *Crossing the threshold of hope*.

In response to a question about the papacy, John Paul II tells us that, as he said in his inauguration homily, we should not be afraid, specifically we should not be afraid of the truth about ourselves. Fundamentally we should not be afraid because God is our Father:

> Because the Pope is a witness of Christ and a minister of the Good News, he is a man of joy and a man of hope, a man of the fundamental affirmation of the value of existence, the value of creation and of hope in the future life.[17]

Asked about how he himself prayed, the Holy Father replied: 'in his concern for all the Churches every day the Pontiff must open his prayer, his thought, his heart to the entire world. Thus a kind of geography of the Pope's prayer is sketched out. It is a geography of communities, Churches, societies, and also of the problems that trouble the world today. In this sense the Pope is called to a universal prayer in which the *sollicitudo omnium ecclesiarum* (concern for the Churches; 2 Cor 11:28) permits him to set forth before God all the joys and hopes as well as the griefs and anxieties that the Church shares with humanity today.'[18]

WOMEN

From the beginning of his pontificate John Paul II gave special attention to the place of women in the Church and in the world. He outlined some of his basic insights on Christian feminism in his catechetical series on the Theology of the Body (1979–84). But his most developed thinking on this issue was given in *Mulieris dignitatem*, his apostolic letter on the dignity of women, published on 15 August 1988. His 1994 *Letter to women* would draw out some of the practical implications of this feminism with regard to women in public life.

From the point of view of creation and redemption, John Paul II says, man and woman are of equal dignity. Revelation teaches us how a woman, Mary, was at the centre of the greatest event in human history, the incarnation of the Word. John Paul II says that whenever there are relationships of domination of women, this is contrary to the Gospel message and is the result of sin. It is sin that fractures that community of persons that God has intended 'from the beginning', a relationship which reflects the radical equality of man and woman as images of God. Society should safeguard the distinctive vocation of women which results from their 'personal originality'. On the other hand, he continues, women should not try to appropriate male characteristics which go contrary to their own 'feminine originality'.

17 *Crossing the threshold of hope*, p. 22. 18 Ibid., p. 83.

In writing about Christ's relationships with women, John Paul II shows that they were counter-cultural, in that he gave women a status which was denied them under Jewish law. He uses the story of the woman taken in adultery (Jn 8:3–11) to illustrate the irresponsibility of the man, who was at least equally guilty, and draws an analogy with the situation today when a woman is abandoned with an unwanted pregnancy, and the man is unwilling to accept responsibility for it.[19] John Paul II says that the self-giving love of Jesus, which the holy women encountered in him, was one of the reasons why they accompanied him throughout his ministry and remained faithful to him on Calvary when all his male disciples had fled.

Drawing on a theme from his encyclical *Redemptoris Mater* (Mother of the Redeemer),[20] John Paul II says that motherhood is not just a biological reality, but something with a moral and religious meaning as well. For it was through motherhood that humanity was given its Saviour. Motherhood is always related to the covenant which God established with the human race through the motherhood of the Mother of God.[21]

As regards the relationship between men and women in marriage, John Paul II writes that marriage can only be understood on the analogy of Christ the Bridegroom and the Church as Bride (cf. Eph 5:25–32); that there has to be a mutual subjugation between husband and wife out of a self-giving love for each other. Any idea of the wife being subject to her husband is contrary to Gospel values. Referring to the 'feminine genius', he says that woman was the one in whom love first took root. Thus 'the human being is entrusted by God to woman in a particular way'.[22]

John Paul II clarified in *Crossing the threshold of hope* that his Marian piety was also an attitude towards woman as woman.[23] Everything he wrote in *Mulieris dignitatem*, he says, he felt from the time he was very young, and he suggested that this was perhaps influenced by the climate of the time when he was brought up – a time of great respect and consideration for women, especially for women who were mothers. In contemporary society, however, where these attitudes had eroded, woman had become, he affirmed, above all else, an object of pleasure.[24] In the middle of all this, he continues, an authentic theology of women is being reborn. 'The spiritual beauty, the particular genius, of women is being rediscovered ... And for this purpose we must return to the figure of Mary. Mary herself and devotion to Mary, when lived out in all its fullness, becomes a powerful and creative inspiration'.[25]

19 Cf. Weigel, pp 578–80. **20** John Paul II, Encyclical Letter, *Redemptoris Mater*, 25 March 1987. **21** Cf. John Paul II, Apostolic Letter, *Mulieris dignitaterm* (The dignity of women), 15 August 1988, 18–19. **22** Cf. *Mulieris dignitatem*, 30. **23** *Crossing the threshold of hope*, p. 216. **24** Cf. ibid., p. 217. **25** Ibid.

WORK IN THE HOME

An integral part of the defence of the family and family values for John Paul II was the need for society to recover an awareness of the exceptional importance and dignity of a mother's work in the home. While recognizing the equal right of women with men to work in external professional activity, he said it was imperative to identify the reasons why domestic work had a higher priority in terms of fundamental values. Woman, he reminded us, is 'the heart of the family community. It is she who gives life, it is she who is the first educator'. In the same way that the heart is essential to the human organism, 'she who is the heart of the family cannot be missing from it.'[26] What the Church asks first of all, he continues, is that 'all the activity of a woman in the home, as mother and educator, be fully esteemed as work. This important work', John Paul II warned, 'cannot be socially scorned, but must constantly be reaffirmed in its value, if society does not wish to act against its own interests'[27] because, among other things, the vocation of mother is integrally united to the vocation of transmitting 'the truths of the faith and ethical values' in the home.

'Doubt is frequently cast', he continued, 'on this natural mission of the woman-mother by positions which emphasize the social rights of women. At times their professional work is seen as social advancement, while total dedication to family matters and the education of children is held to be a renunciation of the development of their own personalities.' While proclaiming that the equal dignity of women with men justifies their access to all public responsibilities, he nevertheless strongly reaffirms that

> the true advancement of women demands of society a particular recognition of maternal and family responsibilities because they constitute *a value superior* to all other public tasks and professions … Children have a particular need of the dedication of a mother in order to develop as persons who are responsible, religiously and morally mature and psychologically well-balanced. The good of the family is so great that it urgently requires of today's society *a reaffirmation of the value of maternal duties*, in the sphere of the advancement of women and among those who hold that they must do remunerative work outside of the home.[28]

Roundly proclaiming the mother's work in the home as superior to all other external professions is a strongly counter-cultural statement, but a necessary one if the importance of the family is to be truly recognized. In 1981 John Paul

26 John Paul II, Address, 13 June 1987, no. 4. **27** Ibid., no. 5. See also John Paul II, Encyclical Letter, *Laborem exercens*, 19, 14 September 1981. **28** Address, 13 June 1987, no. 7 (italics in the original).

II had already called for a 'renewed theology of work' to shed a deeper light on the 'original and irreplaceable meaning of work in the home and in rearing children'.[29] Thus he says the Church

> can and should help modern society by tirelessly insisting that the work of women in the home be recognized and respected by all in its irreplaceable value ... Furthermore, the mentality which honours women more for their work outside the home than for their work within the family must be overcome. This requires that men should truly esteem and love women with total respect for their dignity, and that society should create and develop conditions favouring work in the home.[30]

APOSTOLATE WITH YOUTH

As we have seen, pastoral outreach to young people was a priority with Karol Wojtyla as priest and bishop. Very soon after his election as Pope he started to promote ways of continuing this apostolate. He celebrated a special Mass each year during Advent and Lent for the university students of Rome, as he used to do in Krakow. This started off in a small way but within a few years, St Peter's basilica was full of students on these occasions to hear John Paul II speak to them about making good use of these penitential seasons. A particular characteristic of these events were the large numbers of students who received the sacrament of reconciliation from priests dotted all around the basilica.

And then there was the idea of World Youth Day. This, John Paul II affirmed, was the outcrop of his experience at St Florian's and the young people he kept in contact with as priest and bishop in Krakow. From the beginning, on his pastoral visits as Pope to the different countries, there was always an apostolic encounter with youth. Then, for Palm Sunday 1985, taking advantage of the fact that 1985 was being celebrated as International Youth Year, he invited young people to come to Rome for the first World Youth Day. About 250,000 young people turned up, a clear indication that this was a pastoral event with a future. It was to be celebrated with the Holy Father every two years in different cities around the world, and in the intervening years in the local dioceses. Thus there was a World Youth Day in Buenos Aires in 1987, in Santiago de Compostela in 1989, in Czestochowa in 1991, in Denver in 1993, in Manila in 1995, in Paris in 1997, and back in Rome in 2000 for the Jubilee Year.

29 *Familiaris consortio*, 23. **30** Ibid.

John Paul II prepared the first World Youth Day by writing an Apostolic Letter to all young people.[31] In this letter he tells young people that in them there is hope because the future belongs to them; that youth is a time to take a decision about a path in life, but especially a time to discern what Christ is asking of them. It is a time to ask themselves the question, 'What must I do so that my life may have full value and full meaning?'[32] The fundamental question of youth, he tells them, is the question of conscience and its authenticity.[33] Conscience is the measure of human dignity; to develop one's conscience authentically is the true measure of a human personality's development. Here the commandments of God take on their full significance when seen as an expression of the commandment of love, which opens the human person to God and to neighbour. This allows the young person to appropriate the full meaning of that special glance of Jesus at the young man ('And Jesus looking upon him loved him' [Mk 10:21]) who asked, 'Good Teacher, what must I do to gain eternal life?'(Mk 10:17).

A characteristic of John Paul II's addresses to young people was the very direct way he spoke to them about Christ. He opened the scenes of the Gospel to them, showing them the richness of the personality of Jesus, his tender love for every individual, and his desire to depend on each one of us to bring about the redemption of man. He also spoke very clearly to young people about sexual morality. At a meeting in Paris in 1980, he was asked: 'In questions of a sexual nature the Church has a rather intransigent attitude. Why? Are you not afraid, Holy Father, that young people will move further and further away from the Church?' John Paul II replied:

> If you think of this question deeply, going right to the heart of the problem, I assure you that you will realize only one thing, which is that in this domain the only demands made by the Church are those bound up with true, that is, responsible, conjugal love. She demands what the dignity of the person and the basic social order require. I do not deny that they are demands. But that is the essential point, that man fulfils himself only to the extent that he knows how to impose demands on himself. In the opposite case 'he goes away sorrowful', as we have just read in the Gospel. Permissiveness does not make men happy. The consumer society does not make men happy. It never has done.[34]

What was extraordinary about the World Youth Days was the size of the attendance at these events, despite, at times, a lot of negative media speculation in preparation for them. For example, the cynics in France were aston-

31 John Paul II, *Apostolic Letter to the Youth of the World* (31 March 1985). **32** Ibid., no. 3. **33** Cf. ibid., no. 16. **34** Ibid., p. 111.

ished that one million young people would turn out at the Longchamp racecourse in Paris in 1997 to meet John Paul II. And the fact that between five and seven million gathered in Manila in 1995 left the secular world astonished at the charisma of this Pope.

PAPAL JOURNEYS

One of the most striking aspects of the papacy of John Paul II was his pastoral journeys to practically every corner of the earth. These grew out of his experience of parish visitation during twenty years as bishop in Krakow. There he found it was important to visit the parish communities personally in order to foment unity with the centre.[35] The presence of the bishop in a parish enabled the people to experience a deeper sense of Christian unity and made them feel at home in the Church as a whole. It made Christian communities aware of the Good Shepherd. As John Paul II explained: 'The notions of episcopal service put into effect at Krakow were just as valid in Rome for the pontifical ministry.'[36]

John Paul II's pastoral trips were always a great blessing for the countries he visited. They were an occasion of grace that brought about many conversions, and resulted in an increase, sometimes quite significant, in the number of priestly vocations. He made 107 pastoral trips outside Italy (visiting 129 countries), and 146 within Italy.

FUNERAL MASS

On Saturday 2 April 2005 Catholics and many others in different parts of the world followed very closely the reports from Rome about the Holy Father's deteriorating health. It was clear to everybody that within a matter of hours he would meet his heavenly Father. People would have reflected on an extraordinary twenty-six year papacy which in some way affected them all personally. Perhaps more than anything else, it was his personal witness to the value of suffering which impressed and encouraged them, especially during the last decade of his life. Now he was preparing to begin his new, definitive life with God. At 9.30 p.m. Archbishop Sandri announced to the gathered crowds in St Peter's Square: 'The Holy Father has returned to the house of the Father,' and intoned the *Salve Regina* which was taken up by crowd.

The news of the death of John Paul II left a deep impression on people. Perhaps the most striking was the reaction of those who decided that somehow

35 Frossard, p. 28. **36** Ibid., p. 198.

they had to get to Rome for the funeral services of the Holy Father, without any knowledge of where they might stay. The very next day, Sunday 3 April, people began to arrive in Rome by the tens of thousands, many of them young people. It is estimated that some three million people descended on the city of Rome over the next week, coming from all parts of the world. They had come to pay honour to a man whom they personally regarded as a saint. In so many ways, through his teaching, his pastoral visits, his very illnesses, he had reflected the face of Christ for them with a clarity which they had never previously experienced. For most of the youthful pilgrims to Rome, the figure of John Paul II was, in fact, for them, the history of the Catholic Church.

That same Sunday, 3 April, the body of John Paul II, vested in red, was laid out in the *Sala Clementina*, one of the audience halls in the papal apartments, where firstly cardinals paid their respects, followed by members of the Roman Curia, government representatives and others. On Tuesday 5 April the Pope's body was carried to St Peter's basilica, where it lay in state awaiting the funeral Mass on Friday. By this time a vast throng of hundreds of thousand had gathered in St Peter's Square and environs, which was characterized by a remarkable spirit of patience and prayerfulness. Some people queued for as long as twenty hours to be able to pray for a brief fifteen or twenty seconds before the remains of John Paul II. Significantly a very high proportion of those waiting in the seemingly never-ending queue were young people. Different banners among the crowds expressed people's affection for the dead Pope, one of which proclaimed *Santo subito* – Make him a saint now.

During the week before his burial, pilgrims kept pouring in. To facilitate the vast crowds, St Peter's basilica was kept open all day and all night, except for a brief three-hour period in the early morning to facilitate essential cleaning. When the basilica was finally closed on the Thursday evening, some two million people had been able to pay their last respects to the dead Pope. One of the more remarkable sights in Rome during those days was the presence of many priests, wearing a purple stole, hearing confessions all along the Via della Conciliazione, on both sides of the street. Long queues of penitents formed in front of these impromptu confessionals to prepare themselves sacramentally for John Paul II's funeral Mass. The author of the apostolic exhortation *Reconciliatio et paenitentia* (Reconciliation and penance), John Paul II's 1984 document on the promotion of the sacrament of confession, would have been particularly gratified with this aspect of the funeral arrangements.

On Friday 8 April, the day of the funeral Mass, crowds gathered from early dawn. It is reckoned that up to a million people were present in St Peter's Square and environs. In addition, the Roman authorities had erected large televisions screens in a number of open-air venues across the city to facilitate the huge crowds following the ceremonies. There were over two hundred nations officially represented at the funeral – kings, queens, presidents, prime ministers – the greatest representative congregation in human history.

All the College of Cardinals, vested in red, concelebrated the Requiem Mass with Cardinal Ratzinger, the chief celebrant. In a homily which celebrated the faithful priesthood of John Paul II, Cardinal Ratzinger lauded the unreserved self-giving of his long life, especially during his twenty-six years as Vicar of Christ and bishop of Rome. Ratzinger's homily was very simple but powerfully evocative and in a very real sense responded to the spiritual needs of the huge congregation; he was interrupted ten times by applause. He said: 'Today we bury his remains in the earth as a seed of immortality – our hearts are full of sadness, yet at the same time of joyful hope and profound gratitude.'[37] In the pause after the distribution of Holy Communion, and before the final prayer, the crowds spontaneously called out *Magnus*, *Magnus*! (Great, Great), indicating that they wanted John Paul II to be known as John Paul the Great, a title given to only two other Popes – St Leo I (440–61) and St Gregory I (590–604). Shouts of *Magno, Il Grande, Santo subito*, echoed round St Peter's Square and in the surrounding streets for several minutes.[38]

In the case of John Paul II, Pope Benedict XVI waived the normal five-year waiting period before causes of beatification can begin; in his case it was opened on 28 June 2005.

37 Cardinal Joseph Ratzinger, Homily, 8 April 2005. **38** Cf. Weigel, *God's choice*, pp 94–103.

Epilogue

OUR REVIEW OF the lives of ten priests, spread throughout the centuries, leaves us in no doubt that the priesthood is a specific response to a definite call from God. Not only were these men concerned to develop the Christian lives of those already in the Church, but they also devoted considerable energy to making converts to the faith, to the 'One True Fold' as Newman explicitly defined this work. Whether it was Chrysostom recovering Catholics who had been tainted with Arianism, or Newman bringing his Oxford undergraduates to their spiritual home, or Archbishop Lamy converting the Navajo Indians of the Southern Rockies, the motivation was always the same – to bring people into the fullness of truth in the One, Holy, Catholic, and Apostolic Church.

These men had very clear objectives because they were convinced about their vocation. We do not find here any semblance of the crisis of identity which hit many priests in the aftermath of Vatican II. In fact they had so little time to think about themselves, they were so busy working as priests that it never occurred to them to doubt their vocation. Apart from Newman, there was no crisis of vocation, and the story of that crisis, the *Apologia pro vita sua*, has become one of the great spiritual biographies of Christian history.

Most of the priests we have reviewed are beatified or canonized saints. The Church in this way has recognized the holiness of their lives and the fruitfulness of their priesthood. While the Church has proposed the Curé of Ars as the patron of priests, it does not necessarily mean that his spirituality should be imitated in every detail. Certainly priests will be inspired by his prayer life, his love for the Eucharist and his devotion to our Lady. They will also feel challenged by his daily catechetical schedule, and his exceptional dedication to the ministry of the confessional. Reflecting on this latter aspect of the Curé's priestly ministry, John Paul II saw it as a clear example for priests of the generous commitment they should make to the administration of the sacrament of reconciliation. He said that the priest fulfils 'an essential part of his ministry, by voluntarily making himself "a prisoner of the confessional."'[1] Benedict XVI, in his letter to priests on the occasion of the jubilee year 2009/10, emphasized this point also in relation to Jean-Marie Vianney:

1 *Gift and mystery*, p. 58.

> In France, at the time of the Curé of Ars, confession was no more easy or frequent than in our own day, since the upheaval caused by the Revolution had long inhibited the practice of religion. Yet he sought in every way, by his preaching and his powers of persuasion, to help his parishioners to rediscover the meaning and the beauty of the Sacrament of Penance, presenting it as an inherent demand of the Eucharistic presence. He thus created a '*virtuous circle*'. By spending long hours in the church before the tabernacle, he inspired the faithful to imitate him by coming to visit Jesus with the knowledge that their parish priest would be there, ready to listen and offer forgiveness.[2]

Each of these priests reflected Christ in his own unique way – they were truly icons of Christ. The priest is the visible representation of Christ in history – man needs this perceptible icon of the Lord down through the centuries. The priest as icon and representative of Christ has a long history in the tradition of the Church, beginning with the New Testament where Christ is seen as the image of the Father. By virtue of sacramental ordination the priest acquires an ontological identification with Christ which objectively imprints Christ's image on his soul, irrespective of his personal moral qualities. However, to be a true icon of Jesus, the priest has a duty to be spiritually assimilated to Christ so that in his behavior he increasingly reflects his objective identity. The more a priest is identified with Christ, the more fully will he make him present in the community entrusted to his care.

The exercise of the priestly ministry, especially in the celebration of the sacraments, receives its saving effects from the action of Christ himself who becomes present in them. But the effectiveness of the priest's pastoral activity is also deeply influenced by his level of holiness. This was clearly stated by Vatican II:

> The very holiness of priests is of the greatest benefit for the fruitful fulfillment of their ministry. While it is possible for God's grace to carry out the work of salvation through unworthy ministers, yet God ordinarily prefers to show his wonders through those men who are more submissive to the impulse and guidance of the Holy Spirit and who, because of their intimate union with Christ and their holiness of life, are able to say with Saint Paul: 'It is no longer I who live, but Christ who lives in me' (Gal 2:20).[3]

We have seen this reality at work with exceptional clarity in the lives of the priests we have considered in the foregoing chapters. Precisely because they

2 Benedict XVI, Letter proclaiming a year for priests, on the 150th anniversary of the 'dies natalis' of the Curé of Ars. 3 *Presbyterorum ordinis*, 12.

were men of remarkable holiness, the Holy Spirit was able to work with freedom in their souls. As a consequence, they had great pastoral ambitions and dedicated themselves totally to achieving them. Each, in his own way, is an example of what holy priests should be. Clearly they are very different in personality and background, but all have the common denominator of deep holiness, profound apostolic zeal, and the fortitude necessary to overcome all the obstacles they encountered in doing God's will.

They were truly configured to Christ the Good Shepherd in their pastoral work and in their teaching. They showed zeal to spread the kingdom of God on earth through the many apostolic initiatives they undertook.

People who are really searching for God expect the priest to reflect the holiness of Christ, to somehow be better than themselves, so that he can bear the burden of their weaknesses. We have seen that the priests we have considered were men of exceptionally rich human personalities. Their closeness to God did not in any way stifle their human development. On the contrary, it stimulated the growth of the human virtues to their full potential.

People have a right to expect priests to be understanding, affable, and accessible – these are human qualities which reflect Christ and draw people to him. The priest's human personality should be a bridge to link people to Christ.[4] One characteristic that stands out in all our priests is their fortitude. Whether it is John Fisher standing up to the naked aggression of Henry VIII, Oliver Plunkett facing execution, or Clement von Galen confronting Hitler – they were all endowed with the courage to defend God's law even in the most extreme circumstances. In this context we cannot forget the fortitude of John Paul II in his dealings, as bishop, with a communist regime over a period of twenty years.

Our priests were all effective communicators – some of them, like John Chrysostom, John Henry Newman, and Josemaría Escrivá were outstanding. Apart from theological erudition, their preaching had a profound effect on people because of their ability to explain difficult truths in accessible language, and because the sentiments of their preaching reflected their own holiness. Every priest has to make the effort to be a good communicator so that his message comes across as credible and compelling despite all the competing messages in the airwaves. In the present cultural environment, where people are constantly bombarded with audio and visual images of very different provenance, often hostile to Christian values, it is difficult for the priest to make his voice heard above all the static. He has to have confidence in his message so that he can speak persuasively about the things of God.

It is inevitable that the priest will always be, to some extent, a sign of contradiction as Christ was. Since the priest is an instrument of redemption, he has

4 Cf. John Paul II, Apostolic Exhortation, *Pastores dabo vobis*, 43 (25 March 1992).

to challenge people with the full truth about their lives for their own good. We have seen how this was the case in the lives of each one of the priests reviewed.

Because of his fidelity to preaching Christian moral values, John Chrysostom provoked the anger and resentment of the Empress Eudoxia in Constantinople. In revenge she negotiated John's banishment and exile to the most remote and most inhospitable corner of the empire. In the case of John Fisher, Henry VIII could not tolerate that he would continue to defend the validity of Queen Catherine's marriage, or that he would refuse to take the oath of supremacy which would recognize Henry as head of the Church in England. Fisher had to be liquidated because of his stand, a result which was achieved through the judicial murder of the bishop of Rochester.

In fact all of these priests had to suffer to fulfil God's will in relation to the specific vocation given to each. Newman's conversion to Catholicism caused him immense pain and suffering, because of the way he was treated by family and friends, and because of all he lost as a consequence of his conversion – career, prestige, separation from Oxford, etc. But in the end, he recovered his good name in England as a result of the publication of the *Apologia pro vita sua*, and regained his status in the Church by being made a cardinal by Leo XIII.

When we consider the life of Cardinal von Galen, we see that from the moment he became bishop in 1933 he joined battle with the state about the new German paganism based on the theory of race. For the rest of his life he fought like the colossus he was, against the evil of National Socialism, and used the pulpit, pastoral letters, and every other means at his disposal to expose the nefarious purposes of the Nazi regime, especially in relation to the Catholic faith. He knew he was taking his life in his hands in doing so, but his love for Christ and for the Christian faith gave him the courage to speak out clearly.

For a long period of years, Josemaría Escrivá had to suffer constant calumnies against himself and the organization which he founded, Opus Dei. At one stage he was reported to the Vatican on a charge of heresy for teaching what is now the common doctrine of the Church about the vocation and mission of the laity. He never allowed these accusations to colour his attitude to the people responsible, but suffered in silence while defending the charisma entrusted to him by God.

UNITED TO CHRIST

As a consequence of ordination the priest is united to Christ by means of an irreversible bond. His soul is marked with a permanent seal configuring him to the Lord, which enables him to act *in persona Christi Capitis* (in the person of Christ the Head), the ultimate source of the dignity of the priest. The sacred character affects the priest so deeply that his whole being is directed to a priestly purpose. He is always God's minister – just as Jesus Christ was always a priest and always acted as a priest.

Often today the service of the priest takes place in a secularized society where there is a gradual decline in the sense of the sacred and a progressive elimination of religious values. Such a society has all the more need of the sign value of the visible priesthood, of this witnessing to the unseen world of the supernatural. This is particularly so in a society where communication of ideas by means of visual images is so important.

Priests are, in a very real sense, an extension of Christ's sacred humanity, because they continue to perform in souls the same miracles he worked while on earth – restoring spiritual sight to the blind, giving back supernatural life to those who have died through sin, nourishing hungry souls with the Eucharistic bread. At a human level, the personalities of our priests are also attractive. They are big-hearted men, generous to a fault, who worked with a tireless dedication for the good of others. Many of them faced enormous challenges, yet they responded to them with great courage and immense faith in God.

In the lives of the priests we have considered, it is clear that there was a deep sense of fulfillment because they gave themselves fully to God and to their responsibilities in the Church. This point was illustrated by John Paul II in an address he gave to priests in Columbia in 1986:

> You are asked for what you can truly give: the Word of Salvation, the sacraments, the love and the grace of Christ, the service of guiding towards a more Christian life, worthy and human. If you are authentic bearers of these gifts, you will see that your life is fully fulfilled, and you will try to respond each day better to this task, with the respect and the love that ought to be given you by the clear knowledge that the Lord, in spite of our weakness, has placed in our hands a treasure of incalculable value (cf. 2 Cor 4:7).[5]

VOCATIONS

The priests we have reviewed were very committed to the task of promoting vocations to the priesthood. In his many travels to different countries, John Paul II invariably spoke about the nurturing of vocations through prayer, Eucharistic adoration, and the direct invitation to young men to consider a call to the priesthood. We think too about St Josemaría Escrivá, who during his life

5 John Paul II, Address to the priests of Colombia, 1 July 1986.

called nearly a thousand men to the priesthood. We remember how St John Fisher set up a new college in Cambridge University with the express purpose of preparing men for the priesthood. Archbishop Lamy built a seminary in Santa Fe for those vocations which proceeded from the local Christian Brothers' schools. After many years relying on volunteer priests from France, he saw that in the long term the priesting of his diocese would have to come from home-grown vocations, an objective which he achieved in due course.

We have seen how all these priests enriched the living tradition of the Church. Each of them made their own particular contribution to our understanding of the vocation and mission of the clergy in the Church and society. This is precisely what Pope Benedict XVI proposes as the main objective of the current jubilee year for priests. While new insights are constantly given to the Church about the nature of priesthood through the light of the Holy Spirit, our understanding of God's works is also enhanced by reflection on Church history.

In our review of the lives of this group of priests, we have observed how they responded to the specific needs of their times, with energy and initiative, ready to find appropriate pastoral solutions. We can learn from their indefatigable preaching of the Gospel, their committed efforts to acquire personal holiness through their priesthood, and their willingness to accept the Cross generously in the demands of their vocation. Their lives will always be an inspiration for priests because, in spite of their limitations and defects, they give a vision of priesthood based on the eternal priesthood of Christ, which is always challenging and uplifting, and which is valid for all time (cf. Heb 13:8).